Emergency Planning for Nuclear Power Plants

Emergency Planning for Nuclear Power Plants

Paul Elkmann

CRC Press
Taylor & Francis Group
Boca Raton London New York

CRC Press is an imprint of the
Taylor & Francis Group, an **informa** business

CRC Press
Taylor & Francis Group
6000 Broken Sound Parkway NW, Suite 300
Boca Raton, FL 33487-2742

First issued in paperback 2021

© 2017 by Taylor & Francis Group, LLC
CRC Press is an imprint of Taylor & Francis Group, an Informa business

No claim to original U.S. Government works

Version Date: 20160726

ISBN 13: 978-1-03-224227-9 (pbk)
ISBN 13: 978-1-4987-5457-6 (hbk)

DOI: 10.1201/9781315399140

Publisher's Note
The publisher has gone to great lengths to ensure the quality of this reprint but points out that some imperfections in the original copies may be apparent.

Library of Congress Cataloging-in-Publication Data

Names: Elkmann, Paul, author.
Title: Emergency planning for nuclear power plants / Paul Elkmann.
Description: Baton Rouge, Fl : CRC Press, [2017] | Includes bibliographical references and index.
Identifiers: LCCN 2016028954 | ISBN 9781498754576 (hbk)
Subjects: LCSH: Nuclear power plants--Law and legislation. | Nuclear energy--Law and legislation. | Nuclear power plants--History. | Radioactive pollution--Law and legislation. | Liability for nuclear damages. | Emergency management--Law and legislation.
Classification: LCC K3990 .E45 2017 | DDC 363.17/996--dc23
LC record available at https://lccn.loc.gov/2016028954

Visit the Taylor & Francis Web site at
http://www.taylorandfrancis.com

and the CRC Press Web site at
http://www.crcpress.com

Contents

List of Figures and Equations

List of Tables

Preface

Welcome to this book about emergency planning for power reactors; I greatly appreciate each and every one of you. The radiological emergency preparedness community is changing, as many long-time practitioners are retiring and being replaced by recent graduates. I was practicing health physics in the early 1980s, and my emergency preparedness career largely began with Chernobyl. The people I learned from had their start not many years earlier with Three Mile Island, and for the most part they have already left the field. The defining experience for today's emergency planners will be Fukushima Daiichi.

I wrote this book to fill a void in training new emergency planners. There are currently very few formal training opportunities in radiological planning, and those that exist tend to focus on the planning standards. I do not know of any comprehensive training that surveys essential topics across the entire discipline. I hope this book at least partly fills that gap and provides a more comprehensive discussion of all of the relevant topics than has been available previously.

This book is not intended to be a primer on compliance with the regulations governing emergency preparedness for power reactors. Instead, this book introduces readers to the essential concepts and terminology used in radiological emergency preparedness, so they can apply those concepts to the specific programs with which they are associated. One cannot help but run into regulations along the way, but they should not be the primary emphasis or dominate the discussions.

Radiological emergency preparedness can be approached from a plant operator's perspective or from a health physicist's perspective. Whenever possible, I have presented the material from a health physics point of view. I think that it is important to emphasize radiological aspects, because it is ultimately the properties of radiation that cause us to need emergency preparedness for reactors. Although it is important to have a good understanding of current emergency preparedness, I have also tried to provide the historical basis for current developments. It is my strong belief that the practical application of these topics depends on understanding why we now do what we are doing.

As with any topical survey book, the author is challenged in picking the topics that will be of most use to the reader. There is not currently an established syllabus that represents a standard for a first course in the material, the way there is in many other disciplines. I have tried to present radiological emergency preparedness as a coherent discipline, rather than as a series of somewhat-related tasks to be performed. The choices were mine, based on nearly 30 years of experience in radiological response. If I failed to address an important topic, the failure is also mine.

Some subjects are not discussed in great detail and may be somewhat simplified; some details may be inaccurate or may become inaccurate between my writing and your reading. I apologize in advance for any errors I have included. I have endeavored to present the positions of the various agencies and entities involved in emergency preparedness as fairly and accurately as possible, and source documents are referenced whenever possible. I am responsible for my own opinions on various topics, which should be clearly distinct from the positions of others.

I have provided as complete a bibliography as possible, which I hope proves useful to the reader.

1 Overview and History

INTRODUCTION

Emergency preparedness is the discipline that ensures an organization's readiness to respond to an emergency in a coordinated, timely, and effective manner. Radiological or nuclear reactor emergency planning is a subdiscipline that ensures a readiness to respond when that emergency originates from or includes a nuclear power reactor. The concepts and discussion in the book also apply to some degree to accidents involving low-power test reactors, to fuel cycle facilities, and to nonreactor installations possessing a large enough inventory of radioactive material to require a site emergency plan. This is a resource book that serves as an introduction to the technology of planning for, and responding to, incidents at nuclear power reactors. However, radiological response is closely related to all-hazard response, and radiological emergency planners should also have some familiarity with the generalized topic of emergency planning.

The terms *incident*, *emergency*, *disaster*, *catastrophe*, and *calamity* are frequently used virtually interchangeably, particularly by the media and by individuals (including emergency responders) speaking to the media. All of these terms refer to an unexpected event or condition with the potential to cause injury or death, harm, and/or physical damage. "Unexpected" in this sense refers to being unable to predict in advance the specific time the condition might occur or appear, not to an inability to predict the general nature and probability of the event, although for any particular incident type both could be true. An emergency responder or response manager should be able to use these terms with precision, for they denote a progression increasing in both scope (more persons at risk) and consequences (greater injury or damage). The following definitions are taken from the technical literature:

Incident—(1) An occurrence that requires action by emergency services personnel (Incident Command System, National Fire Academy, Federal Emergency Management Agency). (2) An occurrence or event, natural or human-caused, that requires an emergency response to protect life or property (USDHS, 2003c).

Accident—(1) Any unintended event, including operating errors, equipment failures, or other mishaps, the consequences or potential consequences of which are not negligible from the point of view of protection or safety (IAEA, 1999b). (2) Any accident involving fatalities or activities from which a release of radioactive material occurs or is likely to occur and which has resulted or may result in an international transboundary release that could be of radiological safety significance for another state (IAEA, 1986).

Emergency—(1) A serious situation or occurrence that happens unexpectedly and demands immediate action (*American Heritage Dictionary of the English Language*, 4th ed., 2000). (2) Any occasion or instance that warrants action to save lives and to protect property, public health, and safety (FEMA, 1996c). (3) As defined by the Stafford Act, "any occasion or instance for which, in the determination of the President, Federal assistance is needed to supplement State and local efforts and capabilities to save lives and to protect property and public health and safety, or to lessen or avert the threat of a catastrophe in any part of the United States" (USDHS, 2004).

Disaster—An occurrence of a natural catastrophe, technological accident, or human-caused event that has resulted in severe property damage, deaths, and/or multiple injuries. A "large-scale disaster" is one that exceeds the response capability of the local jurisdiction and requires state, and potentially federal, involvement (FEMA, 1996c).

Catastrophe—Any natural or manmade incident, including terrorism, that results in extraordinary levels of mass casualties, damage, or disruption severely affecting the population, infrastructure, environment, economy, national morale, and/or government functions. A catastrophic event could result in sustained national impacts over a prolonged period of time; almost immediately exceeds resources normally available to state, local, tribal, and private-sector authorities in the impacted area; and significantly interrupts governmental operations and emergency services to such an extent that national security could be threatened (USDHS, 2004).

As can be seen from these definitions, not all incidents are emergencies, all emergencies are not disasters, and not all disasters become catastrophes, although mismanagement by responders can turn one into another. As a natural progression, a calamity would be an extraordinary incident of severe disruption that overwhelms response from the local through the national levels and is extranational (involving more than once country) in scope. This progression of severity also implies a progression in response, with an incident generally being within the capabilities of a single local jurisdiction, management of an emergency requiring several local jurisdictions to work together, a disaster requiring the aid of substantial state resources, and a catastrophe requiring substantial state and federal resources.

Emergencies, disasters, and catastrophes of all sizes occur routinely around the nation. Some are large-scale natural events, such as floods, tornadoes, earthquakes, and wildfires; some are local events, such as house fires and pipeline explosions; and others involve technological events such as the release of hazardous materials. Although the time and place of individual disasters are random, in many areas they occur frequently enough it is certain that over a relatively short period of time—say, a few years—disasters will occur. In many places, most or all of the likely disasters can be anticipated and steps taken in advance to protect people and property from their effects. The ability through experience to predict the kinds of incidents an area is likely to have gives rise to emergency planning. This is also true of highly unlikely events, some of which may never have occurred but whose consequences are sufficiently calamitous and widespread to deserve anticipation and contingency planning. This book is primarily concerned with the response to emergencies at commercial light-water nuclear reactors, a rare event that nevertheless can be anticipated and whose probable scope can be modeled.

WHY PLAN? SOME HISTORICAL CONTEXT

Emergency response is concerned with managing command-and-control, personnel, facilities, information, and equipment resources to maximize the protection of affected and potentially affected members of the public from some significant or widespread hazard. Emergency preparedness is concerned with providing the needed resources and maintaining them in a state of readiness to initiate a rapid response when required. Assuming that the capabilities exist, an effective emergency response depends on two factors: the speed of communication and the speed of transportation. When the hazardous event or condition occurs, potential responders have to recognize the hazard and be notified to assemble, and persons at risk must be notified to escape. If the condition travels or expands at a speed faster than, or comparable to, the speed of communication then neither the responders nor at-risk populations have sufficient advance notice to do anything except limited *ad hoc* and rather local actions with no coordination with other persons in the same situation. Only if communication outpaces the spread of the hazard can responders assemble sufficient resources to attack (mitigate) the hazard and enable persons not yet affected to flee before its arrival. Prior emergency planning is largely ineffective if decision makers and those organizations providing resources cannot be informed about the hazards and magnitude of an event in time to make and implement practical decisions that have an actual effect on the safety and health of the affected population.

Similarly, if the speed of transportation is slower than, or comparable to, the speed of the hazard, then there is high likelihood that even with advance warning the hazard will overtake the fleeing population. The speed of transportation also affects the ability of predesignated responders to assemble and to move to where the actions are required to be taken. In cases such as floods, large-scale fires, or releases of poisonous chemicals into the air, where the only possible protective action is evacuation, the effectiveness of preplanned actions is undermined when people move more slowly than does the hazard.

The dependence of effective emergency action on speedy communications and transportation in part explains the hierarchy of local, state, and federal efforts in emergency preparedness. From the time of the settlement of America through roughly the era of World War I, most catastrophic events were natural phenomena, such as floods, hurricanes, fires, tornadoes, and blizzards. When news moved at the speed of a person's walk, or when on horseback, an immediate response was only possible from persons within a few miles of the event. To send for help even 20 miles away meant someone coming perhaps 48 hours after the messenger set out. This alone limited practical emergency planning to the village or town level, because even persons in the same county were too far away to provide quick assistance. Planning at the state and national levels essentially did not exist, both because of political and cultural notions about separation of powers (especially in the earliest years of the American republic) and because of the knowledge gap created by the need to hand-carry messages.

Local notification was generally limited to the range of a bell tower (perhaps a mile or so in radius). The railroad and the telegraph were the first significant advances in transportation and communication, but their practical effect in emergency preparedness was minimal. Messages still had to be hand-carried to the telegraph office, telegraph equipment was owned by businesses and not individuals and most towns had only one telegraph office, people still had to walk or ride animals to railroad terminals, and both telegraph lines and railroad tracks could easily be disrupted by natural disasters. The introduction of radio (both as a widespread commercial service used by the general public and for point-to-point communication by emergency services), the telephone, and at about the same time the automobile had significant effects on the viability of emergency planning. For the first time there existed viable notification technologies that were in significant use by the general population and which provided relatively fast communications over wide areas. The automobile provided a means of escape for the population that was much faster than anything previously available. In addition, unlike the telegraph and railroad, neither radio nor automobiles had the physical restrictions that limited the usefulness of the older technologies.

The industrial revolution had been underway for more than 100 years by the time of World War I. Although hazardous materials were in use in a variety of industries, such as mining and smelting, kerosene production, dye-making, and gunpowder production, the amounts were relatively small and so were the populations that could be affected by their release. Following World War I, new chemicals were invented, and progressively more massive facilities were built to produce them. Beginning in the 1920s and over the subsequent 40 to 50 years, the toxicity of chemicals significantly increased, chemicals began to be much more widely used (for example, as fertilizers and in the production of plastics, another invention of the 1930s and 1940s), and much more of the population became the potential targets of a chemical release.

New industries and facilities based on radioactive material arose beginning in the early 1940s (for military uses) and later in the 1950s (for civilian uses). Although radioactive materials had been known since the end of the 19th century, and their potentially dangerous effects were recognized by the early 1920s, the creation and storage of large inventories of radioactive materials, often in conjunction with chemically toxic materials, presented fundamentally new hazards to the population.

Providing for emergency planning, event response, and post-event reconstruction is not among the enumerated powers of the federal government according to the Constitution; therefore, according to a strict constitutional interpretation, doing so is (was) a function entirely reserved to the states. During the first half of the United States' existence, there was a political and legal consensus about strictly prescribed roles for the federal and state governments that was largely supported by national leaders of the time (the Civil War notwithstanding). Since that time, national leaders of all political viewpoints have slowly but steadily became less concerned with certain of the historic limitations on the federal government and have come to a common viewpoint that emergency preparedness and response are aspects of the common defense clause of the Constitution. The author could speculate that much of the changes in these attitudes were facilitated by the same advances in communication technology that made it possible for state and federal capitals to know immediately about events that previously would have taken weeks to be communicated. It would be accurate to state that the basic documents concerning the federal role in emergency preparedness response do not clearly articulate why this has become a federal function in the absence of specific constitutional authorization.

Beginning with the Great Depression and continuing for most of the rest of the century, the general public and its elected leadership have gradually became more concerned with protecting the lives and the livelihoods of individuals from both physical and societal disasters; these attitudes grew out of some of the same religious and cultural movements that also resulted in the founding of the American Red Cross, temperance, and Prohibition. As a result of the confluence of changing ideas about the role of government and the individual's right to protection, over the last 100 years a moral and legal consensus has emerged that holds that government at all levels has a duty to actively limit the occurrence of disasters where this is practical, must respond forcefully to protect the population when disasters do occur, and must compensate or otherwise aid disaster victims to make an affected area whole again after the disaster abates. In addition, the consensus holds that possessors and operators of potentially hazardous facilities have a duty to protect both their employees and the general public from the possible harm associated with those facilities or the materials they contain. This duty is partially expressed by requirements that local governments and possessors of designated quantities of hazardous materials (typically, but not always, industrial-scale users) preplan for actions to take in the event of an emergency. Operators of facilities containing hazardous materials (including nuclear power reactors) also have other incentives to do advance planning to prevent, contain, and respond to emergencies at their facility, such as receiving lower rates from insurers and limiting their potential legal liability under tort law.[*]

OVERVIEW OF RADIOLOGICAL CONCEPTS

Radiological emergency preparedness is intended to protect people from radiation originating from uncontrolled radioactive sources and radioactive material, rather than from radiation-producing machines. Commercial nuclear power reactors would not be potential threats to the health and safety of the public around them except for the radioactive properties of their fuel and the large inventory of radioactive materials that develop in their coolant systems. The accidents of concern are therefore ones that allow radioactive material to escape into the environment. The proper public health response to an accident is selected based on radiation exposure to the public and on its consequences. This operational focus on radiation exposure consequences requires emergency planners and event responders to be familiar with radiological concepts, units, measurements, and terminology. This discussion of radiological concepts is intended as an introductory overview for readers unfamiliar with the radiological sciences. It is brief and necessarily omits a great amount of the technical detail not required to understand and implement public protection schemes. Readers who

---

[*] Torts are civil wrongs recognized by law as grounds for a lawsuit. These wrongs result in an injury or harm constituting the basis for a claim by the injured party. The primary aim of tort law is to provide relief for the damages incurred and deter others from committing the same harms. Among the types of damages the injured party may recover are loss of earnings capacity, pain and suffering, and reasonable medical expenses. They include both present and future expected losses. The numerous specific torts include trespass, assault, battery, negligence, products liability, and intentional infliction of emotional distress. Torts fall into three general categories: intentional torts (e.g., intentionally hitting a person), negligent torts (e.g., causing an accident by failing to obey traffic rules), and strict liability torts (e.g., liability for making and selling defective products). Intentional torts are those wrongs that the defendant knew or should have known would occur through their actions or inactions. Negligent torts occur when the defendant's actions were unreasonably unsafe (Cornell Law School, Legal Information Institute, http://www.law.cornell.edu/wex/index.php/Tort).

are already familiar with radiation and health physics concepts do not require this section. Many of the detailed health physics calculations are not discussed because most emergency planners do not require that level of health physics proficiency. Additional information about radiological concepts can be found in many introductory health physics textbooks. Readers can also find information on the websites of the Nuclear Regulatory Commission (www.nrc.gov), Environmental Protection Agency (www.epa.gov), Health Physics Society (www.hps.org), National Council on Radiation Protection and Measurement (http:/www.ncrponline.org), and Conference of Radiation Control Program Directors (www.crcpd.org).

Radioactive materials are substances that create or emit radiation. At its simplest, radiation is a directed flow of energy. The energy can be carried on a particle as momentum (mass times velocity) or can be carried by an electromagnetic wave. To complicate the situation further, if particulate radiation is an ion, meaning that it carries an electric charge, it has electrical interactions all along its path at atomic distances that can disrupt other atoms.

Although there are many forms of radiation, four forms are of primary interest in radiation protection at commercial nuclear power plants, three of which could reach the public after a major accident. The radiations of interest are designated alpha (α), beta (β), and gamma (γ); alpha and beta are particulate radiations that carry an electric charge, whereas gamma radiation is an electromagnetic wave that does not have a charge. The fourth radiation, neutron (η), is also a particle that does not carry an electric charge. An alpha particle consists of two protons bound to two neutrons (identical to a helium nucleus, at a +2 charge); alpha is a massive and heavy subatomic particle with a very short range, delivering a large amount of energy. The range of an alpha particle in air is up to a few inches and is a few millimeters in soft tissues (skin and organs). A beta particle is a free electron, a very light subatomic particle at a –1 charge; it delivers intermediate amounts of energy per length along a relatively long path. The range of a beta particle in air is up to a few meters and is a few centimeters (1 to 2 inches) in soft tissue. A gamma "particle" is an electrically neutral photon packet that delivers a relatively small amount of energy per length over a very long path. The range of gamma radiation in air is tens to hundreds of meters, and, except for very low energy radiation, gamma completely penetrates through a body. The characteristic range of a radioactive atom is one factor in establishing how hazardous it is to humans: Very short range is not an external hazard because its range is shorter than the thickness of dead skin, medium ranges can be hazardous to the skin and for a small depth below the skin but not to organs well inside the body, and the longer ranges are hazardous throughout the body because of their very high penetrating power.

At the atomic level, when radiation collides with a target atom it is either absorbed or scattered (i.e., bounces off). Absorption only occurs if the remaining energy corresponds to an open energy shell or excitation energy. If the incoming radiation does not have the correct amount of energy for absorption then it is scattered; the exact angle of scattering is determined by the angle of incidence, radiation energy, and electric charge. Each change in direction causes a loss of energy; in some cases of very large changes in angle, particulate radiation can also create a gamma as it turns. Incoming radiation is continuously losing energy through scattering interactions until it eventually gives up enough energy to allow absorption to occur. Charged particulate radiation also loses energy through the interaction of its electric charge with atoms along its path; this kind of interaction does not change the path or direction of the radiation because it is not close enough for the interacting atom to be a target. Radiation energy is measured in electron volts (eV); a more practical unit for radiation protection is the kiloelectron volt (keV), or 1000 electron volts; 1000 keV is a megaelectron volt (MeV). The radiations that are caused by nuclear processes have characteristic energies between 20 keV and approximately 3500 keV.

At the biological level, radiation injures people by depositing energy in cells which damages cellular DNA and internal structures. This damage comes from direct impingement against cellular structures and from collateral chemical damage induced by the free radicals (charged molecules) in cellular fluids that are created by ionization along the radiation path. In radiation biology, no consensus has been reached with regard to how many radiation hit events a cell can survive. The amount of effective damage is a function of the radiation rate (interactions per unit time), the radiation type, the radiation energy, and the cell type. If the radiation events are sufficiently far apart in time, cellular repair processes may negate the damage. The repair processes are not perfect; they also provide opportunity for an incomplete or faulty cellular repair that may kill essential cells, reduce or change their function, or alter their reproductive cycle (leading to cancer formation).

The word *exposure* has two uses in radiation protection. In the more common, colloquial usage, you are exposed to radiation whenever you are close enough to a radiation source for the associated radiation to reach you. This usage simply denotes that radiation interactions are possible, without quantifying those interactions in any way. The term also has a more technical meaning related to the amount of energy that is available to be deposited in the body.* The unit of radiation exposure is the röntgen (R, also referred to as *roentgen*), which represents a specific quantity of ionization in air (note that this discussion uses traditional radiation units rather than SI [metric] units, because traditional units are mandated in the United States). The actual amount of energy absorbed by the body is referred to as the *absorbed dose*, measured in rads (ergs/gram tissue), which is essentially a calorimetric measurement. The quantity used most frequently in radiation protection is the rem, which reflects the amount of biological damage done by the absorbed dose. The precise value of the rem varies with the radiation type, the target organ, and other factors. One rad of alpha radiation results in the most rems (internal dose only, as the external skin dose will be zero), 1 rad of gamma radiation the fewest rem, and beta radiation intermediate between them.

In terms of biological damage, roentgens, rads, and rems are large units and represent a significant exposure and dose. The working units are typically the milliroentgen (mR, or more commonly mR/h expressed as a rate) and mrem. In each case, milli indicates 1000th, or 0.001 times. It should be noted that the roentgen is only defined for gamma radiation. Portable radiation survey instruments are typically calibrated to measure mR/h for gamma radiation over a specific energy range in keV. Radiation protection personnel typically treat mR and mrem as interchangeable and often refer to mR/h as the *dose rate*, when it is the *exposure rate*. This is because for gamma radiation 1 R produces 0.96 rem, which is rounded up to 1. For purely external exposure this imprecise use of units does not have any practical effect. That is not true for the dose delivered by radioactive material taken into the body.* Because the rem does not measure a physical quantity, there are no portable survey instruments that read in rem or mrem/h.

One might infer from the periodic table of elements that each element exists in only one form, which turns out not to be true. An element is defined by the number of protons in the nucleus and the number of electrons in the shell, which in a nonionized state are equal. No mention is made of the number of neutrons, which do not contribute to the electrical properties of the element. It has been found that most elements exist with a range of neutrons in the nucleus; each different number of neutrons is referred to as an *isotope*. The number of possible isotopes varies with atomic number, so that the higher number elements (e.g., iron compared to oxygen) have many more isotopes than do the lower numbered elements. Thus, what distinguishes U-235 from U-238 is that they have different numbers of neutrons. The total number of protons plus neutrons is called the *atomic mass*, although protons and neutrons do not weigh precisely the same. The atomic mass is used to distinguish among isotopes; the 235 in U-235 is the atomic mass. Although all of the isotopes of a given element have the same chemical properties, such as density, melting point, etc., they do not have the same nuclear properties. In particular, they vary in their ability to capture incipient radiation and in how much energy is required to eject a neutron (which also produces neutrinos and gamma radiation). These differences explain why the amount of U-235 in reactor fuel is important. Isotopes are either stable or unstable; the unstable ones are *radioactive*.

One of the defining characteristics of radioactive material is that it is inherently unstable and over time naturally transforms completely from one element of the periodic table to another element. Each isotope has a unique characteristic transformation rate that can be anywhere between a

---

* Also see 10 CFR 20.1003 and ICRP (1977a, 1979, 1980, 1981).

fraction of a second to billions of years. This transformation rate is referred to as the *activity* of the isotope. These transformations, random quantum effects that occur atom by atom, are called *decays* or *disintegrations*. Each decay takes the atom to either a lower atomic mass (isotope of the same element) or a lower atomic number (isotope of a different element). A decay always results in emitting radiation of a specific type and energy (this property is useful in identifying isotopes through spectroscopy). Some decays eject neutrons, and some cause a proton to transform into a neutron plus a neutrino and gamma radiation. Most radioactive materials undergo a defined series of decays until they finally decay to a stable isotope; this series is called a *decay chain*, and the isotopes produced through decay are the *daughter products*.

If it were possible to produce a completely pure sample of a radioactive isotope, that sample would immediately begin to decay at its characteristic activity. Because of the random nature of decay, it is not possible to know the exact number of atoms that have decayed at any future time, but it is possible to calculate the expected average number of decays. In practice, health physicists tend to speak of the amount of original isotope that is present at any specific time, rather than the amount of transformed material. The activity represents the number of atoms still available for decay and is measured in curies (Ci). Because radium, specifically Ra-226, was one of the first radioactive elements to be produced, the curie was defined in terms of the number of decays per second in a pure 1-gram sample, which is 3.7E10 disintegrations per second. The curie is a large unit—1 Ci of most isotopes would produce radiation exposure rates that would be considered hazardous to people. The most common working units are the microcurie (μCi, 1.0E-6 Ci) and picocurie (pCi, 1.0E-12 Ci; also 2.22 disintegrations per second); some plant applications also use the millicurie (mCi, 1.0E-3 Ci). The inventories of radioactive material in reactors are frequently expressed in megacuries (MCi, 1.0E+6 Ci). A calculation of remaining activity could be made using any arbitrary endpoint. For a variety of practical reasons, the calculation is usually done based on the time required for half of the initial sample to decay away, and the characteristic decay time is the *half-life* of the isotope. Extensive standard tables of the half-lives of radioactive isotopes are available in handbooks and the scientific literature.

In general, two categories of radiological measurements are made: (1) radiation exposure and (2) the number of decays. Instruments (i.e., meters or survey meters) in this second category register the number of discrete radiations that trigger the detector. For a variety of reasons, instruments do not detect every radiation that passes through the detector, depending on the type of radiation and its energy. Each discrete event is a *count,* and the instrument typically measures either the count rate, usually expressed in counts/minute, or the total number of counts occurring during the set counting time. A true activity can be calculated from the count rate, given certain parameters that describe the detector. These parameters include the detector geometry factor and the detector response efficiency for radiation at the energy of interest. For practical reasons, a detector is usually calibrated using a specified isotope, often Cs-137, with a known energy, and it is simply assumed that the calculated detector efficiency applies to radiation at all other energies. If the measured count rate is known to be from a single isotope, then it is possible to calculate the exposure rate from the count rate. If there is a mixture of isotopes, or the source isotope is unknown, it is not possible to calculate an exposure rate.

When one makes any radiological measurement, the instrument measures not only the radiation from the intended source, sample, or location but also any other radiation that may be present. This other radiation causes the measurement to be higher than the true count rate or exposure rate. Sometimes this other radiation comes from other radiation sources in the area, but most often it comes from radiation that is found throughout the environment. Environmental radiation is referred to as the *background* because it is always present. The background in any one area generally varies only a small amount, but backgrounds can vary significantly throughout the country. These variations are caused by the thickness of the atmosphere (e.g., mountains have higher background rates than do seacoasts) and partly by the kind of rock that underlies the area (e.g., rocks enriched in radium or uranium have higher background rates). A background measurement must be made before making any radiological measurement and the total value adjusted by the background to obtain the true measured value.

A *survey* is a radiological measurement made to identify the total radiation present in an area, or emanating from an object, without regard to the specific source. A typical application would be to measure the radiation in a plant room to establish worker protection requirements or to measure the contamination on the exterior of a package being shipped to comply with regulations governing the shipment of radioactive materials.

Radiation originating from radioactive material taken inside the body is referred to as *internal* radiation. The most important intake route for members of the public during a radiation accident is through the lungs (breathing) and, to a much lesser extent, the digestive system (stomach and intestines) from radioactive material in the food chain. Radioactive material can also be absorbed through the skin or through open wounds, but these modes are more likely to be a concern in protecting emergency workers rather than for the general public. The amount of radioactive material initially taken into the body depends primarily on its solubility in blood, and the distribution of radioactive material inside the body depends on the affinity of organs for the chemical form of the radioactive material. When radioactive material enters the body, it decays radiologically and is eliminated biologically through excretion processes. These are separate elimination processes that proceed in parallel, resulting in a total elimination time that is faster than either one by itself. Each combination of organ and radioactive material has a characteristic elimination rate that follows the same mathematics as radiological decay. Biological elimination is usually described by the *biological half-life*, which is completely governed by the element, not by the isotope. The combination of radioactive and biological decay results is described by the *effective half-life*, a quantity that is shorter than either the biological or radiological half-lives alone. For large organs, internal radiation has the greatest dose effect on the organ in which the material collects, whereas for small organs the greatest effect is on nearby organs.

For emergency preparedness purposes, the most important organ-level effects of radiation on the human body are direct radiation injury and an increase in an individual's likelihood of experiencing a variety of cancers (the overall risk of cancer for men is about 45% and for women 38%) (NCI, 2006). Radiation injury can include reddening and blistering of the skin, cataract formation on the eyes, suppression of red blood cell formation, damage to the intestinal tract leading to bacterial infections in the bloodstream, and, in extreme cases, the direct killing of essential nerve cells. The appearance of a radiogenic cancer is delayed from the initiating cellular damage, with each type of cancer having a characteristic delay period ranging from 3 years to roughly 40 years; for example, leukemia is the earliest occurring of the radiogenic cancers, typically appearing 3 to 5 years after the precursor radiation damage. It is worth noting that not all cancers, even in persons with occupational or accidental exposure to radiation, are radiogenic in origin. Some cancers are more likely to be radiogenic than others, and for any single individual cancer it is generally impossible to prove a definitive cause.

The dose equivalent to individual organs is calculated by multiplying the activity (in μCi) resident in the organ by a dose conversion factor that depends on the length of the exposure period. The usual practice is to calculate the dose that an organ receives for 50 years after the depositing of radioactive material in the organ and then assign that entire dose to the year in which the intake occurs. In practice, most radioactive materials are not resident in the body for 50 years, and the exceptions are not typically released in power reactor accidents. A dose equivalent calculated for 50 years of exposure is referred to as the *committed dose equivalent* (CDE). Tables of CDE dose conversion values can be found in standard dosimetry references (e.g., USEPA, 1988, 1993). The thyroid organ dose plume phase and relocation Protective Action Guides (FEMA, 1982; USEPA, 1992) are based on the committed dose equivalent, but these were eliminated in the 2013 interim USEPA Protective Action Guides (USEPA, 2013).

The most important means of protection against radiation dose are time, distance, and shielding. Dose is reduced or prevented by spending as little time in a radiation field as possible. Dose is reduced by staying as far away from a radioactive source as possible. Dose is also reduced by placing absorbing materials (*shielding*) between the radiation source and the at-risk individual. The central principle of radiation protection is expressed in the acronym ALARA, which refers to "as low as reasonably achievable" radiation doses. This principle applies to accident or emergency situations as well as routine operations and underlies radiation protection for the public as well as for emergency workers.

An important working assumption in radiation protection is that any dose of radiation has a potential to increase an individual's risk of cancer, with progressively greater risk with greater dose.* This has been shown to be true for chronic exposures of 50 rem or more and is extrapolated to lower total doses where the effect has not been clearly demonstrated. This model, the *linear no-threshold model*, is the basis for regulatory radiation dose limits. The actual risks of cancer for individuals chronically exposed to low (less than 10 rem) radiation doses remains unknown and may remain unknowable because of the very large populations needed to settle the question with statistical certainty.

Radiation doses delivered in a single event over a short period, such as a few hours or less, are described as *acute* exposures, whereas exposures that continue over an extended time, such as weeks, months, or years, are described as *chronic*. Discernible changes in human cells have never been observed for acute doses of less than approximately 10 rem. The range of doses less than 5 rem (5000 mrem) can be described as being in the regulatory range because 5 rem dose equivalent is the regulatory annual limit for occupational exposure. The range of 5 to 25 rem can be described as the extraregulatory range because doses in this range can be permitted under some (rare) circumstances. Cellular level changes can be observed from radiation doses in the range between 10 and 100 rem, but no acute radiation injury occurs even in radiosensitive individuals. In the range of 100 to 250 rem, radiation injury occurs with the initial effects being suppression of new red blood formation and damage to the cells lining the intestines. Acute radiation doses of 250 rem or greater could be fatal to the most radiosensitive individuals, and damage to red blood cell-producing marrow and the intestines becomes progressively greater with dose, until 50% of individuals exposed to 450 to 500 rem do not survive 30 days following exposure without extensive medical treatment. When modern medical treatment is available, 50% of individuals acutely exposed to approximately 500 to 600 rem survive at least 30 days. Individuals who do not survive radiation exposure at these doses most commonly die from a combination of anemia (a lack of red blood cells and depressed oxygen transport in the blood) and bloodborne infections resulting from destruction of the protective barrier of cells in the intestines complicated by suppression of the immune system. As dose continues to rise, nerve cells and more other radiation-resistant cells begin to be killed; doses near 1000 rem are generally not survivable regardless of medical treatment.

OVERVIEW OF REACTOR PLANT DESIGNS

Radiological emergency planners need to be familiar with the design of the plants they are planning for, understanding both normal operations and the emergency reactor protection systems. Employees of nuclear power licensees and regulatory authorities are generally provided extensive training in reactor design and systems. This overview description is intended for readers without any previous experience with operating nuclear reactors of any type. It is necessarily brief and very simplified, omitting many important reactor systems and details. Readers familiar with nuclear power plant design do not require this section.

---

* It should be understood that radiation, as well as a wide variety of natural and manmade chemicals, is known to increase an individual's risk of cancer. Aside from any accidental contact, individuals experience baseline levels of exposure to cancer-promoting agents that are present in their environment at all times, the amount of which varies with where they live, what they do for a living, and the foods they eat. This baseline level is referred to as *background*. No person, anywhere, can live in total isolation from cancer-promoting agents. In the case of radiation, the components of background include common diagnostic and therapeutic medical procedures (such as dental x-rays), radiation produced outside the Earth in the solar system, secondary interactions of cosmic rays with Earth's atmosphere, primordial radioactive materials distributed throughout rocks and soils, and radioactive gases, such as radon, produced by the transformation of radioactive elements found in rocks and soils.

FIGURE 1.1   Arkansas Nuclear One nuclear power station.

All commercial power reactors currently in operation in the United States are *light-water reactors*, meaning they use very clean ordinary water as a moderator and coolant (see Figure 1.1).* These power plants have two basic designs: *boiling water* and *pressurized water.* Roughly two-thirds of operating plants in the United States are of the pressurized design and one-third of the boiling water design. Pressurized water reactors (PWRs) represent about 60% of operating units in the world and boiling water reactors (BWRs) about 21%, with the remainder being reactor types not currently used in the United States.

Both types of plants have at their center a cylindrical metal pressure vessel with rounded ends, about 20 feet across and 60 feet long, which contains a symmetrical vertical array of zirconium alloy tubes called the *fuel rod*, with each tube containing a long stack of uranium oxide ceramic pellets. A pressurized water reactor contains 80 to 100 metric tons of uranium, and boiling water reactors contain about 140 metric tons. There are 15 isotopes of uranium, and natural uranium ore is approximately 99% ^{238}U and 0.7% ^{235}U, with the remaining 0.3% split among the other isotopes. All of the uranium isotopes of interest for power production are pure alpha-particle emitters with half-lives between 100 million and a billion years, with complex chains of beta-gamma-emitting daughter isotopes. The uranium used in a commercial reactor core is concentrated to be at about 3% isotope ^{235}U by weight with virtually of the rest being isotope ^{238}U; the precise enrichment varies somewhat between the two reactor types and between individual core loads.

Uranium *fissions* (breaks apart) when it absorbs a neutron of the right energy, producing a spectrum of lighter radioactive isotopes called *fission products* or *fission fragments*. The neutron-rich environment of an operating reactor induces the transformation of initially non-radioactive metals in steel reactor components into radioactive metals through a process known as *neutron capture* or *neutron activation*, transforms some of the stable hydrogen and oxygen in the water surrounding the fuel into their respective radioactive isotopes, and transforms impurities in the water, such as corrosion product metals from the metal pipes connected to the reactor. The newly produced fission fragments primarily stay in the zirconium fuel rods during normal operation, although very small amounts of pin-hole

---

* A heavy-water reactor uses a moderator whose water is enriched (is more common than would be found in nature) in the isotope ^2H (hydrogen-2) instead of the more common ^1H.

leakage into the water coolant commonly occur over time. Because of these processes, the water surrounding an operating reactor quickly builds up a radioactive inventory which is controlled through water cleanup systems. A 1000-megawatt-electric operating core contains roughly 1.64E+9 Ci of the 33 radioactive isotopes most important to health (see Table 2.2 in McKenna and Glitter, 1988).

The tubes of uranium fuel are gathered together in square groups called *assemblies* or *bundles*, each assembly being made up of some number of individual fuel pins. A fuel pin is a zirconium tube confining a single vertical stack of uranium fuel. Cruciform-shaped control rods are placed between the bundles, which control reactor power by regulating the flow of neutrons through the reactor. Also located between the fuel bundles are neutron detectors, as well as power (boiling water reactor) and temperature (pressurized water reactor) detectors. The entire collection of fuel bundles, control rods, physical supports, and associated internal sensors is referred to as the *core*. In addition to control rods, pressurized water reactors also regulate power by dissolving boron, a low-density element with good neutron capture properties, in primary coolant water, and boiling water reactors regulate power by controlling the water flow through the reactor using dedicated recirculation pumps.

Neutron-induced fission occurring inside fuel rods produces the neutrons that are required to continue reactor operations, plus heat. Fuel rods typically operate at 600°F to 650°F. High-pressure water is forced from the bottom of the core through to the top, flowing around the fuel assemblies and the control rods, absorbing heat from the fuel. This flow is typically measured in millions of pounds mass per hour of water.

BOILING WATER REACTORS

In a boiling water reactor (Figure 1.2), the internal pressure allows water flowing past the fuel rods to boil and become steam. This steam passes through water-separating and steam-drying stages to produce a steam vapor with essentially no entrained liquid water. The steam bubbles up and collects in the reactor vessel head, and the pressure forces it through steam lines to the steam turbine, which drives the electric generator. This steam does include radioactive gases and radioactive isotopes of

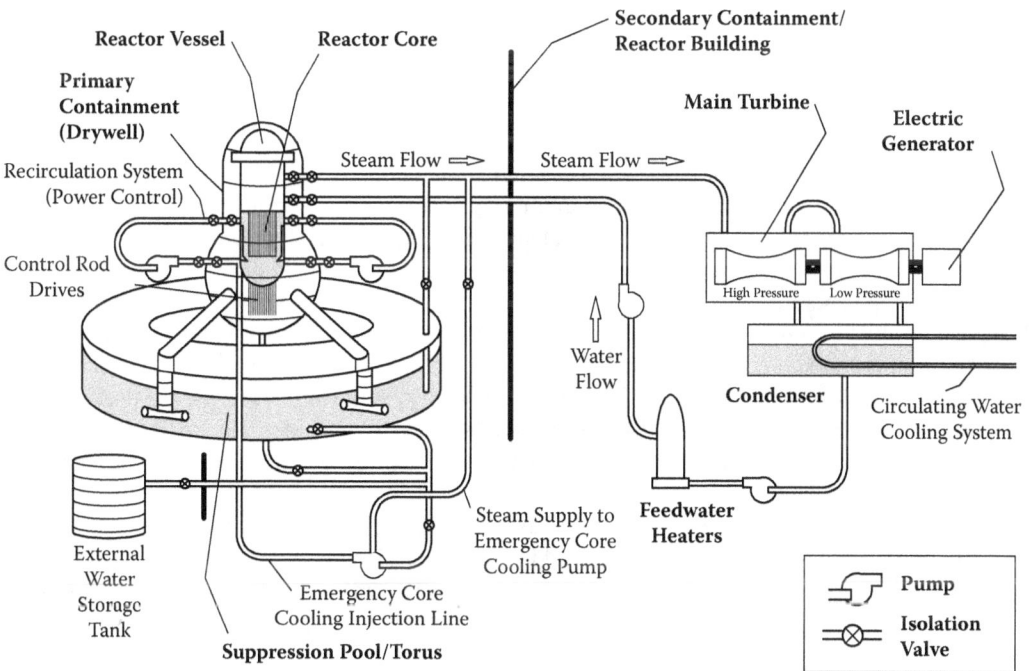

FIGURE 1.2 Diagram of a typical boiling water reactor.

hydrogen, oxygen, nitrogen, krypton, and xenon, so access to the steam lines and the area around the turbine must be controlled during operation. Steam is exhausted from the turbine into a condenser, which cools it so the steam is converted back to water that is injected back into the reactor vessel; the condenser is cooled by a secondary cooling system, often referred to as the *service water* or *essential service water.* This forms a closed steam cycle whose primary waste products are noncondensable radioactive gases such as krypton and xenon. Between startup and about 70% power, power is controlled by the positions of the neutron-absorbing control rods located throughout the reactor core; above 70% power, power is controlled by the flow rate of water through the reactor core which is controlled by the two reactor recirculation pumps. This allows for a rapid and precise control of reactor power.

A boiling water reactor has a very large pool of water called the *suppression pool*; in older boiling water designs, this pool is called the *torus*. The pool is normally kept at a volume of around 80,000 ft³ of water. Newer boiling water designs have a second pool of water that can be used to supplement the suppression pool; the upper pool replenishes the lower pool using gravity-fed lines that do not require pumps. The suppression pool is designed to receive high-pressure steam either from the reactor coolant system pressure relief valves or from a large loss-of-coolant accident. In either case, high-energy steam is vented or exhausted below the water level, transferring the heat to the pool water, condensing the steam, and trapping radioactive material in the pool. The condensation prevents primary containment pressure from reaching its failure limit. The pool also provides a source of water to make up to the reactor in the case of a large loss-of-coolant accident which drains other sources of injection water.

The reactor vessel is housed in a small primary containment structure called the *drywell*. The drywell is the primary containment structure designed to isolate a reactor line breach from the environment. The drywell is often depicted as an inverted light bulb with a spherical bottom section and an upward cylindrical extension, because that is how older boiling water reactors were constructed. More recent reactors are housed in drywells that look like truncated pyramids. Large pipes called *downcomers* connect the drywell to exhaust ports in the suppression pool. If a steam line breaks (or a water line, allowing coolant to flash to steam), the higher pressure in the drywell forces the steam down through the downcomers into the suppression pool. The drywell is located in the *reactor building*, a multistory structure that constitutes *secondary containment*; while the reactor is in operation, secondary containment is maintained at a negative pressure relative to the environment to prevent the leakage of radioactive gases.

Boiling water reactors have a high-pressure emergency core cooling system referred to as either *high-pressure core injection* or *core spray*, depending on the reactor design; the high-pressure system typically uses a steam-driven turbine and pump that take steam from the main steam lines. The various low-pressure cooling systems include *reactor core isolation cooling*, *core sprays*, and *residual heat removal*. The reactor core isolation cooling system also features a steam-driven turbine and pump. There are two identical core spray systems that run on electric motors, and two identical residual heat removal systems, each of which has two electric motors (two subsystems per system). The initial source of water for all emergency core cooling systems is the *contaminated water storage tank* or *refueling water storage tank*, both very large tanks; the storage tank volumes would only be completely drained in the event of a large-break loss-of-coolant accident, allowing the core cooling systems to switch to either the drywell sump or the suppression pool as a secondary source of water.

If there is enough steam, or if the steam break goes on long enough, eventually noncondensable gases build up in the primary containment and in the suppression pool air space. These gases cause drywell pressure to increase, which threatens drywell integrity unless they are vented. The temperature increase caused by steam in the drywell also contributes to the pressure rise and necessitates drywell cooling.

---

* The essential service water system rejects heat to the ultimate heat sink for the plant.

The spent fuel cooling pool at a boiling water reactor is normally located in the reactor building above the drywell. The spent fuel pool is generally a rectangular pool of water sufficiently deep to provide 25 to 30 feet of water above the top of the stored fuel assemblies. During refueling operations the drywell and reactor heads are removed and the reactor cavity flooded up to a level equal to that of the spent fuel cooling pool. A refueling bridge moves across the fuel pool and reactor cavity; the fuel handling grapple is attached to the bridge and is used to move single fuel assemblies from the reactor to the spent fuel storage pool and back. The fuel assemblies being handled remain far under water at all times to provide radiation shielding. Even though newly stored fuel has a contact (surface) radiation exposure rate greater than 10,000 R/h, this depth is sufficient to maintain near-background levels of radiation above the pool and in nearby working areas; there is sufficient margin that several feet of pool inventory would have to be lost before surface radiation exposure rates begin to rise. Note that although the spent fuel storage pool is located in the reactor building, it is not inside secondary containment.

Noncondensable gases in the condenser, primarily radioactive krypton and xenon, are drawn off into the *offgas treatment* system. This system filters radioactive iodine and other volatile fission products and delays the noble gases so that radioactive decay reduces the amount of radioactive material released into the environment. After being run through delay lines these gases are exhausted to the atmosphere via tall (generally 100 meters) chimneys called *stacks*. At rated power, a typical boiling water plant typically exhausts between 800 and 1000 Ci/s through its stack. The main stack also discharges from the reactor building and turbine building ventilation, which usually involves a negligible amount of radioactive material as compared to the offgas system; these ventilation systems are usually not filtered but are delayed.

The two ventilation systems intended for use during an emergency are the *standby gas treatment* and the *hardened vent*. Standby gas treatment draws on the reactor building and the main steam line tunnel; at some sites, it can also draw on the suppression pool air space. Standby gas treatment is a low-flow system (10,000 ft³/min as compared to greater than 100,000 ft³/min for reactor building ventilation), but it is exhausted through a pre-charcoal particulate filter, a charcoal bed filter for iodine and the volatile isotopes, and a 99.99% efficient HEPA filter. The hardened vent, a dedicated pressure relief system for the drywell and suppression pool air space, is an unfiltered pipe that releases directly to the atmosphere* and is intended to save primary containment from failure. Although it may be counterintuitive, the reasoning is that an intact containment structure provides protection to the environment by holding a release for radioactive decay and steam quenching and by allowing natural removal mechanisms to deplete the available radioactive material (i.e., surface plate out). An intentional, controlled release through the hardened vent causes radiation exposure downwind of the plant, but the amount of exposure can be controlled by venting when the wind is not traveling toward population centers, and whatever radiation exposure occurs is less than that caused by the catastrophic failure of the containment and the total release of the radioactive gases inside. The controlled aspect of the release allows protective measures to be taken prior to the release, whereas a catastrophic failure cannot be predicted and protective measures cannot be taken prior to the release.

Attributes that distinguish a boiling water reactor include the following:

- Operating temperatures and pressures are lower.
- Control rods are inserted from the bottom and are operated individually.
- Power is controlled by control rod position and by changing the water flow through the core.
- The turbine is driven by radioactive steam produced in the reactor.
- Water pools condense the steam from reactor line breaks and control primary containment pressure.

---

* There is currently debate within the Nuclear Regulatory Commission about whether to require boiling water reactors to retrofit filters to hardened vent systems, as one of the responses to the Fukushima Daiichi disaster.

- A single system of low pressure pumps and heat exchangers can be used to provide decay heat removal during shut down, cooling to the spent fuel storage pool, and cooling to the suppression pool.
- The single high-pressure emergency core cooling injection system has a steam-driven pump.
- There are three low-pressure emergency core cooling injection systems; one has a single steam-driven pump, one has two electric pumps, and the third has four electric pumps.
- An emergency pressure relief system can reduce primary containment pressure, although this causes an unfiltered radioactive release to the environment.
- Spent fuel storage pools are located above the reactor on the top floor of the reactor building.

PRESSURIZED WATER REACTORS

In a pressurized water reactor (Figure 1.3), the internal pressure is controlled so that water flowing past the fuel rods is superheated but is not allowed to form steam; during normal operations, the coolant always remains in the liquid phase. The superheated water flows through the interior tubes of large vertical heat exchangers called *steam generators*. A steam generator is a large cylindrical vessel with many (inverted) U-shaped tubes inside. Some reactor designs use straight tubes; coolant enters from the top and flows downward, and water exits from the bottom (called *once-through steam generators*). High-pressure, high-temperature primary coolant flows through the tubes, and the tubes are surrounded by water supplied from the condenser by the main feedwater pumps. The cooler feedwater flows past the tubes containing superheated primary coolant, and this secondary water is allowed to boil to steam. This steam is dried in the same way that steam is dried in a boiling water reactor. The only differences between a steam generator and any other heat exchanger found in a plant are its size and that the cooling water in heat exchangers is not allowed to flash to steam.

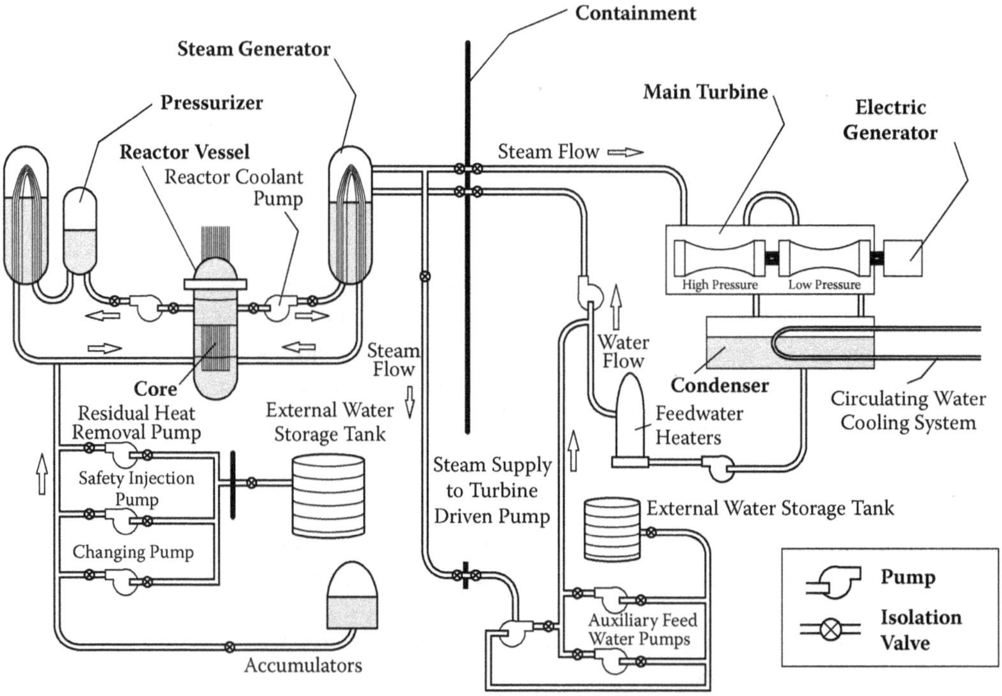

FIGURE 1.3 Diagram of a typical pressurized water reactor.

Depending on the specific reactor design there are between two and four steam generators; each steam generator loop has a *hot leg* carrying the higher temperature water from the reactor to the steam generator and a *cold leg* carrying cooled primary coolant water back to the reactor. A reactor coolant pump provides the flow in each steam generator loop.

A steam generator cannot be completely filled with water, as there has to be room in the vessel for steam to form; this requires that water temperature and pressure in the steam generator vessel be less than reactor coolant temperature and pressure. A typical operating water level is around two-thirds of the U-tube height. If the feedwater going into the shell side of the steam generator is cut off, all of the remaining water will quickly boil off, a situation called *going dry*, leaving the tubes to be cooled by air. The pressure differential between the high-pressure coolant and the air promotes tube breaches. Because air does not conduct heat as efficiently as does water, the tubes heat up, which also promotes tube failures. In addition, if a tube leak occurs under water the radioactive materials in the primary coolant are at least partially scavenged (which does not affect radioactive gases).

The steam cycle is identical to that of a boiling water plant, in that the steam drives a turbine that drives an electric generator, the steam is quenched to water in a condenser, and condenser water is pumped back to the steam generator to form a closed steam cycle. Reactor power is primarily controlled by changing the concentration of neutron-absorbing chemicals, such as boron and lithium. The reactor control rods have relatively little effect on reactor power above lower-power operations (20% power or more). An emergency shutdown is typically accomplished by *emergency boration*, which injects water highly enriched in boron in parallel to inserting all of the control rods. A full shutdown of a pressurized water reactor is generally referred to as a *reactor trip*.

The reactor is housed in a cylindrical building referred to as *containment*; a pressurized water reactor containment is much larger than the typical boiling water reactor drywell. Unlike most boiling water reactors, it is generally possible to enter the containment during at-power operations, although the high radiation (both gamma and neutron) dose rates make entries uncommon.

The water volume in the primary loop is normally a closed loop. Water is removed through the chemical volume and control system to be filtered, collected in the volume control tank, and injected back into the reactor by two normal charging pumps. When the reactor is shut down (i.e., not making steam), heat is removed by the residual heat removal (RHR) system, which runs primary water through shutdown heat exchangers and then injects water back into the primary loop using two residual heat removal pumps. The RHR pumps are low-pressure pumps. High-pressure emergency water injection into the core is provided by two safety injection pumps. There are also water accumulators in containment that inject water into the core in an emergency; the motive force is provided by high-pressure nitrogen.

Although a break in the secondary loop does not directly threaten the integrity of the reactor core, it does take away the ability to remove excess heat from the system. In general, adequate core cooling can be maintained by one steam generator. If the main feedwater cannot be maintained during an emergency, there are three auxiliary feedwater pumps that draw either on a large external water tank or on the *service water* (equipment cooling water) supply system as a source. There are typically two motor-driven auxiliary feedwater pumps and one turbine-driven pump. The turbine-driven pump runs on steam taken from the steam generators; the reactor decay heat is sufficient to continue to make steam for some time after the reactor is shut down.

In normal operation essentially none of the volatile or particulate radioactive species cross from primary coolant to secondary-side steam. The secondary-side steam is not radioactive. Pressurized water reactors also build up noncondensable radioactive gases in the primary coolant, and these are removed through the reactor coolant cleanup system and vented to gas decay tanks. The plant periodically releases radioactive gases after they undergo several days of radioactive decay. At rated power, a typical pressurized water plant typically exhausts between 500 and 800 Ci/s, usually through a rooftop vent.

A pressurized water reactor is designed to isolate systems containing radioactive material from systems containing nonradioactive steam and water. One incident of concern is when coolant tubes in the steam generator develop leaks or entire tubes rupture completely. Radiation monitors on the steam lines coming out of each steam generator are capable of detecting even very small amounts of radioactive material and alerting operators to leaks. Although a reactor can remain within its operating license conditions with a small enough leak, the operator is likely to perform an orderly shutdown of the plant if this were to occur. It is not possible to repair a defective steam generator tube, so the tube would be permanently sealed (*plugged*) before the plant was put back into operation. Larger leaks would constitute an emergency condition and result in a rapid reactor shutdown.

Pressurized water reactors also store their spent fuel in spent fuel cooling pools, which have characteristics similar to those found in boiling water reactors. The size of the pool, amount of water above the stored fuel, fuel capacity, heat loading, fuel pool cooling systems, and other design features are the same. The primary difference between how the two plants store spent fuel lies in the location of the pool. Whereas the storage pool in a boiling water reactor is typically at the top of the reactor building, in most pressurized water reactors the pool is typically situated in a separate building, physically distinct from the reactor containment building and auxiliary systems building. During refueling operations the space above the reactor is flooded to allow rods to be lifted out of the reactor without producing unacceptable radiation doses in nearby spaces. A *fuel transfer canal* or *fuel transfer tube* connects the flooded reactor vessel with the adjacent fuel building, allowing a single fuel assembly to be moved from one building to another. When the assembly is in the fuel building, a refueling bridge and grapple mechanism are used to move it in the pool and set it into the appropriate holding rack.

Attributes that distinguish a pressurized water reactor include the following:

- Operating temperatures and pressures are higher.
- Releases of radioactive materials to the environment are lower.
- Control rods are inserted from the top and typically operate in groups.
- Power is primarily controlled by regulating the concentration of boron (a neutron absorber) in the coolant.
- A pressurizer maintains primary coolant pressure to keep the coolant in the liquid phase.
- Heat is transferred from the radioactive primary coolant system to the nonradioactive secondary coolant system in the steam generators.
- The turbine is driven by nonradioactive steam produced in the steam generators.
- Separate emergency systems provide water to the reactor core and to the steam generators.
- Spent fuel storage pools are generally in their own buildings, not part of the reactor building.

Commercial power reactors are largely operated using detailed written procedures. This involves a hierarchy of normal and surveillance procedures, abnormal operating procedures, emergency operating procedures, emergency plan implementing procedures, and, finally, severe accident (management) guides. As an incident or event departs from normal operating conditions, operators transition to preplanned procedures for bringing the condition under control and, when necessary, shutting down the reactor. Abnormal operating procedures generally address predicted and analyzed conditions caused by unexpected losses of operating plant equipment and are designed to protect plant equipment; some abnormal conditions are also entry conditions for the formal declaration of an emergency. Emergency operating procedures are generally designed to protect the reactor core, water injection systems, and containment structure from failure, containing any radioactive materials from breached plant systems within plant buildings. Severe accident (management) guides assume damage to the reactor core and are designed to protect the containment structure from failure, in addition to preventing or limiting the release of radioactive material into the environment.

FISSION PRODUCT BARRIERS

Radioactive materials are isolated from the public by protective barriers designed into the reactor and its supporting systems. The three primary fission product barriers are (1) the integrity of the metal fuel rods containing reactor fuel and associated fission products, (2) the integrity of the closed-loop reactor coolant systems that keep the fuel rods surrounded by water at all times, and (3) the integrity of the thick containment building that surrounds the reactor pressure vessel and most radioactive water systems. Sometimes the integrity of the individual ceramic uranium fuel pellets inside fuel rods is included as a fourth barrier. The public cannot be exposed to radioactive materials unless all three fission product barriers are simultaneously breached in some way.

Two fission product barriers are associated with water level in the core. A boiling water reactor is operated with almost 16 feet of water above the fuel, and a pressurized water reactor is operated with the entire pressure vessel filled with liquid water. When an operating boiling water reactor core is starved of water to replace steam production or a pressurized water reactor loses water from the primary coolant systems, the vessel water level may be reduced to below the top of active fuel (the heating zone). A combination of air and steam surrounding the core is less efficient at transferring heat than is water, and the excess heat remains in the fuel rods, heating the uranium fuel and the metal rod. This process has positive feedback and increases in rate over time. Eventually the ceramic fuel pellet melts and the metal rod fractures, releasing the radioactive inventory into the core environment.

Containment structures are thick and robust, designed to handle the high-pressure consequences of a large break in coolant systems. For uncontrolled radioactive material to reach the atmosphere, either it must bypass the containment structure or the containment structure must fail. A containment bypass occurs when a line containing radioactive coolant or steam fails to isolate on demand, allowing primary coolant or steam to flow directly to the atmosphere through a pipe break outside the containment structure. A bypass requires at least two valves (and often more) in a single pipe line to simultaneously fail in the open position (most valves are designed to fail closed). Every steam, liquid, and pneumatic line passing through the containment structure wall has an inboard (inside containment) and outboard (outside of containment) isolation valve, and the valves are operated from different power and control circuits to reduce the likelihood of a failure to isolate.

Containment structures are designed to hold the steam from a large break in piping attached to the reactor vessel. The possible failure paths include leakage from seals around personnel and equipment hatches and around electrical and sensor lines passing through the containment wall. In the very unlikely condition where an accident causes the containment pressure to exceed design pressure, emergency operating procedures direct purging or venting of containment to control pressure. The actual estimated breaking pressure of containment is twice to three times the design pressure.

GENERAL EMERGENCY PREPAREDNESS HISTORY

From before the founding of the American republic until roughly the middle of the last century, the story of public emergency preparedness efforts was the story of local emergency preparedness, involving the establishment of local police, fire, and ambulance services and (later) public hospitals. The federal government had neither a policy nor a funding interest in emergency preparedness, and the involvement of the states was generally very limited. The only federal efforts of note in this area were the establishment of coastal lighthouses and the Coast Guard's role in maritime rescue, both of which date from the earliest years of the republic. Nongovernmental organizations became heavily involved in public safety toward the end of the 19th century and in the early years of the 20th century as evidenced by the emerging roles of the American Red Cross, Salvation Army, and similar charitable organizations in disaster response and post-disaster congregate care; the American Red Cross' role in developing and promoting first-aid training for the public; and the involvement of the American Red Cross and Young Men's Christian Association (YMCA) in developing and teaching water safety.

As the public's perception of the role of government during emergencies evolved, a more proactive approach was demanded. The federal government first addressed hazard-specific controls and disaster recovery, rather than an active emergency response. This led to legislation such as the following:

- Flood Control Act of 1934, giving the U.S. Army Corps of Engineers authority over flood control projects
- Disaster Relief Act of 1950
- National Flood Insurance Act of 1968
- National Environmental Policy Act of 1969
- Disaster Relief Act of 1970, following Hurricane Camille
- Flood Disaster Protection Act of 1973
- Disaster Relief Act of 1974 (Public Law 93-288)
- Stafford Disaster Relief and Emergency Assistance Act of 1988 (Public Law 100-707)

The Disaster Relief Act of 1974 established the current system of presidential declarations for emergencies and disasters. The Stafford Act (1988) declaration of policy stated the following:

> The purpose of this subchapter is to provide a system of emergency preparedness for the protection of life and property in the United States from hazards and to vest responsibility for emergency preparedness jointly in the Federal Government and the States and their political subdivisions. The Congress recognizes that the organizational structure established jointly by the Federal Government and the States and their political subdivisions for emergency preparedness purposes can be effectively utilized to provide relief and assistance to people in areas of the United States struck by a hazard. The Federal Government shall provide necessary direction, coordination, and guidance, and shall provide necessary assistance, as authorized in this subchapter so that a comprehensive emergency preparedness system exists for all hazards.

Federal efforts to provide for active emergency preparedness and planning were slower to emerge than provisions for post-disaster recovery. The initial efforts were largely driven by the perceived need for the population to recover from a large-scale conventional or nuclear weapon attack, whereas later efforts were part of the initial establishment of federal environmental protection schemes, including the creation of resources to respond to accidental large-scale chemical releases. More recently federal emergency preparedness has become more focused on responding to small-scale (community-level) attacks such as could be mounted by nongovernmental extremist groups. Significant federal actions have included the following:

- Creation of the Office of Civilian Defense (1941), whose mission mainly included preparing the populace for possible invasion and for spotting enemy aircraft and submarines
- Creation of the Federal Civil Defense Administration (1950), whose mission was to prepare the populace for attack by nuclear weapons, including protection from radioactive fallout from nuclear weapons used elsewhere in the world, and which was intended to be done primarily through a combination of massive survival material stockpiles, large-scale urban evacuations, and a series of fortified buildings (bomb shelters) scattered around the country
- Creation of the Federal Disaster Assistance Administration under the Department of Housing and Urban Development (1960), whose mission was to provide financial assistance and loans to populations affected by major disasters
- Creation of the National Response Team (1968), providing for a combined federal response to oil discharges and releases of hazardous substances[*]

---

[*] Chemical emergency response as a separate specialization largely arose in the 1970s and 1980s with creation of the first "hazardous materials" teams. The first requirements to consider the effects of chemicals (among other hazards) in federal projects were contained in the National Environmental Policy Act (NEPA) enacted in 1969. The first legal requirements regarding chemical emergency planning were contained in the Comprehensive Environmental Response, Compensation, and Liability Act (CERCLA) enacted in 1980.

- Creation of the National Oil and Hazardous Substance System (1970), whose mission was oriented toward identifying pipelines, terminals, and petrochemical storage facilities and planning for, and responding to, large-scale oil spills
- Creation of the Environmental Protection Agency (1970), among whose missions was to establish federal standards for occupational and accidental radiation exposure
- Creation of the Federal Emergency Management Agency (FEMA) (1970), whose mission was to provide training in emergency management to all levels of government and to coordinate the use of federal assets when large-scale emergency response was required; at first, FEMA was solely focused on the response to natural disasters, with the Departments of Defense and Energy responsible for responding to other kinds of events
- Creation of the National Response Center (1974), whose mission was to act as a clearinghouse for information about hazardous material shipments and to act as a limited source of technical information to local first responders during hazardous material incidents
- Creation of the Federal Preparedness Agency under the General Services Administration (1976), taking over the functions of the former Office of Emergency Preparedness[*]
- The Comprehensive Emergency Response, Compensation, and Liability Act (1980),[†] which provided federal authority to respond to the threatened or actual release of hazardous chemicals that could endanger the public or the environment; the Act also established legal requirements to remove hazardous materials when facilities are closed and to identify abandoned hazardous sites, as well as funded remediation of abandoned sites
- Federal Radiological Preparedness Coordination Committee and Regional Assistance Committees (1982)[‡]
- The Superfund Amendments and Reauthorization Act (SARA), Title 3 (1986), which introduced the concept of "reportable quantity" of hazardous material, required annual public reports of hazardous materials by industry and plant, specified training requirements for hazardous material responders, required local hazardous material emergency response plans, and required establishment of state and local hazardous material planning committees[§]
- Creation of the Department of Homeland Security (2003), among whose missions are to identify, evaluate, and provide capabilities for the nation as a whole to respond to a variety of natural, manmade, or external threats[¶]

Historical plans for the use of federal government assets to support state and local response to emergencies have included the following:

- National Oil and Hazardous Substances Pollution Contingency Plan (1969)
- Radiological Incident Emergency Planning, Fixed Facilities and Transportation: Interagency Responsibilities (GSA, 1975)
- Federal Response Plan for Peacetime Nuclear Emergencies (Interim Guidance) (GSA, 1977)
- Radiological Contingency Plan (Carter, 1980)
- Revised Federal Radiological Emergency Response Plan (1986), which introduced the concept of lead (or principal) federal agency
- Radiological Emergency Preparedness Planning (Reagan, 1988b)

---

[*] By Executive Order 11921, June 11, 1976; for more information, also see Executive Orders 10242, 10952, 11051, and 11795.
[†] CERCLA is also commonly called the "Superfund Act."
[‡] Also see 44 CFR 351.10 and 351.11.
[§] SARA Title 3 is also referred to as the Emergency Planning and Community Right-to-Know Act of 1986. The materials subject to reporting include extremely hazardous substances (Sections 301–304), hazardous substances (Section 304), chemicals defined as hazardous by the Occupational Safety and Health Administration (Sections 311–312), and generally toxic chemicals (Section 313, including radioactive materials).
[¶] Created by H.R. 5005, The Homeland Security Act of 2002. Also see Executive Order 13284.

- Federal Response Plan for Natural Hazards (1990)
- Federal Response Plan (1992, revised following Hurricane Andrew)
- Revised Federal Radiological Emergency Response Plan (1996)
- Critical Infrastructure Protection (Clinton, 1996)
- Management of Domestic Incidents, Homeland Security Presidential Directive 5, required development of the National Incident Management System (USDHS, 2003a)
- Critical Infrastructure Identification, Prioritization, and Protection (USDHS, 2003b)
- National Preparedness (USDHS, 2003c)
- National Response Plan (effective 2005), as required by the Homeland Security Act of 2002, which introduced the "incident of national significance" concept (USDHS, 2004)
- National Response Framework (2008; currently under revision), which introduced concepts such as emergency support functions and core capabilities (USDHS, 2008a)

As the federal government became more involved in emergency planning and response, the need developed for single points of contact at the state level to assist in coordinating emergency plans, impose standards and procedures, provide training to local jurisdictions, obtain and maintain specialized equipment, administer grants, and provide status reports to federal officials. Consequently, states organized formal emergency management agencies generally beginning in the 1950s (for example, the Texas state emergency management agency was organized in 1951), and essentially all states had organized emergency response agencies by the late 1960s.

EVOLUTION OF RADIOLOGICAL EMERGENCY PREPAREDNESS

Section 161, General Provisions, of the Atomic Energy Act of 1954 states the following:

> In the performance of its functions the Commission is authorized to ... (p) make, promulgate, issue, rescind, and amend such rules and regulations as may be necessary to carry out the purposes of this Act,

which gave the Commission (originally the Atomic Energy Commission, later the Nuclear Regulatory Commission as a result of the Energy Reorganization Act of 1974) the authority to prescribe conditions and rules for licensing and operating commercial nuclear power plants and other uses of radioactive byproduct material; the regulation of natural radioactive materials (such as radium or thorium) and regulation of radiation-producing machines was reserved to the states. The only specific mention of radiological emergency preparedness in the Atomic Energy Act of 1954 is Section 103.f, which stated:

> Each license issued for a utilization facility under this section or section 104.b shall require as a condition thereof that in case of any accident which could result in an unplanned release of quantities of fission products in excess of allowable limits for normal operation established by the Commission, the licensee shall immediately so notify the Commission.

The Atomic Energy and Nuclear Regulatory Commissions promulgate regulations through the Code of Federal Regulations (CFR). Title 10, "Energy," Parts 0 through 199, are assigned to the Commission. Of particular note regarding emergency planning are Parts 50 and 100; Part 50 pertains to operating reactors and Part 100 contains the requirements for reactor siting under which most operating reactors were licensed. The Commission issues a license to each company operating a nuclear power reactor for each individual reactor that meets all of the requirements of 10 CFR and may include additional license conditions to address site-specific issues raised during the licensing process. Part 100 introduced the concepts of "low population zone," "exclusion area," and "maximum credible accident" and placed restrictions on the minimum distance from the reactor to the nearest offsite population centers. A *low population zone* is defined as the area in which the total number and density of residents provide reasonable probability of taking appropriate (offsite) protective measures in the event of a serious accident. A *population center* is defined as 25,000 or more residents. For design evaluation purposes, the outer boundary of a low population zone was limited to an individual exposure of 25 rem whole body dose or a thyroid organ dose of 300 rem over the first 2 hours of a release from a maximally credible accident. Additional guidance on complying with the radiological components of the reactor siting criteria was provided in Technical Information Document 14844 (DiNunno et al., 1962).

CONTENTS OF EMERGENCY PLANS

During its first 15 years, the Commission required as a license condition that power reactor license operators have a site-specific emergency plan but had no other generic emergency preparedness requirements, and the Commission did not place much emphasis on reviewing or inspecting licensee emergency plans. The first significant step in establishing additional licensee emergency preparedness was Appendix E to Part 50 of Title 10 of the Code of Federal Regulations (abbreviated as 10 CFR 50, Appendix E, or just Appendix E), which took effect in December 1970, providing minimum standards for the contents of the emergency plans submitted by license applicants and in use by reactor licensees. These emergency plan requirements included provisions for a cooperative interface between reactor licensees and supporting offsite agencies and officials, because in 1970 the Atomic Energy Commission had regulatory responsibility for all offsite activities supporting the onsite emergency plan.

Appendix E originally consisted of four sections, addressing requirements for the preliminary safety analysis report, the final safety analysis report, and the required contents of emergency plans. The required content of an emergency plan includes descriptions of the licensee's (1) emergency organization, including delineation of authorities; (2) means to assess the condition of the reactor, including emergency action levels; (3) means for assembling the organization when needed; (4) means to notify offsite authorities regarding the emergency, including the need to take preplanned protective actions; (5) routine distribution of emergency planning information to the potentially affected population; (6) emergency facilities and equipment, including provisions for medical support; (7) program to train its emergency organization, including provisions for drills and exercises; (8) program to maintain a current and effective emergency plan; and (9) means to recover from an accident. Appendix E was later amended to require that licensees submit detailed emergency plans and implementing procedures to the Nuclear Regulatory Agency.[*] In 1991, it was amended to require that licensees provide real-time computer data for selected parameters important to assessing the reactor status and to supporting dose assessment (Emergency Response Data System, or ERDS).[†] The data system was required to be operational at each commercial nuclear power plant by February 1993.

In conjunction with 10 CFR 50, Appendix E, the Commission published *Guides to the Preparation of Emergency Plans for Production and Utilization Facilities* (USAEC, 1970), providing instructions to licensees about implementation of Appendix E. Four years later this was followed by the *Guide and Check List for the Development and Evaluation of State and Local Government Radiological Emergency Response Plans in Support of Fixed Nuclear Facilities* (NRC, 1974), which provided the first guidance on the structure, content, and evaluation of the offsite emergency plans necessary to provide medical, fire, and law enforcement assistance to power plants and to implement protective actions for members of the public. This document was superseded in 1978 by the *Planning Basis for the Development of State and Local Government Emergency Response Plans in Support of Light Water Nuclear Power Plants* (NRC, 1978a), which was the product of a joint Nuclear Regulatory Commission and Environmental Protection Agency task force, primarily in

---

[*] 45 FR 55402, effective November 3, 1980. The submission of plans and procedures was required by January 2, 1981. Also see NRC (1980d).

[†] Also see NRC (1989b) and NRC (1991a).

response to a 1976 petition from the Conference of Radiation Control Program Directors (CRCPD).[*] The CRCPD had petitioned the Nuclear Regulatory Commission to make a determination of the most severe accident basis for which radiological emergency response plans should be developed by offsite officials, and this document introduced the concept of plume (10 mile) and ingestion (50 mile) emergency planning zones.

The earlier 1970 guidance to licensees regarding the contents of emergency plans was updated in the Regulatory Guide *Emergency Planning for Nuclear Power Plants* (NRC, 1977a). This regulatory guide provided licensees the staff's position regarding how licensees should meet review criteria for the emergency plan section of preliminary (reactor applicant) and final safety (operating reactor) analysis reports. The guide discussed in detail the general structure of plant indications and events suitable for entering an emergency condition, site-specific emergency classification schemes, protective measures for employees and the public, organizational control of emergencies, and the range of supporting information required to be in a licensee's emergency plan. The basic structure of the original Regulatory Guide was later adopted (and considerably expanded) to form NUREG-0654 (NRC, 1980c). Regulatory Guide 1.101 is currently in its 5th revision (NRC, 2005e); revisions 3, 4, and 5 communicated the NRC staff's acceptance of specified emergency action level schemes as acceptable alternatives to the NUREG-0654 emergency action levels.

REACTOR ACCIDENT CONSEQUENCE STUDIES

Efforts to model the consequences of major reactor accidents predate operation of the first commercial power reactors and have been updated periodically since then. These studies have proved to be problematic for the Commission because of the calculation limitations of severe accident modeling at the time and the manner in which anti-nuclear power activists have used their conclusions. In WASH-0740 (USAEC, 1957), the Commission estimated that the "maximum credible accident" would produce up to 3400 deaths, 43,000 radiation injuries, and $7 billion in property damage (in 1957 dollars). This study used extremely unrealistic assumptions about the amount, type, and chemical forms of the released radioactive materials which were generally taken from atomic weapon fallout studies; it also used the worst possible weather conditions and did not assume containment structures or some of their associated safety systems. Furthermore, due to the limitations of then-available computing machines, the environmental transport and population models were very simplistic and unrealistic.

WASH-0740 was updated by WASH-1400 (NRC, 1975b), which was the first systematic application of probabilistic risk assessment and fault-tree analysis to nuclear power plants. Probabilistic risk assessment is a system of applying statistical information about the failure modes of individual components in a system to derive probability estimates of system-level failures. The study also included reactor containment buildings in the assumed reactor design, considered the effects of some containment safety systems (such as containment sprays), used improved environmental transport models, and, because of the increased computing power of computers, used more complete models than the previous study. WASH-1400 analyzed nine accident categories and divided accidents into early-release and late-release scenarios, terminology that largely shaped the emergency preparedness framework that currently exists and formed the technical basis for the methods found in NUREG-0150 (NRC, 2002h), currently in its fifth revision by the Nuclear Regulatory Commission in its response to reactor emergencies.

WASH-1400 was followed by *Calculation of Reactor Accident Consequences* (NRC, 1982b), a study specific to the Indian Point Energy Center, and by NUREG-1150 (Kouts et al., 1990; NRC, 1990c). Licensees had been required in 1988 by Generic Letter 88-20 (NRC, 1988c) to examine their vulnerability to severe core damage accidents using probabilistic risk assessments, and NUREG-1150 used these site-specific risk analyses to refine accident probabilities, using updated environmental

---

[*] The CRCPD is a nonprofit professional organization primarily consisting of senior radiological public health officials from the states and territories.

transport models and considering the effects of offsite protective measures (shelter and evacuation). It estimated the average probability of a fatality due to an early-release accident at a pressurized water reactor as 2.0E-8/reactor-year and at a boiling water reactor as 5.0E-11/reactor-year. The probability of a death due to cancer due to an accident was estimated at 2.0E-9/reactor-year for a pressurized water reactor and 4.0E-10/reactor-year for boiling water reactors. The radioactive inventory and release fraction assumptions used in NUREG-1150 formed the basis for NUREG-1465 (Soffer et al., 1995).

The most current consequence study is *State of the Art Reactor Consequence Analyses* (NRC, 2007f). The code is specific to two selected reactor sites and includes consideration of the effects of specific emergency preparedness activities on population dose. The results were published as NUREG-1935 (NRC, 2012h), with supporting technical information in NUREG/CR-7110 (NRC, 2013f). The overall conclusions were that (1) existing resources and procedures can stop an accident, slow it down, or reduce its impact before it can affect public health; (2) uncontrolled accidents take much longer to happen and release much less radioactive material than earlier analyses suggested; and (3) the analyzed accidents would cause essentially zero immediate deaths and only a very, very small increase in the risk of long-term cancer deaths. Also see NUREG/BR-0359 (NRC, 2012d).

Another study that may be of interest for emergency preparedness is NUREG-2161 (Barto et al., 2014), which provides consequence estimates of a hypothetical spent fuel pool accident occurring at a specific reference plant. The study compares high-density and low-density loading conditions and assesses the benefits of post-9/11 mitigation measures. The study concludes that spent fuel pools are robust structures that are likely to withstand severe earthquakes without leaking, with results that are comparable to past analyses.

THREE MILE ISLAND ACCIDENT AND REGULATORY RESPONSE

The major event largely responsible for the current emergency preparedness regulatory structure was the Three Mile Island accident which began on March 28, 1979 (Figure 1.4). During the accident, a significant portion of the reactor core overheated then melted, leaving a thick bed of slag or rubble in the bottom of the reactor vessel. Radioactive gases collected in the containment structure

FIGURE 1.4   Photograph of the Three Mile Island site.

through an open vent path, and during the accident hydrogen gas produced as the core melted ignited. During the month following the accident, approximately 15 Ci of ^{131}I and 300 Ci of ^{133}Xe were released, and several months later 43,000 Ci of noble gases (primary krypton isotopes) were vented to the atmosphere. Several post-accident studies concluded that the average radiation exposure to members of the public living near the reactor due to the accident was approximately 1 mrem.

Although no mandatory offsite protective actions were implemented during the accident, the governor of Pennsylvania did issue an advisory suggesting that pregnant women and children voluntarily leave a 5-mile-radius area around the reactor site. With a large population living in the vicinity of the reactor, not only did large numbers of women and children evacuate but also many others, creating concerns about "shadow evacuations" (defined as a voluntary self-evacuation from areas not recommended for protective action), which continue to the present. For additional information regarding the accident and response, the reader may refer to several available references (e.g., NRC, 1979k; Presidential Commission, 1979; Rogovin and Frampton, 1980; Walker, 2004). More than 13 health effect studies have been conducted among the population living around the Three Mile Island reactor (e.g., Hatch, 1991; Howe, 1991; Jablon et al., 1991; NCI, 1990; PDH, 1985; Tokuhata, 1981).

Executive Order 12130 (Carter, 1979b) established the President's Commission on the Accident at Three Mile Island, which also became known as the Kemeny Commission, after its chairman. The Commission's report was due to President Carter 6 months from its first meeting, and was delivered October 30, 1979. The report addressed public health affects, assessed emergency response activities, examined the role of the utility and its suppliers, assessed the training of plant operators, assessed the role of the Nuclear Regulatory Commission and the regulatory and oversight environment, and addressed the distribution of information to the public during the accident. The report made findings and recommendations concerning each area it examined. With regard to emergency preparedness, the recommendations included (1) a state emergency plan approved by the Federal Emergency Management Agency as a prior condition to siting a reactor; (2) the Federal Emergency Management Agency having primary responsibility for federal radiological planning; (3) predetermined scenario-based protective action schemes (such that each general accident type was a scenario; for example, a steam generator tube rupture coincident with gap-level core damage); (4) Protective Action Guides reduced from the current (1979) values; (5) expanded medical research into radioprotective drugs for issuance to the general population; (6) expanded public education efforts regarding reactor design and operation and the health effects of radiation; (7) evaluation of relative risks of early mass public evacuation from areas close to the site; (8) improved integration of federal technical support and assets for radiological monitoring; and (9) a streamlined and centralized process for communicating information and protective action decisions to the public. Another recommendation was abolishment of the five-member Commission heading the Nuclear Regulatory Commission, in favor of a single administrator. Although the accident resulted in many changes to reactor design, procedures, training, and operation, it also caused a major reassessment of the effectiveness of the emergency preparedness planning efforts of licensees and offsite authorities. Most of the current regulatory basis documents in emergency planning are direct consequences of this reassessment. Coincidently, a GAO report, *Areas Around Nuclear Facilities Should Be Better Prepared for Radiological Emergencies*, was also issued that year (GAO, 1979).

A complete list of regulatory documents issued after Three Mile Island is far too extensive for a short historical survey, but the major emergency preparedness documents include the following:

- *Criteria for Preparation and Evaluation of Radiological Emergency Response Plans and Preparedness in Support of Nuclear Power Plants*, Revision 1 (NRC, 1980c)
- *Functional Criteria for Emergency Response Facilities* (NRC, 1981f)
- *Clarification of TMI Action Plan Requirements* (NRC, 1980a) and Supplement 1 (NRC, 1983a)
- *Methodology for Evaluation of Emergency Response Facilities* (NRC, 1981i)
- *Guidelines for Preparing Emergency Procedures for Nuclear Power Plants* (1981g)

Among the regulatory consequences of Three Mile Island were abolishment of unique site-specific emergency classifications, mandatory adoption of standardized emergency action levels, mandatory plume and ingestion planning zones, onsite technical support centers and operations support centers, near-site emergency operations centers and unified facilities for dissemination of official information to the media, emergency preparedness planning standards, planning basis document NUREG-0654 (NRC, 1980c), requirements to submit updated emergency plans and implementing procedures to the Nuclear Regulatory Commission, developing evacuation time estimates and continuing to submit changes to these documents as they were made, and the 15-minute requirement to notify offsite authorities of a licensee's emergency classification or protective action recommendation. Revision 0 of NUREG-0654 was issued for interim use and comment in January 1980, and the document was renumbered to Revision 1 when it was issued in final form in November 1980. NUREG-0654 was initially incorporated by reference into federal regulation by both the Nuclear Regulatory Commission (for reactor licensees) and FEMA (for offsite jurisdictions in the plume phase emergency planning zone). The Nuclear Regulatory Commission removed NUREG-0654 from regulation in 1983 while retaining it as the basis for reactor licensing decisions concerning emergency preparedness, but FEMA and its successor agency, the Department of Homeland Security, have not done so for offsite authorities.

Prior to the Three Mile Island accident, licensees were required to submit emergency plans and implementing procedures as part of initial plant licensing, but they were not required to notify the Nuclear Regulatory Commission as those plans and procedures changed. Likewise, the Commission did not review or approve (or even require) formal emergency plans by offsite authorities. Following the Kemeny Commission report, the Commission made emergency planning standards (10 CFR 50.47(b)) part of regulation and required that licensees submit emergency plans meeting the standards for agency review and approval. The Commission intended to do the same for offsite plans. Generic Letter 79-063 (NRC, 1979n) stated:

> In addition, applicants are required to make certain emergency preparedness arrangements with State and local organizations to cope with plant-related emergencies outside the site boundary. In this regard, the NRC, in conjunction with several other federal agencies, has attempted, on a cooperative and voluntary basis, to provide for training and instruction of State and local government personnel and to establish criteria to guide the preparation of emergency plans. However, in the past, NRC concurrence in State and local emergency plans has not been required as a condition of nuclear power plant operation. We now are requiring, pending the results of a proposed rule change, that NRC concurrence in State and local emergency response plans be obtained as a condition for issuing an operating license.

CREATION OF THE FEDERAL EMERGENCY MANAGEMENT AGENCY

Before the Commission could implement review and approval of offsite emergency plans, the authority for offsite radiological planning was transferred to the Federal Emergency Management Agency. FEMA became an independent federal agency on April 1, 1979,[*] created to combine the many emergency preparedness, disaster planning, disaster response, and post-disaster management and recovery functions of numerous federal agencies. A primary impetus to create FEMA was the National Governors Association, which wanted to reduce the number of federal agencies that states had to deal with in the area of disaster response at a time when the federal government was making its initial large-scale efforts in this area. Executive Order 12148 (Carter, 1979c) formally transferred the emergency management and response functions of numerous agencies to FEMA. Originally, FEMA was not intended to have oversight of offsite emergency preparedness for nuclear power plants, but after the reports of several post-Three Mile Island commissions and review groups, including the Kemeny Commission, the President transferred offsite emergency preparedness oversight to FEMA on December 7, 1979. The division of emergency preparedness

---

[*] See Executive Order 12127 (Carter, 1979a).

oversight responsibilities between the Nuclear Regulatory Commission and FEMA is governed by the Memoranda of Understanding that was dated November 1, 1980 (FEMA/NRC, 1980), revised April 9, 1985 (FEMA/NRC, 1985), revised June 17, 1993 (FEMA/NRC, 1993), and again revised in 2000.

One curious and very unusual aspect of the transfer of responsibility for oversight of offsite radiological emergency planning to FEMA was that it was communicated in a statement by President Carter released by the Office of the White House Press Secretary on December 7, 1979; however, President Carter did not issue a formal Executive Order or Presidential Directive concerning the transfer of responsibilities between federal agencies, and no *Federal Register* notice was made. None of the usual processes for directing federal action apparently were followed in this instance, and primary documentary evidence does not exist. Although the division of regulatory responsibility is universally understood and has since been codified in Memoranda of Agreement between the Nuclear Regulatory Commission and FEMA (currently, the Department of Homeland Security), no legal document apparently exists directing this division. The Commission, also departing from its normal regulatory practices in the 1979 to 1980 time frame, did not issue generic communications to licensees concerning the change in regulatory authority for offsite emergency preparedness. Generic Letters issued by the Nuclear Regulatory Commission in November 1979 required licensees to take certain actions regarding offsite emergency preparedness, and related Generic Letters issued in March 1980 and thereafter have addressed actions to be taken jointly by the Commission and FEMA. There was no formal or generic communications to licensees to notify them of the transfer of responsibility.

The Federal Emergency Management Agency became part of the Department of Homeland Security in March 2003, essentially as a whole organization retaining its existing structure according to Public Law 107-296 (Homeland Security Act of 2002) and Executive Order 13284 (Amendment of Executive Orders, and Other Actions, in Connection with the Establishment of the Department of Homeland Security) issued in 2003. In 2006, elements of the former Federal Emergency Management Agency, including the (offsite) Radiological Emergency Preparedness program, were moved from FEMA into the Department of Homeland Security, Preparedness Directorate, Office of Infrastructure Protection, Chemical and Nuclear Preparedness and Protection Division. The Post-Katrina Emergency Reform Act, signed October 4, 2006, significantly reorganized FEMA within the Department of Homeland Security, restored some of the elements previously transferred, provided additional authorities, and partially restored its status as an independent agency headed by a director appointed by the President.

EVACUATION TIME ESTIMATE STUDIES

Another requirement stemming from the Kemeny Commission recommendations was to prepare site-specific evacuation time studies for the emergency planning zones immediately surrounding each plant. This requirement was communicated to licensees in Generic Letter 79-067 (NRC, 1979e), and completed studies were required to be submitted by August 1, 1980 (NRC, 1980j). At that time, the evacuation time estimates (ETEs) were intended for use primarily by offsite officials in making protective action decisions for the public. After a licensee recommended areas where action was needed (i.e., having doses above predetermined Protective Action Guides), offsite authorities were to evacuate those areas where the evacuation could be largely completed before plume arrival, as determined by evacuation time estimate study, and to shelter-in-place all other locations. The prevailing protective action decision philosophy at the time was not to take action without confirmation of a radiological release detectable offsite. In the early to mid-1980s, evacuation time studies were commonly used as the basis for protective action decisions; however, over time evacuation time estimates became less useful as an integral part of protective action decision making, and by the mid- to late 1990s essentially none of the offsite jurisdictions continued to use them for their original purpose. The decline in evacuation time study utility for active decision making occurred for several reasons: (1) dose assessment models had improved, (2) licensees and offsite authorities shifted from sector-bearing protective action schemes to geographical subzone protective action schemes, and (3) the studies were not being maintained current with changes to populations and road networks.

Another major factor in the decline in using evacuation time studies to make protective action decisions was a significant change in protective action philosophy toward a concept of early evacuation based on plant conditions, primarily relying on the core damage state, without requiring a release to occur and without requiring detection of a plume in the environment. This change de-emphasized shelter as a protective action option, as research indicated that for some accident scenarios the public was better protected by evacuating, even through a radioactive plume, than by sheltering in their homes. Because shelter was viewed as generally less protective than evacuation and emergency plans required evacuation earlier in the accident sequence than previously, the length of time to complete evacuation became less of an issue, thus lessening the immediate value of the evacuation time study. Although this philosophical change occurred slowly over several years, aspects were expressed in documents such as Information Notice 83-28 (NRC, 1983b), Information Notice 92-08 (NRC, 1992h), NUREG/BR-0150 (NRC, 2002h), and NUREG-0654, Revision 1, Supplement 3 (NRC, 1996b). NUREG-0654 Supplement 3 was widely viewed by both licensees and offsite authorities as the Commission repudiating the concept of shelter as an effective protective action. Although the official regulatory position of the Commission never changed and guidance documents always included at least a brief mention of shelter as a protective action, by the early to mid-1990s Commission staff were consistently informally communicating a view that shelter was not an important part of a licensee's protective action scheme. Predictably, licensees reacted by removing requirements to evaluate shelter as a protective option from their protective action procedures, did not practice shelter evaluations in drills and exercises, and rarely trained staff about it. Licensees, in particular, came to see shelter as an offsite authority decision driven exclusively by extraordinary external safety concerns (blizzards or earthquakes) and not as a protective strategy for radiological releases. This perception caused some licensees to remove shelter as a practical protective action option and directly led to the Commission's Regulatory Issue Summary 04-13 (NRC, 2004a), in which the Commission staff returned to a view that shelter could be an effective protective action and licensees were required to evaluate it.

Commission regulations required evacuation time studies as part of the licensing basis of all new reactors going into commercial service in 1981 and thereafter, and required all existing licensees submit current time studies to the Commission. However, although the Commission reviewed the initial evacuation studies, no evaluation standards were implemented, and the studies did not receive regulatory approval; furthermore, regulation did not require the studies be updated with the federal census cycles. The Commission staff established an informal expectation that licensees should update their evacuation time study following a 10% change in the baseline population and tried to influence licensees to update their studies following the 1990 and 2000 census, with limited success. Licensees and offsite authorities were provided guidance for preparing evacuation time studies in USEPA (1978), Perry (1980), Urbanik et al. (1980, 1992), and FEMA (1993). Previous guidance was updated in NUREG/CR-6863 (Dotson and Jones, 2005a).

One current area of controversy is whether the Department of Homeland Security (FEMA) and/or the Commission should prescribe the models used to perform evacuation time estimate studies and establish performance criteria for evacuation estimates, such that reactors would not be permitted to be sited in areas not capable of being fully evacuated in a predetermined number of hours (and any existing reactors in such locations would be required to cease operation). Another issue is *population creep*, in which what was a low population density area when the reactor was constructed no longer has a low population density, essentially because of the services and benefits offered by local government due to the tax revenues from the reactor licensee. In some areas where reactor sites are not far from major metropolitan areas, the expansion of suburbs into previously rural areas has also increased the population of the emergency planning zone while not expanding the local road network at the same pace.

The Commission has attempted to make evacuation time estimates relevant again to the protective action decision-making process in changes to Appendix E to 10 CFR Part 50 that were implemented in November 2011, with various effective dates to December 2014. These changes

- Required updates to every evacuation time estimate study following each decennial census. Previous to this change, no updates were required, although some licensees had updated their reports.
- Required that evacuation times be considered in the required reevaluation of protective action strategies in conjunction with the revision to NUREG-0654 that was issued in 2011 (NRC, 2011c).
- Required that each licensee annually estimate changes in the population in the emergency planning zone, and compare those changes against pre-established criteria that would trigger an evacuation time estimate study revision between decennial censuses.

The Commission recognized that evacuation time estimate studies had essentially lost all of the value they once had and is attempting to return the industry to the way they were used in the 1980s.

PLANNING STANDARDS (10 CFR 50.47(b))

Although there is no clear documentation of the basis for the 16 emergency planning standards found in 10 CFR 50.47(b) (45 FR 55409, August 8, 1980), together they are the basic performance elements the Nuclear Regulatory Commission and Federal Emergency Management Agency (the responsibility for offsite emergency preparedness having been moved to FEMA prior to promulgating 10 CFR 50.47(b)) consider necessary for conducting an effective emergency response. These functions include assignment of functions and roles, effective organizational interfaces, standard emergency action level and classification schemes, effective means for licensees to notify and communicate with offsite authorities, distribution of information to potentially affected residents, adequate emergency facilities, adequate means to assess accident consequences and arrive at protective action recommendations and decisions, radiological controls for emergency workers, medical support for contaminated and injured persons, response organization training, periodic proficiency drills, and maintenance of the emergency plans and procedures. The planning standards were developed in parallel with NUREG-0654 and form the primary divisions within the guidance document; standard 50.47(b)(1) is equivalent to NUREG-0654 Planning Standard A, standard 50.47(b)(2) to NUREG-0654 Planning Standard B, etc. 10 CFR 50.54(s)(1) required licensees to submit to the Nuclear Regulatory Commission emergency plans and implementing procedures meeting the planning standards of 10 CFR 50.47(b) and requirements of Part 50 Appendix E for all offsite agencies in the designated emergency planning zone, and 10 CFR 50.54(u) required licensees to submit the licensee emergency plans and implementing procedures meeting the same standards. In both cases, the updated emergency plans and procedures were required to be in effect no later than April 1, 1981. Although NUREG-0654 is being revised, with a projected implementation date sometime in 2017, its underlying reliance on the planning standards has not changed. The revision team did not identify any necessary deletions or additions to the existing planning standards.

RADIATION PROTECTION AND PROTECTIVE ACTION GUIDES

Prior to 1960, the federal government published standards for radiation protection but did not have enforceable rules and regulation. These standards were contained in a series of handbooks published by the National Bureau of Standards* (e.g., NBS, 1959). The Federal Radiation Council was established in 1959 to provide recommendations to the President for federal policy on radiation matters

---

* Currently know as the National Institutes of Standards and Technology (NIST).

affecting health, and the first federal radiation protection requirements for occupational radiation exposure and exposure to members of the public were promulgated in 1960 (FRC, 1960). The duties of the Federal Radiation Council were transferred to the Environmental Protection Agency (EPA) upon its creation in 1970, and the EPA continues to have sole federal authority to set radiation exposure and intake limits, which are primarily implemented by the regulations of the other federal agencies, including the Occupational Health and Safety Administration, the Department of Energy, and the Nuclear Regulatory Commission. The 1960 general radiation protection standards were revised in 1987 (USEPA, 1987).

Although radiation protection guidance for population fallout shelters and for reclaiming land contaminated by the radioactive fallout from a nuclear attack goes back to Defense Department publications of the 1950s, the first guidance for responding to peacetime radiological accidents was that of the Federal Radiation Council (FRC, 1964, 1965). These reports introduced the dose avoidance concept (i.e., the dose expected to be received if no action is taken) and the term *Protective Action Guide* (PAG). The EPA consolidated and updated previous radiological response guidance in the *Manual of Protective Action Guides and Protective Actions for Nuclear Incidents* (USEPA, 1975; also referred to as the *PAG Manual*), which was the first comprehensive document addressing actions to protect both emergency workers and the public. The *PAG Manual*, including its later revisions (USEPA, 1980b, 1992), incorporated Food and Drug Administration recommendations (USFDA, 1982), which were later revised (USFDA, 1998). A draft revision to 400-R-92-001 was published in 2010, and a final "interim for use" version was published in April 2013.

The 1980 *PAG Manual* introduced the concepts of *early phase, intermediate phase*, and *late phase* of an accident. The early phase was up until the reactor was stabilized and any releases had concluded and dissipated. The intermediate phase was from the end of the early phase until all potentially contaminated land had been surveyed and environmental samples collected. The late phase was for any post-accident remedial actions that might be required. The 1980 manual included early phase Protective Action Guides of 1 rem whole body dose and 5 rem infant thyroid dose. The 1992 manual kept those numerical values, although the way dose was calculated had changed with updates to internal dosimetry models, and the thyroid value was changed from the infant to the adult. The 1992 manual also introduced relocation criteria of 2 rem whole body dose in 1 year and 5 rem whole body dose over 50 years. Relocation was intended to protect members of the public in areas that were contaminated but did not meet the initial evacuation criteria or it was discovered after the fact. The 1992 manual also introduced Protective Action Guides for potentially contaminated foods but not for drinking water.

The 2013 interim-for-use manual kept the 1 rem whole body dose guideline for the early phase but removed the 5 rem thyroid criteria. The reasoning was that the thyroid dose contributed to the whole body dose and so the single criteria bounded both. To date, the author is not aware of any states that have dropped the thyroid dose from their protective action schemes. The other significant change in the 2013 version was the inclusion of a protective standard for drinking water.

CHERNOBYL DISASTER AND POTASSIUM IODIDE

A major event in the history of nuclear power, the disaster at Chernobyl, Unit 4, occurred on April 26, 1986. This plant was located in the central part of the Ukraine, at a multi-reactor unit site. This accident released essentially the entire core of a large reactor into the atmosphere in a very high plume. The plume reached the upper atmosphere, allowing the radioactive material to be caught in the jet stream and eventually to be distributed around the world. The winds over the initial several days were toward the northwest, and the accident was not discovered until the radioactive plume reached nuclear power plants in Sweden. The plume was sufficiently radioactive that it caused alarms to go off on installed environmental monitors located outside of the plant. The Chernobyl plume could be compared to the atmospheric nuclear weapons testing of 25 years earlier. A sufficient amount of radioactive material was released to be detected in air and water samples taken in the continental United States for several weeks following the accident.

Very little of the Chernobyl experience applies directly to U.S. reactor designs or emergency planning because of the significant differences in reactor design, most notably a different system of moderation (e.g., charcoal vs. water), a lack of a reactor containment structure, major differences in safety systems, and very different emergency preparedness philosophies. From an emergency preparedness perspective, the major lessons from the Chernobyl accident concern the effectiveness of potassium iodide as a radioprotective agent (including its adverse affects and effects on children), the effectiveness (or weaknesses) of existing radioactive transport models in predicting the distribution of the released radioactive material, and additional information about the entry of deposited radioactive materials into the food chain. On June 25, 1986, the Food and Drug Administration issued a Comprehensive Policy Guide, Section 560.750 (USFDA, 1986). This guidance introduced the concept of derived intervention levels for measuring (bulk) radioactive contamination and largely informed the FDA's later 1998 guidance on radioactive contamination of human foods and animal feeds.

The Food and Drug Administration had concluded in 1978 that potassium iodide (KI) was both safe and effective under some circumstances for blocking the uptake of radioactive iodine by the thyroid. In 1982, the FDA promulgated final recommendations on the use of potassium iodide by the general public, recommending 130 mg/day for those persons (and children above the age of 1) projected to receive at least 25 rem committed dose equivalent (CDE) to the thyroid. Data from the post-Chernobyl use of potassium iodide throughout Europe was used extensively by the FDA in an updated guidance (USFDA, 2001), which prescribed 130 mg potassium iodide per day for persons greater than or equal to 40 years projected to receive greater than or equal to 400 rem CDE to the thyroid at greater than or equal to 10 rem CDE for persons between ages 19 and 40 and at greater than or equal to 5 rem CDE for persons 18 years and younger. Children should receive between 16 mg and 65 mg potassium iodide per day depending on age and body weight. The next year, FEMA revised the federal policy on the use of potassium iodide (FEMA, 2002a) based on the new FDA guidance. Although potassium iodide is taken orally and is generally available in pill form, in 2005 the FDA approved an oral solution of 65 mg/mL concentration to give to children.

The Nuclear Regulatory Commission changed 10 CFR 50.47(b)(10) in 2001 to require that issuing potassium iodide be considered as an offsite protective actions for the public (NRC, 2001a). The Commission made stocks of potassium iodide available at no charge to those states and tribes who elected to distribute potassium iodide to the populations within a nuclear power plant plume phase (10 mile) emergency planning zone as a protective measure. Thirty-four states have populations within an emergency planning zone; as of January 2007, 21 states had requested or received potassium from the Commission. In 2005, the Commission also made the pediatric potassium iodide solution available to participating states and tribes as part of the distribution program. The specifics of distributing potassium iodide to the public were left to the local jurisdictions, with some electing to pre-distribute to individual households, while others maintain local stockpiles for distribution at evacuation shelters.* The public distribution of potassium iodide remains a controversial issue today, as Section 127 of the Public Health, Security and Bioterrorism Preparedness and Response Act of 2002 requires states and tribes within 20 miles of a nuclear power plant to stockpile potassium iodide for distribution to the public during an accident.

EMERGENCY PLAN EXERCISES

Per 10 CFR 50, Appendix E, IV.F(2), the Nuclear Regulatory Commission requires reactor licensees to periodically conduct exercises that

---

* Details about the Commission's potassium iodide distribution program can be found in SECY-97-124, *Proposed Federal Policy Regarding Use of Potassium Iodide After a Severe Accident at a Nuclear Power Plant*; SECY-97-245, *Staff Options for Resolving a Petition for Rulemaking (PRM-50-63) Relating to a Re-Evaluation of the Policy Regarding Use of Potassium Iodide (KI) After a Severe Accident at a Nuclear Power Plant*; SECY-00-0037, *Status of Potassium Iodide Activities*; SECY-01-0069, *Status of Potassium Iodide Activities*; and SECY-01-0208, *Status of Potassium Iodide Activities*; as well as other Commission documents.

… shall test the adequacy of timing and content of implementing procedures and methods, test emergency equipment and communications networks, test the public notification system, and ensure that emergency organization personnel are familiar with their duties.

Exercises are scripted simulations of degraded plant conditions sufficient to require the activation of all emergency response facilities. They require the active participation of those offsite agencies in the plume phase emergency planning zone having a role in the licensee's emergency plan. Department of Homeland Security (FEMA) evaluation requirements state that, "All exercises must simulate an emergency that results in offsite radiological releases that would require response by offsite authorities." Reactor licensees had been conducting emergency plan exercises prior to 1979 but according to site-specific schedules, without the required participation of offsite agencies and without formal (independent) evaluation of licensee and offsite agency performance.

After the publication of NUREG-0654, licensees and offsite jurisdictions began conducting routine annual joint offsite emergency preparedness exercises. Beginning in 1982 and 1983 these exercises were evaluated jointly by the NRC and FEMA. The NRC amended its regulations in 1988 (implemented in 1989) to reduce the evaluation frequency for reactor licensees and offsite agencies to biennial while continuing to require that reactor licensees conduct at least an annual large-scale integrated drill (offsite agencies being encouraged, but not required, to participate "off-year"). From the early days of the exercise program, reactor licensees were unhappy with requirements that exercises result in severe core damage and significant offsite releases because such scenarios (1) were unrealistic in the degree of damage necessary to plant systems, (2) did not allow plant systems to operate as designed, (3) were difficult to model and control, (4) never rewarded participants for innovative thinking or good performance, and (5) resulted in the "negative training" of participants. An important justification for reducing exercise evaluation to every other year was to address licensee concerns regarding exercise scenarios. The "off year" scenarios were required to practice "management and coordination of emergency response, accident assessment, protective action decision making, and plant system repair and corrective actions" (10 CFR 50 Appendix E, IV.F(2)(b)) but did not have to reach the General Emergency classification or simulate a radiological release, and they could allow operating staff to resolve problems (have success paths) rather than have controllers intervene.

With the development of practical commercial computers, during the 1970s some reactor licensees installed control room simulators that exactly mimicked the layout and controls of their reactor control room. When the controls of the simulated control room were manipulated, the underlying computer models produced a response similar to that of the actual plant, allowing reactor operators to be trained on abnormal and emergency situations not encountered during routine plant operations. NUREG-0737 (NRC, 1980a) required reactor licensees to begin licensed operator testing in a control room simulator by October 1981 (for a reactor built after 1981, before loading fuel). In the early 1980s, the control room operations part of an emergency plan exercise was typically done in the working control room using scripted messages and individual controllers for each reactor operator. This method of drill control did not permit actual operation of plant controls. Plant reference simulators are designed and required only for use in operator training; the Commission has never required (and does not currently require) the use of simulators to conduct exercises, and it does not require that simulators model conditions beyond those of design basis accidents. However, reactor licensees have found simulators to be better venues for conducting emergency plan exercises than the working control room, minimizing distractions in the working control room while allowing a better evaluation of the control room crew. By approximately 1990, essentially all reactor licensees were conducting their emergency plan exercises using their plant reference simulator. With the NRC's introduction of the Emergency Response Data System in 1989–1990 to support its emergency response operations, licensees began creating links from their simulators to the NRC Emergency Response Data System (ERDS) and using them in emergency plan exercises.

The FEMA evaluations were initially conducted according to the Procedural Policy on Radiological Emergency Preparedness, Plan Reviews, Exercise Observations and Evaluation, and Interim Findings,[*] which defined *areas recommended for improvement*, *areas requiring corrective action*, and *deficiencies*. By the 2000s, the evaluation categories consisted of *areas requiring corrective action*, *deficiencies*, and the added *planning issues*. Deficiencies indicated planning issues or performance that called into question the presumption of reasonable assurance that appropriate measures could be taken to protect the health and safety of the public, and required re-demonstration through a remedial exercise. An area requiring corrective action was required to be demonstrated or corrected prior to or at the next biennial exercise. A planning issue was a problem with an emergency plan or implementing procedure that did not call reasonable assurance into question but did have to be corrected in a reasonable period of time. In June 2015, FEMA replaced the term *deficiency* with *Category 1 finding* and the term *area requiring corrective action* with *Category 2 finding*, without changing the definitions.

Appendix 2 of the August 5, 1983, memorandum listed 35 offsite demonstration objectives and set in place the basic FEMA evaluation scheme used until 2002. The evaluation objectives were modified slightly and updated in Guidance Memorandum EX-3 (FEMA, 1988), which divided the objectives into three categories:

1. Category A. Core objectives that are scenario independent (1 to 15)
2. Category B. Scenario-dependent objectives (16 to 25)
3. Category C. Other objectives to be demonstrated at least once every 6 years (26 to 36)

Examples of Category A objectives include direction and control, communications, plume dose projection, and alert, notification, and emergency information. Category B examples include implementation of protective actions, relocation centers, and decontamination centers. Category C examples include recovery, reentry, and relocation; evacuation of onsite personnel; and unannounced and off-hours exercises. Guidance Memoranda EX-1, EX-2, and EX-3 were superseded by FEMA REP-14 and REP-15 (FEMA, 1991b,c). REP-15 retained 34 objectives and three categories—13 demonstrated every exercise by every organization, 9 demonstrated every exercise by some but not all organizations, and 11 demonstrated by every applicable organization within a 6-year evaluation cycle (now 8-year cycle).

After more than 17 years using essentially the same evaluation scheme, offsite agencies were discontented with FEMA and had the perception that the evaluation scheme was rigid, prescriptive, often applied harshly by evaluators with insufficient experience and expertise, and not sufficiently accounting for site-specific differences. This perception, in conjunction with the appointment of James L. Witt[†] as director of FEMA and the Clinton–Gore "Reinventing Government" initiative, led to a significant revision of the exercise evaluation scheme (FEMA, 2002b). The 2002 evaluation scheme replaced the 34 objectives with 6 exercise evaluation areas, each one with between 3 and 9 sub-criteria, for a total of 32 evaluation elements. One essential feature of the revised evaluation scheme was replacement of the specific evaluation checklists, which had often been treated as "all or nothing" by exercise evaluators, with broader, narrative-style evaluations that relied to a greater degree on the evaluator's experience, training, and judgment regarding the significance of performance problems.

One area of exercise evaluation that has changed is the requiring of off-hours drills and exercises. NUREG-0654 Planning Standard N, Exercises and Drills, N(1)(b), states in part, "Each organization should make provisions to start an exercise between 6:00 p.m. and midnight, and another between midnight and 6:00 a.m. once every six years," and this requirement was implemented from

---

[*] By memorandum, FEMA Deputy Associate Director, State and Local Programs and Support, August 5, 1983.

[†] Mr. Witt having previously served as Director, Arkansas State Emergency Management Agency, and as a County Judge in Yell County, Arkansas.

about 1982 to 1994. In 1994 and 1995, FEMA relaxed its policy of requiring actual demonstration of off-hours (e.g., between 6:00 p.m. and 6:00 a.m.) response, allowing offsite agencies to show compliance by providing rosters of sufficient depth for greater than 24-hour coverage (this had already been a requirement) in conjunction with records proving the ability to contact their staff off-hours. Reactor power licensees generally continue to have 6-year objectives to conduct one off-hours exercise, although by 2000 they had discontinued the practice of conducting off-hours biennial exercises evaluated by the NRC. However, the issue of whether to require off-hours demonstration continues to draw attention, as illustrated by the following (FEMA, 2002b):

> We sought comments about whether FEMA should begin exercises on weekends, holidays or off-hours. The comments from the emergency management community were uniformly negative. Some commenters responded that emergency management has advanced to the level that off-hours response to actual incidents is routine. Other commenters felt that the cumulative burden of actual off-hours responses and off-hours exercises on volunteers was too great. The NRC staff, on the other hand, suggested that off-hours and unannounced exercises were helpful since actual events often happen in the off-hours. Evaluation Criterion 1.b of Planning Standard "N", as interpreted by subsequent guidance, requires off-hours exercises. Additionally Planning Standard "N" suggests that some exercises should be unannounced. In light of this language, FEMA believes that the new exercise evaluation criteria should provide for off-hours and unannounced exercises, but will defer consideration of a standard until it has finalized a policy on granting exercise credit for participation in actual emergency response activities and equivalent drills and exercises. We believe that many OROs will be able to demonstrate their ability to mobilize personnel quickly at any time of the day through documented performance in actual emergency responses and other equivalent drills and exercises. This is the reason that Planning Standard "N" suggests unannounced and off-hours exercises. We will publish the proposed credit policy and off-hours, unannounced exercise criteria in the Federal Register for comment before we implement them.

Although evaluated emergency plan exercises after 1982 were required to result in significant radiological releases, there were few other requirements regarding scenario selection and design. The Department of Homeland Security (FEMA) had always been heavily involved in the selection of offsite objectives for evaluated exercises to ensure that all offsite agencies with a role in the licensee emergency plan are tested on all applicable evaluation criteria over the 6-year cycle. Historically, this has meant FEMA has specified, in advance, target protective actions for target jurisdictions in the plume phase emergency planning zone to be met by the exercise scenario. The NRC has never been involved in scenario design to the same level of specificity; its sole criteria regarding scenarios has historically been that they test "major portions of emergency response capabilities" (10 CFR 50.47(b)(14)) over the 6-year cycle. The definition of what a "major portion" consists of was left to the reactor licensee and offsite authorities. Although some licensees had routinely included security events in their range of exercise scenarios (especially following the February 1993 Three Mile Island intrusion), following the terrorist attacks against the United States in September 2001 the Commission recognized the integration of security and emergency plans as a "major element" requiring exercising (NRC, 2011b). The Commission took the position that exercises should have a range of radiological consequences taken over time:[*]

> The staff should coordinate with DHS to develop emergency planning exercise scenarios which would help avoid anticipatory responses associated with preconditioning of participants by incorporating a wide spectrum of releases (ranging from little or no release to a large release) and events, including security-based events. These scenarios should emphasize the expected interfaces and coordination between key decision-makers based on realistic postulated events. The staff should share experiences of preconditioning or "negative training" with DHS.

---

[*] See NRC (2006j) and associated Staff Requirements Memorandum dated June 29, 2006.

The nuclear industry created a pilot project to demonstrate how to design and conduct an exercise based on a site attack scenario, and each site ran a demonstration exercise in 2008 and 2009. The NRC, FEMA, and others observed these demonstration exercises and participated in some of them, but did not inspect or formally evaluate them. Each security-based exercise was considered to be a licensee off-year exercise. The NRC subsequently included a number of changes to the required exercise program in the rule change implemented in November 2011, with an implementation date of December 2015. These changes included the following:

- Implementation of an 8-year exercise cycle
- Requirement for licensees to submit preliminary exercise scenarios to the NRC
- Required variations in the content of biennial exercises, including an exercise based on hostile action, an exercise without a significant radiological release, and an exercise having an unpredictable pattern of emergency classification (rapid escalation)
- Evaluation of the ability to classify every emergency action level over the cycle

OFFSITE AUTHORITIES AND THE "REALISM DOCTRINE"

The Three Mile Island accident had a strong psychological effect on the public's acceptance of nuclear power. There often had been no significant local opposition to a proposed reactor site; however, after 1979, both opposition and interveners became common elements in reactor license hearings. Although there was some regional variation across the country, more such challenges occurred in the New England states than elsewhere. Following the NRC's adoption in 1980 of a requirement for mandatory offsite radiological emergency plans approved through FEMA, local and state governments opposed to licensing a nuclear power plant attempted to use emergency planning requirements to block plant licensing and operation by refusing to develop and submit the required local emergency plans. The working theory was that without an approved emergency plan the Commission's regulations required that an operating license could not be issued. This was referred to at the time as a *captive plant*. The perceived ability to hold plants hostage to emergency planning requirements was attractive to governments who could not prevent the plant from being built through the Commission's public hearing process. The plants most affected by captive plant efforts were Indian Point in New York, Seabrook in New Hampshire, and Shoreham on Long Island in New York.

At Indian Point, local officials in Rockland County refused to participate in radiological emergency planning on the grounds that the State of New York plans were inadequate. With a governor largely supportive of nuclear power, New York developed alternative plans to perform the functions of Rockland County, which were approved by the Commission in 1983. The Seabrook plant is located on the New Hampshire coast, a narrow strip between Massachusetts and Maine. Governor Dukakis of Massachusetts did not believe that state beaches could be safely evacuated under any emergency plan, so in 1986 he directed state agencies to refuse to cooperate with emergency planning for the site. A similar situation existed at Shoreham, in Suffolk County, New York. Construction on the Shoreham plant was completed in 1982, and in early 1983 Suffolk and Nassau Counties declined to participate in emergency planning on the grounds that the existing road system was inadequate to support evacuation (the fact that New York City was very near presented additional challenges). Also in 1983, Governor Cuomo directed that the State of New York also refuse to participate in planning for the Shoreham site. Although the station did not have an approved emergency plan it was granted a low power operating license in 1985. Ultimately, the Seabrook plant was granted an operating license in 1990 and a deal was reached between the State of New York and Long Island Light to close Shoreham, which operated for 1 day.

As part of the licensing actions related to Seabrook and Shoreham, the Nuclear Regulatory Commission promulgated the "Realism Doctrine" in 10 CFR 50.47(c)(1) and 10 CFR 50 Appendix E, Section IV.F (effective December 3, 1987, 52 FR 42078), and in NUREG-0654, Revision 1,

Supplement 1 (NRC, 1988b). This doctrine assumes that officials who have refused to plan for a radiological emergency will nonetheless take actions to protect the public during an actual emergency. NUREG-0654, Supplement 1, states in part,

> Assumptions: … In an actual radiological emergency, State and local officials that have declined to participate in emergency planning will: (a) exercise their best efforts to protect the health and safety of the public, (b) cooperate with the utility and follow utility offsite plans, and (c) have the resources sufficient to implement those portions of the utility offsite plan where State and local response is necessary.

In addition, Executive Order 12657 (Reagan, 1988b) required FEMA to provide for offsite emergency planning in cases where local or state official declined to participate. The Order states in part,

> This Order applies whenever State or local governments, either individually or together, decline or fail to prepare commercial nuclear power plant radiological emergency preparedness plans that are sufficient to satisfy Nuclear Regulatory Commission ("NRC") licensing requirements or to participate adequately in the preparation, demonstration, testing, exercise, or use of such plans…In carrying out any of its responsibilities under this Order, FEMA … (2) shall take care not to supplant State and local resources. FEMA shall substitute its own resources for those of the State and local governments only to the extent necessary to compensate for the nonparticipation or inadequate participation of those governments, and only as a last resort after appropriate consultation with the Governors and responsible local officials in the affected area regarding State and local participation; and (4) shall assume for purposes of Sections 3 and 4 of this Order that, in the event of an actual radiological emergency or disaster, State and local authorities would contribute their full resources and exercise their authorities in accordance with their duties to protect the public from harm and would act generally in conformity with the licensee's radiological emergency preparedness plan.

NUMARC EMERGENCY ACTION LEVELS

The concept of "emergency action levels" as thresholds for recognizing the onset of an emergency condition predates the Three Mile Island accident; however, each reactor site originally developed their own unique emergency action level and event classification scheme. This situation proved confusing to local, state, and federal responders during the Three Mile Island event and during other events in the 1970s. During the wholesale overhaul of emergency preparedness programs that followed the Three Mile Island accident, the NRC recognized the potential for site-specific emergency action level and classification scheme terminology to create confusion and delay in an emergency response. The Commission therefore required implementation of a standard, four-tier classification system (Notification of Unusual Event, Alert, Site Area Emergency, and General Emergency) and required all licensee to develop emergency action level thresholds based on common guidance and terminology. This guidance was initially provided in NUREG-0610 (NRC, 1979c) and then adopted essentially unchanged as Appendix 1 of NUREG-0654/FEMA REP-1, Revision 1 (NRC, 1980c). Appendix 1 of NUREG-0654 defined the radiological significance of each classification category and listed conditions which, if they occur, should result in declaring that category; these example conditions were primarily event based or scenario based. In hindsight, the major drawbacks of these emergency action levels were that they required the plant operator to have at least a general knowledge of the type of accident that was occurring, the emergency action levels had no bases justifying their numeric values or their association with a particular classification category, and the use of broad, undefined, terminology forced plant operators to do considerable interpretation with regard to the intent and meaning of the examples. NUREG-0654 introduced the concepts of *fission product barriers*, *potential loss of a barrier*, and the *loss of a barrier* without providing any clear details for implementation. Anecdotal evidence (discussion with some of the participants) suggests that the NUREG-0610 scheme, which was adopted into NUREG-0654, was largely the work of a small group of Commission staff working over a weekend against a short deadline to present a proposal to the FEMA/NRC working group responsible for writing NUREG-0654.

In 1988, the Nuclear Management and Resources Council (NUMARC)* began work on an alternate emergency action level scheme. This resulted in the document NUMARC/NESP-007, Revision 2 (NUMARC, 1992), which was subsequently accepted by the NRC as an acceptable emergency action scheme in Revision 3 of Regulatory Guide 1.101, *Emergency Planning and Preparedness for Nuclear Power Reactors*, in 1992. The essential elements of the NUMARC scheme are (1) symptom-based and barrier-based action levels should be used wherever possible, (2) higher classification clearly equates to higher risk to the public, (3) decisions are made rapidly using readily observable indications or obtainable information, (4) precursor events to dominant core damage scenarios result in classification, and (5) administrative reporting elements that do not represent a degradation of plant safety should be removed. Broadly, the NUMARC emergency action scheme uses four recognition categories: (1) abnormal radiation levels and radiological effluents, (2) fission product barrier degradation, (3) hazards and other conditions affecting plant safety, and (4) system malfunctions. Within each category are initiating conditions that provide the threat condition, and emergency action levels within each threat condition give the measurements indicating that the threat exists. NUMARC/NESP-007, Revision 2, was generally applicable only to operating reactors. Its philosophy was applied to the refueling and shutdown modes of reactor operation, to permanently defueled reactors, and to dry-cask fuel storage facilities. It was reissued as Nuclear Energy Institute (NEI) 99-01, Revision 4 (NEI, 2003). The Commission accepted NEI 99-01, Revision 4, as an acceptable alternative basis to NUREG-0654 emergency action levels in Regulatory Guide 1.101, Revision 4, and provided guidance for changing between approved emergency action schemes in NRC (2003g, 2004f, 2005a,n). Revision 5 of NEI 99-01 was issued in 2008, and Revision 6 was issued in 2012. There are currently no operating plants still licensed to the NUREG-0654 emergency action levels and may not be any licensed to NUMARC/NESP-007, Revision 2 (NUMARC, 1992). Generic guidance for developing emergency action levels for next-generation or advanced reactor units can be found in NEI (2009b).

HURRICANE ANDREW, TURKEY POINT, AND THE POST-DISASTER REACTOR RESTART PROCESS

Another significant event that affected the relationship between the Nuclear Regulatory Commission and the Federal Emergency Management Agency was Hurricane Andrew, which came ashore in South Florida on August 24, 1992. The hurricane affected the Turkey Point Nuclear Generating Station and its surrounding area. The event is discussed in Information Notice 93-53 (NRC, 1993b), which states, in part,

> On August 24, 1992, Category 4 Hurricane Andrew hit south Florida and caused extensive onsite and offsite damage at Turkey Point. ... Hurricane Andrew is historic because this is the first time that a hurricane significantly affected a commercial nuclear power plant. The eye of the storm, with sustained winds of up to 233 kilometers per hour (km/h) [145 miles per hour (mph)] and gusts of 282 km/h (175 mph), passed over the Turkey Point site and caused extensive onsite and offsite damage. The onsite damage included loss of all offsite power for more than 5 days, complete loss of communication systems, closing of the access road, and damage to the fire protection and security systems and warehouse facilities.

Post-hurricanes concerns of the Commission included pre-hurricane preparations, the timing of a reactor shutdown in advance of a hurricane, the adequacy of licensee communication systems to offsite authorities, and the impact of a hurricane on non-safety-related systems. Information Notice 93-53, Supplement 1 (NRC, 1994b), specifically addressed the reliability of communication systems. Following the hurricane there was a concern over the need for electric power in hurricane-damaged

---

* NUMARC was an industry trade group that was the director predecessor to the current Nuclear Energy Institute. NUMARC was itself preceded by an earlier nuclear industry trade group named the Atomic Industrial Forum.

areas; after repairing some exterior damage to the plant within a few days, plant staff began to bring the reactor back to power (reaching a few percent of rated power) with the knowledge and approval of the NRC. When FEMA learned of the reactor startup, they raised objections with the Commission on the grounds that if an accident occurred then local officials could not effectively warn the public and take appropriate protective actions because of the severely damaged local infrastructure. Subsequently, the Commission asked the plant to voluntarily shut down, which it did. The Commission and FEMA established an *ad hoc* working group to review the status of offsite emergency response in Florida before allowing Turkey Point to restart. The important emergency preparedness outcome from this experience was the establishment of a formal consultation process between FEMA and the Commission governing the restart of reactors following major natural disasters or other events affecting offsite emergency preparedness. This process was documented in a 1993 revision to the FEMA/NRC Memoranda of Understanding[*] and subsequently in Chapter 1601 of the Commission's *Inspection Manual* (NRC, 1997e) and in Administrative Letter 97-03, Plant Restart Discussions Following a Natural Disaster, dated March 28, 1997. The FEMA/NRC Memoranda of Understanding can be found in 44 CFR Part 353.

The memorandum was updated and reissued in 2012, primarily to expand the process to apply to a nuclear power plant that is not shut down (see also NRC, 2006c, 2010b). This expansion was requested by FEMA based on their experience with Super Storm Sandy on October 29, 2012, during which only three New England power plants shut down (Nine Mile Point, Indian Point, and Salem), and the August 23, 2011, earthquake which caused an alert at the North Anna Station and notifications of unusual events at 12 other nuclear plants and extended across the entire eastern half of the United States.

The current process is that for anticipated events, such as hurricanes, the Commission staffs its emergency response centers as a precaution and dispatches liaisons to the FEMA regional response centers and to the affected state emergency operations centers. Throughout the event, both the Commission and FEMA monitor the reactor status and onsite and offsite capabilities. If significant damage is reported offsite, especially to emergency warning systems and to designated evacuation routes, then FEMA initiates a disaster-initiated review through a request to the Commission and notification to the affected states and local jurisdictions. If the reactors are shut down, the Commission agrees to prevent them from starting until the review is complete and it has been established that offsite capabilities are adequate. If the reactors remain operating, the Commission agrees to require them to shut down, pending review and verifying that offsite capabilities are adequate. Technically, the Commission does not exercise operational control over the reactor units, so if a licensee were to not shut down when requested or begin to restart without permission, the Commission would use its authority to issue Orders to the licensee or to revoke their operating license. A review typically requires 2 to 3 days of direct observation of the status of offsite facilities and capabilities before a decision is reached as to whether or not to allow restart. If offsite capabilities are badly damaged, the hold order could conceivably be lengthy. Additional information can be found in FEMA (2011a).

THREE MILE ISLAND INTRUSION EVENT AND THE DESIGN BASIS THREAT

Although licensee security programs were fundamentally changed after September 11, 2001, a significant precursor event for nuclear power plants occurred on February 7, 1993, when an individual drove a station wagon through the protected area fences surrounding the remaining operating reactor at Three Mile Island and hid for several hours in the plant. It was later determined the individual was alone, unarmed, and disoriented. Although there was no actual threat to plant systems during this event, it highlighted a significant plant attack vulnerability. The event is discussed in NRC (1993g,h). Information Notice 93-94 states, in part,

---

[*] See also Revision 0 published as FR 82713, dated December 16, 1980, and Revision 1 published as 50 FR 15485, dated April 9, 1985. A subsequent revision occurred in 2002.

The performance objectives of Title 10 to the Code of Federal Regulations (10 CFR) Part 73 do not specifically address preventing a vehicle from forced entry through the protected area barrier and that there is no NRC guidance specific to performance standards for a security response to such an intrusion. Notwithstanding this, the TMI Unit 1 assessment system was not effective in observing the intruder/ vehicle penetrating the protected area barrier. Although the protected area detection system functioned (alarmed) as designed, the use of a land vehicle reduced the available time that security personnel had to respond and significantly affected their strategy toward protecting vital areas. ...

The above items illustrate a broad spectrum of activities that were not anticipated or covered by procedures. While it cannot be expected that every variable of a security event can be anticipated in advance, there may be some lessons learned from the event that can be applied generally. On the basis of the NRC incident investigation team findings with respect to this event, the NRC staff is considering the need for additional regulatory actions.

The event did have emergency preparedness implications, as the security response took priority and post-incident evaluations identified adverse impacts on some essential emergency preparedness functions, such an inability to notify offsite authorities due to closing security barriers to the control room. Although the Commission recognized the adverse emergency preparedness conditions that occurred in this event, it can be argued that the Commission failed to take action for another 10 years to ensure that implementation of licensee security plans did not prevent effective implementation of their emergency plans.

Based on this event, and a vehicle bomb explosion at the World Trade Center in New York City in February 1993, the Commission modified its design basis threat (NRC, 1994d) and required licensees to install vehicle barrier systems and establish stand-off distances to prevent unauthorized vehicles from approaching the reactor protected area. The primary concern was limiting damage from a bomb concealed in a vehicle but the potential for an adversary force using a vehicle to breach the protected area was also considered. The stand-off distance was subsequently revised again after the attacks of September 11, 2001.

REVISED REACTOR OVERSIGHT PROGRAM

The Nuclear Regulatory Commission's program for inspecting reactor licensees, including in the emergency preparedness area, remained largely static over the period between the Three Mile Island accident until the introduction of the revised reactor oversight program (ROP) in April 2001.[*] The program introduced three safety barriers, seven safety cornerstone areas (one cornerstone being emergency preparedness), a color-coded risk-informed approach to regulatory significance, and an agency action matrix that determined agency action based on a combination of the number and safety significance of licensee deficiencies. Key concepts included assessing licensee performance by blending numerical performance indicators with active inspection, the use of probability-based risk information to focus on high-risk issues, and licensee implementation of robust corrective action programs (which had previously existed for about 6 years) capable of identifying performance problems at a low level then effectively correcting them.[†]

---

[*] See SECY 98-132, *Plans to Increase Performance-Based Approaches in Regulatory Activities*; SECY 98-144, *White Paper on Risk-Informed and Performance-Based Regulations*; SECY 99-007/007A, *Recommendations for Reactor Oversight Process Improvements (Follow-Up to SECY-99-007)*; SECY 00-146, *Status of Risk-Based Performance Indicator Development and Related. Initiatives*; and SECY 01-0114, *Results of the Initial Implementation of the New Reactor Oversight Process*.

[†] In the NRC *Inspection Manual*, see Chapter 0305, *Operating Reactor Assessment Program*; Chapter 0308, *Reactor Oversight Process Basis Document*; Chapter 0308 Attachment 3, Appendix B, *Technical Basis for Emergency Preparedness Significance Determination Process*; Chapter 0608, *Performance Indicator Program*; Chapter 0609, *Significance Determination Process*; and Chapter 0609, Appendix B, *Emergency Preparedness Significance Determination Process*.

The revised reactor oversight program changed the emphasis of Commission inspections to verifying the licensee's implementation of the most essential emergency functions and ensuring that corrective action program processes are identifying, and correcting, emergency preparedness performance problems. Some previous inspection elements, such as observation of control room operator performance in a drill and emergency response facility tours to determine facility operability, were discontinued; new inspection elements included a review of alert and notification system testing methods, a review of the tests to determine the licensee's ability to staff and activate emergency response facilities during an emergency in accordance with their emergency plan requirements, and extensive reviews of corrective action program documents (drill reports, audits, assessments, and post-incident evaluation reports). Although the Commission's evaluation of emergency plan exercises continued essentially unchanged, the emphasis shifted to verifying that the licensee's evaluation team adequately identified all significant performance deficiencies and entered them into the corrective action system.

Prior to the revised reactor oversight program the Commission had an enforcement policy that defined how enforcement (i.e., sanctions) was taken against non-compliant licensees. The enforcement policy assigns violations of NRC requirements by Severity Level (I though IV, with I being the most severe) and provides for issuing fines (*civil penalties*) to licensees. The reactor oversight program introduced the concept of *findings*, a citation against a self-imposed standard that was not a violation of NRC requirements and removed the link to civil penalties for most findings and violations. The Severity Level scheme was retained for violations that prevent the Commission from performing its regulatory function, such as failing to report certain conditions to the Commission, and for violations that have actual consequences, such as causing an actual radiation exposure above regulatory limits. Findings and violations were assigned a four-color scheme (red, yellow, white, and green) in order of higher to lower severity. It also introduced the significance determination process (see Chapter 0609 and Appendices A through M in the *Inspection Manual*); emergency preparedness issues are assessed using Appendix B, most recently revised in September 2014.

With regard to emergency preparedness, the program introduced the concept of *risk-significant planning standards*, defined as those planning standards that directly affect the ability to implement measures to protect the health and safety of the public: classification (10 CFR 50.47(b)(4)), notification to offsite authorities (10 CFR 50.47(b)(5)), dose assessment (10 CFR 50.47(b)(9)), and processes for licensee protective action recommendations (10 CFR 50.47(b)(10)). Although all of the planning standards remain important, failures or performance deficiencies related to the risk significant standards result in more significant consequences for the licensee. The emergency preparedness performance indicators (NEI, 2009c) are drill and exercise performance, alert and notification system reliability (essentially taking over a metric that had been reported to FEMA for many years), and emergency response organization participation in drills and exercises.

The Commission's increased interest in alert and notification systems for the general public, an area largely left to FEMA prior to 2002, has particularly impacted reactor licensees and has caused increased interagency consultation with the Department of Homeland Security (FEMA).

POST-9/11 SECURITY ENVIRONMENT

Although the September 11, 2001, terrorist attacks in the United States did not involve radioactive material or nuclear power reactors in any way, they did change how the Nuclear Regulatory Commission, Federal Emergency Management Agency, and, later, Department of Homeland Security viewed potential threats to nuclear power plants and other locations that store significant quantities of radioactive material. As a direct result of the attack, the Commission issued Orders to reactor licensees on February 25, 2002, April 29, 2003, and June 20, 2006, that affected licensee emergency preparedness.[*] The Order details are not available to the public, but they

---

[*] Additional orders affected only licensee security organizations.

generally required changes to emergency action levels, changes to on-shift emergency responders, enhanced or alternative emergency response facilities, enhanced schemes to contact off-duty emergency response personnel, greater integration between licensee security and emergency plans, and enhancements to mitigation strategies for certain plant events. The Orders were followed by Commission inspections to verify the effectiveness of the required actions.

Within the Commission, the emergency preparedness inspection program was moved in 2004 from the Office of Reactor Regulation to the newly created Office of Nuclear Security and Incident Response. The Commission also conducted studies related to the ability of containment structures to withstand airliner impacts (essentially updating previous work on the impacts of smaller airliners) and studies of the effectiveness of the available protective action scheme, and it reevaluated the emergency preparedness (EP) planning basis. As a result, the Commission concluded the following:

> Whether the initiating event is terrorist based or a nuclear accident, the EP planning basis provides reasonable assurance that the public health and safety will be protected. EP plans have always been based on a range of postulated events that would result in a radiological release, including the most severe.

In 2005, the Commission issued Bulletin 2005-02 (NRC, 2005f), which asked reactor licensees to implement specific emergency action levels related to site threats and attack based on those found in NEI 99-01, Revision 4 (NEI, 2003), as augmented by Orders; to implement prompt notification to the NRC following a credible threat with a more limited notification scope; to staff alternative emergency facilities prior to and during a security-based event; to routinely include significant security-based events in the drill and exercise program; and to enhance onsite protective actions by evacuating and dispersing key personnel and sheltering personnel in hardened facilities or away from potentially threatened areas. Licensees were asked to implement these measures, including making necessary changes to their emergency plans and emergency action plans, no later than January 20, 2006, and were asked to respond to the Commission regarding their current capabilities and planned actions.

Complementing the Commission's actions, the Department of Homeland Security identified 17 critical infrastructure sectors, including commercial nuclear power, with the intent of conducting systematic emergency preparedness evaluations of each sector (USDHS, 2003b). Because of the relatively advanced state of radiological emergency planning and preparedness as compared to other sectors, between 2005 and 2008 the Department conducted site-specific comprehensive emergency preparedness reviews and vulnerability assessments around operating commercial reactors with an emphasis on the preparedness of offsite authorities in the emergency planning zones. The purpose of these reviews were to evaluate the interface between the licensee staff and local emergency preparedness agencies and law enforcement agencies and to evaluate their respective capabilities. These analyses resulted in detailed gap analysis and recommendations for improving the preparedness planning for all affected agencies. The results were also considered in drafting the rule-making plan that led to the emergency preparedness rules implemented in 2011.

PUBLIC ALERTING SIREN SYSTEMS

The question of how to best warn members of the public about an emergency and the need to take protective action predates radiological emergency planning, going back to the period of 1940 to 1945. At that time, notification systems were based on electromechanical outdoor sirens or steam-powered whistles, which conveyed information about the emergency by changing the tone of the siren. Because there was no capability to disseminate situation-specific instructions, the public was trained to take specific actions according to the siren tone, such as report to an air raid shelter or douse the building lights. As information delivery systems became available, siren systems began to function as alerting or notifying systems not intended to convey instructions but to direct the public's attention to mass communication systems that could distribute specific emergency information or instructions.

The Commission requires all power reactor licensees to demonstrate that an adequate system exists to warn the public in the emergency planning zone of an emergency. The design objective is for the primary system to warn essentially 100% of the public in the emergency planning zone within 15 minutes of the decision to activate the system. There is no specific requirement to provide warning to the public outside of the emergency planning zone, although in practice the actual range of the system is greater than the defined planning zone boundary. The licensees are not required to own or operate the system, and the decision to activate the system must be made by offsite authorities. Some licensees have the capability to activate the alert and notification system for testing purposes and as a backup in case offsite officials are unable to activate the system from their designated control location. The radiological emergency warning system (sirens) are permitted, but not required, to be used for other warning purposes at the discretion of local authorities; the primary other purpose is to warn residents of tornadoes and other severe weather.

The Federal Emergency Management Agency has the authority to determine whether an alert and notification system provides adequate coverage in the emergency planning zone, and licensees must submit their system design to FEMA for review and approval before implementing the system. The design requirements for alert and notification systems can be found in FEMA (1980d, 1985b). The most important criteria for outdoor warning sirens is that the range of a siren is defined as the distance at which the effective sound level is greater than 60 dBC for areas with population densities less than 2000 persons/mile^2 and 70 dBC for areas having population densities greater than 2000 persons/mile^2.

The FEMA approval is documented in licensee-specific alert and notification system design reports. The design report includes sound propagation studies and modeling, along with operating, maintenance, and testing procedures. Any change to the warning system, including changes to applicable procedures, must be approved in advance by the FEMA regional office having jurisdiction. The Commission inspects licensees to ensure that the alert and notification system is maintained and operated in accordance with design report commitments. The states provide an annual report of siren testing performance to FEMA, with a goal of maintaining siren performance at greater than 90% operability (as determined by the routine testing program).

The basic construction and operation of siren systems have changed very little from the 1950s through the present. Beginning in the early 1990s, multiple electronic-speaker alerting systems became available, their advantages being scalability (adding power or range by adding speakers) and simpler construction (omnidirectional without rotation). Some speaker systems had the capability to broadcast short recorded messages (some systems in the 2000s have the capability to broadcast live messages). Sirens, including speaker systems, continue to have multi-tone capability, and some local emergency plans continue to assign meanings to the different tones, although for the most part there are only minimal efforts (at best) to educate the public about the tone alert scheme. Where tone alert schemes continue to exist they are generally tested using only a single tone.

A majority of current siren systems work on AC power supplied by the local electric power grid, although some are DC systems working on batteries, and a small number are supplied with back-up solar power. The vulnerability of siren systems to electric power outages has been recognized for decades but had not been an issue in prior widespread blackouts, such as the Northeast blackout of November 9, 1965; New York City blackout of July 13, 1977; U.S. West Coast blackout of December 22, 1982; U.S. West Coast blackout of July 2–3, 1996; U.S. West Coast blackout of August 10, 1996; and the Ontario and U.S. North Central blackout of June 25, 1998 (see U.S.–Canada Power System Outage Task Force, 2004). Federal design standards for siren alerting systems have never required that systems remain operable during electric grid failure conditions. Guidance in this area is given in Eisenhower (1955), in DCPA (1977), and in FEMA (1980d, 1983, 1985b, 1991a). CPG 1-14 (FEMA, 1991a) and CPG 1-17 (FEMA, 1980d) are currently in revision by the Department of Homeland Security; because REP-10 (FEMA, 1985b) implements CPG 1-14 and CPG 1-17, it will be revised to be consistent with those documents.

Backup power for siren alerting systems became a significant issue for the public after the electric power blackout on August 14, 2003, which affected a total of approximately 50 million people in seven U.S. states and a Canadian province. The blackout took 265 power plants offline, including 9 U.S. and 11 Canadian nuclear plants. Eight of the U.S. plants entered their lowest (least significant) emergency condition as a result of losing offsite power, a condition that increases the effect of failures in plant backup emergency diesel generators. In addition,

> The electrical disturbance on August 14 had a significant impact on seven [nuclear power] plants that continued to remain connected to the grid. ... Sixty-four nuclear power plants experienced non-significant transients caused by minor disturbances on the electrical grid. These plants were able to respond to the disturbances through normal control systems. ... Twenty-four nuclear power plants experienced no transient and saw essentially no disturbances on the grid, or were shut down at the time of the transient. (U.S.–Canada Power System Outage Task Force, 2004, p. 119)

Offsite alerting siren system for all of the U.S. plants that tripped were also made inoperable by the power blackout, so mobile loudspeaker systems were the only available means had it become necessary to alert the public to an emergency. One of the affected plants was the Indian Point site in New York, located about 25 miles north of New York City along the Hudson River. This site had been contentious since its construction more than 20 years earlier and in recent years had experienced more problems with the public and offsite officials as a result of poor operating performance (e.g., a single steam generator tube failure of 146 gal/min on February 15, 2000, that increased the plant's radioactive effluent, causing the licensee to declare an Alert emergency classification), the expansion of New York's suburbs northward into the area near the plant, and the relocation of prominent national politicians to the area. The Energy Policy Act of 2005 required all nuclear power plants having population densities of 1.5 million within a 50-mile radius to have siren altering systems with 100% backup DC power by January 30, 2007; the only plant meeting this criteria was Indian Point. Although there is no current regulatory requirement for alternative siren system power (except at Indian Point), licensees and offsite emergency planners widely anticipate that the revised CPG 1-17 will require backup power, and many licensees are currently installing DC-based systems (AC-powered battery chargers). The NRC has encouraged this perception and trend, in part by Commissioner-driven requests to licensees for information about the status of upgrades to siren power systems.

The Commission required all power reactor licensees to formally designate backup methods to warn members of the public of an emergency in the event that their primary method (e.g., outdoor warning sirens) does not function. This requirement (Appendix E to 10 CFR 50, Part IV(D)(4)) was part of the final emergency preparedness rule that went into effect in 2011. The rule required that licensees having a FEMA-approved backup method in December 2011 implement that method no later than December 2012. Those licensees not having a FEMA-approved backup method in December 2011 had until June 2013 to submit a revision to their alert and notification system design to FEMA and until June 2015 to implement the backup method (after receiving FEMA approval). This requirement was essentially met before it was implemented, and FEMA certified to the Commission in January 2013 that all licensees had acceptably designed backup methods of notifying the public.

EMERGENCY BROADCAST AND EMERGENCY ALERT SYSTEMS

The Control of Electromagnetic Radiation (CONELRAD) system, established in 1951, was the first national emergency communications system (Truman, 1951). It utilized two AM radio channels and was designed as a one-way communications system used exclusively by the President to provide information to the public in case of a "dire emergency"; it could only be used by federal authorities. Television stations did not participate in CONELRAD and participation was optional for radio stations. Its use of only two AM frequencies was to prevent radio stations from being used as guidance beacons by incoming enemy missiles.

The Emergency Broadcast System was established by the Federal Communications Commission (FCC) in 1963, again with the primary purpose of providing a direct means for the President to communicate to the public during a condition of war or emergency. All FCC radio and television licensees were required to participate in the system as a license condition (requiring purchase of special encoding/decoding equipment for signal authentication). The system allowed the use of existing station AM and FM frequencies (because missile guidance at the time no longer depended on radio broadcasts), used a two-tone alert signal, and allowed state and local authorities use of the system to broadcast localized alerts. The Emergency Broadcast System was an analog system requiring active operator control. Activation tones were initiated at predesignated "point of entry" stations that cascaded through the radio and television system, followed by an informational message to be read in live-time by each individual station operator. CONELRAD was officially replaced by the Emergency Broadcast System in 1976 by the FCC through a Memorandum of Understanding with the National Weather Service (amended in 1982 to include FEMA). The Emergency Broadcast System featured random weekly tests, a practice that continues to the present. Executive Order 12472 (Reagan, 1984), assigned FEMA responsibility to develop and provide policy and management oversight of the Emergency Broadcast System, and to advise and assist private radio licensees of the FCC in developing emergency communications plans, procedures, and capabilities.

In 1994, the FCC replaced the Emergency Broadcast System with the Emergency Alert System, whose primary purpose remains to provide the President a national communication capability during a national crisis, although none of the national communication systems has been used for this purpose to date. The first-ever test of this capability was conducted on November 9, 2011. State and local jurisdictions continue to have access to the Emergency Alert System to transmit local emergency information. All radio and television licensees were required to participate in the Emergency Alert System as a license condition. Cable television systems with 10,000 or more subscribers were required to participate by December 1998; digital television, digital cable, and satellite radio providers were required to participate in the Emergency Alert System by December 2006; all direct satellite service providers by May 2007; and video dial-tone services by July 2007. The Emergency Alert System differs from the previous system in that it is a digital system allowing for computer-based controls. It does not require human operators to function, uses the same initiation tone as does the National Weather Service weather radio system, and is capable of targeting messages to as small an area as individual counties. The system also has the capability to interface with digital pagers and other electronic devices.

A related technology is Wireless Emergency Alerts (WEAs), also known as the Commercial Mobile Alert System (CMAS). Emergency alert information is distributed to cellular telephones, but phone users have to activate this feature on their phones. The system became operational in 2012. Among other features, it allows emergency messages to be sent to at-risk geographical areas. In theory, messages could be sent to individual cell phone repeater towers. Emergency messages appear as texts on all phones connected to the targeted towers.

Emergency warning systems continue to be of national interest. Executive Order 13407 (Bush, 2006) requires the Secretary, Department of Homeland Security, to inventory, evaluate, assess, maintain, and protect the public alert and warning infrastructure in the United States, including interoperability among emergency communication systems. The Secretary was required to issue implementing guidance within 120 days and to make annual reports and recommendations to the President.

HOMELAND SECURITY EXERCISE EVALUATION PROGRAM

The Homeland Security Exercise Evaluation Program (HSEEP) was developed as a result of Homeland Security Presidential Directive 5 (USDHS, 2003a). Specifically, HSEEP implements Section V.A.6, which required facilitation of the development of national standards, guidelines and protocols for incident management training and exercises. HSEEP (implemented in 2007 and revised in 2013) provides a standard process and method for developing, conducting, evaluating, and critiquing drills and exercises, as well a standard method for after-action reporting that can be applied to drills and to events. HSEEP implements the National Response Framework and National Preparedness System, and supports the National Preparedness Goal and National Exercise Program. All federal entities are required to use HSEEP; states, local governmental jurisdictions, and the private sector are encouraged to use HSEEP but are not required to use it, in a manner similar to the National Incident Management System (NIMS) and the Incident Command System (ICS). The program is based on the core capabilities and capability targets in the prevention, protection, mitigation, response, and recovery mission areas. *Core capabilities* are defined as the critical elements necessary to execute the specific mission areas. It is intended to be an "all-hazards" approach to maintaining preparedness, applicable to training for any kind of emergency situation. One of its primary strengths is that it creates a single set of terms and definitions, so that emergency preparedness staff across the government can accurately communicate.

EMERGENCY PREPAREDNESS RULEMAKING, NOVEMBER 2011

The Commission has periodically made small revisions to its regulations pertaining to emergency preparedness. However, an extensive revision was made in November 2011, after a multi-year effort. The purposes of this revision were to formalize requirements put into place by Commission Order after the events of September 11, 2001, and to implement improvements to the regulatory scheme identified in a 2005–2006 internal review. This review was directed by the Commission as described in a staff requirements memorandum dated December 20, 2004, and the results are documented in NRC (2006j). The subsequent rulemaking plan was approved in a staff requirements memorandum date January 8, 2007.[*]

Elements of the rule pertaining to an enhanced safety–security interface include the following:[†]

- Enhanced emergency action levels for hostile action events
- Implementation of alternative facilities where the emergency response organization could be assembled if primary onsite facilities are not accessible, such as in hostile action events
- Identification of all functions that the licensee would rely on offsite authorities to accomplish, with particular attention to coordination of effort with offsite authorities during a hostile action event
- Implementation of schemes to protect vital plant personnel (e.g., plant operators) in the event of a hostile threat or hostile action event at the site

Elements of the rule identified as safety enhancements during the staff review include the following:

- A required licensee analysis of the emergency response duties of on-shift staff to identify conflicting duties
- Implementation of a multi-year scheme for conducting NRC-evaluated biennial exercises with required variations in the simulated scenario events

---

[*] Documents related to this change can be found on the www.regulations.gov website under the docket, NRC-2008-0122. These documents include the technical basis for the rule, dated May 18, 2009; SECY-09-0007, *Proposed Rule Related to Emergency Preparedness Regulations*, dated January 9, 2009; and SECY-11-0052, *Final Rule: Enhancements to Emergency Preparedness Regulations*, dated April 8, 2011. The final rule was published in the *Federal Register* as 76 FR 72595, dated November 23, 2011.

[†] The security-related elements of the rule addressed interim measures required by Order EA-02-26, *Interim Safeguards and Security Compensatory Measures*, dated February 25, 2002, and by Bulletin 2005-002, *Emergency Preparedness and Response Actions for Security Based Events*, dated July 18, 2005. The technical basis for the security-related elements is documented in SECY-02-0104, *Plan for the Comprehensive Review of Safeguards and Security Programs for NRC Licensed Facilities and Activities*, dated June 14, 2002, and SECY-03-0165, *Evaluation of Nuclear power Reactor Emergency Preparedness Planning Basis Adequacy in the Post 9/11 Threat Environment*, dated September 22, 2003. The only document that is currently publicly available is Bulletin 2005-002.

- Designation and implementation of backup means for notifying the public of a radiological emergency
- Requiring that licensees have the capability of declaring an emergency classification within 15 minutes of conditions occurring that required classification (both initial event recognition and upgrade to more serious classifications as conditions changed)
- Requiring that licensees periodically update their initial evacuation time estimate studies
- Clarifying the process for making changes to the approved emergency plan; in particular, that changes requiring advance approval from the Commission were to be submitted as amendments to the operating license

The requirement for varying biennial exercise scenarios was a response to the Commission's observation that licensee performance in exercises was not a good predictor of licensee performance in actual events. The Commission identified that licensees often had problems performing the key emergency response functions of classification and offsite notification that they did not have during exercises. The Commission concluded that one cause was that exercises had become too predictable and therefore exercise participants could anticipate the necessary actions, thus improving their apparent performance. The requirement that licensees be capable of classifying an event within 15 minutes of receiving indications formalized criteria that had been Commission policy since the mid-1980s but had previously not been enforceable.

The various requirements of the November 2011 rule had implementation dates between 2012 and 2015 as described below:

- Use of the license amendment process for changes to the emergency plan requiring NRC approval (February 21, 2012)
- Submission of a summary of the licensee's evaluation of the impact of changes to the emergency plan not requiring the prior approval of the NRC (February 21, 2012)
- Incorporation of updated emergency action levels for security events and hostile action (June 20, 2012)
- Establishing the ability to classify all emergency action levels within 15 minutes of the onset of conditions requiring classification (June 20, 2012)
- Implementing a range of onsite protective actions to protect vital personnel from hostile threats or hostile action (June 20, 2012)
- Implementation of a mustering facility for the relocation of onsite emergency response organization staff (e.g., technical support center and operations support center) in the event that the site is not accessible (June 20, 2012)
- Submission of an updated evacuation time estimate study based on the 2010 census (December 23, 2012)
- Implementation of a backup alert and notification system capability if approved by FEMA before December 23, 2011 (by December 23, 2012)
- Submission of an analysis of the capability of the on-shift emergency response organization to perform their functions without conflicting duties (December 24, 2012)
- Submission to FEMA of a revision to the site alert and notification system design report to include a backup notification method if a method has not been approved before December 23, 2011 (by June 24, 2013)
- First annual evaluation of the impact of changes to emergency planning zone population (December 31, 2013)
- Identification of the functions expected to be performed by offsite agencies, including as part of the response to a hostile action (June 23, 2014)
- Implementation of an alternate facility for the relocation of onsite emergency response organization staff with capabilities to communicate with licensee emergency response

facilities, perform notifications to offsite authorities if required, and perform engineering assessments (December 23, 2014)

- Implementation of a backup alert and notification system capability as submitted to FEMA by June 2013 (365 days after receiving FEMA approval and not to exceed June 22, 2015)
- Conduct of an NRC-evaluated biennial exercise based on a simulation of hostile action (December 31, 2015)
- Implementation of an 8-year exercise cycle in which a variety of required scenario variations are demonstrated, including variation of scenarios to prevent participant preconditioning (January 1 of the year in which the licensee conducts its first hostile-action-based biennial exercise)

ACCIDENT AT FUKUSHIMA DAIICHI, JAPAN, MARCH 2011

The Fukushima plant on the northeastern coast of Japan consisted of six General Electric boiling water reactor units. At the time of the accident, units 1, 2, and 3 were operating, and units 4, 5, and 6 were in maintenance outages. The event began with a 9.0-magnitude earthquake (Richter scale) on the afternoon of March 11, 2011. The earthquake caused the three operating units to automatically shut down. The plant lost offsite power as the local electric grid collapsed, and the plant emergency diesel generators automatically started to supply vital power.

Approximately 45 minutes later, a tsunami struck the plant; this tsunami was smaller than the protective sea wall built around the site and did not cause any significant damage. Approximately 1 hour after the earthquake, a 14-meter (46-feet) tsunami struck the plant; this wave was taller than the protective sea wall and destroyed the emergency diesel generators and their fuel tanks. Unit 1 had a steam-powered isolation condenser and Units 2 and 3 had steam-powered emergency core cooling systems available. Battery rooms were flooded on Units 1 and 2, but Unit 3 had battery power for about 30 hours. The reactor vessel level on Unit 1 reached the top of active fuel level after about 3 hours; it is thought that the core had completely melted by about 16 hours after the reactor scram. Unit 1 experienced a hydrogen explosion in the service building on the second day. The steam-driven emergency core cooling system on Unit 2 failed on the third day, and the Unit 2 core was largely melted 30 hours later. The water injection systems on Unit 3 failed about 40 hours into the accident, and the Unit 3 core subsequently melted.[*]

Hydrogen explosions eventually occurred in Units 1, 2, and 3, and a fire occurred in the Unit 4 reactor building. The licensee vented primary containment on Unit 1, and the hydrogen explosion occurred about 24 hours into the event. The explosion on Unit 2 occurred almost 4 days into the event. The licensee vented primary containment on Unit 3, and the hydrogen explosion on that unit occurred 3 days into the event. A Unit 4 hydrogen explosion occurred 4 days into the event, apparently because of hydrogen from Unit 3 that collected in common ventilation ducts and then traveled to Unit 4. The utility eventually injected seawater into the reactor vessels on Units 1, 2, and 3 and continuously sprayed seawater into damaged fuel storage pools to provide heat removal.

Radioactive gases were vented from Unit 1 to the atmosphere beginning on the second day of the accident. Intentional venting from Unit 3 began on the third day of the accident. Intentional venting to atmosphere from Unit 2 began during the fifth day.

The first 3-kilometer evacuation order was issued 5 hours into the event. The evacuation order was extended the next day to 10 km. This order was further extended to 10 km on the second day and then to 20 km after the hydrogen explosion on Unit 1. On the third day, the government

---

[*] Several detailed event timelines are available online. Some examples include https://en.wikipedia.org/wiki/Timeline_of_the_Fukushima_Daiichi_nuclear_disaster; http://www.scientificamerican.com/media/multimedia/0312-fukushima-timeline/; http://www.livescience.com/13294-timeline-events-japan-fukushima-nuclear-reactors.html; https://www.oecd-nea.org/press/2011/NEWS-04.html; http://www.nei.org/Master-Document-Folder/Backgrounders/Reports-And-Studies/Special-Report-on-the-Nuclear-Accident-at-the-Fuku; and http://www.tepco.co.jp/en/press/corp-com/release/betu12_e/images/120620e0101.pdf.

recommended that persons in a radius of 20 to 30 km stay indoors and 10 days later requested persons in the 20- to 30-km zone voluntarily relocate. It is estimated that 81,000 persons were eventually evacuated from the 20-km area surrounding the plant, in addition to the many other evacuees from the severe earthquake. The licensee originally classified the accident as a 5 on the International Atomic Energy Agency International Nuclear Event Scale, indicating an event with wider consequences than the plant site, which was changed after a month to a 7, a major accident (for the combined Units 1, 2, and 3). Three employees were killed by the tsunami but to date none has died from exposure to radiation.

In the United States, the Nuclear Regulatory Commission activated its headquarters Operations Center on March 11, 2011, to monitor the Fukushima event. This was a completely new level of response by the Commission, which had not previously used the Operations Center to respond to an event occurring outside of the United States. The initial concern was that tsunamis would impact the western U.S. coastline, including two operating nuclear power plants, but no significant tsunami occurred. The Commission also provided information and analysis to other U.S. government agencies and to the states, including the dispatch of personnel to the U.S. embassy in Tokyo. The Operations Center also provided some technical assistance to Japanese regulators. The Operations Center remained fully staffed for several weeks and operated at lesser staffing for some additional weeks.

The Environmental Protection Agency activated its headquarters Emergency Operations Center 4 days after the event began. It also activated the Advisory Team for Environment, Food and Health and the RadNet system, and it deployed portable air sampling systems to the western United States. The EPA also increased operations at the National Air and Radiation Environmental Laboratory. The Advisory Team for Environment, Food and Health is a group of scientists and radiation protection experts whose function in domestic nuclear incidents is to advise the affected states on measures to protect the food supply from radioactive contamination. RadNet (previously called the Emergency Monitoring System) is a system of fixed monitoring stations that collect periodic environmental samples of airborne radioactive material; the stations are typically operated by universities and state public health departments. RadNet increased the sample collection frequency and collected air samples, precipitation (rainwater) samples, drinking water samples, and samples of milk, all of which was analyzed for radioactive material. Although the amount of radioactive material from Fukushima that was detected was far below applicable health standards, radioactive material was detected in the United States, as it had been in 1986 after the Chernobyl event. According to EPA data, the maximum Fukushima samples had concentrations of radioactive material about one-tenth the maximums measured following Chernobyl. In particular, the highest concentration of I-131 in milk was 18 pCi/L at Hilo, HI; I-131 in air was 0.84 pCi/L at Boise, ID; and I-131 in rainwater was 390 pCi/L at Boise, ID (Mosser, 2011). The data collected through RadNet during the Fukushima response is available on an EPA website (www.epa.gov/japan2011/).

The Department of Energy deployed Aerial Monitoring System assets to Japan following the Fukushima event, including fixed-wing aircraft and helicopters equipped with airborne systems for measuring airborne radioactive material (plume) and ground deposition. The first monitoring flights began on the fifth day following the onset of the accident, and 85 flights were conducted over 500 hours of flying time. The Department of Energy also deployed a mobile radiological laboratory and ground survey teams. The ground teams made exposure rate measurements, collected air and soil samples, and surveyed objects and persons for radioactive contamination (Blumenthal, 2012). The Department of Energy also activated the Interagency Modeling and Atmospheric Assessment Center to model airborne and waterborne radioactive plumes from Fukushima using the National Atmospheric Release Advisory Capability (NARAC) atmospheric assessment code.

There were many lessons to come out of the Fukushima accident. Ones on the plant side included the need for more robust (i.e., longer lasting) DC batteries, the need to stage more portable emergency equipment at reactor sites, the need for more robust containment venting systems, and the need for permanent level instrumentation on spent fuel pools. Some of these issues were addressed in Orders issued to licensees in 2012. With regard to emergency preparedness, the accident produced the following recommendations in the United States:

- Multi-unit reactor sites should perform a staffing analysis to determine whether they have enough on-shift staff to handle simultaneous emergencies on all units, with particular attention to severe natural disasters.
- Multi-unit reactor sites should implement dose assessment methods that allow the simultaneous assessment of releases from more than one source.
- Reactor sites should assess power sources for communications equipment to ensure offsite communications during a beyond-design-basis event.

The nuclear industry is addressing the need for additional portable equipment to mitigate the effects of a prolonged beyond-design-basis event through the FLEX program. This program has established two depots of equipment commonly used at nuclear power plants, one at Phoenix, AZ, the second at Memphis, TN. Each depot has a large number of semitrailer-mounted generators, pumps, motors, compressors, hoses, electrical cables, portable lighting, and other equipment that could be useful in responding to a significant event. In some cases, equipment specific to a particular licensee is also maintained offsite as a backup measure. One feature of the FLEX program is that all equipment uses standard fittings and connections, which may require individual plants to make permanent modifications to power and water systems to accept the standard connections. The depots are capable of delivering equipment close to an affected plant within 24 hours of being notified of the event. There is also a drill and exercise program to ensure that licensees and depots are both familiar with the processes for activating the depots, deploying the equipment, and accepting the equipment at the affected reactor site. Each depot has also implemented a preventative maintenance program to maintain, and periodically operate, all equipment to ensure its readiness to be deployed. For more information, see NEI (2012b) and NRC (2011k).

FEMA RADIOLOGICAL EMERGENCY PREPAREDNESS MANUAL

From roughly 1982 through 2012, guidance from the Federal Emergency Management Agency consisted of Radiological Emergency Preparedness (REP) reports, numbered 1 through 22, and a large number of implementing memoranda. FEMA conducted a Strategic Review program assessment in 1996, which recommended (among other things) that the offsite radiological emergency preparedness program be streamlined. The initial effort resulted in the 2002 *Interim REP Program Manual*. This manual combined previous guidance and policy memoranda and other documents and retired some others. The final *REP Manual* was put out for public comment in 2009 (www.regulations.gov; Docket FEMA-2008-0022), and the final version was issued in 2012. The latest *REP Manual* revision as of this writing is dated June 2015, the previous revision being dated June 2013. The intent of the *REP Manual* is that offsite authorities have a single reference document that contains all of the current program requirements so users do not have to discern which FEMA guidance is current and which has been superseded. The *REP Manual* also made an extensive effort to use plain language and to reduce the usage of technical jargon and acronyms that were unfamiliar to many users.

SMALL MODULAR REACTORS

The emergency preparedness requirements developed over the past 35 years have been driven by the significant dose consequences that could result from currently licensed reactors, including the various advanced or passive reactors being constructed today. Another kind of next-generation light-water reactor technology that is in active development will have much different operating characteristics and different radiological consequences. The *small modular reactor* will be an essentially sealed passive reactor with an electric power output of between 100 megawatts electric

(MWe) and 200 MWe, as compared to the current fleet, which has power outputs between roughly 600 and 1300 MWe per reactor unit.[*] These reactors are designed to be constructed in an offsite factory and transported to the operating site for installation. The entire reactor package is designed to be installed underground with little to no aboveground footprint for critical systems. The design concept is that modular reactors will not be operated as single stand-alone units but installed in groups of four or more; the maximum number of units that could be installed at a site is a topic that is still being discussed. It is possible that the total electric output of a modular reactor site could be nearly the same as the total output from a traditional base-load reactor, but the active fuel would be divided among several reactor vessels rather than in a single vessel. A useful overview of current international small reactor designs can be found in IAEA (2014). Some of the important proposed design features include reactor vessels immersed in external water pools, standby pools of water available to completely flood the reactor vessels, and water circulation (heat transfer features) that does not depend on pumps or external electric power.

There are currently three vendors proposing to license modular reactors. Although some of the reactor design parameters are known, none of the designs has been completed, and none has been submitted to the NRC for design certification. The first licensing submission might occur in mid- to late 2016, or it may occur later. The reactor certification process will take 30 to 36 months. The earliest that a modular reactor could go into operation is likely in the 2022–2023 time frame, but it is more likely to be later. A modular reactor would currently have to be licensed under 10 CFR 50, with all of the current emergency preparedness requirements found in Part 50. New licensees would then have to be exempted from individual requirements through the licensing process on a case-by-case basis. The Commission recognizes that all of the current requirements may not be necessary to ensure that adequate measures can be taken to protect public health and safety and is in the early stages of developing a new licensing scheme for modular reactors. Some of the emergency preparedness issues that are unresolved include the following:

- Should specific defense-in-depth attributes be defined?
- Should predefined accident scenarios be used to determine design and siting acceptability?
- Under what conditions should analyses include accidents affecting multiple modules?
- Do current radiological source term models apply to the proposed designs?
- Could a plant be safely built without a pressure-retaining containment building?
- Should the plant exclusion area boundary and emergency planning zone be reduced?
- How large of an on-shift emergency response organization should be required?

The Commission directed staff to draft new emergency preparedness regulations specific to small modular reactors in NRC (2015c) and in a staff requirements memorandum dated August 4, 2015. The Commission specifically directed the staff to develop a performance-based emergency preparedness program to the maximum extent possible. The Commission required staff to provide a rule-making plan and schedule no later than April 2016. The rule-making process typically takes 3 to 4 years, with a subsequent implementation period; it is likely that there will not be effective emergency preparedness rules for small modular reactors until approximately 2021 to 2022.

One of the most contentious decisions that has to be made is determining the size of the required offsite emergency planning zone. The 10 CFR Part 50 and 10 CFR Part 100 requirements currently allow a reactor of less than 300 MWe to have an emergency planning zone of less than 10 miles as determined on a case-by-case basis, but they do not provide guidance about how to determine the appropriate size. Although there are many possible outcomes, in the author's opinion the options

---

[*] Some online reference sites include http://energy.gov/ne/nuclear-reactor-technologies/small-modular-nuclear-reactors; http://www.world-nuclear.org/info/Nuclear-Fuel-Cycle/Power-Reactors/Small-Nuclear-Power-Reactors/; http://www. nrc.gov/reactors/advanced.html; and and https://www.iaea.org/NuclearPower/Downloadable/SMR/files/IAEA_SMR_Booklet_2014.pdf.

are likely to be planning zones of 5-mile radius, 2-mile radius, 1-mile radius, and site-only (i.e., no offsite zone). The site-only option and the 1-mile-radius option could essentially be the same if the owner-controlled area is sufficiently large. One of the unanswered questions is the relationship between the number of installed reactor modules and the planning zone. It is possible that new regulations will allow a site-only emergency plan for a specified number of modules, a 1-mile offsite zone up to an second specified number, a 2-mile zone up to a third specified number of modules, and so forth.*

DECOMMISSIONED PLANTS

The original operating license for a commercial power reactor is for 40 years. In the early 2000s, the Commission created a process to extend an original operating licensee in increments of 20 years, depending on the outcome of inspections related to the management of aging plant equipment. As of this writing, all U.S. plants have either received their extended operating licensee or are in the licensing process to receive it. A few plants have already entered their extended operating phase. It was generally expected by the Commission and by industry that all of the operating plants would enter extended operations and that most would extend their licenses into a second extended operating phase.

From 2012 to 2014, the industry and Commission were caught off guard and essentially unprepared when four nuclear plants decided to permanently cease operations, in one case with only a few months' warning. These plants were San Onofre, Kewaunee, Crystal River, and Vermont Yankee. Each situation was unique. At San Onofre, it was because the cost of maintaining two idle plants for years while fabricating and installing new steam generators† was more than the expected return on investment. At Crystal River, it was because the primary containment building was found to be inadequate when it was opened to replace its original steam generators and the cost of a new containment was more than the expected return on investment. At Kewaunee, it was because virtually all of its contracts to supply electricity expired simultaneously at a time of extremely low natural gas prices, and the prices customers were willing to pay did not support continued plant operation. At Vermont Yankee, the cost of replacing aging plant equipment was greater than the expected return on investment. Prior to these four sites, the most recent reactors to be decommissioned were Zion Units 1 and 2.‡

Permanently Defueled Emergency Plans (PDEPs) have been approved for San Onofre, Kewaunee, Crystal River, and Vermont Yankee, the last being San Onofre in June 2015. Each licensee submitted license amendments to request exception from parts of the 10 CFR Part 50 emergency preparedness

---

* Some useful references related to emergency preparedness for small modular reactors include NRC-2008-0237, *Policy Statement on the Regulation of Advanced Reactors*, May 9, 2008 (73 FR 26349), with additional discussion in a staff memorandum dated March 26, 2008; SECY-08-0130, *Updated Policy Statement on Regulation of Advanced Reactors*, September 11, 2008; SECY-03-0047, *Policy Issues related to Licensing Non-Light-Water Reactor Designs*, March 28, 2003; SECY-10-0034, *Potential Policy, Licensing, and Key Technical Issues for Small Modular Nuclear Reactor Designs*, March 28, 2010; SECY-11-0152, *Development of an Emergency Planning and Preparedness Framework for Small Modular Reactors*, October 28, 2011; Memorandum, G. Tracy to the Commission, "Current Status of the Source Term and Emergency Preparedness Policy Issues for Small Modular Reactors," May 30, 2013; NEI Position Paper, *Small Modular Reactor Source Terms*, December 27, 2012; NEI Position Paper, *Proposed Methodology and Criteria for Establishing the Technical Basis for Small Modular Reactor Emergency Planning Zone*, December 23 2013; and a memorandum from M. Mayfield to the NEI, "Questions on White Paper Describing Proposed Methodology and Criteria for Establishing the Technical Basis for Small Modular Reactor Emergency Planning Zone," June 11, 2014.

† Designing, constructing, and installing new steam generators for the two units would require up to 5 years. The licensee, Southern California Edison, also needed to settle lawsuits with the vendor (Mitsubishi Industries) over who would bear the responsibility and costs because of tube failures in the newly installed generators previously constructed by Mitsubishi; those lawsuits were not expected to be settled for several years.

‡ A partial list of U.S. plants that ceased operations prior to 2000 includes Shippingport, Three Mile Island Unit 2, Rancho Seco, Trojan, Zion, Fort Saint Vrain, Big Rock Point, Lacrosse Boiling Water Reactor, Yankee Rowe, Connecticut Yankee, Humboldt Bay, and Maine Yankee.

regulations. Each amendment request was individually evaluated by licensing reviewers based on a combination of the requirements that apply to independent spent fuel storage locations and the historical precedents created by the exemptions granted to previous licensees. The final licensing decision to grant the exemptions was made by the Commissioners.

One of the issues that needs to be addressed is when licensees can begin reducing their emergency preparedness program prior to receiving an approved PDEP from the Commission. This becomes an issue because the spectrum of possible accidents is greatly reduced when the fuel is out of the reactor vessel and placed in the spent fuel storage pool. Issues arose in this instance when licensees made changes to their final safety analysis report to reflect the current plant condition (e.g., no fuel in the reactor vessel) and then used the revised analysis to support changes in their emergency plan. The licensee correctly used their authority to change the safety analysis without NRC approval, but incorrectly used their authority to make changes to their emergency plan without NRC approval. The problem was that only the Commission can change a licensee's licensing basis; it cannot be changed by a licensee.

The Commission has directed the development of emergency preparedness regulations that define the program that is required after a plant permanently ceases operation until the time that all fuel is permanently removed from the spent fuel pool. The Commission issued an advance notice of preliminary rulemaking in September 2015. The current schedule is to publish a draft regulatory basis for the rulemaking in November 2016, provide the preliminary final rule to the Commission in April 2018, and the final rule in approximately June 2019.

The current emergency preparedness requirements fully apply as long as fuel remains in the reactor vessel. The goal is to define which requirements continue to apply after all fuel has been transferred to the spent fuel storage pool and then to gradually reduce program requirements based on the age of the fuel (i.e., time since operation). The Commission has selected a criteria of uncovered or uncooled fuel requiring 10 hours or more to heat up to the fuel cladding ignition temperature as the time at which the emergency planning zone can be reduced to the owner-controlled area and formal offsite preparedness activities discontinued. The Commission believes that 10 hours is sufficiently long that a licensee can be expected to be able to take effective measures to provide spent fuel pool cooling even in the absence of offsite emergency plans.

NUREG-0654, REVISION 2

NUREG-0654, Revision 1 (NRC, 1980c), is the foundational document that describes the planning required to support a radiological emergency response program and the planning elements to be described in a licensee or offsite agency emergency plan. Both the Commission and FEMA use NUREG-0654 to evaluate new emergency plans and propose changes to existing plans. The Commission and FEMA recognized in 2012 that Revision 1 contained numerous superseded planning elements and did not address guidance and regulations that had been issued in the previous 30 years and agreed to undertake a joint effort to revise, update, and modernize the document to current standards. The revision goals were to simplify and consolidate guidance, maintain the existing onsite/offsite linkage, clarify existing guidance, and to avoid impacting any existing determination of reasonable assurance. It is anticipated that the current portions of some existing guidance documents will be combined into a Revision 2, and the older guidance documents will be retired. The existing supplements to Revision 1 will be combined into Revision 2 and the supplements retired. The regulations.gov docket numbers for Revision 2 are FEMA-2012-0026 and NRC-2015-0133. NUREG-0654, Revision 2, was made available for public comment on May 29, 2015 (see 80 FR 30739). The anticipated release date of the final Revision 2 is mid-2017.

2 Protective Responses

This chapter discusses the theoretical and practical aspects of recognizing emergency events and of determining the protective response to a release of radioactive material. The ultimate goal of an emergency preparedness program is to ensure that adequate measures are taken to protect the health and safety of the public. The first step in meeting this goal is to recognize that an emergency is occurring that requires a protective response. Then, licensees and offsite authorities must have processes that result in implementing the best level of protection for the public and for emergency workers; however, the best protection may not always result in a complete avoidance of radiation exposure and dose.

NUCLEAR REGULATORY COMMISSION SAFETY GOALS AND LARGE EARLY RELEASES

According to the Federal Emergency Management Agency (FEMA), an emergency is a "natural or man-made catastrophe that warrants action to save lives and to protect property, public health, and safety." The U.S. Congress declared in the Robert T. Stafford Disaster Assistance and Emergency Relief Act (1988) that "special measures, designed to assist the efforts of the affected States in expediting the rendering of aid, assistance, and emergency services, and the reconstruction and rehabilitation of devastated areas" were necessary and that a comprehensive emergency preparedness system should be implemented for all hazards. The Nuclear Regulatory Commission (NRC) defines the risk to the public from the operation of a nuclear power plant as the risk from exposure to radioactive materials entering the environment because of routine operations and accidents. The overall risk is calculated using the best-available probabilistic risk assessment and does not include the overall nuclear fuel cycle (whose risk has been evaluated separately), the diversion of special nuclear material, or potential security events or challenges.[*] The Commission's safety goals for the design and operation of a power reactor are that an average person living in a plant's vicinity should not have an incremental or marginal risk of accidental death greater than 1.0E-3 (one-tenth of one percent) times the combined (local) risk of accidental death from other sources; they should not have an incremental risk of death from all radiogenic cancers greater than 1.0E-3 times the overall (local) risk of cancer death due to all other sources of cancer; and the overall societal risk of plant operation should be comparable to or less than the overall risk from alternative means to generate electricity (NRC, 1986g,h).[†] The average risk of accidental death in the United States is 5.0E-4 per person per year as described in NUREG/CR-6595 (Pratt et al., 2004). In addition, during an accident, the risk of fatality within 1 mile should be less than 5.0E-7/year, and the risk of a latent fatality due to future cancers should be less than 2.0E-6/year. For comparison, a risk of 1.0E-6, or "one-in-a-million," is the most common regulatory standard of acceptable risk applied to hazardous materials.

---

[*] The Commission's policy statement on plant safety goals specifically mentions sabotage (i.e., an insider threat). It was promulgated 6 years before the design basis threat was codified, at a time when site attack was considered such a remote possibility that it was not mentioned in the statement. The Commission did not include sabotage in its deliberations based on a lack of basis to calculate the risk; the Commission reaffirmed the continuing lack of a firm basis to calculate an increase in the marginal or incremental risk of a reactor accident due to plant attack or terrorist activity in SECY 03-0165, *Evaluation of Nuclear Power Reactor Emergency. Preparedness Planning Basis Adequacy in the Post-9/11 Threat Environment.*

[†] Also see SECY 89-102, *Implementation of the Safety Goals*; SECY 93-128, *Status of Action Plan for Regulating Fuel Cycle Facilities*; SECY 93-138, *Recommendation on Large Release Definition*; SECY 97-007, *Weekly Information Report—Week Ending January 3, 1997*; SECY 97-208, *Elevation of the Core Damage Frequency Objective to a Fundamental Commission Safety Goal*; SECY 97-287, *Final Regulatory Guidance on Risk-Informed Regulation: Policy Issues*; SECY 98-015, *Final General Regulatory Guide and Standard Review Plan for Risk-Informed Regulation of Power Reactors*; and SECY 98-101, *Modifications to the Safety Goal Policy Statement.*

The Commission's safety goals were updated in the 1990s to include a maximum risk of "large early release" less than or equal to 1.0E-5 per reactor per year. Because residents closest to the plant have the largest individual risk of accidental death, the Commission required the risk of accidental death to be evaluated for persons within 1 mile of the reactor or, if none lived within 1 mile, then at the 1-mile boundary. The Commission required the risk of cancer deaths to be evaluated throughout a region around the plant 10 miles in radius. The Commission also noted that its safety goals are discussed in the context of acceptable risks, not acceptable deaths (outcomes), and that no actual deaths are considered acceptable or permissible. Regarding "large early releases," the Commission has stated

> As a part of a program to implement the Safety Goal Policy, the staff was directed by the Commission to develop a definition for a parameter to be termed a "large release." This would be a major release of fission products to the environment from a severe accident which is coupled with containment failure. Such a large, but exceedingly rare, event would be a surrogate definition for the major accident which would create a public health threat equivalent to the Quantitative Health Objectives (QHOs) in the Commission's Safety Goal Policy. The intent would be that a release of this magnitude or greater would occur with a frequency of less than once in a million reactor-years of operation. ... The ACRS has previously recommended, and the Commission has endorsed, a position that surrogates for the QHOs should be simple and not be so conservative as to create a de facto new policy. In addition, the Commission had recommended to the staff that the large release definition should be related to a dose outside the plant boundary which would cause one hypothetical death per accident. ... Using risk analysis information for a number of plants, ... staff calculations have shown that releases sufficient to cause one fatality would be equivalent to health objective values far less than the QHOs. In addition, calculated health impacts were shown to be very complex functions of the details of the particular plant and of the accident sequence. The goals that the surrogate would be simple, but not excessively conservative, have been elusive. The staff has proposed that, rather than a quantitative definition of a large release in terms of a number of curies or a fraction of core inventory as ACRS has previously suggested, a qualitative definition should be used. The definition proposed by the staff is as follows: "A large release is any release from an event involving severe core damage, reactor coolant system pressure boundary failure, and early failure or significant bypass of the containment.[*]

and in NRC (2002a, Note 3),

> In this context, large early release frequency (LERF) is being used as a surrogate for the early fatality QHO. It is defined as the frequency of those accidents leading to significant, unmitigated releases from containment in a time frame prior to effective evacuation of the close-in population such that there is a potential for early health effects. Such accidents generally include unscrubbed releases associated with early containment failure at or shortly after vessel breach, containment bypass events, and loss of containment isolation. This definition is consistent with accident analyses used in the safety goal screening criteria discussed in the Commission's regulatory analysis guidelines.

Per NUREG/CR-6595 (Pratt et al., 2004), large early releases capable of causing an offsite fatality can potentially occur while the reactor is at power and for 8 days (roughly 200 hours) after reactor power is brought to zero. For an offsite fatality to be "early," the victim must suffer central nervous system syndrome, requiring a release capable of delivering at least 1000 rem/h at a distance 1 mile from the reactor.[†] Radiation dose less than this value may also be fatal, but the fatality does not occur promptly (within the first few days after exposure), thus allowing some opportunity for successful medical intervention.

---

[*] Letter from D. Ward, Chairman, Advisory Committee on Reactor Safeguards, to I. Selin, Chairman, Nuclear Regulatory Commission, "Definition of a Large Release for Use with the Safety Goal Policy," 1992.

[†] Note that this value is based on health physics considerations and is the author's. The Commission has not adopted specific release (in curies) or dose (in rem) values characteristic of a "large" release. The discussion follows from the Commission's definition of large early release.

The meaning of "early" in the context of "large early release" has not been clearly defined for regulatory applications, such as evaluating changes in core damage frequency due to changes in plant configuration. Arguments can be made for starting the early period at the onset of reactor core damage (making the necessary source term available), the declaration time of a General Emergency classification (requiring a recommendation to evacuate the public close to the reactor), the time offsite authorities make an evacuation decision (confirming an evacuation of the public will take place), or the time the public is informed of an evacuation order (implementing the protective evacuation). The author would suggest starting the "early" period at the onset of core damage because this is when the necessary inventory of radioactive material becomes available—theoretically, failures leading to offsite dose can occur at any time after a large radioactive inventory has escaped the reactor core. As currently used, a release becomes "late" (or more correctly "not-early") when evacuation of the close-in public is completed. The best *a priori* estimate of this time is the current site-specific evacuation time estimate study, acknowledging that in any particular incident there could be a lack of available public safety resources to carry out an evacuation, or offsite conditions may not allow evacuation in the predicted time (such as after the passage of a tornado, following an earthquake, or during a blizzard). There are no current NRC or FEMA acceptance standards for evaluating close-in evacuations. Whether or not to prescribe such standards for the evacuation of close-in populations remains a controversial issue, the current majority opinion being not to implement such standards.

DEFENSE IN DEPTH

Based purely on numerical risk models, plants are actually operated at risks 1000 to 10,000 times lower than the Commission safety goals, with the precise value for each plant fluctuating slightly over time as the plant configuration changes. This would suggest, and industry has tried to argue, that emergency planning is not required or, if required, can be greatly reduced from its current level of effort. The Commission and other public safety agencies have not agreed with industry's position, and the present level of required emergency planning is essentially the same as it was immediately following the Three Mile Island accident. The Commission regards emergency preparedness as a rational "defense in depth" measure. Although the Commission has not formally defined "defense in depth," a working definition is

A layered approach to reactor plant design and operation in which regulation, design, construction, operation, testing, and maintenance each forms a separate safety barrier and all act together to prevent accidents from happening and mitigate any accident consequences. Plant locations in low population areas and a preplanned emergency preparedness program further reduce the likelihood of public health consequences should all safety barriers fail.

The emergency preparedness objective is to provide dose savings, and in some cases life saving, for a spectrum of accidents that could produce offsite doses (NRC, 1978a, 1980c). The Commission, the Environmental Protection Agency (EPA), and FEMA have agreed since the mid-1970s that no offsite dose to the public is desirable, that acceptable values for dose to the public during an accident cannot be determined, and that emergency planning efforts cannot be limited to any specific predetermined accident sequence. The Commission agrees that, although severe reactor accidents are highly unlikely, the option of no preplanning for emergencies is unwise and that planning for the worst case (e.g., most dose-producing) possible reactor accident is not warranted. Emergency planning bounds core melt accidents in that planning for accidents of lesser consequences also provide for effective dose reduction in the event of more severe accidents. The Commission considers emergency planning as prudent should a severe accident occur, not requiring inordinate licensee or public resources considering the potential consequences (NRC, 2002a):

In theory, one could construct a more generous regulatory framework for consideration of those risk-informed changes that may have the effect of increasing risk to the public. Such a framework would include, of course, assurance of continued adequate protection (that level of protection of the public health and safety that must be reasonably assured regardless of economic cost). But it could also include provision for possible elimination of all measures not needed for adequate protection, which either do not effect a substantial reduction in overall risk or result in continuing costs that are not justified by the safety benefits. Instead, ... the NRC has chosen a more restrictive policy that would permit only small increases in risk, and then only when it is reasonably assured, among other things, that sufficient defense in depth and sufficient margins are maintained. This policy is adopted because of uncertainties and to account for the fact that safety issues continue to emerge regarding design, construction, and operational matters notwithstanding the maturity of the nuclear power industry. These factors suggest that nuclear power reactors should operate routinely only at a prudent margin above adequate protection. The safety goal subsidiary objectives are used as an example of such a prudent margin.

REASONABLE ASSURANCE

The goal of radiological emergency preparedness is to establish reasonable assurance that adequate protective measures to protect the health and safety of the public can be taken in the event of an emergency. Reasonable assurance is determined by the NRC as described in 10 CFR 50.47(a)(1). FEMA is responsible for determining the adequacy of state and local emergency plans and that reasonable assurance exists that offsite officials can implement those plans and provides findings, information, and recommendations to the Commission. Ultimately, the existence of reasonable assurance, or its lack, is a value judgment based on professional experience and a preponderance of evidence. A finding of reasonable assurance is a prerequisite for licensing a commercial reactor. A reactor may be ordered to cease operation by the Commission if either onsite or offsite reasonable assurance is lost.

Reasonable assurance is that level of resources, preplanning effort, equipment, facilities, training, and practice (drills) that together would seem prudent to a reasonable person,[*] such that the reasonable person would have confidence that protective measures would be successfully implemented for a wide range of accidents under the likely range of environmental conditions. It should provide the public at least the same degree of protection as is provided for all other predictable hazards. The test is one of prudence. Reasonable assurance does not require the level of protective planning necessary to satisfy the most skeptical member of the public and does not require the capability to implement protective actions under the most extreme combination of circumstances imaginable. It does not require offsite authorities to prevent any radiation exposure to members of the public during an emergency, but it does require that they limit any public radiation doses to far below radiation injury thresholds by implementing Protective Action Guides. Offsite authorities may implement Protective Action Guides that are more protective than those recommended by the EPA but may not plan for Protective Action Guides that are less protective.

Reasonable assurance requires a level of protection beyond merely implementing the emergency plan in the most common circumstances. It requires a capability to effectively implement emergency plans under the entire likely range of circumstances that can be reasonably foreseen based on evidence and experience, including the ability to take actions outside of the preplanned zones as necessary. Reasonable assurance provides a high degree of likelihood that members of the public

---

[*] The *reasonable man criteria* is often found in both philosophy and law and describes the position that would be taken or accepted by a hypothetical rational person who is well informed about the subject (although not necessarily an expert) and not driven by emotion. The implication is that a reasonable man would not accept no emergency planning as a responsible action.

will not be injured by exposure to radiation and assurance that many, or most, members of the public will not be exposed to radiation at all. However, it is not a commitment to ensure that all members of the public avoid a radiation dose or contamination during an emergency, under any possible circumstance. The reasonable assurance standard assumes that protective systems (e.g., sirens, radios, buses, roads) can fail and requires a diversity of means, as well as backup capabilities, for the most critical systems and components. One aspect of "reasonable" is the (often unmet) expectation that the public understands that, although all radiation exposure may engender some additional risk, not all radiation exposure results in physical harm.

Reasonable assurance is established based on a licensee complying with its operating license, with Commission regulations and guidance, and with other applicable federal guidance and standards, and it is based on offsite authorities maintaining an adequate emergency preparedness program as evaluated by FEMA. It is maintained and regularly demonstrated through a robust drill and exercise program with periodic (during the 1980s, annually; currently, biennially) evaluation by the Commission and FEMA.

DESIGN BASIS

Design basis refers to the complete set of requirements and performance standards that define how a component, system, structure, building, or entire plant must be constructed to respond to a given situation. The design basis also generally includes those ongoing tests, reviews, and surveillances that will demonstrate that the as-built configuration continues to meet the design criteria. The design basis is primarily used when making licensing decisions about a plant. Only a plant whose design, construction, and operation meet or exceed the design basis is capable of being licensed to operate. The design basis may include requirements for the design of staffing, procedures, training, engineering evaluations, and other programs to ensure that plant personnel are and remain capable of safely operating the plant. All aspects of plant operation have a design basis, whether defined by the Commission or by the licensee, including the emergency preparedness and security programs. A plant is permitted to continue to operate after receiving its license as long as it demonstrates that it remains within its design basis.

A *design basis accident* is a postulated accident that a nuclear power plant must be designed and built to withstand without a loss of the components, systems, or structures necessary to ensure public health and safety. Typically, the design requirement is that, for critical safety functions, a system must be capable of achieving its safety function during the postulated accident even with the failure of any one system component. A design basis accident is used primarily in making licensing decisions, although minimum and maximum operating parameters and equipment testing requirements are derived from the design basis accident. One aspect of remaining within the plant design basis is operating at all times in a plant configuration capable of responding to a design basis accident. Note that a design basis accident is generally not the worst possible accident or the accident with the greatest consequences. The specific design basis accidents that apply to a plant were selected based on the Commission's safety goals and probabilistic risk. One way to look at the spectrum of design basis accidents is that they are the most significant accidents that could occur that are expected to be handled entirely by control room operators without requiring significant additional resources (e.g., implementation of the site emergency plan).

For the most part, a design basis accident does cause implementation of the emergency plan as a measure of prudence, rather than because the additional capabilities are needed to ensure adequate protection of the public. This implementation is a prudent step as protection against the very unlikely situation in which the plant configuration degrades to a beyond-design-basis condition.

EMERGENCY PREPAREDNESS PLANNING BASIS

... the Task Force concluded that there was no specific accident sequence that could be isolated as the one for which to plan, because each accident could have different consequences, both in nature and degree. Further, the range of possible selections for a planning basis is very large, starting with a zero point of requiring no planning at all because significant offsite radiological accident consequences are unlikely to occur, to planning for the worst physically possible accident regardless of its extremely low likelihood. (NRC, 1978a)

Emergency preparedness planning basis refers to the collection of facts, policies, and assumptions that define the minimum and maximum scope of an acceptable emergency preparedness program. The basis in effect is a cost–benefit analysis that predefines where planning is done, the scale of that planning, and the performance objectives the planning must achieve (e.g., how severe an accident must the planning handle). Although neither the NRC nor FEMA has formally defined the radio-logical emergency preparedness planning basis, it broadly consists of the following:

- A spectrum of potential accidents—some result in no core damage, some result in increas-ing core damage, and some have severe core damage.
- Potential accidents are not limited to licensing design basis accidents; more severe beyond-design-basis accidents are considered in the design of the emergency preparedness program.
- Radiological preplanning is done only in designated emergency planning zones.
- Core damage can occur 15 to 30 minutes after a reactor core is uncovered; radiological source terms can include radioactive gases (gap) or gases mixed with fission products (core melt).
- Releases of radioactive material can initiate 30 minutes to a few hours after core damage occurs.
- Offsite authorities have some warning of core damage and prior to the start of a radiologi-cal release, although the warning time may be short.
- The primary options for protective actions for the public are shelter-in-place and evacuation; after 1998, another is issuance of potassium iodide to the public when designated by the state.
- Actions based on the existing emergency plans can be readily expanded beyond the desig-nated emergency planning zone, if necessary.

In addition to defining what the planning basis is, NUREG-0396 discusses the planning basis limits and what the planning basis is not. The expectation is that reasonable, not massive, emergency planning programs are established in emergency planning zones. The planning basis specifi-cally excludes requirements for

- Extensive, large-scale, stockpiles of anti-contamination clothing and provisions for the general public
- Decontamination facilities capable of handling essentially the entire evacuated population and their vehicles and livestock/pets
- New construction of hardened or other specially equipped public shelters; for radiological accident purposes, such facilities could be used in planning where they already exist for other purposes, such as national attack
- Construction of new medical facilities capable of providing treatment of radiological injury on a large (public) scale
- Dedicated permanent emergency stockpiles of non-contaminated food and drink for the general public, or stockpiles of non-contaminated animal feeds for livestock/pets
- Acquisition, staging, storage, or maintenance of sufficient decontamination equipment to provide for the prompt decontamination of land, property, or equipment owned by the public
- Participation by the general public in tests, demonstrations, or evaluations of emergency plan capabilities (e.g., emergency plan exercises)

Following the 2001 terrorist attacks in the United States, the Commission determined that the existing emergency preparedness planning basis remained valid and bounded reactor accidents initiated by site attack. By this they primarily meant that, even if adversaries gain effective control over a reactor, severely damage or destroy accessible safety equipment, and disable or prevent the operation of designed safety systems, then the physics of nuclear fission and heat transfer would prevent them from damaging nuclear fuel faster or to a greater degree than the accidents that are already included in (e.g., bounded by) the current emergency planning basis. Essentially, the planning basis already includes accidents where essential cooling water is removed from the reactor as it operates at full power; taking away cooling water intentionally rather than as the result of a malfunction or pipe break does not worsen the resulting core damage. A terrorist scenario could result in increased radiological risk to the public only if offsite authorities are caught unaware by a major release. The Commission has required addition actions by licensees to address the "caught unaware" aspect of a site attack, making it essentially impossible for offsite authorities not to be informed in time to take appropriate actions to protect the health and safety of the public.

The programmatic and performance elements of the emergency preparedness basis are captured in the 16 emergency preparedness planning standards that were codified in 1981 as 10 CFR 50.47(b)(i) through 50.47(b)(xvi). The planning standards are the essential operational, communication, and planning functions that are considered necessary to organize a successful emergency response to meet the planning basis. Together, the planning standards address routine and emergency response organization staffing, incident command-and-control, accident assessment measures, the range of onsite and offsite protective responses, response facilities, interfacility communications, public notification and information, emergency responder training, drills and exercises of emergency plans and procedures, and ongoing planning functions. The planning standards were largely articulated in Regulatory Guide 1.101 (NRC, 1975a, 1977a), although not called by that name. They form the basis for NUREG-0654 (NRC, 1980c), although NUREG-0654 lists the standards by letter beginning with A, rather than by number.

EMERGENCY PLANNING ZONES

NUREG-0654 defines an emergency planning zone as "the areas for which planning is needed to assure that prompt and effective actions can be taken to protect the public in the event of an accident." Although not explicitly stated in either NUREG-0654 or NUREG-0396, "protect the public" means to limit radiation doses to the public to prevent acute or life-threatening radiation injury, and "effective actions" generally means the ability to evacuate when required. Although initially "when required" meant as indicated by direct in-field radiological measurements, at the current time it primarily means as indicated by computer-based radiological dose projections. "Protect the public" cannot be taken as an absolute certainty that individual members of the public will not receive radiation doses greater than applicable Protective Action Guides. Radiological emergency plans are required by 10 CFR 50.47(c)(2) for reactor licensees and offsite jurisdictions (states, counties, parishes, municipalities, tribes, and federal entities) in identified emergency planning zones. The emergency planning zone concept was introduced in NUREG-0396 in response to confusion on the part of offsite officials after 1970 about where emergency planning was required.

Title 10 of the Code of Federal Regulations, Part 100, promulgated in 1962, governs reactor siting. In Part 100, Section 100.1, Purpose, it states, in part, "Siting factors and criteria are important in assuring that radiological doses from … postulated accidents will be acceptably low … and that physical characteristics unique to the site that could pose a significant impediment to development of emergency plans are identified." Section 100.10 states, "The Commission will take the following factors into consideration in determining the acceptability of a site for a power or testing reactor: … (b) Population density and use characteristics, including the exclusion area, low population zone, and population center distance." The working assumption was that if the number of persons in the area surrounding the (proposed) reactor site was small enough, then offsite authorities would always be able to take effective action in the event of a radiological release. No specific credit is taken in Part 100 for the effectiveness of offsite emergency response actions. The various zones that relate to reactor emergency preparedness are discussed below.

EXCLUSION AREA

Each reactor site is surrounded by an exclusion area or zone, inside of which the licensee has the authority to determine all activities, including the exclusion or removal of all personnel and property. In this case, authority includes an essentially immediate capability to unilaterally impose protective measures in the areas without the need to work through offsite authorities. Public use areas (e.g., parks, roads, railroads, waterways) may be part of an exclusion area provided that agreements are in place to limit or control access as directed by the licensee, and that immediate measures to protect public health and safety will be taken in an emergency. The intent is to prohibit residences in the exclusion area, although there are a small number of reactor sites with residences; in these cases, there are agreements in place for immediate evacuation of the resident population by the licensee. Activities unrelated to reactor operations are permitted in the exclusion area provided there are no significant additional hazards to the public. The licensee must have arrangements in place to evacuate persons engaged in the unrelated activities (for example, farming on leased lands), and persons engaged in unrelated activities should not receive radiation doses exceeding the exclusion area dose limits before they can be evacuated.[*]

The exclusion area must be sized so that a hypothetical adult located along its edge does not receive a dose of more than 25 rem whole body (now TEDE) and not more than 300 rem thyroid organ dose (now TODE and CDE), for a continuous 2-hour exposure. In practice, the exclusion area may be, and often is, larger than is required by regulation. The postulated radiation exposure results from a "major accident," which is not defined but is required to be sufficient to melt fuel. The term *major accident* predates the more modern term *design basis accident*. The procedure for determining applicable limits of a release resulting in both whole body and thyroid organ dose is not given. Although worst-case[†] accident meteorology is generally used in licensing actions, the meteorology to be used in the analysis is not specified in the requirement (the difference between doses calculated using best-case and worst-case meteorology being different by about a factor of 100). The specified radiation dose limits are numerically equal to the occupational dose limits when Part 100 was promulgated in 1962, as found in NBS Handbook 69 (NBS, 1959).

It is curious that, although emergency limits on bone marrow dose were in widespread use in the 1960s and 1970s, the exclusion area calculation does not require this calculation. For the radioisotope mix resulting from melted fuel, occupational limits for whole body and thyroid organ dose are more restrictive than those for skin (organ) dose and eye (organ) dose, so skin and eye dose are not considered when establishing the exclusion area. Typical reactor exclusion areas vary from 1/2 mile to 2 miles in radius. When more than one reactor is sited together, the site exclusion area is the combination of the individual exclusion areas for each reactor. If the reactors are located sufficiently far apart from one another the resulting exclusion zone would be oval in shape rather than circular. Simultaneous releases from multiple reactors are only considered when reactors share interconnected critical safety systems.[‡] The exclusion area must be maintained throughout the operating life of the plant. A licensee desiring to change reactor fuel, operating power, or other reactor

---

[*] See Section 2.1.2 in NUREG-0800 (NRC, 1996j).

[†] Worst-case meteorology generally assumes a very low wind speed and a very stable and concentrated plume of radioactive material (stability class F) directed at the largest population center.

[‡] One might expect the Part 100 exclusion area criteria to be updated as part of the Commission's post-Fukushima actions, but determining the exclusion area for a multiple-reactor site using simultaneous radiological releases from all units is not currently identified as a planned action.

characteristics in a manner that would result in the radiological doses defined in Part 100 occurring at greater distances than provided for in the initial license would have to demonstrate that they have effective control over the larger area before being permitted to proceed.

Low Population Zone

Regulatory Guide 4.7 (NRC, 1998c) states

Locating reactors away from densely populated centers is part of the NRC's defense-in-depth philosophy and facilitates emergency planning and preparedness as well as reducing potential doses and property damage in the event of a severe accident.

The boundaries of the low population zone are calculated using the same radiological limits as the exclusion area, except that the exposure time is over the entire passage of the plume. In the EPA's *Manual of Protective Action Guides* (USEPA, 1992), the "entire passage" time is given as 30 days, allowing for an undetermined delay between core damage and a release to the environment, the purposeful venting of containment several days after core damage, and/or several releases ("burps"). Title 10 of the Code of Federal Regulations, Part 100, does not give population density or numerical population limits for the "low population" zone and does not address the "population" aspect in any way, except that a low population zone is acceptable if it is determined that appropriate protective measures can be taken on behalf of the enclosed populace in the event of a serious accident. A *serious accident* is not defined. The primary differences between the exclusion area and low population zone are that the licensee is not required to have physical control over the low population zone and residences are permitted in the low population zone.

Section 2.1.3.4 of Regulatory Guide 1.70 (NRC, 1978b) states

The low population zone (as defined in 10 CFR Part 100) should be specified and the basis for its selection discussed. A scaled map of the zone should be provided to illustrate topographic features; highways, railways, waterways, and any other transportation routes that may be used for evacuation purposes; and the location of all facilities and institutions such as schools, hospitals, prisons, beaches, and parks. Facilities and institutions beyond the low population zone which, because of their nature, may require special consideration when evaluating emergency plans, should be identified out to a distance of five miles. A table of population distribution within the low population zone should provide estimates of peak daily, as well as seasonal transient, population within the zone, including estimates of transient population in the facilities and institutions identified.

Section 2.1.3.6 states

The cumulative resident population projected for the year of initial plant operation should be plotted to a distance of at least 30 miles and compared with a cumulative population resulting from a uniform population density of 500 people/sq. mile in all directions from the plant. Similar information should be provided for the end of plant life but compared with a cumulative population resulting from a uniform population density of 1000 people/sq. mile.[*]

The standard review plan states that, if a proposed reactor site equals or exceeds these values, then the applicant should consider alternative sites having lower population densities. The standard review plan also states

A site that exceeds the population density guidelines of Position C.3 of Regulatory Guide 4.7 can nevertheless be selected and approved if, on balance, it offers advantages compared with available alternative sites when all of the environmental, safety, and economic aspects of the proposed and alternative sites are considered.

---

[*] Also see Section III of NUREG-0800 (NRC, 1996j).

The regulatory basis for the 30-mile evaluation distance found in Regulatory Guide 1.70 is unclear, and it does not correspond to any other distance used in emergency planning at any time from the 1970s through the present. It is also unclear why the population values of 500 and 1000 persons per square mile were chosen. Appendix A, Table A, of Regulatory Guide 4.7 (NRC, 1988c) includes the 500-person-per-square-mile criterion but uses a 20-mile analysis distance instead of 30 miles.

The low population zone is determined as part of the initial reactor licensing and is not required to be maintained over the operating life of the plant. In particular, the Commission and FEMA do not require offsite authorities to implement policies and restrictions that prevent population growth in the licensed low population zone. In part, the Commission's requirements relating to updating evacuation time estimates is a recognition that population in the low population zone may not be static. There are plants that have historically experienced population creep, such that the effective low population zone has shrunk over time as populations have moved toward the plant.* The effective low population zone has not generally been a controlling issue in the reauthorization of plant operating licenses.

NEAREST POPULATION CENTER

A population center is a municipality (or group of contiguous municipalities) that currently have populations greater than 25,000 or are projected to exceed populations of 25,000 during the life of the plant. The distance from a commercial power reactor to any population center must be greater than or equal to 1.33 times the distance to the low population zone boundary in the same direction. The distance to the population center is considered important; however, the Standard Review Plan states, "Population density is the controlling criteria and in this regard the corporate boundary of the community itself is not limiting. ... Where a very large city is involved, a greater distance than the one and one third factor may be required." There is no documented basis for why the value of 1.33 was chosen for this analysis. The nearest population center is determined as part of the initial reactor licensing and is not required to be maintained over the operating life of the plant. In particular, the Commission and FEMA do not require offsite authorities to implement policies and restrictions that prevent population growth in the surrounding area, so that towns within the 1.33 time exclusion area distance that do not meet the "population center" criteria at initial licensing may meet it at a future time.

PLUME PHASE AND INGESTION EXPOSURE PATHWAY EMERGENCY PLANNING ZONES

Since approximately 1980, plume phase and ingestion exposure pathway emergency planning zones have been established around all commercial nuclear power plants (and at some other nuclear facilities) as required by 10 CFR 50.54(s)(1). The plume phase emergency planning zone is approximately 10 miles in radius, with some variations to account for the boundaries of political subdivisions, significant natural or local topographical features, and the location of access and evacuation routes. The ingestion pathway emergency planning zone is approximately 50 miles in radius and may also be adjusted for the boundaries of political subdivisions and significant natural features. Ingestion pathway control plans may also include significant food processing plants located outside the planning zone but accepting foods from within the zone. Title 10 of the Code of Federal Regulations, Part 50.54(s)(2), allows a 5-mile-radius plume phase emergency planning zone and 30-mile-radius ingestion pathway zone for gas-cooled reactors and other reactors whose thermal power is less

---

* In part, this can be attributed to persons wanting to move nearer to their place of employment, either at the licensee's site or in related employment. It is also often true that the towns (and other taxing authorities) in which the plant resides tend to have more infrastructure at a lower cost than do surrounding areas because of the increased taxes paid by the utility. The improved services and amenities funded by the increased revenue also tend to attract additional residents.

than or equal to 250 megawatts. The Commission has permitted permanently defueled reactors to eliminate their associated emergency planning zones on a case-by-case basis (i.e., by licensing exception) beginning approximately 3 years after ceasing power operations. The elimination of the offsite planning zone is based on there being an essentially complete decay of all iodine isotopes and a reduction in latent decay heat below the threshold necessary to support a zirconium fire if the fuel pool were breached or drained.

Emergency planning zones are based on geographical features, population densities, and population center locations. There are several examples of large population centers bisected by the plume phase emergency planning zone boundary; in most cases, FEMA has required the planning boundary to be adjusted to include the entire affected population center, although for a few very small towns the border was adjusted to exclude the entire town. In any case, to simplify planning requirements and enhance public acceptance, the general policy has been to treat an entire town as an indivisible body and not to allow areas of the town to be subject to differing protective actions. There have been a few examples in the period from 2012 to 2015 of individual FEMA regions allowing reversal of a previous whole-town planning zone; one such example is changes made in 2013–2014 to the boundary through Granbury, TX, in the Comanche Peak emergency planning zone.

The objective of emergency response plans is to provide dose savings for a spectrum of accidents that could produce offsite doses, not to prevent all radiation doses to the public during an emergency. As an alternative to selecting a single emergency planning basis accident, the Commission and FEMA have identified the accident timing, release characteristics, and potential consequences of a spectrum of accidents that require a response. As described in NUREG-0396 (NRC, 1978a), the size of the emergency planning zone was chosen so that

- Doses from all design basis accidents are less than the Protective Action Guides outside of the emergency planning zone.
- Doses from most core melt accidents are less than Protective Action Guides outside of the emergency planning zone.
- For worst-case accidents, life-threatening doses do not occur outside the emergency planning zone.
- The emergency planning zone is useful under unfavorable meteorology for any accident that results in dose.
- Planning by jurisdictions located inside the zone can be readily used as the basis to expand protective actions beyond its boundary on an *ad hoc* basis.

The size of the ingestion pathway zone was chosen so that

- Some of the released iodine will chemically bind into forms that do not enter the food chain.
- Measurable radioactive contamination for worst-case accidents is unlikely to occur outside the ingestion planning zone.
- The likelihood of exceeding food pathway Protective Action Guides at the ingestion zone boundary is comparable to the likelihood of exceeding plume Protective Action Guides at the plume phase emergency planning zone boundary.

Contamination is unlikely to occur outside the ingestion pathway boundary because of the anticipated deposition (fallout) of the heavier isotopes during plume travel,* taking into account the most likely source terms, the effects of wind shifts and of rain, and the effects of terrain on wind patterns. NUREG-0396 estimates that the probability of an emergency somewhere in the United States that

---

* The most significant isotopes for causing radiation dose tend also to be the heavier ones or ones that readily combine with dusts and other environmental chemicals to form heavy particles.

requires actions outside of the emergency planning zone is about 1% over 500 reactor-years of oper-ation (pp. I-9–I-10), with a probability of about 1 in 6000/year for a state affected by 10 reactors, or 1 in 60,000/year for a state affected by a single reactor.* NUREG-0396 noted on page I-41 that an ingestion pathway planning zone for milk and dairy products of about 25 miles in radius would yield a similar likelihood of an accident requiring taking action outside of the planning boundary as does the 10-mile plume phase boundary. The 50-mile radius was eventually chosen based on proposed changes (i.e., more restrictive) to ingestion pathway Protective Action Guides† because milk is not the only product of interest in the ingestion pathway zone and because the 5-to-1 ratio in size from the plume to ingestion pathway boundary is numerically simple and in keeping with traditional safety factors.

Although the Commission and FEMA have high confidence that direct protective measures for the public will not have to be implemented outside of the plume phase emergency planning zone, a key assumption is that protective measures can be readily expanded beyond the planning zone on an *ad hoc* basis when needed. The bases for this assumption include the following:

- Emergency planning zone boundaries and the boundaries of political jurisdictions, includ-ing school districts, are generally different.
- Offsite officials responsible for protective action decisions within the plume phase emer-gency planning zone are often also responsible for areas beyond the zone.
- Because of the distances from the reactor, offsite officials are expected to have longer warning times and more time to consider decisions and communicate decisions to the public, as compared to affected areas close to the reactor site.
- Public alert and notification systems (sirens and tone alert radios) generally have some coverage beyond the plume phase emergency planning zone boundary; public alerting sys-tems for radiological emergencies are often subsystems of more extensive local alerting capabilities. Often, these more extensive systems are used to warn the public of natural disasters, such as tornadoes.
- The annual distribution of emergency planning information to the public generally includes members of the public living outside the plume phase emergency planning zone because distribution is generally by Zip Codes, whose boundaries do not coincide with the emer-gency planning zone boundary.
- The Emergency Alert System (radio and television) stations for a plume phase emergency planning zone usually have extensive coverage beyond the zone.
- Some aspects of the offsite emergency plan, such as congregate care and decontamination facilities, are located outside the plume phase emergency planning zone, so the public officials responsible for those facilities already have some knowledge of local emergency plans.
- Members of the public living outside of the emergency planning zone may have some familiarity with evacuation routes and other emergency planning information from expo-sure to roadway signs and signs posted to inform the transient population within the plan-ning zone.
- Experience gained through a drill and exercise program, including the ingestion pathway, will help offsite officials in expanding protective actions. In part, a county or parish need-ing to make an unexpected protective action decision can receive assistance and expertise from those closer-in counties.

---

* Note that between 1978 (when NUREG-0396 was published) and 2015, approximately 4000 reactor-years have occurred without any activations of emergency plans outside of emergency planning zone boundaries, including during the 1979 accident at Three Mile Island.
† Protective Action Guides for iodine between 1975 and 1978 were 10 rem as calculated for the child thyroid.

Although not explicitly credited in radiological planning, public officials in areas beyond the designated emergency planning zones may also be able to readily expand protective actions because of existing emergency planning for hazardous materials, natural disasters, mass casualties, national attack (terrorism), pandemic, and other emergency planning requirements that have been implemented from the late 1980s onward.[*]

It should be noted that plumes of airborne radioactive material that do not exceed Protective Action Guides at the emergency planning zone boundary will be detectable at much farther distances and will produce measurable contamination outside of the planning zone. Radioactive material is commonly detectable in concentrations approximately five orders of magnitude below the concentration meeting the Protective Action Guides, with a dispersion of about three orders of magnitude over 10 miles for a C to D stability plume. Therefore, a plume causing Protective Action Guides to be exceeded at a 10-mile distance would be detectable by commonly used field survey instruments at a distance of approximately 30 miles from the plant.[†]

The most common standard for determining that radioactive contamination is present is about twice natural background, or concentrations four orders of magnitude below the Protective Action Guides—given a sufficiently long exposure time, the contamination criteria would likely be met at a distance of at least 25 miles from the plant for a plume exceeding Protective Action Guides at 10 miles. Contamination at, or even greatly exceeding, the detection limit, does not pose an immediate radiological hazard and should not drive protective actions for the public during the early phase of a radiological emergency. However, it is likely there will be considerable public concern about any areas that have detectable levels of airborne radioactive material or contamination. Planners and decision makers should anticipate significant pressure to take protective measures for any area affected by radioactive material, not only for those in which the preplanned thresholds for protective actions are exceeded.

Reactor licensees are required by 10 CFR 50, Appendix E, IV(B), to have the capability to assess the consequences of a radiological release. This capability must exist for all radioactive material released from the reactor site and is not limited by distance. The capability to assess is not *ad hoc* and is not limited to consequences in the designated emergency planning zones. The requirement for analysis does not stop at 10 miles. The licensee must be capable of correctly applying the Protective Action Guides to a radioactive plume at any distance and of recommending appropriate protective actions to offsite authorities. The implementation and communication of protective action decisions made by offsite authorities are *ad hoc*, extended as necessary based on existing emergency plans, not the actions taken by the licensee.

EMERGENCY CLASSIFICATIONS

An emergency classification is a brief descriptor applied to an emergency situation that summarizes its seriousness compared to other accident sequences and to the expected consequences. The descriptor provides a simplified way for emergency responders to discuss the situation and, if used correctly, improves communication among onsite and offsite responders. An emergency classification does not represent or describe a specific accident, as many initiating events can lead to the same classification. Because emergency classifications do represent gradations in accident severity, some preplanned actions (notifications, staffing of facilities, relocation of personnel, and onsite and

---

[*] See Section 6 of Homeland Security Presidential Directive 5 (USDHS, 2003a) and Presidential Policy Directive 8 (Obama, 2011). See also FEMA (2010), a previous version of which was titled *State and Local Guide 101*.

[†] Recognize that the Protective Action Guides are expressed in term of radiation dose and not in the derived concentration of airborne radioactive material. The distances are approximate and determined by the author from very rudimentary calculations solely for purposes of illustration. Readers are cautioned to consult appropriate health physics staff and to use site-specific models for the transport of radioactive material when deriving any action levels for use in an actual emergency response.

offsite protective actions) are tied to classification. Both licensees and offsite public information (e.g., press releases) often describe an accident using its emergency classification, although in the author's opinion it is unlikely that the public gains much benefit from the practice. It is appropriate to consider the process of classifying an emergency in a discussion of protective measures because adequate measures will not be taken to protect the health and safety of the public unless the licensee first recognizes the emergency condition and activates their emergency plan.

United States Scheme

Prior to 1979, reactor licensees in the United States were required to have schemes to classify accidents at their facilities; however, these schemes were negotiated between the sites and their surrounding state or states, and there was no uniformity in the classification systems. In particular, federal emergency responders were likely to be unfamiliar with the scheme in use at any particular facility, which created the potential for serious communications problems. Beginning in 1979, the NRC required all licensees to use a standard four-tier classification system (five tiers if "normal operations" is considered a classification[*]), which is described briefly in NUREG-0610 (NRC, 1979c) and more fully in NUREG-0654 (NRC, 1980c). The four standard emergency classifications are, in order of increasing accident severity, Notification of Unusual Event (NOUE), often shortened to Unusual Event (UE); Alert; Site Area Emergency (SAE), sometimes shortened to Site Emergency; and General Emergency. Licensees are required by 10 CFR 50.47(b)(4) to use this classification scheme, which states, in part, "A standard emergency classification and action level scheme ... is in use by the nuclear facility licensee," and by 10 CFR 50, Appendix E, IV(C), which states, in part, "The emergency classes defined shall include: (1) notification of unusual events, (2) alert, (3) site area emergency, and (4) general emergency. These classes are further discussed in NUREG-0654; FEMA REP-1." The classifications were described in NUREG-0654, Appendix 1, and the descriptions were updated in Bulletin 2005-02 (NRC, 2005f); additions to the NUREG-0654 classification descriptions follow.

- *Notification of Unusual Event*—Events are in process or have occurred that indicate a potential degradation of the level of safety of the plant or indicate a security threat to facility protection. No releases of radioactive material requiring offsite response or monitoring are expected unless further degradation of safety systems occurs.
- *Alert*—Events are in process or have occurred that involve an actual or potential substantial degradation of the level of safety of the plant or a security event that involves probable life-threatening risk to site personnel or damage to site equipment because of intentional malicious dedicated efforts of a hostile act. Any releases are expected to be limited to small fractions of the EPA Protective Action Guide exposure levels.
- *Site Area Emergency*—Events are in process or have occurred that involve actual or likely major failures of plant functions needed for protection of the public or security events that result in intentional damage or malicious acts (1) toward site personnel or equipment that could lead to the likely failure of or (2) that prevent effective access to equipment needed for the protection of the public. Any releases are not expected to result in exposure levels that exceed EPA Protective Action Guide exposure levels beyond the site boundary.
- *General Emergency*—Events are in process or have occurred that involve actual or imminent substantial core degradation or melting with potential for loss of containment integrity or security events that result in an actual loss of physical control of the facility. Releases can be reasonably expected to exceed EPA Protective Action Guide exposure levels offsite for more than the immediate site area.

---

[*] "Normal operations" is considered a mode of the NRC's internal emergency response plan, as discussed in NUREG-0728 (NRC, 2005j).

Note that according to the description, accidents resulting in the need to take limited protective actions for the public (e.g., exposure levels exceeding EPA Protective Action Guide exposure levels at the site boundary) are properly classified as Site Area Emergencies. All current site emergency classification schemes require a General Emergency to be declared if radiation doses are measured or projected at EPA Protective Action Guide exposure levels at a site's boundary. This is an internal inconsistency in the Commission-endorsed classification schemes that has existed since NUREG-0610. Although the current classification criteria are very unlikely to be changed, a better fit to the definition of General Emergency would be measured or projected radiation doses exceeding the Protective Action Guides at 2 miles (i.e., sufficiently far offsite to be more than the immediate area).

According to NUREG-0610, each individual reactor was expected to declare one or two Unusual Event classifications each year, an Alert every 10 to 100 years, a Site Area Emergency every 100 to 5000 years, and a General Emergency less frequently than every 5000 years (with life-threatening offsite doses no more frequently than once in 100,000 years). An Alert was expected (on the average) to release less than 10,000 Ci of total noble gases and less than 10 Ci of all iodine isotopes, and a Site Area Emergency less than 1 million Ci of total noble gases and less than 1000 Ci total iodine. In 2007, 64 reactor sites were operating 104 reactors units; according to the NUREG-0610 assumptions, a reactor fleet this size would have approximately 90 Notifications of Unusual Event per year, 1 to 10 Alerts per year, and a Site Area Emergency every 1 to 50 years. In 2004, there were 41 Notifications of Unusual Event and 2 Alerts; in 2005, there were 25 Notifications of Unusual Event and 4 Alerts; and, in 2006, there were 23 Notifications of Unusual Event, 3 Alerts, and 1 Site Area Emergency. It is likely that the actual number of Unusual Event and Alert emergency declarations is currently far fewer than anticipated in 1980 in part because large numbers of reactor licensees have adopted the NUMARC/NEI emergency action levels, which reduced the number of classifiable conditions, as well as (in some cases) raised thresholds for entering an emergency condition.

The 2006 Site Area Emergency was the first at that classification since the February 1993 vehicle intrusion event at Three Mile Island Unit 1; see Information Notice 93-94 (NRC, 1993g). Since the current classification scheme was implemented there have been zero General Emergency declarations by U.S. reactor licensees. It is likely that if the current classification scheme had existed at the time, the Three Mile Island Unit 2 accident would have been classified as a Site Area Emergency.

INTERNATIONAL SCHEME

In 1989, the International Atomic Energy Agency and the Organization for Economic Cooperation and Development (Nuclear Energy Agency)* jointly developed the International Nuclear Event Scale, as a means to report safety-related events to the International Atomic Energy Agency and its member countries (see Table 2.1). The scale uses a nine-tier classification scheme, from least significant to most significant, and is intended to apply to any incident involving radiation or radioactive material, including accidents occurring during the transport of radioactive materials or waste. The scale refers to all events not involving reactor or fuel damage as *incidents* and to those resulting in reactor core damage or fuel damage as *accidents*. The classification of a particular event depends on the number of failed safety systems (barriers, degradation of defense in depth), the onsite radiological impact and reactor or fuel damage, and the offsite radiological impact. An International Atomic Energy Agency pamphlet (IAEA, 1999c) states, in part,

> Although the Scale is designed for prompt use following an event, there will be occasions when a longer time-scale is required to understand and rate the consequences of an event. ... The Scale does not replace the criteria already adopted nationally and internationally for the technical analysis and reporting of events to Safety Authorities. Neither does it form a part of the formal emergency arrangements

---

* The OECD/NEA is an international cooperative effort among the nations of Europe, headquartered in Brussels, Belgium.

TABLE 2.1
International Nuclear Event Scale

Scale Number	Classification	Description
Out of scale	—	Events of no safety relevance
0	Deviation	Unexpected events of no safety significance
1	Anomaly	Event outside of authorized regime (technical specification violations)
2	Incident	Events with safety system failures or individual radiological overexposures
3	Serious Incident	Events with no remaining safety margin or acute radiological health effects
4	Accident without Offsite Risk	Significant reactor damage, release at or near Protective Action Guides, fatal radiological dose
5	Accident with Offsite Risk	Severe reactor damage, partial implementation of offsite protective actions
6	Serious Accident	Severe reactor damage, full implementation of offsite protective actions
7	Major Accident	Severe reactor damage, large radiological release with widespread health and environmental effects

that exist in each country to deal with radiological accidents. … It is not appropriate to use the Scale to compare safety performance among countries. Each country has different arrangements for reporting minor events to the public, and it is difficult to ensure precise international consistency in rating events at the boundary between level 0 and level 1. The statistically small number of such events, with variability from year to year, makes it difficult to provide meaningful international comparisons.

According to the International Atomic Energy Agency,

- The 1986 accident at Chernobyl would have been classified at Level 7 (Major Accident).
- The 1957 accident at the Kyshtym reprocessing plant in Russia, which required offsite evacuation, would have been classified at Level 6 (Serious Accident).
- The 1957 accident at Windscale (since renamed Sellafield) in Cumbria, U.K., and the 1979 accident at Three Mile Island would have been classified at Level 5 (Accident with Offsite Risk).
- The 1973 accident at Sellafield, which released radioactive material onsite, and the 1980 accident at the Saint Laurent reactor in France, which resulted in a damaged reactor core but no offsite release, would have been classified at Level 4 (Accident without Offsite Risk).
- The 1999 inadvertent criticality event at Tokaimura in Japan was classified at Level 4.
- The 1989 fire at the Vandellos plant in Spain, which severely damaged reactor safety systems but did not result in core damage, would have been classified at Level 3.

Governmental agencies in the United States did not participate in drafting the event scale and at first (per Commission letter to licensees, August 1990) did not support its use. A change to this position occurred in 1992 via a Generic Letter (NRC, 1992f) that communicated the Commission's decision to report reactor events to the IAEA using the International Scale if they were associated with an emergency classification of Alert or higher. The Commission committed to evaluate the event, complete the associated rating form, and submit the rating form, rather than having licensees make the IAEA report. The Commission would make the rating form public but would not necessarily allow the licensee or offsite agencies to comment on the proposed rating. In addition, the Commission would delay performing the rating using the International Scale for at least a week after the event to prevent any confusion between the emergency classification and the international scale rating. The Commission reaffirmed its use of the International Scale in SECY 95-098 (NRC, 1995e).* Between 1992 and 2001, the Commission rated 20 events at United States reactors, resulting in 3 events rated at Level 2, 4 rated at Level 1, 8 at Level 0, and the rest as out of scale. In 2001, the Commission decided to increase its participation in the International Scale, electing to rate and report all reactor, fuel cycle, nuclear materials, and radioactive materials transportation events (NRC, 2001b). This change was communicated to licensees in Regulatory Issue Summary 01-01 (NRC, 2002c).

Emergency Action Levels

Emergency action levels are sets of individual indicators or thresholds that, when they occur, require entry into an emergency classification; the emergency classification entry may then require additional actions depending on the severity of the event. The Commission does not clearly define "emergency action level" in its documents, and an inconsistent use of the term in regulation and guidance documents has often contributed to its misunderstanding. The following definition is from NUMARC/NESP-007 (NUMARC, 1992):

> ... a formal set of threshold conditions that require plant personnel to take specific actions with regard to notifying state and local governments and the public when off-normal indications or events are recognized ...

Commission regulations pertaining to emergency action levels are (underline added by author):

> 10 CFR 50.47(b)(4) states, in part, "A standard emergency classification and action level scheme, the bases of which include facility system and effluent parameters, is in use by the nuclear facility licensee."

10 CFR 50, Appendix E, IV.B, states, in part (underline added by author),

> The means to be used for determining the magnitude of and for continually assessing the impact of the release of radioactive materials shall be described, including emergency action levels that are to be used as criteria for determining the need for notification and participation of local and State agencies, the Commission, and other Federal agencies, and the emergency action levels that are to be used for determining when and what type of protective measures should be considered within and outside the site boundary to protect health and safety. The emergency action levels shall be based on in-plant conditions and instrumentation in addition to onsite and offsite monitoring.

10 CFR 50, Appendix E, IV.C, states, in part (underline added by author),

> Emergency action levels (based not only on onsite and offsite radiation monitoring information but also on readings from a number of sensors that indicate a potential emergency, such as the pressure in containment and the response of the Emergency Core Cooling System) for notification of offsite agencies shall be described.

In addition, NUREG-0610 (NRC, 1979c, p. 1) and NUREG-0654 (NRC, 1980c, pp. 1–3) state, in part (underline added by author),

> Four classes of Emergency Action Levels are established which replace the classes in Regulatory Guide 1.101, each with associated examples of initiating conditions. The classes are: Notification of Unusual Event, Alert, Site Emergency, General Emergency.

---

* Also see NRC Generic Letter 92-09, *Limited Participation by NRC in the IAEA International Nuclear Event Scale*; NRC Information Notice 2009-27, *Revised International Nuclear and Radiological Event Scale User's Manual*; NRC Regulatory Issue Summary 02-01, *Changes to NRC Participation in the International Nuclear Event Scale*; SECY-01-0071, *Expanded NRC Participation in the Use of the International Nuclear Event Scale*; SECY-11-0105, *Proposed Minor Revision to Management Directive 5.12, International Nuclear Event Scale Participation*; and SECY 92-225, *NRC Participation in World Use of the International Nuclear Event Scale*.

In the author's opinion, the Commission blurred or confused the functions of emergency classification, recognition schemes to identify accidents requiring an emergency response, and the implementation of protective action schemes for onsite and offsite persons in their original inception through the use of the same terminology to describe diverse emergency functions. Title 10 of the Code of Federal Regulations, Part 50, Appendix E, IV.B, is particularly confusing in this regard. Although the regulatory documents remain essentially unchanged from the Three Mile Island period, through years of use and subsequent development of alternative emergency action level schemes it is clear the Commission intended emergency action levels to refer solely to schemes to recognize or identify accidents and as entry conditions into emergency response plans and procedures. Although the four emergency classifications are occasionally referred to as emergency action levels in guidance documents, there are no examples of this later than the mid-1980s, and more current usage is unambiguous.

When the regulation states, "emergency action levels that are to be used for determining when and what type of protective measures should be considered," then usage has established an intent that licensees establish recognition thresholds (e.g., measured or predicted radiation dose, radiation monitor thresholds or alarms) which will be used to make protective action recommendations to offsite authorities. Some of these decision parameters may duplicate thresholds found in emergency action levels and some parameters are likely to be unique to the protective action decision process. In any case, determining protective measures is an emergency plan function that can only occur after the emergency has been recognized and categorized and the emergency plan has been entered. Because emergency action levels as they are currently understood are precursors to determining an initial or upgraded emergency classification, this usage should be considered as distinct from the protective measures process.

NUREG-0654 (NRC, 1980c, p. 26) states,

> For this reason, licensee emergency planners must recognize the importance of prompt accident assessment at the source. The criteria in this document reflect the identification and classification of accidents and the notification of offsite agencies by the facility licensee consistent with NRC rules as set forth in Appendix 1. Emphasis on inplant identification of potential hazards is a change from the previous emphasis in many licensee response plans on measurement of actual levels of radioactivity before notifications of offsite organizations are made and actions to protect the public recommended.

NUREG-0654 Emergency Action Levels

Prior to 1979, each licensee created its own scheme to recognize and identify the need to enter the emergency plan, to take onsite protective actions, and to recommend protective measures for the public to offsite authorities. The initial Commission guidance on emergency action levels is contained in NUREG-0610 (NRC, 1979c); NUREG-0654, Revision 1, Appendix 1, *Basis for Emergency Action Levels for Nuclear Power Facilities* (NRC, 1980c); and NUREG-0818 (NRC, 1981c). Emergency action levels are often referred to as either "event-based" or "symptom-based," meaning the reactor operator is required either to recognize and diagnose the accident sequence ("event") or to recognize and respond to an abnormal indicator (usually a plant instrument or alarm, a "symptom"). The connotation is that event-based emergency action levels require more information to diagnose than do symptom-based indicators and generally take longer to analyze. NUREG-0654 provides 16 to 18 example initiating conditions indicative of an emergency for each emergency classification; although these initiating conditions are a mix of event-based and symptom-based indications, the whole is more weighted toward event-based initiators. The example Site Area Emergency and General Emergency indicators are more event based than are the Unusual Event and Alert indicators. The NUREG-0654 emergency action levels are often characterized as "deterministic," meaning the operator must apply a lot of individual judgment to the situation, resulting in a high degree of variability among control room crews or an overall lack of predictive power in the emergency action level scheme. NUREG-0610 and NUREG-0654 were also widely regarded among licensees as using loose, poorly defined, or undefined terminology. One example is the introduction of the term "loss or potential loss a fission product barrier" at the Site Area Emergency and General Emergency classifications; although there was some understanding at the time of what the fission product barriers were (although no regulatory definition), there was no guidance about how to determine the "loss" or "potential loss" of a barrier.

In addition, NUREG-0654, Appendix 1, provided example emergency action levels but the text implied that the list was not necessarily comprehensive nor complete. Licensees had no way of knowing, or of demonstrating to licensing officials, that their proposed classification scheme bounded the spectrum of events that could require entry into the emergency plan, creating a high degree of regulatory uncertainly as well as a potential for the public to be at risk from events not properly captured in the event scheme. Some minor modifications were made to the NUREG-0654 scheme in the 1990s; specifically, the Commission allowed licensees to remove an emergency action level-initiating condition for the transportation of an injured and contaminated person to an offsite facility.

NUMARC EMERGENCY ACTION LEVELS

Beginning in 1988, the nuclear industry began development of an alternative means to comply with Commission regulations pertaining to emergency action levels. NUMARC emergency action levels are emergency action levels based on the resulting document, NUMARC/NESP-007 (NUMARC, 1992). Sometimes the term is applied to schemes based on the various revisions of NEI 99-01 (NEI, 2003, 2008, 2012a). NUMARC/NESP-007 was endorsed by the Commission as acceptable for use in Regulatory Guide 1.101 (NRC, 2003c). Revision 4 of NEI 99-01 (NEI, 2003) was endorsed by the Commission as acceptable for use in Regulatory Issue Summary 03-18 (NRC, 2003g), Regulatory Issue Summary 03-18, Supplement 1 (NRC, 2004f), and in Regulatory Guide 1.101 (NRC, 2005e). The Commission's endorsement of Revisions 5 and 6 of NEI 99-01 were not communicated to license holders through generic Commission communications. NEI 07-01 (NEI, 2009b) was developed to address the development of schemes for the advanced reactor designs expected to be licensed after 2010. The industry developed its alternative scheme because it was concerned that (NUMARC, 1992, p. 2-1),

> ... initiating conditions and Emergency Action Levels are defined differently; terms like symptom, event, and barrier-based initiating conditions need to be defined and applied uniformly; some plants integrate their emergency operating procedures with their Emergency Action Levels, and some do not; some plants have applied technical specification operating mode considerations to their event classifications, some have not. Some initiating conditions have been misclassified, some have not been classified at all, and some events should not be classified as emergencies.

The NUMARC emergency action levels are characterized by grouping into recognition or hazard categories (abnormal radiological levels, degraded fission product barriers, hazards affecting plant safety, and safety system malfunctions), higher level emergency action levels that typically have several potential initiating conditions, and reactor mode[*] dependency for power operations, and they have a well-developed basis document that informs how they are used. The emergency action levels are weighted toward symptom-based conditions and the protection of fission product barriers, with less dependency on event-based emergency action levels. There are generally fewer individual plant initiating conditions in the NUMARC system than were in the older NUREG-0654

---

[*] The reactor modes are typically Operating (1), Hot Standby (2), Cold Standby (3), Cold (4), and Defueled (5). The mode is determined by reactor temperature and neutron flux; in boiling water reactors, it is also determined by the mode switch position.

system, and the NUMARC system eliminated some events from the classification scheme.[*] The NUMARC scheme further refined the concept of fission product barriers by providing a matrix of initiating events that indicate when each barrier is "potentially lost" and "lost." The concept of challenges to fission product barriers as a reduction in the safety margin of the plant was extended to all emergency classifications in the NUMARC scheme, not only the Site Area Emergency and General Emergency as was the case in the NUREG-0654 scheme.

The three fission product barriers applicable to emergency action levels are fuel cladding integrity, reactor coolant system integrity, and primary containment integrity. The fission product barriers are mentioned in the NUREG-0654 emergency action levels under the General Emergency classification as "Loss of 2 of 3 fission product barriers with potential loss of the third barrier." The NUMARC classification scheme gives example initiating conditions (instrument readings, sample results, or observed condition) indicative of potential losses and losses of each barrier, but like the NUREG-0654 scheme does not provide general criteria used to validate that all indications of potential loss and loss of fission product barriers have been identified and included in the emergency action levels. In the NUMARC system, either a potential loss or loss of the primary containment boundary requires an Unusual Event classification; potential losses and losses of the reactor coolant and fuel cladding barriers do not have Unusual Event criteria because precursor events in these barriers result in classification under the system malfunction recognition category, as discussed in NUMARC/NESP-007 (NUMARC, 1992, p. 5-17).

A potential loss or loss of either reactor coolant system or primary containment integrity requires an Alert classification because these barriers have a greater immediate contribution to public risk than does the containment barrier. Both the fuel cladding and reactor coolant system directly confine radioactive material; conversely, problems with primary containment without a simultaneous loss of control over radioactive material does not result in any risk to the public. The potential loss or loss of any two barriers requires a Site Area Emergency classification because there has been a loss of control over radioactive material and the public's safety margin has been significantly reduced (to only one barrier). The loss of any two barriers and challenge (potential loss) of the third requires a General Emergency because significant core damage has occurred or is likely, because there is a loss of control over radioactive material, and radioactive material is actively entering the environment (generally in an uncontrolled way) or it is highly likely to enter the environment. The high-range or accident-range primary containment radiation level is a unique indicator of fission product barrier status, in that a sufficiently high radiation level results in declaring all three barriers potentially lost or lost; this is because there is such a large radioactive source term in containment, with a potential for severe offsite consequences, that offsite protective actions are considered to be prudent.

The NUMARC scheme requires that a potential loss or loss of a fission product barrier be treated as if it had already occurred if the loss is "imminent," which is defined as a progression that will result in the loss within 2 hours and it is not anticipated that the condition can be mitigated, stopped, or prevented in that time (NUMARC, 1992, p. 5-17). In the NUMARC scheme, the primary threshold for the Unusual Event classification is operation outside the plant's safety envelope as defined by the plant technical specifications, events not covered by the technical specifications whose operational risk (probabilistic risk assessment) is about the same as operating outside the plant safety envelope, and selected events that are precursors to more serious safety conditions. The thresholds for Alert classification are hazards that affect plant safety systems, events that require additional plant monitoring, or events that require the response of additional plant staff beyond the operating crew. The Site Area Emergency and General Emergency thresholds are based on the severity and extent of challenges to the fission product barriers, using current plant conditions and projections of future radiological conditions (offsite dose).

---

[*] The Commission permitted the removal of seven Unusual Event emergency action levels, an Alert, and a Site Area Emergency from the original NUREG-0654 scheme. This was communicated in EPPOS-1 (NRC, 1995b).

NEI 99-01 (NEI, 2003) introduced new recognition categories—cold shutdown/refueling, permanently defueled station, and independent spent fuel storage installations—and modified some security-related emergency action levels based on post-September 11, 2001, Commission Orders, Advisories, and Guidance. Additional modifications were made to the security emergency action levels after NEI 99-01 was adopted based on NRC Bulletin 2005-02 (NRC, 2005f).[*]

Licensees began adopting NUMARC emergency action levels in 1993. Between 1993 and 2006, numerous examples were identified of NUREG-0654 scheme licensees implementing (cherry-picking) individual emergency action levels from the NUMARC scheme without adopting the entire scheme. This resulted in hybrid classification schemes that were neither NUMARC nor NUREG based. The Commission's expectation is that licensees maintain an internally consistent emergency action level scheme based on either the NUREG or NUMARC guidance documents as stated in Regulatory Guide 1.101, Revision 4 (NRC, 2003c):

> In Revision 3 to Regulatory Guide 1.101, the NRC stated that "Licensees may use either NUREG 0654/FEMA-REP-1 or NUMARC/NESP-007 in developing their EAL scheme but may not use portions of both methodologies." The staff stated in EPPOS No. 1, "Emergency Preparedness Position (EPPOS) on Acceptable Deviations from Appendix 1 of NUREG-0654 Based upon the Staff's Regulatory Analysis of NUMARC/NESP-007, 'Methodology for Development of Emergency Action Levels,'" that it recognizes that licensees who continue to use EALs based upon NUREG-0654 could benefit from the technical basis for EALs provided in NUMARC/NESP-007. However, the staff also recognized that the classification scheme must remain internally consistent. Likewise, licensees can benefit from guidance provided in NEI 99-01 without revising their entire EAL scheme. This is particularly so in regard to adopting guidance on EALs for cold shutdown and refueling modes of operations or for Independent Fuel Storage Facilities. However, the licensee needs to ensure that its EAL scheme remains internally consistent (i.e., the EALs making up the scheme are integrated so as to cover the spectrum of conditions that may warrant classification in a logical manner).

The Commission addressed this issue in RIS 05-02 (NRC, 2005a) and RIS 07-01 (NRC, 2007b).

EXPECTATIONS FOR CLASSIFYING AN EMERGENCY

Commission regulations require that a licensee recognize an emergency condition and declare an appropriate emergency classification. The expectation is that when a licensee receives indications that require an emergency declaration, they will immediately recognize the indications, promptly analyze applicable emergency action levels, and enter the appropriate emergency classification as soon as possible. Determining the correct classification is considered so important the senior licensee official (usually the operations crew shift manager) should do nothing else while analyzing plant conditions and emergency action levels. There are few competing plant or emergency planning priorities considered to be important enough to interrupt or delay the proper determination of an emergency condition. The regulatory requirements related to classifying emergency conditions include the following:

- 10CFR50.47(b)(2), which states, in part, "On-shift facility licensee responsibilities for emergency response are unambiguously defined, adequate staffing to provide initial facility accident response in key functional areas is maintained at all times, timely augmentation of response capabilities is available and the interfaces among various onsite response activities and offsite support and response activities are specified." (See also 44CFR350.5(2).)

---

[*] The new emergency action levels communicated in Bulletin 2005-02 were expected to be adopted by licensees using both NUREG-0654 and NUMARC emergency action schemes. This is one of the few examples where the Commission has allowed the mixing of emergency action schemes.

- 10CFR50.47(b)(4), which states, in part, "A standard emergency classification and action level scheme, the bases of which include facility system and effluent parameters, is in use by the nuclear facility licensee." (See also 44CFR350.5(4).)
- 10CFR50 Appendix E, IV(B), which states, in part, "including Emergency Action Levels that are to be used as criteria for determining the need for notification and participation of local and State agencies, the Commission, and other Federal agencies. ... The Emergency Action Levels shall be based on in-plant conditions and instrumentation in addition to onsite and offsite monitoring."
- 10CFR50 Appendix E, IV(c)(2), which states, in part, "Licensees shall establish and maintain the capability to assess, classify, and declare an emergency condition within 15 minutes after the availability of indications to plant operators that an Emergency Action Level has been exceeded and shall promptly declare the emergency condition as soon as possible following the identification of the appropriate emergency classification level."

A requirement to have the capability to classify within 15 minutes is not precisely the same as a requirement in every case to actually classify within 15 minutes, although the distinction is subtle. Although there can be acceptable reasons that an event is not classified within 15 minutes of initial indications being available, for the most part a licensee not making a 15-minute classification in an actual event will be a risk of Commission enforcement actions. A capability standard is properly understood as a design criteria for the system associated with classification. This system has numerous components that work together to achieve the designated performance standard (e.g., declaration within 15 minutes). They include the following:

- Detector hardware, such as sensors, radiation monitors, security cameras, and alarms
- Computer systems, such as a plant safety parameter display system or meteorology displays
- The availability and operability of analytical equipment, such as radiochemistry laboratory instruments, or computer-based engineering analysis programs, as applicable
- Communications systems that allow information to reach the decision maker in a timely manner
- The design of the decision system, the emergency action levels, including their degree of completeness
- The design of procedures and job aids to implement the emergency action levels
- The staffing and conduct of plant watches, which can detect events not readily recognizable by installed sensors
- Control room staffing, which ensures the availability of persons to react to plant sensors and alarms.
- Operator and emergency response organization training on the emergency action level scheme, including drills and exercises to maintain proficiency

All of these components must interact such that under reasonable anticipated circumstances there is high confidence that each indicator will lead to the appropriate classification within 15 minutes. All components must allow for timely event recognition in the plant control room. Because command-and-control (i.e., decision-making authority) may be transferred between licensee emergency response facilities during an event, system components must also support the ability to perform classification at remote locations, when the decisions are not necessarily being made by licensed plant operators. A capability would not exist to classify an emergency action level indicator if it could be successfully analyzed in 15 minutes in the control room but could not be analyzed within 15 minutes at any other licensee location.

An unstated implication of this is that no indicator should be designed to require more than 15 minutes to analyze; an analysis might not meet this criteria if the person needed to perform the analysis was not available at all times on-shift, or if the analysis could not be performed quickly.

One can think of a capability as having a performance distribution over the number of persons who need to implement it—the function must be designed for all persons to be capable of success. A capability is therefore maintained and demonstrated by the organization being capable of meeting the design criteria. A capability is not necessarily determined to be lost (invalidated) by a single failure to meet the design criteria; a determination of loss of capability should be based on a pattern of failures over time. For emergency action levels, these failures tend to occur in training and in drills and exercises and should be entered into the corrective action system for tracking, analysis, and action.

There are two parts to meeting the design criteria for classification. One is that the correct classification must be reached, and the other is that it must be reached in the time standard. Arriving at the correct classification is not merely declaring the correct one of the four classifications (Unusual Event, Alert, Site Area Emergency, General Emergency), but it is also declaring the classification based on the correct indicator. Selecting the correct emergency action level indicator is important because it shows that plant operators have a good understanding of the situation, including recognizing the conditions that warrant an escalation in classification; conversely, use of the wrong indicator may cause plant operators to focus their attention on the wrong parameters and so miss conditions that warrant escalation.

The expectation that the senior licensee official must analyze conditions and declare an emergency within about 15 minutes of appropriate indications or information being available goes back to the 1980s as an informal and undocumented NRC position prior to the 15-minute classification capability regulation.* This expectation was first formally incorporated into emergency preparedness programs in 2000 as part of the reactor oversight program (ROP). In particular, this expectation became one of the metrics in the performance indicator for drill and exercise performance (DEP). Although in an event there may be situation-dependent reasons that may justify exceeding 15 minutes, this flexibility is not allowed in the performance indicator evaluation standard. The reason is that the performance indicator reflects the performance of the program, not individual performance, and is used to evaluate the overall health of the licensee's capability. The response bands have been chosen to allow some variability in performance without penalizing the licensee; in this case, the Commission established that a success rate of less than 90% indicated that classification design criteria may not be met (i.e., sets the threshold for additional Commission inspection). The assumption is that if a licensee remains in the "licensee response band" (i.e., greater than 90%) then the licensee's emergency plan, plan implementing procedures, and training and evaluation program are probably adequate to ensure that appropriate measures would be taken when necessary. In other words, it provides objective evidence that the licensee has likely implemented NRC requirements and guidance in an acceptable manner.

The Commission requirement is that an emergency classification must be made as soon as the senior official determines the classification that should be declared, without any delay. Furthermore, the decision is made when the senior official has determined which emergency action level indicator applies and at what emergency classification—the classification time does not depend on when the official verbalizes their decision, on when they log the decision, or when they brief the decision to their staff/crew. Classification is made when an observer could reasonably conclude from their actions that the official knows the emergency classification level. For example, if a shift manager has an event in progress and requests on-shift emergency response organization members to report to the control room, it is likely that classification has occurred, even if it has not been verbalized. Likewise, if a shift manager directs a shift communicator to prepare an emergency notification form with a specific classification and emergency action level, but does not announce this to the control room staff, classification has already occurred; otherwise, the manager would not know what information to put on the form. This distinction becomes important because time clocks for other required activities start with classification.

---

* This regulation took effect in June 2012.

A plant whose systems are seriously degraded will likely meet the entry criteria for several different emergency action levels. The senior official is expected to identify the indicator that best describes the plant's situation and declare the highest classification among all of those that apply. For example, if Notification of Unusual Event and Alert emergency actions both apply, the Alert should be declared. When more than one emergency action level at the same classification level applies, it is generally expected that the first-occurring be selected, unless there is a significant reason to select the second event. In any case, for the purposes of the 15-minute classification capability, the clock starts with the first indications, regardless of when the emergency action level is met that is recorded as the basis for classification. For example, if the leak rate from the reactor coolant system is determined to exceed the Alert threshold and 5 minutes later a containment radiation monitor exceeds the fission product barrier Alert threshold, the 15-minute clock began with the leak rate calculation. It would also be more proper to classify based on the leak rate, but classification on the radiation monitor could be acceptable with justification (with 10 minutes remaining on the clock to make the classification).

Some emergency action levels are constructed with internal clocks; that is, an emergency condition does not exist until the malfunction or adverse condition exists for the specified time period. For fires, this time period is often 10 minutes in NUREG-based schemes or 15 minutes in NUMARC/NEI schemes; similarly, clocks for loss-of-power action levels could be up to 4 hours. With these emergency action levels, when an indication or information about the initiating event is available the internal clock must expire before the emergency condition exists, with the additional 15-minute analysis period being permitted before declaring the emergency condition. The Commission generally expects that for these kinds of emergency action levels the licensee will recognize the applicable emergency action level while still in the internal clock phase and will declare the appropriate emergency classification promptly with essentially no need for an additional analysis period. Also, should the senior official determine that the initiating event cannot or will not be mitigated before the clock expires, the official should then immediately declare the emergency. An emergency action level is imminent when it becomes unavoidable, regardless of the amount of time remaining on the classification clock. For example, for an emergency action level of a fire within the protected area burning 15 minutes or greater, if the official determines after 8 minutes that the fire will burn for at least 15 minutes and cannot be extinguished sooner, then the emergency action level is met (the licensee can wait until the 15 minutes has elapsed but should not). In such cases, it is permissible (and encouraged by the Commission) to declare the emergency condition before strictly meeting all of the conditions in the initiating condition (that is, the required time has not yet elapsed). Although for the most part the Commission discourages classifications before the initiating conditions are met, imminent and unavoidable events form the exception.

Licensees have historically struggled to recognize the fission product barrier emergency action levels because they often do not clearly identify and track the fission product barrier potential losses and losses that occur (in drills and exercises and in events). In some cases, the correct emergency classification and emergency action level were entered but were based on an incorrect determination of the fission product barrier potential loss and loss indications. The best practice is for senior licensee officials to treat the potential losses and losses of fission product barriers as serious events in their own right, tracking, logging, and announcing them in the same manner in which they track, log, and announce emergency classifications. Visual displays of fission product barrier status aid in recognizing when emergency action levels are met.

NOTIFICATIONS FROM LICENSEES TO OFFSITE AUTHORITIES

The adequate protection of the public requires timely protective action decisions by the designated legal authority (offsite agency). This is only possible if the legal authority receives timely information about the emergency condition from the reactor licensee. Title 10 of the code of Federal Regulations, Part 50.47(b)(5), requires that, "Procedures have been established for notification, by the licensee, of State and local response organizations." Appendix E to 10 CFR 50, Part IV.D(3), requires that, "A licensee shall have the capability to notify responsible State and local governmental agencies within 15 minutes after declaring an emergency." The performance standard is that offsite officials are notified as soon as possible, but not to exceed 15 minutes, from the time the licensee command-and-control individual declares an emergency or determines a protective action recommendation. Acceptable means of notification include electronic worksheets or forms, paper worksheets sent by facsimile followed by a verbal confirmation, paper worksheets read over the telephone by a communicator followed by a facsimile copy, paper worksheets transferred by runner or courier, or other technological means worked out between the reactor licensee and the applicable offsite authorities. Notification is complete when the information provided by the reactor licensee is transmitted to a designated communication point, where the person receiving the information is not required to be a decision maker (however, in cases where immediate action is required, the offsite authorities must have the capability to analyze the provided information, arrive at decisions for action, authorize appropriate actions, and initiate the public warning system all within 15 minutes of receiving the licensee's information).

The content of the message from the licensee to the offsite official must include the emergency classification, the emergency action level (either by designator or in plain English), the time of classification, whether or not a radiological release is in progress, and whether protective actions are recommended. The site and offsite officials may elect to include additional information in the message; however, the design of the notification process should ensure that at least the minimum required information is reliably transmitted within 15 minutes. Licenses would be advised to track the time that the required information is delivered during all drills and exercises to assure themselves that their process is, and continues to be, adequate.

CHANGES TO EMERGENCY ACTION LEVELS

Reactor licensees are permitted to make changes to their emergency plans, emergency action levels, and emergency action level schemes according to the requirements of 10 CFR 50.54(q):

(2) A holder of a license under this part [10CFR50], … , shall follow and maintain the effectiveness of an emergency plan that meets the requirements in appendix E to this part and, for nuclear power reactor licensees, the planning standards of § 50.47(b).

(3) The licensee may make changes to its emergency plan without NRC approval only if the licensee performs and retains an analysis demonstrating that the changes do not reduce the effectiveness of the plan and the plan, as changed, continues to meet the requirements in appendix E to this part and, for nuclear power reactor licensees, the planning standards of § 50.47(b).

(4) The changes to a licensee's emergency plan that reduce the effectiveness of the plan as defined in paragraph (q)(1)(iv) of this section may not be implemented without prior approval by the NRC. A licensee desiring to make such a change … shall submit an application for an amendment to its license. In addition to the filing requirements of §§ 50.90 and 50.91, the request must include … the basis for concluding that the licensee's emergency plan, as revised, will continue to meet the requirements in appendix E to this part and, for nuclear power reactor licensees, the planning standards of § 50.47(b).

(5) The licensee shall retain a record of each change to the emergency plan made without prior NRC approval for a period of three years from the date of the change and shall submit, as specified in § 50.4, a report of each such change … including a summary of its analysis, within 30 days after the change is put in effect.

(6) The nuclear power reactor licensee shall retain the emergency plan and each change for which prior NRC approval was obtained pursuant to paragraph (q)(4) of this section as a record until the Commission terminates the license for the nuclear power reactor.

Prior to November 2011, 10 CFR 50.54(q) stated,

A licensee authorized to possess and operate a nuclear power reactor shall follow and maintain in effect emergency plans which meet the standards in §50.47(b) and the requirements in appendix E of this part. ... The licensee shall retain the emergency plan and each change that decreases the effectiveness of the plan as a record until the Commission terminates the license for the nuclear power reactor. The nuclear power reactor licensee may make changes to these plans without Commission approval only if the changes do not decrease the effectiveness of the plans and the plans, as changed, continue to meet the standards of § 50.47(b) and the requirements of Appendix E to this part. ... Proposed changes that decrease the effectiveness of the approved emergency plans may not be implemented without application to and approval by the Commission. The licensee shall submit, as specified in § 50.4, a report of each proposed change for approval. If a change is made without approval, the licensee shall submit, as specified in § 50.4, a report of each change within 30 days after the change is made.

Prior to 2004, 10 CFR 50, Appendix E, IV.B, stated,

These emergency action levels shall be discussed and agreed on by the applicant and State and local governmental authorities and approved by NRC. They shall also be reviewed with the State and local governmental authorities on an annual basis.

After January 2004, Appendix E, IV.B, stated,

The initial emergency actions levels shall be discussed and agreed on by the applicant or licensee and state and local governmental authorities, and approved by the NRC. Thereafter, emergency action levels shall be reviewed with the state and local governmental authorities on an annual basis. A revision to an emergency action level must be approved by the NRC before implementation if: (1) The licensee is changing from one emergency action level scheme to another; (2) The licensee is proposing an alternate method for complying with the regulations; or (3) The emergency action level revision decreases the effectiveness of the emergency plan.

For the most part, the requirements of 10 CFR 50.54(q) were not changed in the rule that became effective in November 2011; the large paragraph was broken into smaller cohesive ones to improve readability. The essential evaluation standard defining acceptable changes to the plan was unchanged. The new requirements included (q)(3), which required an analysis; (q)(4), which changed the submission process to be a license amendment; and (q)(5), which required submission to the Commission of a report of all changes not submitted to the Commission for approval. Prior to February 2012, the effective date of (q)(3), licensees typically performed analyses of the effect of changes to their emergency plan but there was no requirement for the analysis, and enforcement action could not be taken if the licensee failed to perform the analysis or performed an inadequate analysis. Licensees were in compliance as long as they did not implement a change that reduced the effectiveness of the plan, with or without the supporting analysis.

The significance of the Commission allowing licensees to reduce the effectiveness of their emergency plans using the license amendment process is that all license amendments are published in the *Federal Register* and the public is allowed comment on, and to challenge, the amendment and request a hearing in front of an administrative judge. The previous method did not allow for public notification, comments on, or challenges to the proposed changes to emergency plans.

From 1980 to January 2004, the Commission required licensees to gain the agreement of offsite officials in the initial implementation of their emergency action level scheme and agreement to every subsequent change to emergency action levels. Also, licensees were required to review the entire set of emergency action levels with offsite authorities at least annually to maintain offsite familiarity and understanding and to provide offsite officials an opportunity to propose changes. However, in the late 1990s and early 2000s, several examples occurred of offsite officials threatening to not agree (or to delay agreement) to individual licensee emergency action level changes as a means to gain budget leverage with the nuclear utility. Although this was not a widespread practice, the trend concerned both industry and the Commission. The January 2004 rule change maintained the requirement for the agreement of offsite officials to a new plant's initial emergency action level scheme and agreement for an existing plant to change schemes, and it maintained the requirement for the utility to annually review the emergency action level scheme with offsite officials but removed the requirement that off-site officials provide agreement to every individual emergency action level change.[*]

Section (1) of 10 CFR 50.54(q) defines the terms used in the rest of the regulation. For the first time, the regulation of November 2011 defined the plan:

(ii) *Emergency plan* means the document(s), prepared and maintained by the licensee, that identify and describe the licensee's methods for maintaining emergency preparedness and responding to emergencies. An emergency plan includes the plan as originally approved by the NRC and all subsequent changes made by the licensee with, and without, prior NRC review and approval.

The Commission found it necessary to include this definition because of long-standing confusion among licensees about whether emergency plan implementing procedures were included in the scope of 10 CFR 50.54(q). The Office of General Counsel is the organization within the Commission that interprets regulations, and in the mid-2000s the General Counsel had ruled that the term *plan* as used in regulation meant only the emergency plan and did not include any procedures. This implied that changes to procedures were not required to be reviewed to determine whether the changes reduced the effectiveness of the plan. However, the Commission had also determined that some licensees had moved information required to be part of their emergency plan into some of their implementing procedures. Therefore, the Commission has taken the position in Regulatory Guide 1.219 (NRC, 2011f) that procedures that contain information relocated from the plan are also subject to 10 CFR 50.54(q).[†]

Although 10 CFR 50, Appendix E, IV.B, stated that emergency action level changes were "approved by the NRC," the Commission's practice in the 1980s and 1990s had been to allow licens-ees to make changes to their as-licensed emergency action levels using 10 CFR 50.54(q) and for Commission inspectors to review and evaluate each change after implementation. Only emergency action level scheme changes or changes identified as decreasing the effectiveness of the emergency plan required the Commission's prior approval. This interpretation was challenged in 2000 when the Commission's Office of General Counsel concluded that the Commission was required by its regulations to approve each individual change to licensee emergency actions levels. Because both the Commission staff and industry preferred allowing licensees to make changes to emergency action levels without prior Commission approval, interim guidance was communicated to licensees to continue current practices while the Commission went through the rulemaking process to change the regulation.[‡] Under current regulation,[§]

---

[*] Presumably, the Commission would require offsite agreement to any emergency action level scheme change requiring prior approval, including the inclusion of decommissioning emergency action levels, but this is not clear in regulation, Regulatory Issue Summary 03-18, or Regulatory Issue Summary 05-02.

[†] Appendix E to Part 50, Part V, requires licensees to submit changes to the emergency plan and implementing proce-dures to the NRC within 30 days of implementation, which includes changes to emergency action levels. In late 2015, the Commission issued an Enforcement Guidance Memorandum that gave licensees permission to no longer submit procedure changes (i.e., would not take enforcement action when procedures were not submitted). However, the 10 CFR 50.54(q)(5) requirement to submit summaries of the change impact analysis still applies to those procedures for which an analysis is performed. Licensees that can demonstrate that specific procedures do not contain relocated emergency plan information can elect to discontinue performing the change analysis for those procedures and discontinue submitting analysis summaries to the Commission. However, they remain at risk if they implement changes to the procedures that do not continue to correctly implement requirements of the emergency plan.

[‡] See SECY 01-192, *Rulemaking Plan: Revision of Appendix E to 10 CFR Part 50*; SECY 02-130, *Status of Proposed Amendments to Emergency Preparedness Regulations in 10 CFR 50 Appendix E*; SECY 03-067, *Proposed Amendments to 10 CFR Part 50, Appendix E Relating to (1) NRC Approval of Changes to Emergency Action Levels (EAL) Paragraph IV.B. and (2) Exercise Requirements for Co-Located Licensees, Paragraph IV.F.2*; and SECY 04-211, *Final Amendments to 10 CFR Part 50, Appendix E, Relating to (1) NRC Approval of Emergency Action Levels Paragraph IV.B, and (2) Exercise Requirements for Co-Located Licensees Paragraph IV.F.2*.

[§] See Regulatory Issue Summary 03-18 (NRC, 2003g).

- All reactor licensees may change individual emergency action levels using 10 CFR 50.54(q).
- Licensees with NUREG-0654 emergency action schemes must receive prior Commission approval to change to either NUMARC scheme or to add shutdown mode emergency action levels to their scheme.*
- Licensees with NUMARC Revision 2 schemes may implement shutdown mode emergency action levels or revise their scheme to NUMARC Revision 4 using 10 CFR 50.54(q).
- All licensees implementing decommissioning emergency action levels must receive prior Commission approval.
- All licensees may implement independent spent fuel storage installation emergency action levels using 10 CFR 50.54(q).

PROTECTIVE ACTION GUIDES

The ultimate purpose of recognizing an emergency condition and entering the correct emergency classification is to ensure that appropriate protective actions are taken, both onsite for emergency and non-emergency workers (employees) and offsite for members of the general public, including the non-residential transient population. The emergency preparedness function is focused on the protection of people, not the protection of plant equipment. The protection of the reactor core is an essential activity for the onsite emergency organization, not because repairing or replacing the core is expensive but because when the core's integrity is maintained the radiological threat to members of the public is reduced or eliminated.

Evacuating before a radiological release arrives is the most effective possible protective action for the public, as it completely protects an individual from radiation exposure. Although there are concerns about a radiological release catching up with, and enveloping, members of the public as they evacuate, radiological models show that evacuees have a lower overall radiological risk from evacuating through a plume than they would have from sheltering in place for an extended time. The efficiency of early evacuation must be balanced against the disruption that evacuation causes in individuals' lives and against the risks they incur in evacuating. Evacuating a member of the public who is unlikely to be at radiological risk may not be protective of their overall safety. The Protective Action Guides promulgated by the Environmental Protection Agency are the tool that balances radiological risk and physical risk.

EPA 400-R-92-001 (USEPA, 1992, p. 1-2) states,

> During a nuclear incident, when the source of exposure of the public is not under control, the public usually can be protected only by some form of intervention which will disrupt normal living. Such intervention is termed protective action. A Protective Action Guide (PAG) is the projected dose to reference man† or other defined individual, from an unplanned release of radioactive material at which a specific protective action to reduce or avoid that dose is recommended.

In 2013, the EPA published the *PAG Manual: Protective Action Guides and Planning Guidance for Radiological Incidents* for interim use and public comment (USEPA, 2013), which includes the following statement:

> PAGs are guides to help officials select protective actions under emergency conditions during which exposures would occur for relatively short time periods. They are not meant to be applied as strict numeric criteria, but rather as guidelines to be considered in the context of incident-specific factors. PAGs do not establish an acceptable level of risk for normal, nonemergency conditions, nor do they represent the boundary between safe and unsafe conditions.

---

* There were no remaining licensees with NUREG-0654-based emergency action levels as of 2013.
† The term *reference man* refers to a person with the anatomical and physiological characteristics of an average individual and whom is used in calculations assessing internal dose. The calculation of radiation dose due to the inhalation or ingestion of radioactive material (one aspect of estimating overall dose during an accident) depends heavily on reference man values for respiration, organ mass, and other biological factors.

The current federally recommended Protective Action Guide for the early phase of an accident (as found in the *PAG Manual*) is evacuation beginning at 1 rem total effective dose equivalent (TEDE) and in all cases where evacuation is safe before 5 rem. Administration of potassium iodide to the public is recommended at a projected thyroid dose of 5 rem based on the child thyroid, for those states electing to provide potassium iodide to the general population. The intermediate phase relocation protective guide is 2 rem TEDE calculated for the first year of exposure or 0.5 rem/year calculated for any subsequent year. The food interdiction Protective Action Guide is a calculated 0.5 rem/year TEDE or 5 rem/year to any individual organ, unless the withdrawal of food would cause a public health problem (e.g., no viable replacement food supply is available).

The 1992 evacuation Protective Action Guide based on thyroid dose has been eliminated because the EPA determined that 1 rem TEDE bounds 5 rem thyroid committed effective dose equivalent (CEDE). The previous relocation Protective Action Guide of 5 rem TEDE calculated over 50 years has been eliminated because the EPA determine that 2 rem in the first year bounds the 50-year dose. The current Protective Action Guides are based on TEDE and CEDE dose conversion factors based on ICRP Report 60 (1991) instead of ICRP Report 30 (1981).

The Federal Radiation Council and later the EPA[*] were given authority to determine exposure limits for radiation and radioactive material. As the principal federal agency planning for radiological emergencies, FEMA directed the EPA in 1982 to develop Protective Action Guides for use by federal agencies (FEMA, 1982). The EPA used the following principles to determine the federally recommended Protective Action Guides:

- The decision to implement a protective action should be based on an evaluation of the radiation dose that would be received if the action is not taken.
- Avoid acute or prompt health effects (10 rem).
- Although the generally accepted value for a lethal acute whole body radiation dose is between 400 and 500 rad without medical treatment, it is estimated that 1 to 2% of an exposed population would experience prompt radiation injury at an absorbed dose of about 50 rad. Prompt injury includes damage to cells in the blood, damage to the cells of the digestive system, skin reddening, eye injury, or temporary or permanent sterility. Damage could occur to a fetus following exposures of 10 rad.
- Provide adequate protection against cancer and genetic effects (0.4 rem).
- EPA 400 used risk factors of 2.8E-4 fatal cancers per rem of exposure for adults, 4.8E-4 fatal cancers per rem for young children, and between 1.4E-3 and 2.8E-3 future fatal cancers per rem for a fetus exposed in the womb. These were taken from the National Research Advisory Committee on the Biological Effects of Ionizing Radiation (1980). The Environmental Protection Agency's upper limit for acceptable lifetime risk is 1.0E-4, which is comparable to the NRC's health goal for latent fatalities multiplied over a 50-year period $(50 \times 2E-6 = 1E-4)$.[†]
- Optimize the cost of protective actions vs. avoided dose (1 rem).
- EPA 400 used a range of $400k to $7M per life saved by protective action, equivalent to $200 to $1200 per rem of avoided dose. The report assumes evacuation costs of $185 per person over a 4-day evacuation period.
- The risk of taking a protective action should not exceed the risk from receiving the avoided dose (0.03 rem).
- EPA 400 assumed an evacuation round trip of 100 miles, a risk of fatal cancer of 3E-4/person-rem, and a fatality risk of 9E-8 deaths per person-mile.
- Protective Action Guides are independent of particular accident sequences and source terms.

---

[*] For authorities, see Section 274.h of the Atomic Energy Act as amended, 44 CFR 351.22(a), and Executive Order 12656 (Reagan, 1988a).
[†] See Appendix C to EPA 400 (USEPA, 1992).

These principles are similar to those recommended by the World Health Organization (WHO, 1982, 1987):

- All of the countermeasures that can be applied to reduce the exposure of members of the public after an accidental release of radioactive materials carry some detriment to the people concerned, whether it is a risk to health or some societal disruption. The decision to introduce countermeasures should be based on a balance of the detriment which it carries and the reduction in the exposure that it can achieve.
- Nonstochastic effects should be avoided by the introduction of countermeasures to keep individual doses below the thresholds for those effects.
- Individual risk from stochastic effects should be limited by introducing countermeasures that achieve a positive net benefit to the individuals involved. This can be accomplished by comparing the reduction in individual dose (and therefore risk) that would follow the introduction of a countermeasure with the increase of individual risk resulting from introduction of that countermeasure.
- The incidence of stochastic effects should be limited by reducing the residual health detriment. This source-related assessment may be carried out by cost-benefit techniques and would be similar to a process of optimization in that the cost of the health detriment in the affected population is balanced against the cost of further countermeasures.

The World Health Organization (WHO, 1982) states

Within a broad range of projected doses, a number of specific dose levels can be set as reference levels. These reference levels can be fixed to set off emergency interventions in the event of an accident. The lower reference level corresponds to dose levels below which it would not generally be appropriate to take a given action. This level would thus be generally applicable and only when its value is exceeded should an assessment be initiated with a view to decision-making.

The upper reference level corresponds to the expected dose value above which remedial measures would be virtually certain to be applied in all cases. This value is much more difficult to define precisely than the previous one, since the effectiveness of a countermeasure is variable and depends on various parameters.

The *PAG Manual* (USEPA, 2013) reduced the guiding principles to the following:

- Prevent acute effects.
- Balance protection with other important factors and ensure that actions result in more benefit than harm.
- Reduce the risk of chronic effects.

Similar principles have also been adopted outside of the United States; for example, the German Commission on Radiological Protection (GCRP, 2014, p. 8) states,

The competent authorities should make sure that protection strategies for emergency exposure situations are developed in advance as part of emergency preparedness, and that they are justified, optimised and, in the event of an incident, implemented in a timely manner. To this end, appropriate responses to an emergency exposure situation should be planned using postulated events and corresponding scenarios based on risk analyses with the aim of avoiding major deterministic effects and reducing the probability of stochastic effects resulting from public exposure. Key steps in developing a protection strategy include the three items listed below:

- A reference level of the residual dose is set which primarily refers to the effective dose and combines contributions from all relevant exposure pathways (inhalation, external radiation, ingestion). ... In terms of the residual dose following public exposure, the number of exposed people and level of individual doses both below and above the reference level should be kept as low as reasonably achievable (ALARA principle) when planning the protection strategy to be developed and optimized.

- The results of the optimised protection strategy based on the reference level of the residual dose should be used to develop generic criteria for specific protective measures and other measures known as the projected dose or received dose. General criteria include, in particular, intervention levels for protective measures. If these criteria are expected to be met or exceeded, corresponding protective measures or individual or multiple measures should be implemented.
- Once the protection strategy has been optimised and a series of general criteria for protective measures and other measures have been developed, fixed trigger levels for initiating the various emergency measures of the plan—primarily during the urgent phase of an incident—should be derived in advance. These standard triggers should be expressed in the form of parameters and observable emergency action levels (EALs) or operational intervention levels (OILs).

In general, each individual protective measure and not only the strategy as a whole should be justifiable, meaning that each protective measure should do more good than harm.

Further (GCRP, 2014, p. 25),

When justifying and setting the overarching reference level for the residual (effective) dose in the first year after a major accident at a nuclear power plant, it should be noted that this is a temporally and spatially singular event and the additional radiation exposure it causes should be limited to tolerable and proportionate levels. This requires a weighing up of the gravity of interfering with the lives of the public, which also includes social and economic aspects, against the health risk associated with the additional radiation exposure caused by the accident.

Although protective measures at any point in an accident sequence could be based on the Protective Action Guides, initial protective actions are generally planned to be based on plant conditions. In part, this is because many accident sequences would not have a radiological release in progress when a General Emergency classification is declared, and in part because of the time necessary to do the initial radiological assessment. The Protective Action Guides cannot be used until there are either actual radiation measurements in the environment or radiological assessments result in projected radiation doses offsite. Assessments prepared prior to a release necessarily make assumptions about the release characteristics which may not be accurate when the release occurs. Although licensees must be prepared to make rapid assessments and recommendations, the *PAG Manual* does note that actual accident sequences may progress slowly (compared to those used in training scenarios) and may allow consideration of the Protective Action Guides even in formulating the initial protective action recommendation. The Protective Action Guides have historically been primarily used to expand upon those areas that are initially sheltered (shelter-in-place) or evacuated.

The EPA-400[*] guidance for members of the public during the plume phase of a radiological event was evacuation beginning at 1 rem TEDE and in all cases before reaching 5 rem TEDE, evacuation beginning at 5 rem thyroid CDE and in all cases before reaching 25 rem thyroid CDE, and administration of stable potassium iodide to members of the public at 25 rem CDE when states elect to use potassium iodide as a supplemental protective action. The Food and Drug Administration (FDA) updated the recommendations for issuing potassium iodide in 2001 to the following: (1) adults ages 40 years or greater should be given 130 mg of potassium iodide at actual or projected doses greater than or equal to 500 rem thyroid CDE, (2) adults between ages 18 and 40 should be given 130 mg of potassium iodide at doses greater than or equal to 10 rem thyroid CDE, and (3) pregnant

---

[*] The EPA released a review draft copy of *Protective Action Guidance for Radiological Incidents* in 2007, which was subsequently updated in the 2013 Protective Action Guides.

women and children under 18 years should receive potassium iodide at doses greater than or equal to 5 rem.* Shelter-in-place may be the preferred protective strategy when the radiological release is known to have a very short duration or when the risk of evacuation exceeds the radiological risk from exposure. The implementation of immediate protective measures is based on calculated and projected radiation dose from the time a release starts until the cloud of radioactive material exits the affected area.

The use of dose ranges to trigger evacuation of the public has historically been poorly understood. The 1-rem TEDE and 5-rem TEDE values were chosen to bound evacuation (the same arguments generally apply to evacuation based on thyroid CDE) because of uncertainties in the analysis, to round analysis results to values that were easily recognized and remembered, to bound a range of accident sequences, and to allow for local variation rather than a one-size-fits-all approach. The upper dose limit also represents the dose at which an evacuation delayed because of public safety concerns (e.g., competing or simultaneous natural or manmade hazards) is recommended because the radiological risk generally is larger than the physical risk. The original concept was that states and local authorities would use the methods described in the *Manual of Protective Action Guides* to select appropriate local Protective Action Guide values based on specific local data, rather than simply adopting the more generic national values. In practice, the lower TEDE and thyroid CEDE Protective Action Guide values have become the only values used in determining protective actions, and the offsite legal authorities did not adopt the ranged approach at the working level; although there may be mention of the range of Protective Action Guides in the emergency plan, this range is not generally trained upon and not implemented in procedures for protective action decision making. Local authorities did not perform the Protective Action Guide assessments originally envisioned in the *Manual of Protective Action Guides*, using locally applicable values for costs and benefits. The concept of a range of Protective Action Guides was not implemented by offsite authorities for reasons of simplicity of implementation, ease of training and evaluation, and for reasons of public confidence.

The EPA-400 Protective Action Guides for relocating members of the public out of a contaminated area[†] are 2 rem TEDE projected to be received during the first year of exposure, or 500 mrem TEDE (1/2 rem TEDE) projected to be received during the second year of exposure, or 5 rem TEDE projected to be received over 50 years of exposure. The requirement for protective measures is met if any of the three conditions is met independently of one another, rather than when all of the conditions are met simultaneously. For most postulated reactor core damage sequences the first year of exposure action guide is most likely to be exceeded. The analysis should consider all pathways except for consumption of contaminated food. These pathways include direct radiation from contaminated surfaces, radioactive material resuspended in air and subsequently inhaled, and accidental ingestion of contaminated soils and plants. Although the contamination around dwellings and businesses can be affected by decontamination procedures and is affected by natural weathering and sequestering processes, Protective Action Guides for relocation should not assume any source reduction except through natural decay, which is accounted for in the long-term dose conversion factors. A relocation decision is always based on a calculated future radiation dose but is based on actual measurements of deposited radioactive material. Because actual plumes of radioactive material will consist of complicated and unpredictable mixtures of radioactive isotopes, the dose from each individual isotope is calculated then summed to obtain TEDE. The only practical difference between evacuation and relocation is that relocated persons will have somewhat more time to gather

---

* Section 127, Public Health Security and Bioterrorism Preparedness and Response Act of 2002, P.L. 107-188, provides guidelines for states and local agencies to acquire potassium iodide (KI) from the Strategic National Stockpile for distribution to members of the public located between 10 and 20 miles from a commercial power reactor. Also see USDHS (2005).

† Relocation applies to those areas where evacuation did not occur (the population may have sheltered in place or had no protective measures taken), and the contamination was discovered or measured only after passage of the radioactive plume. Evacuation areas that are also contaminated above relocation Protective Action Guides are controlled using reentry and return criteria.

needed belongings and to leave the affected area than do evacuees, since their immediate health is not threatened; neither evacuated nor relocated persons will have future access to their property for an undetermined amount of time.

AVAILABLE CHOICES FOR INTERVENTION (COUNTERMEASURES)

The immediate protective actions (countermeasures) available for reducing the radiation dose to members of the public include advising the public to remain indoors with active warning devices (radio, television), radioactive prophylaxis, active shelter-in-place, evacuation, decontamination, relocation, and the control of access to radiologically affected areas. Longer-term protective measures include food controls and decontamination of property. The immediate protective actions available for reducing radiation doses to emergency workers include contamination protection, respiratory protection, radioactive prophylaxis, personal decontamination, and decontamination of structures and property. In this context, *shelter-in-place* involves keeping people in one place inside a solid structure (usually a home, business, school, or other predesignated indoor assembly area) with doors and windows closed, ventilation systems shut down, chimneys closed or sealed as much as is practicable, people remaining in inner rooms or areas, and the possibility of applying improvised respiratory protection (e.g., masks, wet handkerchiefs).

Remaining indoors does not require sealing the building or discontinuing ventilation and is intended to make the population ready to take protective actions if it becomes necessary, as well as to limit or reduce accidental interference by unaffected persons with ongoing evacuations (including shadow evacuations).* Shelter is intended as a dose-reducing measure, while remaining indoors is intended as a preparatory or precautionary measure to facilitate future distribution of public information, instructions, and warnings. NUREG-0654, Supplement 3 (NRC, 2011c) refers to remaining indoors as "monitor and prepare."

Radioactive prophylaxis is medical treatment to prevent or reduce radiation dose from internal contamination, primarily caused by breathing in radioactive material carried in an airborne plume. The best known of these treatments is potassium iodide, a nonprescription drug determined in 1978 by the FDA to be safe and effective in blocking or reducing the uptake of radioiodine by the thyroid. Radioiodine is not present in large concentrations in normal reactor coolant but would be present in large quantities if fuel rods are damaged or the fuel melts. Iodine is a concern in the atmosphere, but deposited iodine is also a concern because it rapidly transfers to milk in both cows and goats. The FDA published final recommendations for the administration of potassium iodide to emergency workers and to the public in June 1982, and the recommendations were revised in 2001. The current federal policy regarding the use of potassium iodide was published by FEMA in 2002 (FEMA, 2002a).† Potassium iodide is the only prophylaxis treatment approved for the general public. Potassium iodide is highly effective in blocking the uptake of radioiodine when taken between about 30 minutes before exposure and about 30 minutes after exposure, with some (reduced) benefit gained by taking it up to 4 hours after exposure. However, potassium iodide protects only one organ from internal contamination and then only against a limited number of chemicals; it is most effective against iodine but also offers limited protection against chemically similar species, such as cesium. It does not protect in any way against external radiation sources and does not provide

---

* *Shadow evacuations* are defined as voluntary, spontaneous, undirected, evacuations by persons for whom protective actions have not been implemented. It is *not* used to describe persons who spontaneously evacuate when other protective measures have been ordered by public authorities (e.g., evacuate when shelter has been ordered).

† For additional information regarding the NRC's position on potassium iodide and its program to make potassium iodide available to those states requesting it, see SECY 97-124, *Proposed Federal Policy Regarding Use of Potassium Iodide After a Severe Accident at a Nuclear Power Plant*; SECY 98-016, *Specific Domestic Licenses of Broad Scope for Byproduct Material*; SECY 00-0037, *Status of Potassium Iodide Activities*; SECY 01-0069, *Status of Potassium Iodide Activities*; SECY 02-0089, *Revised Draft NUREG-1633 and Public Information Brochure on Potassium Iodide (KI) for the General Public*; and NUREG-1633, *Assessment of the Use of Potassium Iodide (KI) As a Supplemental Public Protective Action During Severe Reactor Accidents*.

any significant protection to organs other than the thyroid. In addition, the thyroid has a weighting factor of only 3% in contributing to the TEDE (i.e., whole body dose), making it the least significant individual organ among the group. There are four types of thyroid cancer, three of which are readily treatable and have high survival rates and the fourth type being very rare but more malignant. Patients can survive the removal of the thyroid, if it is necessary, although this necessitates permanent medication.

Some states[*] have elected to incorporate the distribution of potassium iodide to the public into their strategies for responding to a radiological release from a nuclear reactor. The Commission initiated a program to provide potassium iodide to those states requesting it in 2002.[†] The Commission revised the requirements of 10 CFR 50.47(b)(10) effective April 19, 2001, to require licensees to consider potassium iodide in their range of protective actions when their states elect to provide potassium iodide to the public (NRC, 2001a).

The Public Health Security and Bioterrorism Preparedness and Response Act of 2002 required state and local governments to distribute potassium iodide tablets to populations within 20 miles of a nuclear power plant and directed the National Academy of Sciences to study the expanded distribution of potassium iodide (see National Research Council, 2004). The Department of Health and Human Services published implementation guidelines on August 29, 2005. The Act included a waiver provision that was invoked by President Bush on January 22, 2008, through the Director of the Office of Science and Technology Policy.[‡]

Chelating agents have the properties of strongly binding metallic ions in a complex that is both less chemically active than is the free ion and rendering the metal more water soluble, greatly increasing its elimination rate through the kidneys compared to its natural or unchelated rate. In general, chelating agents are organic compounds. In 2003, the FDA has determined that three drugs are safe and effective chelating agents for treating internal radioactive contamination: Prussian blue for cesium and thallium and calcium and zinc trisodium (also known as Ca-DPTA and Zn-DPTA) for the transuranic elements plutonium, americium, and curium.[§] Although not currently approved for chelation therapy, the compound sodium alginate is known to increase the excretion rates of iodine, strontium, barium, cadmium, and radium, and there is some evidence for the chelating effectiveness of calcium gluconate, D-penicillamine, ammonium chloride, sodium bicarbonate, and dimercaprol (e.g., Marcus, 2004). Chelating agents are only administered to patients with very significant internal uptakes of radioactive material because of their potentially toxic side effects; they are generally only administered in a hospital setting under direct medical supervision. In theory, chelating agents that have been developed for mercury, lead, iron, cadmium, arsenic, chromium, antimony, copper, etc., would be effective in reducing radiation doses from radioactive isotopes of those elements; of the group, isotopes of lead, iron, cadmium, chromium, and antimony are the most likely to be found in the source terms from power reactors.

Relocation is the medium- to long-term (i.e., weeks to months) removal of populations from radiologically affected areas after the plume's passage, generally based on direct environmental radiation measurements and derived intervention levels, rather than on dose projections. The populations in areas requiring relocation either would been issued the protective actions of remaining indoors or sheltering or had no previous protective action requirements. Because areas requiring relocation are often only identified through post-accident environmental monitoring, they represent

---

[*] As of December 2015, these states were Alabama, Arizona, California, Connecticut, Delaware, Florida, Illinois, Maryland, Massachusetts, Michigan, Minnesota, Mississippi, New Hampshire, New Jersey, New York, North Carolina, Ohio, Pennsylvania, South Carolina, Tennessee, Vermont, Virginia, Washington, West Virginia, and Wisconsin.

[†] See SECY-01-0208, *Status of Potassium Iodide Activities*, and SECY-06-0142, *Options and Recommendations for Repleneshing Expired Potassium Iodide (KI)*.

[‡] See *Interagency Technical Evaluation Paper for Section 127(f) of the Bioterrorism Act of 2002*, Federal Radiological Protection Coordinating Committee Subcommittee on Potassium Iodide; transmitted by letter from V.E. Quinn, Chair, Federal Radiological Protection Coordinating Committee, to Dr. John H. Marburger III, Director, Office of Science and Technology Policy, dated October 2,3 2007.

[§] See FDA press releases P03-69, September 12, 2003, and P03-75, October 2, 2003.

the difference between dose projections (which are models) and dose reality. Affected people are described as being relocated rather than evacuated because evacuation is generally considered a more immediate countermeasure taken early in the emergency event. A *derived intervention level* is a threshold for action in units of a readily measurable physical quantity, usually an exposure rate (mR/h) or measured radioactive contamination (in μCi/m^2), calculated from a threshold for action of a fundamental nonmeasurable quantity, usually TEDE in rem, that implies the fundamental action threshold has been exceeded.

Whenever an accident progresses to a Site Area Emergency or General Emergency classification, local emergency response plans call for implementing access control schemes at predefined control points around the nuclear plant. This is done to control and keep clear the evacuation routes needed to implement protective actions, to maintain unimpeded access to the affected area by emergency services such as fire departments and ambulances, and to prevent additional radiation exposure to members of the public heading toward the affected plant (including curious, sightseers, potential criminals such as looters, and persons wanting to provide or sell impromptu news coverage of the event). After the accident situation stabilizes, local officials may authorize a program of *reentry*, the temporary and controlled admittance of emergency workers and selected members of the public into the controlled area to perform vital or necessary functions. Persons authorized to reenter must typically be trained to the level of occupational radiation workers and be given dosimetry, and they often would be accompanied by radiation survey technicians. Temporary entries would typically be on the order of hours, rather than days. Reentry may be appropriate to perform search and rescue, stabilize or make safe broken utility infrastructure (e.g., water mains, electrical lines, natural gas lines, pipelines), fight fires or contain nonradiological hazardous material releases, shut down potentially dangerous industrial plants, or feed or remove livestock and animals. Reentry may also permit members of the public brief visits to secure their homes, retrieve pets or medicine, and obtain the supplies necessary for an extended absence.

In the early hours of a serious radiological accident, respiratory protection generally refers only to self-contained breathing apparatus, which provide breathing protection factors of at least 1000 (that is, the breathed contaminant concentration is less than 1000 times smaller than the exterior airborne concentration of the contaminant). Self-contained breathing apparatus is widely available among emergency services. Many or most emergency personnel have been trained in their use, it is portable, and replacement air bottles can generally be used with a wide variety of equipment. The disadvantages are that the bottles provide only short-term (30 to 45 minutes) protection, in conjunction with the masks and backpacks the bottles are heavy, and self-contained systems are not suitable for use in vehicles. Other, even more protective systems of respiratory protection, such as supplied air face masks, full body suit with supplied air lines, and full body suit with rebreathing units, have the disadvantages of being rare, being difficult to deploy in the field (e.g., require special compressors and power), having few personnel trained in their use, or requiring substantial maintenance when in long-term use.

After the plume passes, the primary inhalation threat becomes resuspended radioactive material—that is, longer-lived radioactive species deposited on the ground and vegetation, and to a lesser extent on buildings, that are lifted back into the air by winds. The typical assumption is that the airborne radioactive concentration in units of μCi/m^3 is no greater than 1.0E-6 times the radioactive ground contamination in units of μCi/m^2, averaged over 24 hours. To limit the inhalation of resuspended radioactive material, respiratory protection less protective than self-contained breathing apparatus may be acceptable, ranging from industrial dust masks, to half-face canister respirators, to canister-type full-face respirators (often called *gas masks*). The advantages of these forms of protection are that they are very widely available, are relatively lightweight, do not require frequent exchanges, and require relatively little training in their use. The use of respiratory protection is governed by rules of the Occupational Safety and Health Administration and by equipment certifications provided by the National Institute for Occupational Safety and Health (some kinds of equipment were formerly tested and certified by the Mine Safety Administration). The National Institute for Occupational Safety and Health has not certified any respirator cartridges as being effective for the removal of radioactive iodine and therefore no mask or respirator may be used for the sole purpose of protecting against iodine inhalation.

PROTECTIVE MEASURES ON LICENSEE SITES

10 CFR 50.47(b)(10) states, in part,

> A range of protective actions has been developed for the plume exposure pathway emergency planning zone for emergency workers and the public. ... Guidelines for the choice of protective actions during an emergency, consistent with Federal guidance, are developed and in place.

and 10 CFR 50, Appendix E, IV.B, states, in part,

> ... including ... levels that are to be for determining when and what type of protective measures should be considered within and outside the site boundary to protect health and safety.

NUREG-0654 (NRC, 1980c) states,

> NRC and FEMA agree that licensees of nuclear facilities have a primary responsibility for planning and implementing emergency measures within their site boundaries. These emergency measures include ... protective measures and aid for persons onsite ... (Section 1.H, p. 25)

and

> Each licensee shall establish the means and time required to warn or advise onsite individuals who may be in areas controlled by the operator, including ... (b) visitors, ... (d) other persons who maybe in the public access areas on or passing through the site or within the owner controlled area ... (Criteria J.1, p. 59).

Reactor licensees have the primary responsibility for protecting members of the public who are on their property unless agreements are implemented with offsite authorities to perform this function; any such agreements must be capable of notifying the public in about the same time as would the licensee (between 15 and 45 minutes from declaration of an emergency classification requiring action, or the decision to clear the site as made by the command-and-control position), and personnel must be trained, equipped, and drilled. The public includes licensee employees who are not part of the immediate emergency response effort, regardless of whether or not they have radiation worker training. It also includes licensee employees not having protected area access, employees not normally working at the nuclear power station (e.g., electrical switchyard workers), licensee contractors and vendors (e.g., sandwich truck driver, vending machine delivery person, air conditioning mechanic), postal or commercial delivery service employees, and members of the public not affiliated with the power station who are granted access to the owner-controlled area for recreational purposes such as boating, fishing, or hunting. Some licensees rent space or buildings in their owner-controlled area to unaffiliated businesses or allow community groups occasional use of their facilities. Many licensees lease sections of their owner-controlled area for crops or grazing. Some licensees have established campgrounds on their property, used by the temporary workers (and their families) employed during reactor refueling and maintenance. For additional information, see Information Notice 2002-014 (NRC, 2002f).

Although many licensees remove the public from the exclusion area after a Site Area Emergency classification (also licensee employees not responding to the emergency), some are not committed by their emergency plan to remove or exclude the public until a General Emergency classification is made. It should be noted that conditions on or at the exterior boundary of licensee property could exceed federal Protective Action Guides while remaining within the definition of a Site Area Emergency; licensees not committed to the exclusion of the public until the General Emergency are still responsible for assessing onsite dose and taking appropriate protective actions for the public whenever Protective Action Guides are exceeded, regardless of less restrictive emergency plan commitments.

Following the terrorist attacks of September 11, 2001, several states deployed National Guard troops to reactor sites for extended periods (up to several months) or augmented site security with state highway patrol or police personnel. In some areas, local authorities greatly increased patrols on or near licensee sites by county sheriffs or other local law enforcement agencies. Regulatory Issue Summary 02-21 (NRC, 2002g) discussed the status of these personnel from an emergency preparedness perspective. During a radiological accident they could be considered as non-essential members of the public and evacuated, but during a radiological event resulting from site attack they should be considered as essential emergency workers and their dose controlled using emergency worker exposure control requirements. In all events, National Guard and law enforcement personnel remain under the authority of appropriate offsite authorities who are ultimately responsible for their deployment, protection, and evacuation. RIS 02-21 recommends that whenever possible National Guard troops augmenting site security and offsite law enforcement personnel be treated as members of the public from a radiological control perspective and their doses controlled under 10 CFR Part 20 guidelines for members of the public. When Guardsmen and law enforcement personnel are treated as occupational and emergency workers, the licensee is required to provide the same radiation safety and site access training as provided licensee employees or is required to verify that offsite personnel have received equivalent training.

The means employed to warn onsite individuals usually include a combination of plant public address systems (sometimes extended to remote plant buildings), fixed onsite warning sirens or electronic speakers, and sweeps of station buildings and the owner-controlled area by the security staff. Some licensees have patrol cars or other vehicles equipped with mobile public address systems or bullhorns. Some licensees have arrangements with offsite officials to fly over the owner-controlled area using helicopters equipped with mobile public address systems. At one reactor site where bow hunting is permitted, hunters are issued emergency response notification pagers when they enter the hunting area. In addition to providing protective measures and aid to persons onsite during an emergency, licensees have a duty under 10 CFR 50.47(b)(7) to provide information to members of the public entering licensee-controlled areas about how they would be warned in an emergency and what actions they could be required to take. This information usually takes the form of fliers or handouts given to non-employees when they pass through a staffed security checkpoint, augmented by large permanent signs in areas generally accessible by the public.

OFFSITE PROTECTIVE MEASURES

Reactor licensees are required to recommend appropriate protective actions for members of the public in the plume phase emergency planning zone to offsite authorities, based on their best radiological analysis of the situation. The protective measures scheme used by licensees to recommend offsite actions is always negotiated between the licensee and offsite authorities and applies federal guidance to local situations. Therefore, protective measures schemes vary widely among reactor licensees and may be implemented based on local Protective Action Guides different from the values recommended by the EPA's *Manual of Protective Action Guides* (e.g., Kansas). Local protective action schemes may not implement higher Protective Action Guides than recommended by federal guidance. In states where potassium iodide has been stockpiled for distribution to the public during a radiological emergency, the licensee's protective measures scheme may include conditions for the licensee to recommend the general distribution of potassium iodide to offsite officials. Licensees *recommend* action to offsite authorities, except for those portions of a licensee's owner-controlled area where alternative protective measures have not been provided; *only the controlling legal authority (offsite governmental entity) can take and implement protective actions affecting the public.*

A reactor licensee is responsible for analyzing the effects from radioactive materials released by the site wherever they are transported and the licensee's responsibility does not end at the plume phase emergency planning zone boundary. The licensee is required to recognize conditions requiring protective actions at any downwind distance (this analysis is not limited to the plume phase emergency planning zone), arrive at an appropriate protective measure recommendation as soon as practicable after recognizing the conditions, and communicate the recommendation to offsite authorities within 15 minutes. The recommendation should be based on the best available technical information and analysis, taking into account known factors affecting offsite safety (such as road conditions, severe weather, or flooding) when possible. When licensees implement acceptable protective action schemes, adherence to their procedures becomes the standard for making accurate or acceptable recommendations. Although there is no explicit regulatory requirement governing the time allowed for a licensee to determine a protective action recommendation after recognizing conditions that require protective measures, the NRC and FEMA have historically communicated an informal expectation that licensee decisions about protective measure recommendations are completed within about 15 minutes of the onset of conditions. Licensees are required by regulation to notify offsite authorities of classifying an emergency condition within 15 minutes of making the classification—because emergency notification forms (whether paper or electronic) contain sections for communicating protective action recommendations, at least the initial protective action recommendation must be complete in time to make the associated notification of an emergency condition. For those reactor sites making protective action recommendations at the Alert or Site Area Emergency classification in accordance with their agreements with offsite agencies, the appropriate protective action recommendation must be developed to meet the required 15 minute notification.

There is no specific FEMA requirement governing the timeliness of protective action decisions by the controlling legal authority, but again an evaluation standard of 15 minutes from the time of receiving the licensee's protective action recommendation has historically been used during emergency plan exercises. Commission regulations require that notification of a protective action decision be made to essentially 100% of the affected population within about 15 minutes of the decision being made.

The Commission views licensee protective action recommendations as being fundamentally independent from, and made in parallel with, protective action assessments made by offsite authorities. A protective action recommendation is a communication of the licensee's best estimate of where radiological risk exists and where it does not. This recommendation should be based on a combination of good analysis and professional judgment. It is not appropriate for licensees and offsite authorities to collaborate to formulate licensee recommendations, for offsite authorities to negotiate with licensees about the content of licensee recommendations, or for offsite authorities to suggest recommendations the authorities may favor. Licensees should be aware of the protective action decisions implemented by offsite authorities but should not base subsequent recommendations on those decisions. A licensee should not catch up with more extensive protective action decisions already implemented by the legal authority, even when allowed by procedure; licensees should not provide authorities the recommendations they have already decided to implement in situations where those decisions are not supported by radiological analysis. Although harmonization between the licensee and offsite officials is generally desirable, there may be situations where the licensee's recommendation and the authorities' decision will differ. The Commission recognizes that it is more important that the licensee accurately characterize the radiological risk than that the recommendation and the decision be in harmony.

Offsite authorities are not required to have a licensee protective action recommendation before making a protective action decision, and they are not required to follow licensee recommendations when they are provided. Examples are found in the exercise history of local officials whose decisions are less extensive than the measures recommended by the licensee, as well as decisions that are substantially more extensive (in both timing and affected areas). Only the designated legal authority may make and implement a protective action decision applying to members of the public outside of the licensee's property. The designated legal authority is either the governor (or the governor's legally defined designee, such as a state Homeland Security director or state Emergency Management Agency director) or the elected executive (commissioner, judge, sheriff) of a county or parish, depending on the state constitution. There is no current legal authority for federal executives (President, Vice-President, Secretary of Homeland Security, Director of the Federal Emergency Management Agency, or principal federal official under the National Response Plan) to make, implement, direct, or override the protective action decisions of local jurisdictions. Also, state and local authorities cannot delegate their legal authority to federal officials.

The Commission evaluates the protective measures recommended by the licensee to offsite officials during an event, will independently evaluate the event, and may develop protective action recommendations that differ from the licensee's based on their evaluation. The Commission may discuss their protective action recommendations with the designated legal authority, primarily at the state level. However, federal executives and principal federal agencies cannot require the designated legal authority to implement their protective action recommendations when those differ from those determined by the legal authority.

In states where the governor is the designated legal authority, local jurisdictions are required to implement protective action decisions made by the legal authority, which are not optional. For example, the governor or their designee or representative is the legal authority in states such as Illinois, Nebraska, Kansas, Missouri, Mississippi, Louisiana, Washington, and Arizona. In states where the local executive is the designated legal authority, the governor, state Department of Homeland Security, state Emergency Management Agency, or state health department, may recommend protective actions based on the licensee's recommendations or their own technical analysis, but their recommendations are optional and not legally binding on local authorities. For example, California, Texas, Arkansas, and Iowa are states in which local executives are the designated legal authority.

In some states, the designated legal authority may require and enforce evacuation decisions, including the forcible removal of the civilian population if necessary, while in other states evacuation orders are voluntary. Members of the public volunteering to remain in an area designated for evacuation assume all risks from radiological exposure. Even in states where the evacuation is voluntary, local authorities can implement mandatory access control measures and prevent members of the public from entering (or reentering) areas designated for evacuation, even when those persons volunteer to assume the risks of entry.

Typical preplanned protective actions that may be implemented at the Site Area Emergency classification include the following:

- Close recreational facilities, parks, and schools in the emergency planning zone and other public facilities with long lead times for implementing evacuation; some offsite jurisdictions close lakes and parks immediately adjacent to reactor sites at an Alert classification due to their close proximity (essentially contiguous) to licensee property.
- Remove food animals from open pasture and place them on stored (covered) food and water.
- Staff access control roadblocks as a precautionary measure (not necessarily implementing access control).
- Staff emergency congregate care shelters and other facilities for receiving the public as a precautionary measure (not necessarily opening the facilities to the public).
- Start shutdown processes for large industrial facilities located in the emergency planning zone, as a precautionary measure to allow the evacuation of plant staff if required.
- Sound public warning sirens and issue public warning messages asking the public to tune to the Emergency Alert System (monitor and prepare).
- When a radiological release is occurring, evacuate the public from an area around the reactor site 2 miles in radius.

Typical preplanned protective actions that are implemented at the General Emergency classification include the following:

- Implement emergency planning zone access control.
- Open congregate care facilities and public decontamination centers.
- Sound public warning sirens and activate the Emergency Alert System to provide emergency information to the public.
- Issue evacuation orders for radiologically affected areas (generally a minimum area 2 miles in radius around the reactor site and 5 miles in the downwind direction).
- Issue shelter-in-place orders for radiologically affected areas in which evacuation is not warranted or in which evacuation cannot be safely accomplished (e.g., competing disasters).
- Embargo home-grown food crops from gardens and fields, embargo home-processed dairy products (especially milk), and prohibit fishing and hunting in the emergency planning zone.
- Recommend the taking of stockpiled potassium iodide (when predistributed to the population) or make stockpiled potassium iodide available (when stocked at a central distribution location).

The philosophy of the NRC and FEMA regarding evacuations is that

- The immediate or initial preplanned evacuations should be performed based on plant conditions (e.g., a likely or confirmed severe core damage sequence) without requiring definitive evidence of, or confirmation of, a radiological release.
- The minimum possible area consistent with federal radiological guidelines should be evacuated.
- Evacuation orders should be expanded to as far away as necessary based on projected dose without requiring evidence of, or confirmation of, a radiological release, or based on a confirmed radiological release that has not yet reached the at-risk populations.
- All members of the public in and near the emergency planning zone not affected by an evacuation order should stay indoors and near an information source and should prepare to evacuate if necessary.

Protective actions are typically recommended in at least a three-sector section because the true wind direction throughout the affected area is not known, the true plume location is not known prior to environmental monitoring, and because plumes do not travel in straight lines because of terrain effects. A *sector* is a wedge-shaped geographical area whose outer edge covers 1/16 of the perimeter of a circle (22.5° of arc), so a three-sector-wide section covers 3/16 of the 5-mile radius perimeter. The wind direction is not truly known because the onsite meteorological tower only provides an approximation of offsite conditions that is valid for 1 to 2 miles downwind. In addition, there may be significant uncertainties about wind persistence times (e.g., stability in the wind direction). Licensees with the capability to obtain wind data from multiple meteorological towers in the emergency planning zone may be capable of making more precise recommendations (e.g., two sectors or a single sector). Close to the reactor site, an individual sector is very thin, and as downwind distances increase the off-center sectors provide a margin of time to implement protective actions when wind directions change. Some licensees have implemented a protective action scheme that includes a four-sector-wide downwind area when the downwind wind direction is along a sector boundary line. In this regard, NUREG-0654, Supplement 3 (NRC, 2011c) states in Section 2.5 that, "it may be appropriate to include more than three downwind sectors in an expanded evacuation," based on site-specific wind persistence studies. Also, "modifications may be appropriate for areas where the typical site meteorology includes wind direction shifts on a timescale that is shorter than the ETE [evacuation time estimate] for downwind 2- to 5-mile sectors."

PROTECTIVE MEASURES GUIDANCE

The current guidance for protective measure strategies during a General Emergency is found in NUREG-0654 Supplement 3 (NRC, 2011c). This guidance states that protective action recommendations are appropriate only after a General Emergency classification is made. The guidance recognizes that protective measures are unlikely to be necessary for protecting public health and safety unless the affected reactor is experiencing a severe accident; however, it is prudent to implement such measures for any emergency serious enough to be characterized as a General Emergency even when a severe accident is not in progress. Tying protective measures to the General Emergency classification simplifies decision-making and encourages uniformity in response across the country, which is an advantage for state and federal responders.

The *minimum recommended protective measure* is a 2-mile radial evacuation with active shelter-in-place in the downwind direction to 5 miles. This minimum applies when the emergency is not a rapidly progressing severe accident, and there are no impediments to evacuation. Impediments could include dangerous natural phenomena (e.g., tornado, blizzard, hurricane), damaged or destroyed evacuation routes, or hostile actions occurring at or near the licensee's site.* Where impediments do exist, the guidance recommends shelter-in-place in a 2-mile radius and downwind to 5 miles. If the impediments are removed while the conditions causing the General Emergency remain (the classification will likely not be exited for a considerable time) then the 2-mile-radius area should subsequently be evacuated. If the impediments are removed after the conditions causing the General Emergency no longer exist, then additional actions should only be taken if the relocation criteria are met. In all cases, *monitor and prepare* is recommended for all areas of the emergency planning zone not affected by either evacuation or shelter-in-place.

A rapidly progressing severe accident is defined as an accident with a rapid loss of containment integrity (i.e., containment barrier loss) and a loss of ability to cool the core. It includes accidents in which containment integrity is bypassed or immediately or quickly lost with concurrent core damage. Core damage may be indicated by a loss of the fuel barrier or by site-specific calculation using reactor vessel level, drywell or containment radiation monitors, reactor coolant or containment atmosphere samples, or other indications. It is intended to denote a large early release situation (see Chapter 3). The guidance recommends either shelter-in-place or evacuation for the 2-mile-radius area and for downwind areas to 5 miles, the choice depending on the evacuation time estimate study results, along with shelter-in-place for populations in the downwind distance from 5 miles to 10 miles. Evacuation is recommended if the areas can be evacuated in less than or equal to 2 hours; otherwise, shelter-in-place is recommended. When shelter-in-place is recommended, authorities should evacuate the areas as soon as it becomes safe to do so, assuming that the conditions causing the General Emergency remain; this evacuation should be staged such that the public in areas at the highest risk should be evacuated first, then the lower risk areas.†

The previous guidance for protective strategies was found in the 1996 version of NUREG-0654, Supplement 3 (NRC, 1996b). This guidance was intended for severe accidents and not necessarily for all General Emergency conditions. As stated in the later Supplement 3 (NRC, 2011c),

---

* The response to hostile actions could be an impediment because incoming law enforcement units and fire and medical vehicles could be impeded and delayed by the outflow of evacuating vehicles, particularly near the site where there may be a limited number of roads.

† The NRC (2011c) introduced the concept of staged evacuations, such that the highest risk area is evacuated first, then successive areas from higher to lower risk. The successive aspect of the evacuation is intended to prevent evacuees close to the plant from being impeded or delayed by evacuees starting farther out in the evacuated area. This contrasts with earlier strategies in which all evacuees were started at the same time. Specifically, "The evacuation should proceed from the areas that are most at risk. The evacuation may involve a 2-mile radius unless field monitoring data show otherwise (e.g., at a site with an elevated release point where contamination may begin beyond 2 miles). Lateral evacuation (e.g., travel perpendicular to the direction of the plume) may be considered where the roadway network is conducive, as it may reduce public exposure. ... In any case, the determination of evacuation routes and timing should be based on release information, field monitoring data, and ORO [offsite response organization] resources."

The 1996 version of Supplement 3 noted that the guidance was to be used to develop PARs in response to severe accidents. In practice, this was translated into the expectation that protective actions would be recommended and implemented during any General Emergency. Although a General Emergency is a serious event and warrants protective action, it is not necessarily synonymous with a "severe accident" as that term is used in nuclear power plant accident analyses.

The 1996 guidance proposed a minimum offsite protective action recommendation of evacuation the public within a 2-mile radius of the affected reactor plus evacuation of populations between 2 and 5 miles in a three-sector-wide section centered on the prevailing wind direction. All persons in the emergency planning zone not included in the evacuation area were to be directed to go indoors and monitor the Emergency Alert System for further instructions. The minimum (or default) protective action recommendation was to immediately evacuate the public nearest the reactor site when a core damage sequence is in progress, even before the start of a radiological release. This is because they are likely to receive the highest radiation dose, have the least warnin0g of a radiological plume, have the least warning of changes in meteorology, and would gain the most advantage from even short travel distances. Although not explicitly credited in the analysis, a radial (vs. downwind-only) strategy also guards against an upwind exposure from circulating wind patterns caused by large buildings, significant natural terrain features, or natural diffusion during calm conditions. The close-in radial evacuation coupled with evacuation along the more distant downwind direction is often referred to as a *keyhole evacuation*, often shortened to just *keyhole* because, when plotted on a map with the three-sector-wide downwind extension, the resulting boundary line forms the shape found on physical locks.

In 2004, the Commission directed a study to determine whether changes should be made to NUREG-0654, Supplement 3. The objective was to investigate whether alternative, possibly nontraditional, protective action strategies could reduce the dose to the public during severe accidents, as compared to the existing strategies. A generic model emergency planning zone was used for the evaluation with an assumed population of 80,000 persons and average U.S. meteorology (represented by Moline, IA). The analyzed scenarios included rapid and slowly developing releases, accidents without containment failure, and a range of evacuation times between 4 and 10 hours; NUREG-1150 (NRC, 1990c) source term assumptions were used. The major interim conclusions from the study include the following:

- Evacuation remains the major element of a protective action strategy.
- Precautionary protective actions at the Site Area Emergency classification may be prudent, especially at sites with long evacuation times.
- Staged evacuation strategies usually offer improved dose savings to the overall population.[*]
- Shelter-in-place followed by evacuation is more protective for large early release (fast breaking) accidents at sites with long evacuation times.
- Other strategies that could provide dose savings generally require extensive low-traffic road networks which do not exist around sites with moderate to large populations. Very rural sites which do have such road networks also typically have very low evacuation times, which cannot be significantly improved upon using alternative strategies.

There is no explicit regulation that requires protective action recommendations or decisions at the General Emergency classification; the FEMA link is in the exercise evaluation methodology rather than in 44 CFR Part 350. The initial protective action guidance in NUREG-0654, Appendix 1 (1980, p. 1-16), stated, "State and/or Local Offsite Authority Actions: … (3) Recommend Sheltering

---

[*] A staged evacuation has the inner ring (0 to 2 miles) completely evacuate first while all other areas shelter-in-place, then the middle ring (2 to 5 miles) completely evacuates while the outer ring continues to shelter-in-place, then finally the outer ring evacuates. The primary benefit is that evacuation routes remain clear so that the most exposed persons are not stopped or held back by traffic simultaneously evacuating from areas further away from the plant site.

for 2 mile radius and 5 miles downwind and assess the need to extend distances." The July version of NUREG-0654, Supplement 3, stated, "The guidance in Appendix 1 to NUREG-0654 ... was intended to apply only until a determination was made that substantial core damage sequences were in progress or projected." Historically, the 1996 version of NUREG-0654, Supplement 3, had been understood by most licensees as abandoning previous guidance regarding shelter-in-place as a protective action, although this is not stated in the text. This understanding was promoted by a variety of informal (i.e., unwritten and undocumented) contacts between the Commission staff and industry between 1994 and 2000, during which time the staff communicated a diminished emphasis on shelter as a viable protective strategy.

An August 2003 NRC inspection revealed that for a particular licensee the recommendation of shelter-in-place as a protective action was prohibited by station procedures even when it was more protective than evacuation; the licensee had removed shelter-in-place as an option because the legal authority (state) had communicated that they would never implement shelter-in-place, and the licensee desired to harmonize their scheme with the state's. This finding, and similar cases discovered because of subsequent requests for information to licensees, led to Regulatory Issues Summary 04-13 (NRC, 2004a), which restated the Commission's position that temporary shelter-in-place is the most protective action for some kinds of radiological releases, particularly for radiological releases of very short duration or during particularly dangerous external conditions. Shelter-in-place may be followed by evacuation or relocation following cessation of the release. This had always been the Commission's official (documented) position from 1980 onward and was discussed in the 1996 version of NUREG-0654, Supplement 3. RIS 04-13, Supplement 1 (NRC, 2005b) again restated the Commission's view that protective action schemes are required to have a diversity (i.e., several) of potential protective actions, which must include shelter-in-place as one option. The RIS required that shelter-in-place be included, in part, because it was specifically described in the (then-current) 1992 EPA *Manual of Protective Action Guides*. Licensees were required to include shelter-in-place as an available protective measure regardless of whether local and/or state emergency plans included it as an option; this was an exception to the Commission's general practice at that time of accepting any licensee scheme of protective actions that implemented a scheme negotiated with offsite authorities. Prior to the 1996 version of Supplement 3, the guidance was to evacuate when environmental monitoring detected radioactive material in concentrations that would result in radiation doses approaching the Protective Action Guide, and criteria were not provided for a shelter-in-place recommendation.

Reactor licensees originally communicated protective action recommendations to offsite officials in terms of *range and bearing*—that is, sectors and downwind distances. The sectors have letter designators, A through R, skipping I and O, which can be mistaken for numbers. Sector A is centered on north and the letters proceed in sequence in the clockwise direction. Recommendations were given in circles or wedges whose radius is the reactor site boundary (sometimes the exclusion area boundary), 2 miles, 5 miles, and 10 miles, which also established the pattern for performing radiological assessments. Offsite officials generally make protective action decisions in terms of predefined geographical areas or zones that generally follow established political (e.g., township) or geographical (e.g., road, river) boundaries; these zones are often wider than three sectors across. The primary purposes of using geographical zones are to simplify communicating to the public, to implement consistent protective actions across a single political jurisdiction (e.g., a city), and to simplify non-evacuation protective measures, such as establishing access control points. Particular emergency planning zones may have between 5 and 20 predefined geographical zones. Where offsite officials prefer protective actions to be communicated by their licensees in terms of defined zones, licensee protective action recommendation schemes may be defined in terms of offsite zones. When geographical zones are used to implement protective actions the actual shape of an evacuated zone may not resemble a keyhole even when the keyhole concept is used to generate the licensee's protective action recommendation. Predefined geographical zones are not ordinarily used to implement post-plume agricultural controls.

Evacuation through a radioactive plume is a more effective protective action option than is shelter-in-place for a *prolonged* period, although shelter may be more protective for a short time. The kinds of buildings used for shelters range from thin metal walls, to wood-and-gypsum (dry-wall) residential construction, to substantial concrete or stone commercial buildings. Of these, only concrete or stone buildings provide any substantial radiological protection due to the density of the materials, which block about three-quarters of the external gamma radiation. All buildings provide some protection from the airborne plumes, although this protection depends on how airtight the building is and the number of air exchanges per hour. The number of air exchanges depends on the building design and construction, the ventilation system, ventilation system flow rates, infiltration through the walls, and how the ventilation system is operated (e.g., the season). Because no residential or commercial building completely prevents air exchanges, the protection from airborne radioactive materials steadily decreases over time until eventually there is no submersion protection when the concentrations in exterior and interior atmospheres become equal. The *Manual of Protective Action Guides* states, "Sheltering is usually not appropriate ... for exposures lasting longer than 2 complete air exchanges of the shelter," and states that houses without fans running typically have 1 to 2 air exchanges per hour, while buildings have about 5 air exchanges per hour while fans are running. A building's protection from airborne radioactive materials therefore lasts between 18 and 45 minutes (for two air exchanges), depending on construction and season.

Precautionary steps to protect livestock and to isolate potentially contaminated agricultural products do not directly derive from the federal Protective Action Guides. The removal of livestock from open pasture and covering of open sources of feed and water (to the extent practicable) is usually directed at the Site Area Emergency and General Emergency classifications because these actions may take a long time to accomplish, and farmers or ranchers may not be willing to protect themselves by evacuating until they know their livestock is protected. An immediate embargo on consumption of foods produced in the emergency planning zone is put into place because of the uncertainties regarding whether radioactive materials will be released to the environment; when the release will occur, its duration, and its path; and the very high potential economic and health impacts.

PROTECTIVE ACTION RECOMMENDATIONS AND WIND SHIFTS

A protective action recommendation depends on the current wind direction at the time the recommendation is developed, for both initial default recommendations and dose-projection-based recommendations. However, wind directions are often not stable, and both licensees and offsite authorities may have to periodically evaluate the existing situation and make changes or updates. Changes in wind direction do not affect protective measures implemented in all sectors (e.g., radial, circular, 360°) but will affect those in the downwind keyhole.

An important rule of thumb is to *never change an existing recommendation or action to a less restrictive measure while the emergency condition remains*. That is, one cannot change an area ordered to evacuate into one with only shelter-in-place or one in which protective measures are canceled (i.e., effectively allowing the return of the public while the event is still in progress). Although changes in the wind direction may in fact eliminate the immediate radiological risk in some areas, the confusion created by reducing a measure already communicated to the public will undermine the entire protective measure scheme. In addition, allowing movement toward the plant site in some areas while at the same time requiring movement away in others will cause communication issues with responders, confusion at control check points, and confusion with the public about whether they are protected. The public will interpret such changes as indicative of officials who do not understand the situation or who do not understand how to protect the public. Furthermore, there is no guarantee that the winds will not shift back into those areas in which protective measures are relaxed, putting the population there at higher risk.

If there is no radiological release in progress when the wind shifts, then the existing protective action recommendation should be expanded to include the new sectors or geographical zones. This should be an automatic action because there is only the reactor core condition to indicate risk to the public, not actual data. If there is a release in progress when the wind shifts, the situation becomes more complicated because the avoided dose must be considered. This should *not* be an automatic action because actual data are available for evaluating the risk. The data may include active radiation monitors, active or passive effluent samplers, and in-field measurements (e.g., radiation exposure rates, air sampler surveys, contamination surveys). NUREG-0654, Supplement 3 (NRC, 2011c) addresses this issue in Section 2.6 and in the attached Protective Action Strategy Development Tool. Section 2.6 states, in part,

> If the licensee believes that containment may fail, it should pursue the expansion of PARs. Finally, if a radiological assessment shows that an ongoing release or containment source term is not sufficient to cause exposures in excess of EPA Protective Action Guidelines, licensees should not expand PARs based only on changes in wind direction.

The Strategy Development Tool addresses the expansion of existing protective action recommendations in flow chart box 6, which reads, "GE [General Emergency] conditions remain?" The accompanying note states, in part,

> If the conditions that caused the GE declaration have been mitigated (i.e., core cooling is restored), it may not be necessary to expand the PAR to evacuate downwind sectors upon completion of the initial staged evacuation. However, if GE emergency action levels are still met expansion of the PAR to the downwind sectors may be appropriate.

The Commission staff currently interprets Supplement 3 with an emphasis on "if GE emergency action levels are still met"; however, one can read that interpretation as being inconsistent with the text of Section 2.6, particularly, "when radiological assessment shows an ongoing release or containment source term is not sufficient to cause exposures in excess of EPA protective action guidelines, it would be inappropriate for licensees to expand PARs based only on changes in wind direction." An intermediate interpretation might be to assign the flowchart note to the control room and Section 2.6 to the technical support center or emergency operations staff, as appropriate. The fundamental conundrum is that, when General Emergency conditions no longer remain,* by definition the Protective Action Guides cannot continue to be exceeded; one cannot expand recommendations only to areas where the Protective Action Guides could be exceeded as the wind direction changes if no Protective Action Guides can be exceeded anywhere. If the Protective Action Guides were exceeded at any location, then one could not conclude that General Emergency conditions did not continue to exist, because one of the applicable emergency action levels is that Protective Action Guides are (or are projected to be) exceeded at the site boundary. The logical outcome of this emphasis is that as wind direction changes the Commission expects licensees to expand protective measures into areas where radiological assessment shows there is insufficient radiological risk to justify those measures, or perhaps no risk at all. Commission staff consider it appropriate to use radiological assessment to expand protective measures outward when projected doses result in a wider area requiring protection than does the plant-condition-based evaluation but do not consider it acceptable to use radiological assessment to prevent unnecessary protective measures.

In the context of whether General Emergency conditions remain after initially occurring, recall that for a radiological threat to actually exist the three fission product barriers must be threatened, even if classification was made on a different emergency action level. For a loss of the fuel barrier, restoration of vessel water level, restoration of core cooling, etc., may limit or prevent additional fuel damage; however, it will not remove the damage already done and may not prevent the movement

---

* Even though the site may remain at the General Emergency classification level.

of radioactive material from the currently damaged fuel to the drywell/containment or the environment. For the reactor coolant system barrier, it may be possible to restore physical integrity and prevent any additional contaminated water or steam from reaching the environment; however, such mitigation is probably only possible in containment bypass scenarios where repair crews do not have to enter primary containment. For the containment barrier, isolation of the breach may be possible, depending on its size and location. In any event, a radiological release sufficient to cause Protective Action Guides to be exceeded at the site boundary, a half-mile or more from the reactor building, is going to have much higher radiation doses at the breach point, likely higher by factors of 10 to 20 or more. That means that the local radiation exposure or dose may be too high to allow the repair to occur, even with the dose limits that are appropriate for emergency workers. In the author's opinion, the removal of General Emergency conditions prior to the reactor being shut down, depressurized,[*] and put onto shutdown cooling is likely to be only possible in situations where the accompanying radiological release never exceeds the Protective Action Guides. The consequence, perhaps unintended, is to reduce the efficacy of radiological assessment and to greatly deemphasize the importance of radiological assessment in developing protective action recommendations and actions.

POTASSIUM IODIDE AS A PROTECTIVE MEASURE FOR THE PUBLIC

The federal position on the use of potassium iodide as a supplemental protective action during a radiological event is that, "KI should be stockpiled and distributed to emergency workers and institutionalized persons for radiological emergencies at a nuclear power plant and its use should be considered for the general public within the 10-mile emergency planning zone (EPZ) of a nuclear power plant" (FEMA, 2002a). Potassium iodide has been stockpiled for use by emergency workers essentially everywhere since the early 1980s. The stockpiling of potassium iodide for use by institutionalized (generally meaning hospitalized or incarcerated) members of the public has been relatively rare, partly because typical institutional construction provides much greater protection against radiation than do most residential buildings and because of a reliance by local authorities on special population evacuation strategies. States that have elected to include potassium iodide as a supplemental protective action generally maintain a single stockpile, which is distributed to congregate care sites when needed, although potassium iodide has been distributed directly to households at a few reactor sites.

The primary reasons for maintaining a central stockpile are for ease of receipt and resupply, having control of distribution (i.e., ensuring administration of the correct dose per person per day), having the ability to register and subsequently track the persons taking potassium iodide for medical follow-up and post-emergency studies, and to ensure availability when needed (households may dispose of, lose, or consume the potassium iodide so that it is not available when needed). The primary reasons to distribute potassium iodide directly to households is to give the public a feeling of confidence and individual control over the emergency situation and to allow the public the option of bypassing congregate facilities. Based on the long national experience with natural disasters, local authorities are not required to have prestaged congregate care facilities capable of housing 100% of an emergency planning zone's population. A drawback of the central stockpile model for potassium iodide is that facilities may not be configured to rapidly deal with large numbers of persons who only want potassium iodide but do not plan on staying at the facility—this could overwhelm both the radiological monitoring function and the administrative staff at the facility, causing a strong negative reaction or response by the public. For practical reasons, when potassium iodide is distributed at congregate care facilities it must be essentially available to anyone who requests it for reasons of public confidence; its administration probably cannot be effectively limited to only evacuees from the emergency planning zone. Because it can be expected that some persons not affected by protective action orders will still desire potassium iodide during an accident situation, a stockpile whose size is closely matched to the emergency planning zone population may be quickly exhausted.

---

[*] That is, brought to a system pressure equal to atmosphere pressure, thereby making offsite releases impossible.

When potassium iodide is used as a protective measure for the general population, it is most protective when taken prior to the arrival of a cloud of airborne radioactive material; when this is not possible, it should be taken as soon as possible afterward, preferably within 4 hours of exposure. When potassium iodide is stockpiled for distribution at evacuee reception centers it will not be possible to take potassium iodide prior to breathing in radioiodine; evacuees who have not been exposed to radioiodine before arriving at the reception center should not be issued potassium iodide as it will then be unnecessary.

Once taken, potassium iodide provides thyroid protection for about 24 hours (USFDA, 2001). Potassium iodide is effective against both the inhalation and ingestion of radioactive iodine; however, it is not recommended for long-term use. When radioactive iodine has entered (or may enter) the food chain, food control measures are more effective in preventing radioactive iodine uptake than the prolonged use of potassium iodide. Although pregnant women may safely use potassium iodide, they should not take more than a few doses because of the risk of affecting the normal fetal thyroid development; infants requiring potassium iodide should receive it directly rather than through breast milk.

Regulatory requirements associated with protective measures for the public include the following:

- 10 CFR 50.47(b)(4), which states, "State and local response plans call for reliance on information provided by facility licensees for determinations of minimum initial offsite response measures." (See also 44CFR350.5(4).)
- 10 CFR 5.47(b)(9), which states, "Adequate methods, systems, and equipment for assessing and monitoring actual or potential offsite consequences of a radiological emergency condition are in use." (See also 44CFR350.5(9).)
- 10 CFR 50.47(b)(10), which states, "A range of protective actions has been developed for the plume exposure pathway EPZ for emergency workers and the public. In developing this range of actions, consideration has been given to evacuation, sheltering, and, as a supplement to these, the prophylactic use of potassium iodide (KI), as appropriate. Guidelines for the choice of protective actions during an emergency, consistent with Federal guidance, are developed and in place, and protective actions for the ingestion exposure pathway EPZ appropriate to the locale have been developed." (See also 44CFR350.5(10).)
- 10 CFR 50 Appendix E, IV(B), which states, in part, "The means to be used for determining the magnitude of and for continually assessing the impact of the release of radioactive materials shall be described, including emergency action levels that are to be used as criteria for determining the need for notification and participation of local and State agencies, the Commission, and other Federal agencies, and the emergency action levels that are to be used for determining when and what type of protective measures should be considered within and outside the site boundary to protect health and safety."

The phrase, "consistent with Federal guidance," as used in 10 CFR 50.47(b)(10), generally means consistent with the EPA's *Manual of Protective Action Guides and Protective Actions for Nuclear Incidents* (USEPA, 1992) or the *PAG Manual: Protective Action Guides and Planning Guidance for Radiological Incidents* (USEPA, 2013).

EVACUATION TIME ESTIMATE STUDIES

Licensees are required to submit an evacuation time estimate (ETE) study as part of their initial emergency plan by Appendix E to 10 CFR 50, Sections III and IV, which state,

> The ... applicant shall also provide an analysis of the time required to evacuate and for taking other protective actions for various sectors and distances within the plume exposure pathway EPZ for transient and permanent populations.

Also, according to NUREG/CR-6863 (Dotson and Jones, 2005a, p. 1),

> The purpose of the evacuation time estimate is to provide a tool for preplanning, as well as protective action decision making. The evacuation time estimate identifies potential challenges to efficient evacuation, allowing mitigative measures to be preplanned. Decision makers use the evacuation time estimate when considering protective action decisions regarding whether an evacuation should be implemented.

These studies are compilations from statistical and computer models which together estimate the time required to evacuate permanent and transient populations from the plume phase (10-mile) emergency planning zone. The models generally address daylight and night scenarios and areas with significant transient populations (e.g., ocean beaches) also evaluate peak season and off-season populations. In locations where seasonal environmental conditions (e.g., heavy snow or blizzards, hurricanes) affect the outcome, the scenarios bound the identified environmental conditions. The evaluation identifies the time required to evacuate even under conditions in which the public would not actually be evacuated because of excessive physical danger. Even though the emphasis of an evacuation time estimate is on land evacuation, the study should also address the evacuation of lakes, rivers, and the ocean, as applicable to the site.

The starting point for an evacuation time estimate is an analysis of the evacuation demand (population and vehicles) against the roadway capacity available under each scenario. The analysis variables can include population distribution (geographical, age, special population), warning schemes, hazard type, times to depart, wind directions, weather conditions, achievable road speed under specified weather conditions, distribution of vehicle types (e.g., passenger vehicles vs. commercial vehicles), average number of passengers per vehicle, the time of day, day of week, seasonal changes in land use (e.g., school sessions, planting and harvest), and traffic accident probability, among many others. "Special populations" or "special facilities" include schools, churches, daycare centers, hospitals, nursing homes, prisons, and special event facilities (e.g., major football stadium, concert hall, amusement park). In rural areas, the need to transport animals and large agricultural equipment may impact road availability. Some variables can be estimated with some accuracy (e.g., population and age distributions obtained from Census Bureau data), whereas many others are represented by measured or assumed distributions. The results of each scenario are therefore generally mean values with an associated standard deviation or confidence interval that combines all statistical errors. All assumptions should be stated, justified, and documented. Each type of analysis is performed for wind blowing into each of the 16 sectors of the emergency planning zone to determine the average condition and worst-case condition.

The transient population is defined as visitors, tourists, persons in recreational areas, shoppers, persons employed in the evacuation area who live elsewhere, and any other people temporarily visiting the area. In some areas, this group also includes hikers, campers, recreational or commercial boaters, and hunters. The effect of seasonal recreational vehicles on road usage may also have to be considered. Transients should be appropriately counted or located for each scenario; for example, transients may be at shopping and recreational centers in daylight scenarios but in hotels and camping areas at night. Evacuation studies should also account for persons who live in the evacuation zones and work outside the emergency planning zone but would need to return home to evacuate family members, or they should account for the special transportation needs of these stranded family members if the returning family member is refused entrance into the evacuation area.

When road capacity is greater than demand no significant delays should normally be expected. Even when there is in generally excess capacity, local bottlenecks can develop, or a more careful analysis may show capacity is not as great as initially assumed. When demand is larger than capacity, then additional time is required to account for traffic-related delays, or mitigating actions must be taken to temporarily increase road capacity. For example, alternatives may include conducting a staged evacuation, reprogramming stop lights, or implementing countervailing traffic patterns in which normally inbound lanes carry outbound traffic on selected routes.

Shadow evacuations are defined as a spontaneous and voluntary evacuation by persons outside of a designated evacuation zone. Shadow evacuations impact the evacuation time estimate when the shadow evacuees are using the same routes as the primary evacuees, potentially overloading what otherwise would be sufficient road capacity. Shadow evacuees may also interfere with primary evacuees at intersections and by delaying their access to the evacuation routes. NUREG-6864 (Dotson and Jones, 2005b) states that shadow evacuations occur in about one-third of all evacuations.

It has been observed that when an affected population is given the choice a small number of persons consistently refuse to evacuate their property. This often occurs in states where the controlling legal authority lacks the legal authority to compel evacuation. Although this phenomenon is an operational concern, and offsite emergency response plans should address the situation, it is not a concern in developing the evacuation time estimate. When models assume complete evacuation, the results bound a real situation in which most people evacuate and a small number do not.

The original, 1980s-era philosophy was that the evacuation time estimate studies would be actively used by offsite officials when developing protective actions for the public. This was because protective action guidance at the time was to only evacuate those areas for which the evacuation could be complete before arrival of the radioactive plume. Evacuation time estimates were rarely used as operational tools in the period from 1995 to 2014 (e.g., in association with the 1995 version of NUREG-0654, Supplement 3), and the perceived emphasis was on evacuation for all circumstances, although some older emergency plans continued to reference them in this capacity. In part, the 2011 revision to Supplement 3 was driven by the Commission's interest in restoring evacuation time estimates as an operational resource. The usefulness of the studies to identify impediments to evacuation was considered to be a secondary benefit; informal discussions indicate that local officials rarely, if ever, actually improved their road network for the purpose of improving evacuation times based on the identified bottlenecks or impediments.

Although an evacuation time estimate is a licensing basis document, NUREG/CR-6863 (Dotson and Jones, 2005a) cautions against performing a worst-case analysis that results in an overly conservative estimate; *worst case* in this context means to assign to every variable the value that results in the most negative overall outcome, as compared with assigning the most representative or most likely value. A worst-case or conservative evacuation estimate could cause offsite authorities to not order an evacuation when evacuation is the best (i.e., most dose saving) alternative; this could happen if authorities erroneously believe the population could not be evacuated before the arrival of a radioactive plume, when a more realistic assessment would show that evacuation could be completed. In theory, a worst-case-only evaluation could also cause authorities to change road networks or make other expensive capital improvements that actually have very little benefit to public safety and may mask or cause local officials to not recognize improvements that would benefit public safety. An evacuation time estimate study should not be designed to support the *a priori* conclusions or convictions of offsite authorities and should not be used as a tool to extract concessions from licensees.

The submission of an evacuation time estimate is a requirement for a reactor power licensee to be issued an initial operating license and are considered one element of providing reasonable assurance. The expectation of the Commission and FEMA was that evacuation time estimate studies would be updated following each decennial Census Bureau report, although few licensees voluntarily updated their studies. The Commission also expected that an evacuation time estimate study would have sufficient information to identify actions that could be taken to significantly improve evacuation times, although FEMA does not require the identified actions to be taken. Although every reactor licensee is required to ensure that an evacuation time estimate study is performed, and the study becomes part of the licensee's licensing basis and emergency plan, there are no regulatory acceptance standards for adequacy; that is, regardless of how long an evacuation requires (for a particular scenario), the reactor operating license will be issued as long as there is an overall finding of reasonable assurance that adequate measures can be taken to protect the health and safety of the public during an emergency.

The general refusal of licensees to voluntarily update their estimates led to the requirement in Appendix E, Part IV, implemented in November 2011, for all licensees to update their evacuation time estimates by December 2012 using the 2010 census data and to perform a new analysis following every subsequent decennial census. The regulation also required each license to perform annual analyses of population changes in the emergency planning zone to determine whether the current analysis required updating, commencing in 2013. The Commission expected that the annual review would be done by licensee staff using locally generated data, such as utility records, tone-alert radio distribution records, construction permit data, and the like; however, the initial experience through 2015 is that the reviews have mostly been done by a single contractor who depends on extrapolated Census Bureau data. The original guidance for preparing evacuation time estimates was found in NUREG-0654, Appendix 4 (NRC, 1980c). Additional guidance was published in NUREG/CR-4831 (Urbanek and Jamison, 1992), which was updated in NUREG/CR-6863 (Dotson and Jones, 2005a) and NUREG-6864 (Dotson and Jones, 2005b).

A common error made by reactor licensees and offsite authorities is a failure to address the time required to implement "other protective actions," which are alternatives to evacuation or complement evacuation. Planning standard 10 CFR 50.47(b)(10) requires licensees to be capable of recommending a range of protective actions appropriate to the emergency planning zone. The time estimate study should identify the specific actions that together constitute the local range of protective action options and should discuss the implementation times and impediments for each. Where the local emergency plan calls for actions specific to special populations, the expected times to implement these actions should also be evaluated. The relative times to implement the range of potential protective actions should then be used to reevaluate the overall proposed protective action schemes.

POST-PLUME PROTECTIVE MEASURES FOR THE PUBLIC

Relocation is defined as the medium to longer term removal of persons who were not initially evacuated as protection against chronic (low-level) radiation exposure, especially caused by deposited radioactive material. This material may be ground surfaces, on occupied buildings, on commercial buildings, or on other surfaces to which people are routinely exposed. One method for determining those areas requiring relocation is to collect a small number of surface contamination samples* soon after the radiological plume passes and to analyze these samples using gamma spectroscopy to identify the fission products actually present. Existing radiation dose models can calculate the gamma exposure rate that would be measured when those fission products are present at concentrations meeting the relocation Protective Action Guides. This calculated value is often referred to as a *derived intervention level* and becomes the operating limit used in radiation monitoring; it may change over time to account for fission product radioactive decay. Offsite monitoring teams can quickly identify areas from which the public may have to be relocated by comparing the local gamma exposure rate to the derived exposure limit; the measurement is made at waist height using ion chamber instruments which are relatively insensitive to other types of radiation. Because some accidents may deposit significant amounts of radioactive material whose characteristic radiations are primarily alpha or beta, the initial operating limit for surveying the emergency planning zone may have to be increased somewhat, because the laboratory analyses necessary to correctly measure these isotopes and calculate the true operating limit may take several days. It is generally preferable to relocate some persons from contaminated areas and later release the area based on more accurate laboratory results than to allow persons to remain in contaminated areas for days or weeks and then discover that they should have been relocated. Relocation protects the public from long-term or chronic radiation exposure, and short-term radiation doses can be expected to be well below the emergency Protective Action

---

* Note that, during and immediately after passage of a plume, environmental monitoring teams are largely confined to existing roadways and samples are unlikely to be collected in agricultural areas.

Guides; this gives the relocated persons more time to gather their belongings, prepare their property, and make arrangements for animals. Although the EPA *Manual of Protective Actions* typically anticipates that evacuated persons will be gone for up to a week, relocated persons likely will relocated for much longer periods. Post-plume environmental monitoring is likely to identify some evacuated areas that are sufficiently contaminated such that return will not be permitted in the short term, but the entire evacuated area will not be contaminated to that degree.

Reentry is defined as temporary activities performed in a controlled or restricted contaminated area by persons who are not radiation workers. Some essential operations may still be required in areas that have been evacuated. Typical examples are firefighting, law enforcement, mitigating hazardous conditions such as open natural gas lines or broken water mains, staffing chemical or other large (hazardous) industrial operations that cannot be shut down, repairing damaged utility infrastructure, repairing damaged public infrastructure, feeding or milking livestock that could not be evacuated, and decontamination efforts. These activities may require members of the public to reenter the evacuated area to perform tasks that are not directly part of the emergency response. Reentry would require some level of radiation training and would be performed with dosimetry, radiation monitoring, and decontamination, generally using occupational (non-emergency) radiation dose limits. Workers reentering a restricted area would typically be permitted to work for a specified time then leave the area, and they would not be permitted to permanently occupy buildings in the restricted zone. At all times workers should apply the "as low as reasonably achievable" principle to their work activities in contaminated areas.

Return is defined as the permanent lifting of evacuation (plume phase) or relocation (post-plume) orders allowing the reoccupation and use of property in the restricted zone, including the abandoning of access controls. This would generally occur after some appropriate period combining natural decay and mechanical or chemical decontamination and is more likely to occur after weeks of restrictions rather than only a few days. The lifting of access restrictions does not imply a complete removal of contamination or a zero residual radiation dose rate; in the short term, restoring a contaminated area completely to its prior (pre-plume) condition is likely to prove impossible. Although return is often thought of as being an unrestricted condition, it is likely that land use and agricultural restrictions would remain for some time after return is permitted.

The Protective Action Guides for agricultural products are briefly discussed in Chapter 5.

EMERGENCY NOTIFICATION TO THE PUBLIC

Achieving actual dose savings for the public requires making appropriate protective action decisions and the public correctly implementing those decisions. Implementation requires the public to be warned of the emergency condition and then being informed about the actions they should take. Public warning and public notification refer to different functions, although the terms are often incorrectly used as synonymous. *Warning* means to get the public's attention, usually through an audible or visual signal that does not transmit instructions; *notification* means to provide instructions and information using appropriate communication systems and devices. The public has been notified when they receive specific instructions that apply to their situation—do nothing, remain indoors and monitor the Emergency Alert System, shelter-in-place using active dose reduction methods, obtain or use potassium iodide, evacuate, or take some other actions.

The primary Commission requirement regarding public warning and notification is found in 10 CFR 50 Appendix E, IV.D(3), which states that, "each nuclear power reactor licensee shall demonstrate that administrative and physical means have been established for alerting and providing prompt instructions to the public … (within 15 minutes of the time that State and local officials are notified that a situation exists requiring urgent action)." The associated FEMA exercise evaluation criteria require that offsite officials reach an appropriate protective action decision and initiate the warning and notification process, both within 15 minutes of receiving the licensee's protective action recommendation.

A variety of methods are acceptable to warn and notify offsite persons. FEMA (1985b, p. E-3/4) states, "A fully effective alerting system may employ ... a combination of ... fixed sirens, mobile siren vehicles, tone alert radios, aircraft, automatic telephone dialers, modulated power lines, and police, fire, and rescue vehicles or personnel."* The minimally acceptable system design objectives are to (1) have a capability to produce both an alert signal and an informational message throughout the 10-mile EPZ within 15 minutes, (2) ensure direct coverage of essentially 100% of the population within 5 miles of the site, and (3) ensure 100% coverage within 45 minutes for those persons in the EPZ who many not have received the initial notification.

The two principal means of warning in widespread use are outdoor sirens and warning (tone alert) radios placed in individual households and other high-value locations. Sirens are required to have a sound output greater than 70 decibels (dB) in areas where the population density is greater than or equal to 2000 persons per square mile and greater than 60 dB in areas of lesser population density. For all siren systems, the effective siren output must be greater than 10 dB above any expected ambient background, including any applicable background noise. In some low-population areas, outdoor warning sirens are only installed in towns, and warning radios are the primary method to warn the rural population. Special radio-activated warning devices are used to warn visually impaired or hearing-impaired persons. In essentially all cases, automated systems are backed up by *mobile route alerting* (public address systems mounted on fire or law enforcement vehicles or, in a few locations, on helicopters).

Siren systems are generally manually triggered from a local or county dispatch center, usually a 911 system or law enforcement dispatch center with continuous staffing, with control signals transmitted either by radio or through a permanent cable. The radio-based systems are more common. When an emergency planning zone encompasses multiple counties (or parishes), each county typically has separate siren control points, which are often redundant to one another and could control the entire system if necessary. Although operation of a the public warning system is the responsibility of offsite authorities, many systems also feature additional backup control capability located at a reactor licensee facility, such as at the emergency operations facility; this additional control capability may be used to conduct periodic system testing. Current siren systems generally consist of rotating electromechanical sirens (older equipment), stacks of electronic speakers (newer equipment, which may or may not have a rotating head), or combinations of the two. FEMA guidance for warning system testing† is found in REP-10 (FEMA, 1985b) and dates from the period when electromechanical sirens were the only equipment available; the minimum acceptable testing program consists of a communications and control system test (silent test) every 2 weeks, a low power/short-cycle sounding test (growl test) every calendar quarter, and a 3-minute full cycle sounding test annually. Electronic speaker-type sirens are not usually configured for growl tests. Warning system reliability is acceptable when the percentage of sirens with successful tests is greater than or equal to 90%, averaged over a year. Individual tests may fall below the 90% threshold without threatening the reasonable assurance determination. Specific commitments regarding siren testing and maintenance programs are found in a licensee's FEMA-approved site-specific design report and may also be found in the licensee's emergency plan.

The original guidance for implementing public warning systems was NUREG-0654, Appendix 3, *Means for Providing Prompt Alerting and Notification of Response Organizations and the Population* (NRC, 1980c). This appendix also included requirements to activate the public warning system during emergency plan exercises and to conduct post-activation telephone surveys to establish or confirm acceptable siren coverage; these requirements were generally dropped in approximately 1995, although the surveys continue to be a local commitment at a few sites through the present.

When warning radios are used as the primary or secondary warning system, a "best effort" is required to identify those locations (e.g., households, businesses, public buildings) that require the warning. Every identified location is required to be offered a warning radio, although members of

---

* See also FEMA (1980d, 1983b).
† Requirements for testing the emergency alerting system are set by the U.S. Federal Communications Commission.

the public cannot be required to accept a warning radio. The radio should be offered at no charge to the public and should be operable as distributed; an annual radio maintenance program must be offered to refresh batteries and replace broken radios. An accurate register must be maintained listing the addresses of people to whom radios are supplied and those who refused the radio; access to this register should be controlled to prevent the release of personally identifiable information. Tests of the warning radios should be conducted at least monthly; in many locations, the warning radios are activated using the National Oceanic and Atmospheric Administration (NOAA) National Weather Service radio warning system. Although regulatory requirements exist for the timeliness of notifications from licensees to offsite authorities, and from offsite authorities (the legal authority) to the public, there are no timeliness requirements or performance standards for the completion of protective actions. For example, there is no enforced maximum acceptable evacuation time.

CONGREGATE CARE AND PETS

The treatment of pets at congregate care facilities during evacuations is a currently a significant issue in emergency preparedness for all kinds of initiating events. Prior to 2006, no congregate care facilities operated by the American Red Cross accepted pets (except guide animals for the blind and other service animals), and neither did many facilities run by other organizations. With a presumption that any evacuation would be short (i.e., no longer than 3 or 4 days), the standard advice was to lock pets in a single room with an adequate supply of food and water to last until the evacuees were able to return. This became a serious practical issue during Hurricanes Katrina and Rita in 2005, as many persons in Louisiana and Texas refused to evacuate from their homes without their pets. Evacuees who had left pets behind could not readily return to retrieve or feed those pets. The situation resulted in the Pets Evacuation and Transportation Standards Act of 2006,* which required FEMA to require that state and local emergency plans include provisions to evacuate animals and authorized FEMA to fund the provision of congregate care facilities capable of handling animals.

RADIOLOGICAL PROTECTION OF EMERGENCY WORKERS

One premise of assigning an individual duty as a radiological emergency worker is that the emergency functions they perform is sufficiently important to justify assuming the risk associated with radiation exposure. An individual who does not understand that they may receive a radiation dose as a result of being an emergency worker and who is not willing to receive that dose will not be a worker that can be counted on. Workers should understand their functions as they relate to providing for the health and safety of the public and accept the need to perform those functions.

Emergency workers in a radiological emergency are pre-designated and trained to perform emergency functions while potentially receiving radiation exposure or dose. The licensee's emergency response organization will all be trained as radiation emergency workers, but only some offsite responders will receive this training. Most offsite emergency responders are not day-to-day occupational radiation workers as are utility workers, and they do not receive routine radiation safety training as part of their employment. All offsite radiological emergency workers are required to

---

* Public Law 109-308, October 6, 2006, 120 STAT.1725. The law states, in part, "SEC. 2. Standards for State and Local Emergency Preparedness Operational Plans ... Section 611 of the Robert T. Stafford Disaster Relief and Emergency Assistance Act (42 U.S.C. 5196) is amended— ... (B) by inserting after paragraph (1) the following: '(2) The Director may make financial contributions, on the basis of programs or projects approved by the Director, to the States and local authorities for animal emergency preparedness purposes, including the procurement, construction, leasing, or renovating of emergency shelter facilities and materials that will accommodate people with pets and service animals.' ... Section 613 of the Robert T. Stafford Disaster Relief and Emergency Assistance Act (42 U.S.C. 5196b) is amended— ... (2) by inserting after subsection (f) the following: '(g) STANDARDS FOR STATE AND LOCAL EMERGENCY PREPAREDNESS OPERATIONAL PLANS.—In approving standards for State and local emergency preparedness operational plans pursuant to subsection (b)(3), the Director shall ensure that such plans take into account the needs of individuals with household pets and service animals prior to, during, and following a major disaster or emergency.'"

be trained on the effects of radiation to about the level of licensee general employee training, in addition to any other specialized skills they require (e.g., firefighting, law enforcement, electrical maintenance). Emergency workers receive radiation training appropriate to their function and task and to their potential level of risk. The available options for protecting emergency workers from excessive radiation exposure in real time are

- Personal self-reading dosimetry (may or may not have dose or dose rate alarms)
- Radiation monitoring and survey instruments (in some cases, permanently installed instruments can be read remotely at emergency operation centers)
- Alarming air samplers
- Anti-contamination clothing or equipment
- Personnel, vehicle, and equipment decontamination stations
- Temporary or special radiation shielding
- Respiratory protection
- Blocking agents for intakes of radioactive material (primarily potassium iodide)
- Occupational and emergency dose limits
- ALARA principle (radiation doses are "as low as reasonably achievable" for the conditions that are present)

During emergencies, it is always the expectation that emergency workers who are required to be exposed to radiation minimize that exposure as much as possible (the ALARA principle) by taking advantage of shielding and managing stay times (exposure). An emergency worker who has an assigned post or position cannot effectively manage the distance between themselves and the radiation source to reduce their exposure. One emergency management goal is to keep individual emergency worker doses within the Commission's routine annual occupational dose limits of 5 rem TEDE (whole body, including the trunk and upper limb segments), 15 rem CDE to the lenses of the eyes, and 50 rem CDE to the skin.* Calculations show the 5-rem TEDE limit is likely to be the most restrictive limit during a power reactor accident because the associated fission products produce more deep-penetrating gamma radiation and higher energy beta radiation than the lower energy beta radiation and alpha radiation, which causes eye and skin dose. When lower (within occupational limits) doses are not practicable, the *Manual of Protective Action Guides* (USEPA, 1992, p. 2-10, Table 2-2) provides guidance for controlling emergency worker doses of an upper limit of 10 rem TEDE for protecting valuable property, and an upper limit of 25 rem TEDE for life saving and the protection of large populations; the same values are found in the 2013 *PAG Manual* guidance. Saving or protecting large populations includes actions to mitigate, reduce, or terminate a radiological release. In all cases, only the lowest practicable dose should be received, and an unnecessary dose is to be avoided.

The *Manual of Protective Action Guides* implies that emergency radiation workers may be directed to perform activities resulting in radiation exposures up to 25 rem TEDE; that is, activities that result in actual radiation doses above occupational limits and up to 25 rem are not required to be voluntary. Doses greater than 25 rem TEDE may be authorized for life-saving missions and the protection of large populations only when the emergency worker is a volunteer† and is fully aware of the additional radiation risks involved in the mission. Licensees and offsite response agencies

---

* Routine occupational dose limits are found in 10 CFR 20, Subpart C, § 1201. Prior to 1993, the 5-rem limit applied only to a whole-body deep dose with separate limits on the annual intake of radioactive material that were not combined into a single integrated dose. Prior to 1993, there existed a lifetime whole body dose limit calculated by $(5N - 18)$, where N equals the radiation worker's current age in years. OSHA regulations for general industrial use of radioactive materials (29 CFR 1910.1096) still contain the older radiological limits; 29 CFR 1910.1096(p) requires industrial users with Nuclear Regulatory Commission licenses to follow Commission radiation protection requirements (10 CFR Parts 19 and 20) in lieu of 29 CFR 1910, even when the Commission requirements differ.

† Some licensees and offsite authorities restrict activities expected to result in doses of more than 25 rem TEDE to volunteers of age 40 and above, on the presumption that workers of those ages are past their reproductive years and the possibility of radiation-induced genetic effects is greatly reduced.

whose workers could reasonably become involved in life-saving missions should have procedures in place to identify volunteers and brief them regarding the additional radiation-induced risks they may incur. ICRP Report 26 (ICRP, 1977a) states that no emergency worker should receive more than 10 rem TEDE during any single emergency event and not more than 25 rem TEDE emergency dose over a worker's lifetime. Additional information can be found in Information Notice 84-40 (NRC, 1984c). Title 29 of the Code of Federal Regulations, Part 1910.120(a)(1)(v), states in part that OSHA's requirements for training apply to "Emergency response operations for releases of, or substantial threats of releases of, hazardous substances without regard to the location of the hazard," where radioactive material is considered to be a hazardous material (i.e., it is listed on the EPA hazardous substance registry for CERCLA).

The working radiation dose of each emergency worker is controlled through a combination of administrative dose limits and turn-back exposure rates. An *administrative limit* is an applied dose control limit that is lower than the applicable regulatory limit. Administrative limits are warning levels designed to ensure that employees do not accidentally exceed the regulatory limits; in an emergency, they allow responsible officials the opportunity to determine whether additional dose is justified based on the functions being performed by the person receiving the dose while the employee still has dose margin. Administrative limits are generally established only for cumulative radiation exposure or dose.

A *turn-back exposure rate* or dose, applied only during emergency conditions, is a measured radiation exposure rate or dosimeter deep-dose equivalent (DDE) dose that requires the emergency worker to leave the area and report on the as-found conditions to the authorizing official. A turn-back DDE or exposure rate is applied to limit the emergency worker's chances of exceeding their authorized dose, where the authorized dose may be above regulatory limits under some situations. Operating and occupational radiation protection procedures are not necessarily suspended during an emergency, except as specifically provided for in the appropriate emergency plan and implementing procedures (e.g., a suspension of radiation work permit requirements).

When assigning doses above 10 CFR 20.1201 occupational dose limits, licensees must clearly document the basis for the dose (property or life saving/populations) to ensure that the correct dose limit is applied. The licensee should also determine in advance of the exposure the doses that are expected during the assigned tasks, including all assumptions, and record why lower doses are not practicable. Both the predictive doses and the actual dose received should be well documented. A licensee may determine that a particular task is sufficiently important to warrant requiring the additional dose but should document their reasoning in this regard.

In addition to routine occupational dose limits, in 1993 the Commission created an extraordinary individual dose limit called the *planned special exposure*. The planned special exposure limits are applied separately to each type of dose limit and are five times the applicable occupational dose limit per lifetime, with no more than an additional one times each occupational dose limit received in a single year. Emergency workers who are also occupational radiation workers have their individual special exposure bank reduced by the doses they receive during an emergency response, as 10 CFR 20.1201(b) states, "Doses received in excess of the annual limits, including doses received during accidents, emergencies, ... must be subtracted from the limits for planned special exposures." Although the regulation does *not* state that the planned special exposures must be voluntary, there are some indications that this may have been its intent, including the statement that "the individuals involved must be ... informed of the estimated doses and associated potential risks ... before permitting an individual to participate in a planned special exposure." In this regard, Commission regulation and the *PAG Manual* may not be inconsistent, such that licensees should document in their procedures whether they will use planned special exposures during emergencies. Planned special exposures do not apply to minors or to declared pregnant workers.

In practice, an emergency worker could receive 30 rem TEDE of involuntary radiation dose during an emergency—5 rem of annual occupational dose plus an additional 25 rem for critical life-saving or tasks protecting large populations or terminating a radiological release. Note that a worker receiving 30 rem TEDE would exceed the normally allowed one times their annual occupational dose and completely deplete their allowed lifetime special exposure dose limits. This situation refers only to those doses planned to be received. Because of unexpected and rapidly changing conditions, emergency workers may receive doses different from those that are planned, including workers who are not expected to exceed their occupational limits. Any actual dose received above occupational limits during the emergency is still subtracted from the individual's planned special exposure "bank," regardless of whether it was planned or unintended. Prior to 1993, EPA 520/1-75-001 (USEPA, 1975) permitted emergency workers to receive doses to 100 rem (whole body) for lifesaving activities.

Both men and women are occupational radiation workers and may be emergency responders, including women who are (or may be) pregnant. An embryo or fetus is a special case of a member of the public. A declaration of pregnancy is completely voluntary; a women who chooses not to declare a pregnancy cannot have her occupational dose limited by management differently than provided for other workers for the sole purpose of protecting her unborn child, including during assigned emergency response activities. In such a case, she assumes all associated risks to her child (see 10 CFR 20.1208). Training on this subject is required to be provided as part of annual radiation worker training, including for emergency responders. There is no regulatory requirement to exclude a declared pregnant worker from a licensee or offsite emergency response organization, although it may be generally prudent to assign a declared pregnant worker to a shielded location, such as the control room, technical support center, or emergency operations facility. Title 10 of the Code of Federal Regulations 20.1208(b) states, "The licensee shall make efforts to avoid substantial variation above a uniform monthly exposure rate to a declared pregnant woman." EPA 400-R-92-001 (USEPA, 1992, p. 2-10) states, "To assure adequate protection of minors and the unborn, the performance of emergency services should be limited to nonpregnant adults."

PERSONAL DOSIMETRY

Every emergency worker is issued both passive integrating dosimetry* and personal self-reading dosimetry. Licensee workers may be issued either electronic self-reading dosimeters or the older, pencil-style ion chamber or quartz fiber type dosimeters, although electronic dosimetry is now more common even at licensee emergency response facilities. Electronic dosimetry is essentially universal for survey and repair teams entering plant buildings. Offsite workers are generally issued pencil-type self-reading dosimeters because offsite agencies do not have the infrastructure that supports electronic dosimetry systems. Because quartz fiber dosimeters are designed to different sensitivities, often emergency workers are issued two dosimeters, one reading in the lower range (below 500 mrem total exposure) and the other to a higher range (often to 5000 mrem/5-rem exposure or 10,000 mrem/10-rem exposure). The normal practice is for emergency workers to read their dosimeters every 15 to 30 minutes and to keep running written records of their dosimeter readings.

It is not generally necessary to measure emergency worker exposure more precisely than to the nearest 1 to 5 mrem (0.001 to 0.005 rem). The detection sensitivity of electronic, ion chamber, and quartz fiber dosimeters are about the same, with the higher intrinsic sensitivity of solid state detectors being compensated for by the larger detection volume of the pencil-type detectors. The typical 0 to 200 mrem (civil defense) pencil-type dosimeter can be accurately read to about the nearest 2 to 3 mrem, with higher dose dosimeters having correspondingly higher minimum readings.

Self-reading dosimeters measure exposure (essentially only gamma radiation dose), but emergency worker dose limits are in rem TEDE (the sum of external and internal doses), creating a problem when applying self-reading dosimetry to controlling individual worker dose because

---

* Passive integrating dosimetry typically serves as the legal dose of record and is carried by an individual throughout the emergency. Typical passive devices measure exposure to beta and gamma radiation and include film badges, thermoluminescent dosimeters (TLDs), optically stimulated dosimeters, and other solid-state detectors. Neutron dosimetry is not usually used. Passive dosimetry requires specialized equipment to read and does not warn the wearer when exposure limits are exceeded.

self-reading dosimeters cannot measure TEDE. The most accurate solution is to collect a representative air sample of the plume to which the worker is exposed, perform an isotopic analysis, calculate the resulting inhalation dose factors, calculate the ratio of dose from inhaled radioactive material (using reference man respiration rates) to external dose, then adjust the self-reading dosimeter by the resulting ratio. Theoretical calculations of this adjustment ratio range from 3 to 10 depending on the assumed initial core inventory, the core damage state, and time after reactor shutdown; a value of 5 is a good average estimate. The worker's dose is estimated by multiplying the dosimeter value by the adjustment ratio so that the estimated dose is always greater than the measured exposure. One problem with this adjustment is that the worker is unable to differentiate between gamma radiation shine from a nearby cloud of radioactive material (outside the cloud with zero inhalation dose) and submersion in a cloud of radioactive material (inside the cloud with inhalation dose) without a survey meter with a beta/gamma window. Another problem is that the measured exposure depends on the average gamma energy of the mixture of radioactive materials and the inhalation dose dosimetry adjustment factor depends on the mixture of radioactive materials, both of which change over time because of radioactive decay. Licensee and offsite agency procedures may specify a single value for the dosimetry adjustment factor, but because of the time-dependent aspects calculating an event-specific adjustment factor becomes important. When a representative air sample has been obtained and analyzed, the appropriate adjustment factors can be calculated for the entire emergency event.

POTASSIUM IODIDE FOR EMERGENCY WORKERS

As previously discussed, potassium iodide is an approved protective measure against radioactive iodine and may be taken by emergency workers. Although Protective Action Guides for the use of potassium iodide by the general public are suggested by the U.S. Food and Drug Administration and by the 1992 *Manual of Protective Action Guides* (EPA-400) there is no explicit guidance for administering potassium iodide to emergency workers. Section 2.6 of the 2013 *PAG Manual* discusses the protection of response personnel but the discussion is limited to dose limits and does not address potassium iodide. EPA-400 states on pages 2-11 and 2-12, "… Stable iodine is also recommended for blocking thyroid uptake in personnel involved in emergency actions where atmospheric releases include radioiodine…" The federal position is that potassium iodide is a drug with potential harmful side effects, therefore Commission licensees should evaluate and document the need for potassium iodide, then issue potassium iodide only to those emergency workers requiring it. While licensees are required by 10 CFR 50.47(b)(10) to include potassium iodide as one of a range of protective measures, individual emergency workers may decline to use it. In general, emergency response organizations do not screen responders in advance for iodine allergies which would indicate a greater risk from taking potassium iodide, and the legal consequences of excluding workers from performing emergency services based on their identified iodine sensitivity are unclear. Many power reactor licensees have selected 25 rem thyroid CDE as their protective measures limit for administering potassium iodide to emergency workers; offsite agencies generally have much lower administrative limits for potassium iodide than do reactor personnel—many offsite responders issue potassium iodide as a precautionary measure whenever there is any detectable airborne iodine present.

RESPIRATORY PROTECTION FOR EMERGENCY WORKERS

Planning standard 10 CFR 50.47(b)(10) requires that licensees provide a range of protective actions for emergency workers. Title 10 of the Code of Federal Regulations, Part 20.1702(a), requires licensees to use respiratory protection to reduce an employee's exposure to airborne radioactivity to concentrations less than that requiring posting as an airborne radioactive materials area, subject to maintaining exposures ALARA.* There are no explicit regulations requiring emergency personnel to be respiratory qualified, although 10 CFR 50.47(b)(8) and 10 CFR 50.47(b)(15) may apply; (b)(8) states, "Adequate emergency facilities and equipment to support the emergency response are provided and maintained," and (b)(15) states, "Radiological emergency response training is provided to those who may be called upon to assist in an emergency."

Emergency workers who are issued respiratory protection must be enrolled in a routine respiratory protection program. The essential elements of an acceptable program include an overall plan and assigned responsibilities, approved and maintained implementing procedures, initial and requalification training for workers and evaluators, periodic (usually annual) medical surveillance of workers, availability of a range of protective equipment (including a range of sizes), mask fit testing of workers, routine inspection and operational testing of respiratory protection equipment, routine monitoring of the work environment to identify and assess hazards, and an independent quality assurance program. The medical evaluation and fitting testing requirements make it difficult for a licensee to issue *ad hoc* respiratory protection in an emergency to persons not part of a routine program. It may be possible to do a prompt medical evaluation, but it is generally not possible to ensure a proper mask fit without proper facilities.

For routine plant operations, the Commission accepts half-face air-purifying respirators (with filter cartridges rated for the specific hazard), full-face air-purifying respirators, supplied-air hoods, and self-contained breathing apparatus (SCBA). In general, all equipment that is used must be National Institute of Occupational Safety and Health (NIOSH) certified; however, NIOSH does not have test methods for some kinds of respiratory equipment, such as supplied-air encapsulating suits or filter cartridges specific to radioactive iodine—these applications are permitted provided the user (licensee) does not apply a dose reduction factor in calculating the worker's internal radiation dose. Devices that rely on filter cartridges may only be worn in areas known not to be immediately dangerous to life and health (IDLH) (e.g., an oxygen-deficient atmosphere) and which cannot become immediately dangerous to life and health.

Regulatory Guide 8.15 (NRC, 1999a, p. 12) states

> The equipment preferred for emergency entry into an unassessed environment … is the open-circuit self-contained breathing apparatus (SCBA) operated in the pressure-demand mode, with a minimum rated service life of 30 minutes. Also acceptable are a combination full-facepiece pressure demand supplied air respirator with an auxiliary self-contained [escape] air supply of at least 5 minutes duration and a positive-pressure, closed-circuit (recirculating) SCBA with a minimum rated service life of 30 minutes. … Other equipment may be designated for emergency use against airborne radioactive material. An example would be air-purifying respirators … organic-vapor cartridges or canisters may be used for whatever protection they provide.

Further (NRC, 1999a, p. 3),

> The NRC suggests, consistent with the OSHA Act, that a monthly visual inspection of SCBAs is sufficient, and that an operational test (i.e., pressurizing the regulator, testing the low-pressure alarm) need only be done quarterly. Other devices stored for emergency use should be visually inspected monthly, but only need to be thoroughly examined two or three times per year.

---

* Depending on the situation, the licensee may also be subject to 29 CFR 1910.120, Hazardous Waste Operations and Emergency Response, and 29 CFR 1910.134, Respiratory Protection. For most applications, respiratory protection programs that meet the requirements of 10 CFR 20, Subpart H (§§ 1701 through 1705), also meet the requirements of 29 CFR 1910. NRC respiratory protection requirements take precedence over OSHA requirements if the device is (1) used to protect against the radiation risk from inhaling radioactive materials, (2) used to protect against the associated chemical risk produced by a material that is also radioactive (e.g., isotopes of uranium), or (3) when plant conditions generally present an increased radiation risk to employees. OSHA rules take precedence whenever the atmosphere also contains non-radioactive hazards or the atmosphere is oxygen deficient.

Workers enrolled in a respiratory protection program must receive vision screening as part of their medical qualification. Prior to the year 2000, the wearing of contact lenses in full-face respiratory protection equipment was prohibited because of the potential for a displaced lens to block air flow into the mask; at that time, all users who required prescription lenses were required to obtain and have available eyeglass kits that mounted inside the facepiece so that vision was maintained and there was no interruption of the face-to-mask seal. NUREG-1736 (Zelac et al., 2001) and NUREG/CR-0041 (Steinmeyer, 2001) currently state, "It is vital that a respirator wearer be able to see clearly. … Vision spectacle kits specific for each respirator type are available and contact lens are allowed to be used." Workers are required to be fit-tested and perform any hands-on respirator training using the vision correction they would use in an emergency. Workers cannot be required to use contact lenses with respiratory protection and should not use contact lenses if these are not their normal means of vision correction (i.e., there must be an established fit and comfort level with vision correction to be effective during emergency conditions).[*]

---

[*] For additional information regarding respiratory protection programs and emergency use, see NRC (1984e, 1997d, 1998h, 1999a) and Steinmeyer (2001); ANSI Standard Z88.2-1992, Standard for Respiratory Protection; and ANSI Standard Z88.6-1984, Respiratory Use—Physical Qualifications of Personnel.

3 Core Damage and Related Concepts

INTRODUCTION

This chapter discusses reactor core states, radioactive material inventories, severe accidents, the world experience with reactor accidents, accident sequences, the sources of radiological releases, mechanisms for depleting radioactive source terms, and plant monitoring systems used for assessing accidents. The purpose of emergency planning for commercial nuclear reactors is to avoid as much radiation dose to the public as possible under the circumstances of a specific accident. An important aspect of preplanning is establishing the means to detect abnormal amounts of radioactive material and analyze its likely consequences. Predicting future consequences from releases of radioactive material involves both the direct measurement of radiation and the indirect modeling of its movement through the environment. The resulting dose analysis is not accurate in every detail but when done properly provides a sound technical basis for selecting from among the available protective action strategies. This chapter primarily discusses the assessment of damage to the reactor core and aspects of modeling the behavior of radioactive material in the environment.

The total effective dose equivalent radiation dose to a member of the public from a commercial power reactor accident is the sum of the external doses and the committed dose equivalents received from internally deposited radioactive material. The total effective dose equivalent is estimated at predetermined locations and distances in the environment and does not represent the assumed actual dose of any individual member of the public. Dose estimates (or estimates using different core damage or meteorological assumptions) are intended to provide offsite authorities a basis for selecting among options for taking protective actions. Although the goal is to provide as accurate a radiological analysis as possible, in practice the underlying assumptions often tend more toward "worst case" than "most likely"; therefore, members of the public will likely receive less actual radiation dose than is estimated for their location.

The deep-dose equivalent (external dose) is primarily delivered by gamma (γ) radiation originating in airborne radioactive material within the range of the highest energy gamma radiation in the radioactive mixture, with a small contribution from higher-energy beta (β) radiation. This effective distance is typically between 100 and 150 yards.[*] The maximum effective range in air of beta radiation originating from the radioactive material typically present in a power reactor accident is about 35 feet. The deep-dose equivalent at a point in the environment is calculated by multiplying the concentration of each individual radioisotope by an external dose conversion factor;[†] the conversion factor takes into account all of the radiation energies from the isotope and their effective distances. A uniform distribution of radioactive material throughout the effective radius is assumed; this assumption overestimates the likely external dose at locations very near the edges of a radioactive plume. The deep-dose equivalent is the sum of all individual isotope deep-dose equivalents for both gamma and beta radiation. If a direct air sample has been collected, then an actual distribution of radioactive material can be used; otherwise, the analysis uses predetermined distributions of radioactive materials for the different stages of core damage.

---

[*] The intensity of 3.0-meV gamma radiation in air at standard temperature and pressure (STP) conditions is reduced by 99% at about 328 feet.
[†] External dose conversion factors can be found in USEPA (1993).

An individual does not have to be surrounded by radioactive material (i.e., in the plume) to receive an external dose from the radioactive material in the plume. Given the range of gamma radiation in air, a member of the public could be as far as 150 yards away from the plume and still be irradiated at a low dose rate. Gamma radiation originating in radioactive material not near the person receiving the dose is referred to as *shine*. Models of the behavior of radioactive material in the environment vary in their treatment of external exposure along the physical edge of a radioactive plume; the model output is usually an exposure rate or total integrated dose estimate map that rarely distinguishes the physical location of radioactive material from its associated gamma shine. Some models simply do not calculate radiation exposure rates or deep-dose equivalent for locations outside the plume of radioactive material.

The estimation of dose from an internal uptake of radioactive material is complicated and involves many assumptions, some of which are not accurate for specific individuals. Internal dose is estimated by multiplying the concentration of each individual radioactive isotope by a dose conversion factor* and by an exposure time. The dose conversion factor includes models about breathing rates, the biological efficiency of absorbing radioactive material into the body, the destination organs into which radioactive material is ultimately deposited, radioactive decay, and biological processes for eliminating isotopes from the body. As with external radiation, either a measured or a calculated distribution of radioactive isotopes can be used to perform the analysis, and the overall internal dose is the sum of the individual internal doses from each isotope in the distribution.

Because radioactive material enters the body more effectively by breathing than through other pathways, generally only the inhalation dose is calculated. In general, the radioactive isotopes released from a damaged power reactor core are not radioactive species or in chemical forms that have significant direct absorption through the skin.

GENERAL METHOD

The general method for generating a protective action decision is as follows:

- Estimate the radioactive source term based on the core damage state.
- Multiply the source term by a release rate determined from an effluent radiation monitor.
- Apply meteorological dispersion factors to estimate radioactive material concentrations.
- Multiply concentration by isotopic dose conversion factors to obtain gamma exposure and dose rates.
- Multiply dose rates by exposure time to get dose.
- Compare the dose estimate to established Protective Action Guide action thresholds.
- Adjust the release rate as needed to match the estimated gamma exposure rates to measured gamma exposure rates as observed by environmental monitoring teams.

DEFINITIONS

FUEL DAMAGE

Fuel damage is perforation of the fuel cladding that permits the release of fission products into reactor coolant.

CORE DAMAGE FREQUENCY

Core damage frequency expresses the likelihood that, given the way a reactor is designed and operated, an accident could cause the fuel to be damaged. The estimated frequency of core damage accidents in the U.S. reactor fleet is 1 in 10,000 reactor-years (Deutch et al., 2003). A single

---

* Internal dose conversion factors can be found in USEPA (1988).

reactor operating at power for 12 continuous months represents one reactor-year; with an average U.S. fleet capacity factor of 89.6% (NEI, 2006a) and 165 operating reactors, each calendar year currently represents approximately 148 reactor-years. The theoretical expected core damage frequency is approximately once every 67.7 years. WASH-1400 (NRC, 1975b) estimated the frequency of a worst-case reactor accident at approximately one per billion reactor-years, or with the current U.S. fleet once every 600,000 years. Through the end of 2005, the worldwide reactor fleet has operated for about 12,000 reactor-years (UIC, 2006). Commercial reactors are allowed to operate with very small amounts of fission products in the coolant but are required to shut down the reactor when fission product concentrations reach or exceed critical values that are set far below concentrations that could threaten public health and safety. Core damage represents a loss of the fuel integrity fission product barrier but by itself is not sufficient to threaten the public as long as the coolant system and containment barrier remain intact. In most reactor events, core damage would be a problem for the reactor's operators and owners but not for the public living near the plant.

REACTOR FUEL

Commercial power reactors are fueled with a large number of upright tubes (*fuel rods*) that are generally fabricated of stainless steel alloys containing zirconium; the alloy is often referred to as *Zircaloy*. Each tube is filled with ceramic uranium fuel pellets that are enriched in the isotope ^{235}U. For ease of handling, these individual tubes are bundled together in fuel assemblies, and each assembly has a square matrix of fuel rods. The metal alloy tube surrounding and confining the fuel pellets is the *cladding*. The cladding holds the fuel pellets in a rigid geometry, collects the fission gases produced during power operation, and provides an effective surface to transfer heat from the fuel pellets to the moderator (water). The fuel rods in boiling water reactors are designed to facilitate the formation of steam bubbles along the surface of the rods so the upper third of each rod is in contact with steam rather than water; these fuel rods are designed to produce most of their nuclear power and heat at the bottom of the rod. Pressurized water reactors are operated to prevent boiling in the reactor vessel, and the fuel rods are designed to transfer heat more evenly along their length.

A new, unused fuel assembly contains refined uranium and a small amount of natural uranium, an alpha emitter whose isotopes all have very long (millions of years) half-lives. Within its metal cladding tube, the unused fuel presents essentially no radiation protection hazard. When placed in an operating reactor, the fission process produces neutrons, causing the transmutation of non-radioactive atoms in structures and components into radioactive isotopes and also producing fission fragments, the remains of split uranium atoms. The curve describing fission fragment formation has two peaks, one between atomic numbers 85 and 105, the other between atomic numbers 130 and 155, both peaks having abundances (conversion efficiency) between 0.1% and about 8%. Some of these fission fragments are gases, primarily isotopes of krypton and xenon, although there are also volatile nuclides such as iodine and cesium. The gases escape the individual fuel pellets and collect in empty spaces engineered into the fuel rods; the remaining nuclides are particulates that remain trapped in the pellet ceramic or in the metal of reactor components.

ISOTOPES OF INTEREST IN REACTOR ACCIDENTS[*]

A very large number of radioisotopes are produced in an operating power reactor. Although theoretically one could analyze the contributions of each one to radiation dose, in practice the set is too large to work with conveniently. The usual practice is to concentrate on the most significant isotopes; however, there are various ways to define *significant*.

---

[*] This section was developed using data from Lin (1996), Neeb (1997), McKenna and Glitter (1988), Unterweger et al. (1992), USDHEW (1970), and www.periodictable.com. The dispersion calculations were performed by the author using a simplified straight-line Gaussian model.

TOTAL CORE INVENTORY

One way to rank isotopes is by the total activity in the core. In this respect, the most significant isotope is ^{239}Np at about 1.63E6 Ci (for a 1000-MWe reactor), followed by approximately equal activities of ^{133}I, ^{133}Xe^m, ^{135}Xe, ^{99}Mo, ^{140}Ba, ^{140}La, and ^{134}I, all at about 1.6E5 Ci, then a group consisting of ^{91}Y, ^{132}Te, ^{132}I, ^{91}Sr, and ^{103}Ru, all at approximately 1.2E5 Ci. A group of isotopes consisting of ^{89}Sr, ^{131}I, ^{144}Ce, ^{88}Kr, ^{87}Kr, ^{133}Xe^m, ^{129}Sb, ^{106}Ru, ^{85}Kr^m, and ^{131}Te^m have core inventories of between 1E3 and 1E4 Ci. The isotopes ^{134}Cs, ^{90}Sr, ^{136}Cs, ^{95}Zr, and ^{135}I have core inventories between 1E3 and 1E4 Ci. The isotopes ^{60}Co, ^{85}Kr, ^{54}Mn, ^{125}Sb, ^{3}H, ^{99}Tc, and ^{129}I have core inventories of less than 1E3 Ci.

HALF-LIFE

One can rank isotopes by their half-lives, either longest to shortest or shortest to longest. Some might rank the longest lived isotopes as more significant because they are present the longest. Others consider the shorter lived isotopes as being more important because they tend to contribute more to dose. Beginning with the shortest lived, the most significant is ^{134}I, with a half-life of 0.875 hours. The isotopes ^{87}Kr, ^{132}I, ^{56}Mn, ^{88}Kr, ^{129}Sb, ^{85}Kr^m, ^{135}I, ^{135}Xe, and ^{91}Sr have half-lives between 1 hour and 10 hours. Of this group, ^{135}Xe^m has the largest initial inventory, and it takes about 20 days for the entire core inventory to decay. However, even though ^{91}Sr has a somewhat lower initial inventory (1.1E6 Ci vs. 1.7E6 Ci for ^{135}Xe^m), it takes longer to completely decay away. A total core inventory less than or equal to 1E-10 Ci was chosen as representing the complete decay of the initial isotopic inventory.

The isotopes ^{24}Na, ^{133}I, ^{131}Te^m, ^{140}La, ^{239}Np, ^{99}Mo, ^{132}Te, and ^{127}Sb have half-lives of between 10 and 100 hours. For this group, ^{239}Np has the largest initial inventory, at approximately 1.64E6 Ci; it takes about 125 days for the entire inventory to decay away. In this group, ^{127}Sb is present the longest, taking about 175 days to completely decay. The isotopes ^{133}Xe, ^{133}Xe^m, ^{131}I, ^{131}Xe^m, ^{140}Ba, ^{136}Cs, ^{51}Cr, ^{129}Te^m, and ^{103}Ru have half-lives of between 100 hours and 1000 hours. For this group, ^{131}Xe^m has the largest initial inventory, at approximately 1.7E5 Ci; it takes about 600 days to completely decay away. In this group, ^{103}Ru is the longest lasting; approximately 0.0025 Ci is still present after 1000 days.

The isotopes ^{89}Sr, ^{91}Y, ^{95}Zr, ^{58}Co, ^{57}Co, ^{144}Ce, ^{54}Mn, and ^{106}Ru have half-lives of between 1000 hours and 10,000 hours. In this group, the isotope with the highest initial inventory is ^{91}Y, at 1.2E5 Ci; approximately 1 Ci is left after 1000 days. The isotope in this group that is present the longest is ^{106}Ru, which is reduced to approximately 3900 Ci after 1000 days from an initial inventory of 2.5E4 Ci; it takes about 5500 days to decay to 1 Ci.

The isotopes ^{3}H, ^{134}Cs, ^{22}Na, ^{125}Sb, and ^{60}Co have half-lives of between 10,000 and 100,000 hours. In this group, ^{134}Cs has the highest initial inventory at approximately 7500 Ci; after 6500 days, the inventory is reduced to approximately 19.2 Ci, and after 9750 days the inventory is approximately 1 Ci. In this group, there is approximately 58.5 Ci ^{60}Co remaining after 6500 days; the inventory of ^{60}Co is reduced to approximately 1 Ci after 18,000 days. The isotopes ^{85}Kr, ^{90}Sr, ^{137}Cs, ^{99}Tc, ^{135}Cs, and ^{129}I, have half-lives greater than 100,000 hours. In this group, ^{137}Cs has the highest initial inventory at 4700 Ci; after 40,000 days, there is still an inventory of approximately 380 Ci, and the total inventory of ^{137}Cs is reduced to 1 Ci after about 135,000 days. This is also the isotope having the largest remaining inventory of the group after 40,000 days. ^{90}Sr is the other significant isotope in this group, remaining at 40,000 days and being reduced to 1 Ci after about 125,000 days.

EXTERNAL RADIATION DOSE FACTOR

Direct external radiation from a plume of radioactive material is a major contributor to the radiation dose to the public during a release of radioactive material. Seven isotopes deliver greater than or equal to 1 R/h external radiation exposure from a total activity of 1 Ci: ^{24}Na at 1.919 R/h, ^{134}I at 1.573 R/h, ^{132}I at 1.421 R/h, ^{60}Co at 1.369 R/h, ^{136}Cs at 1.273 R/h, and ^{88}Kr at 1.025 R/h. The isotopes ^{135}I, ^{59}Fe, ^{58}Co, ^{54}Mn, ^{87}Kr, ^{91}Sr, ^{133}I, ^{137}Cs, ^{103}Ru, ^{131}I, ^{132}Te, ^{135}Xe, ^{140}Ba, ^{57}Co, ^{106}Ru, ^{99}Tc, ^{99}Mo, ^{133}Xe^m, and ^{133}Xe each deliver between 0.1 and 1.0 R/h external exposure, with ^{135}I having the greatest exposure rate at 0.862 R/h. The isotopes ^{134}Cs, ^{95}Zr, ^{144}Ce, and ^{51}Cr each deliver between 0.01 and 0.1 R/h external exposure, with ^{134}Cs delivering the most exposure at 0.07 R/h.

Although it is useful to consider only the magnitude of the direct radiation exposure factor, the actual exposure (dose) delivered also depends on initial core inventory, decay rate, total release rate to the environment, and downwind dilution factor (i.e., dispersion). Consider a hypothetical release that is measured 0.5 miles from the release point in an atmosphere with C stability class (i.e., a dispersion factor of 6E-5 using data from *Turner's Workbook*). The total release rate is 1E6 µCi/s,[*] and the hypothetical member of the public is exposed for 1 hour. All isotopes are present in the ratios found in the initial reactor core inventory (a very simplified and unrealistic assumption), and in-flight decay and other removal mechanisms are not considered. In this example, six isotopes deliver between 1E-6 and 1E-5 R/h: ^{134}I at approximately 6.5E-6 R/h, ^{140}La at 5.6E-6 R/h, ^{132}I at 4.7E-6 R/h, ^{133}I and ^{88}Kr at approximately 2E-6 R/h, and ^{91}Sr at 1.3E-6 R/h. Ten isotopes each deliver between 1E-6 and 1E-7 R/h, seven isotopes deliver between 1E-8 and 1E-7 R/h, and five isotopes deliver less than or equal to 1E-8 R/h. The total external exposure rate for this release is approximately 2.8E-5 R/h (note that this value does not include the submersion dose from the eight Kr and Xe isotopes).

INHALATION DOSE FACTOR

A significant amount of the dose delivered to the public in a hypothetical reactor accident is due to the inhalation of radioactive materials. ^{144}Ce, ^{129}I, ^{106}Ru, and ^{91}Sr have inhalation dose conversion factors (in rem/µCi breathed) between 0.1 and 1.0 rem/µCi, with ^{144}Ce delivering the highest dose at 0.256 rem/µCi. ^{134}Cs, ^{60}Co, ^{137}Cs, ^{103}Ru, ^{95}Zr, and ^{59}Fe have inhalation dose factors between 0.01 and 0.1 rem/µCi breathed, with ^{134}Cs delivering the highest dose at 0.0318 rem/µCi. ^{32}Te, ^{133}I, ^{125}Sb, ^{129}Te^m, ^{22}Na, ^{136}Cs, ^{140}Ba, ^{90}Sr, ^{238}Np, ^{131}Te^m, ^{54}Mn, ^{135}Cs, ^{140}La, ^{58}Co, ^{127}Sb, ^{135}I, ^{99}Tc, ^{24}Na, and ^{99}Mo have inhalation dose factors between 0.001 and 0.01 rem/µCi breathed, with ^{132}Te delivering the highest dose at 8.68E-3 rem/µCi. ^{57}Co, ^{129}Sb, ^{132}I, ^{56}Mn, ^{134}I, ^{51}Cr, and ^{3}H have inhalation dose factors between 1E-4 and 1E-3 (0.001), with ^{57}Co delivering the highest dose at 9.17E-4 rem/µCi. The eight Kr and Xe isotopes are not considered because they each have essentially zero uptake fractions in the lung.

Although it is useful to consider only the magnitude of the inhalation dose conversion factor, the actual dose delivered also depends on the initial core inventory, decay rate, total release rate to the environment, downwind dilution factor (i.e., dispersion), and order in which isotopes are released from the fuel. Consider the previous 1E6-µCi/s release rate with all isotopes present in the ratios found in the initial reactor core inventory. In this case, three isotopes deliver greater than 0.1 rem: ^{144}Ce at approximately 0.57 rem, ^{91}Sr at 0.34 rem, and ^{91}Y at 0.11 rem, totaling 1.02 rem/h. ^{106}Ru, ^{131}I, ^{103}Ru, ^{133}I, ^{132}Te, ^{140}Ba, and ^{140}La each deliver between 0.01 and 0.1 rem/h, with ^{106}Ru delivering the most at approximately 0.09 rem. The total dose from this group is approximately 0.3 rem/h. The five isotopes ^{134}Cs, ^{99}Mo, ^{137}Cs, ^{132}I, and ^{131}Te^m deliver inhalation doses between 1E-3 and 1E-2 rem/h; the total dose from this group is approximately 0.016 rem. Eight isotopes each deliver inhalation doses between 1E-4 and 1E-3 rem/h: ^{129}Te^m, ^{134}I, ^{95}Zr, ^{90}Sr, ^{136}Cs, ^{129}Sb, ^{60}Co, and ^{127}Sb. The total dose for this group is approximately 4.4E-3 rem/h. The remaining six isotopes each deliver between 4E-5 and 5.4E-11 rem/h, for a total dose of 6.4E-5 rem/h. In this example, the total inhalation dose rate is approximately 1.5 rem/h.[†]

---

[*] The distance of 0.5 miles is a representative distance for the nearest member of the public to a reactor at most sites; a release rate of 1E6 µCi/s under most conditions will produce a radiation exposure rate of about 1 mR/h.

[†] An accident producing this dose rate would require declaration of a General Emergency classification based on exceeding a projected 1 rem/h at the site boundary and would require protective actions to be taken offsite. However, the expected inhalation dose at 2 miles would be 0.15 rem/h, which does not exceed Protective Action Guides. The dispersion factor at 2 miles is 5E-6 compared to 6E-5 at 0.5 miles.

The most likely reactor accidents will release only the radioactive gases stored in fuel assemblies and will not release radioactive materials from within the ceramic fuel pellets. Correcting the above example to remove the refractory fission products, three isotopes deliver inhalation doses greater than 0.01 rem/h: [131]I at 0.17 rem, [133]I at 0.07 rem, and [91]Sr at 0.036 rem. If significance is defined as delivering dose at greater than or equal to 1E-4 rem/h, the remaining significant isotopes are [132]I at 1.86E-3 rem, [134]Cs at 6.8E-4 rem, ^{137}Cs at 3.13E-4 rem, and [91]Y at 1.16E-4 rem. The remaining 17 isotopes each deliver from 8E-15 to 9E-5 rem, or a total dose for the group of approximately 2E-4 rem/h. The above calculations used a release rate of 1E6 µCi/s; all dose values simply increase by a factor of 10 for rates of 1E7 µCi/s, by 100 for rates of 1E8 µCi/s, etc.

LIMITATIONS ON MEASUREMENT

The previous discussion assumed that an analyst had information about all of the isotopes that are present in a reactor. In practice, this is not the case during at least the initial several days of an accident. In an actual event, information will only be readily available for γ-emitting isotopes, and only those with characteristic energies above 100 to 200 keV. This partially explains why ^{131}I is considered to be such a key isotope, while [133]I, which has about the same dose impact, is essentially ignored. [133]I is a γ emitter with a characteristic energy of 56 keV, which is very difficult to measure. Analysts will depend on plant effluent radiation monitors and on in-field exposure rate (e.g., mR/h) measurements; in either case, the measured values are input into dispersion models that have a pre-established, assumed distribution of isotopes. The isotopes that are carefully tracked during an event and considered key are those that rank highly in all of the above attributes, total core inventory, half-life, external exposure, inhalation dose, and ease of measurement. Therefore, the key isotopes are typically considered to be ^{60}Co, [91]Sr, ^{131}I, [134]Cs, [136]Cs, and [137]Cs.

SOURCE TERM AND CORE INVENTORY

The starting point for analyzing the consequences of a damaged power reactor is understanding the accident source term. NUREG-1228 (McKenna and Glitter, 1988, p. 1-2) states that, "This characterization of radionuclides that may be released to the environment, in conjunction with release rate and height, is referred to as the 'source term.'"* The source term is the collection or distribution of the radioisotopes that exists at the transition from the reactor site to the environment, along with their initial concentrations. The transition point to the environment could be the top of a chimney, vent, or stack; it could be a hole in the side of a plant building such as an engineered blowout panel; or it could be a damaged seal, such as the gasket surrounding the external hatch of a reactor containment building. The source term is not necessarily the distribution and concentration of radioisotopes measured in reactor coolant or in containment structure atmosphere samples, because both natural and engineered processes act to change and deplete the reactor coolant distribution before it reaches the environment.

The isotopes with the most significant contribution to early health effects were identified in WASH-1400 (NRC, 1975b) and are shown in Table 3.1. These values are similar to those used in the accident models described in NUREG-0925 (NRC, 1983e) and NUREG/CR-3108 (Wilson et al., 1983). These assumptions are considered by the Nuclear Regulatory Commission (NRC) to have a probable error of less than 25%. The inventory of long-lived (half-lives of 10 years or more) isotopes is proportional to the burn-up factor or the length of time the core has been in operation. The inventory of short-lived (half-lives of 30 days or less) isotopes is proportional to the core power density, and the inventory of activation products found in core components is proportional to the average reactor power level.

---

* NUREG-1228 (p. 1-2) also states, "To be useful, these [radiological consequence] projections should be based on a best-estimate assessment of the source term and not on artificial assumptions intended only for licensing purposes. ... These assumptions should not be used to characterize an actual accident."

TABLE 3.1

Total Curies of Radioactive Isotopes Available in a Reactor Core (While Operating, per Megawatt Electric)

Isotope Group	Total Activity (Ci)
Noble gases	520,000
Halogens (iodines)	715,000
Alkali metals (cesium)	15,200
Tellurium group	177,500
Strontium group	367,700
Noble metals (Ru, Rh, Mo, Co)	295,000
Cerium and transuranic metals	1,760,000

Source: Data from NRC, *Source Term Estimation During Incident Response to Severe Nuclear Power Plant Accidents*, NUREG-1228, U.S. Nuclear Regulatory Commission, Washington, DC, 1988.

TABLE 3.2

Total Curies of Radioactive Isotopes Available in a Reactor Core (Immediately After Reactor Trip/Shutdown)

Group	Class	Isotopes	Total Activity (Ci)
1	Noble gases	^{85}Kr, ^{85}Kr^m, ^{87}Kr, ^{88}Kr, ^{133}Xe, ^{133}Xe^m, ^{135}Xe	3.84E8
2	Halogens	^{131}I, ^{132}I, ^{133}I, ^{134}I, ^{135}I	7.71E8
3	Alkali metals	^{134}Cs, ^{136}Cs, ^{137}Cs, ^{86}Rb	2.18E7
4	Tellurium	^{127}Sb, ^{129}Sb, ^{127}Te, ^{127}Te^m, ^{129}Te, ^{129}Te^m, ^{131}Te^m, ^{132}Te	2.13E8
5	Strontium	^{89}Sr, ^{90}Sr, ^{91}Sr, ^{92}Sr	3.57E8
6	Noble metals	^{58}Co, ^{60}Co, ^{99}Mo, ^{105}Rh, ^{103}Ru, ^{105}Ru, ^{99}Tc^m	5.94E8
7	Lanthanides	^{241}Am, ^{242}Cm, ^{244}Cm, ^{140}La, ^{141}La, ^{142}La, ^{95}Nb, ^{147}Nd, ^{143}Pr, ^{90}Y, ^{91}Y, ^{92}Y, ^{93}Y, ^{95}Zr, ^{97}Zr	1.54E9
8	Cerium	^{141}Ce, ^{143}Ce, ^{144}Ce, ^{239}Np, ^{238}Pu, ^{239}Pu, ^{240}Pu, ^{241}Pu	2.15E9
9	Barium	^{139}Ba, ^{140}Ba	3.38E8

Note: The group numbers, classes, and isotopes are as given by NRC, *Accident Source Terms for Light Water Nuclear Power Plants*, NUREG-1465, U.S. Nuclear Regulatory Commission, Washington, DC, 1995.

Although there is variation and some minor disagreement among the different sources regarding the total radioactive inventory of a reactor, a 1000-MWe reactor core contains about 4.2E9 Ci of total activity, with inventories of each critical isotope being between 5E4 and 1E9 Ci. One source[*] proposed the data shown in Table 3.2 as the typical core inventory at 30 minutes after reactor shutdown (taking radioactive decay into account). If 100% of this inventory was released at a constant rate over 24 hours under constant meteorology, the author calculates that a hypothetical person located 1 mile downwind would receive approximately 8.18E18 rem deep-dose equivalent (DDE) and 2.4E4 rem committed effective dose equivalent (CEDE).[†]

---

[*] Presented in training material for NRC Course P-300, Accident Progression Analysis, Idaho National Engineering and Environmental Laboratory, 2001. The table applies to a reactor of 3300 MW-thermal. The approximate decay periods (in days) for each group are (1) 0.118, (2) 8.04, (3) 0.121, (4) 3.21, (5) 1.06E4, (6) 7.29E-3, (7) 1.58E5, (8) 1.38, and (9) 12.8.

[†] Calculated using a straight-line Gaussian model with a C stability class.

The isotopes that contribute most to external dose are ^{24}Na, ^{110}Ag^m, ^{134}I, ^{132}I, ^{60}Co, ^{136}Cs, ^{124}Sb, ^{88}Kr, ^{131}Te^m, and ^{54}Mn. Those contributing most to internal doses are ^{154}Eu, ^{152}Eu, ^{90}Sr, ^{129}I, ^{144}Ce, ^{106}Ru, ^{60}Co, ^{91}Y, ^{110}Ag^m, and ^{131}I.* The normal concentration of most nuclides in reactor coolant water during power operation is between 0.1 and 0.001 μCi/g, with pressurized water reactors having somewhat higher concentrations on average than boiling water reactors of the same power rating.† The normal coolant concentrations of the transuranic metals may be as low as 1.0E-8 μCi/g (their concentration is not readily determined because alpha emitters are not detected by gamma spectroscopy).

While a reactor is in operation, the noncompressible radioactive gases produced by the fission process must be continually removed. In boiling water reactors, this occurs in the condenser when steam is cooled back to water; the radioactive gases are drawn off and discharged through a chimney (*stack*) or roof vent. In pressurized water reactors, small amounts of gases pass through defects in the steam generator tubing, but most of the gases are removed by the chemical volume and control system. They are then discharged through the gaseous radioactive waste system either through a vent at the top of the containment structure or from a small site stack. Depending on the reactor design, site-specific systems, and specifics about the fuel being used, a typical plant discharges between 800 and 1000 μCi/s to the environment; boiling water designs generally have higher discharge rates than pressurized types of the same power rating. Commercial reactors have operating limits for the maximum amount of radioactive material released offsite and maximum release rates‡ that are generally about 5.0E4 μCi/s (measured by a beta–gamma detector calibrated to noble gases, often to ^{133}Xe^m), although a few plants have limits in the range of 1.0E5. Discharges at rates exceeding these limits for more than a few minutes (often, 15 minutes) indicate emergency conditions.

The normal environmental radiation background rate around most commercial reactors is between 20 and 40 μR/h. During normal operations, if radioactive water or steam lines are breached, the radioactive material released to the environment would not be detectable at the site boundary using most portable survey equipment (generally limited to about 0.25 mR/h or 250 μR/h); this includes reactor coolant water with a normal concentration of nuclides.

CORE STATES

Fuel damage is defined as any perforation of the cladding that permits the release of fission gases or fission products. It can result from physical strain of the fuel assembly or from fuel overheating. A radioactive release cannot occur unless the physical barriers that isolate the activity from the environment are all breached. These are generally considered to be the integrity of fuel cladding,§ the integrity of the reactor coolant system, and the integrity of the primary containment. Some texts also describe fuel pellet integrity as a fourth barrier, but the ceramic matrix only acts as a barrier for some particulate fission products and for heavy metals. The overall core state is the state of fuel cladding averaged across all of the fuel assemblies. The status of each fission product barrier is determined by several predefined, measurable, parameters; when a threshold value is reached in any parameter, the associated barrier is considered to be challenged. A barrier may be *potentially lost* or *lost*, depending on the parameter and value; any potential loss or loss of a barrier means the barrier is outside of its design parameters and constitutes an emergency condition. Simultaneous potential losses or losses in multiple barriers are more serious, meriting a higher emergency classification, because the plant's margin for preventing a radioactive release is more seriously degraded.

---

* Data sources are *Radiochemistry in Nuclear Power Reactors* (Lin, 1996) and Health Canada (1999). The isotopes listed have the highest individual gamma exposure factors and internal organ doses; for specific accident sequences, other nuclides may contribute more to the projected dose because of their greater abundance in the reactor's inventory.

† Also see ANSI (1984b).

‡ Typically found in the Radiological Environmental Technical Specifications (RETS), *Technical Requirements Manual*, or *Offsite Dose Calculation Manual Guidance* (Meinke and Essig, 1991).

§ *Cladding* refers to the zirconium–aluminum alloy tubing that surrounds the fuel pellets and holds them in a rigid configuration. The cladding provides a smooth surface, generally free of defects, to facilitate heat transfer from the fuel to the surrounding coolant.

The four generally used terms that describe the condition of a reactor core (by increasing severity) are *normal, gap release, in-vessel fuel melt*, and *ex-vessel fuel melt*. NUREG-1465 (Soffer et al., 1995) defines the phases of a severe accident as *coolant activity release, gap activity release, early in-vessel release, ex-vessel release*, and *late ex-vessel release*.

In normal power operations, the peak centerline fuel pellet temperature is between 1700°F and 3500°F, depending on reactor type and fuel design, whereas the outer clad skin temperature is about 600°F. Although the cladding may contain or develop pinhole leaks from manufacturing, at this temperature no additional cladding defects are expected to form. The permissible concentration of nuclides in coolant is controlled by the site technical specifications; because of the importance of iodine in Protective Action Guides, one common measure of overall activity in coolant is *dose equivalent iodine* (DEI), a calculation that takes the concentrations of all iodine isotopes present and converts them to an effective concentration of ^{131}I having the same dose consequence. A typical limit on activity in coolant (for boiling water reactors) is a DEI less than 4.0 µCi/g; if this limit is exceeded, operators have 48 hours to correct the condition; otherwise, operators are required to have the reactor subcritical within the next 12 hours.

When fuel cladding exterior temperatures approach 1300°F, defects begin to form in the metal fuel cladding, and these defects are widespread when surface temperatures reach 2100°F; these temperatures are not sufficient to damage or deform the ceramic fuel pellet. Cracks and pinholes in the cladding allow the built-up radioactive gases to escape the fuel rod into the surrounding reactor coolant; essentially all of the gases have escaped by the time surface temperature reaches 2000°F. In addition to the noble gases Kr and Xe, some volatile elements, such as cesium and iodine, that are at the surface of the fuel pellet may also escape. Between 1000°F and 2200°F, the noble gas, iodine, cesium, and tellurium isotope groups are released from the fuel. The fuel condition that allows radioactive gases and volatile elements to escape the fuel rod into the coolant is referred to as a *gap release*. Following a gap release into coolant, the typical concentration of noble gases, iodine isotopes, cesium, and volatile species is between 1.0E2 and 5.0E4 µCi/g, with between 3% and 5% of the total available isotopic inventory being released; up to 80% of the inventory of specific radioactive gases and volatile isotopes may be released. High cladding temperatures tend to develop in regions or zones of the core and do not usually occur homogeneously across the core at the same time; however, the discussion in NUREG-1228 (McKenna and Glitter, 1988) assumes rupture of 100% of the fuel rods during a gap release. Table 3.3 compares the fraction of total core inventory of some important groups of nuclides released from fuel rods during a gap release, as described in several Nuclear Regulatory Commission reports: NUREG-1228 (McKenna and Glitter, 1988), NUREG-1465 (Soffer et al., 1995), and NUREG-5942 (Carbajo, 1993).

After the fuel cladding fails at about 2200°F, the rate of release of fission products from the ceramic fuel increases with temperature, the rate doubling with every 180°F to 200°F. Between fuel cladding temperatures of 2200°F and 2800°F, the strontium and barium isotope groups are released from the fuel; above about 2800°F, the noble metal, lanthanide, and cerium isotope groups are released. Also, when the fuel cladding exterior temperature increases to 3000°F, the fuel pellets begin to physically deform, with melting (liquefaction) occurring by 4500°F. NUREG-0772 (Lorenz et al., 1980) and NUREG-1228 (McKenna and Glitter, 1988) assume that after the cladding exterior temperature

TABLE 3.3
Comparison of Gap Release Fractions Used in Regulatory Guidance

Nuclide Group	NUREG-1228	NUREG-1465	NUREG-5942
Xenon, krypton	0.03	0.05	0.022–0.05
Iodine	0.02	0.05	0.03–0.05
Cesium, rubidium	0.05	0.05	0.028–0.058
Tellurium, antimony, selenium	1E-4	0	0

TABLE 3.4

Comparison of Fuel Melt Release Fractions Used in Regulatory Guidance

Nuclide Group	NUREG-1228	NUREG-1465	NUREG-5942
Xenon, krypton	1.0	0.95	0.73–0.95
Iodine	1.0	0.25	Not discussed
Cesium, rubidium	1.0	0.2 BWR, 0.25 PWR	0.21–0.44
Tellurium group	0.3	0.05	0.005–0.1
Barium, strontium	0.2	0.02	0.03
Ruthenium, molybdenum, cobalt	7E-3	2.5E-3	1.1–1.5E-3
Lanthium group	1E-4	2E-3	0
Cerium group	1E-4	5E-3	0

Note: Table values for NUREG-1465 and NUREG-5942 are for the *early in-vessel* melt category. NUREG-5942 has lanthium and cerium only released during late in-vessel and ex-vessel melt sequences. NUREG-1228 also has the category *grain boundary release*, which begins at local surface temperatures of 3000°F (this category has release fractions of 50% for Xe, Kr, I, and Cs; about 1% for Sb, Ba, and Mo; and less than 1E-3 for Ru and Sr). According to NUREG-1228, the uncertainty regarding release rates from melting fuel is no better than a factor of 10. *Abbreviations:* BWR, boiling water reactor; PWR, pressurized water reactor.

reaches 3600°F the remaining inventory is released at 10% per minute. Regions of the core where melting occurs collapse, forming a molten mixture called *corium*. When corium has formed, a corium–water steam explosion becomes a major concern for operators, as is a hydrogen explosion inside containment (the hydrogen is liberated during a zirconium–water reaction at the metal cladding surface). Table 3.4 compares the fraction of total core inventory of some important nuclides released from fuel during a fuel melt event, as described in several NRC reports: NUREG-1228 (McKenna and Glitter, 1988), NUREG-1465 (Soffer et al., 1995), and NUREG-5942 (Carbajo, 1993).

After water is removed from a fuel assembly, the cladding may reach about 4000°F in about 15 minutes, which forms the basis for several emergency preparedness decision and notification requirements. There is no essential difference between in-vessel and ex-vessel core melt, except that in the latter case the reactor vessel also fails, allowing the corium to escape the vessel.

Fuel damage can only be directly assessed by sampling liquid reactor coolant, in normal operations and during accidents. A sample of normal reactor coolant has a contact radiation exposure of at most a few mrem/h, depending on sample volume. Process radiation monitors provide secondary indications. In boiling water reactors, these include main steam line radiation monitors and reactor water cleanup system radiation monitors; in pressurized water reactors, they include main steam line radiation monitors (to detect steam generator leaks) and letdown radiation monitors. Process radiation monitors are effective in detecting small leaks (slow releases from one or two fuel rods) but are not very effective in assessing more general fuel damage, because (1) the detector saturates at a relatively low dose rate, (2) there is an automatic isolation signal at a relatively dose rate, (3) abnormal operating procedures direct operators to manually isolate the line monitored by the radiation detector, or (4) some other isolation signal causes an isolation of the line being measured. The containment or drywell atmosphere of many reactors can be sampled, but this may require resetting interlock signals, placing jumpers across circuit boards, and manually opening valves in the reactor buildings; automatic containment atmosphere process monitors are physically located outside of the containment structure and are automatically isolated on containment isolation signals. Atmosphere samples and monitors are very indirect indicators of the core state because some radioactive isotopes released from the core remain mostly in liquid coolant and do not readily become airborne, because containment sprays and other mitigation systems change the airborne isotope mixture compared to what was released from the fuel and atmosphere samples can only be collected for loss-of-coolant accidents. The core state can also be inferred from reactor water level, primarily in boiling water reactors, using the rule of thumb that gap releases occur 15 minutes after the core is uncovered and fuel melting begins about one-half hour after core uncovery (see above discussion); rules of thumb may be highly inexact and are not descriptive of any actual accident sequence, but they may represent all the information that is available.

Most reactor sites have developed site-specific, accident-range radiation monitor curves to estimate core damage based on drywell and containment radiation dose. Section A.4, *Evaluation of Containment Radiation*, of NUREG/BR-0150 (NRC, 2002h) contains similar generic curves. Fuel damage can be inferred from the response of accident range monitors only when the reactor coolant system is breached (a loss-of-coolant accident) because the calibrations are valid only for a uniform or well-mixed submersion in a site-specific noble gas/iodine mixture. Often, curves are given by the licensee that differentiate between gap release and fuel melt conditions but the average radiation energies and decay characteristics of these mixtures are significantly different. The monitors can only be accurately calibrated for one level of core damage, and care must be taken when assessing core damage based on monitor responses to understand the basis for the monitor calibration. Although the accident range monitor curves read into the mR/h range, they cannot be used to evaluate fuel damage below about 1% of the core because high-range monitors utilize built-in *keep-alive* radiation sources that prevent them from reading less than about 1000 mR/h. Reactor containments and drywells also have two installed operating-range radiation monitors, which typically have ranges limited to between 100 and 1000 mR/h, depending on their physical location in primary containment; these monitors respond (increase) to fuel damage even when the reactor coolant system is intact but cannot be used to evaluate the damage. Operating-range containment radiation monitors also respond to reactor coolant system breaches with routine levels of radioactive material but will become saturated (read off-scale) before the activity in the coolant reaches the high end of the allowed operating band. A response on operating-range radiation monitors cannot be used to differentiate between an intact and breached radiation coolant system, and additional confirming indications are required such as the response of containment atmospheric monitors, humidity or hydrogen sensors, containment temperature sensors, or the filling of containment sumps. Because of the keep-alive radiation sources, any response on accident-range monitors above their baseline indicates a breach of the radiation coolant system.

CORE DAMAGE FREQUENCY

Core damage frequency is a term for a mathematical construct used by reactor licensees and the Commission to characterize the safety of a particular configuration of plant equipment. The configuration describes the mode of reactor operation, and the equipment (both safety-related and balance of plant) currently available to respond to an emergency. The core damage referred to is not actual core damage but rather a probability function that the reactor will reach the beginning of core degradation (the start of a core damage sequence); the analysis assumes that, once started, a core damage sequence cannot be mitigated before the damage occurs. For example, in boiling water reactors, the core damage is assumed to occur if the reactor vessel water level lowers to the top of active fuel, even though this level would have to be sustained for 15 to 30 minutes before fuel would actually rupture. The Commission's *Reactor Safety Goal Policy Statement* (NRC, 2000e) includes a secondary goal of maintaining the core damage frequency of each reactor at less than 1E-4 per reactor-year of operation.[*] It should be emphasized that core damage frequency is a mathematical concept not tied directly to any physical quantity, that core damage frequency is used to determine the acceptability or risk of changes to the reactor plant, and that the core damage frequency value does not drive any emergency preparedness function or decision-making process.

---

[*] Also see NRC (2002a).

In practice, the *conditional* or *marginal* core damage frequency is used in regulatory analyses, safety analyses, and real-time risk management computer software to control the allowed reactor plant configuration. The conditional core damage frequency represents the difference in risk between the planned or actual plant configuration and an ideal plant configuration with all systems operational. The plant is allowed to remain operating as long as the conditional core damage frequency remains within a prescribed band. Typically, conditional core damage frequencies in the range of 1E-5 or lower are permissible as long as the resulting overall core damage frequency remains less than 1E-3 to 1E-4.

It is not possible to always maintain the reactor plant in the configuration giving the lowest core damage frequency because plant equipment requires scheduled preventative maintenance and must be periodically run to demonstrate its continuing ability to operate. Some of the riskiest plant configurations are during plant startup and shutdown and while fuel is being loaded and unloaded from the reactor, all of which must be done to operate the reactor.

SEVERE ACCIDENTS

NUREG-1228 (McKenna and Glitter, 1988) states that the fuel cladding surfaces in an uncovered core heat up at 1°F/s because air and steam are much poorer conductors of heat than water. As long as neutrons continue to flow through the core, fissions continue and undissipated heat builds up in the cladding. NUREG-1228 states

> The consensus is that even for the worst accident analyzed, if the plant safety systems work as designed, less than 20% of the fuel pin cladding will fail, releasing a large fraction of the gap in those pins. ... This type of accident (within plant design limits) would result in release of considerably less than 20% of the gap from the reactor coolant system. Therefore, any accident that releases more than 20% of the gap from the reactor coolant system is considered a *severe accident.*

The terminology used to quantify fuel damage during a severe accident is site specific, imprecise, and often confusing. The most frequent unit used to express core damage is *percent fuel damage*, which correlates most closely with the percentage of the core that has sustained damage beyond a gap release. Another common convention is that a release (into reactor coolant, not necessarily to the atmosphere or the environment) of 10% of the gap inventory is equivalent to the release of 1% of the fuel inventory.

Reactor licensee emergency operating procedures are designed to save the core and prevent significant fuel damage; abnormal and emergency operating procedures are primarily designed for analyzed accidents and maintain the plant within its design basis. Since 1990, reactor owner groups and licensees have developed severe accident management guidelines (SAMGs) and strategies[*] that address issues beyond-design-basis events. The severe accident strategies assume a substantial loss of reactor water level and significant (greater than 20%) fuel damage (i.e., loss of reactor coolant system integrity and loss of fuel cladding integrity), and their goal is to save primary containment and to prevent large radioactive release to the environment. The Commission has identified three broad categories of severe accident strategies:

- Replenishing batteries, borated water, compressed air, and other resources that support operation of safety systems
- Innovative uses of plant systems not designed to supply water to the core or to remove decay heat (e.g., fire suppression pumps)
- Defeating interlocks and signals meant to protect plant equipment

These categories can be applied to the functions of reactivity control, reactor coolant inventory, heat removal, and containment integrity. Current industry efforts are aimed at developing additional low-power, shutdown (decay heat only), and fuel building strategies.

---

[*] Also see IAEA (2004).

The Commission identified a need for licensees to prepare for severe accidents in an NRC policy statement (1985e). This was followed by Generic Letter 88-20 (NRC, 1988c), which states

> The NRC will evaluate licensee IPE submittals to obtain reasonable assurance that the licensee has adequately analyzed the plant design and operations to discover instances of particular vulnerability to core melt or unusually poor containment performance given a core melt accident. Furthermore, the NRC will assess whether the conclusions the licensee draws from the IPE regarding changes to the plant systems, components, or accident management procedures are adequate.

Licensees were initially expected to submit Individual Plant Examination (IPE) reports by the end of 1991. Individual Plant Examination reports were only required to assess the implications of failures and events internal to the reactor plants. The Commission required an additional assessment of severe accident vulnerabilities due to external events (primarily hurricanes, tornadoes, and flooding) in a 1991 supplement to Generic Letter 88-20. All assessments of external events were expected to be submitted by the end of 1998; none of the severe accident analyses was required to address malevolent acts or site attack scenarios. In the author's opinion, from 1985 to 1991, the Commission clearly intended to develop and promulgate additional regulations requiring licensees to implement a severe accident response program and include these elements in its inspection program.

In 1994, the Nuclear Energy Institute proposed to the Commission that reactor licensees commit to implementing a voluntary severe accident management program. This approach was accepted by the Commission in a 1995 letter to the Nuclear Energy Institute and confirmed in SECY-95-004 (NRC, 1995i).* The Nuclear Energy Institute committed to the Commission that every reactor site would implement such a program no later than December 1998. The reasons why the Commission accepted a voluntary industry initiative to implement severe accident management instead of the formal regulatory program it previously had intended are unclear, but by 1993 (and continuing throughout the remainder of the decade) the Commission was facing budget reductions, and it had already reduced the scope of its evaluation of Individual Plant Examinations of External Events (IPEEEs). Reactor licensees benefited from this approach because the Commission did not impose new regulations and did not incorporate severe accident management into its inspection and drill programs. In particular, licensees did not want the inspection of drills to verify a licensee's ability to implement severe accident procedures, because the plant reference simulators in use during the mid- to late-1990s were incapable of modeling severe accident core melt sequences and simply ceased operating outside of design-basis plant conditions. Although the core thermodynamic and heat transfer models incorporated into current plant reference simulators are much improved compared to those of the 1990s, current simulators generally are not designed to operate in the severe accident regime because the NRC agreed not to require demonstration of these capabilities. As of 2015, reactor operators were not being tested by the Commission regarding their knowledge of severe accident procedures as part of their individual license examination, and reactor licensees were not required to demonstrate implementation of their severe accident management strategies as part of their routine drill and exercise program.

ACCIDENTS INVOLVING STORED IRRADIATED REACTOR FUEL

All currently operating U.S. power reactors store the most recently irradiated fuel rods in deep (about 40 to 50 feet) water pools, which resemble large open rectangular swimming pools. These fuel pools generally contain between two and four complete core loads. The oldest fuel assemblies are 8 to 10

---

* See also *Integration Plan for Closure of Severe Accident Issues* (SECY-88-147); *Status of Implementation Plan for Closure of Severe Accident Issues, Status of the Individual Plant Examinations, and Status of Severe Accident Research* (SECY 94-166, SECY-95-004); *Status of the IPE and IPEEE Programs* (SECY-96-051); *Status of the Integration Plan for Closure of Severe Accident Issues and the Status of Severe Accident Research* (SECY-96-088, SECY-97-132, SECY-98-131); and *Severe Accident Issue Closure Guidelines* (NEI, 1994).

TABLE 3.5
Inventory of Some Isotopes in a 1000-MWe BWR One Year
After Adding Fuel

Nuclide	Curies *1E7	Nuclide	Curies *1E6	Nuclide	Curies *1E5
^{241}Pu	2.19	^{106}Ru	9.31	^{95}Zr	5.10
^{137}Cs	1.97	^{134}Cs	5.80	^{238}Pu	4.54
^{90}Y	1.39	^{85}Kr	1.33	^{242}Cm	3.50
^{90}Sr	1.38	^{95}Nb	1.11	^{241}Am	3.21
^{144}Ce	1.13			^{60}Co	2.85
				^{91}Y	2.21
				^{244}Cm	2.19
				^{240}Pu	1.30

Source: NRC, *Technical Study of Spent Fuel Accident Risk at Decommissioning Nuclear Power Plants*, NUREG-1738, U.S. Nuclear Regulatory Commission, Washington, DC, 2001, p. A3-4.

years old; because of delays in providing a permanent fuel repository, many licensees have reconfigured their fuel pools to hold more used fuel than they were originally designed for (referred to as *re-racking*). Most licensees have now moved, or are in the process of moving, their oldest fuel rods, which date back to original operation, to air-cooled semipermanent storage casks (independent spent fuel storage installations, or ISFSIs) located outside elsewhere on the licensee's property.

Accidents that result in damage to the fuel stored in fuel pools are possible. These accidents develop more slowly than in operating reactors because the latent heat in fuel rods drops rapidly after reactor shutdown. Catastrophic events are unlikely but possible, primarily including natural phenomena such as earthquakes and tornadoes; beginning in 2001, concerns have been raised about aircraft impacts against fuel pools. The worst-case analyzed accidents can have dose consequences comparable to operating reactor accidents (that is, protective actions are required in the emergency planning zone), and the accident probability is about the same as for operating reactors. The major concern for fuel in its initial 36 months of storage is a zirconium fire; this condition can occur if cooling water is removed and the rod is steam or air cooled. In either case, the fuel surface temperature becomes very high (greater than 2200°F) because the heat transfer coefficients of air and steam are so much lower than that of liquid water, and the metal rapidly oxidizes. The zirconium reaction is exothermic (i.e., produces more heat than the heat of combustion) and produces flammable free hydrogen.

The radioactive isotopes with the highest dose rates also tend to be short lived (i.e., 100% of all iodine in fuel rods has decayed by 7 months after reactor shutdown). Fuel pool accidents are dominated by isotopes that are longer lived (greater than 3-month half-lives).[*] A typical fuel pool has an inventory of more than 40 isotopes with a total radioactive material inventory of about 7E7 Ci. A typical fuel pool source term is given in Table 3.5. Some expected release fractions for a severe fuel pool accident are shown in Table 3.6. These release fractions would be expected for a fuel pool where the stored fuel assemblies remain mostly to fully covered by water. Radioactive gases and volatile particulates are not effectively absorbed into water, and virtually all of these isotopes escape the pool.

The least likely fuel damage accident is to fuel transferred from fuel pools into independent spent fuel storage installations. This is primarily because the fuel rod internal decay heat has decayed enough that external plant cooling systems are not required to maintain fuel integrity. Fuel

---

[*] Most power reactor licensees do not have dose assessment computer software that correctly models the fuel pool source term. Although a case could be made that this is not in compliance with 10 CFR 50.47(b)(9) in that the licensee may not possess "adequate methods ... for assessing ... actual or potential offsite consequences" of a fuel pool not in use, the historical NRC practice has been that this does not constitute a deficient dose analysis program.

TABLE 3.6

Expected Isotopic Release Fractions from a Fuel Pool Accident

Nuclides	Fraction	Nuclides	Fraction
Krypton	1.0	Strontium, barium	0.002
Iodine[a]	1.0	Ruthenium, molybdenum, cobalt	2E-5
Cesium, rubidium	1.0	Lanthium, zirconium, niobium, curium, americium, cerium, plutonium	6E-5
Tellurium, antimony	0.02		

Source: NRC, *Technical Study of Spent Fuel Accident Risk at Decommissioning Nuclear Power Plants*, NUREG-1738, U.S. Nuclear Regulatory Commission, Washington, DC, 2001, p. A4-6; NRC, *A Safety and Regulatory Assessment of Generic BWR and PWR Permanently Shutdown Nuclear Power Plants*, NUREG/CR-6451, U.S. Nuclear Regulatory Commission, Washington, DC, 1997.

[a] Assuming an initial inventory of 5.65E8 Ci of all iodine isotopes, less than 1 Ci of ^{131}I (half-life of 3.1 days) remains after 7 months, and all other iodine isotopes have half-lives at least 9 times shorter than ^{131}I.

transferred into spent fuel storage installations must have decayed for at least one year; in practice, they have generally decayed at least 5 and often more than 10 years. All fuel located in spent fuel storage installations can be cooled indefinitely by air* without any expected structural degradation, though the on-contact dose rates remain dangerous to personnel health and safety, and so the fuel must be isolated and shielded. Although there are several designs for spent fuel storage installations, all of them feature a multi-ton semipermanent, steel-lined, sealed (inaccessible) concrete storage cask that contains from one to four fuel assemblies; the concrete is sufficiently thick that exterior gamma radiation dose rates require only minimal radiological controls. The storage casks are then located on reactor licensee property away from the operating reactor to eliminate the potential for the cask to be damaged by failures of plant equipment;† at some sites, the storage casks themselves are placed inside reinforced bunkers to further increase their security and reduce accessibility.

Because of their structural strength, individual storage casks are most likely to be affected by only the most powerful earthquakes. The design criteria for casks and storage bunkers make it very unlikely that floods, hurricanes, tornadoes, or other kinds of catastrophic natural events would have any impact. The confined fuel assemblies have generally already lost their most volatile isotopes prior to being loaded into casks

WORLD REACTOR ACCIDENT EXPERIENCE

It is difficult to concisely describe the world's experience with reactor accidents to date. This is partially because of philosophical and technical differences regarding the meaning of the term *accident* and partially because there are no reliable reference documents that summarize either national or international accident reports for any but single-year periods. What can be generally said is that (1) radiation injuries and accidents involving x-rays and radioactive materials (primarily isotopes of radium) first occurred somewhere around 1905 (including events related to medical treatment);

---

* The need for storing reactor fuel outside of water-filled fuel pools had been anticipated by at least 1981; see ANSI/ANS-18.1-1984, *Design Criteria for an Independent Spent Fuel Storage Installation (Dry Storage Type)*, and Regulatory Guide 3.60, *Design of an Independent Spent Fuel Installation (Dry Storage)*. Although guidance and regulation have provided for independent wet storage—such as ANSI/ANS-2.19-1981, *Nuclear Fuel Facilities—Spent Fuel Storage Installation, Site Selection and Design of an Independent Spent Fuel Storage Installation (Water-Pool Type)*, and Regulatory Guide 3.49, *Design of an Independent Spent Fuel Storage Installation (Water-Basin Type)*—all licensees to date have installed dry or air-cooled storage facilities. The first licensed spent fuel storage installation was in 1986 at the Surry Plant in Virginia.

† Although there have been proposals to establish semipermanent, independently operated or consortium-operated spent fuel storage installations away from specific licensee properties that would receive and store fuel as an interim step before final geological disposal, no such interim repositories have reached the siting or licensing stages.

TABLE 3.7
Summary of Radiation-Related Accidents through 2005

Event	Number	Fatalities	Injuries
Power reactor accidents	2	41	438
Research reactor accidents	4	6	9
Naval reactor accidents	3	18	80
Non-reactor criticality	19	15	27
Irradiator accidents	31	8	39
Criminal use of radioactive material	5	4	1
Totals	64	92	594

Note: Reactor accidents only include those that resulted in abnormal radiation dose; for example, they do not include the Fermi Unit 1 accident
of 1966 or the Browns Ferry Unit 1 fire in 1975. A large number of
lost radioactive sources, accidental dispersals of radioactive material
(e.g., incident in Goinna, Brazil), and other accidents with medical
radiation-producing machines are not included. The term *injuries*
refers only to non-fatal examples of acute radiation syndrome and
does not include non-radiological burn or mechanical injury.

(2) the first accidents involving experimental, test, or military reactors occurred somewhere around 1950; (3) the first accident in a civilian commercial power reactor resulting in fuel damage was in 1966; and (4) there have been four reactor accidents that resulted in radiologically significant offsite releases—Windscale, Three Mile Island, Chernobyl, and Fukushima Daiichi. One unofficial source has provided the breakdown of radiation accidents through 2005 shown in Table 3.7.

NUREG-1437 (NRC, 1996f) discusses the following fuel melt accidents: Fermi Unit 1 (Newport, MI), Saint-Laurent (France), National Research Experimental (NRX) reactor (Chalk River, Canada), Experimental Breeder Reactor (Atomic City, ID), Heat Transfer Reactor Experiments (Idaho Falls, ID), Westinghouse Test Reactor (Waltz Mill, PA), and the Oak Ridge Research Reactor (Oak Ridge, TN). Report LA-3611 (Stratton, 1967) discusses 36 criticality incidents or accidents that occurred worldwide between 1949 and 1965.

A chronological listing of reactor accidents that resulted in damaged fuel, including those at experimental and test reactors, is given below. The list does not include operational events at reactors that did not result in core damage and is not a list of declared emergencies. The list does not discuss the numerous non-reactor radioactive material incidents that resulted in personnel injuries or fatalities.

- *NRX reactor* (Chalk River, Canada; INES 5; December 12, 1952)—An unplanned high-power excursion occurred with a subsequent hydrogen explosion in the balance of plant systems; 1E4 Ci were released into cooling water.
- *Windscale* (Cumbria, England; INES 5; October 10, 1957)—During annealing maintenance on a non-power reactor the graphite moderator caught fire, and the fire was not extinguished for 24 hours. Twenty percent of the core was damaged, and about 8.24E4 Ci were released[*] (mostly iodine). Worker doses were 150 times occupational limits, and offsite doses were retrospectively calculated at 10 times maximum allowable lifetime dose limits for the public. No evacuation of the public was performed. Restrictions were placed on milk produced in an area of 500 km^2 for about 2 months, and radioactive iodine was found in samples taken outside this area; ^{131}I was measured in milk at concentrations of up to 5.0E4 Bq/L.

---

[*] The estimated releases include 18,000 Ci ^{131}I, 850 Ci ^{137}Cs, 240 Ci Po^{210}, 105 Ci ^{89}Sr, and 7.5 Ci ^{90}Sr (the midpoints of the estimate ranges are given) (Eisenbud, 1987). The release duration was 21 hours.

- *NRX reactor* (Chalk River, Canada; May 24, 1958)—A fuel rod fire occurred during refueling, causing building and site contamination.
- *SL-1 reactor* (Idaho National Laboratory, Idaho Falls; January 3, 1961)—An inadvertent criticality during maintenance resulted in a steam explosion. Three fatalities occurred (one victim lived for 90 minutes after rescuers arrived). The deceased workers' bodies measured greater than 100 R/h on contact; 99.9% of the radioactive inventory was released, consisting of about 80 Ci. Measured exposure rates were from 25 R/h at the reactor building wall to greater than 1000 R/h at the reactor vessel; the reactor building was essentially a corrugated tin building not designed as a containment structure. Twenty responders received radiation doses in excess of 1 rem, three of which exceeded 25 rem.
- *Fermi Unit 1* (liquid metal reactor; Newport, MI; October 5, 1966)—A sodium coolant malfunction resulted in melting two fuel assemblies and damaging two more; no radioactive release was detected.
- *Chapelcross reactor* (Dumfries and Galloway, Scotland; May 1967)—A cooling channel blockage (broken-off piece of zirconium) resulted in one fuel assembly catching fire.
- *Swiss research reactor* (Lucens, Vaud, Switzerland; January 21, 1969)—A loss-of-coolant accident resulted in a steam explosion, but no radioactive release was detected. The reactor was located underground, and the contamination was contained in the sealed cavern.
- *KS150 reactor* (Plant A1; Jasloveske, Bohunice, Czechoslovakia; INES 4; February 22, 1977)—Fuel was damaged when the reactor was restarted after fueling because of foreign material left in a fuel assembly.
- *Three Mile Island Unit 2* (Middletown, PA; INES 5; March 28, 1979)—A failed reactor coolant system component followed by mistakes by operators led to a loss of coolant, uncovering of the core, fuel damage, and a hydrogen explosion in containment. About 2E6 Ci of noble gases were intentionally vented (0.9% of inventory), and between 15 and 20 Ci of iodine were vented (3E-5%) of inventory). Three plant workers each received about 4 rem, and members of the public within 8 miles received from 0 to 8 mrem. According to a health study conducted in 1997, there were no detectable health effects in the surrounding population.
- *Reactor A2* (Orleans, France; INES 4; March 13, 1980)—An inadvertent power excursion resulted in fuel damage, and the release of 8E10 Bq to the environment.
- *RA2 facility* (Buenos Aires, Argentina; INES 4; September 23, 1983)—An inadvertent criticality while refueling an experimental test reactor resulted in the release of 3E17 Bq; one operator received a fatal dose of 2000 rads, and 35 other persons each received between 1 and 35 rads.
- *Chernobyl Unit 4* (Prypiat, Ukraine; INES 7; April 26, 1986)—An improperly performed safety test resulted in an uncontrolled power excursion and a steam explosion in the core, followed by complete core meltdown and a graphite moderator fire; operators intentionally disabled some required safety systems prior to conducting the test. The reactor building (not designed as a containment structure) was completely destroyed. The accident resulted in 28 radiation fatalities in 91 days; 238 persons were treated for acute radiation syndrome, 710 persons had measured or estimated doses greater than 50 rads, 20,000 persons had measured or estimated doses between 25 and 50 rads (including stabilization and cleanup activities through 1988), and 130,000 persons received doses in excess of ICRP radiation safety limits for the general public. About 4000 cases of thyroid cancer occurred in children as a result of the accident, with 10 fatal cases.
- *THTR-300 high-temperature gas reactor* (Hamm-Uetrop, Germany; May 4, 1986)—Cladding damage to a fuel pebble that became stuck in a refueling channel caused a radioactive release detectable offsite.
- *Greifswald nuclear power station* (Greifswald, Germany; November 24, 1989)—Equipment failure during a test of safety systems caused overheating in 10 fuel assemblies (similar to Chernobyl in that some safety systems were intentionally defeated prior to the test).

- *Reactor 1, Shika Nuclear Plant* (Ishakawa Prefecture, Japan; June 18, 1999)—An operator error while inserting control rods resulted in three rods being withdrawn, causing an inadvertent power spike.
- *Paks nuclear power plant* (Paks, Hungary; INES 3; April 10, 2003)—Thermal shock to an irradiated fuel assembly being handled after removal from the core caused rods to rupture, spilling fuel pellets into a tank.
- *Fukushima Daiichi Nuclear Power Plant* (Fukushima, Japan; INES 7; March 11–20, 2011)—Extensive core damage in multiple reactors and spent fuel pools following a station blackout caused by a very strong earthquake and a subsequent tsunami. The tsunami flooded the emergency diesel generators and caused the vital emergency power buses to be deenergized. Reactor damage occurred after the station batteries were exhausted.

The four accidents with the most effect on offsite populations were Windscale (the plant was later renamed Sellafield), Three Mile Island, Chernobyl, and Fukushima Daiichi. Table 3.8 compares some nuclides in the radioactive releases to the environment from these accidents.

The *Additional Report of the Japanese Government to the IAEA, Second Report* (Nuclear Emergency Response Headquarters, 2011) estimated that during the first 4 days of the Fukushima accident 4.60E6 Ci ^{131}I were released to the atmosphere, along with 4.87E5 Ci ^{134}Cs and 4.05E5 Ci ^{137}Cs; the total estimated ^{131}I release was later revised to 2.7E4 Ci. An IAEA report (IAEA, 2015b) estimated that the ^{134}Cs and ^{137}Cs releases to the environment from the Fukushima accident were ~14% of the total release from Chernobyl, and the total activity deposited on the ground was 4.6% of the deposition from Chernobyl. The World Nuclear Association estimated in 2015 that 4.33E6 Ci ^{131}I had been released from Fukushima into the atmosphere and 4.05E5 Ci ^{137}Cs. TEPCO, the operator of Fukushima, estimated in 2012 that 2.54E7 Ci ^{131}I had been released into the atmosphere and 2.16E7 Ci of noble gases, primarily ^{133}Xe. Estimates are that 20% of overall releases to the atmosphere from Fukushima came from Unit 1, 40% came from Unit 2, and 40% came from Unit 3, with Unit 4 contributing almost a negligible amount. The calculated Chernobyl release fractions are shown in Tables 3.9 and 3.10, and the estimated Fukushima release fractions are shown in Table 3.11.

The Windscale and Fukushima accidents resulted in significant discharges of radioactivity into the oceans. The primary discharges at Windscale were from water injected into the graphite pile to suppress the fire which was then routed through a discharge canal, into a nearby river, and into the Irish Sea. Discharges from Fukushima were a combination of leaks from the internal structure and discharges from water pumped or sprayed into the reactor core to stabilize the damaged fuel.

TABLE 3.8
Total Airborne Releases (Ci) of Selected Radioisotopes at Four Reactor Accidents

Nuclide	Windscale	Three Mile Island	Chernobyl	Fukushima
^{133}Xe	3.80E5	1.00E7	1.80E8	5.50E8[a]
^{131}I	2.74E4	1.40E2	4.70E7	4.30E6
^{137}Cs	1.40E3	0	2.30E6	4.14E5
^{90}Sr	5.4	0	2.70E5	4.03E3
^{239}Pu	54	0	810	0.09

Source: Data from SCK•CEN (Mol, Belgium) and from Povinec et al. (2013); some unit conversions by the author.

[a] It is estimated that 100% of the ^{133}Xe inventory in Units 1, 2, and 3 escaped to the atmosphere; the value is calculated from NUREG-1228 (McKenna and Glitter, 1988) assuming three 1000-MWe units.

TABLE 3.9

Estimated Release Fractions of Selected Radioisotopes from the Chernobyl Unit 4 Accident

Nuclide	Fraction (Percentage of Core Inventory)	Nuclide	Fraction (Percentage of Core Inventory)
^{85}Kr	100	^{137}Cs	33
^{133}Xe	100	^{140}Ba	4.6
^{131}I	50–60	^{89}Sr	4.6
^{99}Mo	30–50	^{90}Sr	4.6
^{103}Ru	30–50	^{95}Zr	3.5
^{106}Ru	30–50	^{141}Ce	3.5
^{132}Te	25–60	^{144}Ce	3.5
^{134}Cs	33		

Source: OECD, *The Chernobyl Accident Source Term*, Organization for Economic Cooperation and Development, Paris, France, 1996.

TABLE 3.10

Estimated Release Fractions of Iodines, Telluriums, and Cesiums by Reactor Unit

Isotope Group as Defined by NUREG-1465	Unit 1	Unit 2	Unit 3
Iodine	0.7%	0.4%	0.4 –0.8%
Tellurium	1%	0.4–3%	0.3–0.6%
Cesium	0.3%	0.3–6%	0.3–0.6%

TABLE 3.11

Estimated Release Fractions of Selected Radioisotopes from Fukushima Units 1, 2, and 3

Isotope	Release (Percentage of Total Inventory)	Isotope	Release (Percentage of Total Inventory)
^{131}I	2.6%	^{90}Sr	0.03%
^{134}Cs	2.4%	^{238}Pu	1E-6%
^{137}Cs	2.2%	^{240}Pu	1E-6%
^{89}Sr	0.03%	^{241}Pu	1E-6%

Source: Povinec, P.P. et al., *Fukushima Accident: Radioactivity Impact on the Environment*, Elsevier, Amsterdam, 2013.

It is difficult to estimate the total amount of radioactive material discharged into the ocean as a result of the Windscale accident, in part because the majority of the available data are for the larger airborne discharges and in part because the site has continued to be used until the present day. For example, the Sellafield site released 158 Ci of ^{137}Cs into the Irish Sea in 2011, ~52 Ci ^{90}Sr, and ~2.6 Ci ^{134}Cs, according to the Radiological Protection Institute of Ireland (McGinnity et al., 2012). It is

TABLE 3.12
Isotopic-Specific Release Fractions into the Oceans

Stagnant Water		Direct to the Ocean	
Isotope	Percentage (%) of Total Core Inventory (Units 1–3)	Isotope	Percentage (%) of Total Core Inventory (Units 1–3)
^{89}Sr	1.2	^{54}Mn	0.016
^{90}Sr	1.6	^{60}Co	0.11
^{99}Tcm	0.58	^{90}Sr	1E-5
^{115}Sb	0.015	^{125}Sb	2.8E-4
^{131}I	32	^{134}Cs	0.49
^{134}Cs	20	^{137}Cs	0.5
^{136}Cs	17	^{144}Ce	3.0E-5
^{137}Cs	20		

Source: Povinec, P.P. et al., *Fukushima Accident: Radioactivity Impact on the Environment*, Elsevier, Amsterdam, 2013.

estimated that about 6.5 Ci ^{137}Cs were discharged from Windscale during the entire year (1957) in which the fire occurred. Other important isotopes discharged during the accident were ^{95}Zr, ^{95}Nb, and ^{106}Ru/^{106}Rh (Jeffries, 1968; Mauchline and Templeton, 1963).

According to the Japan Atomic Industrial Forum (JAIF) Earthquake Report #250, the Fukushima site released a total of 7.33E5 Ci to the ocean between March 21 and July 15, 2011. The French Radioprotection and Nuclear Safety Institute estimated in 2011 that a total of about 7E5 Ci of ^{137}Cs alone had been released to the ocean, about 5% of the estimate of the total radioactivity released to the atmosphere. The second Japanese Government Report to the IAEA estimated that through April 6, 2011, Fukushima released a total of 1.27E5 Ci of all isotopes to the ocean. TEPCO estimated in 2012 that releases to the ocean totaled 2.97E5 Ci ^{131}I, 9.46E4 Ci ^{134}Cs, and 9.73E4 Ci ^{137}Cs. Other estimates of releases to the ocean are 1.08E5 to 1.07E6 Ci ^{137}Cs (Buesseler, 2014), 2.52E4 Ci to 1.08E5 Ci ^{137}Cs (Dietzel and Kriest, 2012), and 2.7E3 Ci ^{90}Sr (Povinec et al., 2012). Some published values of the fractions of specific isotopic inventories released to the ocean are given in Table 3.12.

DAMAGE TO REACTORS FROM SITE ATTACK

There have been concerns about the possibility of armed attacks against nuclear power plants since at least 1993, when an intruder drove through fences at Three Mile Island, and these concerns were compounded after the 9/11 airliner attacks in the United States. Since 2001, both generic and specific vulnerability studies of nuclear power plant designs have been conducted by the Department of Energy, Department of Homeland Security, and the Nuclear Regulatory Commission, primarily to determine whether containment structures could withstand the impact of large aircraft or missiles. Although the specifics of these studies are classified or sensitive and are not available to the public, the Commission has publicly discussed their conclusions: Containment structures are in general strong and robust, and the likelihood of both damaging the reactor core and releasing sufficient radioactive material into the environment to affect public health and safety is very low.

Similar studies have been conducted on behalf of the nuclear industry by the Electric Power Research Institute (EPRI, 2002), which reached similar conclusions. These studies are also not available to the public but the threat basis has been described: a fully fueled (23,980 gallons of aviation fuel) Boeing Model 767-400 weighing approximately 400 tons at an impact speed of 350 mph. The aircraft is 201 feet long, with a wingspan of 170 feet. Each of its two engines weighs 9500 pounds, and the engines are located 15 meters apart so that only the fuselage and one engine are assumed to impact the structure (the other engine being deflected by the curvature of the structure). The study assumed the aircraft and engine struck perpendicular to the containment building center-line. The analysis of fuel pool integrity assumed the aircraft and engine made a perpendicular hit at the mid-point of the fuel pool wall. The models are primarily based on a 1988 study by Sandia National Laboratory in which a 27-ton (54,000-pound) F-4 Phantom fighter plane was propelled into a 3.7-meter (145-inch) thick reinforced concrete wall at 480 mph.[*]

ACCIDENT SEQUENCES

The four emergency classifications are arranged in a pyramid configuration, with many emergency action levels that result in classifying a Notification of Unusual Event and very few that result in classifying a General Emergency. Although there are almost infinite combinations of plant equip-ment failures that could result in an emergency classification, there are only three severe accident categories that can result from those combinations: a reactor coolant system break inside contain-ment, a steam line break outside containment with a failure to isolate (stop) steam flow, and a break in a liquid recirculation line outside containment with a failure to close the recirculation line.

The reactor coolant system break inside containment can lead to an unfiltered and unmonitored release directly to the atmosphere if the containment structure breaks or any external hatch seals fail. A filtered and monitored release may occur from containment into plant buildings (secondary containment) if piping or electrical penetration seals fail or some lines fail to isolate (i.e., because all containment penetrations have at least two isolation valves arranged in parallel, both the inboard side and outboard side values must fail). Valve failures in containment purge and vent lines could also create a path for radioactive material to reach the environment.

An unisolated steam line break can lead to an unfiltered and unmonitored release if it occurs in the steam tunnel or if the plant turbine building has lost integrity. A steam break around the turbine generator and condenser leads to a filtered and monitored release through turbine building ventila-tion. A steam generator tube rupture is a special case of a steam line bypass accident that may be unfiltered and unmonitored if the steam line safety valves lift; otherwise, the release is filtered and monitored.

A reactor coolant system break inside containment causes containment building sump pits (an engineered safety feature) to fill with contaminated water from condensed steam. When the refu-eling water storage tank (or other large external water sources used to inject water into the core through safety injection systems) are emptied or exhausted, a water circulation path is established from sump pits through heat exchangers external to containment, back into the reactor core, and out the reactor coolant system breach to the sump pit. This water can contain a large inventory of radio-active material if core melting has occurred. A recirculation line break outside of containment puts this contaminated water into other plant buildings and creates a release path to the environment.

SOURCES OF RELEASES

Radioactive releases to the environment can originate from the reactor primary containment, from the spent fuel cooling pool, from systems that process and transfer radioactive waste, or from areas where processed radioactive waste is stored. Although the available radioactive material inventory

---

[*] Numerous references state that 96% of the aircraft's kinetic energy was dispersed by the destruction of the aircraft and 4% was absorbed by the concrete wall. Unlike reactor containment structures, the concrete used in this test did not have embedded steel rebar. The Sandia report is not available to the public. See also Sugano et al. (1993) and Hessheimer and Dameron (2006).

and source terms are different for each release pathway, the emergency response to the release component of the accident is the same: (1) maintain situational awareness using available installed radiation monitoring systems, (2) perform local radiation surveys, (3) dispatch environmental survey and monitoring teams, (4) collect site and environmental samples, (5) estimate the resulting potential dose to the public using appropriate radioactive material transport models and real-time meteorology, and, for the licensee, (6) when appropriate, communicate protective action recommendations to offsite authorities.

Processed radioactive waste is generally made up of suspensions, resins, and slurries containing long-lived (half-lives greater than several months) radioactive solids and metals stored in drums, barrels, or a larger volume high-integrity container (often a cylindrical polyethylene container holding about 200 to 300 ft^3 of waste). This waste has undergone weeks to months of radioactive decay, and the source term is greatly reduced from what was present when the waste was collected. Waste of this type presents a local radiation hazard but under normal conditions there is no potential to affect the public. If a container seal fails, the physical form of this waste limits its mobility, although it could cause a local airborne radioactivity area resulting in some localized radioactive material contamination and potentially intakes of radioactive material by nearby workers. Any release of radioactive material from stored waste sufficient to cause a radiation dose to the public (beyond or away from the licensee's property) requires a catastrophic event that simultaneously breaches multiple containers, such as a tornado or major fire. The radioactive material would move directly from the breached containers into the atmosphere without any delay, filtration, or reduction mechanisms and would not be measured by plant radiation monitoring systems. Releases of this kind would not usually be expected to result in offsite protective actions, although detectable offsite contamination may be possible.

Plant systems that collect, process, filter, and hold radioactive waste can contain radioactive gases, liquids, resins, slurry, suspensions, and solids of half-lives greater than a few hours. The radioactive materials are confined in piping, ducts, filters, holding tanks, and processing tanks and have undergone hours to weeks of radioactive decay. Plant areas around these pipes, filters, and tanks present local radiation hazards but under normal conditions there is no potential to affect the public; seal leaks in piping carrying radioactive gases and unsealed open tanks holding radioactive resins, slurry, and solids both may require airborne radioactivity controls. A release of radioactive material sufficient to cause a radiation dose to the public requires more than minor failures or breaches of waste system piping, ducts, and tanks. Radioactive gases are immediately discharged to the environment through plant ventilation systems, while radioactive material from other physical forms are collected and discharged after drying, which allows solid materials to become suspended in air. Most radioactive gases would be delayed but not filtered or reduced, whereas most aerosols and particulates would be both delayed and filtered prior to release. Releases through engineered plant ventilation systems are measured by plant radiation monitoring systems. Most releases from plant radioactive waste systems would be short, less than 30 minutes, because the affected tank or piping volume is small or because automatic systems or plant operators isolate the breach, or both. Releases of this kind would not be expected to result in offsite protective actions, and those involving radioactive gases would not result in offsite contamination.

The spent fuel cooling or holding pool (often just called the *fuel pool*) holds highly radioactive fuel assemblies after they are removed from the reactor, with isotopes of half-lives ranging from hours to millions of years. The pool water provides cooling to dissipate decay heat in the assemblies, provides radiation shielding to personnel working around the pool, and filters radioactive material released through minor defects in fuel cladding. Because of the water and the thickness of concrete used in pool construction, there is not normally a radiation hazard near the pool. Small amounts of radioactive gases may be present near the pool during routine operations because of fuel defects but in insufficient concentrations to be either a local or environmental hazard. Similarly, low concentrations of radioactive solids are found in the pool water but at insufficient concentrations to be a radiation hazard.

A release of radioactive material sufficient to cause a radiation dose to the public requires either direct physical damage to fuel rods or an extended loss of the pool's ability to remove decay heat. Direct physical damage could occur if a fuel assembly drops while being moved,* if the assembly is incorrectly lowered into its holding rack, or if a sufficiently heavy foreign object drops into the pool onto one or more stored assemblies. A fuel pool could lose the ability to remove decay heat if the entire pool cooling system (usually two or more redundant sets of pumps and heat exchangers) fails, allowing the pool water to heat to boiling, which can lead to localized steam cooling of fuel assemblies, a zirconium–water reaction, and rupture of the fuel. A loss of pool cooling is particularly significant within the first months after fuel is removed from the operating reactor. The same result would occur if there is a catastrophic failure of fuel pool integrity, allowing pool level to fall below the top of stored fuel; a loss of pool integrity also causes very high radiation levels around the reactor site because of the loss of radiation shielding material. Direct physical damage would normally affect one or at most only a few fuel assemblies, and the primary hazard would be from radioactive gases not being absorbed by the water; a release of this kind would be expected to be of short duration, a few minutes or less, as the gases are fully discharged and would primarily be a hazard to plant workers. An extended loss of fuel pool cooling, whether from a cooling system or pool integrity failure, affects the entire fuel rod inventory, and all assemblies aged (approximately) 36 months or less are at risk of structural failure; a release of this kind could be similar in both duration and concentration (though not in source term isotopes) to that caused by damaged fuel in the operating reactor, with additional complications from the very high radiation conditions onsite.

All reactors are designed with at least one filtered plant ventilation system that collects radioactive gases and aerosols from the fuel pool area; the filters remove essentially all of the radioactive iodine, volatile gases and aerosols, and radioactive particulates (with an initial removal efficiency of at least 99.99%), leaving only the noble gases. In boiling water reactors, the entire reactor building is kept at negative pressure relative to the environment and acts as a secondary containment structure; the structural integrity of the building is protected by blow-out panels designed to rupture at an interior overpressure of a few psig, creating an unmonitored, unfiltered pathway to the atmosphere; these panels are often located in the fuel pool area. Even though boiling water reactor fuel pool areas are very large spaces, a loss of fuel pool cooling scenario can result in pool boiling, with resulting overpressures sufficient to cause a loss of the blowout panels. Except for designed accident-range radiation detectors, working-level area radiation monitors on the adjacent refuel floor do not have sufficient measuring range and will become saturated (off-scale on the high end) during an accident.

Gaseous releases from one to a few fuel assemblies with an intact pool would not be expected to result in offsite protective actions, and radioactive contamination would not be expected offsite. For loss of fuel pool cooling and loss of pool integrity scenarios, radiation doses could be sufficient to warrant protective actions for the public, and in the case of boiling water reactors where blowout panels are lost protective actions would be expected.

DRYWELL AND CONTAINMENT RADIATION MONITORS

Containment structures for both boiling water and pressurized water reactors generally have two ranges of installed radiation monitors, with at least two instruments in each range (each one powered from a different vital electrical bus). Operating range detectors are usually unshielded quenched Geiger–Mueller detectors with a top detection range of 10,000 mR/h (100,000 mR/h at some plants); in radiation fields above their top range, the detectors become saturated and either

---

* All operations involving handling spent fuel rods are performed under many (15 to 25) feet of water because of the potentially lethal radiation hazard. Spent fuel rods are never allowed to be exposed to air. Fuel assemblies transferred to dry independent spent fuel storage facilities are loaded into their storage casks underwater, sealed, then drained and dried; the multi-ton concrete and steel casks provide radiation shielding comparable to the depth of water in the fuel pool.

read zero (on older model instruments) or continue to read at their maximum value. Accident range detectors can be shielded Geiger–Mueller instruments but may also be shielded sodium iodide (NaI) crystals sized between 4 and 16 in.^{2}. Although accident range detectors may have lower detection limits less than 1 R/h, they are generally installed with radiation sources that ensure constant readings between 1 and 2 R/h during normal operations; their maximum ranges are typically 10,000 to 100,000 R/h. Normal operating range detectors and accident range detectors are typically installed in different areas of the containment structure to minimize the possibility the detectors will be destroyed; therefore, even when the normal operating range detector response overlaps the accident range detector range, the readings are not directly comparable because of differences in detector geometry, and they cannot be used to validate one another; this is especially true when the monitors are of different physical type (Geiger–Mueller vs. sodium iodide).

Accident range monitors are calibrated to a site-specific average energy that corresponds to the average energy of an assumed nuclide mix at a stated time after the accident (details and assumptions are found in the site's final safety analysis report; see Chapter 5), and the detector does not provide accurate indications for other accident sequences or times. The calibration must consider both the containment geometry and shielding. The average radiation energy of a loss-of-coolant accident (reactor coolant system breach) is nearly constant for the initial 2 to 3 hours after fuel damage, decreases over the following 24 hours, and then as short-lived high-energy nuclides decay off begins to increase again. Between 2 and 24 hours after fuel damage, the accident range monitors tend to under-report actual dose rates; thus, concentrations of airborne radioactive material derived or calculated from containment dose rates are also less than what is actually present.

Accident range detectors typically receive a live source calibration only when they are installed and may not be subsequently live-tested in their installed configuration. Live source calibrations are often done with ^{137}Cs (662 keV) or ^{60}Co (1332 and 1173 keV) sources due to their ready availability at accident ranges; care must be taken with these live calibrations because the dominant energies of cesium and cobalt may not closely approximate the average energies of the site-specific accident source term.

Containment monitors are useful only for loss-of-coolant accident sequences (reactor coolant system breaches inside primary containment). For containment bypass scenarios with severe fuel melting, an increased radiation response is expected on all of the normal and accident range detectors because of the release of radioactive material from the fuel into the coolant system, but this increase cannot be used to diagnose the core status because the accident range calibration assumes an equal concentration of airborne radioactivity throughout the containment volume, which is not the case when the material remains confined in coolant system piping. No significant additional response should be expected on these monitors for containment bypass with low to moderate fuel damage, or no damage at all.

Accident range radiation monitors are used (1) as recognition or entry conditions for emergency action levels, (2) to estimate the amount of core damage, and (3) to bound the public health consequences of a release of airborne radioactive materials to the environment. Most sites have prepared site-specific core state curves based on generic vendor-supplied curves; the Commission uses similar generic curves that are not site specific.[*] These curves give an analyst a rough idea of core state, but they must be used with care and with an understanding of their limitations: (1) they do not apply when the reactor coolant boundary inside the containment structure is intact, (2) they do not apply to containment bypass scenarios, (3) the minimum monitor reading (in R/h) may be above the low end of the curve (the keep-alive source may mask and overstate the true radiation reading), (4) the curves assume a 100% transfer of nuclides from coolant to atmosphere (although this may not be true), (5) the curves assume a homogeneous nuclide mixture in containment (although this may not be true), (6) when curves are provided that take into account containment or core sprays it is often to determine whether or not the sprays are effective, and (7) the effects of isotopic decay and source depletion are not considered.

---

[*] For example, see NUREG-0150, *NRC Response Technical Manual*, Revision 4, Figure A.5, p. A-30.

FUEL STORAGE POOL RADIATION MONITORS

Boiling water reactors usually have radiation monitors installed on the refuel floor with at least two ranges, one instrument for normal operations and one for accidents; the normal range instrument typically reads from below 1 mR/h to a maximum of 1000 mR/h, whereas the accident range typically reads from 1 to 1E6 mR/h. Pressurized reactors with separate fuel buildings usually have only installed accident range monitors. Both reactor types typically have two instruments in each range, fed from different vital or essential power sources.

Normal ventilation from pressurized reactors has installed process radiation monitors that normally automatically isolate on signals slightly above background (between 5 and 10 mR/h). These detectors are frequently scintillation detectors; high-range detectors may be shielded with calibration adjustments to compensate for shielding absorption. The fuel building release path effluent monitor is generally calibrated to noble gases, as it is assumed that the 25 feet of water over the fuel racks will absorb all particulates (all halogens are either very reactive with water or have such half-lives that there is essentially no inventory left 200 days after they are removed from the reactor). These systems are designed to detect a gap release from a small number of fuel assemblies as scrubbed by the water overlay (e.g., a fuel rod dropped onto a small number of racked assemblies during handling).

Boiling water reactor refuel floors are normally exhausted via the plant chimney, and pressurized water reactor fuel handling buildings normally have their own engineered vent to the environment. Care must be taken not to use main chimney or stack effluent monitor readings when assessing the consequences of a fuel handling accident when the associated radiological release is not exhausted through the chimney; in boiling water reactors where the refuel floor is exhausted through the plant stack, the main stack noble gas monitor results require adjustment to compensate for the different source term (while iodine is present in stored fuel assemblies the iodine monitor channel should not require compensation).

Most plants also have a radiation detector installed on the fuel bridge. This bridge is a moveable platform spanning the fuel storage pool that supports the fuel assembly grapple and the fuel handling operator's grapple control station. It may also be equipped with an array of underwater lights and inspection cameras, as well as remote-telemetry electronic dosimeters. The fuel bridge monitor is generally a mid- to high-range Geiger–Mueller instrument with a local display and a high dose rate alarm. It is designed to alert workers on the fuel bridge when the grapple lifts too high (in case the upper limit switch fails) so they can secure the fuel assembly in a safe position and exit the area before receiving a radiation overexposure. This monitor may not always be connected to the normal plant radiation monitoring system, may not be recorded by the plant computer, and may not feed an alarm in the plant control room.

SOURCE TERM DEPLETION

Source term as used in dose assessment refers to the inventory and concentrations of radioactive material that survive the transit from the core to the environment. Therefore, the source term that is available to produce a radiation dose to the public is reduced from the inventory initially released from reactor fuel. The depletion and reduction mechanisms include the natural processes of diffusion, radioactive decay, particulate settling, and chemical scavenging and the technological processes of filtration, rainout (washout from sprays), and flooding. Although it occurs, credit is not given for the retention of radioactive material in primary coolant as an inventory reduction process.[*]

---

[*] NUREG-1228 (McKenna and Glitter, 1988) states that "a comparison of available computer projections shows dramatically different plate-out (reactor coolant system retention) for different chemical forms and events." NUREG-0956 (Silberberg et al., 1986) states that "primary retention factors cannot be used rigorously as a multiplier of accident source term nor can they be combined linearly with other retention factors." Therefore, reactor coolant system retention generally will not be considered. However, for bypass accidents, system retention is the only reduction mechanism, and a reduction factor typical of those predicted by computer codes for this accident will be used (RDF of 0.4).

Diffusion describes the tendency of a gas or vapor to expand to fill up the available space, which tends to reduce its average density or concentration; this is especially true as superheated water under pressure flashes to steam at normal atmospheric pressure. *Particulate settling* describes the tendency of larger and heavier particulates, especially those of 1-μm diameter or larger, to settle out in the absence of significant air currents. *Chemical scavenging* describes chemical reaction processes and bonding that result in some radioactive species becoming bound to surfaces and airborne dusts because of their chemical properties, rather than because of their radiological properties. This can be particularly important with the halogen species and with chemical forms that readily react with hydrogen, fluorine, boron, and some other highly reactive chemicals typically found as additives to reactor coolant.

Filtration describes any process where the gas or vapor is made to flow over, past, or through a high-efficiency particulate filter, charcoal bed, resin bed, impaction line, or other mechanical device that removes radioactive material by mechanical or chemical means, absorption, or adsorption; a holdup or decay line acts to increase the time required for effluents to reach the plant chimney, creating time for increased radioactive decay; therefore, these system features are not filters. *Rainout* describes the physical interaction of airborne radioactive material in vapors, particulate, and contaminated steam with water; the water spray or mist physically removes the material through impact (agitation), dissolves the radioactive material, and then traps it, or it causes the material to adhere to non-radioactive particles (i.e., dusts) in the air. In plant buildings, the water is supplied by engineered sprays (core sprays, drywell sprays, containment sprays). Water can also be sprayed on external plant vent or release points using *ad hoc* procedures (e.g., fire hoses); when the radioactive plume moves through natural rain (or snow) essentially the same process depletes the plume and concentrates particulates on the ground closer to the plant. When radioactive gases or steam can be exhausted or bubbled under water, the cooler water quenches and absorbs some steam. Some radioactive material dissolves in the water, and some radioactive particulates are ejected from the effluent stream and become trapped in the water (they do not have enough energy to become airborne). The process of removing radioactive material by exhausting it through water is often referred to as *scrubbing*. A similar effect occurs when steam and hot gases are vented through ice condensers, producing water and acting as a physical filter.

Flooding describes the ability to trap radioactive materials, primarily particulates and halogen and not radioactive noble gases, within the damaged reactor core by covering the core with water (unrelated to the water's core cooling function). The inherent decay heat of a damaged core will still drive steam production, which facilities radioactive material becoming airborne, but a layer of water greatly reduces the rate of transfer to air. Some radioactive species will also dissolve in the water.

NUREG-1228 (McKenna and Glitter, 1988) estimated that natural processes (the interaction of diffusion, decay, settle, and plate-out) remove about 60% of aerosols and particulates over 30 to 60 minutes and remove about 94% over 12 or more hours. Most of the benefit of natural processes occur in the initial 24 hours, after which the marginal rate of inventory reduction decreases significantly. Sprays increase the early removal effectiveness from 60% to 97%. Bubbling radioactive steam through water, such as a torus or suppression pool, reduces aerosols and particulates by between 95% and 99%, depending on the water temperature. The water in a steam generator has a 50% reduction factor (the steam generator is less effective at scrubbing than is the torus because of its much smaller water volume and its higher water temperature). These estimates of plume reduction apply only to a single puff or bubble of radioactive effluent that is subsequently not affected by any other process.

Settling and deposition are assumed to not have a significant effect on radioactive material in transit, such as through a fan or ventilation system, due to the relatively fast transit times as compared to the settling velocity of about 1 cm/s. Scavenging can occur while material is in transit but estimates are not available regarding its efficiency, which is assumed by NUREG-1228 and NUREG-1465 (Soffer et al., 1995) to be small. Decay will be significant only for those nuclides whose half-lives are on the order of a few (less than 10) minutes, due to the relatively short transit times as compared to their half-lives.

Sprays achieve an activity reduction by a factor of 20 in the first hour of operation, after which the marginal rate of continued reduction begins to decrease. After 24 hours, the overall reduction may be on the order of 500. When sprays have been secured, the remaining decay heat may be sufficient to cause material previously removed by spraying to become resuspended in containment and available for release.

The initial effectiveness of filtration trains* is very close to 100% for particulates and halogens, particularly for high-efficiency filters (99.999% effective), and effectively zero for radioactive noble gases; as the filter media become coated, flow through the filter decreases and differential pressure increases until the filter ruptures. As charcoal traps halogens, its adsorption efficiency decreases until it has essentially no removal capability left. Temperature and humidity also affect the effectiveness of charcoal, with higher temperatures and more liquid content tending to impair halogen removal and decreasing its overall removal effectiveness.

It is difficult to calculate the depleted environmental source term starting from knowledge of the core state because it is often not known (or knowable) what removal processes are present. Also, interactions and synergies between various processes and the accident chemistry are unknown, there is a continuing input of new radioactive material mixing with previous (partially depleted) material, and there may be an outflow of radioactive material through design basis leakage or an active containment breach. Simply put, the radioactive material inventory in reactor coolant or the containment air space is usually not close enough to steady-state conditions to allow a useful prediction. From an operational perspective, any technological actions that deplete the radioactive source term are desirable, whether or not their results are detectable or quantifiable.

RELEASE POINTS (AIRBORNE PATHWAYS)

Boiling water reactors are generally designed with a single elevated plant stack (chimney) which receives air flow from all of the engineered plant ventilation systems; this stack is the release point for all routine plant effluents. The stack is described as *elevated* when it is at least twice the height of nearby plant buildings; the stack is also considered *isolated* if it is located a distance at least twice the height of plant buildings away from the nearest plant building. A typical boiling water reactor stack is between 60 and 110 meters high and 2 to 3 meters in diameter, and it has a normal operating gas flow of greater than 100,000 cfm.

Pressurized water reactors are generally designed with three routine plant effluent stacks (often called *vents*): one for the combined primary containment and the auxiliary systems building pathway, one from the turbine building, and one from the fuel building. These stacks are typically attached to the building and are of low height (from roof-height vents to chimneys of less than 10 meters), and they have normal operating flows much smaller than in boiling water reactor designs (10,000 to 50,000 cfm). Engineered release points have installed radiation monitors and go through high-efficiency particulate filters (>99.9% effective) and charcoal filtration beds. Boiling water reactors also are designed with two independent low-flow (10,000 cfm) monitored backup filtration systems (*standby gas treatment systems*) that draw from the torus (suppression pool) air space and primary and secondary containments. Release point filtration systems are highly effective in removing radioactive halogens (iodine and cesium) and particulates, but they do not remove radioactive noble gases (krypton and xenon).

The primary source of radioactive gases released from boiling water and pressurized water reactors during normal operations is the steam condenser. During an accident, radioactive effluents continue to flow through the engineered release point while a normal steam-flow path still exists (i.e., main steam line isolation valves are open). If the containment structure cannot be isolated, breaches

---

* Assumes a train that consists of an electric dryer system to remove small amounts of suspended liquids or vapors, a preheater, a high-efficiency particulate pre-filter, a charcoal filter bed at least 6 feet long, and a high-efficiency particulate post-filter.

in any steam or water system that flows between containment and the plant building may create an open path to the environment (i.e., *containment bypass scenarios*). The inability to close both main steam isolation valves in the same steam line, followed by a steam line rupture in the steam tunnel or turbine building, is one such scenario. Other systems that can create bypasses include exhausts from steam-driven turbines, containment sump recirculation lines, and the shutdown cooling (pressurized water reactors) or residual heat removal (boiling water reactors) systems. A few older boiling water reactors (e.g., Dresden Units 2 and 3) also have a once-through emergency heat exchanger (isolation condenser) located in containment that rejects decay heat directly to the environment—a tube leak in this heat exchanger allows radioactive material in the reactor coolant to flow directly to the environment. Steam line pressure relief valves at boiling water reactors discharge inside the drywell to the water-filled torus or suppression pool, but safety relief valves at pressurized water reactors discharge directly to the environment. During a steam generator tube rupture event, this could provide an unmonitored, unfiltered pathway for contaminated steam.

During loss-of-coolant accidents, failures in engineered penetrations through the containment wall can create unmonitored release paths, such as primary and emergency air lock seals, seals around personnel and equipment hatches, and seals around piping and electrical lines. Pressure-driven, non-specific, design basis leakage from steam-filled containment structures also provides pathways directly to the environment; depending on the containment's design, from 0.5% to 1% of the containment cavity volume may escape per day. NUREG-1228 assumed non-specific leakage rates of 0.10% to 0.25% per day for pressurized water reactor containments (large/dry) and 0.5% leakage per day for boiling water reactor drywells (wet well) and primary containment structures.[*] Note that at the time NUREG-1228 was written all operating boiling water reactors used either Mark I or Mark II containments, Mark III design plants had not yet gone into operation; NUREG-1465 (Soffer et al., 1995) did not address the subject of containment leakage.

Pressure spikes can occur in drywell or containment structures when high-pressure coolant flashes to steam after a reactor coolant system break, after a steam line break inside containment, or after a hydrogen burn or detonation (the standard curves for hydrogen burns are based on low-pressure or near-atmospheric events and may overestimate the amount of hydrogen required under high-pressure conditions). Pressure spikes may directly damage the containment structure, causing cracks and holes that allow the escape of trapped radioactive gases; depending on containment design, the final safety analysis report safety limit is between 20 and 60 psig, with structural failure expected at pressures approximately double the safety limit value (newer plants typically have lower safety limits than older plants). With containment coolers in operation it is likely that containment safety limits would not be challenged until several hours into a loss-of-coolant accident. A hole in the containment structure 2 ft^2 or larger is considered to be catastrophic containment failure; a typical accident analysis assumption is that following catastrophic damage 100% of the available (existing) radioactive material inventory in containment is discharged to the environment over one hour (not including any additional radioactive inventory added to containment during that hour). A failure to isolate containment due to the failure of seals in a through-wall valve is assumed to result in releasing 100% of the existing radioactive material inventory from containment over the subsequent 24 hours; this is equivalent to a hole of 8 in.^{2}

Boiling water reactors are designed with an unmonitored, unfiltered emergency vent pipe[†] connecting the primary containment to the environment which is used to relieve containment pressure before it reaches the structural safety limit. It is considered sufficiently important to prevent a structural failure of the containment that pressure is relieved regardless of the radiation dose to the public delivered by the released radioactive material. Pressurized water reactors have monitored and filtered containment purge systems that can be used to relieve containment pressure, but emergency use of these systems requires defeating interlocks and isolation signals or placing jumpers in

---

[*] Many computer-based dose assessment programs do not model passive containment leakage. The NRC's radiological assessment model (RASCAL 3.X) uses a default containment leakage value of 0.2% per day.

[†] At most boiling water reactor sites, this emergency pressure relief is referred to as the *hardened vent*.

control boxes, so they cannot be operated immediately in the same manner as the hardened vent. Emergency venting may cause very high radiation conditions along the ventilation ducts that connect containment to the atmospheric vents because of shine from the radioactive material being exhausted; after the venting is complete, these radiation conditions may persist for an extended period of time because of fission product plate-out on the interior duct surfaces and the collection of radioactive material at duct connections and elbows.

LIQUID RELEASES

Liquid and sludge-like radioactive material is generally produced by plant radioactive waste systems that filter and remove radioactive material from reactor coolant or store or process the material downstream of the filter. This radioactive material contains a relatively high concentration of longer lived activation product isotopes, such as cesium, cobalt, iron, manganese, tellurium, and zirconium. At some plants, this material is periodically discharged from the plant into surface waters, to either an onsite settling pond or a lake, river, or ocean. A few plants (e.g., Palo Verde in Arizona) are zero release sites, which do not have any engineered liquid discharge points. The greatest potential radiation dose to humans from liquid plant effluents is from drinking after the direct uptake of effluents by a surface water supply system; washing and bathing with contaminated water produce a much smaller dose. Pure surface water supply systems are relatively rare and are not commonly located within miles of nuclear power plant outfalls. Most water systems are capable of being isolated for up to several hours without appreciable impact on system performance. Another concern is the transfer of radioactive material into home-grown (garden) food after plants are watered by contaminated surface water. Compared to airborne effluents, liquid effluents

- Have a very low total radioactive content.
- Are released at relatively low flow rates and volumes.
- Come from a small number of sources (primarily storage tanks), primarily located below grade with no ready release paths.
- Have high engineered and natural mixing (dilution) rates.
- Present little opportunity for direct radiation exposure (shine) because of the low concentration and high self-shielding.

As with engineered airborne release paths, intentional liquid releases require multiple valves to be aligned to the open position (system valves are normally closed, with at least one valve locked closed), and all release paths must have installed radiation monitors.

PLANT PROCESS RADIATION MONITORS

Process radiation monitors are installed on plant liquid and gas lines, primarily to detect breaks and failures in the system during normal operation. They often are Geiger–Mueller instruments with relatively low ranges, the high values being 100 to 1000 mR/h. These detectors are generally unshielded and are susceptible to radiation shine from nearby pipes, tanks, lines, or equipment rooms; monitors located near external walls also can experience shine from an external radioactive plume. Because many of these monitors are in plant radioactive waste systems handling mostly longer lived nuclides, they are frequently calibrated to either ^{137}Cs or ^{60}Co. Most process monitors input into automatic line or ventilation isolations that occur at low radiation levels. They may not remain representative under accident conditions (calibrations, temperatures, pressures, or flow rates). Some process monitors used in plant emergency action levels (e.g., failed fuel monitor) may automatically isolate, or be isolated manually as directed by emergency operating procedures while still on-scale. As count rates increase, instrument dead-time correction becomes a problem and can cause the detector to under-report actual radiation conditions by as much as 25% to 30%.

Plant effluent monitors are a special case of process monitor. Many plant monitors are high-range Geiger–Mueller instruments with parallel detectors for noble gases, iodine/halogens, and particulates; older scintillation-type detectors are often found abandoned in place because they proved to be unreliable. Low-flow pumps pull from the vent or chimney effluent stream and direct flow in parallel past the separate detector channels. Each channel is calibrated to a marker isotope. Channels may read in counts per minute (requiring a manual conversion to activity units) or in µCi/cc or µCi/s, or the plant computer may provide conversions so that results are simultaneously available in multiple units. The plant computer may also apply an adjustment factor to the raw count rate to correct for differences between the average energy of the marker isotope and the calibration source. Plant effluent monitors can have the following problems: (1) because they are high-count-rate instruments, dead time correction can create a significant under-reporting of the true count rate; (2) the detectors are often unshielded or partially shielded, leaving the detector susceptible to radiation shine from the effluent stream where both the vertical and horizontal plume components act as line sources; (3) because the detectors rely on air pumps, a loss of power to the pump or a pump failure causes the radiation monitor to be unreliable; and (4) because the sampling lines are open to the environment they are susceptible to changes in environmental conditions (low and high temperatures, rain, snow, and dust loading). Plants with chimneys located away from plant buildings can have the associated effluent monitors housed in a remote building away from the actual chimney, resulting in long runs of small-diameter piping with bends and elbows that deplete particulate and halogens from the effluent through impact against the bend walls; they also require a constant effluent temperature and are particularly affected by cold winter temperatures (leading to under-reporting of release rates).

Older plants may be equipped with emergency air sampling systems that automatically redirect flow from the chimney air sample pumps through activated charcoal canisters or cartridges as the concentration of radioactive material in the effluent increases. The systems are not designed to sample containment or drywell atmospheres. Although the systems are essentially identical, they have different names because they were made by different vendors; two common ones are the wide-range gas monitor (WRGM) and separate particulate, iodine, and noble gas (SPING) monitors. These systems automatically isolate the normal (low-range) effluent monitoring channel when the mid-range detector reads on-scale (there is some range overlap between the low- and mid-ranges). The systems feature a mid-range charcoal filter and a separate high-range filter (again, with a range overlap between mid- and high-range detectors). These systems do not have a real-time measurement capability. The charcoal canister must be physically removed and analyzed by spectroscopy; a two-person team requires 30 minutes to exchange sample canisters and under accident conditions team members may incur a substantial radiation dose. The used charcoal cartridge will contain substantial radioactivity, and a heavily shielded transport container is required. There may be flow time restrictions on the system that require a minimum sample time of between 8 and 12 hours. One design quirk is that, as effluent concentration falls, the system cannot automatically realign to its normal detection mode; it requires a local reset. Alignment to the normal operating mode can cross-contaminate the detector with higher level activity from the accident unless the system is well purged (usually with nitrogen).

IN-PLANT AIR SAMPLES

During an accident, radiation protection technicians or chemistry technicians are likely to be dispatched to collect manual in-plant grab samples because process monitors are not designed to sample the atmospheres of plant buildings. This information is primarily used to plan radiation protection actions for emergency workers, although it could provide an input to offsite dose assessment. The most commonly used instrument for air sampling is a low-flow (<5 cfm) sampling pump with a 4- to 5-inch sampling head; all sampler heads have a particulate prefilter (paper or fiberglass) and a cartridge of absorbing media. The most common absorber is activated charcoal, which has a high affinity for noble gases and radioisotopes over a wide variety of environmental conditions.

When iodine is known or suspected, the media may be silver zeolite,[*] which is much more effective at adsorbing iodine than is charcoal. Activated charcoal is often preferred over zeolite because of cost—charcoal is around $1 a cartridge vs. $40 to $50 per cartridge for zeolite (the price fluctuates with the price of silver). Grab air samples are desirable because they provide the best estimate of the conditions workers will be exposed to and may provide a better estimate of the environmental source term than does a reactor coolant sample or containment/drywell atmosphere sample. Problems with grab air samples include (1) dust or (non-radioactive) particulate loading on the prefilter, which both degrades the absorption media's ability to collect radioactive material and introduces self-shielding for the beta–gamma counting of the filter, leading to an underestimate of the airborne radioactive material concentration; (2) although the sample may be collected in 5 minutes or less, sample analysis requires 30 minutes to a few hours;[†] (3) the technician collecting the sample may incur a substantial radiation dose; and (4) there may be difficulties in making or obtaining high-activity air sample calibration sources for onsite counters, leading to inaccurate or uncertain measurements.

Neither charcoal nor zeolite are particularly effective in collecting radioactive noble gases. The best method for collecting these gases is a *sample bomb*, which is a vessel evacuated to less than atmospheric pressure. The sample is collected when the collection valve is opened, allowing the empty vessel to be filled with the sample gas. A common collection vessel is a sealed cylindrical Marinelli beaker in sizes between 1 and 5 liters. Collection may be through a particulate prefilter to screen out any halogens, iodines, or fission product particulates, so that only the noble gases are collected. Marinelli beakers are commonly used to count radioactive liquids and solids, but obtaining calibration sources for an accident mix of noble gases may be a problem.

A plant is likely to have a few portable continuous air monitors, which are mostly used during plant outages and have local displays and alarms (i.e., they are not connected to the plant computer system). Emergency response facilities, particularly the ones located onsite, will often have installed continuous air monitors, located in the facility proper or sampling from the facility ventilation system. Portable monitors may be used in the plant under accident conditions but they are bulky and heavy (usually mounted on a large wheeled cart), the technician putting them into service may incur substantial radiation dose not justified by the data acquired, and (as noted) they usually lack a remote data capability. Continuous air monitors intended for routine plant operations may not be capable of measuring accident condition concentrations (i.e., they may go into saturation at concentrations much above the upper alarm threshold).

POST-ACCIDENT MONITORING SYSTEMS

After the Three Mile Island accident, all power reactor stations were required to install or design the capability to collect post-accident reactor coolant (liquid) samples; this requirement was intended to address the difficulties the licensee and Nuclear Regulatory Agency had understanding reactor core damage during the March 1979 accident. The initial requirements to install a post-accident sampling capability were contained in NUREG-0578 (NRC, 1979l) and NUREG-0660 (NRC, 1980g). NUREG-0737 (NRC, 1980a) required that by January 1, 1982, all licensees must have the capability installed to promptly obtain samples under accident conditions without incurring radiation doses to plant workers greater than 3 rem whole body and 18.75 rem to the extremities. Licensees were required to have the capability to sample the primary coolant and containment sump and containment

---

[*] For a discussion of historical problems with silver zeolite, see NRC Information Notice 86-043 (NRC, 1986f). The same event is also discussed in Gavila (2003a).

[†] The minimum measurement sensitivity and the amount of time required to analyze a sample of radioactive material is determined by the square of the background (i.e., no sample present) radiation count rate. The onsite beta–gamma counters require a relatively low radiation background to obtain an accurate measurement, even when located inside a substantial radiation shield; under accident conditions, the external radiation count rate may become too high, effectively making the counters inoperable for all except the highest activity samples.

air. The systems were to be designed so that samples could be collected and analyzed within 3 hours of the decision to initiate sampling. "Accident conditions" in this context referred to Regulatory Guide 1.3 (USAEC, 1974a) or 1.4 (USAEC, 1974b) releases of fission products. Secondary conditions included the following: (1) the design must not depend on operating a system previously isolated from the reactor, (2) a backup grab sample capability must exist when inline instrumentation is used, and (3) the samples obtained must be representative of the reactor coolant and containment atmosphere. Regulatory Guide 1.97, *Instrumentation for Light-Water-Cooled Nuclear Power Plants to Assess Plant and Environs Conditions During and Following an Accident* (Revision 0, 1975; Revision 2, 1980; see also NRC, 2006a) also has design requirements for post-accident sampling systems. To ensure that licensees maintained and could operate post-accident sampling systems, NUREG-0654 (NRC, 1980c), Planning Standard N(2)(e)(2), required an annual demonstration drill including actual use of the system to collect a liquid sample; site technical specifications required quarterly surveillances to ensure the sampling equipment remained operable.

At lower levels of fuel damage the post-accident sampling system collects an undiluted reactor coolant sample of at least 100-cc volume; at higher fuel damage levels, when large reactor coolant samples pose a radiation hazard for the collecting technician, a diluted sample of 3- to 5-cc total volume is collected (diluted at 50 to 1 or more). Bulky shielded transport containers (referred to as *pigs*) were required for even a small diluted sample of coolant from a severely damaged reactor because of on-contact radiation dose rates calculated at greater than 1 R/h. These sampling systems featured long runs of high-pressure, small-diameter pipe, with significant amounts of lead and concrete shielding. Most licensees experienced problems with dilution systems and in maintaining isolation and flush valves. The calibration of radiation counting systems for non-operating source terms and the extremely high count rates expected from even small-volume samples also caused problems.

The Westinghouse Owners Group assessed the technical basis and effectiveness of post-accident sampling (WOG, 1998), and the owners groups for other reactor vendor types performed similar analyses at about the same time (e.g., CEOG, 1999). The industry generally concluded that relevant direct reactor coolant and drywell/containment atmosphere sample information could not be collected in a sufficiently timely manner during an accident to guide real-time emergency response decision-making and that indirect measures of core damage were sufficient for licensees to carry out their safety responsibilities. In addition to timeliness issues, there were technical questions about whether post-accident sampling systems collected representative reactor coolant and drywell/ containment atmosphere samples, about the effectiveness of distilled water flushing, about whether sample materials remained trapped in elbows and turns along piping runs, about uncertainties in measuring flow rates, and about possible cross-contamination between sample runs. After containment isolation occurs, manual actions (such as pulling reactor protection system fuses or installing jumpers on circuit boards) were required to defeat the isolation signals and allow containment isolation values on the sample lines to be opened.

In addition to ongoing valve maintenance issues, the long piping runs required long purge times (15 to 30 minutes). Although the sampling stations were heavily shielded to reduce radiation dose to the chemistry technician collecting the sample, the piping runs were often either not shielded or received much less shielding, so when the system was operated other areas of the plant (reactor building) would also potentially have much higher radiation doses. At many plants, particularly boiling water reactors, the post-accident system sampling room was a permanent contaminated area. The sampling team was required to dress in anti-contamination clothing (sometimes double sets of clothing) and remain in the area for up to an hour.

Both industry and Commission staff questioned whether the post-sampling system results were meaningful for emergency response purposes and their usefulness in site remediation. The primary use of post-accident chemistry reports was to compute the percentage of cladding damage and melted fuel; however, these percentages are not directly used (and often not even indirectly used) in the assessment of potential dose to the public and generation of protective actions, and they do not result in any specific emergency response actions. As discussed previously, even accurate knowledge of radioactive material concentrations in reactor coolant and the containment atmosphere does not readily translate into accurate knowledge of the radioactive release source term. The Commission agreed, and beginning in 2002 it permitted licensees to remove liquid and atmosphere sampling systems from technical specifications. Most, although not all, licensees have now either abandoned such systems in place or have taken them out of their licensing basis (and emergency plans) but have the systems in standby for possible use.[*]

---

[*] Also see Generic Letters 82-05 (*Post-TMI Requirements*), 83-36 (*NUREG-0737 Technical Specifications*), and 83-37 (*NUREG-0737 Technical Specifications*); Industry/TSTF Standard Technical Specification Change Traveler TSTF-413, *Elimination of Requirements for a Post Accident Sampling System (PASS)*; and the model safety evaluations 65 FR 65018 (2000), 66 FR 66954 (2001), 67 FR 13027 (2002), 68 FR 10052 (2003), and 68 FR 25664 (2003).

4 Basics of Dispersion

INTRODUCTION

The characteristic of nuclear power plants that largely distinguishes them from other kinds of industrial plants is that they release radioactive material into the environment while operating.[*] A nuclear power plant also has a large permanent source term of radioactive material which is well contained but potentially available for release during a serious accident. Therefore, it is important that emergency responders and planners have at least a basic understanding of how radioactive material behaves in the environment. This chapter discusses basic meteorology, the characteristics of plumes of airborne radioactive material in the environment, the technical and environmental mechanisms for plume depletion, dose pathways to humans, and applicable standards.[†]

ROUTINE RADIOLOGICAL RELEASES

Commercial nuclear power plants are permitted to release (vent) radioactive gases into the environment during normal, routine operations. Pressurized water reactors typically release from 500 to 1000 μCi/s, primarily the noncondensable radioactive noble gases krypton and xenon. Boiling water reactors release larger amounts of radioactive effluent than pressurized water units do, typically in a range from 1000 to 3000 μCi/s. Permissible effluent (release) concentration limits are given in 10 CFR 20, Appendix B, Table 2. Individual isotope concentrations that would result in 50 mrem total effective dose equivalent (TEDE)[‡] are calculated for a member of the public assumed to stand continuously at the site boundary exposed to radioactive releases for 8760 hours (1 year). Mixtures of radioactive isotopes are calculated using the ratio rule.[§] For most plants, a radiological release at the technical specification limit will not be detectable offsite using standard survey instruments, although a lengthy release would be detectable by the more sensitive environmental thermoluminescent dosimeters; this is a longer term detection, as the dosimeters are typically collected and analyzed quarterly.

In practice, most reactor units keep their ongoing routine releases to between 1% and 10% of their permit limits. Originally, the station technical specifications provided administrative controls to ensure that the plant remained within its permit limits; the effluent release limits may have subsequently been relocated to the Technical Requirements Manual (TRM), Radiological Environmental Technical Specifications (RETS), or the Offsite Dose Calculation Manual (ODCM) in accordance with Generic Letters 89-01 (NRC, 1989d) and 95-10 (NRC, 1995f).[¶] Many technical specification limits are also incorporated into site emergency action levels for recognizing the onset of emergency conditions.

---

[*] It is not universally true that nuclear reactors and nuclear fuel facilities are the only plants that release radioactive material. For example, a coal-fired power plant has a relatively high site area radiation dose due to the radium (^{226}Ra, ^{228}Ra) found in coal, along with the radon (^{222}Rn) that is a daughter decay product of radium. Similarly, radium and some other trace radioactive materials are released in the plant effluent after the coal is burned (assuming no gas capture technology is used).

[†] This chapter primarily addresses airborne releases. It draws heavily upon TID-24190 (Slade, 1968), NUREG/CR-3332 (Till and Meyer, 1983), and from Regulatory Guide 1.145 (NRC, 1979a).

[‡] Individual isotopic limits are based on the maximum permissible dose to the public from plant operations.

[§] The ratio rule is $\Sigma(\chi/\text{limit})_i \leq 1$, where χ (chi) is the concentration of each individual isotope and therefore each (χ/limit) is the fraction of each individual isotope compared to its individual concentration limit. If, for a release consisting of ^{85}Kr, ^{85}Kr^m, ^{133}Xe, ^{135}Xe, and ^{131}I, the respective concentration to limit fractions are 0.6, 0.15, 0.33, 0.2, and 0.05, then the summation has a value of 1.33; Although no single nuclide exceeds its individual release limit, the mixture exceeds limits because the summation is ≥1.0.

[¶] For more information about RETS/ODCM requirements, also see Generic Letter 79-003 (NRC, 1979j); Generic Letter 79-006 (NRC, 1979b); NUREG-0472, *Standard Radiological Effluent Technical Specifications for Pressurized Water Reactors*; and NUREG-0473, *Radiological Effluent Technical Specifications for Boiling Water Reactors*.

Dose assessment activities generally begin when the on-shift or augmented organization recognizes that radioactive material effluent release rates are trending toward the Technical Specification limits. The analysis that is generally referred to as *dose assessment* uses real-time meteorology and plant instrument readings coupled with mathematical models of how gases and particles move through the atmosphere to predict the radiation effects on the affected population, assuming that protective measures are not taken. It is a decision-making tool to help appropriate officials determine the appropriate protective measures for the public. The original assessment models required hand calculations, then pocket-calculator calculations; these took about 10 to 12 minutes to perform even with extensive simplification and extensive use of generic parameter graphs. This essentially became the basis for the industry-standard dose assessment performed every 15 minutes. The 15-minute expectation was never written into regulations or even guidance documents but has shown up in many licensee procedures and may have been incorporated into Institute of Nuclear Power Operation (INPO) guidance in the 1980s.

Dose assessment is performed for the atmospheric or planetary boundary layer, that part of the troposphere that is immediately above the surface. The atmospheric boundary layer extends from the surface upward to a (variable) height of a mile or two, its upper boundary formed by the first atmospheric inversion layer. Below the inversion layer air temperature decreases with altitude, while above the layer temperature increases with altitude; average wind speed generally increases with altitude both above and below the inversion layer. Winds above the inversion layer are disconnected from winds in the atmospheric boundary layer and often have different directions. An inversion layer always exists above the atmospheric boundary layer, although its height changes as a complex function of local air temperature, barometric pressure, humidity, wind direction, and the influence of larger scale zones of low and high pressure. The inversion layer tends to reflect a rising plume back on itself and prevent the transportation of airborne radioactive material into layers above the atmospheric boundary layer. In most dose assessment methodologies, the plume concentration is not reduced to account for the relatively small amount of radioactive material that penetrates the inversion layer. Radioactive material that penetrates the inversion layer eventually falls back into the atmospheric boundary layer and is deposited on the surface in directions and at distances that can be very different from those projected from conditions in the atmospheric boundary layer; emergency preparedness models do not calculate the effect of this radioactive material on population dose or the food chain.*

DISCUSSION AND DEFINITIONS

There is no regulatory definition of the term *plume* as it applies to airborne radioactive material in the environment. An airborne plume can be defined as a mass of air contaminated by radioactive or toxic materials that moves through the airborne and ground surface environment under the influence of ambient meteorology. A liquid plume would be a mass of contaminated water that moves through either a geological formation under the influence of ambient hydrology or a marine (ocean, bay, estuary, river, or lake) environment under the influence of ambient currents and flow path obstructions.

Radiation shine refers to gamma (γ) radiation exposure received at a distance from the plume due to radioactive material contained in a plume. It is typically effective at distances up to 1/2 mile from plume surfaces. The term is also used to refer to a radiation exposure due to standing on a (uniformly) contaminated surface after deposition. Although shine is most often from an overhead

---

* Atmospheric models calculate transport and dispersion in multiple layers of the atmosphere to altitudes of a few hundred kilometers (called *mesoscale* models). Most models of this sort are maintained by research universities and national laboratories; they require simultaneous information about meteorological conditions at many locations across a region and run on supercomputers. The data requirements of these models are clearly outside the capabilities of first responders to an emergency. The 2009 mesoscale model used by the U.S. government is the National Atmospheric Release Advisory Center, part of Lawrence Livermore National Laboratory.

plume, it can also be received by persons ahead of a plume as the front edge moves toward them or by persons along the side of a plume. The half-value layer thickness for a 700-keV γ^* in air is 100 meters; 1/2 mile is therefore about 8 half-value layers of air, which achieves a radiation dose reduction of 99.65%. Shine is not an issue for alpha (α) or beta (β) radiation because of their limited range in air (from fractions of a centimeter to a meter mean free path).

Submersion refers to beta and gamma radiation exposure received due to being surrounded by a radioactive material contained in a plume. Submersion typically includes skin dose (β; skin dose equivalent, SDE), deep dose from external sources (deep-dose equivalent, DDE), and inhalation dose (committed effective dose equivalent, CEDE). Alpha radiation is only a CEDE (lung) component of submersion because it cannot penetrate the skin or lens of the eye.

The long-term[†] radiation dose to humans is delivered through several routes, vectors, or pathways, which include shine, submersion and inhalation, skin contamination, ground contamination, post-plume inhalation of radioactive material resuspended from the ground into air, radioactive decay to longer lived daughter isotopes, and radioactive material that enters the food and water supplies. Reactor licensees are supposed to estimate the overall radiation dose or exposure to the affected population from a radiological accident,[‡] although no standard methods exist to perform this calculation. There is also considerable disagreement among health physicists about whether the concept of population dose (cancer risk per person-rem received) is valid. In any case, a practical integrated dose cannot be calculated until after a substantial number of environmental samples have been collected, so the impact of contaminated food pathways can be included in the estimate.

A release point (e.g., building opening, stack, chimney, safety relief valve) is considered *isolated* if it is located sufficiently far away from plant buildings to be unaffected by building wake effects (usually at least 100 yards).[§] A release point is *elevated* when it is at least twice the height of all nearby structures (2.5 times per Regulatory Guide 1.145) (NRC, 1979a). A release point is considered to be *ground level* if it is not elevated, regardless of its actual height above grade.

The *effective stack height* is the maximum distance above grade reached by the effluent stream. It adds the vertical effluent travel distance to the physical stack height and accounts for vertical momentum driven by ventilation fans, differences between system and atmospheric pressure, and the heat buoyancy of gases. The effective stack height generally cannot be determined in real time and may not be predictable at all; it is not necessarily the same as the greatest visible height of a plume. Regulatory Guide 1.145 states that, as long as the licensee can demonstrate that vertical effluent velocity remains constant during an accident, the licensee may determine and use an appropriate effective stack height for accident calculations; also see Regulatory Guide 1.111 (NRC, 1977c).[¶] Effective stack heights have been measured at between two and ten times the physical stack height. The most common equations for calculating plume rise can be found in Briggs (1969) and Slade (1968). According to NUREG-3332 (Till and Meyer, 1983), the effluent temperature does not contribute significantly to plume rise under most routine conditions, but this may not be true when the effluent is superheated contaminated steam.

A ground-level release point is easier to construct than an elevated chimney and is less of a direct radiation source during normal operations. Its disadvantages include that a radioactive plume touches down almost immediately (very short downwind distance), the plume tends to be partially entrained in building wakes, site personnel receive higher radiation doses, and the plant area is more

---

[*] This is approximately the average effective gamma energy for a gap accident mix in the first few hours after reactor shutdown.

[†] *Long term*, as applied to radiation dose, is typically 50 years.

[‡] Per NUREG-0654 (NRC, 1980c), Element M(4), "Each plan shall establish a method for periodically estimating total population exposure." For methods to estimate long term doses, see Federal Guidance Report Number 11, EPA-520/1-88-020 (USEPA, 1988), and the *FRMAC Assessment Manual*, Volumes 1 and 2 (USDOE, 2003, 2010a).

[§] Do not confuse this use of the term *isolated* with its more normal plant usage meaning *closed* or *plugged*.

[¶] Effective stack height is the parameter used on all dispersion nomograms, graphs, and curves. Formulas for effective stack height and plume rise are discussed in TID-24190 (Slade, 1968, pp. 190–198).

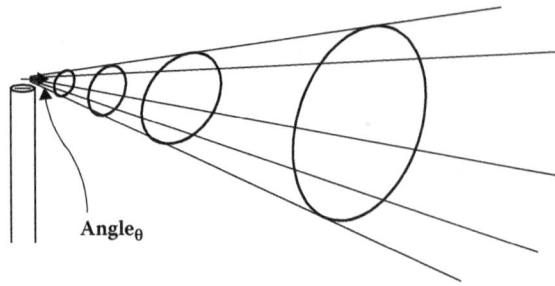

FIGURE 4.1 Plume diagram.

heavily contaminated. Flush-mounted release points on plant buildings under some conditions may cause effluents to initially flow opposite (upwind) from the prevailing surface wind direction due to counterflow along the roof in the turbulent wake above the building.* An elevated release point avoids building wake effects, has longer touch-down distances, and results in more dispersion with less dose. The disadvantages include that the chimney is a vertical line source that can become a radiation hazard to employees, wind speeds at the chimney mouth tend to be higher than at the surface so the plume reaches the public faster, and plumes tend to be more narrow and compact. Under some conditions the plume can be released above an inversion layer. For stability class B, ground touchdown is less than 100 yards for effective stack heights of 50 meters or less, and an effective 100-meter stack has touchdown at about 300 yards (1/6 mile). For stability class D, ground touchdown is less than 100 yards for effective stack heights of 20 meters or less, and an effective 100-meter stack has touchdown at about 900 yards (just over 1/2 mile). For stability class F, an effective 100-meter stack has touchdown at about 2200 yards (1-1/4 miles).

GAUSSIAN DISPERSION EQUATION

When a small discrete volume of airborne radioactive material is released into the atmosphere under completely calm conditions, it forms a ball at the release point that tends to want to spread out (diffuse and disperse) simultaneously in all directions, so that over long enough times the atmosphere is thoroughly mixed and the concentration of radioactive material becomes equal everywhere. When horizontal winds are present the puff cannot move against the wind, so it travels away from the release point in the average wind direction and natural dispersion happens only along the axis perpendicular to the direction of travel, forming an expanding conical shape with its apex at the release point and its long axis parallel to the ground. In a world with purely horizontal winds that are all at a constant speed, the angle at the apex of the cone is determined only by the wind speed (see Figure 4.1).

The Gaussian dispersion equation is shown in Equation 4.1:

$$C(x,y,z) = \frac{Q}{2\pi\pi_y\sigma_z u}\exp\left(-\frac{y^2}{2\sigma_y^2}\right) \times \left\{\exp\left(-\frac{(z-H)^2}{2\sigma_z^2}\right) + \exp\left(-\frac{(z+H)^2}{2\sigma_z^2}\right)\right\} \qquad (4.1)$$

where

C = Ground-level concentration at a receptor point downwind.
Q = Emission rate (μCi/s).
u = Average wind speed (m/s).
x = Downwind distance.
y = Off-centerline distance (m).
z = Vertical direction.

* See Turner (1970, p. 32).

H = Effective stack height (m).

σ_y, σ_z = Standard deviations of wind direction in the horizontal and vertical directions, respectively.

It describes the concentration of radioactive material in such an ideal world, where the horizontal wind direction is nearly constant, the wind directions and speeds at all heights and all distances are both constant and equal, there is no vertical wind flow, and the plume flows over a perfectly smooth and flat frictionless horizontal plane parallel to the wind direction. The equation applies to buoyant plumes, which are at higher average temperature and lower average density than the surrounding atmosphere. The equation is already simplified because it calculates the concentration at the ground surface ($z = 0$) assuming the person (receptor) is farther away than the plume touch-down point.

The Gaussian dispersion equation is derived from statistical fluid flow theory, treating the air as a fluid in motion. Technically, the model is valid only under the following conditions:

1. Diffusion occurs at an equal rate at all locations (called *homogeneity of turbulence*).
2. There is steady-state input of radioactive material (i.e., constant release rate).
3. There are long diffusion times (i.e., several hours).
4. There are steady-state wind conditions (i.e., direction and speed; this is usually true below the mixing height).
5. The only removal mechanism for radioactive material is dispersion.
6. The plume is perfectly reflected from all boundary layers without any losses or transmission (i.e., both the ground surface and the upper boundary layer or mixing layer or inversion layer).

The equation also requires the atmosphere to transport the pollutant but not have the transport processes altered by the pollutant (i.e., no chemical or heat interactions occur between the chemical form of the radioactive material and the atmosphere that change wind flow characteristics). The homogeneity of turbulence requirement leads to a need to characterize the spatial stability of the atmosphere, which essentially allows the derivation of σ_y and σ_z to solve the equation.

Obviously, the Gaussian equation cannot be solved analytically for any real-world event, because the boundary conditions do not apply in the real world. The homogeneity of turbulence condition is essentially never met, none of the input parameters is actually steady state, radioactive material is removed from the plume by several means, reflection is both imperfect and not without losses, and model projection times are not nearly long enough. To make the equation usable, the assumption is made that the volume of atmosphere in which the plume is dispersing is locally stable, stationary, and homogeneous, with σ_y and σ_x dispersion rates that are equal and have a fixed relationship to σ_z.

The Gaussian equation becomes undefined as the wind speed goes to zero (a *calm*). In practice, this occurs when the wind speed falls below the lower response limit of the anemometer. When this occurs, dose assessors should use a site-specific predetermined, non-zero value. NUREG-3332 (Till and Meyer, 1983) suggests an arbitrary value such as 0.1 m/s, or a value that is 1/2 the anemometer measurement threshold (suggested for sensitive instruments with thresholds of 0.5 m/s or less). Another difficulty is that as wind speed becomes sufficiently small, wind direction becomes undefined (or incapable of being measured, which has the same effect). NUREG-3332 suggests that for short-duration (a few minutes) calms, the previous wind direction be continued, and for longer duration periods of calm the historical site-specific wind rose should be used to assign the most probable direction. Under these conditions, the direction vector associated with any positive (i.e., non-zero) environmental measurements obtained using sensitive radiation survey instruments (e.g., µR survey meter, pancake Geiger–Mueller probe, portable Reuter–Stokes pressurized ion chamber) taken 1/4 to 1/2 mile away from the release point may provide the best estimate of wind direction. One problem with Gaussian plume models is that it is impossible to select a single representative wind speed for the surface layer, because of how wind speeds increase with altitude due to surface friction (Turner, 1994).

ATMOSPHERIC STABILITY

Atmospheric turbulence affects the rate at which a plume spreads horizontally and vertically. Turbulence is generated by a combination of air volume parcels moving vertically upward or downward driven by temperature differences between the parcel volume and the overall atmosphere and by local changes in wind direction caused by the interaction of surface winds and terrain (roughness, valleys, obstacles). The atmosphere at any point in time can be described in general terms as being unstable, stable, or neutral. In an unstable atmosphere, air temperature decreases with altitude more rapidly than the dry adiabatic lapse rate,[*] and vertical motion and turbulence are enhanced. In a stable atmosphere, air temperature decreases with altitude less rapidly than the dry adiabatic lapse rate, and vertical motion and turbulence are resisted and damped. In a neutral atmosphere, the air temperature decreases with altitude at nearly the same rate as the dry adiabatic lapse rate.

The atmosphere's stability is of great interest to emergency preparedness practitioners because it controls the width, radioactive material concentration, and meandering of a radioactive plume and has a significant influence on its effective height. Stable atmospheres produce plumes of narrow width, less meander, lower altitudes, and higher concentration (i.e., radiation dose). Unstable atmospheres produce wide plumes with considerable meander and local variability in position, with higher altitudes having the lower average concentration (radiation dose). The meteorological parameters that characterize atmospheric stability are therefore closely tracked by dose assessment staff, by staff responsible for directing environment measurement activities, and by staff responsible for protective action recommendations and decisions.

To simplify technical usage, the stability or instability of the atmosphere has been categorized by six (sometimes seven) representative stability classes, labeled A through F (or G), where class A has the greatest dispersion and most variability in plume position, and class F has the least dispersion and least positional variability. The original definition of six stability classes—from A (most unstable) through F (most stable)—was developed by Pasquill (1961) using concentration data and meteorology from aerosol studies conducted mostly at the Idaho National Engineering Laboratory. Pasquill's original method combined solar radiation (amount of sunshine), wind speed, and degree of cloud cover to determine stability class. Pasquill's work was extended by Gifford (1962), which resulted in the commonly used method based on temperature differences. Regulatory Guide 1.145 (NRC, 1979a) added stability class G to Gifford's method to address stable and low-wind-speed accident conditions. Assumptions are made that stability is the same throughout the atmospheric boundary layer, that no turbulent transfer occurs between layers of dissimilar stability, and that wind direction does not vary with altitude within the atmospheric boundary layer.

To be useful, there has to be a way to select the representative stability class during an event, preferably a general method derived from a measured atmospheric parameter (or set of parameters) that is systematic and reproducible. It is impractical to require each licensee to have measurement systems and meteorological personnel continuously on shift to make real-time physical turbulence measurements; such a measurement requires onsite radar or sounding systems and highly trained personnel to interpret the data. In practice, stability class is inferred either from temperature gradients (ΔT) between points on a meteorological tower or from the rate of change in horizontal wind direction (σ_θ) calculated from the instantaneous (1- to 10-second intervals) wind direction measured at several heights on a meteorological tower. These measurement-based methods replaced an earlier method that relied on subjective judgments about the degree of day and night cloud cover.

NUREG-3332 (Till and Meyer, 1983, p. 2-23) states: "The ΔT method is probably most appropriate when measured over relatively low height intervals, such as from 10 m to 60 m above the ground and for the consideration of releases near ground level. Measurements through deeper atmospheric layers

---

[*] The dry adiabatic lapse rate is the rate at which a volume of air cools as it rises in the atmosphere when that volume contains less water than its saturation capacity, assuming that heat is not allowed to enter or leave the system. This rate is −0.9877°C/100 m (about −0.01°C/m). A volume of air meets the definition of dry as long as its temperature is above the dewpoint temperature.

TABLE 4.1
Determining Stability Class from the Temperature Lapse Rate

Description	Category	ΔT (°C per 100 m)
Extremely unstable	A	$\Delta T < -1.9$
Moderately unstable	B	$-1.9 < \Delta T < -1.7$
Slightly unstable	C	$-1.7 < \Delta T < -1.5$
Neutral	D	$-1.5 < \Delta T < -0.5$
Slightly stable	E	$-0.5 < \Delta T < +1.5$
Moderately stable	F	$+1.5 < \Delta T < +4.0$
Extremely stable	G	$+4.0 < \Delta T$

Source: Data from Turner, D.B., *Workbook of Atmospheric Dispersion Estimates*, U.S. Department of Health, Education, and Welfare, Cincinnati, OH, 1970.

do not properly reflect changes nearer the surface. ΔT is a poor indicator of unstable conditions and should not be considered the best stability indicator for evaluating diffusion from elevated release points (at heights above 100 m). ΔT is probably most useful in estimating turbulent intensity during low-wind-speed, stable conditions because the measurement is unaffected by instrument response to wind speed." Regulatory Guide 1.145 (NRC, 1979a) states that only the ΔT system should be used to determine stability class. ANSI/ANS-2.5-1984, *Standard for Determining Meteorological Information at Nuclear Power Sites*, states that a σ_θ scheme for horizontal stability can be used in conjunction with a ΔT scheme for vertical stability. For other stability classification schemes, see the discussion in NUREG-3332, pp. 2-18 to 2-27. The NRC did not endorse ANSI/ANS-2.5-1984, so it can only be used by reactor licensees after obtaining site-specific approval from the Commission, although it is curious that NUREG-3332 does provide a σ_θ-based method for determining stability class (see Tables 4.1 and 4.2). Note that many reactor licensees do not collect temperature data at a 100-m height and should therefore adjust their site-specific data table appropriately. Also, the many licensees who calculate ΔT in temperature units of °F rather than °C should make appropriate unit adjustments.

TABLE 4.2
Determining Stability Class from the Standard Deviation of the Wind Direction (σ_θ)

Description	Category	σ_θ Value
Extremely unstable	A	$\sigma_\theta > 22.5°$
Moderately unstable	B	$22.5° < \sigma_\theta < 17.5°$
Slightly unstable	C	$17.5° < \sigma_\theta < 12.5°$
Neutral	D	$12.5° < \sigma_\theta < 7.5°$
Slightly stable	E	$7.5° < \sigma_\theta < 3.8°$
Moderately stable	F	$3.8° < \sigma_\theta < 2.1°$
Extremely stable	G	$2.1° < \sigma_\theta$

Source: Data from Till, J.E. and Meyer, H.R., Eds., *Radiological Assessment, A Textbook on Environmental Dose Analysis*, NUREG/CR-3332 (also ORNL-5968), U.S. Nuclear Regulatory Commission, Washington, DC, 1983, p. 2-25.

Studies have been done to characterize the frequency at which the various stability classes occur in nature.[*] Although there is site-specific variability, the results appear to be sufficiently independent of site location (including sea or lake coast sites vs. inland sites) to allow some generalization. Using the ΔT method, class D occurs about one-third of the year, followed somewhat closely by class E, with class A occurring between 15% and 20% of the year. Classes B, C, F, and G together prevail for less than 25% of the year, and classes F and G both are more common than B and C (class B occurs the least frequently). When the σ_θ method is used, the stability class frequencies take on a bell-shaped distribution, with some sites having class D as the most common condition and others having class E predominating. With the σ_θ method, class C goes from being sixth most common to third, occurring about 25% of the year, and classes A, B, F, and G together occur somewhat less than 20% of the year.

Environmental studies show that unstable conditions occur most often during daylight, stable conditions occur mainly at night, and neutral conditions are most likely around dawn and dusk. Stability class A has a bell-shaped frequency distribution curve that rises at about 0600 hours, peaks at about 1200 hours, and tails off at about 1400 to 1500 hours, with a constant (very low) frequency from about 1600 hours through 0600 hours the next day. Stability class C has a frequency curve shaped like a two-humped camel. The first hump occurs between 0400 and 1000 hours, peaking at about 0700 hours, and the second hump occurs between 1400 and 2000 hours, peaking at 1700 to 1800 hours. Stability class G has a two-state frequency curve in which the hours 1700 through 0600 have almost the same probability, and the daylight hours 0700 through 1600 have an occurrence frequency about one-fourth the rest of the day. The time-of-day frequency of stability class B is a mix of the A and C probabilities, and the temporal frequencies of classes E and F strongly resemble the class G probability. Class D, being the most common atmospheric condition overall, has a time-of-day probability curve that is most independent of the hour.

SURFACE ROUGHNESS

Alternatives to the Pasquill–Gifford stability classes include roughness length and the Obukhov length (also called the Monin–Obukhov length). Both are mathematical parameters expressed in units of length (meters), rather than a physical quantity. The roughness length (z_0) is a measure of the friction between a moving plume and the surface over which it flows. The roughness length of an area or object is approximated by its physical height divided by a value from 10 to 30. Roughness lengths less than 0.13 m are considered to be smooth; those greater than 2.5 are rough. Rough surfaces inhibit or prevent laminar flow across them. The roughness length is used to compute the friction velocity, which is a component of the Obukhov length, which represents the height above which buoyant turbulence is more significant than mechanical turbulence.[†] The Obukhov length is generally used in non-Gaussian dispersion models to describe atmospheric stability; it is positive for stable atmospheres, negative for unstable ones, and at or near zero for neutral ones. The Richardson number describing atmospheric flow is given by height (elevation) divided by Obukhov length. The Obukhov length is generally assumed to be constant in the surface layer, at least on the scales normally applicable to nuclear power plant dose projection.

VARIABILITY IN PLUME POSITION

Plume meander is defined as the curved, nonlinear, non-idealized path actually taken by a radioactive plume as it is acted upon by atmospheric forces, as compared to the idealized straight-line instantaneous or time-averaged dominant wind direction. As a plume meanders downwind, the

[*] For one example, see Sejkora (2005). This paper discussed the annual and temporal frequencies of stability classes measured over 3 years at the Calvert Cliffs, Nine Mile Point, and Pilgrim stations.
[†] See AMS (2000).

combination of small continuous shifts in real plume location (centerline) coupled with constant lateral (horizontal or *y*-direction) diffusion tends to fill in gaps caused by the curves in the path. Because of this, the plume footprint looks more and more like a smooth conic figure as the averaging time increases (a figure that gets proportionally wider with increasing downwind direction) and the radioactive concentration becomes more uniform. The plume half-width* is most narrow for stability class F and most wide for stability class A. Even when the average wind direction is stable, the true or actual plume path forms an irregular curve centered on the average direction of travel; although this plume is often drawn as a sine curve, the actual path is more complicated and unpredictable. Each bend or curve in its path is caused by a localized eddy current, where an eddy is a localized, self-contained zone of turbulence whose characteristics differ from those of the overall atmosphere—for example, the bulk properties of the general wind field (a dust devil in the desert is a good example of a localized eddy). Eddies arise from irregularities in terrain (e.g., valleys, hills) and from temperature gradients produced by differences in surface heating and cooling rates; the factors that influence this are surface roughness (e.g., buildings, vegetation cover, paving) and surface reflectivity (e.g., water, sand, rock).

An eddy of about the plume width or larger is required to change the overall direction of the plume. The path curvature is related to the lateral distance between the plume centerline and the center of the eddy. As a plume moves farther downwind, larger eddies are required to affect its course. Eddies on the order of the plume half-width or smaller tend to disrupt the internal structure of a plume and tear it apart; in theory, an eddy of the correct size at the correct location could cause a plume to split. A small eddy located far downwind has little or no effect on the time-averaged concentration or, therefore, the calculated dose. Eddies are sufficiently coherent that they can be an effective barrier to diffusion. The plume centerline does not generally remain at its release height. For ground-level releases, the plume lifts off the surface, becoming buoyant. In the absence of buoyant turbulence, elevated releases tend to sink.

PUFF RELEASES

The protective measures schemes used by licensee and offsite authorities often distinguish between puff releases and longer term, more continuous, stream-like releases. A *puff* is modeled as a single, discrete ball or sphere of contaminated air, with a center point that moves according to the dominant winds while simultaneously smoothly expanding in radius according to the diffusion equation (the inhibiting effect of trying to disperse against the wind is ignored; in reality, the puff would look more like an expanding cigar truncated on the upwind side). A radioactive release is a puff if it is completely contained in one time-averaging period and both the preceding and following time averaging periods have no associated radioactive release (or at least none above routine operating levels). This definition works well for 15-minute time-averaged data but would become problematic if practical time averaging were available on the hour or multi-hour time scale. One possible solution is to require that a puff release cannot last longer than the time allowed to recognize the release, for the licensee to transmit protective action recommendations to offsite authorities, and for the authorities to initiate public warning—a time of about 30 minutes. A puff release is most likely to result from the rupture of a liquid or gas storage tank or from a system failure where operators can readily close an isolation valve. It can also result from operators intentionally cycling vents to control containment pressure or the periodic opening and closing of a pressure relief value around its pressure-control threshold. Because puff durations are typically much shorter than the time required to implement an evacuation of the public, the preferred protective action for puffs is shelter-in-place, because building walls provide more shielding and radiation dose reduction than do automobiles or being outdoors.

---

* The plume half-width is the lateral (perpendicular from the direction of travel) distance at which the radioactive material concentration is 50% of the centerline concentration; this distance is at about 0.67σ for the Gaussian (normal) distribution.

PARAMETER TIME AVERAGING

The time over which meteorological parameters is averaged has a significant impact on the dose values that are calculated by an atmospheric dispersion model. Longer averaging times better meet the Gaussian equation boundary conditions. The averaging times necessary to meet Gaussian boundary conditions lengthen in parallel with the downwind distances at which projections are made; to obtain the most accurate results, averaging times should be at least as long as the time required for the plume to traverse the area of interest. One implication of this is that Gaussian plume projections using 15-minute time-averaged parameters should not be regarded as reliable for distances of 5 miles or more, and projections for a distance of 2 to 5 miles along the plume centerline vector may not be highly reliable at low to moderate wind speeds.

Most licensees average wind direction[*] over a very short time (less than 15 seconds), an intermediate time (either 1 minute or 5 minutes), and a long time (15 minutes[†]). Other meteorological parameters, such as wind speed, are usually only reported at very short or intermediate times and are not time averaged. Regulatory Guide 1.145 (NRC, 1979a) discusses the use of hourly averaging of wind speed, wind direction, and measures of atmospheric stability; however, this is in reference to radiological consequence modeling for plant licensing purposes, not for real-time accident assessment. Regulatory Guide 1.23 (NRC, 2007c) discusses the time averaging of meteorological parameters in Section 6, which states in part,

> The digital sampling of data should be at least once every 5 seconds. The digital data should be (1) compiled as 15-minute average values for real-time display in the appropriate emergency response facilities (e.g., control room, technical support center, and emergency operations facility), and (2) compiled and archived as hourly values for use in historical climatic and dispersion analyses. The hourly values may be generated by (1) averaging all the samples taken during the hour, (2) using one 15-minute value per hour (if the same 15-minute period is used each hour), or (3) averaging all of the 15-minute values recorded during the hour. For precipitation, the hourly value should represent the total amount of precipitation (water equivalent) measured during the hour.

With regard to emergency response purposes, this revision also states in Section 8:

> Special Considerations to Support Emergency Preparedness: In order to identify rapidly changing meteorological conditions for use in performing emergency response dose consequence assessments, 15-minute average values should be compiled for real-time display in the appropriate emergency response facilities (e.g., control room, technical support center, and emergency operations facility). All the meteorological channels required for manual input to the dose assessment models should be available and presented in a format compatible for input to the models (e.g., wind speed is displayed in the proper units; atmospheric stability is displayed as a ΔT value versus a Pasquill stability class, etc.).

Although the above statements are not specifically limited to wind direction, most licensees have not revised their regulatory commitments from Revision 0 (1979) to Revision 1 (1982) of Regulatory Guide 1.145, and 15-minute averages are not commonly available for any other meteorological parameter.

Mixing real-time and time-averaged parameter data is a continuing problem when calculating Gaussian plumes because true Gaussian models are steady state with respect to both meteorology and source term, not only with respect to a subset of meteorological parameters. No licensee calculates time-averaged release rates, which have instantaneous or very short reporting times and can exhibit great period-to-period variability or bounce (monitor values may appear more stable

---

[*] By convention, wind direction is always stated in compass direction *from*, where true north is always 0°/360°, so that a wind out of the northwest would be from 315°.

[†] NUREG-0654, Appendix 2, "Meteorological Criteria for Emergency Preparedness at Operating Nuclear Power Plants," requires that Class A models shall use actual 15-minute average meteorology (NRC, 1980c, p. 2-3).

during exercises because most plant computer simulations are limited to no shorter than 1-minute time increments). Although Gaussian models are essentially always run using time-averaged wind direction, they are not typically run using time-averaged wind speed (most licensee data systems do not calculate a time-averaged wind speed parameter). Some models require air temperature data to calculate effective stack height, and although this parameter is also not time averaged it typically changes sufficiently slowly (no faster than the time-averaging period for wind direction) that modeling is not affected.

In the author's opinion, most reactor licensees using Gaussian plume models have not been provided sufficient procedural guidance for selecting a representative release rate and may not have adequately addressed the mixing of real-time and averaged parameters in training for their dose assessment staff; this problem does not apply in the same way to licenses using puff-vector-type models. The current radiological release rate does not always lead to the best-estimate offsite dose, particularly when the release rate is cyclical or highly variable. When the release rate is decreasing, performing dose assessments based on the current value generally leads to underestimating the overall dose to the public over the entire exposure period. The best-estimate release rate for a Gaussian plume is always obtained by dividing the integrated area under the curve formed by the release rate graph by the total elapsed time of the release, and this is almost always impractical to do effectively while the release is actually in progress, because although plant computers effectively display parameter trends and current values they lack the ability to calculate an integrated parameter value. When the release rate is increasing from its pre-accident value, the current/maximum value should be used to ensure that an upper bound is calculated for the offsite dose. When the release rate reaches a plateau, the best estimate is obtained by multiplying the maximum release rate by the ratio of the time the rate has held at the plateau value to the overall release time.* When the release rate is dropping, the best dose estimate is obtained by using the release rate that is midway between the peak value and the current value. For a cyclical release (e.g., a sine curve caused by a cycling safety relief valve), the best estimate is the average between the peak and valley values. For more complicated combinations of peaks and valleys, the best estimate is obtained by taking the average of the highest peak release rate and the lowest valley in the release rate curve (excluding the initial, pre-accident value).

DOWNWIND DISPERSION

Diffusion is the physical process that results in the average concentration of airborne radioactive material being reduced due to migration from regions of high concentration into regions of lower concentration (or no concentration). Pure diffusion takes place when there is an absence of outside forces (i.e., no wind field) and is governed by random Brownian motion. One can draw a parallel that diffusion is driven by an internal pressure, somewhat similar to partial pressures in gaseous mixtures. *Dispersion* is the combined effect of all the physical processes that act to spread or disperse airborne radioactive material into regions in which it is not initially present, including processes that remove or eliminate radioactive material from the plume. A major component of dispersion is the downwind transport of the airborne radioactive material under the influence of the wind field. The reason why the Gaussian equation does not contain a term for σ_x is that the diffusion time in the *x*-direction (downwind) is long compared to the transport time.

Dispersion factors (see Table 4.3) are usually given in terms of $\chi u/Q$ because the ground-level radioisotope concentration is equal to $(\chi u/Q) \times$ (release rate, in µCi/s) × (wind speed, in m/s). The dose equation is linear with respect to $(\chi u/Q)$. Notice that class F plumes produce about 100 times as much dose as class A plumes. For class B through class E plumes, the dose at 10 miles is 0.5% to 1% of the radiation dose delivered at the site boundary.

---

* This ratio goes toward 1 if the plateau release rate is maintained over a long enough period of time.

TABLE 4.3

Dispersion Factors as a Function of Stability Class and Downwind Distance

Distance (miles)	Class A	Class B	Class C	Class D	Class E	Class F
0.5	6.6E-6	3.0E-5	7.6E-5	2.1E-4	4.2E-4	9.6E-4
1	1.0E-6	7.4E-6	2.1E-5	7.0E-5	1.4E-4	3.3E-4
2	5.5E-7	1.9E-6	6.1E-6	2.4E-5	5.0E-5	1.2E-4
3	3.9E-7	8.4E-7	2.9E-6	1.3E-5	2.8E-5	6.8E-5
4	3.0E-7	4.8E-7	1.7E-6	8.5E-6	1.9E-5	4.6E-5
5	2.5E-7	3.3E-7	1.2E-6	6.1E-6	1.4E-5	3.3E-5
7	1.9E-7	2.5E-7	6.3E-7	3.7E-6	8.4E-6	2.2E-5
10	1.4E-7	1.8E-7	3.3E-7	2.3E-6	5.1E-6	1.4E-5
15	9.9E-8	1.3E-7	1.8E-7	1.2E-6	3.1E-6	8.4E-6

Source: Data from Turner, D.B., *Workbook of Atmospheric Dispersion Estimates*, U.S. Department of Health, Education, and Welfare, Cincinnati, OH, 1970.

MIXING LAYERS

The mixing height is defined as the vertical height (altitude) of the atmospheric boundary layer over which an emitted or entrained inert nonbuoyant tracer will be mixed (by turbulence) within a time scale of about one hour or less. Other terms that mean essentially the same include *inversion lid*, *inversion height*, and *limit of mixing*. When a plume of radioactive material remains far below the mixing height, it shows a Gaussian vertical concentration distribution, truncated at the bottom by reflection from the ground that exhibits a typical distribution tail at the top. As the plume continues to rise and the plume top reaches the mixing height, reflection from the inversion layer combines with ground reflection to widen and lower the peak concentration and to eliminate the tails. Theoretically, given sufficient release duration and mixing time, the vertical concentration of airborne radioactive material will become equal throughout the mixing layer. Those atmospheric layers above the mixing zone are usually characterized by relatively little turbulence and variance. A temperature inversion generally marks the boundary between successive layers in the atmosphere.

A *fumigation* or *inversion* condition occurs when the mixing height is the same as, or is only a short distance above, the physical stack height. A semi-fumigation condition occurs when the mixing height is sufficiently below the effective stack height. This very low mixing height lid rapidly forces the plume to the ground (faster/closer than would be expected from the stability class acting alone) and results in very complete turbulent mixing in which the average (vertical) concentration of the plume is the same between the ground and the mixing height. Fumigation causes the highest radiation doses to occur close to the release point (i.e., onsite). Phenomena that result in inversions include (1) the Earth's surface rapidly radiating heat on a clear night so the ground surface and the adjacent air layer cool faster than does air at higher altitude, because the ground has a greater heat capacity than does air; and (2) an advection inversion resulting from a surface or horizontal inflow of cold air into an area of higher temperature, such as air blowing across cold ocean waters and cooling before reaching land, then displacing warmer surface air.

When the mixing height is below the physical stack height, the plume is constrained and reflected upward by the inversion lid. The heavier particulate material breaks through the barrier before the halogens and the gases, but at a distance further downwind than would be expected. The ground deposition pattern becomes stratified by particle density, instead of all of the isotopes being well mixed together as would be expected from a plume in contact with the surface.

EFFECTS OF BUILDINGS

The Gaussian equation describes the concentration of a steady-state plume moving through an unobstructed atmosphere. One way the real world differs from an idealized environment is in the size and variety of buildings that interact with a plume.* Large buildings can have a significant impact on transport patterns close to the site and cast shadows that affect downfield transport. The combination of a depressed concentration of radioactive material immediately downwind behind a building, along with the vortexes produced by horizontal flows around the building, is referred to as the *building wake*. Building wakes produce local distortions to plumes which disappear at sufficient distances downwind as the plume reattaches to itself.

The expected ground-level plume concentration at 10 km (6.2 miles) downwind differs by factors of two to three, depending on whether or not building wake effects are considered (Walsh and Jones, 2002). Because radiation dose is linear with respect to radioactive material concentration, this implies that the delivered radiation dose varies by similar factors. Protective action recommendations and decisions are generally made based on projections and measurements of TEDE and thyroid CDE at downwind distances of 2 miles, 5 miles, and 10 miles. Because building wake effects result in actual concentrations being lower than would be expected without the building in place, a protective action recommendation based on a dose analysis that does not include building wake effects could lead to prematurely taking protective measures for the 5- to 10-mile region of the emergency planning zone.

When a plume impinges on a building (assuming a wind direction not too different from perpendicular to the building face because accurate calculations become even more complicated when the wind direction is toward a corner), the plume is separated into several zones:

1. At a height sufficiently above the building there is no effect on the plume (perhaps twice to three times building height).
2. Along the front edge of the building roof, the wind vertically deflected from the building face lifts and forms a bubble whose vertical height depends strongly on wind speed and whose depth depends on wind speed, angle of attack, and the details of roof construction (e.g., flat roof vs. inclined upward or downward); inside the bubble, a clockwise vortex sets up parallel to the face. The plume is carried over the bubble and depending on the building's depth may or may not touch down on the roof. Any persons (or an air sampler) on the building roof would measure radiation shine but a substantially reduced (or perhaps no) concentration of radioactive material.
3. Winds deflect horizontally around the building face and form several local layers or zones in which the winds spiral or corkscrew around a horizontal line parallel to the ground. There may be several of these zones which set in front of the building (upwind direction) and run parallel to each other while maintaining their separation. These zones of horizontal flow wrap around the building but are pushed out and away from the building's sides by building shadow (if the incident wind direction is not perfectly perpendicular to the building face) and by downward vertical flow off the building roof (at the ends of the vortex bubble). This zone of split flow (some carried to the left side of the building, some to the right) comes together and reattaches at a distance behind the building determined by building height, wind speed, and incident wind direction. The concentration of radioactive material and associated radiation dose in these zones could be higher than the conditions if

---

* *Meteorology and Atomic Energy* (Slade, 1968) states in Section 5-5: "The use of conventional diffusion formulas for the calculation of concentration fields produced by sources on or near buildings often gives misleading answers. Such formulas contain the implicit assumptions that the flow field has straight streamlines that are parallel to each other and the ground. Although this is reasonably accurate for flow over level uniformly rough ground, we know that flow near buildings contains curved streamlines, sharp velocity discontinuities, and highly nonhomogeneous and nonisotropic turbulence."

the building were not present, as radioactive material diverted horizontally by the building face is added to radioactive material carried by the those elements of the plume that do not impact the building.

4. Behind the building is a cavity zone in which the winds are not synchronized or attached to the overall dominant wind flow. For a building with less depth, the roof vortex bubble extends downwind past the roof edge, and the cavity is defined by the reattachment of the side flows around the building and downward flow that no longer has the bubble to maintain it. For a building with more depth, the roof vortex bubble is not as deep as the building, so the cavity length strongly depends on roof height. In this area, there may be localized upward vertical spiral flows. The cavity zone is approximately five times as long as the average building height for winds perpendicular to the building's face and becomes less deep as wind impacts at shallower angles up to about 30° from perpendicular, after which corner effects begin. Winds that impact on a corner produce a deeper cavity zone whose size is proportional to the total surface area of both the building faces adjacent to the corner. Inside the cavity zone, concentrations of radioactive material are significantly reduced from the average plume concentration and are highly non-uniform, and in some locations the concentration may be zero. Except very close to very large buildings, direct radiation measurements (shine) made inside the cavity zone would be somewhat reduced compared to measurements made in the plume but not significantly so.

5. Downwind past the cavity zone the several split or diverted plume flows come back together and the plume concentration again becomes uniform. Immediately past the cavity zone is a zone of turbulent wake as disconnected vertical and horizontal flows interact in a complex way before being smoothed out by the dominant wind flow (plume). The concentration of radioactive material in this zone is non-uniform. Direct radiation measurements in this zone should be nearly the same as in the uniform plume.

Building wakes can produce a peculiar and counterintuitive phenomenon if a plume is released into (becomes entrained in) the cavity zone—for example, when the release point is a vent flush with the roof line and located in the roof vortex zone. Because of eddy counter flow along the sides of the building it is possible for radioactive material to migrate in the upwind direction along the windward face of the building where it otherwise would not be found. This effect is more likely at lower wind speeds. The interaction of several building wakes located closely together is not well understood. This phenomenon may be of practical significance because upwind migration may cause some released radioactive material to become entrained in building fresh air intakes, such as for the reactor control room or site emergency response facilities, exposing plant emergency workers to radioactive material. Plant repair and survey teams would normally be expected to move about the reactor site by routes that avoid entering the radioactive plume to limit radiation dose to emergency workers; plant staff who are not familiar with the upwind flow phenomenon may not take this potential source of dose into account when routing emergency teams.

A plume impinging on a circular structure produces smoother horizontal diversionary flow than from a rectangular structure, where it more closely follows the building wall structure. This is particularly true for cylindrical structures much taller than their diameter, such as typical pressurized water reactor containment buildings. The associated building wake cavity is parabolic in shape and slightly wider than the building at its widest point, and it is shorter than the cavity from a rectangular building with an incident face the same width as the (circular building's) diameter. The circular cavity may be about three-quarters as deep as the cavity from a similarly sized rectangular building. The cavity from a cylindrical structure also differs from a rectangular structure in that the cavity contains two counter-rotating horizontal vortexes, separated by a line parallel to the wind direction going through the building midpoint. If the release point is on the roof of a cylindrical structure, radioactive material can be found upwind at the structure's base at distances from one-third to one-half the building diameter.

Cylindrical natural draft water cooling towers are not uncommon structures at power plant sites; these towers are about 350 feet in diameter and 500 feet tall with a several-story-tall base structure about 700 feet across. They are sufficiently tall compared to the effective release height that the downwind cavity depth and shape are solely a function of tower and base structure diameters. Because these towers are so wide and are located so close to the engineered release points, they have significant impact on plume characteristics when the wind blows toward them. A cooling tower is wider than the impinging plume under some stability class conditions, especially class D and higher. When a plume impinges on a cooling tower, a component splits and travels around the tower and forms a classical parabolic wake before the horizontal plume section reattaches. However, a natural circulation tower exerts a strong suction flow through the base structure while it operates, such that a component of the plume is entrained in the suction flow, traverses the tower, and is ejected with the tower's effective release height. To the author's knowledge, there is no analytical method for estimating the fraction of plume activity that becomes entrained in the tower. With effective tower stack heights of 1500 to 5000 feet, this release component is likely to be above the atmospheric mixing layer, with a wind direction one to three compass sectors (20° to 70°) different from the surface winds. This secondary plume will be initially reflected upward from the inversion boundary, and plume surface touchdown may not occur for 5 or more miles along the new wind direction vector.

Contemporary dose assessment models used at sites with natural draft cooling towers do not model plume entrainment into the tower air flow and are incapable of simultaneously modeling a surface plume and a plume in the inversion layer. Cooling towers are not constructed with installed radiation monitors, so plant personnel have no means to identify or quantify the entrainment of radioactive material into the tower's air stream. Plants that utilize natural draft towers do not have meteorological instruments that measure wind speed and direction at or above the tower height. While a cooling tower operates, there is a substantial amount of water moving vertically within the tower, and it would be expected that particulate radioactive material in the plume would be virtually eliminated by the impact of water flowing downward through the tower and leaving a release consisting of halogens and radioactive noble gases. The plume reduction fraction (effectiveness) of this process has not been investigated.

Tall, solid fencing creates a vertical vortex similar to the face of a rectangular building and could affect a plume if located sufficiently near the release point. The downwind cavity from such a fence is about 1-1/2 times the fence height tall by about 12 times fence height deep, so for a 6-foot fence the depletion zone is 9 to 12 feet tall by about 75 feet deep.

TERRAIN EFFECTS

The Gaussian equation calculates the concentration of a steady-state plume moving across an empty, flat geometric plane that is completely smooth and has no variation in elevation. This situation does not hold for any real site, even on the flattest of Midwest plains or on the open Western prairie. The term *terrain effects* broadly describes any process that influences or changes the mean centerline position of a plume from its theoretical wind vector when the process is related to variations in terrain elevation or terrain type (e.g., land vs. water). Terrain can also be characterized as being simple, of intermediate complexity, or complex.[*] Terrain with vertical variation no higher than the physical stack height is considered simple, terrain with height variation no higher than the effective stack height has intermediate complexity, and terrain whose height varies more than the plume height (effective stack height plus any plume rise or buoyancy) is considered complex. Terrain effects can change the expected path or course of a plume without affecting concentration or dose rate; can concentrate the plume in unexpected locations, leading to higher than projected dose, deposition, and contamination rates; or can unexpectedly disperse the plume leading to lower than projected

---

[*] For additional information see, among others, Egan and Snyder (2002), Wallace and Hobbs (2006), and Whiteman (2000).

dose, deposition, and contamination rates. Frequently, all of these effects occur essentially simultaneously at different locations along the plume length. There are no rapid or simple techniques or rules of thumb available that allow an analyst to estimate the effect of terrain on a particular plume, particularly when working with a Gaussian plume model.

The plume's position is most affected by slope, obstacles, and channels, and real terrain often consists of combinations of these characteristics. Although slopes are often associated with obstacles, this is not always true. Slopes tend to affect plume position because they are frequently associated with diurnal flow patterns, in which predominant winds are upslope (anabatic, flowing toward the highest point) during daylight hours and downslope (flowing toward the lowest point) at night. Downslope flow is often accompanied by an inversion layer at or near the ridge top. These flow patterns are largely the result of differences in solar heating during the day and differences in (thermal) cooling at night. This is a predictable and stable pattern that can dominate all other wind patterns at a site and is typical of canyons, passes, and river valleys with steep or high walls. Although there is no good definition of a *valley*, the defining ridges should be at least twice the effective stack height for strong channeling effects to occur. The cross-distance of the valley floor should not be more than a few miles. The nighttime downslope winds often are at a higher wind speed than are the daylight upslope winds. A weaker, slower, and more dispersed opposite counterflow often develops above a valley rim for both up-valley and down-valley winds, and, if the plume escapes, the valley carries it along the opposite direction vector.

Obstacles typically include individual hills, bluffs (especially along rivers), ridges, and mountains. Obstacles act as impediments that, when they are small enough, separate and divert surface flow, rather like a large boulder in a swiftly flowing river. Surface flow cannot divert around a sufficiently wide obstacle (e.g., perpendicular to the wind direction vector), such as a tall ridge many miles long; instead, the wind flows up and over the top, causing an overshoot and eddy along the obstacle's crest, similar to that along the roof line of a wide rectangular building. Individual hills act like very large buildings, forming a downwind wake, leeward cavity, or zone of turbulence in which plume concentrations are depressed and beyond which the plume generally reattaches and radioactive material concentrations are similar to upwind of the obstacle. Ridges and bluffs, if sufficiently high, cause a significant diversion of the plume (perhaps as much as 50% of the concentration) in flows along and parallel to the face and can create cavity zones along the crest, due to the wind being required to arc to flow over the obstacle.

Tracer* studies suggest that the atmosphere over bodies of water is less stable for the same ΔT value than would be predicted by standard stability class tables, and that other methods of estimating stability (e.g., U.S. Geological Survey method, or σ_θ) may be more accurate in characterizing over-water atmospheric stability. Dabberdt (1986) states in part, "Inland, stability frequently is established by thermal stratification that can be attributed to temporal variations of the temperature of the earth–air interface relative to a nominally steady air temperature well above the surface. The overwater situation is essentially the opposite (i.e., near-constant water temperatures and variable air temperatures) … the delta-T scheme of the NRC is also inherently faulty; in this case the role of mechanical forces is ignored in characterizing stability." Skupniewicz (1986) also concluded that the Pasquill–Gifford stability class models (the method required by the NRC) does not accurately characterize dispersion over water. The effective roughness length of a large lake, bay, or ocean is shorter (the surface is rougher and has stronger mechanical interactions with the atmosphere) at the same wind speed than for land because of wind-driven waves and swells. Plume meander also causes greater horizontal dispersion without strongly affecting vertical dispersion and more strongly affects over-water plumes than over-land plumes (where the channeling effect of terrain may overcome meander).

---

* The case of plume travel over ocean without sea breeze effects is not discussed because there are essentially no current commercial reactor sites located on bay shores where such plumes could be expected to return to land. For discussions of plume dispersion over water see, for example, Skupniewicz and Schacher (1986), Spangler and Johnson (1989), and Dabberdt (1986).

SEA AND LAND BREEZES

The onshore and offshore wind patterns that can occur along the coasts of very large bodies of waters are a special kind of terrain effect. The direction of these winds is driven by the temperature difference between water and land, and a smaller body of water is necessary to establish the pattern as the water–land temperature difference increases. These conditions are most typical along the ocean shores and the Great Lakes and are more frequent during the summer than during other seasons.

A *sea breeze* is a wind blowing off the water toward land, replacing columns of inland air that are rapidly rising because of stronger daylight surface heating of the land as compared with water. A sea breeze is almost always accompanied by a very low mixing height (fumigation lid), which increases the radiation dose close to the reactor site. Inland penetration is 3 to 5 miles where terrain permits, as determined by the distance at which the warming effect of the land is sufficient to dissipate the low fumigation layer. A plume introduced under the fumigation lid becomes entrained in the column of heated air that breaks through the fumigation layer. The high-altitude return flow (back toward the sea) is generally at a higher wind speed than the onshore flow and has a directional offset because wind directions at altitude are different than at the surface. When it is over the ocean, the plume cools and falls to the surface, where it becomes entrained again in the onshore winds, repeating the pattern some distance from the original plume source. The winding pattern (see Figure 4.2) can be either up-coast or down-coast, depending on the wind direction, creating complex corkscrew patterns that are not readily predictable by analytical methods. This combination of onshore flow, vertical lofting, offset return flow, cooling, and entrainment creates plume stripes separated by areas with essentially no contamination and no population dose. The centerline distance between successive "stripes" is on the order of 1/2 to 1 mile. In general, the radiation dose (concentration, contamination) delivered in stripes successively farther from the source decreases due to decay time and dispersion, but not in a readily predictable ratio compared to the original plume concentration.

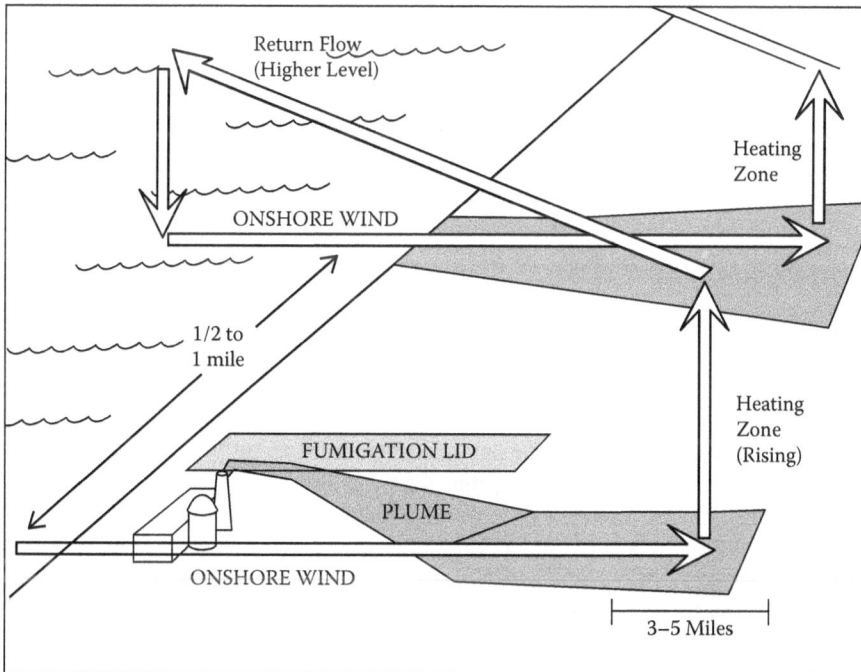

FIGURE 4.2   Illustration of the sea breeze/lake breeze plume pattern.

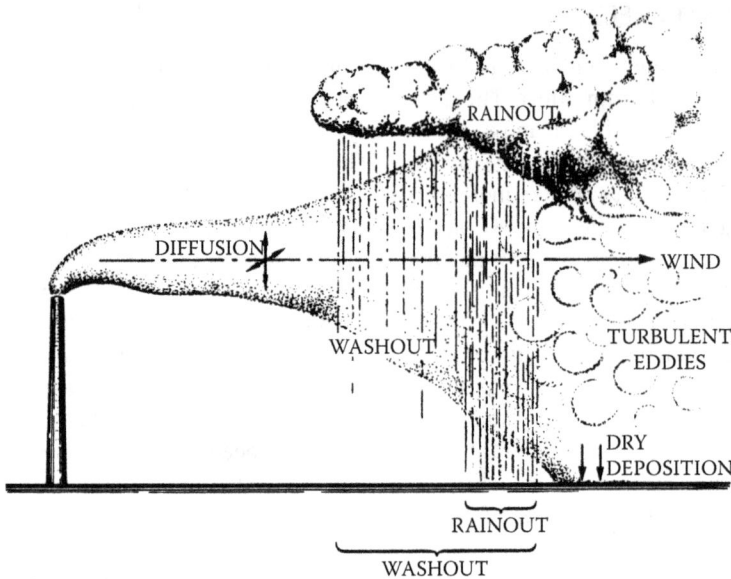

FIGURE 4.3 Illustration of processes for plume depletion. (From Till, J.E. and Meyer, H.R., Eds., *Radiological Assessment, A Textbook on Environmental Dose Analysis*, NUREG/CR-3332, U.S. Nuclear Regulatory Commission, Washington, DC, 1983.)

A *land breeze* is essentially the identical effect occurring at night, with the coastal winds flowing out to sea, where the lofting is driven by the warmer water and the cooling occurs inland over the cooling land. Although the circulation pattern is opposite for the land breeze situation, there is no significant difference in plume path and contamination zones. Shair et al. (1982) estimated that pollutants carried out to sea by a land breeze have mean stay times between 10 and 16 hours before being returned to land on the next day's sea breeze.

To provide representative meteorological measurements for the entire area of interest, multiple measurement sites are needed: one site at a shoreline location (to provide a 10-meter stack height/ plume height wind speed), several additional inland sites perpendicular to the orientation of the shoreline to provide wind speed within the thermal barrier, and a method to estimate the thermal barrier altitude height. Where terrain in the vicinity of the shoreline is complex, measurements at additional locations, such as bluff tops, may also be necessary

MECHANISMS REDUCING PLUME CONCENTRATION

A plume of radioactive material released from a point source (e.g., a stack, vent, chimney) becomes undetectable using the most sensitive portable survey and sampling equipment at some range downwind from the release point. At some additional distance it becomes undetectable even with standard radiochemistry analysis methods (at standard counting times for environmental analysis). This occurs because of processes that act to reduce the plume concentration to essentially zero. These processes include diffusion, radioactive decay, dry deposition (settling), turbulent eddies, washout, rainout, plateout, and the trapping of plume materials on vegetation and other surfaces, as illustrated in Figure 4.3.

Diffusion alone will eventually result in the plume extending to near infinity at a nearly zero average concentration (e.g., below detection limits), although this occurs after a very long time and at a long distance away from the reactor site.* Because one of the Gaussian assumptions is that the

---

* For example, radioactive iodine released into the atmosphere during the Chernobyl accident could be readily detected in air and rainwater samples collected in central North America for about 20 days after the accident. (During the 1986 accident, the author operated an Environmental Radiation Ambient Monitoring System station in Iowa.)

plume is an essentially weightless aerosol that does not interact with its environment, the model must be adjusted for gravitational settling. Settling affects the larger and heavier particulates first, resulting in a ground deposition pattern with a higher relative abundance of heavy fission products (e.g., ^{60}Co, ^{137}Cs, ^{54}Mn, ^{90}Sr) closer to the release point as compared to the deposition pattern at points farther away. Radioactive decay is a significant removal mechanism; for a 10-mph wind, more than half of the released material with a half-life of 30 minutes (or less) will be removed by decay alone before it arrives at the emergency planning zone boundary.

Dry deposition occurs in the bottom few meters of the plume, where the radioactive material comes into direct contact with the surface and obstacles (e.g., buildings, structures, trees). At very small particle sizes, Brownian motion dominates the settling process; for very large particle sizes, particle weight is most important. Dry settling is usually discussed in term of a *deposition velocity* (v_t), expressed in units of m/s. This is a descriptive parameter and should not be understood as an actual, measurable velocity associated with any component or particles within the plume. Because of its definition, it happens to have units that can also describe a physical velocity. Deposition velocity is defined as the ratio of the deposition rate for a particle of specified diameter (often 1 or 10 μm) to the ground-level air concentration of that particle; for some applications, this parameter is divided into total (t), vegetation (v), and dry (d, bare ground) components.

The deposition velocity is largely determined experimentally from air samples collected at 1 meter above the surface, compared to collected surface samples, and reported values in the literature are generally between 1.0E-02 and 1.0E-06 m/s.[*] The distribution of velocities has an observed minimum (lowest rate of deposition) for particles 0.3 μm in diameter, and the rate of deposition increases for both larger and smaller particle diameters. For particulate plumes, the surface roughness also influences the deposition velocity, with increased deposition occurring with increased vegetation cover and structures. Deposition onto surfaces with significant vegetation cover is about five times higher than deposition onto bare soils. There is considerable uncertainty about the deposition values that should be used in models because observed deposition velocities vary by factors of ten or more for the same meteorological conditions, and similar studies often report different deposition velocities. Under most conditions, the deposition velocity also changes with downwind distance from the source, with the highest deposition rate being closer to the release point. The rate falls off semi-exponentially with increasing distance because the settling rate is proportional to the plume concentration, which also decreases with distance. Chemical reactivity also affects deposition rates, with inactive or inert material depositing at slower (or less) rates than do active materials (such as halogens) (Slade, 1978). NUREG-3332 also notes that, because deposition velocity is a function of wind speed, slower deposition rates are expected as wind speed increases. The effect of wet surfaces on settling and deposition velocity is unclear, such as a plume released after a passing rain (where the plume is essentially dry and does not experience washout/rainout).

Turbulent eddies are entrained in the overall plume and tend to enhance diffusion, resulting in local concentrations of radioactive material that are lower than average concentrations at the same downwind distance. The effect of eddies is somewhat dependent on particle size and weight, with lighter and smaller particles responding faster and to a greater degree than do heavier and larger particles.

Washout and *rainout* are terms for essentially the same physical process, distinguished by different endpoints (rainout may also be called *sweepout*). In both cases, the plume is affected by rain falling through the plume from above; the droplets collide with particulate radioactive material, forcing it downward and out of the plume's diffusion zone. There is some evidence that small particles, less than 1 μm in diameter, are essentially unaffected by these processes as they are carried along with the backwash of air pushed out of the way by falling water droplets. The plume is rarely entrained in the cloud because clouds often form just above an inversion layer boundary that the

---

[*] NUREG-3332 (Till and Meyer, 1983) gives average deposition velocities as 10^{-2} for elemental iodine, 10^{-3} for aerosols about 1 μm in diameter, and 10^{-4} for organic iodine.

plume cannot penetrate. The result is that the initial plume volume is depleted of radioactive material and less radiation dose is delivered farther downwind than would have been delivered without the rain. The difference between washout and rainout is that in washout the rain does not reach the surface (ground); this process transfers radioactive material into the (uncontaminated) region of air beneath the plume and above the ground. If the plume has made contact with the ground, washout causes the lowest region, stratus, or zone to have higher concentrations than the upper zones.[*] Although washout does not eliminate airborne radioactivity, it still reduces the downwind dose as compared to having no rain because the closer radioactive material is to the surface the faster it is removed through other removal processes. Rainout describes the situation when the rain reaches the surface, carrying removed radioactive material with it; this process permanently (ignoring resuspension) removes the radioactive material from the plume but greatly increases local external (deep-dose equivalent) radiation exposure derived from direct exposure to contaminated surfaces. Surface areas that are more contaminated, having higher surface activity per square meter than the average amounts of deposition, are often referred to as *hot spots*.

Experimentally derived washout coefficients must be applied to a specific release event with caution, as they are generally derived from long-term climatology and not from short-term meteorology. Experimental data show that particulates are scavenged one to three times more effectively by snowfall than by rain at the same precipitation rate (e.g., water mass). Data using pure, dry (no water vapor) iodine and bromine gases indicate that plume scavenging by snow is less effective than by rain, but the gases are scavenged more effectively by snow when iodine is comingled with water vapor. *Plate-out* is the removal of radioactive material from a plume through contact with objects (generally vertical surfaces), where the removal is due to chemical processes or electrostatic attraction, instead of gravity.

The previously discussed processes are very efficient at removing larger diameter particulates but have limited effect on smaller or fine particulates. In some cases, smaller particles aggregate (or coagulate) together after collisions caused by Brownian motion, only falling out of the plume when the conglomerate reaches a critical weight. Larger particles can also break apart, refreshing the amount of fine particulates available in the plume. Vapors (e.g., isotopes of the halogen series) may become aerosols because of chemical interactions or because of electrostatic interaction with dusts and other fine particulates in the plume.

PLUME MITIGATION OR INTERVENTION

The removal processes previously discussed are all natural effects that do not require human intervention. Many reactor licensees now lay down an external water curtain at or above the release vent as a preplanned action or strategy to mitigate a radioactive release. The purpose of this action is to reduce the concentration of particulate fission products in the plume as much as possible at the source, reducing the dose to the downwind general public and emergency workers. Experimental data using hydrogen fluoride suggest that 10% to 50% of the radioactive material can be removed from a plume by deploying a water curtain near the release point (Meroney, 1989). Caution should be exercised in applying these reduction factors to reactor accident scenarios because (1) some of the observed plume reductions were caused by chemical reactions between hydrogen fluoride and water that would not occur in a reactor accident, (2) the experiments employed water spray nozzles and equipment optimized for producing a water curtain rather than the fire-hose nozzles licensees plan on employing, and (3) the water delivery systems were placed to maximize their effectiveness. Although the effectiveness of this strategy cannot be known prior to its employment, this uncertainty should not prevent a licensee from evaluating its use (or any other reasonable mitigation strategy) in the event of an actual radioactive plume.

---

[*] When the rain ends, diffusion and Brownian motion cause the concentration of radioactive material throughout the plume to again become (more) uniform, given sufficient mixing time.

There are potential problems with this strategy that should be considered as part of accident pre-planning and in developing implementing procedures, including (1) whether the water curtain can be deployed close enough to the vent to encompass the entire plume, (2) dilution of the water curtain by turbulent flow (building wakes), (3) resultant extensive external contamination of plant buildings and ground surfaces (which can become significant long-term area sources of gamma radiation), (4) lack of control over potentially contaminated runoff water (which at some sites is collected by storm sewers and discharged directly to the environment), (5) availability of suitable-length hoses and water connections near engineered release points, and (6) potential for significant individual radiation doses to the firefighters, plant operators, and other plant workers who have to lay the hoses and operate fire hoses and related equipment in close proximity to a radioactive plume. In some drills and exercises where this strategy was simulated, plant engineers questioned whether the material strength and supports for interior ventilation system ducting were sufficient for the weight of water that could be entrained. The effectiveness of an external curtain of water may also be dependent on wind direction, as the plume is carried over or away from plant buildings (and spray heads) and because water sprays may be shortened or blown back for some wind directions. Licensee and dose assessment methods do not model the effect of external plume mitigation strategies.

RADIATION DOSIMETRY MODELS ASSOCIATED WITH DOSE PROJECTION

A dose projection prepared for purposes of making protective response decisions does not represent the expected actual dose to any actual members of the public and cannot be used to derive overall population doses (i.e., the person-rem delivered during the accident). Dose projection systems do not account for the shielding provided by buildings or terrain and generally overestimate actual doses by 25% to 50%, at least during the initial few hours of a release.

The standard external dosimetry model (DDE) for submersion dose is the *semi-infinite plume*, where radioactive concentrations in the plume are assumed to be essentially homogeneous, thoroughly mixed, and evenly distributed, and the cloud is sufficiently larger than the mean free path of the highest energy gamma photon present for the accident of interest. If the cloud is not larger in any dimension than the mean free path, then the approximations do not work and the calculated dose is much larger than the actual dose, which could happen close to the point for very stable meteorology. If this condition is met for gamma photons, it will also be met for beta radiation, and all radiation energy emitted in the cloud is absorbed by the target individual who is located at the geometric center of the cloud. For ease of calculation, the target is placed in the center of a sphere equal in radius to a multiple of the longest mean free path. Three to four mean free path lengths provide a good approximation of the total dose. After the dose to the target is calculated, the result is divided by two to model an immersed individual standing on solid ground (any contribution from radioactive material deposited on the virtual surface are ignored in this calculation, as are the very small differences caused by removing the cloud at the target individual's feet rather than waist). Dose conversion factors should be used to correct for the effects of radiation scatter and absorption in air.

A semi-infinite model underestimates radiation dose when the plume is overhead with little or no submersion and overestimates dose close to the source when the plume is not large compared to the gamma mean free path. The semi-infinite model provides a good approximation for beta radiation when the plume is more than 20 to 40 meters wide (NRC, 1983i). Note that the plume half-width (more similar to a radius than to a diameter) must be larger than this distance for centerline dose calculations to meet the isotropic and homogeneous conditions. The highest energy gamma photons for most reactor accident source terms are typically between 2 and 4 MeV, with corresponding mean free paths between 10 and 100 meters; therefore, a plume half-width greater than 300 to 400 meters (in rough terms, 1/4 mile) is required for accurate centerline calculations. For 700-keV gamma, the ratio of finite plume to infinite plume centerline dose ranges from 0.06 for $\sigma_y = 10$ m to 0.8 for $\sigma_y = 400$ m.

In the cases of both beta and gamma photons, it is likely true that the accuracy of calculated doses is better near the plume centerline than it is near the edges of the plume. Because the isotropic and homogeneous conditions are not met near the edge of the plume, the semi-infinite model tends to overestimate dose in this region. Practically, dose projection methods are most likely to predict a wider plume than is actually present, and environmental monitoring teams would be expected to measure dose rates half (or less) as compared to computations or projections.

The normal practice (see the Introduction in USEPA, 1993) for calculating dose from a contaminated surface is to model an individual (standard reference man) standing on an infinite plane whose surface is uniformly contaminated by the nuclide of interest or in which a uniform layer of earth overlies an infinite plane of uniform contamination (e.g., for material mixed to various distances into topsoil). The normal practice for calculating dose from immersion in contaminated water is to model an individual submerged in an infinite volume of uniformly contaminated water. Typically, the doses received outdoors in an urban area are about half those received in a flat, open area because of the presence of building materials between the individual considered and some part of the radioactive cloud (IARC, 2000).

DOSE REDUCTION FROM BUILDING WALLS

Residential and commercial buildings provide significant dose reduction through shielding while a plume of radioactive material is overhead (that is, at a minimum height above roof elevation). In this case, external gamma radiation is the only effect of interest. Residential and commercial buildings reduce the overall radiation dose received from a plume of radioactive material as compared to the dose that would have been received outdoors, even when the building is submerged in the plume. The amount of protection is initially equal to the absorption factor of the building's wall (i.e., radiation shielding value), although this protection factor decreases at a rate proportional to the rate of air exchange into the building. After two to three air exchanges, there is essentially no remaining protection, because the atmosphere inside the building is in concentration equilibrium with the plume outside the building. For normal residential construction, two to three air exchanges occur over about an hour; therefore, persons sheltering in buildings should be evacuated (when projected doses exceed Protective Action Guides) no later than approximately an hour after plume arrival, even when they must travel into or through a radioactive plume, because no further radiation dose will be avoided if they stay.

NON-GAUSSIAN PLUME MODELS

Non-Gaussian plume models are inherently more descriptive of reality in that they do not require the input parameters to be constant (steady-state). Most models divide the plume into a series of puffs or release periods, move each piece individually within the wind field, calculate the dose at defined receptors, and sum the results over the release period. The methods differ in the statistical distributions used to describe each series (some use a Gaussian, some may use other statistics) and the applied boundary conditions. Because all of the methods are numerical integrations of inexact equations, the accuracy of the models is related to modeling parameters such as the number of cells in the modeling grid, the method of numerical integration (again, the more accurate the method, the longer the computation time required to achieve it), the degree of truncation and when in the model it is applied, and the number of meteorological datasets that are included. A brief discussion of the major models is given below.[*]

---

[*] For a discussion of the various non-Gaussian models in use, also see Section B.1 of Regulatory Guide 1.111 (NRC, 1977c).

SEGMENTED GAUSSIAN MODELS

The segmented Gaussian plume considers the plume as multiple independent elements (plume segments or sections), each of which is allowed to have its own release rate and meteorology. The dose contribution of each segment is calculated only from the radioactive material that enters the environment during that segment instead of during the entire release duration. As more segments are run, the results of each segment are superimposed to form the overall plume plot. This allows the model to account for changes in wind direction and release rate, although under rapidly changing meteorology it will underestimate dose close to the release point and overestimate dose farther away (especially more than 5 miles downwind). Each individual segment is still calculated as a truncated Gaussian plume.

LAGRANGIAN MODELS

A Lagrangian dispersion model mathematically follows pollution plume parcels, as those parcels move under the influence of a wind field; each parcel can represent a large number of physical particles. The path of each parcel is calculated independently in a moving frame of reference, using a Monte Carlo (random walk) simulation. A Lagrangian model is an open boundary model in that it does not require conservation of mass—a parcel is removed from the model when it randomly undergoes radioactive decay or deposits on a surface. A Lagrangian model calculates the concentration of radioactive material at any point in the wind field from the paths of all parcels that survive to that distance. The model requires an assumption that parcels are released independently and that parcels do not interact with each other. The utility of the model depends heavily on the completeness and accuracy of the three-dimensional flow and turbulence fields used to perform the calculation. One difficulty with the model is that it requires transformations of real-time wind field parameters measured in a fixed frame of reference into analogous parameters usable in a moving frame of reference.[*] In Lagrangian particle models, individual particle trajectories can be calculated with great accuracy, and plume mixing by atmospheric motions is simulated by adding a random component to the wind vector. These random components are constrained by their standard deviations (σ_u, σ_v, σ_w) and their respective Lagrangian time scales, $T_L(x;y;z)$. These turbulence parameters have to be derived from the wind and temperature fields and rely on idealized conditions. Numerical errors manifest in these models as statistical fluctuations of particle density, translating into fluctuations of concentration fields if the number of particles is too small or becomes too small in a part of the calculated plume (Seibert, 2000).

EULERIAN GRID MODELS

An Eulerian dispersion model is similar to a Lagrangian model in that it also performs a Monte Carlo simulation of a large number of pollution plume parcels moving under the influence of a real-time wind field. The most important difference between the two models is that the Eulerian model uses a fixed three-dimensional Cartesian grid as a frame of reference rather than a moving frame of reference. In Eulerian models, the most important source of numerical errors is the advection scheme; these advection models suffer from numerical diffusion and phase errors. Another major source of errors is the treatment of plumes whose size is too small to be resolved by the grid. Either a more or less complicated submodel has to be used, or severe artificial diffusion takes place. Problems may also occur in strongly deformational flows, as plumes become more and more elongated and finally become much narrower than a one-grid distance.[26]

---

[*] For additional information, see texts on atmospheric pollution dispersion such as Arya (1999), Jorgensen (1997), and Thielen et al. (2007).

K-THEORY MODELS

The diffusion in Eulerian dispersion models is calculated using *K*-theory, which takes its name from the diffusion constants (K_x, K_y, K_z) in the respective *x*, *y*, and *z* directions that result from solutions of the differential equation describing the change of plume concentration over time. The eddy diffusivity functions can be expressed analytically in terms of atmospheric stability, surface roughness, space, and time. These functions result from the assumption that eddy diffusion in a given direction is constant, although diffusion is not required to be equal along each directional axis. The model is frequently simplified further by assuming that vertical diffusion is much greater than diffusion along the other axes and that diffusivity is proportional to vertical height. Gaussian plume models often do not accurately model particle settling and deposition, and they do not consider the vertical gradient in diffusivity ($K_v(z) = K_0 + \mu_z$); these effects become more important as downwind distance increases and eventually dominate diffusion within a plume. *K*-theory models tend to underestimate the concentration of radioactive material near the source, especially in more turbulent (lower stability class) environments; this is one reason why recent environmental transport computer models often couple a Lagrangian model near the source with a Eulerian model farther downwind (Cooper et al., 2003; Smith, 2008).

ERRORS AND UNCERTAINTY IN DOSE ASSESSMENT

A licensee's dose assessment staff often confuses precision with accuracy, the ability of the computer to calculate numbers to an arbitrary number of decimal places with good models and assumptions. The assumptions required to construct and run an accident assessment model (the combination of reactor core damage, in-plant source reduction mechanisms, the release path to the environment, and environmental dispersion) guarantee that the accident you actually get cannot exactly match the computer model you run.[*] All dose projection models suffer from a lack of meaningful validation (e.g., against field data instead of against hand calculations), large mathematical and modeling uncertainties, a strong sensitivity to both source term assumptions and stability class determination, and the possibility of operator error due to model complexity. A frequently repeated assertion is that the best dose assessment is no closer to reality than a factor of two. Table 4.4 summarizes the kinds and magnitudes of errors that can be expected.

Although dose projection models can never completely describe a given accident, dose assessors should not allow uncertainty in their methods to paralyze them into indecision. Some of the model and measurement uncertainties can be worked out in advance and can be reduced through improvements in the model or data acquisition systems—for example, changing from a single meteorological input to simultaneously using multiple met towers. Focusing too much on what one does not know during an event or on data uncertainty can result in dose assessors not making appropriate protective action recommendations because they do not have confidence in their dose projections. During an event, dose assessors and decision-makers need to treat dose assessment results at their face value, considering they are completely accurate. If decision-makers do not have confidence in dose projection results and wait until they receive confirming measurements from environmental monitoring teams, they are likely to delay necessary protective measures and cause members of the public to receive unnecessary radiation dose.

Some good advice to the dose assessor for coping with model uncertainty is found in NUREG-1228 (McKenna and Glitter, 1988, p. 1-3): "If a change in assumptions does not result in a change … by at least one order of magnitude, it is not worth considering because it will provide no useful

---

[*] For example, TID-24190 (Slade, 1968) states, "At these greater distances the cloud will be relatively insensitive to local irregularities but will be affected by major topographical features, gross changes in meteorological conditions, and depletion by ground deposition en route. The combination of uncertainties in these several parameters can produce major uncertainties in the estimate of effects at all distances downwind. The greatest overall uncertainty in estimating the effects of a release arises from the dynamic character of the atmosphere. Frequent shifts of wind direction and changes in stability and wind speed may cause the plume to move toward unanticipated areas."

TABLE 4.4
Contributors to Dose Assessment Uncertainty

Parameter	Confidence	Uncertainty
Instrument measurements (met tower, radiation monitors, flow rates, etc.)	High	Low (<1%)
Source term		
RCS sample	Analysis, high	Analysis 1–10%
	Representation, moderate	Factors 10–100 (possible spiking)
Inferred or calculated	Very low	Factors 10–100 (NUREG-0965)
		Factor 100 (NUREG-1228)
		Factors 1–1000 (NUREG-1465)
In-plant source reduction	Moderate	Factors 2–5
Stability class determination	Moderate	Factors 5–10
Atmospheric transport	Very low	Factors 10–10,000
Radiation dosimetry	Good	5–25%
Operator error	Moderate to high	Factors 0.5–3

information." For decision-making purposes, when reading doses calculated by dose projection models, numerical values in the upper, lower, or mid-range halves of a decade should be considered to be the same. Numbers to the right of the decimal point should essentially be ignored. See Section 4 of NUREG-1465 (Soffer et al., 1995) for an extended discussion of the uncertainties inherent in estimating accident source terms. A discussion of statistical methods for combining errors and uncertainties in dose projection models can be found in NUREG/CR-3332 (Till and Meyer, 1983, pp. 11-18–11-43).

FIELD VALIDATION OF MODEL RESULTS

During the early phase of an event, environmental monitoring teams[*] are dispatched to identify and track a radiological release. These teams are generally equipped with medium-range radiation survey meters and pancake-type Geiger–Mueller count rate meters; some teams are also equipped with μR survey meters and single-channel sodium iodide (NaI) analyzers for in-field iodine analyses. These teams report back three measurements: β-window open exposure (mR/h), β-window closed exposure (mR/h), and the direct (surface) count rate from the air sampler prefilter and sampling cartridge. This information can be used to validate dose projections but only if the model output includes estimates of exposure rate. Many models estimate the TEDE dose rate, but this is not the same as the exposure rate because it includes the internal inhalation dose. The TEDE dose rate can only be compared to the exposure rate when there is essentially no airborne iodine and no fission products. Note that the exposure rate comparison is only valid while other model inputs remain constant; for example, one cannot compare data collected from a plume having a different stability class than the model projection used, and one cannot compare radiation surveys taken under differing precipitation conditions. When valid comparisons can be made, the model can usually be adjusted to fit the environmental data by multiplying the initial release rate (in μCi/s or Ci/s) by the ratio of the observed exposure rate to the predicted exposure rate at a known location, as the exposure rate is linear with respect to release rate. Because of the inherent uncertainties, only one digit past the decimal point should be included when computing this ratio. When data are available from multiple survey points, the best adjustment factor is the average of all individual point ratios.

---

[*] Environmental monitoring teams are often referred to as *field teams*, but this terminology is also frequently applied to onsite radiation survey teams and to plant mitigation and repair teams. To eliminate possible miscommunication during an event, it is recommended that the designation *field team* be limited to onsite teams.

Historically, many reactor licensees implemented methods to reverse calculate (also called *back calculate*) the release source term and release rate from field measurements. In principle, this cannot be done for Gaussian models, at least not while the release of radioactive materials is continuing, because of the requirement for steady-state conditions. Changes in meteorology between the start of the release and the measured exposure are not accounted for, the release duration is indeterminate, and the contribution of ground shine is both unknown and changing. Corrections based on comparing open/closed window air exposure rates are invalid if the accident source term (isotopic mixture) is not the same as the default one programmed into the computer code, because the exposure per curie (Γ) and assumed β exposure rates will be wrong. When the environmental data to be used to reverse calculate the release are collected off-centerline, an additional correction factor must be introduced to correct the data back to their (assumed) centerline values—σ_y must be assumed because it cannot readily be measured in real time in the environment (default values built into computer models are often invisible to the user and cannot be changed). The calculation can only be done if in-flight radioactive decay is considered because the radioactive source being measured in the environment has undergone decay between leaving the plant site and being measured by the survey team. If the measured isotopic ratios are not the same as the released ratio, then a source term correction is meaningless (early in an event the isotopic composition of deposited is not known and will not be for several hours).

The calculation can be done in principle with a variable plume model if corrections are applied for the time at which the radioactive material was released which was measured, later, in the environment. The overall uncertainty of the updated dose projection is much higher than with a forward dose projection—uncertainties in the dispersion model are squared, not doubled, because the uncertainties in the reverse calculation are repeated in the subsequent forward-looking calculation.

LIQUID RELEASES

It is extremely difficult to have a significant accidental or unintentional release of radioactive liquids from commercial power plants; although there have been a few (small) accidental releases of airborne radioactivity from plants, there has never been an accidental release of contaminated liquids because

- The engineered release paths originate at holding tanks that are normally valved in a closed position, and the release paths have multiple valves that must be opened before a path is established to the environment (at some sites these valves are chained closed).
- Radioactive material is generally held in holding tanks for an extended period of time before intentional release (weeks to years), allowing for a significant source term reduction through decay.
- Process radiation monitors are installed along engineered release paths to provide an indication of unexpected flow or (for intentional releases) an indication that radiation release rates are different from the analyzed and expected radiation conditions.
- Above-grade areas of the plant that contain radioactive systems have floor drain lines to catch radioactive liquids resulting from accidental system breaches; these drains direct contaminated liquid (usually, water) to liquid radioactive waste systems for processing.
- Tanks with radioactive liquids have external berms and sumps to contain accidental leaks.
- Most tanks containing radioactive liquids are located below grade so that line, valve, and tank failures do not have a ready flow path to the environment.
- The total amount of radioactive material that can be accidently released to the environment is inherently limited by the volume of the holding tank.
- Some sites are constructed without any engineered liquid release paths.

The same equations that describe a radioactive plume in air apply to radioactive liquids in water. Although stability class is undefined for bodies of water, rivers and lakes have much more turbulence and internal mixing than the atmosphere does because river bottom surface roughness is much greater than land surface roughness. The internal plume eddies produced by river meander also produce more turbulence than does the atmosphere under most stability class conditions. Radioactive liquids released from a reactor site have nearly the same density as the water but are generally at a higher temperature than the ambient water into which it flows, producing a greater effective stack height and more plume buoyancy (lift) in the short range. The isotopes found in typical liquid releases are similar to those found in gaseous releases, although liquid source terms are much smaller in total radioactivity content, both concentration and volume, than are gaseous source terms, except that nonsoluble elements have been removed by precipitation or flocking.*

Real-time monitoring of a radioactive plume in water is essentially impossible because of the lack of ready water transport for radiation monitoring teams and because the self-shielding of water generally prevents effective radiation surveys at the surface. Monitoring is usually limited to sample collection at fixed downstream water supply intakes.

In practical terms, a liquid release inherently has much lower potential consequences to the public than does an airborne release. A liquid radioactive plume entrained in a body of water is not a radiation source that is capable of affecting people on land, even along the shore. Public or private water supplies that draw from wells are not affected by liquid releases. Public water supplies that draw from surface waters generally have a several-hour supply of water held in tanks or water intake treatment ponds, so they can simply close their intake valves and allow the liquid plume to go past. The permissible concentrations of radioactive material in public water supplies is set by the Safe Drinking Water Act (SDWA). The background or natural concentration of radioactive material in public water supplies that draw from surface waters is essentially zero, and SDWA standards for regulated radionuclides are in the range of tens to hundreds of pCi/L; for example, the limit for tritium (^{3}H) is 50,000 pCi/L. So, even if a public water supply does not restrict their intake and draws the entire liquid plume into their system, the resulting concentration in drinking water may not exceed allowable limits (i.e., there is so much dilution because of the water system volume).

PERFORMANCE REQUIREMENTS FOR DOSE ASSESSMENT MODELS

Commercial reactor licensees in the United States are required by 10 CFR 50.47(b)(9) to have adequate methods, systems, and equipment to assess and monitor the actual or potential consequences of a release of radioactive material from the reactor site. The only guidance that describes an acceptable atmospheric transport and diffusion model is found in Appendix 2 of NUREG-0654 (NRC, 1980c). The guidance states that two classes of models are appropriate. The first (Class A) is capable of producing initial transport and diffusion estimates within 15 minutes following classification of an emergency, and the second (Class B) is capable of estimating the surface deposition and relative concentration of radioactive material within the ingestion exposure pathway emergency planning zone. Both models are to utilize real-time meteorology, including 15-minute averages of all parameters reported by the licensee's meteorological measurement systems. A licensee's model must be site specific and based on measurements of atmospheric stability, and it must account for diurnal variation and terrain-induced flows. The model is required to estimate the plume dimensions and the peak and relative concentration at appropriate locations in the plume emergency planning zone. The limitations of the licensee's model must be documented.

Class A models may not include the dose from deposited or resuspended radioactive materials, although Class B models should include these dose pathways. Class A models are often pure dispersion models that do not correct for dry or wet deposition, washout, or radioactive decay. The wind speed is not an important component in Class A models. Release duration and stability class (e.g., diffusion) are more important parameters. This should not be taken to imply that the wind speed is not important or does not impact response operations; wind speed is often linked to stability class.

---

* *Flocking* is coagulating or precipitating material from a suspension by adding chemicals to the mixture.

NUREG-0654 contains very little guidance about performance requirements for Class B models, primarily the following:

- Class B models should have the capability to accept field measurements (exposure rates, air sample results, and measurements of deposited radioactive material).
- Class B models should also be capable of using wind field data from multiple meteorological towers.
- Class B models should provide results that are comparable to Class A models in the emergency planning zone (the transition zone from about 5 to 15 miles downwind).
- Because NUREG-0654 specifies that Class A models need to run in less than 15 minutes, it is implied that Class B models are not required to run in less than 15 minutes.

Although not explicitly stated, other expectations of a Class B model include variable release rate and meteorology (over time), integration over the entire release (and after the active release terminates, the subsequent plume flight time), accounting for plume meander, and that the model calculates to ingestion pathway distances (at least 50 miles). Although it states on p. 2-4, "Additional guidance will be prepared to outline the staff position on dose assessment capabilities to be used for emergency response," this guidance was never prepared.

In the author's experience, neither licensees nor the Commission currently emphasize the class of model used to perform dose assessment, and the Commission has essentially abandoned its previous emphasis on licensees having true Class B models, although it can be argued that having such a model remains a regulatory requirement. Most licensees have models with some Class A features and some (limited) Class B features. Many licensees do not have models that completely comply with the Class A requirements; the models are specifically lacking an output that provides exact plume dimensions and position (plume centerline positions are given, not plume edges) and do not calculate the arrival times for peak concentrations of radioactive material. Licensees rarely completely document their model's basis. The author is not aware of any reactor licensees that simultaneously employ separate Class A and Class B models; if nothing else, the issues associated with training dose assessment staff to properly use multiple independent models are formidable, and the existence of multiple models (and their associated procedures and references) creates anticipated error traps that can easily result in performance deficiencies. For a good survey discussion of the hierarchy of Class A and Class B models, along with suggestions for model selection and performance, see Mikkelsen and Desiato (1993).

USING PROTECTIVE ACTION GUIDES

Plume dispersion modeling, including corrections for the various source-reduction mechanisms, results in a calculated concentration of airborne radioactive materials at a location of interest (usually a defined distance downwind from the release point or source). To obtain a projected dose, the usual method is to multiply the calculated or assumed concentrations by a set of dose conversion factors for each exposure mode (rem-cm^3 per μCi-h in traditional units, or Sv-cm^3 per Bq-h in SI/metric units; for ground shine, the radiation source is surface deposition in traditional units of μCi per unit area), then multiply the result by a projected exposure time (in hours, which in theory could be different times for each individual exposure mode). A dose projection represents the dose that would be delivered to a theoretical unprotected individual who remained at the location of interest throughout the period of airborne exposure and. for some calculations, is also exposed to surface-deposited radioactive material for a specified number of hours thereafter (usually 96 hours or 4 days).

A complete dose projection compares the doses for each applicable exposure mode—skin (SDE), eyes (EDE), gamma radiation submersion doses to internal organs (DDE), gamma and beta exposure from standing on contaminated surfaces, and inhalation and organ doses (CDE, CEDE)—with applicable Protective Action Guides. The locations of interest are typically those that are used to make protective action decisions, such as the plume centerline at the site boundary, 2 miles downwind, 5 miles downwind, and 10 miles downwind.

A Protective Action Guide is a predetermined threshold for action that represents a measure of radiation risk to the public. The United States uses a *dose avoidance* concept to determine the threshold for action that compares the radiation risk from being exposed to the radioactive plume to the risks of taking action, primarily evacuation by personal automobile. When a sufficiently large risk (dose) can be avoided then protective actions are justified; otherwise, actions are not justified. The goal of protective actions for the public is not to prevent any member of the public from receiving a radiation dose. The goal is to prevent members of the public from receiving radiation doses whose risk is greater than the risk from alternative actions, again principally evacuation by personal automobile.

In theory, each dose assessment is forward looking and does not consider any radiation dose already received by the population for whom the assessment is made. In practice, this can lead to an artificial segmentation problem. If the dose projection period (time of exposure) is made sufficiently small (typically 1-hour increments), then no single dose assessment exceeds Protective Action Guides in situations where a longer, integrated projection into the future (typically 2 to 4 hours) does exceed action guides. In the author's opinion, it is often beneficial to simply model the entire radiological release in every dose projection, avoiding any artificial cutoffs imposed by choices in modeling parameters.

As a comparison, the International Atomic Energy Agency has incorporated into its evaluation standards the *dose averted* concept, which combines dose projection with modeling the effectiveness of effluent mitigation strategies. Averted dose is defined as the dose prevented by the application of a countermeasure or set of countermeasures—that is, the difference between the projected dose if the countermeasures had not been applied and the actual projected dose; see the *IAEA Safety Glossary* (IAEA, 2006a). The basis for this concept is an ICRP report (ICRP, 1992), in which the intervention levels at which countermeasures (protective actions) are implemented are expressed in terms of the dose expected to be avoided by the specific protective action (averted dose), rather than the dose that would be received in the absence of the countermeasure (projected dose). Because any form of intervention is associated with its own degree of harm, in terms of health risks, costs, and inconvenience, those actions taken to reduce radiological risk are required to be justified so that the total benefits outweigh the total risks. The levels of dose at which protective actions are introduced, and later withdrawn, need to be optimized to produce the maximum net benefit.

INITIAL AND EXPANDED PROTECTIVE MEASURES FOR THE PUBLIC

In the United States, the implementation of protective measures is tied to both emergency classification and to dose projection. A reactor licensee is required to communicate recommendations for initial offsite protective actions to cognizant authorities within 15 minutes of declaring a General Emergency or within 15 minutes of projecting radiation doses that exceed one or more Protective Action Guides.[*] Exceeding Protective Action Guides is in itself one criterion (emergency action level) for declaring a General Emergency. Because a General Emergency may be declared before a radiological release occurs, the initial protective measure recommendation is often based solely on plant parameters. The most common preplanned initial protective measure is to evacuate a 2-mile radius around the reactor site with the three compass sectors along the plume centerline evacuated to 5 miles; some reactor sites with very low offsite populations have a preplanned initial protective measure of only a 2-mile radius evacuation (a very small number of reactor sites have initial measures of 5 mile or 10 mile radial evacuations, because of the preferences of local offsite authorities).

---

[*] In some site-specific cases, limited protective measures are taken for the public at lesser emergency classifications. In general, these are precautionary actions that require more time than does a general evacuation or shelter order. These preplanned actions include closing beaches and parks (and verifying that the public has left), removing boaters from lakes, readying school buses to remove children from schools, or readying ambulances to remove patients from hospitals.

Once an initial recommendation has been made to take offsite protective measures, changing circumstances may require protective actions to be expanded to previously unaffected areas. Although there is considerable variability in how meteorological and radiological conditions can change, the range of potential outcomes can be summarized as follows.*

When a radiological release has not yet occurred and the wind vector is unstable (moving clockwise or counterclockwise), expand protective measures into adjacent sectors as required (i.e., no dose projection is possible until a release occurs). *When a radiological release is occurring*, the wind vector remains stable, and dose projections indicate that Protective Action Guides are exceeded at the same or a lesser distance downwind (release severity stable, decreasing, or stopped), no additional protective measures are necessary. When the wind vector remains stable and dose projections indicate that Protective Action Guides are exceeded at a greater distance downwind (release severity increasing), an outward radial expansion of existing protective measures into the newly affected downwind areas is recommended.

When, after expanding protective measures from the 2- to 5-mile section to include the 5- to 10-mile section, there is a subsequent change in wind vector, it is recommended to maintain all current protective action recommendations and evaluate the distance at which Protective Action Guides are now exceeded. If the release severity has subsequently decreased, it may be appropriate to recommend new protective measures in adjacent (counterclockwise or clockwise) sectors only for the 2- to 5-mile section along the new vector while maintaining the previous 10-mile recommendation along the original vector. If the release severity has decreased sufficiently, or stopped, no new protective measures may be required in the new downwind sectors.

When the wind vector is unstable (moving clockwise or counterclockwise) and dose projections indicate that Protective Action Guides are exceeded at a distance beyond the current radial evacuation (release severity stable or increasing; Protective Action Guides must currently be exceeded at least 2 miles downwind), it is recommended to maintain all current protective action recommendations and expand protective measures clockwise/counterclockwise to include those radial areas of the newly affected sectors where Protective Action Guides are exceeded. This could result in a discontinuous protective action recommendation in which the newly affected sectors are recommended to be evacuated to distances greater than are recommended for evacuation along the original keyhole vector.

When the wind vector is unstable and dose projections indicate that Protective Action Guides are either not exceeded offsite or exceeded at distances less than the current radial evacuation (release severity stable, decreasing, or stopped; Protective Action Guides are not currently exceeded within the keyhole area), it is recommended to maintain all current protective action recommendations and no new protective measures are recommended.

When, after a change in wind vector not requiring new protective measures because dose projections for areas along the changing wind vector are below Protective Action Guides, the release severity increases so that Protective Action Guides are now exceeded at distances beyond the previous radial evacuation distance, it is recommended to maintain all current protective action recommendations and expand protective measures only along the current (new) wind vector for those sections where Protective Action Guides are now exceeded. This could result in a discontinuous protective action recommendation in which the original keyhole recommendation is maintained, and there is a gap of one or more sectors having no recommended protective measures beyond the initial radial evacuation between the sections evacuated as a result of the original prompt protective action recommendation and the sectors newly recommended to be evacuated after the change in wind vector combined with increase in release severity.

---

* For this discussion, a 2-mile, 5-mile keyhole existing initial recommendation is assumed along a previously stable wind direction vector; for licensees that do not provide protective action, recommendations in terms of the wind compass and range sectors include affected geographical subzones with the emergency planning zone. This discussion is limited solely to expanded or future protective action recommendations and is consistent with NRC Regulatory Issue Summary 03-12, *Clarification of NRC Guidance for Modifying Protective Actions*, in that when an area has been recommended for protective measures the area must not be recommended for a lesser protective measure or removed from protective measures.

The reasoned professional judgment of a dose assessor or accident analyst is often required to properly apply the Protective Action Guides, as recognized in EPA 400-R-92-001 (USEPA, 1992, p. 2-1). When the licensee exercises such judgment to make protective action recommendations for sectors, sections, or geographical areas where radiation doses are projected to be less than applicable Protective Action Guides or to make recommendations that differ from established procedures, the licensee must be able to document a reasonable technical basis for the protective action recommendation they make, especially if they go outside of procedures in making their recommendation. This technical basis should include all available information and be of sufficient depth and complexity to allow future evaluation of the accuracy of the associated recommendation to offsite authorities. The Commission does not generally consider the harmonization of licensee recommendations with current or future offsite decisions or the maintaining of a contiguous or smooth protective action recommendation footprint to be reasonable technical bases for a licensee's protective action recommendations.

METEOROLOGICAL TOWERS AND MEASUREMENTS

Reactor licensees are required to have the capability to measure real-time meteorology and are required to submit annual reports to the Commission that include cumulative meteorological data. This capability supports the licensee's long-term environmental measurement program and provides the data necessary for an effective emergency response program. An adequate meteorological program forms part of the licensing basis for a licensee to meet planning standard 10 CFR 50.47(b)(9) and the requirements of 10 CFR 50 Appendix E, Sections IV.B and IV.E(2). The statements of these requirements include the following:

- "Each licensee shall have the capability of acquiring and evaluation meteorological information sufficient to meet the criteria of Appendix 2. There shall be ... access to meteorological information by at least the nearsite EOF, the TSC, the Control Room, and an offsite NRC center. The licensee shall make available to the state suitable meteorological data processing interconnections which will permit independent analysis" (NUREG-0654, Element I.4, p. 57).
- "Viable backup meteorological sensors; generally either duplicate instruments on the same mast are acceptable; a single independent 10 meter instrument mast is also an acceptable backup even to a 100 meter primary tower" (NUREG-0654, Appendix 2).
- "All instruments must be capable at remote interrogation" (NUREG-0654, Appendix 2). Note that the minimum specified interrogation baud rate has long been superseded by current technology.
- "An onsite meteorological measurements program ... should be capable of providing the meteorological information required to make the following assessments: ... (5) A rapid, conservative assessment by the licensee and other appropriate persons of the radiological consequences of an accidental release of radioactive material to the atmosphere" (Regulatory Guide 1.23).
- "Onsite meteorological measurements should provide an adequate basis for short distance atmospheric diffusion calculations" (Regulatory Guide 1.23).

The primary regulatory source for meteorological requirements is Regulatory Guide 1.23 (NRC, 2007c). According to the Regulatory Guide, the minimum parameters to be measured are wind speed, wind direction, and ambient temperature, and these parameters are to be measured at a minimum of two elevations on a single mast and must meet the following criteria: (1) the lower elevation instruments are 10 meters above ground; (2) the upper instruments are at the height of the plant vent (but cannot be located less than 30 meters above the lower instruments); and (3) for plants with an elevated stack (e.g., 100 meters), additional instruments are required at the stack height. The mast must be placed where plant structures will have little or no influence on the measurement accuracy. The maximum allowable measurement uncertainty is given for wind direction (±5°), for wind speed (1/2 mph), for temperature (±0.5°C), and for the temperature differential (ΔT, ±0.1°C). In addition, the wind speed instrument must be capable of reading speeds less than 1 mph. Although all reactor licensees currently operate their own meteorological stations, Revision 0 of the Regulatory Guide did not require this; the initial requirement was that licensees have the capability to obtain "regional"-scale meteorological data (e.g., for up to 50 miles downwind) as needed during an emergency.[*]

The ANSI standard that applies to meteorological stations is ANSI/ANS-2.5-1984 (ANSI, 1984b). Although the standard largely repeats the information from Regulatory Guide 1.23, there are some significant additions, including the following:

- The dew point or relative humidity must be measured.
- The meteorological tower should not be located downwind of plant heat dissipation systems (e.g., large cooling towers) and should be located away from plant buildings by greater than 10 times the tallest building height.
- Data sampling should be every 60 seconds or more frequently; data averaging should be computed every 30 seconds or more frequently.
- Instrument data uncertainty should be calculated by the root-sum-of-squares method.

NUREG-0696 (NRC, 1981e) and NUREG-0814 (NRC, 1981i) do not directly address the collection of meteorological data, but they do address the archiving and availability of meteorology data:

- The reliability of computer systems must exceed 99% (averaged over a year).
- The system should collect and store at least 2 hours of pre-event data and 12 hours of post-event data (at the routine sampling and averaging times), and up to 2 weeks post-event at a reduced resolution.[†]
- Facilities should be provided in the emergency operations facility for the acquisition, display, and evaluation of all meteorological data pertinent to determining offsite protective measures.
- At least one computer terminal must be dedicated to the display of meteorological information in each technical support center and emergency operations facility.

To meet the current revision of Regulatory Guide 1.23, reactor licensees must have either a single meteorological tower with duplicate sets of meteorological instruments having physically separate power supplies and data channels or single sets of instruments mounted on physically separate primary and back-up meteorology towers. When multiple towers are used, there is no requirement to average or resolve wind speed and direction differences between the towers; in the author's experience, dose assessors generally select a meteorological tower data source and never look at values from the other (usually backup) tower, so that differences between measurements of the same parameter are rarely recognized. NUREG-0654, Appendix 2, requires that the meteorological data selected to analyze atmospheric transport be indicative of the conditions in the plume exposure emergency planning zone. The difficulty in implementing this requirement is that any single meteorological data source only truly represents environmental conditions within a mile or two of that tower, and the accuracy of the representation varies with stability class. Wind speed and direction data correctly represent environment conditions farther away from the tower for stability class F

---

[*] In the current regulatory environment, an onsite meteorological station is considered to be required per Appendix E, IV(E)(2), "equipment for determining the magnitude of and for continuously assessing the impact of the release of radioactive materials to the environment."

[†] The relaxed requirement for longer term data storage reflected the relatively limited storage capacity of computer memory available in the early 1980s and its relatively high cost.

than for stability class A. It would be a mistake for an analyst to assume that the true plume pathway 5 or more miles from an onsite tower is given by the 15-minute average wind direction calculated by the plant computer, even allowing for the changes in wind direction indicated on the tower while the plume is in flight; the flight time in minutes to any downwind distance is calculated by multiplying the wind speed (in mph) by 60 minutes and then dividing by the target distance (in miles).

RELEASE IN PROGRESS

The Commission requires that licensees correctly characterize the impact of environmental releases to offsite authorities. Most licensees have established measurement or radiation monitor thresholds at which they inform offsite authorities that a release is in progress. The threshold is site specific and is negotiated in advance between the licensee and offsite response agencies. A *release in progress* represents a level or concentration of radioactive material in the environment that warrants heightened concern. The release determination is not directly related to the four emergency classifications, although at some sites the release in progress threshold may be numerically identical to emergency action level entry conditions. The release threshold may be "any radioactive atom associated with the accident," may be specific technical specification limits, may be multiples of the Notification of Unusual Event emergency action level, or may be an absolute release rate as high as 1E+5 µCi/s. Although emergency response organization dose analysts often use the term *release* interchangeably to refer to stack or chimney release rates both below and above the release in progress threshold, there is no commonly accepted and recognizable term for effluent concentrations or release rates that are elevated above routine levels but below permissible limits (e.g., technical specifications, *Offsite Dose Calculation Manual* limits). Recognizing that the release in progress threshold has been exceeded is generally the point at which dose analysts are required to evaluate the offsite radiological consequences of an accident. Reaching this threshold does not require that protective actions be taken by the public if the associated projected doses remain less than EPA Protective Action Guides.

The determination of a release in progress is both a technical and a public information problem. In the author's opinion, the technical designation of a release in progress as it applies to the reactor licensee marking the offsite notification form directed to offsite authorities should be separated from the description of radioactive effluents as used in press releases and other communications to the public. It may be acceptable to describe to the public that additional unintended radioactive material is entering the environment due to the emergency, without formally designating a "release" on the notification form. Likewise, when a licensee uses a very restrictive definition of release, it may be appropriate to communicate to the public without using the word *release*. This issue continues to divide licensees (Nuclear Energy Institute), the regulator (Commission), and various state emergency management and radiation health agencies, because there is no formal, documented agreement regarding how the various parties will describe radioactive effluents to the public during an emergency. Reactor licensees are particularly sensitive to differences on this subject because they look for complete agreement and harmony in public communications and dislike not knowing how offsite authorities will describe the situation. When there are disagreements, the licensees' perception is that the public often blames them for understating or overstating conditions, rather than blaming public officials for misspeaking, even when the public officials may be more culpable.

REGULATORY REFERENCES

NUREG-0654 Planning Standard I, "Accident Assessment" (NRC, 1980c, pp. 56–58), contains the minimum acceptable criteria for meeting planning standard §50.47(b)(9).[*] Licensees are required to demonstrate compliance with the NUREG-0654 elements unless they have proposed, and Nuclear

---

[*] NUREG-0654 category A corresponds to 50.47(b)(1), category B to 50.47(b)(2), etc.

Reactor Regulation (NRR) has approved, an alternative means of meeting the planning standard. The five criteria applicable to dose assessment performed by the licenses are

1. Each licensee shall establish methods and techniques to be used for determining the source term of releases of radioactive material within plant systems (I(3)(a)).
2. Each licensee shall establish methods and techniques to be used for determining the magnitude of the release of radioactive materials based on plant system parameters and effluent monitors (I(3)(b)).
3. Each licensee shall establish the relationship between effluent monitor readings and onsite and offsite exposures and contamination (I(4)).
4. Each licensee shall have the capability of acquiring and evaluating meteorological information sufficient to meet the criteria of Appendix 2 (I(5)).
5. Each licensee shall establish the methodology for determining the release rate/projected doses if the instrumentation used for assessment are offscale or inoperable (I(6)).

Relevant standards that apply to dose assessment include the following:

- ANSI/ANS-2.5-1984, *Determining Meteorological Information at Nuclear Power Sites* (ANSI, 1984b)
- ANSI/ANS-3.8.5-1992, *Criteria for Emergency Radiological Field Monitoring, Sampling, and Analysis* (NRC, 1992)
- IEEE N320, *Performance Specifications for Reactor Emergency Radiological Monitoring Instrumentation* (IEEE, 1993)
- ANSI/ANS-3.8.6-1995, *Criteria for the Conduct of Offsite Radiological Assessment for Emergency Response for Nuclear Power Plants* (ANSI, 1995e)
- ANSI/ANS-3.11-2000, *Determining Meteorological Information at Nuclear Power Sites* (ANSI, 2000), and ANSI/ANS-3.11-2005, *Determining Meteorological Information at Nuclear Facilities* (ANSI, 2005)

Fabric filters cannot handle gases at temperatures greater than or equal to 175°. HEPA filters are fabric filters usually used for particles less than 10 μm; HEPA filters remove 99.97% of all particulates 0.3 μm and larger (Koren, 2003).

5 Environmental Monitoring

INTRODUCTION

This chapter discusses the direction and operation of radiological environmental monitoring teams during all phases of a radiological emergency. Environmental monitoring (surveys) generally refers to active radiological measurements taken outside of plant buildings coupled with the collection of physical samples for later isotopic analysis. Permanent plant systems, such as installed process or effluent release point monitors, are not usually considered part of the environmental monitoring effort. A small number of reactor sites operate high-sensitivity, fixed-perimeter radiation monitoring systems, which are considered part of their routine and accident environmental monitoring programs. Radiation measurements are active when they are taken by emergency responders in real time while the event is in progress.

The task of environmental monitoring differs from other aspects of managing a radiological emergency in that directing surveys is more art than science. The unpredictability of an event; the associated limited information, limited resources, and limited access to the affected areas; and time pressure all combine to prevent effective preplanning. Methods exist to plan environment surveys so there is statistical confidence the sample sufficiently represents the entire area of interest;[*] some elements of these methods may be useful in the recovery phase. Computer programs exist to aid in planning radiological surveys; however, these programs are intended to be applied to a site about which much preliminary information is known and whose size is measured in acres to tens of acres, not in square miles to tens of square miles. It would be difficult to apply these statistical methods to an emergency situation because they are primarily intended for water, soil, and fixed contamination surveys, rather than direct exposure rate measurements, and they require a high sample density using grids that are 1 to 10 meters in size.

Radiological measurements made during an emergency are either prospective (real-time or near real-time) or retrospective (after-the-fact analyses of physical media collected during or after the event). Examples of prospective measurements include exposure rates or count rates read from survey meters, count rates from contamination smears, and gross count rates from air sample prefilters and sampling cartridges. Retrospective measurements include post-accident analysis of fixed environmental dosimeters, the analysis of low-volume continuous air samplers (changed every week to month), the isotopic analysis of radioactivity in water or milk, or analyses of soil samples.

Environmental monitoring performed under accident conditions is intended to (1) detect radioactive material that has bypassed effluent monitors or is released past inoperable detectors, (2) make measurements of radioactivity in the environment to verify that adequate measures have been taken to protect the health and safety of the public, (3) confirm the applicability and results of radiation dose models used to predict the consequences of a reactor accident, and (4) ensure that the radiation exposure of plant and offsite emergency workers is understood and controlled within acceptable limits (FEMA, 1990, pp. 1-2–1-4). Survey teams also act as eyes and ears in evacuated areas to identify stragglers, unsafe road conditions, and collateral events (e.g., evacuee automobile accidents, structure fires, gas line ruptures, downed power lines). Survey teams perform essentially the same tasks in accomplishing all of these purposes; the differences are in how the data are used after being collected.

---

[*] For radiological surveys the primary method is the *Multi-Agency Radiation Survey and Site Investigation Manual* (MARSSIM), which addresses survey grid size, instruments, sampling methods, sensitivity of analyses, and radioisotope concentration limits for the unrestricted release of a contaminated site. MARSSIM developed out of work such as IAEA-SM-229/103 (IAEA, 1979) and *A Statistical Methodology for Radiological Surveying* (Leggett et al., 1979, p. 541).

References to radioactive releases made in this chapter generally mean increased levels of radioactive effluent at a concentration detectable by portable radiation survey equipment. This usage may differ from the definition of a release in progress reportable to local authorities. The reader should not conclude from the following discussions of environmental monitoring that radioactive releases are likely or expected during emergencies at commercial reactors. However, it is difficult to usefully discuss environmental monitoring without supposing radiation or radioactive material for survey teams to measure. Although detectable radioactive releases have occurred during emergencies, periods of several years to a decade or more elapse between such events. None of the historical radioactive release events has been at concentrations that warranted protective measures for the public.

ENVIRONMENTAL SURVEY TEAMS*

The primary sources of information about radioactive material concentrations away from a damaged reactor are environmental survey teams deployed by the reactor licensee and by offsite authorities. The most common practice is for the reactor site to dispatch two or three offsite survey teams at an early stage of the event and for the state radiological health agency to deploy additional teams after they arrive (typically two). Licensee and state survey teams generally operate independently from one another, although some coordination is desirable to limit unnecessary duplication of effort and maximize the collected data. In some areas, combined (blended) teams of site and offsite personnel are used.

The primary missions of environmental monitoring teams in the first few hours of a radiological emergency are to determine gamma radiation exposure rates, collect air samples, measure the surface deposition of radioactive materials, and measure contamination; this period is referred to in the *Manual of Protective Action Guides* (USEPA, 1992) as the *early phase* of an event. Environmental monitoring teams should also be equipped to collect soil, vegetation, water, and food-pathway samples, which become more useful in later stages of the event. The emphasis in the first few hours should be on obtaining information useful in making decisions about immediate actions for protecting members of the public from radiation and radioactive material, rather than thoroughly characterizing the environment. After the initial protective actions are taken and the reactor site stabilizes, the mission changes to emphasize the more detailed measurements needed to identify protective measures for the food chain.

These initial measurements are made by ground-based teams, usually riding in trucks or similar large vehicles, although if necessary any sort of vehicle may be put into service. A typical team consists of two persons: a driver and a health physics technician. The driver must be a qualified radiation and emergency worker but does not necessarily require extensive health physics (i.e., radiation measurement) training. Some sites may deploy three-person teams comprised of a driver and two survey technicians. The technicians double as navigators, radio communicators, and log keepers. All team members should receive radiological emergency worker training.

The most common practice is for a reactor site to deploy two teams when a known radiological release is occurring, even when it is within allowable limits, or as an automatic action following declaration of an Alert or higher emergency classification.† These teams are typically staffed by reactor site personnel. Reactor sites are required to have on-shift staffing sufficient for near-immediate

---

* Standard I, "Accident Assessment," Element 7, of NUREG-0654 (NRC, 1980c) requires, "Each organization shall describe the capability and resources for field monitoring within the plume exposure planning zone which are an intrinsic part of the concept of operations for the facility." Element 8 requires, "Each organization, where appropriate, shall provide methods, equipment and expertise to make rapid assessments of the action or potential magnitude and locations of any radiological hazards through liquid or gaseous release pathways. This shall include activation, notification means, field team composition, ... monitoring equipment."

† Recall that an Alert classification is warranted when a reactor's margin of safety has been seriously degraded and radiological releases are either not expected to occur or are expected to be very small compared to Protective Action Guides. Because most reactor events are expected to develop slowly, this practice is intended to ensure that survey teams are available before radioactive releases begin.

environmental monitoring because reactor accidents can occur quickly and may not have readily identifiable precursors. Survey teams could not be deployed in the initial 1 to 2 hours of an event if team members came only from the emergency response organization called to the plant from offsite (home).* Additional teams may be deployed after the site's emergency response organization is mobilized.

In the author's opinion, the minimum radiological and sampling equipment for an environmental monitoring team consists of the following:

- Exposure rate instruments ranging between 0.005 mR/h (5 μR/h)† and 50 mR/h
- Exposure rate instruments ranging between 1 mR/h and 10 R/h (10,000 mR/h)
- Count rate instruments ranging between 0 counts/minute and 1E5 counts/minute with an appropriate selection of probes (Geiger–Mueller, NaI, Ge, etc.)
- High-volume air sampler equipped with a sampling head 5 inches or more across, collecting at no less than 10 ft^3/min, with both silver zeolite (or similar material) and charcoal sampling cartridges
- A variety of sample collection tools (e.g., trowel, spade) and sample containers (e.g., bags, buckets, jars and bottles, Marinelli beakers)
- Personal protective equipment, including self-reading emergency dosimetry, passive dosimetry,‡ anti-contamination clothing, potassium iodide, gloves and booties, and reflective vests for night operations

At least one additional instrument of each instrument type should be fielded for every two survey teams, allowing for an in-field rendezvous to replace a failed instrument rather than requiring a return to base.

The FEMA REP-2 (FEMA, 1980a) guidance recommends equipping teams with a high-range survey instrument whose upper range is 100 R/h. The author's opinion is that a 100-R/h measurement is unnecessarily high for a survey team; a 10-R/h instrument is sufficient to perform the mission and provide a safety margin for protection of team members. A survey team is initially deployed to detect unexpected radioactive material and to support protective action decision-making by the licensee and legal authorities. An initial environmental survey is not a laboratory-grade measurement. At downwind distances of a 1/4 mile or more, *any* radiation measurement in the mR/h range (i.e., greater than 0.001 R/h) indicates a large radioactive release, typically with activity release rates of 1E5 to 5E6 μCi/s, depending on the release height and stability class. Total effective dose equivalent (TEDE) is always greater than or equal to the exposure rate, so the dose cannot be less than the integrated exposure. Because protective actions for the public should be taken at exposure rates of 1 R/h or greater or an integrated TEDE greater than or equal to 1 rem, a survey instrument whose upscale measurement range is 1 R/h is adequate to identify areas for which protective measures are needed. The difference between the 1-R/h protective action threshold and a 10-R/h instrument detection limit provides protection for the survey team. The team should immediately move to a

---

* The minimum number of on-shift operators, mechanics, chemistry, and radiation protection staff is controlled by site technical specifications (the operating license), operations department procedures, the site emergency plan, and (for NRC-licensed operators) regulation. Reactor sites are staffed dayshift Monday through Friday in excess of minimum required staff but otherwise are staffed at or near the minimum required number of personnel. The minimum number of chemistry and radiation protection staff is chosen to ensure simultaneous capabilities to assess an accident's consequences, provide basic health physics protection to emergency workers in the plant, and to allow immediate dispatch of an environmental survey team.

† 10 μR/h may be an acceptable minimum sensitivity because natural background is rarely less than this value. There is no need for field instruments to be more sensitive than the local radiation background. This restriction on sensitivity does not apply to analytical laboratory instruments, which are generally shielded to much less than the local background count rate.

‡ Although film badges would be acceptable for this purpose, most current dosimetry uses thermoluminescent or optically stimulated solid-state materials. The dosimeter should be capable of responding to gamma radiation of energies from about 50 keV through about 5 MeV and should include a beta window. An alpha or neutron dosimeter should not be necessary for environmental teams, although they may be useful for some in-plant repair and mitigation workers.

lower exposure rate area once 1 R/h is detected, so it is unlikely that the team will be exposed to greater than 10 R/h. If the team is actually exposed to greater than 10 R/h, they should already be taking the appropriate action (e.g., leaving the area as quickly as possible consistent with safety), and their passive dosimetry will record their actual cumulative dose. Another lesser, but real, consideration is that survey instruments should be periodically calibrated in all detection ranges, and most organizations lack access to a calibration source of close to 100 R/h.

Some licensees and states equip their survey teams with single-channel or multichannel analyzers, with appropriate scintillation probes (e.g., NaI, GeLi, TaLi). Because radioactive noble gases are not deposited on surfaces or collected in air samples, these instruments allow field analyses of radioactive iodine. The alternative is to take an on-contact frisker (Geiger–Mueller instrument) measurement of the air sampling cartridge.[*] A single-channel analyzer allows a survey team to selectively measure a particular energy range characteristic of a single isotope. Knowledge of the abundance[†] of the measured energy—combined with detector efficiency, the background and sample count rates, and the sample volume—allows the concentration of the isotope of interest to be calculated. When ^{131}I is measured, the characteristic energy is usually near 354 keV. A multichannel analyzer simultaneously measures many energy ranges and allows identification of a large number of isotopes. A common calibration is 2010 channels between 30 and 2500 keV, for an energy discrimination of about 2 keV/channel. Multichannel analyzers employ computer peak-search algorithms coupled with libraries of 200 or more isotopes. The benefit of equipping teams with analyzer instruments is obtaining a faster and more accurate determination of the ^{131}I concentration (the other iodine isotopes from 128 through 132 rarely being measured). The costs or negative aspects of these instruments include the following:

- Team members require additional training to effectively use the instruments.
- The instruments are somewhat more expensive to purchase than typical radiation survey instruments.
- The instruments are more difficult and more expensive to calibrate, requiring more radiological expertise.
- The analysis requires more time and more in-field calculations as compared with Geiger–Mueller instruments (costing additional time and reducing the number of missions per team with higher rates of operator error).
- The minimum detectable activity in each channel requires the analysis to be done in a low-background area, farther away from the radioactive plume (costing additional time and reducing the number of missions per team). The background and sample count times may be longer for GeLi detectors than for NaI detectors (trading better efficiency for better energy discrimination).

The analyzer instruments and detector crystals available in the 1980s and 1990s tended to be highly breakable and not entirely suitable for field operations. This problem has largely been addressed, and current instruments are much more robust. The detectors with the best efficiencies and energy discrimination require cooling, usually with liquid nitrogen; maintaining this cooling

---

[*] A Geiger–Mueller type of instrument does not discriminate between beta and gamma radiation and does not discriminate based on radiation energy. When measuring an air sample cartridge with a Geiger–Mueller instrument, all resulting counts have to be assumed to be iodine or the effective count rate must be reduced according to some predetermined set of ratios. An all-iodine assumption always overestimates the committed dose equivalent (CDE) inhalation dose, potentially by factors of three to ten compared to the true concentration of ^{131}I. When the iodine concentration is overestimated, authorities may take protective measures for the public and for emergency workers when they are not required. When an adjusted count rate is used to calculate an assumed concentration of ^{131}I, the accuracy of the result depends on how closely the actual isotope concentrations match the assumed concentrations. Although the true concentration may still be overestimated with this method, the overestimate is likely to be less than the error from the all-iodine assumption. However, there is a significant possibility with this method that the true concentration will be underestimated. An underestimate could result in protective measures not being taken when they are justified or necessary.

[†] In this context, *abundance* is the fraction of all radioactive decays having the characteristic decay energy.

in the field can present both logistical and physical challenges. Liquid nitrogen can pose a safety hazard for team members, who should receive training in handling cryogenic (low-temperature) materials. Although radiological monitoring for emergency responders not performing environmental surveys is not the focus of this chapter, it is worth noting that FEMA REP-2 (FEMA, 1980a, p. 6-21) recommends that each access control point be provided with one low-range gamma detection device whose maximum range is 50 mR/h or greater for personal protection purposes. This is not a common offsite practice.

BASIC MONITORING CONSIDERATIONS

There should be at least an hour between the onset of a plant transient and significant core damage, even in a fast-moving reactor event. This gives the on-shift emergency response organization sufficient time to recognize the emergency and dispatch survey teams. Although teams could be dispatched after a significant radiological release has begun, this should be very unlikely when a licensee follows the normal practice of dispatching teams at the Alert emergency classification. In the more likely, slower moving event, survey teams would be dispatched hours before the start of a significant radiological release. Even if a release has begun prior to deployment, the survey team assembly point may be sufficiently distant as to not be radiologically affected.

Licensee and offsite survey teams are dispatched in large trucks or sport-utility vehicles; aircraft-mounted instruments will only be deployed for serious accidents and will be operational no sooner than 24 hours into the incident. The use of trucks has two implications for radiation monitoring: (1) survey teams are restricted to the existing road network, and (2) it is possible to over-drive the instruments. The on-road restriction can severely limit where a plume can be detected and the possible traverse* routes, depending on the combination of plume direction and site-specific roads. Road networks may be lacking in rural areas and in the vicinity of terrain obstacles such as rivers, lakes, or reservoirs or ridges and bluffs. Teams may be restricted to paved roads as a personal safety measure in some weather conditions. At many sites, a restriction from gravel or dirt roads would be a major impediment to accomplishing the survey mission.

Over-driving the instruments occurs when vehicle speed is much greater than the instrument response time. Analog and digital radiation survey instruments have characteristic detection or sampling times, and the human eye requires a minimum amount of movement on an instrument display to recognize a change. When a vehicle drives into an increasing radiation field, over-driving delays recognition of changing conditions; the changes are noted at some time and place after they occur. Depending on vehicle speed, delays of only a quarter to a half minute could cause an error in identifying the correct stability class. When team members are close to their radiation exposure limits or when the radiation exposure from the plume is close to team turn-back limits, a delay in recognizing changing conditions results in unnecessary radiation exposure (dose) to the team. Over-driving could also cause a team to completely miss a radiation area, especially when radiation exposure is near the lower detection limit. The author's experience is that survey teams are given designated monitoring location points by the survey manager and drive at or near the posted speed limit when moving between those points. On paved rural roads, the speed limit is usually at least 40 mph and could be as high as 70 mph. The author recommends that survey teams drive between

---

* A *traverse* is a one-way crossing from one side of the plume to the other, from an area of background radiation to the next closest area of background. Ideally, a traverse is perpendicular to the plume's direction of travel to give the most accurate determination of the edges of the plume. In practice, the possible traverse directions are limited by the local road network and are usually not close to a perpendicular (some angle across the plume). FEMA REP-2 (FEMA, 1980a, p. 4-3) states, in part, "therefore, it is necessary to have several measurement points and a traverse of the plume to provide delineation of the actual plume position. After establishing the plume location, an air sample must be collected at or near the plume centerline in order to provide air concentration measurements which can be directly compared with the projected plume centerline concentration, and hence exposure rate." Note that, although dose assessment programs calculate centerline isotopic concentrations internally, this information may not be available to the user for comparison with field measurements.

20 and 30 mph while actively monitoring to limit the effect of over-driving, although reducing the team's speed does reduce the number of missions a team can perform. Team members should remain aware that driving at less than the posted speed can create safety hazards, as can working along a high-speed road; this would not be an issue when an area has been evacuated.

The author recommends that an environmental team begin surveying with a frisker-type (count-per-minute) instrument and low-range (less than 1 mR/h) exposure rate meter as it leaves the team assembly area. These should be window-open measurements. A Geiger–Mueller-type (cpm) instrument is likely to be the most sensitive instrument available to survey teams. Starting out using the low-range detection capability ensures that the team will identify above-normal radiation exposure as soon as it occurs. Many instruments have audio features, especially count rate instruments. When an audio speaker is available, it should be used. Survey team members' ears are more sensitive than their eyes; team members will hear a change in count rate while watching the road, and those changes in count rates are evident to persons lacking extensive radiological training. Survey meter readings on low-range survey instruments should be averaged over 30 seconds, and high-range instruments should be averaged over 10 seconds (FEMA, 1980a, p. 4-20).

When radiation is detected, the survey team should immediately stop and make open- and closed-window measurements, noting the difference between them. If there is little difference, or none, then radiation shine is being detected and the team is not yet inside the plume. If the difference is large (typically, 50% or more of the window-open value), the team is inside the plume. This measurement should be made outdoors (at least with the vehicle window down and the instrument held outside); a survey made inside a closed vehicle could show no difference when one actually exists because the metal and glass block counts from beta radiation.

Emergency response personnel involved in environmental monitoring should establish the initial reporting level before teams are dispatched, preferably in procedures and checklists. The initial reporting level is the measured count rate or exposure rate at which the team immediately communicates the result back to the survey manager. This level is typically either the first non-background measurement or a measurement equivalent to 1 mR/h, but it could be a site-specific value between the two values. Emergency response organizations should not establish their offsite first-contact reporting value above 1 mR/h because this value represents a radioactive release of at least the Site Area Emergency level and offsite protective actions may be warranted (assuming a 1/4-mile or greater distance from the release point). An emergency response organization should establish additional (window-open) survey levels after first contact with a plume that require immediate reporting back to the survey manager; at a minimum, these should include the following:

- 100 mR/h—for many sites, this exposure rate measured at the site boundary is a condition that requires declaration of a higher (more serious) emergency classification (Site Area Emergency vs. Alert)
- 500 mR/h
- 1000 mR/h (1 R/h)—for all sites, this exposure rate measured at the site boundary is a condition that requires declaration of the highest (most serious) emergency classification (General Emergency); protective actions for the public would be required at this level of emergency
- Site-specific turn-back exposure rate—the exposure rate at which a survey team is not authorized to operate and requires immediate removal to a lower-dose zone

The turn-back exposure rate should be sufficiently higher than 1000 mR/h so that an adequate determination can be made of areas requiring protective actions. The author suggests that turn-back rates be set in the range of 1.5 to 3 R/h.

The first task in radiological environmental monitoring is to find the edge of the plume. Locating the edges is an important step in verifying dose projections. The cross-wind distance between edges is directly related to stability class, and stability class has an important effect on dose. The exact location of measurable airborne radioactivity may also be of significant interest to offsite emergency responders and elected officials, and could affect the actions they recommend or take. There is no generally accepted definition of a plume edge, and the topic is not addressed in guidance documents. When survey teams are equipped with µR/h instruments, a value of 50 µR/h (0.05 mR/h) may be considered as the outer edge, as this exposure rate is small enough to be within double or triple natural background but large enough to rule out random fluctuations. When teams are only equipped with higher range survey instruments, the effective lower limit of detection (often 1 mR/h) becomes the plume edge. All organizations that dispatch survey teams should establish their plume edge definition in procedure, and the definitions should be harmonized among organizations to the extent practicable.

Licensee dose assessment computer programs all calculate the expected peak integrated dose and exposure, and they all have some capability to overlay a plume on a local map. However, the graphic display resolution is often not as good as might be desired, and the map is often truncated at 1 mrem or 1 mR/h (or higher); some programs allow the user to set the map truncation value.[*] It may be difficult to directly validate the calculated plume location from environmental survey data made with more sensitive instruments. As survey teams traverse a plume, they may need to identify locations where the dose rate compares most directly with dose projection results.

Count rates greater than 100 to 150 counts/minute or exposure rates greater than about 50 µR/h provide an indication of abnormal conditions with confidence that actual radioactivity has been detected. If all plumes moved in straight lines, a single traverse of the plume would characterize its spread along its entire length. Because plumes meander and twist, the edges must be located at several different downwind distances (minimum of three, preferably more) and on both sides of the plume. The plume must be periodically rechecked to verify that the plume is not moving under the influence of local (downwind) conditions such as wind patterns different than those measured at the site or prominent terrain features.

A survey team should be capable of determining if they are detecting radiation shine (i.e., are in an area not in the plume), are submerged in radioactive material (are in the plume), or are traveling across contaminated ground (the plume previously passed through but is no longer present).[†] This is done by taking window-open and window-closed readings at head or shoulder height, at waist height (1 m), and at ground height (about 2 to 3 inches or 5 to 10 cm) (FEMA, 1980a, p. 4-20). All survey results at all heights should be the same if shine is being detected because the source is at a distance and only gamma radiation is detected. When the team is submerged in radioactive material, the window-open readings at every height should be the same, the window-closed readings should be the same, and the window-open values should be much larger than the window-closed values (factors of two to ten greater). Differences of factors of five (approximately) or more indicate the combination of fuel damage with an unfiltered release pathway. The amount of radioactive iodine and halogens (e.g., cesium) in normal reactor coolant are not sufficient to drive very large differences between open- and closed-window readings. When the primary radiation source is from radioactive material deposited on the ground, the ground-level window-open result is much larger than the window-closed result, the waist level window-open result is larger than the window-closed result (perhaps by 25 to 50%), and the shoulder-/head-level window-open and window-closed results are essentially equal. If a plume deposits radioactive material on the ground, moves away from the area, and then subsequently returns,[‡] the window-open results at every height would be much larger than the associated window-closed result, and all ground-level readings would be higher than waist-level readings, which would be higher than shoulder-level readings.

---

[*] This is different from calculation truncation, which is also usually a variable controlled by the user. The calculation truncation is a dose, dose rate, or exposure rate value below which all results are arbitrarily reported (displayed) as zero.

[†] FEMA REP-2 (FEMA, 1980a, p. 4-6) states: "A single ground level gamma exposure rate measurement does not distinguish between the exposure rate contributions from radionuclides deposited on the ground ... in the overhead gaseous plume, or from ... a ground level gaseous cloud (one in which a person is immersed)."

[‡] This could occur when a new release begins after securing a previous release path or when a continuing plume moves under the influence of shifting wind vectors.

The author recommends that survey teams collect wipe or smear samples at all survey locations beginning about an hour after the start of a radiological release. This time allows a buildup of radioactive material on surfaces so that a meaningful measurement can be made. In the case where contamination builds up quickly, a delay in collecting smear samples is unlikely to have practical effect because protective measure decisions do not depend on the data. Smear samples are most useful in identifying the isotopes released from the reactor; this analysis typically requires instruments available only in a radiochemistry laboratory. Any surface sample collected early in the event is likely to undergo significant radioactive decay before it can be transported to suitable analytical equipment, leaving only longer lived isotopes (those with half-lives measured in days, rather than minutes or hours). Teams should consider taking interior and exterior smears from their vehicle every hour or so after contacting the plume, counting the smears using a count-rate meter; such data have no immediate radiation protection benefit but can be useful to the survey team manager and may be useful when the team finally exits the operational area.

AIR SAMPLING

It is important for survey teams to collect samples of radioactive material in the environment because these provide the most accurate information about the isotopes actually present, as contrasted by those predicted to be present by models. In this context, an air sample is the solid radioactive material collected on a paper prefilter together with gases that adhere or adsorb onto a collection media in a cylindrical cartridge.[*] The filter is mounted in front of the cartridge so that solid material does not deposit on the cartridge face and decrease flow into the collection media. This sampling arrangement effectively collects most radioactive material; however, there is a very low (essentially zero) collection rate of gases that do not adhere well. The normal assumption is that only the noble gases (krypton and xenon) are not collected.

There are many possible arrangements of filter and cartridges. The most common arrangement is for a large filter, often 4 to 6 inches in diameter, and a cartridge approximately 2 inches in diameter by 1 inch thick.[†] Both the filter and cartridge are mounted in a somewhat conical (tapering) sample head that screws into the air pump casing. The most common filters are made from cellulose or from glass fibers on polyester.

The 5-rem committed effective dose equivalent (CEDE) Protective Action Guide for the thyroid is the only protective action threshold intended to protect an organ, and this value is based on exposure to radioactive iodine. Activated charcoal and silver zeolite are the primary media used to sample radioactive gases because they have excellent collection efficiencies for gaseous iodine. The collection efficiency of laboratory-grade charcoal for iodine is about 90%, charcoal impregnated with triethylenediamine (TEDA) has a collection efficiency of about 95%, and silver zeolite has a collection efficiency of effectively 100%.[‡] Silver zeolite is the preferred sampling media for radioactive iodine because of its very high iodine collection efficiency combined with a very low efficiency in collecting noble gases (principally ^{133}Xe, which interferes with the ^{131}I peak at 364 keV). Survey managers

---

[*] A true sample of airborne radioactive material can be collected using a *sample bomb*, an evacuated pressure vessel kept at near vacuum. The sample is collected by opening valves on the vessel and collecting the sample as air expands into the "empty" vessel, driven by the pressure differential. It is common for sample bombs to be plastic cylinders whose volumes are multiples of a liter (e.g., 1 L, 2 L, 3 L). A sample bomb must be matched to the laboratory counting system on which it will be counted, because the sample geometry (size) affects the instrument calibration (the peak search algorithm that converts from detected radioactive decays into concentrations of individual isotopes).

[†] The cartridge thickness is a function of the porosity of media and the pressure drop across the cartridge. The cartridge needs to be thick enough to have a high collection efficiency (all of the constituent radioactive material comes in contact with adsorbing material), yet not so thick to block air flow (burning up the pump motor). In an ideal media, the vertical distribution of deposited radioactive material follows the Gaussian (normal) distribution.

[‡] See, for example, Distenfeld and Klemish (1976). Similar reports include Whittaker and Heck (1965), Ludwick (1969), and Gavila (2003b). (Mention of a commercial product does not constitute endorsement by the author; similar technical reports are available from other manufacturers of air sampling media and equipment.)

should equip environmental teams with both activated charcoal and zeolite cartridges. The author recommends that each team carry enough cartridges to allow the team to collect an air sample every hour in the field, so from 8 to 12 cartridges should be carried; this is more cartridges than would be expected to be needed in a single operating shift. Teams operating away from their normal staging area should have enough cartridges for 3 days of operation; this applies primarily to state survey teams who may have to travel several hours from their normal work location to the vicinity of the reactor, with limited opportunity to resupply. A mixture of about two-thirds charcoal and one-third zeolite should be adequate. The reasons to carry charcoal cartridges include the following:

- Zeolite costs more than charcoal. In the late 1990s, a single zeolite cartridge cost about $35 vs. about $5 for a charcoal cartridge of similar volume.
- The collection efficiency of zeolite is more strongly affected by environmental conditions than is charcoal, particularly high temperatures and humidity.
- Zeolite degrades over time, so the cartridge should not be used past its listed expiration date.

Both charcoal and zeolite cartridges must be tightly sealed prior to use to limit the adsorption of radioactive gases from the environment. An unsealed or poorly sealed cartridge can also become contaminated prior to use while in storage in the survey vehicle.

The author suggests that silver zeolite cartridges are most useful when the release rate is unknown but increasing as measured on exposure rate meters and when concentrations approach protective action thresholds. The increased accuracy of the zeolite cartridge may not be necessary when iodine concentrations are much lower than Protective Action Guides, as indicated by closed-window exposure rates less than 50 mR/h (for gap or more severe fuel damage). The accuracy is also not necessary when concentrations are much higher than Protective Action Guides, as indicated by closed-window exposure rates greater than 200 to 300 mR/h. The range between roughly 50% and 150% of Protective Action Guides is where the added cost of silver zeolite cartridges is justified by their increased accuracy. Silver zeolite cartridges should never be unsealed or used during training, drills, or exercises—only during actual radiological events. When initial samples are collected using silver zeolite cartridges, often the confirmatory or backup samples can be made with charcoal cartridges.

The collection of air samples should be performed

- As close to the plume centerline as possible
- With the sampler positioned 3 to 5 ft off the ground to minimize dust loading
- With the sampler head pointed in the downwind direction
- At collection flow rates between 1 and 5 ft^3/minute
- At a total sample volume between 10 and 20 ft^3
- For total run times between 10 and 15 minutes

A field screening should be performed on the filter and cartridge as soon as possible after collection to estimate the iodine concentration vs. protective action thresholds. When the plume concentration approaches protective action thresholds, the background count rate is too large to measure the sample count rate with any confidence. In essentially all cases where the sample results are of interest, the sample must be removed to a low-background area to allow screening. Different organizations define "low background" differently, but all definitions fall in the range of 50 to 500 counts/minute.

The typical practice is to perform an on-contact frisk of filter and cartridge (on-contact in this case usually means through the plastic bag the sample is stored in). The usual assumption is the cartridge is 100% ^{131}I, although this ignores the other iodine isotopes and always overestimates thyroid dose. A 100% assumption for iodine is more reasonable for a gap release than for a fuel overheat scenario with ruptured fuel cladding; in the latter case, an assumption of 75% iodine (or less) may be more appropriate. There is a divergence of opinion regarding whether to include or exclude the filter when estimating thyroid dose, because some unknown fraction of the iodine is attached to dusts and other particles collected on the filter. Based on discussions such as found in NUREG-1465 (Soffer et al., 1995, p. 12), it might be appropriate to assign about 1% of filter counts to iodine and add them to the cartridge result when estimating iodine. FEMA REP-2 recommends that air samples be transported to an analytical laboratory within four hours of collection (FEMA, 1980a, p. 4-23). In-field spectroscopy is not generally recommended for the reasons discussed earlier in this chapter.

NUREG-0654, Planning Standard I, "Accident Assessment," Element 8, states (NRC, 1980c): "Each organization shall have a capability to detect and measure radioiodine concentrations in air in the plume exposure EPZ as low as 10^{-7} µCi/cc under field conditions. Interferences from the presence of noble gases and background radiation shall not decrease the stated minimum detectable activity." When the minimum detectable activity is calculated with 95% statistical confidence, the minimum detectable activity is given by

$$4.66 \times \sqrt{\frac{\text{Background count rate}}{\text{Detector efficiency} \times \text{Sample volume} \times \text{Unit conversions}}} \tag{5.1}$$

For a background count rate of 50 counts/minute, a collection volume of 10 liters, and a detector efficiency of 25%, the minimum detectable activity is about 6E-9 µCi/cc. If the background count rate is 500 counts/minute with the same volume and efficiency, the minimum detectable activity is about 2E-7 µCi/cc, which does not meet the NUREG-0654 performance standard. The value 4.66 is the Gaussian distribution Z-score for the 95% confidence interval; the value would be lower if less confidence were required (e.g., 90% confidence) and higher if greater confidence were required (e.g., 98% confidence).[*]

Because many of the isotopes found in a radioactive plume have half-lives measured in minutes to hours, the filter and cartridge count rates measured at the low-background location should be adjusted for radioactive decay to obtain the best estimate of iodine concentration. For example, the half-life of ^{134}I is 1 hour, that of ^{132}I is 2.3 hours, and that of ^{135}I is 6.8 hours. As long as the samples are counted within about 30 minutes of collection, decay can be ignored; in any case, the true decay correction factor is unknown, as it is essentially a weighted average of the half-lives of all isotopes present. If the 100% iodine assumption is made, more than 99% of the initial activity remains one hour after collection.

The most common air samplers used by environmental survey teams are powered by the team's vehicle, using battery clips similar to those on jumper cables. The vehicle should be pointed into the wind to the extent practicable. When the vehicle is stopped, a battery in good condition can provide power for one or two air sampler runs; a capacity for three runs should not be assumed (may jeopardize restarting the vehicle). It is usually a good practice to run the vehicle while the air sample is being taken. The next most common air samplers are battery operated; heavy car batteries are often used. Batteries suffer from a variety of problems, such as age-related depletion, voltage output that varies with temperature, and current fluctuations over time and between uses. These effects may cause the sample collection rate to change while the sampler is running. Many survey teams estimate the sample volume by multiplying the sample run time in minutes by the average of the beginning and end sample rates. The least common air samplers are those powered from portable generators. The problems with this arrangement are primarily connected with the generator: its bulk and the space it takes up in the sampling vehicle, its weight and the difficulty in lifting it in and out of the vehicle, and the safety issues associated with keeping a supply of gasoline in the survey vehicle.

Although it is not a problem for survey teams, emergency planners should be aware of problems in creating calibration standards for the laboratory analysis of air sample cartridges. This is important because an accurate isotopic analysis requires a calibration with a source in the same

---

[*] The treatment of instrument counting statistics is beyond the scope of this book, having more to do with health physics than with emergency response. Among the many papers and references available on the topic are Brodsky (1986), Cember (1983), Currie (1968, 1984), and Strom and Stansbury (1992).

position relative to the detector as the sample and one with the same source distribution. In the case of a sampling cartridge, neither a planar source nor a canister with evenly distributed radioactive material accurately represents a sample. The planar source calibration does not occur for self-shielding (attenuation) in the sample, and the evenly distributed canister calibration has too much self-shielding.

CONTAMINATION

Radioactive contamination is radioactive material that has spread beyond the systems and components designed to contain it. The contamination found offsite during or following a reactor accident is essentially always a thin film coating a surface.* Contamination does not occur uniformly; an object impinged by a radioactive plume is likely to have some uncontaminated areas and some areas of contamination. Two nearby objects both impinged by a plume are likely to have different degrees of contamination. Contamination rarely carries significant radiological risk.

If a radiological release has a limited duration (puff) or occurs in a high wind condition, the amount of contamination is likely to be small because the plume passes quickly and there is insufficient time for material to deposit. If a release has a low concentration, the amount of contamination is likely to be small because there is insufficient radioactive material available to deposit. When a release has both a high concentration and a long duration, the buildup of surface contamination is likely to be linear (increasing counts/minute over time). Areas closer to the plant are expected to have higher degrees of contamination than areas farther away, because of longer exposure times (the plume passes earlier) and because heavier isotopes tend to be depleted by gravimetric settling (do not survive to reach great distances).

In operational terms, contamination is typically characterized as loose or fixed. Loose contamination lightly adheres to a surface, is very mobile, and can be readily removed with essentially no residue or remainder. Fixed contamination is tightly bound to a surface, has very little mobility, and may be difficult or impractical to remove. Fixed contamination often undergoes a chemical transformation, such as bonding with rust, or becomes mixed in with a coating material, such as paint.

A smear sample is used to detect loose contamination. This sample is collected using a material to which loose radioactive material adheres when the sample media is rubbed across it with light to moderate pressure. The most common sample media is a 2-inch circle of cloth mounted inside a folder of thick waxed (semi-waterproof) paper. Closing the folder limits migration of the collected loose material away from the sample and provides a place to record important information about the sample (e.g., location, date and time, collector). A smear is typically collected by holding the folder open, pressing two fingers against the back of the cloth surface, and rubbing the sample surface against the surface of interest in an S-shaped pattern. The minimum sample area is 100 cm^2, formed by swiping the S-shaped pattern across an area about 8 inches long by 4 inches wide. Smears are typically counted by being placed in close proximity to a count-rate survey instrument. Environmental survey teams should be capable of collecting large numbers of smear samples.

Total surface contamination is most commonly measured with a count-rate meter, usually an open-window pancake-type Geiger–Mueller. The measurement is taken in close proximity to the contaminated surface (at distances of an inch or two). Fixed contamination is the difference between the total contamination and the loose contamination.

---

* Contamination in reactor components can penetrate beyond the surface layer and become a bulk property of the material; however, this process often takes place in conjunction with chemical processes such as chemical leaching or rusting. Bulk contamination often requires an extended contact with a contaminating material, such as reactor coolant. In the environment, contamination can become a bulk property of soils, driven into the soil by wind or leached by rain. Heavier isotopes settle into ponds, streams, rivers, and lakes, where they are incorporated into bottom sediments by analogous processes. The initial few hours of a reactor accident do not provide enough time for incorporating radioactive material into soil except in the uppermost few millimeters, still essentially a thin film.

Contamination becomes as issue for offsite survey teams because they are working in a contaminated environment after contacting the plume. After a period of time, the team members, the interior and exterior of their vehicle, and their working equipment become contaminated. Contamination is unlikely to occur fast enough or in amounts sufficient to affect the validity of readings from exposure rate survey instruments. The additional exposure rate from all sources (survey team member, vehicle, equipment) is likely to be on the order of the error in reading the instrument (or less, when ambient radiation exposure is in the tens to hundreds of mR/h). When the ambient count rate on a count rate instrument is from tens to a few hundred counts/minute above background, there may be a statistically significant over-response due to contamination sources; because a reference (non-contaminated) instrument is not available, the error cannot be quantified. At count rates of a few thousand counts/minute or greater (typically approaching 1 mR/h), the error is neither statistically nor operationally significant. The accuracy of MicroR exposure rate instruments is likely to be affected in the same manner as are count-rate instruments.

The most significant impact from working in a contaminated environment is the need to prevent the collected samples from becoming contaminated. When the sample collector's vehicle, tools, and gloves may be contaminated, and the sample container has become contaminated through poor handling techniques, it is difficult to maintain sample integrity. Sample contamination leads to higher analyzed concentrations than were actually present, and higher apparent concentrations may cause authorities to take unnecessarily protective measures. Contamination can also introduce isotopes that are not actually present at a sampling site. Because the isotopic distribution affects dose assessment, potentially over- or underestimating the actual dose, this category of contamination may also inappropriately cause change in implemented protective measures. Because the Protective Action Guides for relocating the public away from contaminated ground and for prohibiting consumption of agricultural products are relatively low, a heavily contaminated sample could cause a false positive.

STRATEGIES FOR MANAGING OFFSITE SURVEY TEAMS

It is very likely that a minimum of two offsite survey teams will be dispatched in an emergency before a radioactive release has occurred. In the early stages of an event, survey teams are primarily looking for an unexpected release bypassing plant systems that requires protective measures. The survey team manager needs to ensure that teams are kept generally informed about plant conditions, especially the potential for radioactive releases. It is helpful for teams to know when reactor and containment conditions make a release likely and when plant monitoring systems are unavailable. Team members must remain aware that their detection of radiation may be the first indication available to the emergency response organization and place some urgency on taking measurements and reporting them to the survey team manager.

The survey team manager should deploy one team as close to the site boundary (exclusion area) as possible while remaining offsite and deploy the second team farther out. The close-in team should be between 1/2 mile and 1 mile downwind, the distance at which a ground-level release can be accurately measured. Whenever possible, the close-in team should be no farther away than the distance a plume covers in 15 minutes (e.g., one-quarter wind speed in miles/hour). The second team should be stationed between 1.5 and 2.5 miles downwind, the distance at which an elevated release can be accurately measured. If suitable roads are available, the teams should continually traverse the roads; if there are no close-in roads, or the roads do not form a good traverse, the teams should be placed as close to the reactor site as possible without overlapping routes. The traverse endpoints should be local landmarks or intersections chosen so the survey spans five sectors. The traverse path must be wider than the expected plume width to ensure that the plume edges are discovered. Recall that protective action recommendations are made for areas at least three sectors across (the centerline sector plus the adjacent sector on each side). If possible the traverses of the closer and farther teams should be coordinated so that one team is always near the predicted plume direction. The team manager should avoid as much as possible having both teams simultaneously at their traverse endpoints, a situation that delays recognition of the leading edge of a plume (in the time needed to turn and move back to the center of the traverse, the plume could move past one or both teams).

Survey team managers have been observed during simulations and drills to park their close-in team along the closest offsite road (often at about a mile) at their best-estimate of plume direction (centerline), having the team continuously monitor until making contact with the plume. This is a practice that should be avoided. Survey team managers are generally limited to using plant meteorological towers as their source of wind direction data. Such data are valid only to about a mile for stability class B and C conditions and to no more than 2 miles for class E or F conditions. When a team is parked at a single location for an extended period without movement, they can lose attention and focus, they can fail to make contact with a plume if the meteorological data used by the survey team manager is wrong, and they can fail to make contact with the plume because of intervening terrain features.

After survey teams detect a plume, noting the location of its near edge, they should continue the traverse until detecting the centerline (the area having the highest exposure rate), again noting its location. The traverse continues until exiting the plume on its far side. It is often not useful to collect an air sample immediately upon contacting the plume, in part because the team has to leave the centerline to recognize it (exposure rates must be decreasing) and in part because the leading edge may not be representative of the entire release. If only two survey teams are deployed, the author recommends that one team continue to traverse the plume at downwind distances between 2 and 3 miles, taking an immediate air sample and another every hour or so; the available traverses will depend on the site-specific road network. The second team should traverse the plume with each traverse at a farther distance than the previous. The available traverses will depend on the site-specific road network, and the distance a team moves outward should depend on wind speed; there is no benefit to surveying unaffected terrain that has not been reached by the plume leading edge. There is no benefit to the outer team collecting air samples unless samples collected by the inner team are suspect. The outer team should continue to move outward until window-open survey results are less than 1 mR/h. When time and resources permit, this team should continue moving outward until the plume is not detectable on any available instrument. When the outer team has reached its furthest distance, it can relieve the inner team, which proceeds to survey outward to confirm earlier data. When a two-team survey is performed, the teams are typically under unified command and share common communications, so it is unlikely that data from one team is unavailable to the other.

When four survey teams (often two from the licensee and two from the country/state) are available, two teams should be assigned to traverse the plume and two teams to determining the plume edges as it expands downwind. One team should be assigned to map each edge, making contact with the plume then pulling back away from the plume (minimizing their radiation exposure by not passing through the plume), making contact again at a point farther out and continuing outward to the point when the plume is no longer detectable. The traversing teams should operate as previously described, one team performing a continuous traverse 1 to 3 miles downwind (depending on the local terrain and road network), the other team moving outward with each traverse until the plume is no longer detectable. At least two centerline air samples are needed—one as close as possible to the plant, the other 2 to 3 miles farther downwind. The author has observed that this strategy is commonly employed with licensee/utility teams performing traverses and county/state teams performing the plume edge surveys. Possible reasons for this include that the utility team is equipped with higher range instruments, the utility team has higher individual dose limits and better dosimetry, the utility is better prepared to deal with contaminated personnel and equipment, or utility personnel are more used to working in a radiation environment (e.g., offsite authorities are less willing to expose their personnel to radiation).

Good interorganizational communication is essential to effectively implementing a four-team survey strategy, as these teams are not under a unified command and are unlikely to share communications. The survey managers for each organization need to promptly agree on the teams to perform the traverses and the teams to perform the edge surveys. Each survey team manager needs to know the mission's assigned teams from the other organization, their approximate locations, and the exposure rates they encounter. This knowledge aids survey managers in avoiding duplication of effort (location) to the extent practicable given the site-specific road network. When the surveys teams are not under unified command, their data (survey results) are reported through the organizations to which each team belongs, but there is a potential for data not to be shared across organizations. A common operational weakness is a lack of integration of data of a similar kind generated by different organizations, so the respective dose assessment staff and decision-makers receive partial data rather than a complete picture. This silo effect is one of the problems the Federal Radiological Monitoring and Assessment Center (FRMAC)* is intended to address; however, there are circumstances under which the FRMAC organization may not be activated, and it may not be operational for 24 hours or more into the incident.

In the author's opinion, little benefit is gained by dispatching more than four teams to survey an active radiological plume, even when additional resources are available. Under some circumstances, a fifth team may be useful to survey the leading edge in a manner similar to the teams assigned the plume edges. Because the early emphasis is on centerline exposure rates and air samples, and the road network is likely to be a limiting factor, deploying six or more survey teams would likely lead to duplication of effort and to unnecessary radiation dose to survey team personnel. When additional survey resources can be obtained, it may be prudent to rest them away from the plume, using them as shift relief or to relieve teams that approach their radiation exposure limit. After the plume passes and the reactor is less unstable, additional teams will be needed to collect soil, vegetation, water, crop, and smear samples.

One element of an effective survey strategy is to utilize existing environmental monitoring stations. In particular, the existing low-volume air sampling stations and environmental dosimeters can provide accident specific data. Air samplers are typically exchanged weekly, and dosimeters monthly or quarterly. Very good long-term records are available for each air sampling and dosimeter station, all of which read essentially at background. After the radioactive release is secured and the plume has dissipated, environmental dosimeters and air sampler filters should be recovered as soon as possible from all stations. It should be possible to replace air sampling filters from existing onsite supplies, but replacement dosimeters may not be immediately available. Environmental air sampling stations are not equipped with radioiodine cartridges.

OPERATING IN PUBLIC

Survey teams are most likely to be deployed into the field before conditions develop that require offsite protective actions and before a radiological release occurs. At this stage of the event, the teams are operating in the public domain because there have been no evacuations and no access controls are in place. No emergency in the United States since 1979 has progressed past this stage. Operating teams in public presents a particular challenge in performing their necessary technical function without alarming the public. When an emergency has not resulted in activation of warning sirens, implementation of traffic or access restrictions, or offsite protective measures, much of the public may be unaware of the emergency declaration. Members of the public will be going about their ordinary activities at home and businesses, will be traveling roads downwind of the reactor

---

* The U.S. Department of Energy maintains funds, staffs, trains, and equips FRMAC. The majority of its operational staff and equipment are at Nellis Air Force Base, Las Vegas, NV. FRMAC has an aerial radiation-monitoring capability, and some aircraft are located at Andrews Air Force Base, District of Columbia. When FRMAC is deployed, its staff is augmented with technical staff from the Nuclear Regulatory Commission, Environmental Protection Agency, U.S. Department of Agriculture, Food and Drug Administration, Centers for Disease Control and Prevention, and other federal agencies. In the early and intermediate stages of an incident, FRMAC is managed by the Department of Energy; in the recovery stage, FRMAC is managed by the Environmental Protection Agency, which has statutory authority to determine the long-term radiological remediation criteria for a peacetime radiological incident.

plant, and will observe survey team activities in this context. The public may, or may not, recognize the survey teams as an unusual activity. Some issues that should be considered in event preplanning include the following:

- *When will survey team members don anti-contamination clothing?* Although a cloth coverall may not appear unusual to the public, the Tyvek® or plastic anti-contamination clothing commonly used at reactor sites will appear unusual; the public associates such clothing with hazardous material operations and is likely to become alarmed.
- *When will survey team members don respiratory protection?* A respirator worn in an industrial setting is not alarming to the public, but is it likely to be alarming when worn along a roadside. This is especially true when self-contained breathing apparatus is worn.
- *When and how should survey team members wear dosimetry?* Radiation dosimetry provides no useful information when the team is exposed to only background radiation (i.e., it does not matter if the dosimeter is left in the vehicle or is worn by the team member). Survey team members have the means to immediately recognize exposure to radioactive material, alerting them to don their dosimetry. Self-reading dosimetry prominently worn or displayed by team members may cause the public to conclude that they are being exposed to an unsafe dose of radiation, especially if multiple dosimeters are worn (e.g., low-range and high-range instruments).
- *Should survey team members wear company badges or identification (e.g., site or protected area access badges) while on survey missions?* Because members of the public or press may approach survey team members, the names and badges of team members should be easily visible.
- *How are survey team vehicles marked?* Vehicles with company or governmental logos may not alarm the public who see them. Vehicles marked for emergency or hazardous material response, as an emergency response team, or having similar markings are more likely to be noticed by the public. The public is likely to become alarmed, especially if no information has been released about the emergency.
- *How should operating procedures be modified when other vehicles are present?* Dust clouds raised by vehicles traveling unpaved roads affect air sampling by causing heavy dust loading on the sampling filter.
- *What safety precautions should team members take while working along roads?* Many rural roads have speed limits of 50 mph or more, so other vehicles can be a major personnel hazard. The dust clouds raised by vehicles on unpaved roads diminish visibility and can be a choking hazard. If the team is operating at night, do team members have reflective vests, reflective armbands, spot lights? Such measures provide additional visibility to the teams that is protective but calls attention to team operations.
- *How should team members interact with the public or press?* Planners should consider that the public may be curious about survey team activities and approach them with questions— Where are you from? What are you doing? What's going on? Is there any danger? What should I do? It is unlikely that teams in the field can prevent the public from approaching or observing their activities. When team members refuse to answer or interact, they may cause unnecessary alarm. Team members should be given instructions and training on the information they may provide and information they cannot. Team members should be provided guidance in the event the public or press photographs or records their activities. A job aid or reference card may be appropriate, especially if team members are expected to provide information about how to obtain official information (e.g., local radio station call letters and frequency, rumor control phone number, web address).
- *Are survey team communications capable of being monitored using base station or scanner radios available to the public, and are the communications encrypted?*

OPERATING IN EVACUATED AREAS

FEMA REP-2 (1980a, p. 6-13) states that less effort should be expended in surveying areas where evacuation is complete (or no effort): "Field monitoring efforts should be concentrated at the edges of the evacuated areas because a primary responsibility of the field monitoring is to determine that the evacuated area is large enough." This guidance needs to be understood in the context of the emergency preparedness capabilities and practices of the 1980s, primarily,

- Environmental survey teams were not dispatched until a release of radioactive material was imminent or occurring (i.e., teams were rarely in place before the release started).
- Protective measures for the public near a reactor site were not necessarily recommended immediately upon declaring a General Emergency classification.
- Offsite authorities often required a physical measurement before implementing protective measures for the public (before NUREG-0654, Supplement 3).
- Computer-based plume dispersion models were in their first generation, employed much less comprehensive modeling than is currently available, and were not universally used. Consequently, there was less value in confirming dose projection predictions in the field, and there was much less ability to use survey data to modify dose projections (e.g., increase accuracy based on measurement).

If plant conditions continue to degrade, an emergency classification will be reached that requires protective measures. Current practices will likely cause evacuation of the public within at least a 2-mile radius of the reactor; at some sites downwind, to 5 miles or more. If the REP-2 guidance were strictly followed, one survey team would be positioned to traverse 2 to 3 miles downwind (along the edge of the 2-mile evacuation) and the other team would monitor the three sides of the rectangle extending downwind (beyond the radial evacuation). The 2-mile team would still make initial contact with the plume, but if a closer road were available there would be an unnecessary delay. If an unmonitored* release were in progress, the delay in detection also delays appropriate protective measures. Protective measures (shelter-in-place or evacuation) are taken for areas larger than the plume is expected to impact, so that some members of the public are protected as a precaution, not because they are expected to be exposed to radioactive material. This is done, in part, because of uncertainty in the actual position of the plume and to provide a buffer against future changes in wind direction. A survey team that moves along the protective measures boundary crosses the plume centerline but for the most part is not in contact with the plume. A substantial amount of time could elapse between the inner team contacting the plume and the outer team making contact.

Although having two centerline locations (at 2 miles and 5 miles) provides some indication of plume location, such a survey strategy does not define the plume boundaries along its entire length, does not provide information about plume meander, and does not provide information about the distance at which the plume can be detected. If the plume exceeded Protective Action Guides along the edge of the evacuation zone (i.e., conditions warrant extending protective measures to a further distance), the outer team would not provide the information necessary to identify the protective measures zone unless that team were detailed to follow the leading edge.

SURVEY OPERATIONS IN CHALLENGING SECURITY SITUATIONS

Radiological survey teams are dispatched based on either conditions at the reactor site (higher effluent release rates) or emergency classification (Alert or higher). Prior to 2001, it was assumed that survey teams would be deployed in the same way in essentially any kind of emergency situation.

---

* An unmonitored release is a release of radioactive material not discernable using plant radiation monitors. The release may bypass engineered release pathways (e.g., steam generator safety relief valves that vent directly to the environment), or installed radiation detectors may be inoperative (e.g., from a loss of power, detector or associated cables destroyed by fire).

There was some recognition that unusual unsafe conditions in the survey zone could at least delay surveys, but these were thought to be limited to hurricanes, intense blizzards, and those earthquakes capable of damaging or destroying the offsite road network. At some reactor sites, a major natural disaster could also affect nearby industrial facilities, potentially causing dangerous chemical plumes or other airborne hazards.

After 2001, offsite response organizations have reconsidered deploying survey teams when a major security event is in progress in the emergency planning zone. The general assumption is that the security event is an active threat against the nuclear power facility; however, it is likely that a threat or attack against a facility elsewhere in the emergency planning zone could result in an emergency declaration at a commercial reactor site (e.g., an attack against a nearby oil storage facility). It is also possible that concurrent threats or attacks are made against both the reactor site and some other facility in the area.

There is no current guidance on whether to deploy environmental survey teams when the condition initiating an emergency is a threat or attack against the reactor site. The actions that reactor sites would take in response to a threat or attack would likely preclude survey teams being dispatched from the reactor site; teams would have to be formed from offsite resources (e.g., survey technicians called from home). At some reactor sites, the threat response precludes survey technicians from obtaining their vehicles or survey equipment, which may be stored onsite. The most likely response would be for available survey teams to be assembled at a forward operations post outside the emergency planning zone and held there until law enforcement resources become available as escorts. These teams could come from reactor sites unaffected by the threat or from state agencies, both of which may have long mobilization times. In the author's experience it is impossible at the current time to predict when and how radiological surveys would be performed at any specific reactor site if a security situation exists. The licensee would take many *ad hoc* actions, depending on the specific situation, event timing, and the information known to the site security and operations organizations. A concurrent radiological release would substantially complicate these *ad hoc* actions. It is unclear how both radiological safety and security activities would be performed because none of the hostile-action exercises conducted between 2007 and 2011 included a simulated radiological release; licensees were also required to hold hostile-action-based exercises between 2012 and 2015, and very few elected to include radiological releases as part of the scenario.

POST-PLUME SURVEY MISSIONS

The survey team's mission changes after the active plume has ceased. This means that the physical release path is isolated at its source and the back edge of the plume has traveled downwind and become undetectable. In many emergency preparedness exercises, the reactor coolant system and containment pressures are reduced to atmospheric pressure (zero pressure difference across the containment boundary) by the end of the exercise, perhaps 5 to 6 hours after the initial core damage. This situation may not completely end radiological releases if the release path remains open because decay heat will continue to cause radioactive material to transfer into the environment. The best that can be said of this situation is that the continuing radiological releases will be very small compared to peak release rates and may not be measurable using portable survey meters, especially with the elevated radiation background caused by radioactive material deposited on the ground. Survey team post-plume missions include identifying areas that were not initially evacuated from which the public should subsequently be removed, performing a preliminary deposition survey of the emergency planning zone, beginning the collection of environmental and food samples to determine the radiological impact on the food chain, and beginning the long-term environmental characterization.

Members of the public may not have been initially evacuated because of competing non-radiological safety concerns or because accident consequence models did not identify all of the impacted areas. Relocation could affect persons who initially sheltered-in-place or who were not included in any initial protective actions. The public should be relocated from areas in which the projected 1-year

TEDE dose is greater than or equal to 2 rem. For the expected mix of released radionuclides, this is approximately a 250-μR/h exposure rate (0.25 mR/h). Post-plume relocation decisions are based on direct exposure rate measurements in the environment or from measurements of surface contamination but will not be based on mathematical models. It is acceptable for members of the public to be relocated up to several days into an event because their radiation dose during the survey period will be very much lower than the immediate evacuation threshold.[*] The use of a much lower threshold for relocation is justified, in part, by the much lower travel risk associated with relocation (e.g., fewer vehicles on the road, lower driving speeds, the presence of law enforcement at checkpoints).

Relocation is intended to protect members of the public from external radiation hazards caused by long-term shine from contaminated surfaces. Some additional radiation dose can result from airborne radioactive material or from ingestion, but this contribution is typically much smaller than from external exposure. The relocation screening threshold is referred to as a *derived intervention level*, calculated from an isotopic analysis of deposited radioactive material. It is assumed that members of the public are at their residence the entire year with no absence (i.e., 8760 continuous hours). No credit is given for cleanup or decontamination or for reduction by wind or weather (i.e., the only mechanism is radioactive decay). The 1992 version of the Protective Action Guides included separate derived intervention levels for 1-year, 2-year, and 50-year exposures and the lowest value (most limiting case) was used for the relocation threshold. Analyses of the expected distribution of radioactive materials after most accident sequences predict that the 1-year case will almost always be the most limiting. The 2013 version of the Protective Action Guides eliminated the 2-year and 50-year intervention levels.

EPA 400-R-92-001 (USEPA, 1992) recommends an initial screening threshold of twice background for allowing evacuated residents to return to their residences, although this may not meet the dose-based return criteria. In practice, a screening exposure rate of 250 μR/h is too low because most of the dose is delivered in the first few months following a radiological event because of radiological decay, and dose is not delivered at a constant rate throughout the year. Exposure rates between 1 and 25 mR/h are more likely screening criteria in the first week following an event. Because of radiological decay, the screening criteria decrease over time; that is, the longer the time that elapses between the radiological release and the population survey, the lower the relocation criteria will be. Also, low-contamination areas may be affected by resuspension from nearby more highly contaminated areas (USEPA, 1992, p. 7-4).

RESUSPENSION

Resuspension is defined as the transfer of previously deposited radioactive material into air. It is any process that moves contamination from the ground or other large surface to an airborne state, making the material available again for inhalation or ingestion. The weight, surface area, and chemistry of a particle affect its ability be resuspended, as do external factors such as wind speed and precipitation. The resuspended fraction is estimated to be between 1E-6 and 1E-7 per day of all available source material.[†] These estimates derive from chemical tracer experiments conducted in the 1950s and 1960s (Slade, 1968, Chapter 7) and from post-Chernobyl measurements. Resuspension is more of an issue at the beginning of the post-plume phase than later. This is because of radioactive decay, weathering effects that transfer radioactive material deeper into soils, and the eventual wedging of windborne radioactive material into locations from which it cannot go airborne again. Resuspended radioactive material is expected to be a very minor inhalation or dose hazard.

---

[*] Recall that the purpose of (evacuation) Protective Action Guides is to prevent radiation injury, not to prevent radiation exposure or dose. This is a subtle distinction, particularly for the public, and great care is required when communicating the need for relocation to affected members of the public.

[†] For more information about resuspension, see technical reports such as *Derivation of Effective Resuspension Factors in Scenarios for Inhalation Exposure Involving Resuspension of Previously Deposited Fallout by Nuclear Detonations at the Nevada Test Site* (Kocher, 2009).

The term *weathering* describes the removal of radioactive contamination from vegetation surfaces by wind, rain, and other natural processes excluding radioactive decay. Many crops absorb radioactive material more effectively through surface contact than through the root system; therefore, weathering has a significant effect on the source term available for ingestion. Species of iodine have an uptake rate of about 35% through the leaf (Slade, 1968, p. 373). Weathering half-time estimates are between 6 and 56 days, with 11 days being typical (Till and Meyer, 1983, p. 5-36). Other sources give average weathering half-times as between 11 and 14 days (e.g., FEMA, 1987, p. 2-25). For a more complete discussion of weathering, see Appendix A of FEMA REP-13 (FEMA, 1987).

POST-PLUME PRIORITIES

The immediate priorities for the post-plume phase are performing a driving survey of all roads potentially affected by the plume, sampling crops being actively harvested, sampling from animal forage and feeds being actively fed to food animals, and sampling surface water supplies. A driving contamination survey can be done soon after cessation of the active radiological release. This is a moderate-speed pass along roads in the emergency planning zone potentially affected by the plume to get a quick idea of what is contaminated and what is not (a go/no-go survey). This initial information is used to develop a more detailed and systematic environmental sampling plan. The author recommends a pass at between 20 and 25 mph, performing a continuous survey with a low-range instrument (μR meter or count-rate meter), and collecting road surface smears every half mile; the survey is even more useful if the detector can be maintained near the road surface (say, within 2 feet or so). A single survey team can survey about 7.5 linear mph in this manner. An emergency planning zone with a road grid at half-mile intervals has about 760 mile of roads, requiring approximately 100 team-hours to perform a complete survey. If only three sectors are potentially affected by the release, the driving survey requires about 19 hours, which is less than one shift if three survey teams are available.

Because it takes time for contaminated forage and feed to build up to detectable levels in animal products, milk sampling should begin between 24 and 48 hours after the event, and sampling for meat can be delayed for 48 to 96 hours. If the volume of samples is too high for the available analysis facilities, meat animals can simply be sequestered and not allowed to go to market until sampling can be done. Dairy animals have to be milked, but sequestering or destroying the milk instead of allowing it to go to market is an option; acceptable storage for milk is often in short supply, so sequestering is at most a short-term option.

If the event occurs between planting and harvest, food sampling should be done in the order crops will be harvested. If the event occurs after harvest and before planting, the fields need to be sampled and determined to be uncontaminated before the next planting season (may vary with crop). In either case, there is time to work out an in-depth sampling plan and acquire additional analytical capabilities. There are no public protection issues connected with allowing crops to rot in the field or banning planting, but there are substantial economic and public policy issues. In some cases, using somewhat contaminated fields for non-food crops may be a preferable option to complete abandonment.

IODINE IN MILK

The most immediate food pathway concern is iodine in milk. Milk is a concern because children consume large amounts of milk and are more sensitive to radiation and radioactive material than are adults. Radioactive material enters milk about 4 hours after ingestion by the cow or goat, reaching a peak concentration in about 65 hours (for a single ingestion event); the time of peak concentration is extended if the animals continue ingesting contaminated feed for an extended period of time. Cow's milk returns to normal concentrations of radioactive material about 6 days after its final intake. Goat's milk contains higher concentrations of radioactive material than does cow's milk after the same forage is eaten (goats have a higher stomach-to-milk transfer efficiency).

One dairy cow produces between 17 and 37 pounds of milk per day. Raw milk is typically cooled and stored to between 38°F and 45°F. Shipments from individual farms to processing plants occur every 2 to 3 days. FEMA REP-12 states that in 1981 about 2% of all milk was produced for home use, 1% was processed by the farmer and sold directly by the farmer to consumers, and 38% was sold to processing plants, the remainder being processed for uses other than direct liquid consumption (FEMA, 1987).[*]

Milk monitoring should be performed as close to the producing farm as possible, preferably sampling individual storage tanks at the diary farm. Monitoring should be done before the milk is batched, so the sources of any contamination can be readily determined. Secondary monitoring can also be done at milk transfer points. It is less efficient to sample at the dairy and more efficient to sample large batches, so that fewer samples are collected. The large number of samples will cause the number of available detectors to become a choke point, and some sort of prioritization scheme will have to be worked out to analyze the more likely affected locations first. However, if only a few dairies are actually affected by ground and feed contamination, dairy level sampling will result in a smaller amount of milk that must be diverted or abandoned, thus having less economical impact. Public confidence will demand taking samples of all commercial products to prove that control and embargo efforts are successful. The preferred field method is passing 4 liters of milk through an anion resin, using a 2×2 sodium iodide (NaI) scintillation probe to count the resin (the resin concentrates the iodine and removes interfering isotopes). An alternative method is to immerse the probe in a 20-liter sample, although this method overestimates the iodine concentration due to problems with isotope interferences. A 2-liter sample should be collected at every location for future strontium analysis (the analysis takes approximately 2 weeks plus detector time).

Note that milk transfer points and dairies supplied from farms in the emergency planning zone may be located some distance away, far outside radiologically affected areas. This can present significant logistical and coordination issues in getting survey teams to the necessary locations. The disposal of resins contaminated by radioactive materials may also become an issue because this creates a mixed (chemical and radiological) waste.

The number of required milk survey teams is a function of the number of sampling locations (e.g., farms, transport stations) and the required sampling frequency. A single sample team can survey between 8 and 12 locations per 12-hour shift, or about 30 locations per milk collection cycle. FEMA REP-12 (FEMA, 1987) states that the U.S. Food and Drug Administration (FDA) prohibits dilution of contaminated milk by uncontaminated milk to achieve concentrations below the derived intervention level (i.e., to reach free-release criteria). The FDA recommendations are to embargo milk based on actual evidence of contamination and not solely on dose projections or surface contamination measurements of fodder. Milk above the intervention level will not be allowed into commerce (i.e., it will be diverted or destroyed). The FDA does not currently address holding milk for decay, although this would probably not be possible for fluid milk due to bacteriological concerns; in theory, such milk could be held and processed for non-drinking use. Cesium and strontium isotopes are also of concern in milk, however, for these isotopes cannot occur without iodine also being in the milk.[†] In most accident sequences, the amount of available iodine is much larger than that of cesium, and iodine is simpler to detect. Any milk with measurable iodine should also receive analysis for cesium (by spectroscopy) and strontium (requires chemical processing and separation in a laboratory).

---

[*] Derived intervention levels for milk are as follows: ^{90}Sr, 160 Bq/kg (4.3 pCi/g); ^{131}I, 170 Bq/kg (4.6 pCi/g); ^{134}Cs or ^{137}Cs, 1200 Bq/kg (8.6 pCi/g). Derived intervention levels are applied individually and are *not* summed, averaged, or subject to the $1/N$ rule. For more information see USFDA (2004). Derived intervention level values are calculated for five age groups, from 3 months through adult, assuming a 30% contamination of the diet. Previous guidance (USEPA, 1984a,b) assumed contamination of 100% of the diet. Also see USFDA (1998). Prior to 1998, derived intervention levels were established at preventative and emergency levels; actions were intended to be taken when preventative levels were exceeded provided there was minimal economic and food chain disruption; action was required above emergency levels regardless of cost or disruption.

[†] This is true for damaged fuel in an operating reactor or for stored fuel in the first 3 months after reactor shutdown. The complete inventory (source term) of iodine isotopes is decayed away by 5 months after reactor shutdown.

The available protective measures to prevent contamination of milk include putting food animals onto covered or stored fodder as soon as possible, removing animals from the potentially affected area, quarantining milk for use in non-drinking applications (with radioactive decay), and destroying milk or animals. States typically recommend that all animals be provided stored or covered feed when an accident escalates to the Site Area Emergency or General Emergency classifications. The purpose is to have farmers, dairymen, and ranchers implement measures to eliminate or reduce an animal's intake of radioactive material before the start of a radiological release.

FOOD CROP SAMPLING

If harvest is in progress, food crop sampling should begin within 36 hours of the initiating event, beginning with the first crops to be harvested, starting along the radiological centerline and working outward toward lower contamination areas. Leaf crops should be sampled before root crops. The survey should consist of rapid field measurement with a count-rate meter, bulk or composited gamma spectroscopy, and longer term wet-chemistry methods to quantify strontium uptakes. Gross in-field beta measurements (window-open) will over-respond compared to gamma (window-closed) measurements if the contaminant is only on the surface and not homogeneously distributed. The results of wet-chemistry methods may not be available quickly enough to prevent significant spoilage; it may be ultimately simpler to destroy exposed crops with short storage times. Typical sample sizes include the following:

- One square foot of soil to a 1-cm depth, minimizing collected pebbles and plant matter (a sample of this size is between 1 and 2 lb in weight)
- Approximately 4 kg (9 lb) raw vegetation or animal forage collected over an area of 1 square meter, collected at least 3 cm (1 inch) off the ground
- Approximately 1 gallon of surface water collected about halfway between the surface and the bottom

Assuming that a food sampling team collects a soil sample, surface water sample, two crop samples, and an animal forage sample at every location, with a 10- to 15-minute transmit time between locations, a team can sample 14 to 16 locations per 10-hour shift.

SURVEY TEAM COMMUNICATIONS

Survey teams must be capable of reliably communicating with the survey team manager from locations throughout the emergency planning zone, and for some distance beyond. Because survey teams will likely measure airborne radioactivity until it disperses or decays below the detection threshold, an effective communications radius of 20 miles or more will be needed. The most common arrangement is a primary radio system and a backup cellular telephone, with a radio antenna at the reactor site and a second antenna at the emergency operations facility (in some cases, the emergency operations facility has a landline or fiberoptic cable connection to an onsite radio tower). The radio system usually is capable of transmitting on multiple frequencies, at least one of which is in common with offsite law enforcement or fire departments. Some licensees also provide backup hand-held radios with less range than the primary system with a long antennae mounted on vehicle roofs.

The issue of communications interoperability has received significant attention since 2001, as a lack of communications between offsite agencies and between offsite agencies and the reactor site can hinder or prevent an effective event response. Interoperability is the ability of any one organization in a response effort to directly communicate with any other organization in the same effort, using communications equipment with common characteristics, frequencies, and (for data) computer programs and file formats. However, in the author's opinion, emergency planners need to distinguish between operational and technical communications and provide interoperability only for those functions that require it. Operational communications are between response organizations with tactical missions involving immediate actions to defend or protect persons and critical site infrastructure (including site take-back operations). The onsite organizations performing such missions are operations (including the control room), security, the fire brigade, emergency medical technicians, and the operations support center. The offsite organizations supporting these missions are primarily fire departments, local law enforcement (e.g., sheriff's department, state highway patrol, state police), and ground and air ambulances. Communications interoperability between these organizations allows for the effective coordination of personnel, the sequencing of necessary actions, fire control among law enforcement and security personnel, and the ability to warn of dangerous or changing conditions.

Technical communications concern the coordination, acquisition, and reporting of data not associated with immediate lifesaving or defense of the facility. Such information may require specific training or expertise to interpret, may be subject to misinterpretation, or may alarm untrained persons. In most cases, it is not desirable to broadcast data such as radiation exposure rates, dosimetry results, air sample and frisker count rates, and contamination survey results to all emergency responders. Most emergency responders do not need radiological data to perform their emergency functions, and the radio traffic is an unneeded distraction for them. Many other responders do not possess the background to effectively understand or make use of radiological data, and these individuals would likely be confused. Raw information from survey teams should not be accessible to the public before it is validated and its significance determined. In all cases, there is substantial risk that information could be taken out of context by persons not trained to understand it and without waiting for confirmatory information.

GLOBAL POSITIONING UNITS

Many licensees now equip their environmental survey teams with global positioning units and record the latitude and longitude of each measurement. This may be another example of collecting information simply because it is possible, without identifying a benefit or even a purpose. In the author's opinion, there is no significant emergency response benefit to having this information unless the organization operates a multilayer, real-time global information system. Survey teams are generally directed using a combination of meteorological data, local intersections and road descriptions, pre-established monitoring points, and landmarks. Protective measures are implemented using local landmarks, roads, and geopolitical boundaries so an adequate distance (margin) exists between the plume and the unaffected public. The additional precision of knowing a sample location or a survey team's location to within a few feet adds nothing to the protective measures being taken for the public or for emergency workers.

COMMON PROBLEMS WITH ENVIRONMENTAL SURVEY TEAMS

Prudent emergency planners should design and operate their programs to minimize predictable performance or equipment issues. Drill and exercise experience has identified several common issues that arise in deploying or operating survey teams; examples include the following:

- Failure to accurately communicate measurement units (e.g., disintegrations/minute vs. counts/minute, microrem vs. millirem vs. rem per hour, millirem/hour vs. millirem, cubic feet vs. liters vs. milliliters, inches vs. centimeters, or values reported with no associated unit)
- Poor log keeping that lacks documentation of missions, communications, and measurements
- Failure to use the phonetic alphabet and three-way communication practices
- Unfamiliarity of survey team members with the local road network (e.g., tendency to become lost)

- Unfamiliarity with operating the radio system (e.g., use of the wrong communications frequency)
- Lack of µR/h monitoring capability
- Lack of replacement consumables (e.g., fresh instrument batteries, sufficient sampling gloves, correct sizes of anti-contamination clothing)
- Lack of markings at predetermined monitoring points (adding to difficulties in finding assigned locations)
- Inaccurate maps or maps not updated to current roads
- Vehicles in poor condition (e.g., battery, tires, wiper fluid, exterior windows, interior cleanliness).
- Lack of readily available fuel to support extended operations
- Lack of sample couriers to retrieve samples and transport them from collection vehicles or couriers not being capable of communicating with survey team vehicles
- Cross-contamination between samples due to contaminated tools
- Detector probe contamination due to lack of probe covers or poor monitoring techniques
- Lack of appropriate chain-of-custody records to ensure the correct association between sample results and sample

WORKER SAFETY FOR SURVEY TEAM MEMBERS

Providing an adequate level of personnel safety for survey team members is challenging because of the wide variety of physical hazards they face. In addition to exposure to potentially high concentrations of radioactive material, survey teams operate in inclement weather that may include extreme temperatures, working at night, encountering a variety of driving conditions, or working outdoors in areas with high-speed traffic and uneven footing. It is even possible that they could encounter poisonous animals. Some response organizations (both licensee and offsite) focus solely on radiological safety and do not place sufficient emphasis on other likely hazards that can be easily anticipated. Most of the discussion about protection from radiation applies generally to all emergency workers.

RADIATION DOSIMETERS

Members of environmental monitoring teams are more likely to be exposed to airborne radioactive material than are many other emergency workers. Each team member should be a fully qualified radiation worker with a general knowledge of radiation and its physical and biological properties, and at least one team member (preferably all) must have more advanced training in health physics and in the use of radiation survey instruments. Each team member should carry a passive integrating dosimeter and an active self-reading dosimeter. The integrating dosimeter is the dosimeter of legal record and if a single dosimeter is worn will integrate the worker's individual dose throughout the event. Most integrating dosimeters distinguish between beta (skin) dose, shallow gamma dose, and deep gamma dose. Film badges have essentially disappeared as occupational dosimeters, having been replaced by thermoluminescent and optically stimulated solid-state dosimeters. Integrating dosimeters should be worn in the center of the chest, with the beta-collecting surface facing outward; when anti-contamination clothing is worn, the dosimeter can be worn underneath protective clothing. Survey team members do not require neutron dosimeters and should not require extremity dosimeters (finger rings). Passive dosimeters cannot be read in the field; they require specialized equipment to determine their accumulated dose.

Many reactor licensees routinely provide their employees with digital electronic self-reading gamma dosimeters with ranges from 1E-3 to 1E+2 rem, although their use for offsite survey teams cannot be assumed. These dosimeters are simple and rugged, with dose rates and dose alarms that can be individually set as needed. This type of dosimeter is the best available for all response organizations; however, they are not cost effective for local and state responders who have relatively few personnel and limited health physics and technical resources. State and local radiological respond-ers typically carry two direct-reading quartz fiber electroscopes, often called *pencil* or *CDV dosim-eters.*[*] One pencil dosimeter commonly has a range of 0 to 200 mrem (sometimes 500 mrem), the other dosimeter a range of 0 to 20 rem (sometimes 50 rem or 100 rem).[†] Electroscope-type dosim-eters require charging and zeroing prior to use, tasks commonly performed with a battery-operated charging station. Self-reading dosimeters should also be worn in the center of the chest; because these instruments only detect gamma radiation, the orientation is not important. The author sug-gests that workers record the value from their self-reading dosimeter prior to departing from each designated survey location; when traversing the plume, current dose should be recorded every 15 to 30 minutes, and when encountering exposure rates at (or near) turn-back thresholds. After encoun-tering a radiological plume, team members should report their current exposure values to the survey manager every 30 minutes.

Dosimeters are useful in estimating radiation doses from external radiation. Current standards for radiation protection are based on integrating external and internal dose to calculate a biological risk. There are no instruments capable of directly measuring internal dose; this must be calculated after the fact using whole-body counters and bioassay sampling. Estimates of internal dose can be made from the isotopic analysis of air samples, by applying standard biological models and assumptions; this cannot be done in real time and always lags actual exposure. In the case of emergency environ-mental surveys, isotopic analyses are not likely to be available during the initial 12 hours (first shift) of the incident. The most practical method to control an emergency worker's overall dose is to lower their allowed radiation dose as measured by a self-reading dosimeter. It is possible to calculate a unique dose reduction factor from any specific set of assumed airborne radionuclide concentrations. There is great variability in the assumptions in these calculations and in their results—many dose reduction factors are in the range of 3 to 5, with some organizations using factors as high as 10. The dose reduction factor is used to adjust the external-only radiation exposure limit so that if the adjusted limit is reached the worker is likely to remain below the actual dose limit for integrated dose. For example, if a particular organization has established an external radiation dose limit of 2 rem (2000 mrem) and uses a dose reduction factor of 5 to account for inhaled radioactive material, workers in the field are limited to an apparent dose of 2000 mrem ÷ 5, or 400 mrem, on their dosimeters.

The integrated dose limit for radiation workers is 5 rem (5000 mrem)/year. All reactor licensees have established administrative controls to prevent inadvertent overexposures (radiation dose unex-pectedly exceeding the regulatory dose limit); the most common administrative limits are 1 rem and 2 rem. These limits continue to apply to all emergency responders, and it is expected that all orga-nizations would limit the radiation exposure of their employees to as little as possible. However, it is widely recognized that it may prove impossible to prevent responders from receiving dose exceed-ing routine occupational radiation limits. The *Manual of Protective Action Guides* (USEPA, 1992) recommends a 10-rem limit for workers engaged in recovering vital plant equipment or performing tasks related to protecting the public. Environmental survey teams clearly fall into the category of protecting the public. A 25-rem limit applies to lifesaving activities; there could be circumstances where the 25-rem limit applies to a survey team. Each response organization needs to maintain a continuing awareness of radiation doses incurred by their employees and be able to evaluate future radiation doses based on current data and trends. They need to identify workers likely to exceed routine occupational dose limits and evaluate whether those workers are performing tasks that

---

[*] Such dosimeters are called *pencils* because of their long narrow shape; they are about the length of a common pencil but about three times the diameter. The acronym CDV refers to Civil Defense Victoreen, the major manufacturer of dosim-eters made in the 1950s and 1960s for civil defense use. CDV dosimeters and survey instruments are readily recognizable by their very bright yellow color.

[†] FEMA REP-2 (FEMA, 1980a) recommends that emergency workers be provided with two direct-reading (pencil) dosim-eters of different ranges which together cover the range from 500 mrem (0.5 rem) to 100 rem. The lower range dosimeter should have a maximum value of no more than 20 rem. A permanent dosimeter should also be issued. All dosimeters should meet the standards of ANSI N322-1977 (ANSI, 1977) and ANSI N13.11-1983 (ANSI, 1983, pp. 5–8).

justify receiving elevated doses. Response organizations need to establish a process for evaluating these tasks, documenting the evaluation, and establishing approval from the appropriate command-and-control authority.

POTASSIUM IODIDE

Potassium iodide can reduce an emergency worker's radiation dose from inhalation of radioactive iodine. It also offers a limited (much smaller) amount of protection against cesium and other isotopes that have some affinity for the thyroid gland. Potassium iodide provides a high concentration of non-radioactive iodine that is completely absorbed by the thyroid. For a period of time, the thyroid is saturated and cannot accept the additional iodine made available by absorbing inhaled radioiodine. Because there are no other organs with a similar affinity for iodine, the absorbed radioiodine is excreted rather than remaining in the body.* The greatest protection is achieved when potassium iodide is taken from 45 to 60 minutes before being exposed to radioiodine; less protection is achieved if taken earlier than 60 minutes prior to exposure (the initially absorbed iodine begins to be released, offering binding sites for the radioiodine), and essentially no protection occurs if taken 4 hours or more before exposure. Similarly, some protection is achieved if potassium iodide is taken after exposure to radioiodine, as long as it is taken within the first 4 hours of exposure (non-radioactive iodine competes with radioiodine as far as being absorbed by the thyroid).

It is important to understand that potassium iodide is not a radioprotective drug, in the sense that persons who take it do not become immune to the effects of radiation. There is no protective, dose-limiting, or cell-regenerating effect of any kind against external gamma, beta, alpha, or neutron radiation. There is no protective effect of any kind against gamma or beta radiation originating from radioactive material absorbed in other body organs. The sole benefit to potassium iodide is that one organ, the thyroid, receives less radiation dose from inhaled radioactive material than it would if potassium iodide was not taken. Furthermore, should thyroid cancer occur, the thyroid can be readily removed (a permanent regimen of replacement hormones is required to compensate for the lost thyroid). It should also be noted that potassium iodide has side effects affecting a small fraction of the population, the most common being upset stomach and skin rashes. The side effects are generally mild but in rare cases can be severe enough to require medical treatment. Apparently, children are more susceptible to the side effects than are adults.

The FDA's *Guidance: Potassium Iodide as a Thyroid Blocking Agent in Radiation Emergencies* (USFDA, 2001) can be found on their website.† For emergency workers, the suggested dose thresholds for administering potassium iodide are 500 rem for adults over 40 years, 10 rem for adults 39 years and younger, and 5 rem for pregnant or breast-feeding women.‡

The *Manual of Protective Action Guides* (USEPA, 1992) discusses potassium iodide for the general public and for emergency workers; this discussion is based on the 1982 FDA guidance. The 1992 version of the *Manual of Protective Action Guides* is widely understood to recommend a dose

---

* The physical half-life of ^{131}I is approximately 8 days; the effective biological half-life is just over 3 days. The biological half-life is defined as the time to reduce an initial intake of radioactive material to one-half its initial activity, from the combination of radioactive decay and biological excretion processes. The intake is assumed to be a single acute exposure.

† Previous FDA conclusions about potassium iodide were published in the *Federal Register* on December 15, 1978, and on June 29, 1982.

‡ Current U.S. guidance does not explicitly address the subject of pregnant women as emergency workers. There is currently no legal prohibition against pregnant emergency workers at the federal level, although state and local laws and regulations may address the topic in some locales. A woman who declares a pregnancy under the provisions of 10 CFR 20 has an individual radiation exposure limited to 500 mrem over the pregnancy. An exposure or dose of this degree could be quickly reached in a severe radiation emergency but may not be reached in a less severe accident or one without core damage. A pregnant woman is not required to declare her pregnancy, and when the declaration is not made her individual radiation dose is not limited (she assumes all risk associated with radiation exposure to her unborn child). A woman who elects to not declare her pregnancy presumably could be ordered to receive the same radiation dose during an emergency as any other emergency worker (e.g., to 25 rem); under these circumstances, she may elect to declare the pregnancy rather than accept doses much greater than present under routine plant operations.

threshold of 25 rem (thyroid CEDE) for administering potassium iodide; however, a more accurate reading shows that no specific threshold is given for emergency workers. The 25-rem value applies to administering potassium iodide to the general population.

The most common problems with potassium iodide are as follows:

- Dose estimates are not performed for individual emergency workers who may be exposed to radioiodine; that is, there is no specific calculation that shows a particular worker is expected to exceed the potassium iodide threshold based on expected concentrations of radioiodine and the individual's exposure time (stay time).
- An emergency planning zone dose projection of the centerline dose (or dose rate) at the site boundary is used to justify the decision to issue potassium iodide. The dose projection result needs to be adjusted by the ratio of the expected exposure time of the emergency worker to the release duration time assumed in the dose projection (typical release durations are 1, 2, or 4 hours). This adjustment could result in the dose projection result being increased or decreased, depending on the relative values of each exposure time.
- Radiation doses for emergency workers are derived from air sample data collected closer to the release point (plant) than the distances at which the emergency workers are located. To be accurate, the projected dose should be adjusted by the ratio of the dispersion factor at the distance where the sample is collected to the dispersion factor at the distance where the worker is stationed.

These last two points can be illustrated by the following practical problem. Given a 10-rem CEDE threshold for issuing potassium iodide, a dose projection at 1015 hours predicts a 20-rem thyroid CEDE dose at the site boundary. Should potassium iodide be issued to emergency workers on the plume's edge at a distance of 5 miles?

Solving this problem requires additional information. The dose projection assumes an exposure time of 2 hours, the dispersion coefficient at the site boundary is 3E-5, the dispersion coefficient at 5 miles is 1E-6, the cross-wind (from centerline to plume edge) dispersion coefficient is 0.001, the wind speed is 10 mph and is forecast to remain at that speed the rest of the day, and the emergency workers will be on station for the next 6 hours.

$$\text{Dispersion ratio, site boundary to 5 miles} = 1E\text{-}6 \div 3E\text{-}5 = 0.033$$

$$\text{Centerline to edge adjustment factor} = 0.001$$

$$\text{Effective exposure time} = [6 \text{ hours} - (5 \text{ miles} \div 10 \text{ miles/hour})] = 5.5 \text{ hours}$$

$$\text{Exposure time ratio} = 5.5 \text{ hours} \div 2 \text{ hours} = 2.75$$

The dose projected to the workers is calculated by

$$20 \text{ rem} \times 0.033 \times 0.001 \times 2.75 = 1.8E\text{-}3 \text{ rem (about 2 mrem)}$$

Because the projected dose of 2 mrem is very much smaller than the 10-rem threshold, potassium iodide should not be recommended in this situation.

Employees cannot be required to take potassium iodide. Command-and-control positions may authorize and recommend potassium iodide, but consumption is voluntary. It is important that emergency response organizations accurately track the workers for whom potassium iodide is recommended (along with the basis of that recommendation), those who accept and consume the potassium iodide, and those who refuse and do not take the potassium iodide. Many emergency response organizations do not have an established policy regarding employees who refuse potassium iodide; that is, they provide no guidance or training to event managers as to whether they should allow such employees to continue to be exposed to radioiodine or replace them with workers who have elected to consume potassium iodide. This is a difficult issue, tied up with issues of personal choice, fairness, and the legal obligations of employers to provide a safe workplace. Local and state legal requirements may force the withdrawal and replacement of workers who do not elect potassium iodide. The author recommends that survey teams with members not taking potassium iodide be kept in as low a radiation environment as possible, preferably along the plume side or leading edges. When this is not possible, use such a team as the farther-out team. When no team is available that has taken potassium iodide, use the older team as the close-in survey team and the younger team as the farther-out team.

Respiratory Protection Issues

No consensus has been reached regarding the respiratory protection provided to environmental survey teams, and licensee practices vary. In the 1980s, survey teams were universally provided with full-face respirators and some were given self-contained breathing apparatus. Although this practice appears to be very protective of emergency workers, it actually provides less protection in the field than might be thought. Respiratory protection can be effective at limiting internal radiation exposure while survey technicians are outside the vehicle, and most survey and sampling tasks can be performed safely in a respirator mask with no significant loss of visibility. However, at least one technician is forced to doff their respirator inside their vehicle because it is unsafe to drive in a mask because of the degraded forward vision and insufficient peripheral visibility. Radioactive material enters the vehicle when the doors are opened for egress and ingress or through the vehicle's ventilation system. Also, because vehicles are not airtight, survey technicians are continually exposed to this contaminated air. Because a team is limited by its most radiologically exposed member, the entire team must be withdrawn when the driver reaches his or her exposure limit, even if the rest of the team has been continually using respiratory protection.

Self-contained breathing apparatus air bottles are typically pressurized to between 3000 and 3500 psig. One bottle provides breathing air for 30 to 45 minutes, depending on an individual's physical conditioning and the work being performed. Survey team equipment is often packaged in 2- or 3-foot locker-sized containers, leaving only a limited space in the vehicle for replacement air bottles. Therefore, a survey team wearing self-contained breathing apparatus has an effective mission time limited to 1 to 1.25 hours, even when carrying one full bottle exchange. This time is too short to accomplish much survey work. A licensee that extensively uses self-contained breathing apparatus in plume monitoring would have to devote considerable resources to shuttling new breathing air bottles to their survey teams.

Aside from safety issues associated with reduced vision, respiratory protection masks cause breathing stress and contribute to heat-related injuries. In cold climates, the transition from warm vehicle to winter environment causes fogging and condensation issues in the mask, affecting visibility. Breathing stress is created by the extra work required to pull air through a respirator (not a factor for positive-pressure self-contained breathing apparatus) and over time reduces a worker's effectiveness. Heat stress is created by both the mask and anti-contamination clothing typically worn during an emergency, which can lead to a worker being incapacitated or worse. Self-contained breathing apparatus is bulky and heavy, making it more difficult to move about, introducing a potential for neck injuries, and adding to heat stress when worn with anti-contamination clothing. Self-contained systems cannot be worn in a moving vehicle, and the bottles should be secured while moving, a capability most survey team vehicles lack. The likelihood of respiratory protection contributing to other safety issues should be considered when deciding whether or not to issue respiratory protection equipment to teams.

Licensees have substantial experience in running respiratory protection programs, and their survey team members are likely to have been provided the necessary medical checks, mask fit testing, and equipment training. Licensees also conduct periodic equipment inspections and maintenance to ensure that the equipment continues to provide the same protection as it did when newly purchased.

They also conduct program reviews and audits. Offsite fire departments and hazardous material teams have similar programs. However, the state (and, in some cases, county) agencies charged with post-accident environmental monitoring may not have the same respiratory protection program expertise, or they may lack the necessary equipment (e.g., a fit-test hood). The ability of the sponsoring organization to provide an adequate respiratory protection program should be considered when determining what respiratory protection should be issued to a survey team.

The author recommends that respiratory protection not be issued to teams used solely to track radioactive plumes released from power plants because of the difficulties in using masks and bottles inside vehicles, as well as the additional physical stress. Instead, their cumulative gamma exposure should be closely followed, and their TEDE estimated using predetermined gamma dose to inhalation adjustment factors. Teams that combine plume tracking missions with other kinds of radiological response (e.g., response to transportation accidents) should be given the types of respiratory protection needed for their other response duties.

ANTI-CONTAMINATION CLOTHING

Environmental survey teams should carry a variety of anti-contamination clothing, including disposable gloves, disposable foot covers, and full-body coveralls. Most reactor licensees issue disposable coveralls that are light and fairly puncture resistant, have elastic arm and leg cuffs, come in several sizes, and are reasonably inexpensive. They are usually white, which enhances visibility in an outdoor environment and at night. Some disposable coveralls have chest or arm pockets. Fabric coveralls are heavier and more puncture resistant; they generally lack cuffs and are less inexpensive. A survey team is less likely to carry a variety of sizes when fabric coveralls are used. When fabric coveralls are used, they should be chosen in colors with good outdoor visibility, rather than tan or brown colors that tend to blend into the visual background. Disposable coveralls tend not to breathe well and they trap body heat, which can lead to heat-related illnesses such as heat exhaustion and heat stroke. Fabric coveralls better allow the body to breathe, reducing the rate of heat-related illnesses.

Emergency response organizations should establish guidelines for the use of anti-contamination clothing. There is no reason to don anti-contamination clothing until after a plume has been detected at a sufficient concentration. The most practical thresholds are a pre-established exposure rate or a pre-established count/minute value as measured on a smear sample. A 1-mR/h exposure rate may be appropriate, or a smear at 500 counts/minute (e.g., offscale high on the lowest count-rate meter scale). These values are essentially arbitrary but serve as possible examples. Coveralls and shoe covers should be donned when the anti-contamination threshold is reached. The author suggests that disposable gloves be donned while collecting any sample after determining that the team is submerged in the plume; there is no benefit to gloves if only radiation shine is present.

PROTECTION FROM PERSONNEL SAFETY HAZARDS

Survey team members need to be prepared for the variety of non-radiological hazards that come from working outdoors. The response organizations deploying survey teams should ensure that teams are equipped with

- Heavy work boots with leather uppers above the ankle, thick soles, and an oil-resistant surface*
- Insulated coveralls suitable for winter wear
- Rubber or plastic rain suits, lowers and uppers with hood, all with elastic cuffs

---

* Crush-resistant toes (safety shoes) are not necessary, but many organizations are likely to require this feature. The boots should be water resistant. These boots give good outdoor traction, provide protection against ankle injuries, and provide protection against snakes, scorpions, thistles, and the like.

- Wide-brim hats and salt tablets, suitable for very hot summer conditions
- Reflective vests (yellow or orange) to provide visibility along highways and during night operations; glow sticks or a battery-powered light attached to the vest are also helpful at night
- Four to six highway traffic cones to provide notice to oncoming traffic of a stopped vehicle ahead
- A selection of flashlights and high-power portable lights with stands to aid in night operations[*]
- A well-stocked first aid kit
- Water coolers of at least 3-gallon capacity

Some personal protective equipment must be fitted to individual team members. Response organizations need to consider how to store and maintain outdoor gear so that it is always readily available to immediate responders and to relief shifts.

Power plant workers are often required to wear hard hats and safety glasses and to carry leather work gloves. These are less useful in an outdoor environment. The most likely head injury is running into the team vehicle's raised hatch or window. The most likely eye injury comes from gravel thrown by a vehicle passing at high speed. Leather gloves are hot in the summer and make it more difficult to do many tasks, such as disassembling the air sampler head and removing the filter and cartridge. The author recommends that team members continue to routinely wear safety glasses because there are no negative consequences, that leather gloves be made available for tasks for which wearing them makes sense (such as blister protection when collecting soil samples), and that hard hats not be required outdoors.

In addition to their radiological training, all survey team members need to be well trained in first aid as a contingency, as they operate outdoors with no immediate support. In the 1970s and 1980s, the standard Red Cross first-aid course was structured under the assumption that emergency medical technician or ambulance support would not be immediately available. However, the current standard first-aid course is designed to stabilize the injured person for up to 15 minutes until an ambulance arrives. Environmental team members need to be able to apply bandages and slings and splints and have other more advanced first-aid skills.

APPLICABLE STANDARDS

- ANSI 3.8.5-1992, *Criteria for Emergency Radiological Field Monitoring, Sampling, and Analysis* (ANSI, 1992)
- ANSI 3.8.6-1995, *Criteria for the Conduct of Offsite Radiological Assessment for Emergency Response for Nuclear Power Plants* (ANSI, 1995e)

---

[*] At least three flashlights are needed, with batteries sufficient to change out every light. Portable lights on stands are useful at night because many tasks require two hands, precluding the use of flashlights.

6 Emergency Response Organizations and Facilities

This chapter discusses the composition and role of the emergency response organization and the design and functions of emergency response facilities.

EMERGENCY RESPONSE ORGANIZATION

The formal emergency response organization consists of individuals designated in advance to respond to an emergency and who have been trained and equipped to cope with such a situation. The formal emergency response organization can then make use of the available personnel, regardless of whether the individuals have received formal training on the site emergency plan. The designated organization forms the core of an emergency response and provides direction and structure to other persons who may become involved on a situational basis.

Each reactor licensee designs an emergency response organization that best fits the facility and circumstances, but that organization may change over time. The functions that must be performed by the emergency response organization are listed in Table B-1, "Minimum Staffing Requirements for NRC Licensees for Nuclear Power Plant Emergencies," in NUREG-0654 (NRC, 1980c, p. 37).* Table B-1 specifies the emergency organization primarily in terms of functions to be performed and only secondarily in terms of the number of staff performing those functions. The table acts as a licensing standard against which the initial emergency response plan was reviewed and as a regulatory floor below which a licensee may not fall. The Table B-1 functions include operational assessments of an event, emergency direction and control, offsite notification and communication, radiological assessment, operational accident assessment, plant system engineering, plant repair, in-plant protective actions, fire fighting, rescue operations and first aid, personnel accountability, and site access control.

The positions that comprise the emergency response organization are those described in the licensee's emergency plan. The reactor site must be capable of continuously staffing all emergency response organization positions throughout an extended emergency; in practice, each position is usually staffed four or five persons deep or a pool of similarly qualified persons staffs several positions, with the overall pool being three to four times as large as the total number of positions being staffed.

In most cases, the emergency response staff consists solely of licensee employees, generally those located at the reactor site. This is a choice made by the licensee, not a regulatory requirement. NUREG-0654 and Appendix E to 10 CFR 50 anticipated that licensees would include licensee employees not working at the reactor site in their emergency response organizations as well as non-employee contractor and vendor staff. In part, this reflected how nuclear utilities were staffed and organized in the 1980s; in particular, employees doing engineering, training, and other

---

* The Commission has periodically attempted to reconstitute Table B-1, or at least develop an alternative approach using job-task analysis methodologies. Attempts from the mid-1990s to mid-2000s failed to achieve any substantial results, partly because of a weak regulatory framework in this area and partly because industry participation was voluntary. Industry supported these efforts so long as it appeared they could potentially reduce response organization staffing; cooperation ceased after the industry came to believe that a rigorous review of response organization functions had a substantial possibility of increasing staffing. The regulatory framework in this area is weak in part because there is no regulatory basis for Table B-1; that is, the NRC did not develop a technical analysis of tasks associated with emergency response from which the table is derived. Anecdotal evidence suggests that Table B-1 was the work of a small number of NRC subject-matter experts working under considerable time pressure.

non-operations functions were often based elsewhere and only visited the reactor site periodically. At the same time, many reactor sites had permanent architect–engineer company staff, either directly performing engineering and other technical functions or advising plant staff on plant design and construction. Appendix E to 10 CFR 50, Section IV.A, requires licensees to describe in their emergency plan the roles of headquarters and contract personnel because both were used and needed at the time initial emergency plans were written. Section IV.A does not distinguish between onsite and offsite responders or employees and contractors, in terms of response functions or response times. There is nothing in regulation that prohibits the sharing of personnel among multiple sites owned by the same licensee or among different sites owned by different licensees, as long as the sharing does not reduce the "donating" site's ability to implement its own emergency plan if required. Likewise, uniquely qualified personnel from non-utility organizations could conceivably support a reactor licensee emergency plan.

Licensee emergency organizations are not static, and many have changed over time. Some licensees increased emergency staffing (i.e., added positions in the organization) as they identified performance gaps through their drill and exercise programs or as more staff was needed to support the offsite response. Some staffing increases occurred because of management decisions or as corrective actions for poor exercise performance. Some licensees have also eliminated positions in the emergency response organization, either by submitting amendments to the NRC for licensing approval or through the 50.54(q) process.[*] The licensee's bases for removing positions have included consolidation (i.e., single plant utility merged into a fleet), technological improvements (e.g., dose assessment using computers rather than by hand calculation), and duplication (i.e., personnel unnecessarily duplicating the same job functions).

COMMAND-AND-CONTROL

Command-and-control describes the highest level of operational authority during an emergency event. The command-and-control individual provides direction to an organization's entire emergency response organization and can call upon all of the organization's resources as required to respond to the event. The licensee's command-and-control individual is referred as the *emergency coordinator* in NUREG-0654 but now is frequently called the *emergency director*, and this text will use that terminology. The responsibilities of emergency directors do not depend on accident severity, the degree to which the emergency response organization is activated, the availability of senior plant managers or company officials, or any other factor related to the emergency condition.

The emergency director can have many tasks, among which is a subset designated as *non-delegable functions*. These tasks must be done by the current emergency director and cannot be delegated to, or performed by, any other persons in the organization, including persons otherwise qualified as emergency director (unless they assume the duty). The non-delegable functions are assigned by each emergency plan but typically include, at least, sole authority to declare an emergency classification, sole authority to determine protective action recommendations, sole authority to authorize radiation doses above 10 CFR 20 limits, and sole authority to authorize notifications to offsite authorities, as well as other site-specific functions.

The licensee's operating shift manager always has the initial command-and-control authority. This is because the initial recognition of emergency conditions must occur in the reactor unit's control room. The shift manager becomes the emergency director upon declaring initial entry into the emergency plan at whatever emergency classification is appropriate. The entry into any of the four emergency classification levels is always referred to as having been *declared* by the senior licensee official, a formal action that denotes examination of the range of conditions, deliberation about the

---

[*] Licensees are permitted to make changes to their emergency plans without prior NRC approval as described in 10 CFR 50.54(q) and, as changed after 2011, 10 CFR 50.54(q)(2) to 50.54(q)(4). This is commonly referred to as the *50.54(q) process*, by both regulators and industry.

event and how it fits with the emergency action level scheme, and a decision that entry into the emergency plan is warranted. This action should always be thoughtful and intentional, as it commits the licensee to a set of actions and may commit the resources of non-licensees as well.

The emergency director retains leadership of, and oversight over, the emergency organization until they are formally relieved or until the emergency is terminated. The declaring emergency director typically directs operations throughout a Notification of Unusual Event, the least serious emergency condition, which often lasts only a few hours. At the Notification of Unusual Event classification, a transfer of the command-and-control authority often occurs but only if the event lasts into the next shift; in part, this is because the technical support center and emergency operations facility are not typically activated for events at the Notification of Unusual Event level. The control room emergency director retains operational authority over an emergency event even when more senior licensee officials are present, such as the plant operations manager, plant general manager, or site vice president. If another qualified emergency director is in the control room, the shift manager may turn over command-and-control to them. At a few licensees, a qualified emergency director is called to the control room upon declaration of an emergency to relieve the shift manager, and the second emergency director remains in the control room to direct the on-shift organization.

When several emergency response facilities are staffed, the emergency director in the control room is relieved by the senior licensee official in one of the other facilities. Because additional facilities are only staffed for more serious or complicated events the transfer of command-and-control is intended to allow the shift manager to be more involved in plant operations and to supervise implementation of site abnormal operating procedures and emergency operating procedures. The relief of one emergency director by an emergency director located in another facility (rather than by the oncoming shift in the same facility) is often called *turnover*. The formal transfer of command-and-control requires a structured process in which the shift manager briefs an oncoming emergency director about current and previous plant conditions, equipment issues, known emergency action level thresholds, and current priorities. The oncoming director acknowledges having the personnel and capability to exercise the non-delegable duties, then formally accepts the emergency director responsibilities. The technical support center or emergency operations facility emergency director is not required to be a licensed senior reactor operator because this person does not direct the activities of licensed operators.

The original (early 1980s) design of licensee emergency staffing schemes had prompt staffing of onsite emergency response facilities and delayed staffing of offsite facilities.[*] This led to the shift manager being relieved of the emergency director duties by the senior official in the onsite technical support center and the technical support center manager being relieved by the emergency operations facility manager if the event escalated further. Turnover between the control room emergency director and the technical support center emergency director was expected to occur between 90 and 120 minutes into the event. In an escalating event, turnover between the technical support center emergency director and the emergency operations facility emergency director would occur 90 to 120 minutes after declaration of an emergency classification requiring the emergency operations facility.

Current licensee emergency staffing schemes have simultaneous staffing of all licensee emergency response facilities. When events occur during dayshift,[†] the technical support center and emergency operations facility may be activated essentially simultaneously, but for backshift events the emergency operations facility is often activated first. The technical support center typically activates first during dayshift events because it is faster to walk from plant buildings than to drive to the

---

[*] Onsite facilities were activated following an Alert declaration, offsite facilities following either a Site Area Emergency or General Emergency declaration. Offsite facilities would not be activated if the event never progressed beyond Alert.

[†] *Dayshift* refers to non-holiday work days, Monday through Friday, often starting between 0600 and 0700 and ending between 1500 and 1600. All other times are referred to as *backshift*. In recent years, sites that formerly worked standard 8-hour days for non-rotating technical and craft personnel have begun working 9- or 10-hour standard days. Such sites often have one or two days out of every two weeks off; these standard off days are also backshift, because the licensee will not have their full staffing complement present at the reactor site to staff their emergency response facilities.

emergency operations facility. For backshift events, staff typically reach the emergency operations facility faster from home than they can drive to the reactor site. Most sites now have procedures that allow the control room emergency director to be relieved by either the technical support center or the emergency operations facility, but the site expectation is that turnover will be to the emergency operations facility. Some licensees split the non-delegable functions when the control room is relieved, emergency classification and authorization of radiation dose extension beyond regulatory limits being assigned to the technical support center manager and all other functions being assigned to the emergency operations facility manager. Turnover from the control room typically occurs about 90 minutes after an Alert declaration.[*]

ON-SHIFT ORGANIZATION

The minimum number of staff required to maintain adequate control over a reactor is specified by a combination of regulations,[†] site technical specifications, site emergency plan, and site-specific conduct of operations procedures. The operating staff includes licensed and non-licensed plant operators, radiation protection personnel, maintenance staff, personnel trained for medical and firefighting response, and the site security organization. Some licensees have chemistry technicians on shift. Most on-shift staff perform essentially the same duties during routine and emergency operations, although the operating staff includes some personnel whose emergency function is to provide intrasite and offsite communications (i.e., their emergency duties are different from their non-emergency duties). The personnel immediately available (within a few minutes) for emergency duty are referred to as the *on-shift emergency organization*. At some licensees, the number and composition of the required on-shift operating staff depend on the reactor mode (whether at power or shut down).

The shift personnel designated as facility and offsite communicators often work outside the control room. Many licensees call these communicators to the control room when a Notification of Unusual Event is declared but do not staff the operations support center or recall the emergency response organization. This gives them additional personnel to handle internal and external communications without affecting reactor operations; most licensees also perform extensive internal notifications of emergency events not related to communications required by regulation (for example, to the electrical load dispatcher or the chief nuclear officer). Most conditions warranting a Notification of Unusual Event declaration can be adequately handled by an expanded control room crew and do not require activation of the full emergency response organization.

When an emergency occurs requiring the full emergency response organization, the on-shift emergency organization immediately reports to the licensee's control room and operations support center; the shift manager takes on the interim functions of the technical support center and emergency operations facilities until these facilities are staffed. The operations support center is augmented by radiation protection, operators, and maintenance staff as soon as practicable but is capable of performing (limited) in-plant mitigation and repair activities essentially immediately. One area of difference among licensees is in the status of the on-shift non-licensed plant operators; the non-licensed operators remain under the shift manager's direct control at many, but not all, licensees rather than becoming part of the operations support center. In all cases, operators called to the plant (i.e., not part of the designated operating shift) report to the operations support center.

The NRC does not define the minimum number of necessary on-shift responders but does define the emergency functions the licensee must be capable of immediately performing, as listed in NUREG-0654, Table B-1, "Minimum Staffing for NRC Licensees for Nuclear Power Plant Emergencies." Each licensee determines the distribution of skills and the number of personnel

---

[*] This time may be different for backshift events because some site emergency plans allow a longer staffing time for backshift events than for dayshift events. The longest allowable backshift staffing time among current reactor sites is 2 hours (120 minutes); many sites still have a 1-hour facility activation requirement for dayshift events.

[†] The minimum required number of licensed operations is specified by 10 CFR 50.54(m). Many licensees routinely operate with more than the required staff.

needed to perform the required functions.[*] The functions are assessment of operation aspects, plant operations, emergency direction and control, notification and communication, radiological accident assessment, plant system engineering, repair and corrective actions, in-plant protective actions, fire fighting, first aid, and rescue operations. Current regulations allow some overlap among emergency response duties so that specific staff members may not be uniquely assigned to each function.[†] There are significant differences in how licensees implement these functions; for example,

- The radiological accident assessment function (dose assessment) may be performed by the shift technical advisor, a senior radiation protection technician, or a shift chemist.
- Plant repair and corrective action may be performed by dedicated maintenance personnel or by non-licensed operators with advanced training. Among sites with on-shift mainte-nance staff, some sites train a single craft (e.g., instrument and control technicians) to be minimally proficient at actions in other crafts.
- Fire fighting may be performed by a dedicated site fire department, by a fire brigade made up of non-licensed operators, or by selected maintenance staff.[‡]
- First-aid response may be by dedicated nurses or emergency medical technicians or by first-aid-trained radiation protection technicians, chemistry technicians, plant fire watch, or security officers (not required for rapid response).

AUGMENTED ORGANIZATION

The augmented emergency response organization includes all personnel who are not part of the on-shift organization. In general, this includes everyone assigned to the technical support center, emergency operations facility, and emergency news center, as well as some personnel in the opera-tions support facility. It also includes plant staff that could be assigned to the on-shift organization but are currently off-shift. These persons may be used to relieve the current on-shift organization. The augmented emergency response organization is in place when the technical support center, operations support center, and emergency operations facility (or their designated alternate locations as applicable) are staffed and prepared to assume their emergency functions from the control room. The transfer of responsibilities may not yet have taken place; for example, rapidly changing plant conditions may prevent the emergency director from taking time for a formal transfer of duties.

A licensee's overall emergency response organization should consist of those persons needed to respond to a variety of projected events. No employee should be subject to emergency recall whose position and functions are not described in the site emergency plan. The organization should not include employees lacking defined duties or present merely to provide backup, occasional assis-tance, or peer reviews. The organization should consist of as few persons as possible, as informed by experience with actual events and large-scale (simulation) exercises.

Many licensees distinguish among personnel whose duties are indispensable or critical, technical employees whose duties are desirable, and administrative employees who make emergency response facilities work more smoothly. Critical positions are often also referred to as *minimum staff* posi-tions. Although all licensees have established time goals for the activation of emergency response

---

[*] NRC regulations prior to November 2011 allowed licensees to assign multiple functions to a single responder, under the assumption that different duties would be performed for different emergency conditions (i.e., no single emergency would require multiple duties to be performed simultaneously). Because of a change in regulation, licensees had until December 2012 to analyze specific emergency events and determine whether their current on-shift staffing was capable of performing all necessary functions. Any changes identified in this analysis were to have been implemented before December 2014.

[†] New emergency preparedness regulations implemented from late 2011 to early 2012 require licensees to perform task analy-ses of several emergency scenarios to determine whether the base operating crew can perform all tasks required to respond to the scenarios. When gaps are identified between necessary emergency response organization functions (tasks) and the resources available, the licensee is required to remedy the gaps by adjusting the required tasks or the available resources.

[‡] Prior to 2005, some sites assigned site security officers to the fire brigade. This practice was discontinued after NRC Bulletin 2005-02 (NRC, 2005f), which (among other requirements) prohibited site security staff from collateral duties that affected their rapid responder role.

facilities, most licensees evaluate only the minimum staff positions against this goal. Often, licensees have deleted their previous explicit time goals for achieving full facility staffing; full staffing may not even be tracked at some licensees. It is generally the Commission's position that, because licensees developed the positions in their augmented emergency response organization based on site-specific circumstances, it is assumed that the licensees need every position described in their emergency plans to conduct an effective response; therefore, licensees should put as much emphasis on achieving full facility staffing as they do on achieving minimum (activation) staffing.

Some licensees have established procedures that allow the facility manager to promote an emergency responder who is judged capable of filling a vacant position. This approach necessarily relies on the experience and judgment of the senior licensee official making the decision. In some cases, the promotion is temporary as the responder intended to fill the vacant position is in transit; however, it may be necessary for the promoted individual to fill the role into which he or she has been promoted for the entire shift or event. The practice of on-the-spot promotion allows an emergency response facility to activate under circumstances where activation is otherwise prohibited by procedure. The benefit is that the technical support center or emergency operations facility has more staff to manage the event than does the control room, even when short-handed, and it is vital to relieve the shift manager of administrative burdens. On-the-spot promotion shifts the vacancy downward in the organization; when multiple promotions are done, the organization could arrive at a staffing configuration in which the vacancy is left unfilled (a position whose function does not warrant extensive action to fill). Making multiple promotions within the same functional group does carry a performance risk as it results in essentially an entire group performing tasks or making decisions for which they are not fully trained.

NUREG-0654 divides the emergency response organization into three categories: immediately available (on-shift), available within 30 minutes, and available within 60 minutes. During the 1990s and 2000s, alternative staffing schemes were approved by the NRC for many licensees through the licensing process. There are currently very few, if any, licensees committed to 30-minute responders, and not many licensees are committed to 60-minute staffing. A large number of licensees have received approval for 75- to 90-minute staffing, with all facilities having a single activation time goal (i.e., elimination of the staged response). From a licensee perspective, these changes were primarily made to address demographic changes that resulted in more employees living farther away from their plant. In many cases, the Commission required a larger on-shift emergency response organization to compensate for the delay in transferring emergency functions out of the control room. Some licensees maintain plant staff on the emergency response organization roster who cannot meet the required initial staffing time; these individuals are typically not contacted during the initial call-out and are used as shift relief.

In the author's experience, an emergency response organization member typically receives a signal to report to the designated emergency 10 to 15 minutes after the shift manager declares an emergency classification. Some licensees have a single control room communicator who makes offsite notifications, initiates callout of the emergency response organization, and informs the Commission of the emergency. If callout is not performed until after offsite notification,[*] 20 to 25 minutes could elapse between event declaration and initiation of the signal to emergency responders. If the responder is at home, it can take 5 minutes or more to leave the building due to the person having to, for example, inform their spouse, call for a child sitter, or lock the doors. It can also take 5 minutes or more for the responder to transit from the plant parking lot to their assigned emergency facility. Under these circumstances, a 30-minute responder has no more than 15 minutes of driving time when traveling a distance of 11 miles driving at 45 mph. This puts a practical upper limit of about 10 miles on the distance that a 30-minute responder can live away from the plant. A 60-minute responder can live up to about 30 miles away and still reach the facility on time, and a 75-minute responder can live up to about 45 miles away. The author recommends that licensees assess their callout process to determine a representative or expected elapsed time between the event declaration

---

[*] A period of 15 minutes is permitted by regulation.

and notification to plant employees and use this time to determine a site-specific limit on the effective distance that an immediate responder can live from the site.* Some licensees prescribe the distance that employees can live from the site as a condition of employment; this ensures that senior staff is capable of staffing emergency facilities as required.

DEFINITIONS RELATED TO FACILITY STAFFING

Several terms are used in licensee emergency plans and procedures to describe the status of emergency response facilities. Sometimes these terms are used interchangeably by licensees, obscuring their correct meaning and usage. It may be difficult to determine whether a licensee can comply with the facility staffing goal when these terms are not well defined in the site emergency plan or emergency plan implementing procedures. The author suggests the following definitions:

- *Staffed*—A facility is staffed when designated response personnel are present inside the facility, regardless of their preparedness to perform their designated functions. Some sites distinguish among a facility staffed with essential personnel, a facility staffed with all necessary technical staff, and a facility staffed with all personnel assigned by the site emergency plan.
- *Available*—A facility is available when it has the staff to assume its technical functions from the control room, procedures and other necessary supplies have been obtained, all necessary hardware (e.g., computers, radios, phones) is operable, and communication links have been established to designated counterparts.
- *Activated*—A facility is activated when it is available, when it has received sufficient event data and situational information to prudently perform its assigned technical functions, and when the facility manager has verified facility capabilities. A facility need not have accepted its assigned technical functions from the control room to be activated, but it must be capable of accepting them without delay. Some licensees define activation of the technical support center and emergency operations facility as having accepted transfer of their designated technical functions; these licensees do not define or label the condition of being ready to accept technical functions.
- *Command-and-control*—A facility has command-and-control after it has accepted transfer of its designated technical functions from the control room. When those functions include the emergency director position, the facility has overall command-and-control.

MINIMUM FACILITY STAFFING

The writers of NUREG-0654 expected that an emergency response facility would be activated when all required staff were present and prepared to perform their assigned duties, and that was how licensees operated in the 1980s and much of the 1990s. In those years, an emergency response facility could do nothing until all designated staff were present. Beginning in the mid-1990s, licensees

---

* Licensees can determine an expected or bounding time from declaration to callout signal from the most recent 20 drills in which callout was demonstrated. The classification time and the signal receipt time should both be recorded in participant and controller/evaluator logs. Most licensees conduct quarterly pager system surveillances, and licensees should also be able to estimate classification to signal times from those test records. A sample size of 20 or greater ensures an adequate sample (statistical confidence interval). Some licensees have relocated their emergency operations facility outside the 10-mile emergency planning zone. Licensees should analyze the response time of emergency operations facility staff from home to the facility (independent of their response time to the reactor site) and use this time to set an effective distance limit for immediate responders. Because the emergency operations facility location is going to be closer to some employees and farther from others, some responders are going to have response times to the emergency operations facility that are much longer than their response time to the reactor site (up to 20 or 30 minutes longer). Employees with very long response times to the emergency operations facility might be better assigned to the technical support center (this could become an issue when assignment to the emergency operations facility is related to professional advancement in an employee's non-emergency position).

began looking at staffing schemes that did not require complete facility staffing before transferring emergency functions away from the control room. Both licensees and the Commission had accepted the idea that a partially staffed response facility had more resources than did the control room. The goal became to relieve the control room of non-operational tasks as soon as possible. Licensees believed that reactor operations were improved when senior reactor operators were not required to split their time between reactor control and oversight of the emergency response. The subset of responders required by licensees to exercise emergency response oversight and relieve the control room is referred to as the *facility minimum staff*.

Essentially all reactor licensees have now implemented some version of a minimum staffing concept, where an emergency response facility is activated when all designated minimum staff positions are staffed and prepared to perform their duties, without requiring that all technical staff be present or all staff designated by the site emergency plan. The normal complement of minimum staff is between five and eight persons, roughly one-quarter of full facility staffing. The functions often include at least one person each in facility and/or event command-and-control, emergency action level assessment, radiological assessment, core damage assessment, plant repair and mitigation, internal communications, and external communications.

Licensees have been responsible for identifying the minimum staffing positions in each facility, and there is little consistency in this area. The concept of minimum-staff activation does not appear in any Commission or Federal Emergency Management Agency (FEMA) regulatory documents. There is no regulatory guidance for determining the number and type of minimum staffing positions and no industry guidance. In the author's opinion, the minimum staff concept has generally worked well; however, the experience base supporting the concept is largely limited to drills and a small number of Alert declarations. When minimum staff activation is performed during a drill, responders know that the complete technical and administrative staff is en route and that the time they have to manage the emergency event alone is limited.* The number of useful data points provided by actual events is few because some events occur on dayshift, a period when minimum staff responders can have high confidence that the remaining staff are en route.

Facility minimum staffing positions have been chosen by licensee management using only their experiences and the opinions of subject-matter experts. Although the list of minimum staffing positions is informed by NUREG-0654 Table B-1, actual minimum staffing schemes do not always directly correspond to the table. The author is unaware of any licensees whose minimum staffing positions are justified by a job–task analysis or any other performance-based analysis. Licensees have not validated their minimum staffing positions through their drill programs, and in the author's opinion most licensees have no idea whether their minimum staff could adequately handle an event using only their own resources.

The Commission has essentially accepted two-phase staffing by licensees (i.e., facility minimum staffing followed by full staffing), but FEMA does not practice minimum staffing when activating its own facilities. The concept has also not been widely adopted by local and state officials when activating municipal, county (parish), or state response centers.

KEY EMERGENCY RESPONSE ORGANIZATION PERSONNEL

The concept of *key emergency response organization staff* has become entwined with, and sometimes confused with, the concept of the minimum emergency response organization staff. The key emergency responders are those whose participation in the drill and exercise program is tracked

---

* Drills are typically structured so there is a lengthy period between the simulated failure that results in staffing emergency response facilities and the next significant simulated failure. This practice is often necessary in evaluated exercises to allow for demonstration of offsite objectives, and the design principles are carried forward into other licensee drills, essentially out of habit. Therefore, few drills present technical or protection action challenges that require the immediate attention of the minimum staff. Sufficient time is planned into the drill to allow essentially full facility staffing before any significant activity is required.

by the licensee and periodically reported to the Commission as part of a voluntary industry initiative. An individual is counted as having successfully participated if that person participated in a meaningful activity within the specified reporting period. The definition of *meaningful activity* is structured to drive licensees to increase the number of training drills they conduct, as compared to the period prior to 2001.* These more frequent drills are expected to result in better overall familiarity with emergency procedures and more opportunities to diagnose equipment, training, and procedure issues.

Licensees specify the key response positions for themselves, using the functional definitions found in the technical document NEI 99-02 (NEI, 2000, 2013). The term *key responder* came out of the Commission's revision of the reactor oversight and inspection programs that occurred between 1998 and 2001. Technical document NEI 99-02 is guidance to licensees, not regulation, prepared by the Nuclear Energy Institute and endorsed by the Commission. In theory, a licensee is not required to participate in the overall performance indicator program because it is a voluntary initiative by industry, although a licensee must provide data for all performance indicators if it does participate (i.e., it cannot choose to only partially report). Any licensee that elects not to report performance indicator results would be removed from the reactor oversight program and would receive additional inspection as compared to those licensees who do report the data.

The NEI 99-02 table of key emergency response personnel specifies functions to be tracked, in a manner similar to NUREG-0654 Table B-1. The NEI functions are similar to, but not exactly the same as, the Table B-1 functions. The NEI table explicitly includes more emergency functions than does Table B-1. Specific key positions or key position titles are not used in the NEI table because industry lacks a standard emergency response organization and position titles. Each licensee has had to identify the positions in their organization that most closely match the functions described in the NEI document and justify their selections. In some cases, aspects of a single function are performed by more than a single responder, necessitating tracking all contributors to the function. In addition, the licensee is permitted to designate positions not included on the NEI table as key for their organization, based on their site-specific program and circumstances (however, when additional or extra positions are included, the licensee must justify to the NRC any subsequent reductions in position tracking).

Some licensees allow a single individual to be assigned multiple positions in the emergency response organization, usually based on similarities in required skill sets. One example of this is the operations shift manager (e.g., reactor control room) and the operations advisor in another response facility. In these cases, the licensee is required to define the similar positions in procedures, and the individual's participation is separately tracked for each key position they simultaneously hold; it is possible that one or more of their assigned positions are not among the key positions. Regardless of the number of licensee personnel assigned multiple response positions, the licensee must still show they have sufficient staff at each position to ensure that all positions can be staffed when required (i.e., one position is not shorted when an individual participates in another assigned position).

In the author's experience, licensees do confuse key responders and minimum staff responders. This is occasionally reflected in site procedures and is often revealed in discussions during inspections. For any one licensee facility, the list of key responders could be the same as the minimum staff for that facility, there could be more key responders than minimum staff, or there could be more minimum staff than key responders. There is nothing in the definitions of either requiring similarity. In at least one facility, the operations support center, the number of minimum staff is always larger than the number of key responders; the only key individual is the facility manager, and the minimum staff always includes some number of mechanics (if only the number of maintenance personnel required to be on-shift).

---

* The key emergency response organization member participation metric is one of a number of performance *indicators* which began in 2000. Each metric is assigned criteria that cause additional inspection by the NRC if licensee performance reported in that area is less than or equal to the criteria. Because performance indicators are essentially an inspection and evaluation tool, they do not directly contribute to a licensee's emergency preparedness program and will not be discussed in detail in this book.

EMERGENCY RESPONSE ORGANIZATION DUTY TEAMS

Most licensees have now organized their emergency response organizations into several duty teams, with four or five teams being the most common. Even licensees who respond to actual emergencies via "all call" use duty teams as a management and tracking tool. A *duty team* is a subset of the licensee's overall emergency response roster consisting of one individual from the pool of persons assigned to each emergency response position that is normally staffed. When a response position is normally staffed two or more deep, the team has as many individuals from the pool as there are positions.

The persons staffing the emergency response organization when an event occurs must be currently qualified for their positions and be *fit for duty*, a defined term in regulation and site procedures typically meaning having not consumed alcohol or other substances affecting mental acuity for a specified number of hours and being sufficiently rested to work a 12-hour shift. Five or 6 hours without alcohol is considered fit for duty at most sites; when there is cause to doubt an individual's fitness, a blood alcohol test is given. Licensees generally provide for unexpected events by allowing behavioral observation if a moderate amount of alcohol had been consumed (may also apply to medications that cause drowsiness or affect concentration). Observation is only permitted when the individual has declared the consuming of alcohol and the work (response) is unexpected and unscheduled—generally, any consumption is prohibited in the 5 hours prior to scheduled work.

In addition to fitness for duty restrictions, licensees typically require that emergency responders remain within a specified response time of site.[*] The time requirement is sometimes expressed as a maximum distance. When the licensee's emergency operations facility is located offsite, the restriction for emergency operations facility staff may be in time or miles from the facility.

A licensee could maximize the probability that response facilities are staffed on time and by persons fit for duty by permanently restricting all response organization members from alcohol and placing movement restrictions on everybody. Because these kinds of restrictions interfere with employee's private lives, they are considered burdens. Employees would not accept permanent off-duty restrictions for the entire emergency response organization; the resulting organization would be smaller and have less ability to respond to extended events as compared to actual organizations. The use of duty teams manages the onerous aspects of being a responder by only imposing restrictions 1 week out of 4 to 6 weeks (more often when the position pool is small) and making the restrictions predictable. Only the duty team is required to observe limitations; no off-duty restrictions are imposed on any other emergency response organization members. It is recognized that many, if not most, of the unrestricted responders are also fit for duty and within a reasonable response distance while off-duty. This gives confidence that any gaps in response by the duty team (e.g., personal illness, family emergency, transportation accidents, pager or telephone failures) will be filled by members of other duty teams and the overall response will not be affected. Most licensees set up their paging and telephone notification processes to contact the duty team first when an event occurs that requires a response by off-duty employees. Other qualified responders are often contacted only when the duty team member for their position has not received or accepted the notification within a specified time.

In addition to providing scheduling predictability to manage the burden of being in the response organization, duty team members train and drill together. These common experiences build working relationships, teamwork, and trust and allow issues of personal management style and philosophy to be identified and addressed in advance of an event. When implemented well, common training instills cohesiveness and reduces distracting personality conflicts. Cohesion and working

---

[*] Licensees generally will not put an employee who lives more than a site-specific distance from the plant into their emergency response organization. Although there is no regulatory restriction that prevents licensees from separating the emergency response organization into *on-call* and *relief shift only* divisions, very few licensees have adopted this practice. Placing some individuals in relief shift status would allow the licensee to incorporate subject-matter experts who do not live close enough to meet requiring facility staffing times. Some licensees make living within a specified distance from the site a condition of employment when hiring from outside their immediate area, but this is far from a universal practice (and may not even be consistent within a single utility).

relationships are not built among responders when the licensee implements duty teams but frequently changes team assignments or does not control the level of substitution in training and drills (i.e., too many members of other teams substitute for missing team members).

Duty teams have worked well for the technical support center, emergency operations facility, and emergency news center (joint information center)—facilities where most responders are drawn from site management and professional staff. Teams also work well in these facilities because most positions are single staffed and can have a pool of four to six individuals. The duty team concept has been difficult to apply to the operations support center, a facility staffed primarily by maintenance workers and other technician-level employees. In part this is because management and professional staff are non-union while technicians are often unionized. The operations support center differs from other facilities in that most positions require multiple responders; it is not uncommon to have three to five individuals in each craft required for full staffing (e.g., five mechanical maintenance technicians, five electricians, five radiation protection technicians).

Most union contracts require employees to be paid for remaining in on-call status, which includes remaining fit for duty, having restricted off-duty movement, and carrying company-provided pagers or cellular phones. Because licensees have been unwilling to pay employees to be on call, the duty teams do not include designated mechanical maintenance staff, electrical maintenance, instrument and control maintenance, chemistry technicians, or radiation protection staff. Commonly, the only designated duty team positions in the operations support center are the facility manager and work planners for mechanical, electrical, and instrument/control maintenance. Licensees rely on the relatively large numbers in each position pool to provide enough individuals in each craft to staff the facility.

There are no regulations or requirements that licensees form, use, or respond to with duty teams. Very few sites describe the use of duty teams in their emergency plans or other planning documents, although an argument can be made that duty teams are now part of the licensee's concept of operation for responding to events and therefore should be included in site emergency plans.

EXTENDED EMERGENCY RESPONSE ORGANIZATION OPERATIONS

The Commission requires that licensees have the capability to continuously staff their emergency response organization during an extended event. In the author's opinion, many licensees manage their on-call duty teams well but do not pay sufficient attention to ensuring a relief shift. Licensees are generally aggressive in ensuring that there are no gaps in duty team (e.g., first shift) coverage, so that back-up staff is promptly identified to cover when primary individuals are unavailable. However, in the author's experience, licensees do not identify relief shifts in advance of an event and therefore lack methods to identify gaps in relief shift coverage. The Commission periodically reviews response organization rosters to ensure that a capacity for continuous staffing exists but does not generally require licensees to demonstrate the actual availability of the relief shift; the Commission would issue a violation to a licensee should an event ever occur in which the licensee does not actually fully staff the relief shifts as required by their emergency plan. Because licensees do not track the whereabouts of all emergency response organization members, they are vulnerable to having only the duty team responder available (for any one position), with all other members of the position pool being out of the area or otherwise unavailable (e.g., on medical disability). The problem is exacerbated when the number of qualified persons in a position pool falls below the number of duty teams. The worst case is when only two individuals are qualified for a position, so that maintaining a relief capability requires that neither one may be out of effective response range.[*]

---

[*] When this vulnerability is discovered, licensees often respond that the second individual is within a reasonable response range as long as he or she can return to the site within 6 to 8 hours. A 6- to 8-hour span gives a range of 300 to 400 miles driving, or about 1500 miles if flying. The point licensees often ignore is that a person who has just travelled 6 to 8 hours is unlikely to be sufficiently rested for a subsequent 12-hour shift. Although the regulatory limits on work hours implemented in 2010 do not apply to emergencies, an individual who must travel prior to working a shift will likely have been continuously awake for 20 hours or more by the end of that shift. Although a few exceptional individuals continue to function well after 20 or more hours without sleep, this would not be a prudent planning basis.

The positions most vulnerable to this problem are the command-and-control positions and the senior radiation protection positions. The command-and-control positions are vulnerable because they are filled by a small number of senior licensee officials who are often away for business reasons. The radiation protection positions are vulnerable because they are generally filled by a small number of subject-matter experts who may frequently participate in industry working groups (including consensus standard development) and may be in demand as peers to support training, audits, and assessments for other licensees (or at other sites within fleets).

Licensees must also carefully watch the number of employees in the pools for operations support center positions. There could be a problem when the total number of employees in a particular discipline is less than three times the number required to staff the operations support center.* There can also be problems with the number of employees with special skills or training; in particular, the operations support center may require minimum numbers of employees trained on self-contained breathing apparatus or other special equipment or personnel trained as fire fighters, emergency medical technicians, or hazardous material specialists. When some members of a particular position pool receive additional training but not the entire cohort, and responders are drawn randomly, it could happen that most special skilled employees report for the first shift, leaving few, or none, to staff the relief shift.

ON-SHIFT EMERGENCY RESPONSE ORGANIZATION STAFFING ANALYSES

There had never been a technical basis for NUREG-0654, Table B-1, and Commission staff had been getting a lot of questions about it from the late 1990s into the early 2000s. In 2012, the Commission required commercial reactor licensees to perform two analyses to determine whether their emergency response organizations were adequate to respond to a spectrum of emergency events. Although these analyses were independent of one another, derived from different requirements, and looked at different aspects of plant response, they are likely to be easily confused.

The first analysis was required by Appendix E to 10 CFR 50, IV.A(9), which became effective in 2011. This new requirement caused licensees to evaluate their on-shift organizations to ensure that no individual was assigned multiple functions that needed to be performed simultaneously. The analysis was required to be completed by December 2012, any immediate compensatory measures were required to be in place by January 2013, and permanent corrective actions were to be in place by June 2014. As part of the overall analysis, licensees were expected to perform a job-task analysis of the on-shift organization† and validate that all emergency tasks could be performed in a timely manner. The licensee was expected to use only the organization and staffing that were described in the site emergency plan, and the necessary coping time was determined by the facility staffing times as committed to in the plan. The analysis covered implementation of all existing abnormal event procedures, emergency operating procedures, and emergency plan implementing procedures. The analysis was for all design-basis events described in the plant's site-specific final safety analysis report. Although this was a new requirement, it followed previous Commission practice in that only license-basis events need be evaluated. For plants having multiple reactors, only a single unit need

---

* For example, one site has an emergency plan requirement for nine radiation protection technicians per shift in the operations support center. At one time, the site had only 17 qualified radiation protection technicians employed at the plant. The site complied with the requirement by identifying additional radiation protection technician-qualified employees onsite (i.e., not currently working in radiation protection but maintaining position-specific qualifications) and demonstrating that they could obtain qualified technicians from another (fleet) site within a reasonable response time for second shift staffing.

† The on-shift organization consists of licensed and non-licensed plant operators, maintenance staff, radiation protection and chemistry staff, site security staff, and any other personnel required to be present by plant technical specifications, the conduct of operations procedure, emergency plan, physical security plan, or any other regulatory commitment. These personnel are immediately available to respond to an abnormal condition until the arrival of offsite resources (including off-duty employees).

be analyzed, allowing credit for staff at unaffected units. The requirement for this analysis had been part of the emergency preparedness rulemaking that was implemented in 2011 since its inception in 2008, and was not related to any specific events.

The second analysis was required by a demand for information from the Commission under 10 CFR 50.54(f),* transmitted to licensees in 2012. This demand for information required that licensees analyze the ability of the emergency response organization to function in beyond-design-basis events and specifically required multi-reactor sites to assume that the condition simultaneously affected all reactors (i.e., no credit was allowed for unaffected unit staff). This demand-for-information was one part of the Commission's short-term actions following the events at the Fukushima Daiichi plant in Japan in 2011. Licensees were required to answer some parts of the demand for information by June 7, 2012, and fully answer by October 31, 2012. Because offsite resources may be required to respond to beyond-design-basis events, this analysis could be informed by the results of concurrent analysis to determine the assistance expected from offsite agencies in a spectrum of emergencies, including hostile actions (Appendix E to 10 CFR 50, IV.A(7), implemented 2011).

EMERGENCY RESPONSE ORGANIZATION AND INCIDENT COMMAND SYSTEM

The Commission published a preliminary proposed emergency preparedness rule on March 12, 2008, and a final proposed rule on May 18, 2009. In both cases, it requested public comment on the proposed rules. Although the proposed rules did not include the Incident Command System (ICS),† some respondents advocated the Commission requiring licensees to adopt the Incident Command System, and some advocated a requirement for licensee training on incident command. In both cases, the respondent's reasoning was that licensee use (or awareness) of incident command would improve the ability of onsite responders to work with offsite responders when required. Offsite agencies routinely use incident command in responding to law enforcement, fire, hazardous material, and natural disaster events. The Commission declined to include the Incident Command System in the final emergency preparedness rule implemented in 2011. The NRC based its decision in large part on a lack of legal authority to require private licensees adopt incident command. Homeland Security Presidential Directive 5 (USDHS, 2003a) required development of the National Incident Management System (NIMS) and required federal departments to adopt the system. Because a National Incident Management System essentially already existed, the practical effect of this part of Homeland Security Presidential Directive 5 was minimal. Although federal agencies and departments could be required by the President to implement the National Incident Management System (those not already in compliance), the President lacks legal authority to require either states or private entities to also adopt the system. With regard to the states, Homeland Security Presidential Directive 5 sidestepped the legal authority issue by limiting emergency preparedness grants from the Department of Homeland Security to those states and local organizations committed to the National Incident Management System.

Federal law does not impose a requirement to implement incident command on private entities such as reactor licensees. It can be argued that the Commission could have required that reactor licensees adopt the National Incident Management System as a condition of their license, as the Commission has authority under the Atomic Energy Act to require any license conditions it believes necessary. However, in this instance, the Commission declined to use that specific authority.

Although licensees cannot be required to adopt incident command, the author agrees in large part that licensee familiarity with incident command would be beneficial because there are situations in which licensee responders could be required to interact with an offsite incident command

---

* 10 CFR 50.54(f) states in part that licensees shall submit statements as requested to enable the Commission to determine whether the license should be suspended, modified, or revoked.

† Information about the National Incident Management System and Incident Command System can be found at http://www. fema.gov/national-incident-management-system. Free online training about the Incident Command System is available on the FEMA Emergency Management Institute website, http://training.fema.gov/IS/. These courses provide a history of NIMS–ICS development.

post. Licensees should consider adding an incident command post liaison position to their formal emergency response organization; it may be necessary to have two liaisons—one for plant operations (which typically includes fire fighting) and one for plant security.

There are no requirements preventing a reactor licensee from choosing to implement an emergency response organization using Incident Command System titles and organization, although none has done so to date. Existing emergency response organizations already share some commonalities with incident command, so simply re-titling some licensee positions would accomplish some alignment—for example, from emergency director to incident commander or operation support center manager to operations section leader.

There are also some structural impediments, as the traditional five radiological emergency response facilities do not align well with the incident command post and its four sections (operations, planning, logistics, and administration). Alignment with incident command would require the technical support center to be separated into operations and planning components, and the emergency operations facility to be split among the planning, logistics, and administration sections. The control room aligns with the operations section, as do most functions of the operations support center. In addition, most licensees do not routinely include many of the functions assigned to the logistics and administration sections in their emergency response organizations.

Nothing in regulation or guidance specifies the staff for an individual emergency response facility, nor are position titles specified. It is likely, in the author's opinion, that the existing response facilities could be renamed from their traditional names to conform to the Incident Command System titles; if this occurs, the licensee's emergency plan would have to provide the regulatory tie between the Appendix E requirements and the licensee's actual facilities.

EMERGENCY RESPONSE FACILITIES

The term *emergency response facility* describes any preplanned location from which emergency response functions can or will be performed. Emergency response facilities are operated by the reactor licensee, local and state offsite officials, and federal departments or agencies. The location, staffing, equipment, and functions of each facility are described in each organization's emergency plan, along with the communication pathways among and between emergency response facilities. Although the emergency response facility usually includes pre-planned alternative locations intended to be used if the primary facility is unavailable or becomes uninhabitable, alternative locations for control room operators are not generally considered to be response facilities. This is because the reactor shutdown panels are intended only for the manipulation of a limited number of reactor systems and are not sized or configured to support incident command-and-control functions. They also lack the radiological protection built into the control room, lack access to most plant instruments, and lack the control room's reference library and procedures.

The reactor control room[*] is the initial emergency response facility for any event. The shift manager (senior reactor operator) is responsible for identifying that an event requires entry into the emergency plan and for determining the correct emergency classification; the shift manager becomes the emergency director when a classification is declared. Other licensee emergency response facilities include the technical support center, operations support center, emergency operations facility, and a public information center most commonly called either the joint information center or the emergency news center. The staffing of emergency response facilities is determined by the emergency classification. The purposes of the emergency response facilities include the following:

- Assisting reactor operators in determining the reactor core state and the plant safety status
- Relieving reactor operators of duties not directly related to reactor system manipulations (including the removal of distracting duties and personnel)

---

[*] Some multi-unit sites have a separate reactor control room for each individual reactor; others have a single integrated control room from which each reactor can be controlled.

- Providing additional technical expertise to reactor operators
- Providing comprehensive analyses of plant systems
- Planning and executing plant repairs to restores plant equipment to reactor operators
- Providing for a coordinated licensee emergency response by technical and management staff
- Providing for reliable communications between onsite and offsite emergency responders
- Providing recommendations for the protection of licensee employees and workers, and for potentially affected members of the public
- Providing plant data to the Nuclear Regulatory Commission to support its independent analysis of abnormal plant operating conditions
- Providing essential information about the event to offsite officials and the public

The Commission's requirements for emergency response facilities are primarily found in NUREG-0696, *Functional Criteria for Emergency Response Facilities* (NRC, 1981e); NUREG-0737, *Clarification of TMI Action Plan Requirements*, Supplement 1 (NRC, 1983a); and NUREG-0814, *Methodology for Evaluation of Emergency Response Facilities* (NRC, 1981i).

The essential characteristics of an emergency response facility include sufficient physical space for responders, communications capabilities, means to acquire situational information, information displays, a facility-specific reference and procedure library, and means to control facility access (facility security). Some facilities also require protection from physical or radiological hazards or require specific analytical capabilities such as core damage analysis or dose projection software. Data acquisition methods can include local instrument displays, system-specific data displays (e.g., radiation monitoring system terminal), the plant computer system, weather radios, and log keeping and interactive chronology software such as WebEOC.* Offsite facilities may be able to track event parameters through the Commission's Emergency Response Data System (ERDS; see below for a more extensive discussion).

Emergency response facilities are to be built to the Uniform Building Code, taking into account 100-year environmental conditions (winds, floods, etc.); they are not required to be designed to survive extreme conditions such as direct strike by a tornado or hurricane. NUREG-0696 defined *sufficient space* as having no less than 75 ft^2/person (NRC, 1981e).

REACTOR CONTROL ROOM

The reactor control room contains the instrumentation, controls, and displays for nuclear systems, steam systems, turbine and electrical systems, reactor safety systems, and accident monitoring systems. It also contains alarm panels to alert reactor operators to the starting and tripping of equipment, parameters outside of normal operating setpoints, and other unusual conditions or conditions potentially requiring operator response (each individual alarm is called an *annunciator* because it both lights and sounds an audible alarm). Typical data sources include gauges and displays on permanent control boards, individual plant computer parameter trend displays, and the safety parameter display system (SPDS), which is a set of computer display screens that group the most important parameters for analyzing the core state, usually organized into easily read graphic displays or charts.

Typical communications systems include the plant public address system, operations and maintenance radio channels, operations and management conference lines with emergency response facilities, and dedicated conference lines to offsite emergency response centers (and/or designated contact points). There is also a dedicated phone line for use by the onsite NRC representative (resident inspector). Some licensees use computer-based systems to inform offsite agencies of an event, with telephones or radio systems serving as backup communications methods.

---

* This is one example among several commercially available programs for keeping computer-based logs, displaying event information, and communicating among facilities. No endorsement of this product is intended.

The control room is designed to be inhabited during radiological accidents and has both radiation shielding and filtered ventilation. The control room ventilation system is designed to detect airborne chemicals and radioactive material and has a recirculation emergency mode of operation. In addition, the licensee is required to provide respiratory protection for reactor operators so they can remain at the controls when there is airborne contamination (at least for the time required to bring the reactor to zero power). The most common respiratory protection is self-contained breathing apparatus, although air-line supplied respirators have also been used. During an emergency, an NRC representative (resident inspector) reports to the control room.

TECHNICAL SUPPORT CENTER

The Commission requires a licensee to have an onsite technical support center per Appendix E to 10 CFR 50, Part IV.E(8). The technical support center is responsible for evaluating the reactor core and plant equipment, for devising means to bring the plant into a safe configuration, and for returning necessary plant systems to service so they can be used to mitigate an emergency condition. The technical support center is also responsible for the safety of emergency and non-emergency employees at the site, including radiological protection, non-radiological worker protection, and physical security. The facility implements site accountability, assembly, and evacuation, and it directs any necessary search and rescue.

The technical support center is required to be activated for events at the Alert classification (or higher) and may be activated for events at the Notification of Unusual Event classification at the discretion of the emergency director. Some licensees have also used their technical support centers for planning and response in abnormal circumstances that were not classifiable events (i.e., non-emergencies). The typical facility personnel are site management in operations and maintenance, system engineers (reactor, electrical, mechanical, instruments and control), health physics and chemistry staff, a senior security representative, communicators, and administrative support staff. The technical support center must be capable of relieving the control room of command-and-control, although the current standard practice at many licensees is for event command to transfer directly from the control room to the emergency operations facility.* Some licensees routinely transfer the emergency classification function to the technical support center while transferring the offsite notification and radiological assessment functions to the emergency operations facility. Splitting the classification from the other command-and-control functions introduces a measure of regulatory risk, as a failure to promptly communicate classification to the emergency operations facility could result in failing to make a timely notification to offsite authorities.

Typical data sources include individual plant computer parameter trend displays, the radiation monitor display system (when this is a stand-alone terminal), and the safety parameter display system (including real-time meteorology). Analysis software to determine core state and project the consequences of radiological releases is typically located in this facility.

Typical communications systems include the plant public address system, operations and maintenance radio channels, operations and management conference lines with emergency response facilities, and dedicated conference lines to offsite emergency response centers. Some technical support centers have radio communications with environmental survey teams. There are also dedicated phone lines for use by onsite NRC representatives and responders. The facility will also have access to any installed backup communications methods.

---

* The standard practice in the 1980s and 1990s was to staff the technical support center, transfer command-and-control, and then staff the emergency operations facility only if the situation degraded further (the emergency operations facility is not required at the Alert classification). A second transfer of command-and-control would occur from the technical support center to the emergency operations facility if warranted. In the mid- to late-1990s, the simultaneous staffing of the technical support center and emergency operations facility became standard industry practice. Some licensees adopted the practice of transferring command directly to the emergency operations facility (unless an impediment exists), because multiple transfers of command-and-control introduce possible miscommunications and because the emergency operations facility may be activated first under some circumstances.

The technical support center is designed to be inhabited during radiological accidents and has both radiation shielding and filtered ventilation; at some reactor sites, the technical support center is within the control room envelope (i.e., shares common shielding and ventilation). The ventilation system is designed with a recirculation emergency mode of operation. The facility should also have installed local radiation detectors, a continuous air monitor to detect airborne radioactive material, access control for continuous staff accountability, and the ability to implement radiological controls such as personnel dosimetry, contamination detectors (friskers and portal monitors), and radiological step-off pads. The technical support center is not required to be a dedicated (i.e., single-use) facility, although shared-use facilities are rare; shared use is permitted provided that no alternative usage prevents the facility from assuming its emergency functions in the time required by the site emergency plan.

NUREG-0696 requires that the technical support center be within a short distance of the control room, and it is always located inside the reactor site's protected area. This requirement was intended (in 1980 to 1982) to facilitate direct face-to-face communications between senior staff in the control room and in the technical support center, in part to compensate for the limited data communications capabilities available at that time. In practice, the movement of staff between these two facilities is rare. There are some licensees whose normal practice is for the emergency director (control room shift manager) to perform a face-to-face briefing of the senior technical support center official before that official reports to their facility.

Some licensees have combined the technical and operations support functions at a single location. This arrangement allows for face-to-face discussions among engineers, work planners, and individual operators and plant mechanics. It also reduces the likelihood that technical support and operations support priorities diverge or are misunderstood.

Although the technical support center is designed to remain habitable under a variety of conditions, licensees are required to plan for an alternative location in case it does become uninhabitable due to, for example, high radiation, high temperatures, or loss of electrical power. The alternative location is typically within the protected area, although it is not required to be. Technical support center staff could also disperse to more than one location; for example, some could report to the control room and some to another nearby location. After 2012, licensees have been required to also provide a near-site alternative location to muster technical support center staff in the event that conditions prevent access to the site;* these conditions could include hostile actions or a widespread natural disaster. In the context of a loss of site access, *near site* has been interpreted as being within a 30-minute drive of the site so the primary facility can be quickly occupied after site access is restored. The alternative or backup technical support center is not required to have the same radiation shielding and emergency ventilation as the primary, but it is required to have similar data acquisition and communications capabilities.

During an emergency, an NRC representative (senior resident inspector) reports to the technical support center; if the situation escalates to a Site Area Emergency or General Emergency, then additional NRC technical staff will be dispatched to the facility (arriving in 2 to 10 hours, depending on the reactor site location). The technical support center is required to provide private working or conference space for the NRC.

OPERATIONS SUPPORT CENTER

The operations support center is responsible for implementing strategies to bring the plant into a safe configuration and for returning necessary plant systems to service. This facility works under technical support center direction and provides the skills and resources to perform necessary in-plant

---

* See Appendix E to 10 CFR 50, Part IV.E(8)(d). The alternative location could be at the emergency operations facility or at some other plant building, or it could be an entirely separate facility; this function should be described in the site emergency plan.

work. The operations support center also carries out search-and-rescue and medical missions and supports site assembly and evacuation as necessary. The operations support center does not take command-and-control of an emergency event.

The operations support center is required to be activated for events at the Alert classification (or higher) and may be activated for events at the Notification of Unusual Event classification at the discretion of the emergency director. The typical facility personnel are plant operations and mainte-nance staff, work schedulers and work planners, plant foremen (mechanical, electrical, instrument, chemistry, and radiation protection), mechanics, technicians, and communicators. The facility may have additional support from fire fighters, medical staff, station laborers, warehouse staff, industrial hygienists, and administrative staff.

Typical data sources include individual plant computer parameter trend displays, the radiation monitor display system (when this is a stand-alone terminal), and the safety parameter display sys-tem (including real-time meteorology). Typical communications systems include the plant public address system, operations and maintenance radio channels, and operations and management con-ference lines with licensee emergency response facilities. The operations support center does not typically communicate to offsite agencies. The Commission does not typically send responders to the operations support center.

The operations support center is intended to be inhabited under most radiological conditions but is not required to have radiation shielding or filtered ventilation. Stand-alone operations support centers generally do not have either shielding or ventilation systems, and they rely on local moni-toring and facility relocation to provide radiation protection for emergency workers. The facility should have installed local radiation detectors, a continuous air monitor to detect airborne radioac-tive material, access control for continuous staff accountability, and the ability to implement radio-logical controls such as personnel dosimetry, contamination detectors (friskers and portal monitors), and radiological step-off pads. Licensees are required to provide an alternative location in case the operations support center becomes uninhabitable. The alternative location should be within the protected area. After 2012, licensees have been required to provide a near-site alternative location to muster operations support center staff in the event that conditions prevent access to the site.

There is no regulatory requirement for a separate operations support center. Some licensees have combined the technical and operations support functions at a single location. This arrangement allows for face-to-face discussions among engineers, work planners, and individual operators and plant mechanics. The operations support center is not required to be a dedicated (i.e., single-use) facility; shared use is permitted provided that no alternative usage prevents the facility from assum-ing its emergency functions in the time required by the site emergency plan. The most common alternative uses are as an outage control center or work control center.

EMERGENCY OPERATIONS FACILITY

The Commission requires a licensee to have a near-site emergency operations facility per Appendix E to 10 CFR 50, Part IV.E(8). The emergency operations facility is responsible for evaluating the radiological consequences of an event, for directing and analyzing environmental measurements, for acquiring resources (e.g., personnel or equipment from other utilities), for communications and coordination with other organizations within the licensee's company, for communications and coor-dination with offsite responders, and for recommending appropriate protective measures for the public (again, only the appropriate legal authority may *implement* protective measures). The emer-gency operations facility may also be responsible for the safety of members of the public allowed access to the site-owner-controlled area. The emergency operations facility is required to be acti-vated at a Site Area Emergency or higher classification, although the current industry practice is to activate at an Alert or higher classification. The emergency operations facility must provide working space for those offsite agencies that colocate with the utility. In some cases, offsite representatives act as liaisons; in others, the legal decision-maker relocates to the facility. It is typical to find county or parish representatives present, along with the state radiation protection agency (or representatives of multiple states when the reactor site is at or near a state boundary). Most states direct their environmental monitoring efforts from the emergency operations facility, allowing for direct coordination with licensee surveys and the immediate sharing of radiological measurement data.

Typical data sources include individual plant computer parameter trend displays, the radiation monitor display system, and the safety parameter display system (including real-time meteorology). Analysis software to project the consequences of radiological releases is typically located in this facility. Communications systems include operations and management conference lines with emergency response facilities, dedicated conference lines to offsite emergency response centers, and radio communications with environmental survey teams. There are also dedicated phone lines for use by Commission staff and responders. The facility will also have access to any installed backup communications methods.

The emergency operations facility is not required to be a dedicated facility, although facilities with routine non-emergency uses are rare (the author knows of only one). The facility can be located in the owner-controlled area and is always outside the protected area. NUREG-0696 required the emergency operations facility be within 20 miles of the reactor site (later extended by the Commission to 25 miles). An emergency operations facility located within 10 miles of the reactor is required to provide installed radiological protection (e.g., radiation detectors, shielding, filtered ventilation), and the licensee must also provide an additional facility capable of performing all of the emergency operations facility's emergency functions located between 10 and 25 miles from the site, in the event the primary location becomes uninhabitable. No installed radiological protection is required when the facility is located 10 miles or more from the site (i.e., outside the emergency planning zone), and no alternative facility is required in this case. Most licensees provide local radiation monitoring capabilities (e.g., survey meters, electronic dosimetry, continuous air monitors, decontamination showers, radiological step-off pads) even when they are not required by regulation.

The emergency operations facility was intended to include an analytical laboratory for the prompt analysis of contaminated environmental samples, along with a limited decontamination capability for environmental survey team members or other staff who become contaminated in transit from the plant site. The Commission has allowed licensees to remove their analytical laboratory capabilities over the years (and associated staffing), so that few, if any, laboratories remain today. In most cases, the approved alternative is a contract laboratory, usually located some distance from the reactor site. Licensees do not intend to use their onsite radiochemistry laboratories for this purpose; in any case, there would be considerable logistical difficulties to overcome in trying to transport samples back to the plant during or after a significant radiological release. Onsite laboratories are equipped and calibrated for some environmental samples, principally smears and air samples, but they are unlikely to be calibrated for most environmental media. In the author's opinion, the removal of gamma spectroscopy systems from the emergency operations facility introduces a considerable delay in obtaining the isotopic data necessary to calculate derived intervention levels and other short-term action thresholds.

The original (1980s) concept was that the emergency operations facility and emergency information function would be at the same location. This was to allow the senior licensee official to also act as the principal company spokesperson and participate in news briefings. Licensees gradually abandoned the concept of dual command-and-control and company spokesperson, lessening the value of colocating radiological assessment and public information functions. Most licensees built their initial emergency operations facility on or near their owner-controlled areas (or least nearby in the emergency planning zone), and this caused logistical difficulties because the public information function had to relocate to outside the emergency planning zone as the event escalated to a Site Area Emergency or General Emergency. By the 1990s, most licensees had completely separated radiological assessment and public information and built permanent new centers outside the emergency planning zone. Interestingly, the trend today is again toward colocation of these functions, mostly because many licensees are removing their emergency operations facility to outside the emergency planning zone—the impetus being removal of difficult-to-maintain ventilation systems and no longer having to maintain quasi-duplicate facilities.

If the situation escalates to a Site Area Emergency or General Emergency, Commission managers and technical staff will be dispatched to the facility (arriving in 2 to 10 hours, depending on the reactor site location). A fully staffed site team consists of 20 to 25 responders per shift. The emergency operations facility is required to provide private working and conference space for the NRC.

EMERGENCY OPERATIONS FACILITIES BEYOND 25 MILES FROM SITE

Since the mid-1990s, licensees have increasingly become interested in locating their emergency operations facility far from the reactor site, to the point where changes to Appendix E to 10 CFR 50 effective in 2011 included regulations for distant emergency response facilities. One factor in this interest was the opportunity to use a single emergency response facility for multiple reactor sites (see discussion below), another was the opportunity for reactor fleets[*] to use headquarters staff as emergency responders, and another was the opportunity to redirect site resources to the technical support center. A licensee may implement a distant emergency operations facility if

- It meets all the communications, data acquisition, and radiological assessment requirements of NUREG-0696.
- It can be staffed and activated within the time specified in the licensee's emergency plan.
- Methods are developed to notify headquarters employees to report in an emergency and the methods are routinely tested.
- Designated headquarters staff receive initial and continuing training on their emergency response functions.
- An additional near-site location is provided for use by the NRC (requirement effective 2011; see discussion below).

A licensee must receive approval from the Commission prior to implementing a distant emergency operations facility. In most cases, Commission approval has been delegated to staff; however, in this case, the Commission has specifically reserved the approval to itself (i.e., requiring a vote of the Commissioners). In general, licensees moving their emergency response facilities are not required to prove adequacy through demonstration, but historically the Commission has required licensees to conduct a demonstration exercise as a condition of approving an emergency operations facility 25 miles or more from the reactor site.

EMERGENCY OPERATIONS FACILITIES FOR MULTIPLE SITES

Some licensees have designed single emergency operations facilities that serve multiple reactor sites. These are primarily operated by reactor fleets, although there are historical precedents: Point Beach and Kewaunee stations in Wisconsin shared a single facility located between them, and in the 1980s and 1990s a single facility served Dresden, Braidwood, and LaSalle stations in Illinois. The Point Beach and Kewaunee stations were about 20 miles apart and at one time were operated by different nuclear operating companies; this was a unique situation because each station staffed the facility for its own events rather than having a single organization capable of responding to either

---

[*] A reactor fleet consists of multiple (many) individual reactors owned and operated by a single nuclear operating company. Fleets typically have standardized business practices, equipment, training, and procedures that apply to all of their operating units. They may also share personnel among sites. It should be noted, however, that a nuclear operating company with several reactors is not a single licensee with respect to the NRC, as each individual reactor is issued a unit-specific operating license. Therefore, a company owning 12 reactors at 6 operating sites would be considered to be an amalgamation of 6 licensees, one at each operating site.

station. The Dresden, Braidwood, and LaSalle stations were all operated by a single nuclear utility; the three reactors are located in a triangle configuration with overlapping emergency planning
zones so that a small area south of Morrison, IL, was not in any of the three zones (this allowed the
facility not to require special shielding or ventilation). There were other examples of shared facilities, especially colocated units operated by different companies, such as Indian Point prior to the
mid-2000s when ownership was consolidated.

Combined emergency operations facilities serving multiple reactor sites were first proposed in
the early to mid-1990s by Virginia Power and Light, Duke Energy, and Commonwealth Edison.
The author worked on aspects of the Commonwealth Edison case. The Commission identified in
late 1991 to early 1992 that Commonwealth Edison was unable to activate its four emergency operations facilities within an hour of an emergency condition as required by its emergency plan. This
was because the company relied upon staff from their unaffected reactors to staff an emergency
operations facility. Although some responders had relatively short distances to travel, the farthest
reactor sites were roughly 200 miles apart. The common emergency operations facility for Dresden,
Braidwood, and LaSalle stations could generally (but not under all conditions) be activated as
required, but the facilities for Zion, Byron, and Quad Cities stations could not. The average staffing
times ranged from 90 minutes at Byron to well over 2 hours at Quad Cities, with Zion's times being
between the two.

The initial corrective action was to maintain the existing emergency operations facility staffing
procedure, supplemented by a new, interim facility located at the nuclear division headquarters.
The company's nuclear headquarters was located in suburban Chicago, 50 miles from the closest of
the six reactor sites. A large number of engineering, radiation protection, and other technical staff
worked at headquarters at the time, and these staff could reach headquarters within the required
hour. Headquarters also already possessed the requisite plant computer connections and plant communications capabilities, greatly simplifying the task of meeting data acquisition requirements. The
company implemented a response strategy that required a station control room transfer command-
and-control to the technical support center, which subsequently transferred control to the interim
emergency operations facility at headquarters, which subsequently transferred control to the near-
site emergency operations facility whenever it was staffed. The interim facility staff was smaller
than the full emergency operations facility staff but covered all of the NUREG-0654 Table B-1
functions; the staff was capable of radiological analysis and could effectively respond to an emergency at any unit (e.g., three boiling water reactor sites and three pressurized water reactor sites).

Several years of exercise experience using the interim emergency operations facility led
Commonwealth Edison to propose a permanent single multi-reactor emergency operations facility
in the late 1990s. This allowed the company to discontinue the four near-site facilities and effectively relieved site personnel from any support of the emergency operations facility. Because each
near-site facility also housed a public information facility, a separate licensing action was necessary
to discontinue their news center functions. The Commission approved Commonwealth Edison's
permanent combined emergency operations facility in the early 2000s, after a lengthy licensing
process and a demonstration exercise.

A licensee must receive Commission approval prior to implementing a combined emergency
operations facility. Again, the Commission has reserved final approval to itself. In every case to
date, the Commission has required that the licensee demonstrate by exercise a capability to respond
to simultaneous emergency conditions at two or more reactor sites.

Combined emergency operations facilities have been effective to date, but in the author's opinion
they have some long-term challenges. The viability of a combined emergency operations facility
rests on having a sufficiently large and diverse technical staff, working from a central location.
Overall industry staffing levels have dropped substantially since the mid-1990s, and the composition of headquarters staff has changed. At one time, headquarters staff was primarily technical
personnel, providing a large pool of personnel with previous plant experience. Now, headquarters
are more likely to be staffed with administrative and business personnel, with proportionally fewer

technical staff, and fewer staff overall from whom to draw emergency responders. Such a situation presents a particular challenge in that in the future an emergency response organization will have to provide non-technical (or less technical) staff with the skills necessary to effectively respond to a radiological emergency, and then maintain those skills. Another potential challenge, even for technical staff, is the continuing workplace trend toward mobile work using remote communications technology. As it becomes less important that employees live near their work, it may become difficult to continue to staff a combined emergency operations facility in a timely manner because staff no longer lives close enough to respond quickly.

EMERGENCY NEWS CENTER AND JOINT INFORMATION CENTER

Per 10 CFR 50.47(b)(7), licensees are required to designate the principal points of contact for news organizations, including the location or locations at which information will be made available. NUREG-0654, element G(3)(b), states, in part, that each licensee shall provide space at the near-site emergency operations facility that may be used for a limited number of news media, and G(4)(a) states that each principal organization shall designate a spokesperson who will have access to all necessary emergency information. The most common names for this space are *joint information center* and *emergency news center*; the author will refer to the facility as the emergency news center. The emergency news center is typically staffed by senior company and participating agency officials who act as primary spokespersons for their organizations, along with public information staff, writers, and administrative assistants. Some organizations include technical briefers to explain the details of reactor systems. There may also be information technology staff to assist with computer system and connectivity problems.

The purposes of the emergency news center are to (1) quickly disseminate accurate information about the event, including instructions to the affected public; (2) serve as a single location at which all of the event information is available; and (3) serve as a single location for news organizations to gather. Although the emergency news center is typically maintained by the reactor licensee, it is staffed by all of the participating emergency response organizations. This joint staffing makes it unique among emergency response facilities and presents some unique challenges.

The emergency news center is required to be activated at the Site Area Emergency or General Emergency classifications, although the practice of activating at an Alert classification is now common. The emergency news center is not required to be staffed as rapidly as other response facilities, and staffing times of 2 hours or more are not unusual. Corporate communications departments typically retain responsibility for news releases at the Notification of Unusual Event classification. The corporate communications department is rarely located at the reactor site, even for a utility with a single reactor site, so there may be challenges in clearly communicating event information to the corporate group. The corporate group may also have limited knowledge about the reactor plant, making it more difficult for operators to explain the emergency.

The first news release about an event should always come from the licensee's corporate communications group, with other statements being released by the public information officers at affected offsite agencies. Around 90 minutes into the event would be a normal time for this first message. If the initial classification was an Alert or higher, or if a Notification of Unusual Event escalates, a news release would be issued to announce staffing the emergency news center and give its location. If an event web page or social media feeds have been created, the initial announcement would provide information about how to access information through the internet.

Typical data sources include individual plant computer parameter trend displays and the safety parameter display system, including real-time meteorology. Communications systems include management conference lines with emergency response facilities and dedicated conference lines to offsite emergency response centers. The emergency news center is also likely to have Internet service and connections, videoconferencing capability, cable and satellite television displays, and computer-driven displays.

The emergency news center facility is not required to be a dedicated facility, although facilities with routine non-emergency uses are rare. The facility can be located in the owner-controlled area or anywhere else in the emergency planning zone, although this presents issues of public access and radiation protection. Previous exercise experience has shown that is it highly disruptive to initially staff a near-site news center at the Site Area Emergency classification, only to have to move it shortly thereafter when the event is upgraded to General Emergency. No licensee will continue to operate a news center within the emergency planning zone after near-site evacuations have been ordered and access controls are in place; for example, reporters would be prevented from entering some areas.

The timing of media briefings will depend on the facility staffing time and on how rapidly the media arrive at the facility. In the author's opinion, it would be reasonable for the emergency news center to be capable of holding its first media briefing within about 90 minutes of being staffed; this gives enough time to organize the facility, activate equipment, obtain situational information, and write initial press releases. The timing of subsequent briefings will depend on whether (and how quickly) the event escalates and whether protective measures are implemented for the public. The facility should be organized to quickly obtain information and conduct frequent media briefings while events are escalating and when urgent information needs to be transmitted to the public.

The first few media briefings will likely be presented primarily to local media representatives, because it will take hours for the major news organizations to get their representatives to some of the relatively remote locations. If emergency news centers begin implementing web casts and other remote-viewing technology, that will affect media's access to information, although such distribution approaches are still in the discussion phases at this time and are unlikely to be implemented in the near future.

The joint nature of an emergency news center poses particular challenges in coordinating information between responding organizations. Facility procedures often designate the utility spokesperson as the one to facilitate intra-facility communications and press briefings, but the agency having legal authority offsite may see itself as the natural leader among the organizations. Some participating agencies may not have strong procedures or may not follow established facility procedures. The intra-facility processes by which agencies share and validate information may be *ad hoc* or informal and depend on the individuals present. Problems that could arise at the emergency news center include the following:

- Spokespersons disagree on the details of the emergency during press briefings.
- Spokespersons speak for other agencies (present or those not represented).
- Spokespersons have inaccurate or out-of-date information.
- Spokespersons improvise or provide their personal opinions on events or activities.
- Agencies do not share their information within the facility before press briefings.
- Agencies are not prepared for press briefings.

A hostile action at a nuclear power plant is likely to create additional problems in communicating to the public. This is because the plant security organization and offsite law enforcement agencies will want control over the information released to the public, and the law enforcement agency claiming jurisdiction may change over time. There may also be conflicts among the various law enforcement agencies simultaneously claiming control over information. The degree of information control may limit the information given to the public, or a single law enforcement spokesperson may attempt to represent all of the agencies responding to the event. The extent to which public information will be restricted is not currently known, in part because law enforcement agencies do not have a long exercise history with radiological response programs. The initial round of hostile-action-based evaluated exercises conducted between 2013 and 2015 did not provide definitive answers, as there were some sites at which essentially no information was allowed to be given out and some sites at which a significant amount of information was made available. No clear pattern has emerged as to what law enforcement will allow, as the same information was allowed at some exercises and censored at others. Most of the experience to date regarding the release of information has been with local law enforcement, particularly with county and parish sheriffs. Federal law enforcement agencies, particularly the Federal Bureau of Investigation and the Department of Homeland Security, proved to be very inconsistent in their level of participation in hostile-action-based exercises, so there is very little solid experience to indicate how they would approach public information in this case.

Media experts expect that during a major emergency some reporters will try to evade access controls and travel to the affected plant. Some reporters will try to interview responders traveling to or from near-site emergency response facilities, or they will try to gain entry to near-site facilities. This behavior is expected because of the inherently competitive nature of the news business—reporting directly from the plant is dramatic and may be perceived as enhancing the reporter's credibility, and information obtained directly from an onsite responder may be perceived as being more accurate or authentic than information obtained at a press briefing. The expectation that reporters will not generally conform to public access restrictions is one reason why each emergency response facility requires access control and a security department presence.

It is worth noting that, although reporters, photographers, and other support staff are members of the public for purposes of radiological protection, the emergency news center is intended to be restricted to news professionals. Some (typically local) news organizations will be accredited in advance, and there will be a process to accredit news organizations as their representatives arrive at the facility. There is no provision or intention for members of the general public to have personal access to event briefings or press conferences. This exclusion of the public is one of the issues that will need to be addressed as bloggers, non-news Internet sites, and posters to social media begin to be included in the public information effort.

MEDIA MONITORING AND RUMOR CONTROL

NUREG-0654 requires that the licensee and offsite agencies have processes to receive and respond to questions from the public. This function is often called *rumor control*, although in practice the function is closer to rumor tracking or rumor response. There is essentially nothing that emergency responders can do to control rumors among the general public in real time. The most common method for addressing rumors is a telephone bank that takes calls from the public. The phone number should be established in advance, included in annual distributions of emergency information, and repeated in the initial press releases concerning an event. It should also be prominently posted on any event-related website and in social media feeds. The phone bank may be operated by the licensee or by other responders, although licensees are most likely to be responsible for this function. The phone bank may be colocated with the emergency operations facility or the emergency news center, but this is not a requirement. The rumor control phone bank is not normally considered to be an emergency response facility when it operates at a separate location. If this function is carried out from a location inside the emergency planning zone, it would be subject to relocation if evacuations are implemented.

Some licensees use their existing call centers and customer service representatives to take calls from the public. Phone bank operators have the following functions during an emergency: (1) reassure callers as best they can; (2) answer event questions, depending on their training and available information; (3) direct callers to sources of information, such as websites, press releases, media briefings, and preprinted emergency response information; and (4) identify misinformation that should be addressed by the emergency news center. If responders have established social media feeds, the persons taking calls from the public should also be able to direct the public to information posted on social media. This function is periodically tested during drills and exercises by callers with scripted questions and rumors. There needs to be a rapid method for phone bank operators to record the question (rumor) and tag it with key words so analysts can sort the information and determine the ones that need to be addressed by the public information process.

A related function is identification and correction of misinformation generated by media coverage of the event. This function is often referred to as *media monitoring*. Media monitoring is always done by the reactor licensee and sometimes by other agencies, depending on their resources. The intent is to immediately recognize inaccurate information about protective measures to be taken by the public and quickly recognize other inaccurate information. Traditional media monitoring involves identifying the most important television and radio stations for an area and having staff listen to reporting about the event; it is not unusual for these reports to be recorded. The number of traditional news outlets (i.e., print, radio, and television) may be large, but it is also somewhat predictable, allowing responders to anticipate the resources the monitoring task will require.

With the advent of social media, identifying posts with inaccurate or inflammatory information will become more important and more difficult. There is no simple or quick method for identifying posts pertaining to the emergency situation, and there is no way for responders to ever know that they have identified all of the posts. After the inaccurate posts are identified, then responders have to respond to all of them, which will likely become a very time-consuming task. At the present, organizations that have established social media monitoring as part of their large media monitoring effort typically devote one or two persons to the task, a level of resources that will likely not be near enough to handle a major emergency.

Inaccurate information about protective measures needs to be corrected as soon as possible through *ad hoc* briefings with reports or expedited press releases. Other important information should be addressed during the next scheduled news briefing; in a slower moving event in which news briefings are less frequent, a special news briefing may be required, depending on the nature of the misinformation. The erroneous information is unlikely to be malicious and may result from a reporter's limited knowledge of reactor systems and the unfamiliar terminology used in press releases and briefings. There is a substantial likelihood that reporters will misunderstand technical information or incorrectly report information they do understand (e.g., accidental misstatements). Emergency news center spokespersons and writers can supply unclear information by using industry jargon and acronyms to describe the event, rather than speaking in plain English. Time pressures may also contribute to inaccurate information, as reporters quickly compose their stories and compete to publish them equally quickly; this competition reduces or eliminates the time to review or fact-check a story.

COMMUNICATIONS TO THE PUBLIC USING THE INTERNET AND SOCIAL MEDIA

Emergency news programs have historically been focused on newspaper, radio, and television reporters, because these have been the primary means for distributing news until recently. Emergency news centers are designed to support professional reporters working for these information channels and have relied on a credentialing process to prevent the public's access to media briefings. There is currently a recognition that emergency response organizations also need to communicate with the public through online websites and social media, in part because the public is increasingly using those sources of information. Fewer members of the public now use newspapers or television as their primary source of news and information than in previous years. Radio continues to be important, particularly when people are in automobiles, although this may also be affected as the public is increasingly using mobile media devices in their vehicles.

Many organizations are experimenting with online emergency communications and information, but a successful integrated strategy has yet to emerge. It is already clear that every emergency response organization should have a permanent online presence that is regularly updated; this presence must include a high-quality website belonging to the organization as well as an online identity on popular social sites, similar to the online campaigns of major companies. A regular posting of news, information, documents, maps, and other information encourages the public to visit these websites under normal conditions and may build a familiarity that results in the public viewing the sites as a reliable source under emergency conditions. Some organizations are creating positions for internal bloggers and media posters, whose efforts appear on both the organization's own websites and websites run by others.* The hope is that if these blogs and posters develop an Internet following then they will be viewed as being reliable in the future, rather then biased. Some organizations are attempting to identify outside (non-organization) opinion leaders and are working to build relationships between them and the response organizations, again hoping that these opinion leaders will rely on official information rather than creating misinformation during an actual emergency. One problem in this area is that popular social media websites and individual opinion leaders tend to be transitory, and they fall in and out of favor with the online community, possibly requiring a continual adjustment of an online strategy.

Emergency response organizations are struggling to create methods to identify event-related information published online. The number of existing online forums is already so large that effective monitoring is somewhere between unwieldy and impossible, and as an event unfolds a large number of new websites and comment boards is likely to be created. During the Fukushima radiological event that began in March 2011, all of this occurred within hours of the event and continued for days to weeks.

It is difficult to identify and correct erroneous information circulating on the Internet and through social media. One of many problems is that any significant radiological event will generate a high volume of comments and persons simply expressing an opinion, most of whom are physically far removed from the incident's location and who have no technical knowledge. They may, or may not, review the information provided by the emergency news center. Some persons are likely to choose to create rumors and false information, simply because the effect of misinformation advances their viewpoint, cause, or agenda.

Considerable effort was expended by the Nuclear Energy Institute in 2014 and 2015 to create and promote what they labeled the *emergency news system*, which emphasizes that neither emergency news center staff nor media representatives require a physical presence at a single location to be functional. The Nuclear Energy Institute has also contracted to provide its members with a "dark"† website and social media simulator that will allow emergency news centers to practice their social media interactions in an exercise environment.

BACKUP EMERGENCY OPERATIONS FACILITY

Licensees whose primary emergency operations facility is located inside the emergency planning zone are required to provide a backup facility located outside the planning zone. The backup is not required to be located in a licensee-controlled building, though many are, and is not required to be a dedicated facility, which many are not. The backup facility should not require radiological protection (e.g., filtered ventilation, thick radiation shielding) and should not require diverse building power, although many are equipped with backup power. The facility should be sufficiently large to accommodate all of the persons who normally report to the primary facility, including representatives of offsite agencies. When responders are relocated from the primary facility, it may be acceptable that they are dispersed to two or more facilities, provided that the capabilities of each location are described in the licensee emergency plan. Each backup facility must have sufficient working areas and data acquisition, data analysis, and communication capabilities to support the assigned personnel. The combined capabilities of all backup facilities must be equal to the capability of the primary facility.

---

* Organizations may have difficulty implementing a strategy of internal bloggers for both internal and external reasons. The primary internal reason is that the frequency of blogs often requires that they operate outside of established information control and approval channels, and the blogger must be given considerable trust and independence. The primary external reason is that bloggers who are openly identified as representing organizations, especially government agencies, may be met with substantial suspicion in the online community and will have to overcome considerable distrust and sometimes disinterest. The typical means of doing so (e.g., humor, edgy content, skepticism) may be considered disloyal by the organization the blogger or poster is representing.

† *Dark* in this case means not visible to, or accessible by, the public.

NEAR-SITE FACILITIES WHEN THE EMERGENCY OPERATIONS CENTER IS 25 MILES OR MORE FROM SITE

Since 2011, licensees who are approved to operate an emergency operations facility located 25 miles or more from a reactor site have been required to provide an additional facility for use by the Commission during an emergency. The purpose of this facility is to provide a base of operations for Commission staff to travel to the reactor site and to provide a location to meet with emergency response organization staff from the technical support center. The facility would be required to have sufficient space for a small, currently undefined Commission staff; communications capabilities with all licensee facilities; limited data acquisition capabilities; and limited plant reference documents. The licensee would have to incorporate the near-site facility into their emergency plan. Presumably it would require periodic maintenance and would have to be included in quarterly communication system surveillances. There may be additional licensee activities required to ensure that the facility is continuously available. As of this writing, no new emergency operations facilities have been located outside 25 miles, so some implementation issues remain unanswered. It is not known whether a licensee would have to make provision for other offsite agencies at the near-site facility, how much (if any) radiation protection capabilities the facility would be required to have, and how physical security would be provided. It is unknown if the facility requires backup power. It is unclear whether the licensee would be required to provide staff, although it is difficult to see how the Commission would access and use the facility without some licensee assistance. Although the Commission periodically participates in emergency plan exercises at all licensees, it remains to be seen whether Commission staff would exercise a near-site facility. This is primarily because the Commission typically does not fully staff their site team for exercises and resource limitations may prevent exercise use of a near-site facility. It is possible, even likely, that the Commission would incorporate a near-site facility into its emergency response in an *ad hoc* manner, without having developed response procedures.

LOSS OF EMERGENCY RESPONSE FACILITIES AND ASSOCIATED REPORTING REQUIREMENTS

Licensees are required by 10 CFR 50.72(b)(3)(xiii) to report to the Commission major losses of their capacity to assess emergency conditions, as well as losses of communications capabilities and some losses by offsite agencies of their response capabilities. The Commission created NUREG-1022, *Event Reporting Guidelines*, in 1998 to provide guidance on the reporting of specified conditions to the Commission (e.g., on 10 CFR 50.72 and 50.73). Revision 1 to NUREG-1022 is dated 2000, Revision 2 is dated 2013, and Revision 3 is dated 2014. Licensees have historically had difficulties with the emergency preparedness reporting requirement because NUREG-1022 did not provide guidance regarding losses of assessment capabilities. The Commission allowed licensees to define "major loss of assessment" for themselves, and most licensees failed to create a site-specific definition.[*] Note that a licensee's failure to adequately define major loss is not a regulatory issue as long as the licensee does not fail to report such a loss.

Some licensees have reported emergency response facility maintenance under 10 CFR 50.72(b) (3)(xiii). Furthermore, they have declared the response facilities *unavailable for use* when the facilities could not be secured against airborne radioactivity, particularly onsite technical support centers and near-site emergency operations facilities. Some malfunctions of required control room

---

[*] All revisions of NUREG-1022 included examples of reportable conditions; however, there were very few examples related to emergency preparedness. The common licensee practice was to incorporate all of the examples in any revision of NUREG-1022 into their procedures for reporting conditions to the Commission, but few licensees extended their reportability procedure to include examples not provided for them in NUREG-1022. The immediate impetus for the creation of NEI 13-01 (NEI, 2014) was several violations issued to licensees for the failure to report to the Commission known problems with dose assessment computer programs that occurred from 2010 through 2013, as well as some problems that were determined not to be major losses of assessment capability but had not been properly evaluated by licensees.

ventilation systems have been reported under a different reporting requirement related to exceeding the requirements of plant technical specifications; the actual evacuation of the licensee control room is reportable under different requirements. Operations support centers would only be included in this requirement if the licensee elected to provide them with systems to protect against airborne radioactive material. Examples of reported deficient conditions include outer facility doors with damaged seals, damaged ventilation system isolation dampers, and out-of-specification charcoal filter beds. Some reports were for a few hours of scheduled maintenance on the ventilation system, such as preventative maintenance on fans, blowers, and motors.

The author believes these licensees have taken an unnecessarily conservative view of facility functionality. The site control room and technical support center are required to be designed such that occupants do not receive greater than 5 rem throughout an accident. They are also required to have filtered ventilation systems to reduce or eliminate exposure to airborne radioactivity; see, for example, NUREG-0737, Section 8.2 (NRC, 1980a) and NUREG-0814, Section 2.5 (NRC, 1981i). The inability to seal the facility against airborne radioactivity does degrade the degree of radiation protection offered occupants but does not prevent the facility from being used for its designed emergency purpose.[*]

The author does not agree that the inability to completely protect licensee emergency workers from radiation is, in itself, a loss of assessment capability. If a radiation hazard does not exist at the time an emergency response facility is staffed, the degraded radiation protection capability has no effect on the facility's emergency response functions. If a radiation hazard does exist at the time a facility is staffed, a hazard assessment should be performed by the control room; if airborne radioactivity is present, or if there is a high likelihood that it will be present, an alternative facility should be staffed. Any preplanned alternative emergency response facility should be capable of performing the same essential emergency functions as the primary facility. A gamma radiation field without airborne radioactivity (i.e., radiation shine) exterior to the primary facility may not affect the facility emergency response function if the permanent radiation shielding offers sufficient worker protection.

Licensees have permanently installed radiation monitors in emergency response facilities and perform internal radiation surveys to identify radiation hazards. If a radiation hazard develops after staffing emergency response facilities, the monitor alarms and ongoing surveys should alert staff when radiological conditions change, allowing for evaluation time. Licensee staff can be relocated to planned alternative facilities if necessary. In the author's opinion, an emergency response facility should be declared out of service when

- Environmental conditions could threaten employee safety (e.g., low oxygen level, loss of air conditioning in summer, loss of heating in winter, paint or solvent fumes).
- A lack of power requires extraordinary efforts to provide internal lighting and power.
- Missile, fire, or explosive damage has compromised structural integrity or reduced protective shielding.
- Conditions exist external to the facility that require extraordinary efforts to provide access.
- Other conditions exist that prevent the performance of many or most emergency functions.

Note that *out of service* is not necessarily the same as *cannot perform the emergency function* or [major] *loss of assessment capability*. The emergency function is maintained if (1) the designated alternative or backup facility is immediately available when the primary facility is taken out of service, (2) preplanned actions are available to inform the emergency response organization to staff the alternative or backup facility, *and* (3) the alternative facility has *all* of the capabilities of the

---

[*] The assumption is that the maintenance issue is temporary and is being addressed. NUREG-0696 (NRC, 1981e), NUREG-0737 (NRC, 1980a), and NUREG-0814 (NRC, 1981i) do not permit the control room or technical support center to be designed without airborne filtration. A licensee who has identified a functional inadequacy in onsite facilities and does not promptly initiate repairs may be in violation of 10 CFR 50.47(b)(8).

primary facility. If any of these three conditions is not met when the primary facility is taken out of service, then there is a loss of assessment capability, the extent of which must be evaluated as major or less than major.

Examples of emergency response facilities having high levels of carbon dioxide were identified from 2013 through 2015. The Commission has taken the position that the facility design criteria in NUREG-0696 (NRC, 1981e) only require the facility be designed (and operated) to provide adequate radiation protection to its inhabitants. Other worker safety issues, such as maintaining acceptable levels of carbon dioxide, are properly issues to be handled by the Occupational Safety and Health Administration, not by the Commission. Therefore, although an emergency response facility should be taken out of service and the carbon dioxide levels remediated, the loss of the facility is not reportable to the Commission as long as the alternative facility is available.

Supplement 1 to NUREG-1022, Revision 3 (Lewin, 2013) endorsed NEI 13-01, *Reportable Action Levels for Loss of Emergency Preparedness Capabilities* (NEI, 2014), as an acceptable method for determining whether a loss of assessment capabilities is a major loss that is reportable to the Commission. NEI 13-01 provides a set of generic event reporting criteria; an event that meets one of these criteria constitutes a major loss of emergency assessment capability, offsite response capability, or offsite communications capability. The NEI document defines *backup emergency response facility, compensatory measure, emergency assessment, planned, radiological assessment, restoration time, viable compensatory measure,* and *unplanned,* among other terms. NEI 13-01 was a response to an increasing number of violations issued to licensees for failing to report long-term outages of certain equipment, particularly radiation monitors and seismic instruments, and for failing to report outages of ventilation equipment in emergency response facilities. These are addressed in Table B1, "Unplanned Loss of Emergency Response Facilities and Equipment," and Table B2, "Planned Loss of Emergency Response Facilities and Equipment." Radiation monitor issues are addressed by Table C, "Loss of Radiological Assessment Capability." The difference between Tables B1 and B2 is in the planned conditions of Table B2. Conditions that would be reportable if they were not planned are not reportable when they are planned with compensatory measures in place; this is similar to having a plant configuration that meets an emergency action level not requiring an emergency classification if it is planned and controlled. The NEI document also provides a number of examples that illustrate how to apply the guidance.

BACKUP POWER FOR LICENSEE EMERGENCY RESPONSE FACILITIES

At most licensees, the control room, technical support center, emergency operations facility, and emergency news center are all normally powered from offsite power—that is, externally from the local electrical grid rather than internally from the plant. This may seem counterintuitive at an electric generating station; however, most plant equipment is supplied from offsite power even when the electric turbine is operating. In part, this ensures that equipment and facilities remain functional even when the station is not producing electricity. Although a station could, in theory, supply its own power from the diesel generators when the units are offline, this is not done because the longer run times would cause the generators to be more prone to failure when they are needed during an emergency.

In general, equipment required for the safe shutdown of the reactor is powered from vital electrical buses, as is equipment necessary to maintain the shutdown reactor in a safe condition (e.g., pumps to circulate water to heat exchangers). A vital electrical bus differs from a non-vital (or non-safety-related) electrical bus in that a vital bus has redundant power sources but a non-vital bus may not have redundant sources. Vital buses are normally fed from the ring bus in the plant switchyard, and the ring bus is collectively powered from several offsite power lines. For the most part, a plant is required to maintain at least two independent offsite power lines at all times, though in practice most plants have more than two lines. If offsite power lines are lost or the ring bus trips (drops out), the standby diesel generators auto-start and pick up vital loads. Typically there are two vital buses per unit, with each vital bus feeding one complete set (or train) of emergency equipment. The two trains each have 100% capability, and reactor control can be maintained with either one alone. Most units have two standby diesel generators, but some units were built with three diesels; each diesel is dedicated to one of the vital buses, often with a manual cross-connection capability. Another layer of protection is provided by plant batteries, which maintain vital power for a specified number of hours should offsite power be lost and the diesel generators fail to pick up the load (i.e., the generators may start but an electrical fault could prevent them from connecting to the bus). Non-vital power typically has no backup; when the bus loses its electrical source or trips because of equipment problems, all loads powered by that bus lose power. Plants are not designed to allow non-vital electrical loads to be powered from vital power; in any event, vital power sources do not have sufficient voltage to carry both vital and non-vital loads.

The control room is powered from vital electric buses and so has redundant power. The technical support center is not required to be powered by vital sources; at most, but not all, sites it receives its primary power from non-vital sources. It is not specifically required to have redundant power; however, NUREG-0696 does require that data display and assessment systems in the technical support center have a secondary power system to allow them to recover operability within a short time of losing their primary power source. In theory, this would allow the technical support center to be designed to only supply backup power to data systems rather than the entire facility. In practice, it would be difficult for the facility to perform its emergency functions during a partial blackout, although a few licensees have tried. The author is not aware of any technical support centers that are not fully supplied by alternative power.

Regulations do not specify how backup power is supplied. Possible options are to provide power from multiple offsite power lines (with an automatic line-swap switch), install a local backup generator, or provide high-capacity batteries similar to those used to back up vital power. The backup generator is the most common solution; it is sometimes run from diesel fuel and sometimes from a natural gas supply tank. Because plant security systems also require backup power, a single backup generator at some sites supplies both the technical support center and security. The backup power for the technical support center may also supply the telephone switching centers or the plant computer.

The operations support facility is powered from non-vital sources. It is not required to have redundant electrical power, and data systems in the facility are not required to be capable of recovering from a loss of primary power. A few licensees provide backup power to the operations support facility, sometimes using the same generator as supplies the technical support center. Most licensees plan on relocating operations support center staff if power is lost in the facility. The emergency operations facility is also powered from non-vital sources. It is not required to have redundant electrical power, and data systems in the facility are not required to be capable of recovering from a loss of primary power. Many, perhaps most, licensees do provide backup power to their emergency operations facility, generally with a local diesel generator.

The emergency news center is typically located outside of the emergency planning zone and is completely powered from offsite power sources. It is not required to have redundant or backup power, and data systems in the facility are not required to be capable of recovering from a loss of primary power. When the emergency news center is located in the same building as the licensee's emergency operations facility then it is powered from the same sources.

Although some emergency response facilities are not required to have backup power by regulation, if a licensee chooses to provide backup power, then that capability should be described in the site emergency plan. When the site emergency plan includes commitments for emergency response facility backup power, some conditions that result in backup power not being available could become failures to implement the emergency plan (e.g., maintenance or human performance errors that render the backup power unavailable, inadequate design of the backup power system). Additional information may be found in Information Notice 04-19 (NRC, 2004e).

OFFSITE EMERGENCY RESPONSE FACILITIES

Emergency response facilities are also operated by municipal, county, and state governments. These are discussed briefly below.

INCIDENT COMMAND POST

An incident command post is established when the senior response official needs to be close to the incident site to provide personal oversight and direction to the first responders. An incident command post will be inside the emergency planning zone and may be in the licensee's owner-controlled area. The location may be situational and *ad hoc*, or one or more locations may be preplanned. At some sites, the preplanned location of the incident command post may be in a licensee-controlled building, in the same building as the emergency operations facility (nearby but not colocated), or in nearby buildings controlled by offsite agencies. The primary means of communication is likely to be a variety of first responder radio systems combined with mobile telephone systems. At sites where the locations are preplanned, advance arrangements for communications systems and the acquisition of plant information may be in place. In most cases where the incident command post is planned to be located in a building, it is still supplemented by mobile command and communications vehicles.

Historically, incident command posts have been primarily used by law enforcement, fire, and hazardous material responders. They have also been used for search-and-rescue operations and to respond to events with large numbers of injuries or fatalities. In the power plant response context, the most likely use of an incident command post is during hostile actions in or around the reactor site (e.g., law enforcement activities). The position designated as incident commander depends on local practice but is most likely either the county sheriff or the local fire chief.[20] The licensee typically provides operations, security, and radiation protection liaisons to the incident command post; at some sites, a licensee fire liaison is also dispatched. The Commission would likely dispatch liaisons to the incident command post during an incident in which a post was established.

The term *incident command post* generally denotes only the facility from which the incident commander operates, but the hostile-action-based exercises conducted between 2012 and 2015 showed that many licensees tended to refer to the [incident] staging area as part of the incident command post. Although the two may be located together, for the most part it is desirable that they be separate. The *staging area* is the location to which available resources report, such as unassigned sheriff's deputies (and their vehicles), fire trucks on standby status, ambulances on standby status, bomb squad units, buses, and other vehicles. The physical area of an incident command post is often not large enough to accommodate a large number of vehicles that would potentially hinder access. A large number of unassigned personnel in the incident command post would also create confusion and might divert attention from managing the event. In the National Incident Management System, the incident command post is part of the command section, and the staging area is operated by the operations section.

LOCAL EMERGENCY OPERATIONS CENTERS

Every county (parish) operates a local emergency operations center. In some areas there may also be municipal (city) level emergency operations centers. These centers have functions similar to the licensee's emergency operations facility and track and analyze the emergency situation. They also serve as the primary work area for the local decision-maker (usually an elected official), the local emergency management agency official, and their command staff. A local emergency operations center located inside the emergency planning zone is required to have radiological protection (e.g., ventilation, shielding). Emergency operations centers also have diverse power supplies, typically including an onsite diesel generator (this generator may be shared with hospitals or other facilities that require backup power). The primary means of communications with the licensee is likely to be dedicated telephone bridge lines, and the primary means of communications with local responders is likely to be by radio.

Evacuee Reception Centers

Reception centers are designated to support the evacuation of emergency planning zones. These centers are designed to receive and house evacuees and have the capability to survey evacuees and their vehicles for radiological contamination. They also have a limited capability for the radiological decontamination of the public. Reception centers are typically located in adjacent counties (parishes) outside of the emergency planning zone, so the affected jurisdictions can concentrate on emergency response activities instead of congregate care. Some reception centers may be operated by local fire departments, Red Cross chapters, the Salvation Army, or by other social service organizations. The number and capacity of reception centers are based on having the overall capability to receive and house at least 20% of the emergency planning zone population.[*]

Emergency Worker Decontamination Centers

Some jurisdictions separate radiological monitoring and decontamination functions for the public (evacuees) from monitoring and decontamination for emergency workers. When there are separate survey and decontamination centers they are most often operated by local fire departments. In some locations, the licensee and offsite agencies share a single emergency worker decontamination facility.

State Emergency Operations Center

Every state has a primary state emergency operations center, typically operated by the state emergency management agency. In some states, the emergency management agency reports to the commander of the state's National Guard, and the Guard operates the emergency operations center. In some states, there may be secondary response facilities operated by the health department, the state radiation control agency, or other responding agencies. These centers have functions similar to the licensee's emergency operations facility and track and analyze the emergency situation. They also serve as the primary work area for the state decision-maker, the state emergency management agency director, senior officials of responsible state agencies, and their technical staffs. In some states, the governor has delegated their emergency powers to a designated official, often referred to as the governor's authorized representative. In some states, the governor's authorized representative relocates to the licensee emergency operations facility rather than work from the state emergency operations facility. The Commission would dispatch liaisons to the state emergency operations center during an event in which the state facility was activated.

State Forward Command Post

It is usually not practical to stage operational resources at or near the state emergency operations center because of the distance to the affected reactor. Most states designate a near-site forward command post (the terminology varies by state), which is the operational staging area for state resources, particularly environmental survey teams and mobile radiological laboratories. This may also be the location for mobile communications vehicles and towers, or the location for aircraft

---

[*] The evacuation of pets became a significant emergency planning issue beginning with Hurricane Katrina in 2005, as significant numbers of the at-risk public refused to evacuate because evacuation shelters would not allow their pets. Prior to 2005, there were essentially no provisions to evacuate pets, and shelters would not accept them. Although FEMA subsequently issued guidance intended to expand the number of pet-friendly shelters, the status of pets continues to be an issue. Few shelters were available for pets in New Jersey and New York during and after Hurricane Sandy in October 2012.

supporting the response effort. The state forward command post may be colocated with the emergency worker decontamination center. It is always located outside the emergency planning zone; some states may predesignate more than one forward command post site, which would be activated depending on wind direction during an event.

FEDERAL-LEVEL EMERGENCY RESPONSE CENTERS

Many federal agencies operate permanent and mobile emergency response centers. The ones most relevant to a radiological emergency are briefly discussed below.

NRC INCIDENT RESPONSE CENTERS

The Nuclear Regulatory Commission operates an integrated agency response center at the headquarters complex in Rockville, MD, and can activate regional centers at its offices in Pennsylvania, Georgia, Illinois, and Texas as needed for an incident. Only the appropriate regional center is activated for events with limited offsite impact; both the Maryland and regional centers are activated for more significant events. The Maryland center is continuously staffed and has some non-emergency functions; a licensee's initial report of an emergency condition is normally made to the Maryland center. Regional centers are dedicated facilities but are not staffed until needed.

The Commission's role during an emergency is to monitor data from the event, understand the licensee's actions and recommendations, and provide an independent assessment of the necessary protective measures as requested by offsite authorities. The Commission also provides event information to the Departments of Homeland Security and Energy, and liaisons with other federal emergency response assets. The Commission is responsible for communication to and coordination with emergency response centers operated by FEMA and other federal agencies. The Commission also provides information to the White House and Congress and performs other duties as directed by the President. The chairman of the Commission (or the designated commissioner when the chairman is unavailable) is the senior agency official during significant events, and the regional administrator (or designated senior regional manager) is the senior agency official in events having limited offsite impact.

The Commission will be in one of three modes, depending on the severity of an event, where mode denotes the incident response centers that are activated. In *normal mode*, no event is in progress, or the event is sufficiently limited that staffing a response center is not warranted. In *monitoring mode*, an event is in progress that may degrade a plant's margin of safety or may have a limited off-site impact; in events of this type, a small number of staff will establish communications with the reactor site from the responsible regional Incident Response Center. In *activation mode*, an event is in progress that has significantly degraded plant safety systems or may have a significant impact offsite; in events of this type, both the Maryland and regional centers will be fully staffed and in continuous communications with the affected reactor site. In any event significant enough to warrant consideration of monitoring or activation modes, the permanent resident inspectors assigned to the site will likely go to the control room to provide the Commission the information it needs to make an informed decision on changing response modes. The decision to change modes is generally made by a consensus of senior agency officials.

If the Commission goes to activation mode, it is very likely that a site team will be dispatched to the affected reactor site to supplement and support the permanent resident inspectors. The site team size and composition will vary according to the event but will likely be between 15 and 30 persons (per shift). The initial staffing will primarily be from the responsible regional office, with additional resources drawn from the remaining agency as needed, depending on the event severity and duration. A senior regional manager leads the site team. The deployment time varies from 2 to 12 hours, depending on the distance from the regional office to the affected reactor. The Commission's emergency response philosophy is that the site team takes primary event responsibility upon arrival, with technical analysis and support from agency response centers.

The Commission's emergency response program is primarily designed to respond to a single domestic incident involving licensed radioactive material. Although the primary focus of the Commission's emergency response program is on incidents at commercial power reactors, because these have the most significant potential offsite consequences, the response program is not limited to power reactors. The Commission would also respond to incidents at non-power research and test reactors, non-reactor fuel cycle facilities, licensed waste facilities, large-inventory users of radioactive materials, and events involving the transportation of radioactive materials.

The Commission may elect to staff the headquarters operations center in response to international events such as the emergency at the Fukushima Daiichi plant in Japan. Although the Commission has added some additional detail about the response to international incidents to its response procedures, an actual response is still likely to be unique and *ad hoc* as dictated by the situation.

NATIONAL RESPONSE COORDINATION CENTER

The National Response Coordination Center is a multi-agency command center located at FEMA headquarters. The facility is activated as needed by the FEMA administrator or a delegated senior manager. The National Response Coordination Center provides national-level emergency management coordination and resource deployment; it also disseminates incident information within the federal government.

NATIONAL OPERATIONS CENTER

A continuously staffed center operated by the Department of Homeland Security. The primary focus of the National Operations Center is law enforcement and homeland security-related intelligence. This facility would not normally be involved in a radiological emergency but would have a role if hostile actions were threatened or directed against a power reactor site.

FEDERAL RADIOLOGICAL MONITORING AND ASSESSMENT CENTER

The infrastructure and most of the staffing for the Federal Radiological Monitoring and Assessment Center (FRMAC) is maintained by the Department of Energy, although staff is also provided by the Nuclear Regulatory Commission, Environmental Protection Agency, Food and Drug Administration, Department of Agriculture, and other federal agencies. The center is a mobile interdisciplinary facility with capabilities in direct radiological measurement, meteorology, environmental sample collection, radiological analysis, data mapping, communications, and radiological dose assessment. It is designed to provide local, state, and federal decision-makers with event-specific data to support implementation of protective measures for the public. The physical infrastructure for the center is primarily stored at Nellis Air Force Base, Las Vegas, NV, with an expected deployment time of about 24 hours to most locations in the United States.

In the event that an active radiological release is occurring when or after the center deploys, the center has the instruments and resources to characterize an active plume. However, because of the relatively long deployment time, the center's primary emphasis is more likely to be characterizing deposition patterns from a radiological release and determining the long-term environmental affects. The Federal Radiological Monitoring and Assessment Center also operates helicopter and aircraft-mounted radiation monitoring systems; these aircraft are based at Las Vegas, NV, and Andrews Air Force Base, MD.

The Federal Radiological Monitoring and Assessment Center is located outside the emergency planning zone and may be sited on an *ad hoc* basis. Although there are no formally predesignated locations for deployment of the center, in recent years there have been some efforts to identify locations in the vicinity of each reactor site (as well as other sites with a potential for significant radiological releases). Local and state authorities have surveyed potential assessment center locations in advance because the center requires a considerable space to operate and has non-trivial requirements for power, water, parking, and other resources.

FEDERAL JOINT FIELD OFFICE

A federal Joint Field Office (JFO) is operated and coordinated by FEMA and provides working space for federal agencies supporting first responders and offering federal assistance to affected members of the public. The designated senior federal official works from the Joint Field Office. In radiological events, the Joint Field Office is responsible for coordinating all disaster response and public assistance tasks except for the consequence analysis functions performed by the Commission and FRMAC. This facility may also be referred to as the *Joint Operations Center.*

LICENSEE COMMUNICATIONS TO THE NUCLEAR REGULATORY COMMISSION

The Commission requires that reactor licensees report to the Commission any entry into their emergency plan. The initial report is always made from the reactor control room; if command-and-control of the event is transferred to another emergency response facility and the event subsequently escalates to another classification, subsequent reports may come from another facility. Any required report must be made to a headquarters operations officer, most commonly located at Commission headquarters in Maryland but occasionally located at a backup site (regional office). The many possible responses by the Commission to the reported information include conducting a future event follow-up or review using onsite inspectors, the speedy dispatch of special inspection teams, requests for additional information from agency technical staff, or the activation of emergency response centers.

A licensee must report entry into any emergency classification as soon as possible following notification to offsite authorities, and in any case the reporting time should not exceed 1 hour from the emergency declaration. Making a required report within 1 hour does not necessarily equate to meeting the regulatory requirement, if an unnecessary delay occurs during that hour and the licensee could have made the report sooner without affecting public health and safety.

Telephone conference bridges are the primary means of communication between licensees and the Commission during an emergency.* These bridges are established by the operations officer as needed to support the Commission's level of emergency response. The bridges that apply to reactor licensees are

- *Emergency Notification System (ENS)*—The telephone used to contact the Commission to make any required report is generally referred to as the Emergency Notification System. When entry into an emergency classification is reported, the operations officer may request that the licensee remain on the line (i.e., go to open-line mode), depending on the classification level and reactor's margin of safety. When the Emergency Notification System is continuously staffed, the bridge is dedicated to information about reactor safety and reactor operations and is monitored by headquarters and affected regional office staff. The Commission expects that the licensee's Emergency Notification System communicator is highly knowledgeable about reactor systems and operations and has immediate access to critical reactor data, including alarms, the safety parameter display system (SPDS), and the plant computer system. The licensee's initial communicator will be located in the reactor control room; at some licensees, this communications function is later transferred to the technical support center.

---

* The Commission now has an extensive capability for videoconferencing. Some licensees have a limited video capability, primarily located at their emergency operations facility. Few, if any, licensees currently have the ability to videoconference from the reactor control room or technical support center.

- *Health Physics Network (HPN)*—If the level of radiological safety in the plant has degraded, the Commission may request that the licensee staff the Health Physics Network. The Health Physics Network is always initiated by the Commission, with the request made to the licensee via the Emergency Notification System. The network is always continuously staffed by the licensee and monitored by headquarters and regional office staff. The Commission expects the licensee's communicator to be knowledgeable about general radiation protection, about the licensee's specific radiation protection program, about the plant radiation monitoring system, and about the radiological aspects of emergency response (dose assessment, environmental monitoring, and procedures for emergency worker protection). The licensee's communicator should have immediate access to data from the plant radiation monitoring system, real-time plant radiation and contamination surveys, and environmental assessments. The licensee communicator could be located in the reactor control room, technical support center, or emergency operations facility, although a control room communicator would likely be rare (i.e., present only if the staffing the other facilities is delayed).
- *Safeguards bridge*—The Commission recognized in the early 2000s that there was no established communications protocol in the event of a security-related event. Subsequently, the Commission informally communicated to licensees an expectation that they staff a security bridge upon request. The expectation is that the licensee communicator is a senior security department representative familiar with site security systems and strategies. The bridge uses secure, encrypted communications technology because restricted information may be discussed.

From the early 1980s into the 1990s, the Emergency Notification System and Health Physics Network were dedicated, hard-wired, telephones located in every licensee control room, technical support center, and emergency operations facility. These phones were supplied to licensees by the Commission and were part of the Federal Telecommunications System (FTS), which was phased out in the mid-2000s and replaced by dedicated and leased commercial telephone lines. The old beige FTS phones can still be found at many licensee facilities.[*]

EMERGENCY RESPONSE DATA SYSTEM

Beginning in the early 1990s, the Commission required reactor licensees to install a system that allowed the Commission to monitor a small number of critical reactor and radiological parameters in real time; this system is referred to as the Emergency Response Data System (ERDS). Licensees were required to submit an implementation plan to the Commission by October 1991 and to implement the system by February 1993.[†] The system consisted of a 1064-baud modem supplied by the Commission, dedicated data lines leased by the Commission, and display software developed by the Commission. The original system was capable of transmitting around 100 plant computer points (the points varied slightly from site to site) with update speeds of between 15 and 60 seconds per point. For multi-reactor sites, the system could only report data for a single unit at a time, so the user had to specify the unit supplying the data. The Commission agreed to require the ERDS to be manually initiated at the licensee end because of a limited data display capability at the Commission (no more than four simultaneous feeds) and because licensees did not want the Commission doing widespread, real-time, reactor monitoring; that is, licensees did not want the

---

[*] References that apply to these communications systems include Generic Letter 91-14, *Emergency Telecommunications*; Information Notice 86-97, *Emergency Communications System*; Information Notice 87-58, *Continuous Communications Following Emergency Notifications*; Regulatory Issue Summary 00-11, *NRC Emergency Telecommunications System* (including Supplement 1); and Regulatory Issue Summary 09-10, *Communications Between the NRC and Reactor Licensees During Emergencies and Significant Incidents*.

[†] See Generic Letters 89-15 (NRC, 1989b) and 93-01 (NRC, 1993c); also see Appendix E to 10 CFR 50, Part VI.

Commission using real-time reactor data in inspection and enforcement activities related to reactor operations. Licensees saw the potential for the Commission to question licensee control rooms about small changes in reactor parameters before operators had time to either recognize or evaluate those changes. Consequently, licensees were required to initiate the ERDS within an hour of entry into any emergency classification; for the most part, this capability was incorporated into the reactor control room, although a small number of licensees located the necessary computer equipment in their technical support center.

Initially, only the Commission had access to ERDS data. In the early 2000s, this capability was expanded to include a number of state emergency operations centers. The data feed to the states did not come directly from the licensees; the Commission copied and transmitted the data from its Maryland incident response center.

The Commission requires that licensees train licensed operators using control room simulators that exactly mimic the actual control room configuration and closely mimic plant responses. Licensees are not required to conduct emergency preparedness drills from their simulators, although that has become the universal practice. There are differences in how the ERDS is incorporated into licensees' simulators. For those for which the system is initiated outside the control room, nothing is incorporated; for those initiating the system inside the control room, essentially all have a dedicated terminal in the simulator with the applicable software. All simulators mimic the plant computer to some extent and calculate some data points in addition to those directly displayed on reactor control panels; however, not all simulators have the capability to transmit that data beyond the simulator computer. Some simulators capable of driving onsite data displays (such as at the technical support center and emergency operations center) do not have the capability to transmit that data to the Commission.

The Commission decided to replace the existing ERDS in the mid-2000s. The reasons for the replacement included the following:

- Increasing frequency of modem failures
- Difficulty in obtaining replacement modems as vendors abandoned the technology
- Substantial improvements in communication system speed and capability
- Increased data handling capabilities of new computer systems
- Concerns about the security of data sent by modem

Between 2005 and 2009, the Commission informally discussed modernizing the ERDS with the industry's representative, the Nuclear Energy Institute. The Commission published RIS 09-13, *Emergency Response Data System Upgrade from Modem to Virtual Private Network Appliance* (NRC, 2009c), which announced the Commission's intention to retire the modem-based system and implement an Internet-based system. The Commission also announced an intention to turn off all existing modems in mid-2010. These two announcements were based in part on Nuclear Energy Institute assurances that all reactor licensees would quickly switch to the new system.[*] Some of the essential features of the upgraded ERDS included the following:

- A greatly expanded number of data points, from around 100 to around 1000
- Simultaneous unit capability for multi-reactor sites
- Always on
- Diverse communications path that eliminated the potential for data line failures
- Simplified remote viewing for licensees and states
- Additional cybersecurity features

---

[*] A Regulatory Issue Summary cannot be used by the Commission to issue a regulatory requirement. Therefore, the emergency response data system upgrade discussed in Regulatory Issue Summary 09-13 (NRC, 2009c) was a voluntary initiative. Although the Commission intended the upgrade to be compulsory, it did not change Appendix E to Part 50, issue Orders to licensees, or perform a safety backfit analysis.

The Commission was surprised to find after RIS 09-13 that a significant number of licensees, about 10 of 64, did not plan on immediately upgrading their ERDS connections. This was contrary to the information previously provided to the Commission by the Nuclear Energy Institute. The licensees did not object, in principle, to the upgrade, but they did object to the proposed time frame (e.g., less than 6 months). Those licensees not planning on immediately switching generally had two complaints:

1. There was not sufficient time to comply with concurrent cybersecurity requirements.
2. The upgrade required the licensee to install new computer systems and software, and the proposed timeline did not allow their costs to be put into the normal budgeting cycle of 2 to 3 years.

The Commission did complete the virtual private network (VPN) upgrade to ERDS; however, it took much longer than originally thought. The last reactor licensee migrated in early 2012 and the modems were retired around April 2012.

INCIDENT RESPONSE ELECTRONIC LIBRARY

From the 1980s through the early 2000s, the Commission maintained hard-copy emergency preparedness documents from every reactor licensee in the headquarters and in the appropriate regional incident response centers. The documents included copies of site emergency plans, emergency plan implementing procedures, and excerpts from the site final safety analysis report, site maps, and some reactor system diagrams. These documents were intended as ready references for agency emergency responders in the event of a significant reactor event. The records were obtained from documents submitted to the Commission, either by requirement (e.g., site emergency plan) or voluntarily as part of the licensing process (e.g., site maps, system diagrams). The specific records that were available depended on what the licensee had submitted. By the early 2000s, the Commission was having problems keeping information up to date and was experiencing document storage problems; there was significant internal pressure at the time to reduce the administrative and physical burdens associated with maintaining large volumes of paper plant-specific emergency response information. At the same time, Commission staff did not want to give up having access to plant records in the Commission's response centers.

The Commission published RIS 06-21, *Improving Response Capabilities Through the Use of an Incident Response Electronic Library* (NRC, 2006i), to request that the industry voluntarily submit plant information to the Incident Response Center. This database was also referred to as the *e-Library*. The Commission essentially wanted to transfer the administrative burden from the Commission to the licensees by specifying a set of records the licensees would supply and then maintain. Licensees would bear any costs associated with transferring those records into an electronic (PDF) format. It was hoped that licensees would also commit to regular updates to the information. The Commission considered an expected reduction in the amount of direct licensee support to the Commission during exercises and events to be the primary benefit to the licensee. As stated in RIS 06-21, "The e-Library significantly reduced the need for the licensees to send plant information to NRC during the exercise, reducing the number of questions and requests for information from NRC to the licensee by more than 50 percent."

The Commission met with some initial success in this area, with about half of the licensees supplying data, particularly those in whose exercises the Commission was participating in 2006 and 2007. Since then, however, there has been very little licensee participation, and those licensees who originally submitted information have not updated their information. Currently, the information already in the e-Library is being maintained, and the e-Library program is available in Commission emergency response centers, but in large part the effort has failed. Licensees have not committed to maintaining the data and the available documents are often several years out of date. The Commission has essentially abandoned ongoing efforts to convince industry to support this initiative.

EMERGENCY RESPONSE FACILITY STAFFING

FACILITY STAFFING TIMES

The staffing goals for each emergency response facility are listed in the site emergency plan, with the control room being continuously staffed. The original intent was for some additional radiation protection and maintenance workers to be available on very short notice, 30 minutes, and the rest of the emergency response organization in less than an hour. This situation was the standard in the 1980s and for much of the 1990s, with very few exceptions.[*] Beginning in the early 2000s, the Commission approved extended staffing goals for most reactor sites, generally in exchange for additional required on-shift staffing. Grand Gulf Station was the first site to receive such approval (2002). Licensees were particularly interested in removing the 30-minute responders because they found that few employees lived close enough to their sites to support this requirement; in effect, a 30-minute response requires travel times to the site on the order of 15 minutes, given the time required to send the call-out signal and then leave home after receiving the signal. Although not universally true, the author has observed that more senior reactor site managers tend to live farther from their site than do less senior staff. These senior managers and staff are the same personnel required to staff the technical support center and emergency operations facility.

When licensees activate their emergency response facilities, the time at which each facility is prepared to perform its emergency functions should be compared to its staffing goal in the site emergency plan. The licensee's processes (i.e., procedures, equipment and systems, and training) should be designed so that each facility will generally be activated within its stated goal time. Having the capability to staff emergency response facilities is demonstrated through a pattern of consistently meeting staffing goals, established through routine surveillances. The Commission's reactor oversight program (ROP) has generally established that success rates of 90% are sufficient to establish and maintain capabilities, so a licensee has the capability to staff its facilities in accordance with its emergency plan if each facility meets its associated staffing goal in at least 90% of its tests. Staffing success rates of less than 90% may not result in regulatory action, but, in the author's opinion, the likelihood increases in proportion to the amount by which success rates fail to meet 90%; that is, significant shortfalls result in significant chances of regulatory action.

When an event requiring actual emergency response facility staffing occurs, the Commission will evaluate the facility response times against the staffing times in the site emergency plan. If a licensee fails to meet a staffing or activation time in its emergency plan (i.e., an explicit requirement), they have failed to comply with the emergency plan, a potential violation of 10 CFR 50.54(q) (2).[†] Licensees who fail to meet a staffing or activation goal in their emergency plan may have failed to comply with the emergency plan, depending on the time by which they missed the goal and (sometimes) on which position failed to be staffed on time. Note that the Commission will evaluate the actual staffing of a facility from the time of the declaration requiring that activation or, for a situation in which the shift manager decides to activate without entering the higher classification, from the time the decision is made to staff the facility.

It is worth noting that unless the emergency plan explicitly states that the staffing goal is only for minimum staff personnel (or some other defined group), all staff assigned to the facility must be present to meet the goal. The emergency plan should be sufficiently detailed to allow an evaluation of whether minimum and full staffing requirements were met. If the emergency plan

---

[*] Some very remote plants were initially licensed without 30-minute responders and with facility staffing times in excess of 60 minutes; these licensees compensated for the lack of immediate responders by having large onshift crews. For example, Palo Verde Station, located in Buckeye, AZ, had typical employee travel times in excess of an hour when it was built; this plant was licensed with a 120-minute goal to staff emergency response facilities. Palo Verde is a three-unit site with three independent control rooms; thus, it has a larger on-shift crew than would normally be present in a combined control room (multiple units controlled from a single location). The site also has more radiation protection and mechanics assigned to each unit per shift than would commonly be present at a site with combined reactor support buildings.

[†] 10 CFR 50.54(q), as amended November 2011.

has separate staffing time requirements for minimum facility staff and full facility staff, then failure to accomplish either could be a failure to implement the emergency plan. An emergency plan that includes a staffing goal for minimum facility staff but does not include a staffing goal for full facility staff is at risk of not complying with Commission regulations. It is likely that an emergency plan that would allow a facility to not achieve full facility staffing during an event would be found deficient. In the author's opinion, a licensee that tests the capability to achieve minimum facility staffing without testing the capability to achieve full facility staffing may have a difficult time proving to regulators that they possess the capability to staff in accordance with their emergency plan.

EMERGENCY RESPONSE ORGANIZATION CALLOUT

Licensees must be capable of staffing their emergency response facilities at any time, without regard to emergency classification.* Designated on-shift responders are primarily notified of an event using plant radios and the plant public address system and secondarily by plant pagers, telephones, and other systems. Most licensees use automated systems that simultaneously signal personal pagers, ring the employee's desk telephone, and signal a cellular telephone (whether personal or company-provided). This combination of communication systems should ensure that all on-shift responders are quickly notified to report to their designated response location.† For events requiring activation of all emergency response facilities, the initial on-shift responders should be capable of staffing the technical support center and operations support center and performing an initial damage assessment while other responders assemble from offsite.

When the full emergency response organization is required, a licensee performs either an "all call" recall or a directed or duty team recall to assemble responders, particularly those currently off-duty. An "all call" requires all available emergency responders to report to their assigned emergency response facility as soon as possible. A directed call requires only that designated emergency responders report; the most common directed call is for those emergency responders with the current (usually weekly) duty to respond, with vacant positions subsequently staffed from the remaining organization. The usual practice to fill vacancies is to manually call the roster of persons qualified to fill the vacant position until a replacement is found.

The advantages of performing an "all call" are a high probability that all positions will be staffed within the staffing time goal and the ease in developing and communicating the shift relief roster; the primary disadvantages are the potential for confusion as responders sort out who will fill each position (when multiple qualified staff are present) and the disruption caused by responders who fill neither primary or relief positions. The advantages of a directed call are that the duty team is highly likely to be fit for duty (see below), the entire response organization is not disrupted, and the person assuming each function is clearly identified; the primary disadvantage is there is no immediate backup for duty team members who fail to arrive. Some licensees combine the duty team concept with an "all call" methodology, with the intention that the duty team forms the initial responder core that is supplemented as necessary.

---

* Shift managers are expected to use their experience and professional judgment to determine when they require technical resources beyond those immediately available. The site is expected to have procedures authorizing the recall of appropriate elements of the emergency response organization as needed, in some cases without declaring any emergency classification. There had been previous examples in the 1980s and 1990s of shift managers declaring emergency classifications for the sole purpose of mobilizing the emergency response organization when the declared emergency conditions did not exist (e.g., the emergency action level threshold was not satisfied). This occurred because plant procedures did not authorize the shift manager to staff the emergency response organization without declaring an Alert.

† The plant public address announcement can also create confusion as non-shift emergency responders are also likely to respond, even at the Notification of Unusual Event when response facilities are rarely staffed. This does not present a problem if the site uses the "all call" philosophy but could be confusing when the site uses a "duty team only" philosophy.

The most common method for notifying site responders of an emergency is individual pagers initiated from the plant control room.[*] Most current pagers have a short alphanumerical display capability and licensees generally have adopted coding schemes to inform responders about the emergency. Coding schemes allow licensees to staff for events not resulting in an emergency classification, perform pager surveillances, differentiate between events and drills, and inform responders to staff alternative facilities. At some licensees, site-issued cellular telephones perform the same function as pagers.

Many licensees back up their pager notifications with an auto-dialer system activated simultaneously with pagers. An auto-dialer system is a multi-line, computer-based communications system that reads a database, contacts a responder's telephone, and reads a scenario script.[†] Some systems prioritize business or personal cellular telephones and desk or home telephones depending on time of day (e.g., dayshift, off-shift). Auto-dialers can be configured to specify the order in which emergency response positions are filled and the order in which staff are called for individual positions (e.g., closer-in staff in preference to staff living further away). Such systems are designed to minimize facility staffing times rather than merely achieve the staffing goal. Some auto-dialer systems allow a limited response, such that contacted individuals can indicate whether they are available to respond and fit to accept duty, and they can acknowledge that they are accepting the emergency response duty. Some systems allow responders to input their estimated time of arrival at the site. Auto-dialers are designed so they continue calling the roster for each individual emergency response position until the duty is accepted; a typical system makes one complete pass through the entire response roster (all positions, all individuals) before starting the next pass (skipping any filled positions).

Some licensees expect responders to immediately report to the site without responding to either page or auto-dialer notification. At some licensees, responders call in to indicate acceptance of emergency duty (when possible, a number of unsuccessful attempts is typically specified before departing for the site). The effectiveness of call-in schemes depends on the number of outgoing and incoming phone lines attached to the computer server; if too many lines are dedicated to making calls, a large number of responders are contacted quickly but many incoming calls receive busy signals or are parked on the system.

STAFFING DURING HOSTILE ACTIONS

The ability to staff emergency response facilities is especially challenged when the initiating event is a compromise in the plant's physical security. Broadly speaking, security-related initiating events are divided into two categories: hostile actions and security conditions. *Hostile actions* are active attacks on the reactor site, including armed intruders, snipers, explosives (whether placed or carried in cars, trucks, or boats or hidden in or around plant equipment), and missiles.[‡] Security conditions are any abnormal physical security configuration or event that does not involve an active site attack.[§] In general, the emergency response organization staffs their primary response facilities during security condition events, using their normal processes. This is acceptable because it is unlikely that the response organization will be personally at risk while responding or that a normally available facility would be unavailable. The normal licensee time goals continue to apply to these events.

---

[*] There are ongoing issues regarding site bargaining unit personnel carrying pagers (or any other immediate recall device). These are usually operations, radiation protection, chemistry, and maintenance staff who report to the operations support center. Union contracts generally require premium pay when bargaining unit employees are subject to immediate recall; because licensees are unwilling to pay this premium, few bargaining unit employees are issued pagers.

[†] In this context, a *scenario* is one of several pre-scripted messages that inform emergency responders which facilities to staff. The scenarios accomplish the same function as the coding scheme used for pager notification.

[‡] In this context, a missile can include an aircraft of any size.

[§] The specific configurations and deficiencies that qualify as *security conditions* are defined in each licensee's site-specific physical security plan. These plans fall into a category of sensitive controlled information called *safeguards*.

The staffing response to hostile actions is more complicated. All persons onsite when hostile actions begin are potentially at personal risk. If the initiating event is a threat but not yet an active attack (including tracking an inbound aircraft), there may be time to staff emergency response facilities using normal processes and to evacuate other employees from the site. This may be desirable in part because emergency response facilities are often located away from the plant control room and are strongly constructed structures because of the weight of required radiological shielding. Plant employees who cannot evacuate the site prior to the threatened attack may be directed to tornado shelters or other strongly constructed buildings that offer some additional personal safety.

When there is warning prior to a threatened attack, licensees are required to ensure the ability to shut down the reactors. This means, in part, dispersing critical plant personnel so that no single event can eliminate any vital capability. Single events include explosions, extensive fires, and the impact of large aircraft. Although the plant control room must generally remain staffed, operators would be sent to multiple areas in the plant, preferably near equipment that would need to be locally operated to trip the reactors; local equipment operation could become necessary if the control room is damaged or destroyed, if electrical control or sensor data cables are damaged, if control circuit power or vital electrical bus power is lost, or if the plant compressed air system is damaged. Other personnel, such as plant fire-fighting or emergency medical staff, could also be dispersed to preserve a capability to respond to physical damage and employee injuries.

Off-duty emergency responders and other employees with special or critical skills can be contacted and assembled at an offsite location in parallel with dispersing onsite personnel following a threat. The revision to Appendix E to 10 CFR Part 50 implemented in November 2011 required licensees to identify by June 2012 locations where off-duty staff assigned to technical support center and operations support center could muster if the primary onsite facilities were not available. The mustering location for technical support center personnel was required to be capable of interfacility communications by June 2014 and was required to have a limited capacity to perform engineering assessments of the plant and formulate mitigation strategies. Some licensees already possessed an emergency operations facility located away from the plant site that could be expected to be accessible at all times; those plants whose primary emergency operations facility was onsite would be expected to staff their backup or alternative emergency operations facility location. The assembly of off-duty employees is likely to be most effective when the threat occurs outside of core business hours when most site employees are away from the site.

If the hostile action begins suddenly, without warning, or not enough time remains to safely move employees before the threatened attack begins, the site has few options to ensure the survival of critical personnel or to assemble the site emergency response organization. All employees will be advised to take cover at their current location to the extent possible and remain there until given other instructions. Operators and other employees in power block buildings when the event begins may be protected by the thick walls and large plant equipment, but employees in other plant buildings may have little structural protection. The plant operating shift can gain some information about the location of critical plant staff by running a computer report showing the last security door they entered; this report does not show employees outside the protected area and may only show that employees are somewhere inside the protected area. The use of plant public address systems, phones, pagers, or radio systems to locate employees is not advisable while an active attack is underway because employees could expose themselves to intruders while trying to reach phones, and audible pagers and radios could alert intruders.

During an unexpected active plant attack the control room is likely to be the only operating emergency response facility because responders cannot safety report to the other onsite facilities. Its emergency response capabilities may be very limited because of dispersed personnel, the need to immediately respond to damaged plant equipment, the inability of planned on-shift responders to safety report, or a direct attack on the facility. In the worse circumstance, there may be only a few minutes for the control room to notify offsite agencies of the attack, to notify the NRC, and to initiate the assembly of off-duty emergency responders before losing the ability to communicate, losing power, or being overwhelmed. At least in the short term, the usual emergency response activities will have to wait until sufficient off-duty responders are assembled. Again, this is most effective when the licensee possesses at least one emergency response facility that remains accessible, and the event is outside of core business hours.

Critical plant staff can be assembled when site security has neutralized (or at least isolated) the attackers and local law enforcement personnel have arrived at the site. This includes plant operators, plant fire fighters, and medical personnel and may include mechanics or other special skills as required by the specific circumstances. It is likely that armed security officers will have to sweep plant buildings to find these critical individuals. Other employees, including some emergency response personnel, would likely be left because the initial sweep would be to assemble the employees needed to immediately to stabilize the reactor. Retrieving site emergency responders would not likely begin until after the reactor is somewhat stabilized and law enforcement has established some degree of control over the site. The general evacuation of plant personnel would likely not begin until after the licensee's emergency response is generally in place and there is a high degree of law enforcement control at the site.

TESTING EMERGENCY RESPONSE ORGANIZATION STAFFING TIMES

There is no specific requirement that licensees test the ability of off-duty responders to report to their emergency response facilities. However, most licensees conduct periodic surveillances of their emergency response organization notification systems to identify failures in transmission equipment, inaccuracies in the notification database, and failed receivers (e.g., pagers, cellular phones). As a collateral benefit, these tests also provide a means to estimate the staffing time for each emergency response facility, had the event actually occurred.

Active Tests

The preferred method to test the ability of off-duty employees to respond to emergencies is to conduct an unannounced drive-in drill using the primary notification method; the occasional use of backup response organization notification methods is recommended to validate their design. Many licensees have established a once per exercise cycle requirement for conducting an active response drill of this kind, although some licensees perform this drill annually and a very few do not conduct active response drills at all.

Whether a licensee conducts frequent action–response verification of the ability of off-duty responders to report may depend on the degree to which local offsite plans rely on volunteer emergency workers. Anecdotal evidence suggests that when offsite responders are primarily volunteers, such as volunteer fire companies staffing evacuation shelters for the public, biennial exercises and annual full-scope drills tend to be conducted off-hours. This facilitates offsite participation because volunteers do not need to leave their normal jobs to participate in the drill or exercise. One benefit to the licensee is that, when offsite agencies prefer conducting off-hours drills, the licensee's response must also be primarily from off-duty employees, giving frequent opportunities to evaluate their actual ability to report.

Likewise, experience tends to suggest that when offsite responders are primarily full-time salaried staff, offsite authorities tend to prefer that drills and exercises are conducted during business hours (i.e., dayshift). Dayshift exercises generally require that licensee responders report from their desk, not their home, which does not validate off-duty response times. These licensees in this category depend on numeric analyses of their employees' self-reported drive times to validate their off-hours staffing capability. They also have a diminished ability to detect negative changes in housing and road patterns that could affect their ability to staff response facilities.

Passive Tests

Licensees also conduct passive response surveillances of their systems to notify off-duty emergency response organization members. Passive response surveillances test both signal transmission and reception and require that employees acknowledge receiving the notification signal. Employees are typically asked to estimate the time that it would have taken to report to their response facility after receiving the signal if the event had been real; sometimes the employee feedback is collected in real time, such as a phone call back to the notification system, but sometimes the feedback is collected in the days following the test. The periodicity of these tests varies, with the largest number of licensees performing them quarterly, fewer licensees performing them semiannually, and a few performing them only annually.

Passive response surveillances can provide useful information and can give the licensee information about the ability of off-duty responders to report. Negative or positive trends in aggregate surveillance performance likely correlate with actual response times declining or improving. However, in the author's opinion, licensees often give passive response surveillances more credence or weight than is often deserved. This is because these tests are primarily designed as tests of equipment operability and not as estimators of actual response times. The potential flaws in surveillance design include the following:

- Starting the evaluation time clock with initiation of the notification system
- Starting the evaluation time clock with each individual's receipt of the notification signal
- Allowing individuals to self-report their estimated response time without associated location information
- Not defining *response time*

The Commission evaluates a licensee's response to actual events beginning at event classification. Licensees who do not start their surveillance at event classification often fail to account for the time between classification and initiation of the notification system. This time can be very situation dependent, and few licensees have procedural restrictions to ensure prompt notification to licensee responders.[*] The preferred method for conducting response time surveillances is to begin in the control room simulator, present the operating crew with an event, and have the crew perform all tasks subsequent to classification in real time as they would in an actual event. A less perfect method would be to review records of control room simulator drills over a 2-year period to determine the average time between classification and initiation of the notification system and then add that time to every individual reporting time.

When the surveillance begins with each individual's receipt of the notification signal, not only is the time between classification and initiation not accounted for but also the time between initiating the system and the actual signal is not included. Experience shows that pager and telephone dialing systems do not react immediately to system initiation, and there can be delays in initiating signals from pager and cellular telephone towers. Individual responders may not receive their notification signal until minutes after the system is started.

Individuals may not be skilled at estimating how long it takes to drive from the location where they received the notification system to their assigned emergency response facility. Experience suggests that individuals underestimate their response times more often than overestimating it. The cumulative error is likely to lead a licensee to believe their effective response is faster than it actually is. Individuals are more likely to be more accurate about reporting from home than from other locations.

---

[*] Observation of licensee drills suggests that the elapsed time between classification and initiation of responder notification varies from about 5 minutes to 15 minutes, with occasional examples of delays of 20 minutes or more. Times between 5 and 10 minutes are most common. The variations are primarily due to differences among licensees in personnel assigned the notification task, the physical means for initiating the callout system, and the placement (ordering) of the notification task in licensee procedures. Some variation occurs because of individual differences in proficiency, but a sufficiently large sample of drills should minimize this effect.

There is no possible verification if the only feedback an individual gives is a time in minutes. A well-conducted surveillance includes post-test sampling of the locations from which individuals reported to validate their reported driving times (i.e., comparing the known route and distance at an assumed representative driving time to the reported time). Post-test sampling is not primarily intended to identify employees who report inaccurate driving times; rather, it is a tool that allows analysts to develop a statistical estimate of data validity.

The value of a response time depends on when the evaluation clock is stopped. The evaluation period could be assumed to end at the site (facility) parking lot (arrival onsite), it could be assumed to end at the facility door (simple staffing), or it could be assumed to end when individuals could have been capable of exercising their emergency functions (simple staffing plus initial procedural steps plus data acquisition). Those are very different endpoints, with differences of several minutes between each. Many licensees fail to establish and communicate to employees a consistent definition of response time, so employees choose the endpoint for themselves. It is impossible to perform a valid analysis when the endpoints are unknown.

Experience suggests that employees most often report the time at which they believe they would have entered their response facility (simple staffing). The Commission evaluates emergency response facility staffing based on the time the facility could have exercised its emergency function. This includes the time for individuals to acquire procedures and supplies, turn on equipment and computers, and acquire situational information. If the licensee's surveillance uses a different endpoint, such as the arrival time of the last required minimum staff employee, then they should consider using drill records to estimate their average time between staffing and facility readiness and applying the estimated time to the surveillance.

An analysis of tests of the response notification system may occasionally reveal systemic hardware issues with the ability to contact individual employees. An example would be an employee who cannot receive a pager signal at home because of the location of local pager towers (a dead zone for this system). Although it is desirable for every notification method to reliably reach every employee, there is no requirement for 100% contact of off-duty responders by every method employed. A licensee is in compliance with NRC requirements if overall surveillance results show that adequate (timely) emergency response organization staffing can be achieved, even if specific individuals on the emergency response organization are never contacted or can never meet the staffing goal. The event could occur while they are at work, or at a location other than their house not dead to notification signals. It is the aggregate response that must meet staffing times, not each individual response. Cases of this sort are expected to be rare and highlight the reasons why notification systems should be diverse and consist of parallel landline telephone, cellular telephone, pager, e-mail, and potentially other methods of communication. A diverse parallel communications capability makes it unlikely that any individual is unable to receive all forms of notifications (i.e., experience a complete communications blackout).

7 Drill and Exercise Programs

This chapter discusses licensee drill and exercise programs.

INTRODUCTION

The effectiveness of an emergency response program is maintained and demonstrated through its drill and exercise program. The drill and exercise program validates and informs training, procedures, and methods; ensures that equipment operates; and ensures that emergency response organization members maintain familiarity with their procedures and functions. Drills and exercises tend to be the most significant performance-based elements of the entire preparedness program, where *performance-based* refers to an activity validated by direct observation under conditions that resemble the conditions that could reasonably be expected in an actual event. The difference between performance-based evaluation and other kinds of evaluation is illustrated by the validation of a new procedure—the technical reviewer reading the procedure and its basis document is not doing performance-based evaluation, but the trainer watching an operator out in the plant walk through the procedure is.

Licensee drill and exercise programs have their origins in Planning Standard N of NUREG-0654 (NRC, 1980c) as described in the commitments documented in the emergency plan. Prior to the early 1980s, licensees were required to conduct proficiency drills but each one developed their own unique program; NUREG-0654 standardized programs so that licensees were all doing essentially the same drills.

It may be worthwhile to reflect on the practices that were common in the 1980s. Regulations at the time required an annual integrated exercise evaluated by the Commission and Federal Emergency Management Agency (FEMA). The normal practice was to conduct a preliminary exercise using the same participants 2 to 4 weeks prior to the evaluation. These two exercises were the only large-scale performance-based activities conducted by licensees during the year. Because licensees had not yet implemented duty teams, the roster of exercise participants was open to manipulation so that evaluators frequently saw a licensee's best performers most years and rarely saw the less skilled responders,[*] who received little practice. The preliminary exercise was needed because even skilled or more proficient staff could not be assumed to retain their proficiency between exercises and needed to be refreshed on procedures. The preliminary exercise provided insurance against poor performance when the evaluators were present. The situation for offsite responders was no better; they participated in the preliminary and evaluated exercises but typically did not have an independent training and drill program to maintain proficiency in the period between.

NUREG-0654, Revision 1, makes a distinction between drills and exercises. A *drill* is

A supervised instruction period aimed at testing, developing and maintaining skills in a particular operation. ... A drill shall be supervised by a qualified drill instructor.

A more current definition from the 2013 revision of the Homeland Security Exercise Evaluation Program is as follows:

A drill is a coordinated, supervised activity usually employed to validate a specific function or capability in a single agency or organization. Drills are commonly used to provide training on new equipment, validate procedures, or practice and maintain current skills.

---

[*] Conversely, less-skilled staff rarely had opportunities to gain the experience necessary to become skilled.

Most organizations involved in emergency preparedness have more than one assigned function and have many capabilities. The emphasis in the 1980 definition was on a particular operation. The 2013 wording of "specific function or capability" conveys essentially the same meaning. Both definitions imply a limited activity, testing less than the organization's overall ability to perform all of its functions and capabilities. The intent is that a drill be task based, a demonstration of proficiency at performing a limited number of closely related actions that tend to have a defined starting point and a well-defined goal. A drill is generally not open ended. A qualified drill instructor is a subject-matter expert in whatever task is being tested, someone who is sufficiently knowledgeable to provide proper feedback to participants following each action and capable of identifying gaps in participant knowledge about their tasks.

NUREG-0654, Revision 1, defines an *exercise* as

> An event that tests the integrated capability and a major portion of the basic elements existing with emergency preparedness plans and organizations.

The corresponding 2013 definition is[*]

> Full scale exercises involve multiple agencies, organizations, and jurisdictions and validate many facets of preparedness ... are usually conducted in a real-time, stressful environment that is intended to mirror a real incident ... simulate reality by presenting complex and realistic problems that require critical thinking, rapid problem solving, and effective responses by trained personnel.

The emphasis in both exercise definitions is on *integrated capability*. An exercise causes an organization to demonstrate its ability to perform most, or all, of its assigned functions; the organization must show that it can manage those functions that are performed concurrently and plan for those performed in series. An activity that does not involve multiple agencies, organizations, or jurisdictions is not an exercise because it does not demonstrate the ability to integrate functions and capabilities to work together. One might also add to the definition *multiple response facilities*, because the facets of radiological emergency response are rarely directed from a single location.

Exercises have value when they lead to increases in individual and team proficiency, enhance interorganizational familiarity, identify capability gaps, refine working processes (i.e., procedures), identify inoperable or deteriorating facilities and equipment, and find sources of miscommunication. Drills have value when they lead to increases in individual proficiency; enhance an individual's knowledge of equipment or facilities that are rarely used; identify inoperable or deteriorating equipment; reveal inaccurate, incomplete, or misunderstood procedures; and find sources of misinformation: "A good exercise is not necessarily one where everything goes well, but rather one where many good lessons are identified" (IAEA, 2005b). Neither drills nor exercises have great value when they are performed mostly to meet internal (emergency plan) or external requirements.

REALISM

The claim is sometimes made that, because the postulated failures in an exercise are both individually and collectively unlikely, realism is not possible. The most likely failure is a single failure in a component or piece of equipment, and plants are designed and built to operate with any single equipment failure. *Realism* in a drill and exercise context means that the description of each individual failure and its associated environmental cues are as accurate as can be if it is assumed that

---

[*] The exercises typically run by licensees are somewhere between functional exercises and full-scale exercises as defined in *Homeland Security Exercise Evaluation Program (HSEEP)* (USDHS, 2013). A functional exercise is "designed to validate and evaluate capabilities, multiple functions and/or sub-functions, or interdependent groups of functions. Functional exercises are typically focused on exercising plans, policies, procedures, and staff members involved in management, direction, command, and control functions."

the failure occurs. Although the endpoint may not be believable as a likely situation, each individual step in the sequence should reflect reality to the extent that reality can be known. Any consequences that would reasonably result from the failure must also be accurately portrayed. For example, water from a simulated fire system header break should flow in the right direction, along the right floors, into the right drains, down the right stairs, etc., and affect the right equipment, with cues that reflect the sound of flowing and spraying water and the depth of the water.

CONDUCTING DRILLS AND EXERCISES

Drills and exercises can be at the same time as proficiency tests, teaching moments, and evaluation tools. Aside from having different numbers of participants and involving different locations, an observer would have difficulty in separating one from the other based on the way they are administered and evaluated. At their simplest level all drills and exercises are simulations, comparable in many ways to first-person video games or to improvisational theater. The essential framework is provided by the *scenario*, which functions as a script that dictates when each event occurs in time and sometimes where. The participants, often referred to as *players*, are the actors, the ones who react in real time to the events occurring around them. The role of stage director is filled by the drill or exercise controllers, who implement the scenario. Evaluators fill the role of theater critics, observing the action but separated from it.

The improvisational aspect of a drill or exercise lies in the fact that the participants (actors) do not know the script; they can only react to information they acquire. Success requires that the participants take the steps to acquire information, interpret it correctly, communicate the information within the organization, and take well-reasoned actions in response to the information. A well-made scenario anticipates the most likely reactions and can have several independent branches (sets of data) depending on the participants' choices. Another aspect of improvisation is that the scenario designers (playwrights) do not always anticipate the participants' actions well, leading to gaps in the prepared data, which must be adjusted on the fly. These unexpected participant responses are referred to as *free play*, and they derive from a participant's incomplete knowledge of scenario events, from options built into plant procedures, and from situations outside plant procedures that require creative solutions.

In practice, the scenario is a collection of pre-scripted event messages, datasets, visual and audio cues, and mock-ups that, taken together, simulate a set of abnormal conditions requiring responses from the participants. Some drills and all exercises include a crew of operators working from the plant reference control room simulator; this machine is essentially a much more powerful version of a video game engine, where the output controls indications on a large number of gauges, recorders, digital displays, alarm panels, video display screens, and the simulated plant computer. The simulator is interactive in that the values of all parameters depend in real time on the manipulations performed, or not performed, by the operators.* The simulated plant computer and video display screens are important because these are also the real-time data engine for remote facilities. They allow responders to monitor critical plant parameters and diagnose the current plant condition.

The control room simulator is not the only source of data for the participants. Some information comes from the control cell or simulation cell, and other information is provided directly by controllers. The simulation cell provides information and interactions that would be expected to occur during an event with organizations that are not part of the particular exercise. They could represent licensee staff who are not part of the emergency response organization (e.g., security officer, fire

---

* The models for reactor-core physics, steam flow, containment response, valve response, and the reactor coolant system are dynamic, reacting in real time to the operator's manipulation of plant controls. System parameters that do not have dynamic models either are static (single value) or respond according to preprogrammed values (often a spreadsheet file) independent of operator actions. Plant radiation detector response, meteorology data, fire alarms, and seismic detection system alarms are examples of non-dynamic data.

watch stander), company resources (e.g., control center for distribution of power to the grid), or offsite agencies (e.g., NRC operations center). For the most part, controllers provide direct sensory information to an individual (or small group) at locations where the simulated conditions differ from the actual condition; this usually occurs at plant locations with some kind of local indication independent of the control room. Sometimes the sensory information is negative, as in a lack of the alarms or other conditions that should be expected under the postulated circumstances. Examples of sensory information include the value read on a radiation survey meter, the acrid odor that comes from a charred wire in a breaker or motor, or the lack of noise expected when entering the room where a diesel generator should be running. Controllers may also provide information to entire facilities, such as the sound and motion caused by an earthquake felt by everybody or the loss of lighting caused by a loss of electrical power.

Every scenario event should be included to validate participant knowledge and training, validate the adequacy of procedures or methods, demonstrate functional capabilities, probe for knowledge gaps or latent organizational weaknesses, or maintain drill or exercise momentum. Validating knowledge and probing for weaknesses require that the scenario push participants out of their comfort zones, so they work through rarely used procedures, not just simulate using them.

Some common definitions are

- *Players* are the subjects or participants, the persons who will demonstrate proficiency through their actions during the activity.
- *Controller* is an individual knowledgeable about the scenario design and whose purpose is to provide situation-dependent information to a participant, which becomes necessary when the activity is conducted using equipment, displays, or other data sources that do not react to participant actions and do not reflect how the postulated events would be experienced. A controller engages with participants during the activity to the extent necessary to provide necessary sensory cues.
- *Evaluator* is an individual knowledgeable about the responses expected if the postulated events were experienced and capable of identifying gaps in the participants' knowledge or judgment in reacting to the postulated events. Evaluators may be provided information about the postulated events in advance, but this is not necessary to their function. An evaluator does not engage with participants during the activity.
- *Scenario* is the set of time-dependent, predetermined, conditions, data, cues, visual information, and other inputs provided to participants.
- *Event* is the specific set of information that includes time, place, sensory information, circumstances, and conditions; each event has a discernable start time and physical/sensory indications that allow it to be recognized and allow for a response, even when participants fail to recognize the event or elect not to respond to it.
- *Inject (message)* is a predetermined item of information that is provided at a designated time or place, largely representing information not under the participant's control or information representing the actions of persons not participating in the activity that is necessary to maintain immersion.
- *Cue (message)* is a predetermined item of information that is provided at a designated time or place, largely representing conditions that would be readily apparent to a participant experiencing the postulated events. Cues can communicate unexpected circumstances,* set scenes, set mood (realism), initiate events, provide feedback from actions, force choices or decisions, and allow the meeting of exercise objectives, but they do not provide conclusions or direct action.

---

* Examples include lights not operating when they are expected to be on, water where it is not normally found, higher than normal temperatures in a room, unexpected sounds, the sticking of a valve that is expected to turn freely, and the like.

- *Earned information* is an inject or cue that is provided to participants only after they take, or simulate to take, action that would allow them to acquire the information had they experienced the postulated events. The implication is that the participants could not acquire such information passively but must go to the location where the information would be found or make an effort that would logically reveal the information.
- *Free play* is actions taken or decisions made by participants that are not anticipated by scenario designers or activity taken outside the intended scope. In either case, on-the-spot creation of unexpected cues and inputs may be required.
- *Objectives* are capabilities being evaluated through observations of participant performance. A scenario is adequate when it provides postulated conditions in sufficient detail to allow participants to adequately perform the selected capabilities.* Not every event in a scenario is required to have an associated objective, and the set of objectives selected for any specific activity may be a subset of the overall master capability list.
- *Preconditioning* is the intentional or unintended provision of clues about the scenario to participants in advance of the activity. Preconditioning generally allows participants a greater opportunity to successfully respond to the postulated events than they would have had without the clues. This generally occurs after repetitive training sessions or other activities with the same or similar postulated events that reasonably imply that the participant will be presented with the same challenge.

DRILL PROGRAMS

Licensees are generally only committed to the drill program described in NUREG-0654. This consists of six drills: (1) communications (element N.2.a), (2) fire (N.2.b), (3) medical emergency (N.2.c), (4) radiological monitoring (N.2.d), (5) health physics (N.2.e.1), and (6) liquid sampling (N.2.e.2). The communications drill element describes four separate activities—essentially a monthly drill of the offsite notification capability, a quarterly drill of the capacity to contact federal and ingestion pathway planning zone agencies, and annual drills among the major emergency response facilities and mobile environmental monitoring teams. These verification activities are actually implemented as equipment surveillances and probably belong more to standard H (equipment) than they do to standard N (drills). Most licensees perform a monthly operability check of all phones and other communications systems in their emergency response facilities, which includes more communications capabilities than are required by this standard. All licensees exercise their emergency response facilities more than annually, usually with the participation of offsite agencies, so the annual requirement is easily met; it is not usually treated as a separate requirement to be tracked. Although the standard makes reference to the ingestion exposure pathway emergency planning zone, licensees usually have a very limited role in radiological surveys of the ingestion pathway and so would have very few pre-established communications pathways to maintain.

The fire drill element states that fire drills will be conducted according to plant technical specifications; most plants have subsequently moved these administrative requirements to other documents, such as a technical requirements manual or a similar document. The details are found in the plant fire plan or the training program document for the plant fire department or fire brigade. Virtually all emergency plans contain a statement that fire drills will be performed as described in the fire training program document. The author has found that emergency preparedness program staff generally do not have much awareness of how the fire drill program is being conducted and

---

* If a scenario is compared to the content of a college course, the objectives are like questions on the examination. Generally, there is a fixed set of objectives that apply to all scenarios (e.g., "demonstrate the ability to exercise command and control over the facility") and some that apply to only a specific scenario (e.g., "demonstrate the ability to survey an injured patient for contamination before the patient is transported offsite").

that could create vulnerabilities. Because the fire program is a commitment in the emergency plan, the delay or cancellation of fire drills may represent not only issues in fire protection but also failures to follow the emergency plan. The linkage between the emergency plan and fire plan also creates a requirement that all weaknesses in emergency preparedness functions that occur in a fire drill be critiqued and subsequently corrected; if emergency preparedness program staff are not involved in fire drills, this may not occur.

Fire drills often have some degree of participation by operators in the control room, but their participation is often not as formal as in the operator training program. A controller/evaluator is often not stationed in the control room to provide real-time feedback. Operators may not be required to work through the procedure steps required by the simulated circumstances; thus, the timeliness of activities may not reflect reality. There may be actions required because of the simulated initiation of fire suppression systems such as sprinklers, CARDOX™, or Halon systems. Expected plant announcements to inform employees of protective actions are not usually prepared or performed. Operators are often not evaluated on their performance during fire drills, so knowledge issues may go unrecognized. Many fire drills simulate situations in which a Notification of Unusual Event or Alert would be required, but operators rarely take the opportunity to practice classification or other aspects of implementing the emergency preparedness program during a fire.* The author has observed that operators may not be included in the post-drill critique session because the fire program staff do not necessarily view them as participants in the same manner as they do the fire suppression team (i.e., the drill is not holistic).

The medical emergency drill element requires an annual demonstration of both onsite and offsite capabilities.† The wording of this element is explicit with regard to offsite capabilities, including *local support services* and *offsite elements*, which has led some licensees to misunderstand that their participation may also be required. Because the element specifically states that *offsite portions* of the drill may be performed during an exercise, the language implies that there must be an *onsite portion*; otherwise, the distinction is meaningless. A complete onsite medical drill tests not only the capabilities of the immediate medical responders but also the ability of radiation protection staff to survey the affected individual and the nearby area and to implement appropriate health physics controls. It tests the ability of operators to secure electrical equipment or other potentially dangerous conditions around the injured persons, and it tests communication to the control room and from the control room to appropriate offsite locations. Security staff are often required to control the scene, and security support is required to bring offsite medical teams onsite to evacuate the simulated injured person. This is not integration on the scale of an exercise but is often beyond the scope of a licensee's ordinary drill, which tends to only extend to surveying the affected individual and addressing the immediate medical condition. At some licensees, radiation protection staff are also the immediate medical first responders, which further reduces drill participation.

The onsite and offsite medical activities can be done on separate days and using different medical events, although the author would suggest that this is not the best practice. When these aspects are separated, the licensee loses the opportunity to practice bringing offsite personnel onsite and into radiologically controlled areas and also loses an opportunity to practice communications with offsite authorities. The realism of how a patient is transferred from onsite medical responders to offsite ambulance services (either ground or air) often suffers, as does the implementation of radiological controls for the ambulance.

---

* The author is unaware of any instances in which a licensee included operator performance during a fire drill in their drill and exercise performance indicator results.
† Some licensees and offsite agencies mistakenly believed the drill periodicity was changed to biennial when FEMA changed their evaluation period from annual to biennial in 2002. At least one of the medical facilities described in the licensee emergency plan must be drilled; those licensees with more than one medical facility capable of handling radiologically contaminated patients generally rotate the annual drill among the facilities. A licensee may elect to conduct an annual drill at each offsite medical facility, but this is not required by guidance. This category of drills is often referred to as *MS-1 drills*, referring to a FEMA guidance memorandum dated February 9, 1988.

Many licensees have procedures that require the dispatch of plant radiation protection staff to an offsite medical facility whenever a radiologically contaminated patient is transported. At some licensees plant staff survey and clear the ambulance after the patient has been transferred to the medical facility; at some sites, plant radiation protection technicians support the offsite medical staff in surveying the patient, controlling the radiological boundary, or handling radioactive waste or trash. Where this is the case, the licensee should supply appropriate licensee participants for the offsite portion of the drill so that the tasks described in site procedures are performed. The licensee should also provide appropriate controllers and evaluators and ensure that the performance of licensee participants is documented and critiqued. This is also important because tasks done away from the site at a remote medical facility are performed infrequently, so there are issues with maintaining familiarity and proficiency. Some licensees have not provided such evaluators in the past, incorrectly believing that licensee performance would be included in the FEMA after-action report, which is not the case.

Some FEMA regions have required that the initiating events* for some drills addressing the response to contaminated injured patients occur outside of the licensee's owner-controlled area. Where this has occurred, FEMA has asked for one such drill over a 2- or 3-year period. This is likely more in line with the original intent of conducting offsite medical drills, which, in part, were intended to ensure that medical facilities along transportation routes were prepared to cope with accidents involving the release of radioactive material. The newer practice has created problems for licensees and for the medical facilities, as there is usually no mechanism for a medical facility to request licensee health physics support in cases of radioactive contamination unrelated to licensee activities, and no requirement for a licensee to provide support for an event not involving its personnel or radioactive material (in fact, licensee participation in an actual event of this kind could expose the licensee to legal liabilities should the response be inadequate). The licensee in such a situation is required to follow its emergency plan, which describes its drill program. This could lead to a medical facility needing to perform at least two drills in a year, with additional scheduling and logistical problems.

The radiological monitoring drill element requires an annual demonstration of the ability to collect samples in the environment for radiological analysis. Although the element language does not explicitly mention the detection of radioactive material in the environment, this element is generally understood to include the ability to detect a radioactive plume. Where licensee procedures require distinguishing between radiation shine and submersion in radioactive material, this should be demonstrated. Although the element uses the language "plant environs" and "onsite and offsite," the skill set is the same and the location is not as important.† Licensee survey teams should only be responsible for those environmental samples they are required to collect; for example, if a licensee is not responsible for collecting water samples in an event, then the team should not be drilled on the collection of water, regardless of the element language that states "all media ... water." If a state has more than one reactor site, the element does not require a drill at each site; however, it may be in the state's interest to exceed the requirement so their staff maintains familiarity with the roads and terrain at all sites where they have responsibility. The element does not distinguish between active-plume and post-plume environments, although different tasks would be performed in each phase. In particular, poorly structured drills can reinforce an inaccurate perception that environmental samples should be collected while a plume is active.

Environmental survey teams at some licensees are comprised of radiation protection technicians who are trained in environmental sampling as a collateral duty, although this is not a universal practice. Some licensees pair a radiation protection technician with a driver who may receive limited training in survey techniques, while others do not assign any radiation protection staff to this function and provide enhanced training to non-radiological staff. At least one licensee assigns the same staff to emergency sampling as performs their routine environmental sampling, on the assumption

---

* That is, the circumstances causing the simulated injury and radiological contamination.
† There is value in drilling the survey team and the supporting staff (team director, radio communicator, dose analyst) together in a realistic plume scenario, rather than the survey team in isolation.

that these individuals are well trained in collecting samples.* Some aspects of the environmental survey team tasks will be infrequently performed by whoever is assigned the duty, regardless of their technical background. Licensee evaluators should therefore pay close attention to both survey and sampling techniques because of the higher likelihood of error in one or both areas.

The collection of "all media" often overlooks the value of collecting surface contamination swipes, a task routinely performed in the plant. Although a swipe is unlikely to yield useful information early in a plume because of the time needed to deposit radioactive material on surfaces, over time there will be many readily accessible surfaces, and a gross analysis can be quickly performed. Rough swipes of road surfaces can be particularly informative. The gross beta–gamma count rate from a swipe can be used to extrapolate the deposition expected on soil and vegetation and can be used to quickly identify areas to receive more detailed surveys. Another task that is often overlooked in environmental drills is surveying the team's vehicle and tools for buildup of radioactive contamination.

The vehicles used by environmental sampling teams are rarely equipped with a shielded cargo area because of the necessary shielding weight. The storage area tends to be at the rear of the vehicle, which limits the radiation exposure of team members but is close to the working area when a team is collecting and analyzing samples. If a team collects enough radiologically contaminated samples, the radiation shine from the sample storage area will affect the background count rate of in-field surveys. Although this should not be an operational problem when teams are trained to perform a background count prior to every analysis (it does affect the sensitivity and detection limit of the analysis), the effect is usually not considered in developing drill data, resulting in negative training or a lack of expected realism.

Licensees should have procedures for transferring environmental samples, which potentially contain radioactive material, to couriers or to laboratory staff. If there are issues with laboratories having state or Commission licenses being required to take possession of radioactive material from the reactor licensee, these should have been anticipated and addressed in advance planning. The couriering of samples and transfer to onsite or offsite radiological laboratories is often the part of environmental sampling that is least practiced and most in need of validation. Although the element does not explicitly require this function to be drilled, it may be to the licensee's advantage to establish such a periodicity requirement.

The first health physics drill element (N.2.e.1) is a semiannual requirement; one drill is to be performed between January and June of each calendar year, the second between July and December. The intent is for plant radiation protection staff to demonstrate the on-scene response to abnormal and elevated radiological conditions. The emphasis is on the ability of the on-scene staff to recognize the abnormal conditions and make an appropriate response. Although on-scene responders in an event would be in contact with the radiologically controlled area entry checkpoint and senior radiation protection staff, the drill should not become a test of senior staff's ability to remotely direct the on-scene staff. Typical scenario events could include the rupture of a pipe or tank containing contaminated water or resins, overflow from a tank holding radioactive waste, breakage of radioactive samples, malfunctions of radiographic cameras, malfunctions of detectors and equipment with built-in sources, the failure of installed shielding in plant areas, problems with the retrieval or changing of filters in radioactive systems, and the like. The licensee gains the most benefit from scenario events that occur in well-traveled or frequently occupied plant areas† or ones that simulate problems in infrequently performed tasks having significant radiation protection consequences.

---

* The proficiency issue for such licensees is in handling radiation survey instruments, as routine environmental samples have no detectable contamination or radiation and often do not receive any special handling. There is also the possibility that emergency samples are collected using different volumes, different sample containers, or different procedures. The documentation needed for an emergency sample will also be different. For example, routine environmental samples often do not require the chain-of-custody documents that are necessary for emergency samples.

† *Plant areas* are generally the reactor building, auxiliary building, fuel storage building, or turbine building; however, an acceptable drill can be constructed in any area where radioactive material is used or stored and does not have to be inside the licensee's protected area.

The second health physics drill element (N.2.e.2) is an annual requirement. Although the wording "included in health physics drills" could imply the intent that N.2.e.2 is a subset of N.2.e.1, the two elements are equal in NUREG-0654. The two drill requirements are generally understood to be independent, so that three health physics drills are conducted per year, not two. The language "with actual elevation radiation levels" implies that not only are samples collected but they are also analyzed using appropriate methods. There would be no need to collect a sample with actual radioactive material if no analysis was to be performed, as all of the radiological data associated with the drill could be adequately supplied by a drill controller. The reason for including analysis in the drill is not to demonstrate that the equipment is operable, as most counting room equipment is used frequently and maintained under a quality assurance program, but to demonstrate that the laboratory staff is familiar with emergency procedures, which may require different volumes, counting geometries, calibrations, and isotope libraries from those used in routine operations. Many licensees have removed a dedicated post-accident sampling system from their licensing basis and have discontinued performing this drill.*

DISTINCTION BETWEEN RADIOLOGICAL MONITORING AND HEALTH PHYSICS DRILLS

Some licensees use the terms *radiological monitoring* and *health physics* interchangeably in their drill programs. Many licensees struggle with the distinction between these drills and with the distinctions between the health physics and sampling drills. The author considers elements N.2(d) and N.2(e) to be particularly poorly worded and not clearly expressing their original intent. The author begins with the premise that the original authors of NUREG-0654 intended different capabilities to be tested by elements N.2.d and N.2.e.1; if this premise is false, there is no apparent reason for both elements to exist. As it is, the author cannot provide a satisfactory explanation for their assigning both elements to offsite agencies. The following discussion is intended to apply only to reactor licensees.

One source of confusion is the word "environment" as used in element N.2.e.1. The author believes the word is best understood as the "working environment" for the organization being tested. For licensees, the working environment in which radioactive material is used is primarily inside the protected area. This is also where radiation protection staff is routinely stationed. The "plant environs," the phrase used in N.2.d, should be understood as specifically referring to areas in which radioactive material is rarely (or never) used and is not expected to be found. The phrase "simulated elevated," found in N.2.e.1, implies that measurements are taken in areas that may have a baseline detectable radiation background; therefore, the drill conditions involve *elevated* radiation exposures sufficiently greater than the expected routine operating level to be of concern.† Again, this condition can only be met inside plant buildings and is difficult to meet in areas outside the protected area boundary.

---

* Post-accident samples are rarely collected in time to inform decisions in the first hours of an event. When sample data are available, the data may still be of limited use because they describe the contents of the reactor coolant system and not the radioactive active material being released to the environment (i.e., the data do not account for the depletion and reduction processes that occur). There are also issues with whether the sample is representative and whether the second, third, etc., samples are contaminated by material from the first sample that was trapped or plated onto the sample lines.

† The converse of this is that some areas of the plant do not allow good demonstration of the drill objectives because the background radiation exposures are too high, setting aside the wisdom of allowing plant personnel to receive more than negligible amounts of radiation exposure during training. It would be possible to use a low-radiation-exposure area of the plant to simulate a higher exposure area to manage actual radiation exposure. The author would suggest the drills having the most opportunity to reveal knowledge gaps are those that change the radiation posting requirements: no posting to radiation area or airborne radioactive material area or contamination area, radiation area to high radiation area, and high radiation area to very high radiation area. In this regard, having the initial event occur in a high radiation area is counterproductive because very little in the way of useful radiological response can be demonstrated when the area becomes a very high radiation area, with the possible exception of life-saving activities.

Licensees often have difficulty in constructing health physics drills because element N.2.e.1 contains the phrase "and liquid samples," but "liquid" also appears in element N.2.e.2, making the differences unclear. The author would suggest that the reference to liquids in N.2.e.1 is situational, while the reference in N.2.e.2 is intrinsic to the purpose of the drill. Because unexpected and elevated radiological conditions in the plant often occur because of the failure of barriers confining contaminated liquids, part of the response *may* be to sample* the liquid to gain operational information.

DRILLS AS A COMPONENT OF EXERCISES

The introductory paragraph of element N.2 states that drills must be conducted in addition to the required exercises, and it states that drills are often components of exercises. Element N.2.c (medical) explicitly states that the drill may be conducted as part of an exercise. The guidance simultaneously implies the independence of the drill program, and its dependence on exercises. The primary advantages to conducting a drill within an exercise are efficient use of plant staff, both as participants and evaluators, and the enhanced realism provided by integration of the drill functions into the larger context. The primary disadvantages are that participants could fail to recognize that conditions require the response that constitutes the drill or may elect not to respond to those conditions. Providing a task-knowledgeable drill evaluator is an important part of conducting a drill; during exercises where the pool of controllers is responding in real-time to participant decisions, that knowledgeable person may be detailed to another activity just when he or she is needed at the designated drill location. It is also important for the scenario developer to carefully prepare the drill events so the drill controller has the correct information to drive the drill events and is not creating unanticipated inputs. Licensees may also be challenged to provide a sufficiently thorough evaluation of the drill in the context of a large set of exercise evaluation criteria and a small set of evaluators. It is not usually sufficient for a drill to be subsumed under a single exercise objective that covers multiple activities; each drill should have its own set of several task-centered objectives to ensure that it is properly critiqued.

IMMERSION

Many forms of entertainment require the participant to accept differences between the described situation and how a similar situation would unfold in reality. There has to be some willingness to accept at face value the actions of law enforcement characters in a crime story or to accept the different physics of a science fiction story; otherwise, the story does not work. Even when viewers or readers recognize a lack of reality in how a situation is depicted, they are willing to overlook it within the context of the overall plot or characters. In literature, this is referred to as the *willing suspension of disbelief*. The same concept applies to a licensee's drill and exercise program. The participants (drill subjects) must be willing to accept the reality of a series of very unlikely independent equipment malfunctions or destructive phenomena to demonstrate their mastery of their emergency functions. The ability to accept the unlikely does not in any way imply a belief that the scenario can or will occur, only that they do not let the unlikeliness affect their performance. Acceptance manifests in the urgency with which they respond to the postulated conditions and the seriousness they evidence in making realistic decisions or taking realistic actions, depending on their role in the response effort. A lack of acceptance is manifested by evidencing less urgency than would be required by an actual situation of the same circumstances, a willingness to tolerate sloppy

---

* Virtually any credible source of contaminated liquids in a plant either has an associated process radiation monitor that provides an estimate of the concentration of radioactive material or is routinely sampled and has an actual isotopic analysis report, or both. From a health physics perspective, the area exposure rate in mR/h and the airborne concentration in derived air concentrations (DACs), or DAC-hours, is more important to the immediate response than the liquid concentration. The dose to a person suspected of ingesting contaminated water can be easily determined by a whole body count.

or inaccurate work by themselves or persons under their direction, a lack of seriousness about the postulated conditions, and a lack of thoughtful, deliberate action. It may also be made evident through obvious complaints and sarcastic comments about the situation.

Individuals who suspend their disbelief and make a best effort to act in accordance with the postulated circumstances are *immersed* in the drill or exercise. The more immersed individuals are, the closer their actions or decisions are likely to be to those actions they would take in reality during an actual event of similar circumstances. Correspondingly, a lack of immersion causes participants to react more to the controllers and to the evaluation process than to the postulated circumstances, so they take the actions and decisions likely to lead to a good evaluation rather than those they would likely take in an actual event. A close relationship between responses to postulated events and responses to actual events is necessary for the evaluation process to have validity. Any evaluation process must necessarily assume that observed performance is a valid predictor of performance under actual conditions. The author expects that a lack of good correlation between responses to postulated and actual events is more likely to cause unnecessary corrective actions (e.g., participants are more skilled than is apparent from their performance) than to fail to reveal corrective actions that need to be taken, but there may be examples of the latter as well.

An individual is immersed, or fails to be immersed, in postulated conditions for a wide variety of reasons. Although many of these reasons are individual, personal, and not readily affected by external factors, some are influenced by the drill or exercise design and its implementation. To the extent that scenario design and control promote immersion, they promote more accurate evaluation of performance and training and ensure better familiarity with the duties and functions of the emergency response organization. The scenario designer primarily controls the quality of the scenario. The larger emergency preparedness group has influence over the scope and participation. Immersion is promoted by the participation of all organizational units that would be involved in an event similar to the postulated conditions and having internally consistent data that accurately portray the postulated failures. A scenario detracts from immersion by presenting incomplete information, inaccurate information, physical indications not consistent with postulated failures,[*] indications that fail to have the expected variability of parameters, or unearned information. A poorly organized scenario or one that does not adequately anticipate participant actions causes the unnecessary creation of on-the-spot data that are more likely to be technically inaccurate, further detracting from immersion.

RELATIONSHIP BETWEEN DRILL AND EXERCISE OBJECTIVES AND EXERCISE DESIGN

An objective is an activity or task that the scenario designer intends that the drill or exercise participant perform. The activity could be completion of a procedure, demonstration of task competence, or demonstration of a particular knowledge or proficiency. Examples of activities include the immediate control room response to an unexpected reactor shutdown, dispatching a team of mechanics into the plant, performing a radiation survey in a room where radioactive material is unexpectedly released, or demonstrating proficiency at recommending protective actions to offsite officials. An objective is usually, but not always, tied to an evaluation criterion.

The design and execution of a drill or exercise are informed by the objectives selected for that activity, although the complete design may sometimes require events that do not have corresponding objectives. The scenario design must provide simulated situations that should cause the participants to perform the intended activities and provide sufficient detail and information to allow the participant to be successful. For the most part, participants receive a negative performance evaluation

---

[*] The actual failure mechanism may not be known by the participant and may not be discoverable, but it should always be consistent with how the scenario design has failed the equipment (e.g., motor, value, pump, pipe, tank, or other affected structure). It is poor scenario design to script an equipment failure without a described cause.

if they decide not to perform the activity or demonstrate a lack of proficiency at the activity. Each organization participating in an exercise will have its own objectives, some of which are common among organizations and some unique to each participating agency.

Drill objectives tend to be unique to each individual drill because these are limited in scope and task based, with little overlap between different kinds of drills. Also, drills tend to focus on the proficiency of individuals in the field, not those in response facilities, and do not test the ability of senior staff to make decisions or direct activities. In contrast, there are two categories of exercise objectives: those intrinsic to any exercise and those that pertain to scenario-specific events. The intrinsic category exists because exercises are inherently tests of the ability of different groups to communicate with each other and to coordinate their activities. The decisions of one group often depend on the actions of another or upon information generated by another. Each group must have an individual in command-and-control, and there are common demonstration attributes that apply to these individuals, such as event recognition, delegation, briefings, and the implementation of protective measures. Some other intrinsic objectives are procedurally tied to certain levels of emergency classification, such as the requirement to staff emergency response facilities following declaration of an Alert or (usually) the evacuation of non-essential workers from site following declaration of a Site Area Emergency. Whenever the scenario includes that emergency classification, the related objectives always apply to the exercise.

The Commission defines the principal functional areas of emergency response (the intrinsic objectives) as[*]

- Classification of events
- Notification of offsite authorities
- Assessment of radiological releases onsite and offsite
- Development of protective action recommendations for the public (scenario dependent)
- Dissemination of information to the public
- Engineering assessment and repair plan development
- Implementation of mitigative actions
- Protection of workers, including medical care
- Response to operational transients
- Coordination with offsite response organizations (scenario dependent)

When offsite agencies (counties, parishes, states, some federal agencies) participate in exercises, their objectives are negotiated with the FEMA evaluators during the scenario development phase based on the generic objectives in the *Radiological Emergency Preparedness Program Manual* (FEMA, 2016). The offsite objectives generally control the overall scenario design. In particular, FEMA generally specifies the distance to which Protective Action Guides must be exceeded, whether the radiological conditions require decisions about potassium iodide, the initial and final wind directions (i.e., determining which offsite jurisdictions might be affected), and whether there must be significant depositions of radioactive material. These specifications together define the radiological release that must be designed. The release characteristics define the required reactor core damage, the source term (gap vs. fuel melt), the size and duration of containment breaches, the amount of iodine depletion through water scrubbing, whether the release is elevated or at ground level, and whether the release is monitored or not. Together, these parameters narrow the designer's choice of reactor accident sequences. At every step in the design process, the designer works from consequence to cause; for example, a particular General Emergency classification implies a certain range of Site Area Emergency classification choices and therefore a range of possible Alert classifications. As the designer works backwards, their choice of initial conditions and events expands. The final scenario is the sum of those design choices. The designer is challenged to present scenarios

---

[*] See *Interim Staff Guidance: Emergency Planning for Nuclear Power Plants* (NRC, 2011g, p. 29).

that do not overlap significantly with previous scenarios and provide some level of plausibility. Overlap becomes an issue because the response organization may become accustomed to patterns in the drill and exercise program and come to rely on those patterns rather than accurately analyzing the simulated plant conditions; this could result in poor performance in a real event when that pattern is not present. The degree of situational accuracy and plausibility affects immersion and the enhancement of participant performance.

With the implementation of Appendix E to 10 CFR Part 50, Sections IV.F(i) and IV.F(j),[*] licensees are required to periodically conduct a no or low radiological release scenario and a scenario that stops at a Site Area Emergency classification, both of which are significant departures from previous exercise requirements for a General Emergency classification and a major radiological release. The intent of this change is to reduce a participant's ability to guess or game the scenario and to identify when they take action based on prior experience and preconditioning. The no-release/Site Area Emergency scenario also requires negotiation with FEMA during the scenario development phase to establish when and how FEMA will evaluate the ability of offsite agencies to issue and implement protective actions for the public. FEMA has not agreed to suspend the evaluation of offsite agency capabilities with regard to radiological monitoring, dose assessment, or protective action decision-making when a biennial exercise does not drive these activities. FEMA has given each regional branch chief the authority to decide how to perform these assessments, and it is likely there will be variation among the regions. Some FEMA regions are allowing demonstration by interview and procedure review, but others are requiring out-of-sequence drills.

SCENARIO INTEGRITY

Both drills and exercises need to exhibit integrity to be adequate measures of emergency response organization capability. *Scenario integrity* is established when the drill or exercise participants do not know, and generally cannot infer, the scenario events they will be tested with. The intent is to ensure that participants react to events in essentially real time with performance that closely approximates their responses to a similar event. The discriminating[†] value of a drill or exercise is lost when participants do not perform as they would perform in an event. Scenario integrity is lost when participants have foreknowledge about the events they will be tested with, allowing them an opportunity to prepare to succeed that they would not have when combating an actual event.

For the most part, scenario integrity is preserved by controlling access to scenario information before it is given. It is expected that participants cannot have foreknowledge of information they cannot access. A scenario intended to be given multiple times presents additional challenges because after its first use some members of the organization have knowledge that could potentially be given to subsequent participants. Access controls may include written security agreements, the use of computers not connected to local area networks, and password-controlled files, as well as access controls on network drives or directories, storage of scenario materials in locked rooms with limited access, flags and placards when material is outside of controlled areas, and duplication of manuals offsite away from areas frequented by the participants.

The ability of drill and exercise participants to infer scenario events in advance of their occurring is called *preconditioning*. The inference is not based on knowledge of the as-designed scenario but generally results from overuse of the specific event or emergency action levels over time. Preconditioning allows participants to anticipate the actions necessary to react to the events, generally resulting in better performance than if the participants had been taken unawares by the event. Anticipation allows them time to read and reflect on procedures, obtain references, stage equipment or tools or personnel, perform calculations, hold discussions with other participants, and

---

[*] Beginning in 2012 and required by December 2015, depending on the individual licensee's exercise schedule.

[†] *Discriminating* as in providing an ability to distinguish adequate knowledge and capabilities from inadequate knowledge. One could also say having evaluative or predictive value.

take other useful preparatory steps that perhaps would not otherwise be possible. Preconditioning can mask actual knowledge or proficiency gaps because of the preparatory steps it enables. When training time is limited, the overuse of some events, procedures, and emergency action levels reduces the time available to practice the response to other events, potentially degrading other skills and abilities.

The exercise program in place between 1982 and 2013 essentially tolerated a certain level of preconditioning in defined areas. This was because evaluated exercises (annual to about 1994 and biennial thereafter with a licensee-only exercise in the between year) are jointly evaluated by the Commission and FEMA, and the offsite objectives required by FEMA forced an exercise to escalate to General Emergency and include a significant radiological release. Exercise participants could reliability expect

- To escalate from an Alert to a Site Area Emergency to a General Emergency, without skipping a classification level, allowing them to concentrate on only a few emergency action levels at a time. If the scenario included a Notification of Unusual Event, the operators could know that the next event would result in an Alert classification.
- A separation of at least 90 minutes between the events associated with the Alert and Site Area Emergency classifications, and a separation of at least 60 minutes between Site Area Emergency and General Emergency.*
- Significant (3% to 10%) fuel damage, generally caused by reducing reactor vessel water level to below the top of active fuel. Thus, participants could expect a significant breach of the reactor coolant system.
- Either a failure of containment integrity (with few choices of failure location, depending on the site simulator) or a steam-line break with a loss of the ability to isolate the steam line (i.e., inability to close both the inboard and outboard main steam isolation valves).
- A change in plant and/or meteorological conditions after the General Emergency that requires an expansion of the initial protective action recommendation. The particular change was often a change in wind direction as indicated on the plant meteorology tower, generally driven by a FEMA expectation that releases affect more than one populated area in the emergency planning zone. In cases of plants located along state borders, each state required an opportunity to make a protective action decision.

Because the practice was to conduct a rehearsal exercise prior to every exercise, and because the understanding was that the emergency action levels and release pathway in the rehearsal and exercise had to be different, participants could anticipate much about the release pathway by knowing it could not be the same as the one used in the rehearsal.

Prior to 1999–2000, licensees typically conducted one rehearsal and one exercise a year. The implementation of the reactor oversight program (ROP) caused licensees to increase the number of exercise-level events to three to five per year, largely to maintain the emergency response organization participation performance indicator in the green band. Although there were few constraints on the design of these additional exercises, virtually all exercises conducted from 2000 through roughly 2012 closely followed the previous evaluated exercise model. One could speculate as to why this occurred. In part, it was likely because when offsite organizations participated they wanted to maintain their skills for the next evaluation. In part, it was likely because licensees saw these exercises as maintaining their skills for the next evaluation. In part, it was likely because scenario developers were accustomed to this model and had developmental aids and templates already in use (i.e., it was easier to develop and manage). The end result was that emergency response organizations were as preconditioned in 2010 as they had been more than 20 years earlier.

---

* The primary reason for the timing was to allow FEMA evaluators to observe all of the activities on their evaluation checklists.

The Commission began to identify in the years 2005 to 2010 that licensee performance in drills and exercises was generally good but that licensees were less proficient in their response to actual plant events. The recognition that the existing drill and exercise program was not adequately preparing licensees for real emergencies resulted in the changes to Appendix E to Part 50, Part IV.F(2)(i) and F(2)(j), that were implemented in 2011. One aspect of improving the evaluation value of drills and exercises is diminishing the prevailing preconditioning practices. In particular, licensees will have to

- Drill essentially every emergency action level over an 8-year cycle (limiting the ability to overuse classifications).
- Conduct exercises that are not designed to escalate to a General Emergency.
- Conduct exercises that do not progress systematically from Alert to Site Area Emergency to General Emergency (skip classification levels).
- Conduct exercises that begin or rapidly escalate to at least Site Area Emergency.
- Conduct some exercises that do not have any radiological releases and some with small releases not sufficient to drive offsite protective actions.

Although these requirements apply specifically to only biennial evaluated exercises, licensees who do not incorporate substantial variation in their routine drill and exercise program will likely find that preconditioning leads participants to respond poorly to less predictable scenarios. In particular, a preconditioned expectation that the scenario will escalate through all classifications may cause them to miss jumps where Alerts or Site Area Emergencies are skipped. An expectation that a large radiological release will happen may lead the organization to take preparatory steps shown not to be necessary when the release does not occur.

GROUND RULES

The *ground rules* are the set of instructions that define how a drill/exercise is conducted and define its limits. Usually, one set of rules applies to controllers and evaluators and another set to participants; in part, the function of controllers is to enforce the ground rules that apply to the participants. Typical rules that apply to controllers and evaluators describe the degree of interaction permitted during the drill or exercise, the controller's authority to deviate from the planned scenario, and the response to unplanned events outside the drill or exercise (e.g., trip of the actual plant, actual medical emergency in the plant). Typical rules for participants include which equipment may be manipulated, which communications must be made and which ones skipped (or made to a simulation cell), whether the acquisition and donning of protective clothing must be demonstrated or discussed, whether the acquisition of tools and parts and special equipment must be demonstrated or discussed, and how to acquire the data necessary to respond to the scenario. Examples of properly acquiring data might include instructions for logging into the simulator dataset instead of the live plant computer system or instructions for how a radiation protection technician acquires simulated radiation exposure rates in areas actually at background.

SIMULATION

Simulation refers to the acquisition of information without having completely performed all of the actions necessary to acquire that information in actual circumstances and to a prior agreement within the drill or exercise ground rules to not perform some activity or function that otherwise would be required. Every drill and exercise has some degree of simulation, caused by the drill/exercise scope and resources and sometimes by the need to perform some tasks when the normal conditions are not present. Simulation is not the same as acquiring earned information within the drill or exercise. Simulation is not inherently problematic, but poorly understood or poorly controlled simulation may adversely affect the participant's ability to achieve the drill or exercise objectives. The degree of simulation is always decided by the controller, not by the participant.

The familiarity of plant operators and mechanics with plant equipment is one performance attribute that is often tested during an exercise; however, because the same equipment is necessary for continued plant operation and the equipment is not actually damaged, the actions taken to repair equipment are virtually always simulated.* Operators or mechanics would be expected to go to the actual piece of equipment in the plant (during the exercise) and then describe what actions they would take to diagnose and repair the problem. The operators or mechanics would not be permitted to touch the equipment, open any covers or doors, or apply any diagnostic equipment or tools directly to the equipment. Depending on the ground rules, individuals might be required to have the appropriate test equipment or tools with them, or they may be permitted to show how they could have acquired the equipment or tools. The entire demonstration would actually be a discussion between the individual and the controller (evaluator); the demonstration might be enhanced by drawings or manipulated photographs to illustrate the condition of the equipment as described in the exercise. It would be the controller's task to provide the proper cues (e.g., burnt aroma, blistering on the exterior of a cable) and apply appropriate time delays (e.g., 10 minutes to unbolt a motor). In this context, the results read from test equipment would be earned information but the unbolting of a motor would be simulation, although neither action would actually be performed.

Simulation is sometimes incorrectly understood by participants as permission to skip entire tasks. The evacuation of employees from the licensee's site is a task often misunderstood in this way and serves to illustrate the potential problem. Many emergency plans require that employees not responding to the emergency be evacuated when a Site Area Emergency is declared,† and this task is frequently simulated. Participants often demonstrate making the decision to order the evacuation and take no further action because the activity is simulated. The participants fail to recognize that it is the movement of plant employees not participating in the exercise that is simulated, not the entire activity. Site procedures often direct employees to intermediate assembly areas before evacuating and require the dispatch of radiation protection staff to monitor those assembly areas. Skipping the activity entirely allows the response organization more resources than they would actually have (e.g., radiation protection personnel who ought to be withdrawn from the available personnel pool) and inappropriately relieves the organization of the need to consider the protection of those simulated employees. In general, the exercise emergency response organization should work through as much of the procedures associated with a simulated activity as possible before affecting non-participants, making the appropriate decisions and announcements and directing the dispatch of appropriate staff (and dealing with the reduction in resources).

Simulation of personnel often causes confusion during exercises. Some licensees routinely simulate members of the on-shift emergency organization whose duty stations are outside the control room, such as non-licensed plant operators, chemistry technicians, radiation protection technicians, fire fighters, medical staff, and security officers. This practice creates confusion because task assignments to simulated personnel are often poorly documented, participants are often poor at tracking the locations of simulated persons, participants often fail to demonstrate briefing and dispatching simulated persons according to plant procedures, and participants often fail to demonstrate the proper level of communications with simulated persons (e.g., updates as the plant status changes). Scenario developers do not always develop appropriate exercise control information that accurately depicts the activities of, and information from, simulated persons, so that controllers are often asked for expected responses that are not scripted, creating a potential to misdirect the scenario. Controllers who are not familiar with the tasks assigned these simulated persons may cause additional confusion by generating incorrect responses and allowing tasks to be performed much more quickly than could actually be done.

---

* Unless an out-of-service or training piece of equipment is employed, with the appropriate safety measures.
† The connection is found in NUREG-0654, Revision 1, element J.4.

Participants are generally expected to respond to an exercise with the staffing described in the emergency plan. They are also generally permitted to call out additional resources as needed to address the specific circumstances of the exercise, provided that the proper decisions are made and established procedures are followed. This combination often affects exercise realism when the additional resources are permitted to be simulated rather than being actual persons added to the exercise organization. One possible effect stretching credulity is the instantaneous appearance of resources that ordinarily would take time to arrive, such as calling out three operators from home. Another common issue is that the use of simulated personnel can give the responders essentially unlimited capabilities, especially when relief-shift personnel are not properly tracked and the number of simulated persons is not checked against actual plant rosters. Because exercise organizations typically work every problem in a scenario until they run out of resources, an excessive allowance of simulated persons may prevent them from demonstrating the ability to prioritize and schedule work and differentiate important tasks from those that are unimportant.

DRILLSMANSHIP

Drillmanship refers to the ability of participants to demonstrate to evaluators how they are responding to the scenario inputs. It involves not only demonstrating specific actions but also ensuring that the evaluator understands the basis for those actions and decisions, something that is often not readily apparent from direct observation. Drillmanship often means verbalizing mental activities so that an evaluator understands the underlying reasoning for actions taken or decisions made. When participants must obtain dynamic situation-dependent information from static equipment or devices that do not reflect the scenario (e.g., reading a radiation survey meter, observing the local alarm panel in a plant building), it requires verbalizing the data sources being observed to allow a controller to provide the correct feedback information. Good drillmanship requires precision and the ability to break activities into their component tasks—for example, participants stating the order in which individual meters, lights, annunciators, and breaker positions are observed on a panel instead of stating that they are observing the panel. The former gives the controller opportunity to provide specific symptoms such as amps, volts, light color, or lack of lighting, while the latter could lead the controller to provide unearned information or conclusions.

VALIDATION

Validation is the process of confirming that a drill or exercise scenario is complete and accurate with respect to the input data to be provided to participants, so that the objectives can be achieved. A valid scenario also provides a high degree of realism and requires a minimum of suspension of disbelief. A scenario is complete when it provides the information necessary to implement all necessary procedures and information for the most likely alternative paths. An alternative path is a decision or set of actions that differs from the optimum or expected actions but which could reasonably be expected to occur given the information that will be available to the participants.

Drills are usually sufficiently limited in scope such that an experienced subject-matter expert can anticipate all of the actions the drill participants should take and confirm that accurate and complete scenario information has been developed. An exercise is complex enough and involves so many station departments that one or two persons are unlikely to have sufficient expertise to confirm the accuracy and completeness of the entire scenario. This is particularly true with respect to the simulator control room and operator actions. It is usually important that an exercise be validated at one or more points in the development process. The most reliable validation comes from presenting the scenario to a group of qualified individuals and confirming that their responses are substantially similar to the responses anticipated by the scenario designer. This group of qualified individuals should be similar to the exercise crew in their level of advance information, and they should be presented exercise information in the same manner. Unexpected actions by the validation crew may indicate that incomplete or inaccurate information is present in the scenario and that changes are needed to achieve the desired objectives. Members of the validation crew should not be permitted to take part as participants in the subsequent exercise.

Drill and exercise scenarios both contain a variety of data derived from fixed and portable instruments and meters. Developers need to review reference documents for these instruments to ensure that all provided numerical values are on-scale on the appropriate instrument and that they are presented with accuracy consistent with the measurement. For example, an analog radiation survey instrument can frequently be read to not more than one-third or one-fourth of the smallest division on the meter face; on the lowest scale, that may equate to the nearest 0.1 mR/h, while on the highest scale the same indication may equate to the nearest 50 mR/h.

TRADITIONAL SCENARIOS

A traditional exercise scenario is one designed to reach a General Emergency classification with a large radiological release. These are traditional because every evaluated exercise prior to 2012, and virtually every other licensee exercise conducted between 1980 and 2012, was designed to result in this endpoint. General Emergency classifications indicate core damage sequences with the potential for a release that meets the Protective Action Guides. There are only a few sequences that end with core damage and radiological releases, and licensees tend to alternate between them.[*] For boiling water reactors these are

- Loss-of-coolant accident inside the drywell, followed by a failure of a pipe or electrical penetration in the reactor building (monitored and filtered release, unless the refuel floor blowout panels are los then unmonitored and not filtered)
- Loss-of-coolant accident inside the drywell, followed by initiating the hardened vent to the environment to save containment, with a failure to close the vent line (usually a monitored release, not filtered)
- Loss-of-coolant accident inside the drywell, followed by the recirculation of water from the drywell sump back to the reactor vessel, followed by a break of recirculation water piping in the reactor building (with the failure of both isolation valves in the recirculation line; monitored and filtered release)
- Steam-line break in the steam tunnel or turbine building, with a failure to close either main steam isolation valve in the affected line (or closure of the exterior valve with a failure of the bypass or drain line, may not be monitored, not filtered)

For pressurized water reactors these are

- Loss-of-coolant accident inside containment, followed by a failure of a pipe or electrical penetration in the auxiliary building (monitored and filtered release)
- Loss-of-coolant accident inside containment, followed by a seal failure on the main equipment hatch or exterior personnel hatch (unmonitored release, not filtered)
- Loss-of-coolant accident inside containment, followed by a failure allowing a radiological release through the containment purge system (monitored and filtered release)
- Loss-of-coolant accident inside containment, followed by the recirculation of water from the containment sump back to the reactor vessel, followed by a break of recirculation water piping in the auxiliary building (with the failure of both isolation valves in the recirculation line; monitored and filtered release)

---

[*] Primarily because of the need to avoid preconditioning in evaluated exercises, which can be interpreted as having the same core damage sequence and release path in two successive exercises.

- Steam generator tube rupture, with a failure to close either main steam isolation valve in the affected line and lifting of the downstream safety relief valve (or with rupture of the steam line in the turbine building).

In addition, exercise scenarios for both reactor technologies often include failures that prevent a normal reactor shutdown—*anticipated transients without scram* (ATWS). These events are included in scenarios because the available source term inventory is maintained as long as the reactor is at power and it begins to decay away as soon as the reactor is tripped. Some kinds of failures also result in iodine spikes or other reactor core conditions that enhance fuel damage, making the subsequent large radiological release more plausible. Maintaining the reactor at power also keeps reactor coolant system pressure up, providing a longer period of substantial motive force to maintain the radiological release.

The necessary release characteristics define the necessary amount of core damage in the scenario. A scenario requiring Protective Action Guides to be exceeded 2 miles downwind will likely require the reactor vessel water level to be below the top of active fuel for at least 30 minutes. A scenario requiring Protective Action Guides to be exceeded 5 miles downwind will likely require the reactor vessel water level to be substantially below the top of active fuel for 45 to 60 minutes and may also require a power spike to occur. An elevated release point makes it easier to exceed the Protective Action Guides (boiling water reactors only) as does a stable atmosphere (stability classes D, E, F, or G). A release with no filtration (filter is bypassed, physically degraded, or not operating) is useful when protective actions are required beyond 5 miles from the site. Because isotopes of iodine have larger dose conversion factors than do the noble gas isotopes, a no-filtration scenario is also useful when the evaluation and distribution of potassium iodide are evaluation objectives.

Exercises conducted through 2015 rarely included substantial damage to the spent fuel storage pool. One can expect spent fuel pool events to become more frequent in the future as a result of integrating beyond-design-basis initiatives into the exercise program and because of the need for no-release or low-release scenarios. Fuel pool events may make good design choices because the older cores stored in the pools are substantially less capable of plausibly providing a radiological source term that meets Protective Action Guides while still providing radiation protection challenges to plant personnel and exercising rarely used procedures.

WEAKNESSES

A *weakness* during a drill or exercise is human performance that would have precluded the effective implementation of the site emergency plan had the circumstances occurred. Although this definition is currently used in the reactor oversight program and found in the NRC *Inspection Manual*, Chapter 0609, Appendix B, "Emergency Preparedness Significance Determination Process," essentially the same definition was found in the inspection procedures used by the Commission between 1983 and 1999. The emphasis is on human performance, how well the emergency response organization is trained to perform its emergency functions, and how well it actually performs them. Another way to look at weaknesses is that they represent the inadequate performance of an adequate procedure. The same definition is applied in a licensee's critique of an event for performance that did preclude the effective implementation of the emergency plan when circumstances did occur. The causes of a weakness are generally one or more of the following: (1) emergency response organization training was not performed or was of poor quality, (2) procedures for the deficient function did not exist or were of poor quality (dependent on skill of the craft knowledge), (3) the deficient participant did not refer to the procedure when performing the function, or (4) the deficient participant exhibited a serious error in judgment (poor use of the procedure).

EXERCISE CRITIQUE PROCESS

Appendix E to 10 CFR 50, IV.F(2)(g), requires that all drills and exercises must provide for formal critiques. A critique is a formal evaluation process intended to identify an organization's strengths and deficiencies in the area of emergency response. A critique generally employs a combination of formal performance objectives, feedback from participants, and observations from subject-matter experts to reach a conclusion about the ability of the licensee's organization to implement adequate measures to protect the health and safety of the public had the circumstances occurred. A thorough critique addresses human performance issues, facility and equipment problems, and the adequacy of existing procedures, in addition to identifying gaps in the preparedness program.

The first phase of the critique process is the collection of immediate feedback from the participants, which typically occurs very soon after a drill or exercise concludes. Participants generally debrief as a facility, with the session being led by the senior participating official. The process always includes an open verbal discussion among the participants, although many licensees make written comment forms available as a supplemental measure. All licensees ask each individual participant to contribute comments about the facility's overall performance and also about their own, personal improvement items. Many, but not all, licensees also ask the facility staff to self-grade the evaluation objectives that apply to their facility; there is no single method that is common to all licensees; some begin by grading objectives and others begin with an open discussion. Although any participants are expected to identify any problems that qualify as a weakness, they are generally encouraged to identify any or every problem or issue. Most licensees follow the participant discussion with a preliminary verbal debrief from the designated controllers and evaluators (as applicable) to the participants to identify issues the participants missed. The controller or evaluator debrief consists of first impressions and observations, and at this point in the process it does not represent a formal position or evaluation. If there are other observers present, their comments often follow those of the controller or evaluator; such observers could be members of site emergency response organization teams not participating in the drill or exercise, new emergency response organization trainees, senior plant managers, station quality control or nuclear oversight department staff, members of the site nuclear safety boards, or industry peers.

The second phase of the critique process occurs after the facility is returned to immediate readiness and the participants are dismissed. The lead controller (evaluator) for each facility conducts a formal meeting of the assigned controllers and evaluators to perform an independent grading of the evaluation objectives assigned to each facility. The evaluators are collectively expected to identify any negative performance that qualifies as a weakness, identify negative performance of less significance than a weakness, grade the evaluation objectives using the site-specific criteria, and identify any performance aspects for which evaluation objectives did not exist. The evaluators will typically only grade those objectives that apply to their facility, along with any cross-facility objectives. When the evaluator's grading of the evaluation objectives differs from the participant's, decisions will need to be made about which evaluation to carry forward.

The third phase of the evaluation process is a formal meeting between all of the facility lead controllers and evaluators, usually led by the exercise lead controller (who is often also the lead scenario developer). This meeting may also include some or all of the facility evaluators, as space and time permit. The primary purpose of this meeting is to assign the final grade for each evaluation objective, with a focus on the cross-facility objectives* and on repeat issues from previous exercises (i.e., performance trends). Some licensees assign an overall grade to exercises. The meeting should also determine which issues will be entered into the corrective action program or other work control processes and identify any other information that will be reported to management.

---

* The cross-facility objectives tend to be either tasks that are shared between facilities or objectives related to coordination and communication. Examples of a shared objective are prioritizing the repair of damaged plant equipment or performing radiological assessments. A communication objective might be to accurately communicate plant status information on the operations hot-line.

Some licensees conduct a formal briefing for senior site management following the lead controller meeting which usually occurs a few days to a week following the exercise. This briefing typically includes the results for drill and exercise performance indicator opportunities in the exercise (expected, unexpected, and those that did not occur), performance issues that constituted weaknesses or deficiencies, and other significant issues not as significant as a weakness. The briefing also may discuss issues related to scenario development, exercise control, and failed equipment. This briefing is intended to give management the opportunity to raise or lower the significance of issues, to include additional issues developed from their observations, and to ask questions of the evaluators.

The last phase of the evaluation process is compiling a written after-action report, which typically is completed from 4 to 8 weeks after the exercise. The report draws on information developed in each of the preceding phases and represents the licensee's final evaluation of the exercise objectives. The report format varies widely among licensees. Some common elements include an executive summary, an explanation of the objective grading scheme, a table of objectives and assigned grades, a summary of the as-designed scenario, paragraphs describing activities in each facility, a discussion of cross-facility performance, a list of corrective action program entries or other work-tracking process numbers, and a list or table of less significant performance issues (including low-significance observations). The purpose of the report is to communicate significant issues to senior licensee management for their attention and action and to raise an awareness of issues with other emergency response organization members and teams (those who did not participate in or observe the exercise).

When the Commission observes a biennial emergency preparedness exercise, the inspectors observe, but do not contribute to, the immediate post-exercise facility debriefs. The purpose of observing these discussions is to be aware of the inputs to the licensee's process; this may become important if significant issues are raised but are not properly evaluated (i.e., an actual weakness is evaluated as having lesser significance). Inspectors may not observe the facility-level evaluator meeting and the subsequent lead controller or evaluator meetings.[*] Although some licensees do not hold a routine management briefing following all exercises, it has become a universal practice following an evaluated exercise.[†] Inspectors observe the licensee's briefing to management to understand the weaknesses identified by the site evaluators and the issues that have been or will be entered into the site corrective action system for action. Inspectors independently assess the weaknesses that occur during an exercise and compare their assessment with the licensee's; this comparison generally occurs after licensee management has had the opportunity to discuss the preliminary findings.

REMEDIAL EXERCISES

A *remedial drill* or *exercise* is a drill or exercise conducted to demonstrate the effectiveness of corrective actions following a drill or exercise that exhibited substantial performance issues. Each licensee should establish an evaluation standard defining an unacceptable level of performance, typically expressed in terms of the number of failed evaluation objectives.[‡] There can also be point-based systems and schemes in which objectives are assigned weighting factors. In this context, unacceptable performance means that the ability of the drill or exercise emergency response

---

[*] One reason for not observing the internal evaluation phases of the critique process is that there is a potential for free and candid discussion of issues to be chilled if the regulator is present throughout.

[†] Procedures 71114.01 and 71114.07 define the end of the critique process as the presentation of preliminary evaluation results to site management, a practice that was not widespread among licensees when the procedures were written in 2000. A licensee cannot be required to conform to the requirements of an internal NRC inspection procedure and therefore may elect to not hold a briefing for senior site management. However, if a licensee follows a different process than the procedure anticipates, it will likely delay the inspectors in discussing their observations and will likely lengthen the inspection period. Although the procedures anticipate that this meeting is held during the same week as the exercise, circumstances occasionally cause a delay or the licensee may plan on holding the meeting later if the evaluation is expected to be complex; this can generally be worked out in advance with the inspectors.

[‡] Where *failed* is used as a relative term that depends on a licensee's specific evaluation methodology and how they designate unsatisfactory performance.

organization to implement adequate measures to protect the health and safety of the public is seriously degraded.* An evaluation of unacceptable, whether for an individual, group, function, facility, or for the entire exercise organization, should lead to prompt corrective actions for the identified deficiencies (also referred to as *remediation*).

A remedial exercise is conducted using substantially the same set of emergency response organization participants as participated in the "failed" drill or exercise, presented with a different scenario having the same performance objectives and degree of difficulty. A performance evaluation of adequate or higher during the remedial exercise indicates that corrective actions were successful and the exercise emergency response organization continues to be capable of protecting the health and safety of employees and the public.

The Commission may request a remedial drill or exercise following observation of a biennial exercise, according to the requirements of Appendix E to 10 CFR 50, Part IV.F(2)(f). The specific scope of the remedial drill or exercise would depend on the key emergency response functions that were identified as being inadequately performed. The Commission would base a request for a remedial activity on the following:

1. A significant compromise of the scenario integrity occurred.
2. A scenario did not provide sufficient opportunity for the organization to demonstrate key emergency response organization performance attributes. The as-designed scenario could have been deficient, or unexpected implementation issues could have prevented the demonstration of key skills. Typical implementation issues include unexpected simulator responses and improper direction of the drill or exercises by controllers.
3. The emergency response organization performance was evaluated as being insufficient to ensure that the exercise crew could implement adequate measures to protect the health and safety of employees and the public in the event of an actual event.

The Commission has never formally invoked their ability to require a remedial exercise, in part because licensees have recognized their poor performance and offered to re-demonstrate certain functions on their own. They have in the past been remarkably successful at convincing the Commission to keep serious performance inadequacies out of the enforcement process, an accommodation that would likely not be acceptable today.

---

* The assumption here is that evaluators have identified all performance issues with a substantial impact on health and safety, so the evaluation does not overestimate actual capabilities.

8 Regulatory Environment

This chapter provides an overview of the regulatory environment associated with radiological emergency planning.

INTRODUCTION

The focus of this book has not been on implementing regulations. The author has attempted, as much as possible, to discuss and illuminate the technical concepts that form the emergency planning framework and to provide the basis for emergency preparedness, separate from compliance. However, as much as we might like otherwise, an emergency planner at a reactor licensee needs to have some familiarity with the substance and terminology of regulations to be effective. Similarly, a planner working at an offsite agency needs to be familiar with Federal Emergency Management Agency (FEMA) guidance documents. The discussion below is not intended as a guide to compliance; rather, it provides an introduction to the most important regulatory concepts and processes that a licensee emergency planner may encounter. A discussion of Commission enforcement processes is included because findings are resolved more quickly when the affected licensee planners understand how the regulator approaches issues.

REASONABLE ASSURANCE

The entire emergency preparedness regulatory structure is designed to ensure that there is *reasonable assurance* that adequate protective actions can be taken in the event of a radiological emergency to ensure the health and safety* of the public surrounding that reactor. Reasonable assurance means that the regulators have confidence that emergency conditions will be recognized, plant conditions will be assessed, and appropriate protective actions will be developed and implemented. The "reasonable" part of the standard says that it is acceptable to have less than an absolute confidence that adequate protective actions can be taken. Absolute confidence in preparedness can never be achieved—no matter how dire the circumstances the emergency preparedness system can overcome, one can always conceive of a circumstance just somewhat more dire. The regulator's criteria for having confidence in the ability of a licensee to implement adequate protective actions are intended to equate to the conditions under which a reasonable member of the public would find the arrangements for preparedness acceptable. This reasonable person is not expected to be an expert in the radiological sciences or emergency preparedness; instead, this person has the knowledge that an average layperson would have. It might be characterized as a "preponderance of evidence" standard. At its heart, the reasonable assurance standard is a statement about the costs and benefits of the emergency preparedness system—an amount of risk that a reasonable person can accept for costs they are willing to bear. Some of those costs are monetary (e.g., higher electric utility rates, higher state and local taxes), whereas others are more intangible (e.g., the chance that they will be required to evacuate).

---

* Ensuring the health and safety of the public is not the same as providing absolute protection against radiation exposure. The public's safety is maximized when the least risky action is taken during an emergency. The choice of actions must take into account all potential risks to the public, from radiation, from environmental factors, from transportation, from natural events, etc. Under some circumstances, the least risky action may be no action. There are some doses of radiation that are so unlikely to result in injury (e.g., cancer) that the radiation risk is smaller than risks associated with taking other actions (e.g., accidents during evacuation); this is true even under the linear-no-threshold model of radiation injury.

Reasonable assurance is solely determined by the Nuclear Regulatory Commission (NRC) with input from FEMA. It consists of a series of professional judgments about the ongoing state of onsite and offsite preparedness. The presumption is that compliance with the emergency preparedness planning standards, with any site-specific license conditions, and with agreements among assignees is sufficient to conclude that reasonable assurance exists. Compliance means that plans, procedures, and equipment exist as necessary to implement every planning standard, and all responsible parties are capable of implementing those plans and procedures. Note that an adverse judgment by FEMA with regard to an aspect of offsite preparedness does not, in itself, remove an existing finding of reasonable assurance, because only the Commission can make that determination.*

Reasonable assurance is established when a reactor facility is first licensed by the Commission, and then it must be maintained. The Commission's and FEMA's routine inspection and evaluation programs are designed to validate that reasonable assurance has been maintained and continues to exist. When the inspection program is adequate, a lack of significant regulatory findings provides a basis to conclude that reasonable assurance continues to exist. Reevaluation of reasonable assurance is warranted when there are significant regulatory findings; these findings include losses of planning standard function and deficiencies in offsite plans or performance.

The Commission has processes to identify the regulatory response to losses of planning standard functions, including increased oversight and independent inspection of the extent of causes. What the Commission lacks, in the author's opinion, is a process to formally assess whether to withdraw reasonable assurance following one or more identified losses of planning standard function. Significant emergency preparedness findings do not initiate a reevaluation of reasonable assurance for the affected reactor site. Procedural links do not exist between the Commission enforcement program and the Commission's findings of reasonable assurance; that is, there is no internal Commission procedure that formally invokes the provisions of 10 CFR 50.54(s) based on inspection findings.

A process exists to reevaluate reasonable assurance when offsite deficiencies are identified. FEMA regulations and procedures define the planning and performance issues that warrant designation as a Severity Level I finding† and provide means to inform the Commission of that determination. Implicit in the Level I designation is a judgment that the associated risk is sufficiently low that it is acceptable to allow 180 days to correct the problem before taking regulatory action. FEMA lacks a condition analogous to the Commission's "immediate safety concern"; there is no mechanism for FEMA to conclude that immediate action is required to maintain reasonable assurance and to transmit that conclusion to the Commission for expedited review. A reevaluation of reasonable assurance is also warranted following significant changes in onsite and offsite infrastructure or capabilities. In part, this is the basis for a disaster-initiated review by FEMA.

DOCKET

The Commission assigns each reactor unit a docket number and a license number, both of which are generally used in official correspondence. A two-unit reactor site will have two docket numbers and two license numbers. The docket number is an eight-digit number; for existing Part 50 reactors, this number always starts with 05000---. The docket is a compilation of official communications between the Commission and the licensee. A licensee must put a wide variety of communications to the NRC on the docket, including required notifications (10 CFR 50.72 and 50.73), requests for license amendments, responses to requests for information, responses to proposed enforcement

---

* An adverse FEMA finding offsite would prevent an *initial* determination of reasonable assurance.
† FEMA changed their terminology with a memorandum entitled "New Terms to Classify REPP Exercise-Related Observations and Issues," dated, May 15, 2015. The Level I finding was previously called a *deficiency*, and the Level II finding previously was called an *area requiring corrective action*. Except for the terminology change, there was no change in the criteria for issuing the findings.

actions, etc. Documents that require Commission approval, such as the final safety analysis report or the site emergency plan, are also part of the docket. In general, a licensee is only responsible for, and held to, statements and information that are on the docket. Conversely, a licensee can only use information that is placed on the docket when demonstrating compliance with NRC regulations. All information placed on the docket is required to be complete and accurate in all material respects; that is, the Commission may take enforcement actions against a licensee or an individual, or both, if it determines that inaccurate, incorrect, misleading, or incomplete information has been submitted.

LICENSING BASIS

The Commission's initial finding of reasonable assurance is based on an adequate licensing basis together with the licensee's demonstration that the licensing basis has been implemented in an acceptable manner. The emergency preparedness licensing basis is the set of documents that taken together describe the design and performance criteria for implementing the licensee's overall emergency preparedness program. This includes the most recent Commission safety analysis report approving the site emergency plan; applicable NRC guidance documents; Institute of Nuclear Power Operations (INPO), Nuclear Utility Management and Resources Council (NUMARC), or Nuclear Energy Institute (NEI) documents (depending on the age of the commitment); ANSI standards, and licensee-generated analyses, plans, drawings, calculations, and procedures. The licensing basis includes any site-specific conditions that were included in the original license, as well as any specific voluntary commitments made by the licensee to the Commission from the initial license to the present date. It may also include self-imposed requirements and standards and other emergency preparedness capabilities not required by regulation.* The licensing basis also includes the records of all changes made by the licensee to their emergency plan under the authority of 10 CFR 50.54(q)—that is, those changes not submitted to the Commission for prior approval, as well as the associated analyses that supported the licensee's determinations that the changes did not reduce the plan's effectiveness.

The licensing basis should clearly indicate which guidance documents were used in developing the initial emergency preparedness program and which documents the licensee continues to be committed to implementing. These include the revision of NUREG-0654,† other applicable NUREG documents (e.g., 0696, 0737), and applicable NRC generic communications (Bulletins, Regulatory Issue Summaries, and Regulatory Guides). Where the original guidance documents have been revised since the licensee's initial commitment, the appropriate revision should be indicated.

All operating reactors had an acceptable licensing basis when they received their operating licenses. Emergency planners need to be familiar with their site-specific licensing basis because it is necessary to refer to the licensing basis when determining whether proposed changes to the emergency plan do, or do not, create reductions in plan effectiveness, and inspectors compare a site's actual emergency preparedness capabilities to the capabilities described in its licensing basis as part of confirming a continuing compliance with the planning standards of 10 CFR 50.47(b) and the requirements of Appendix E to 10 CFR Part 50.

---

* Note that, in this regard, Appendix E, Section I(2), states in part, "This appendix establishes *minimum* requirements for emergency plans." Appendix E, Section III states in part, "The plans shall be an *expression of the overall concept of operations*; they shall describe the *essential elements of advance planning* that have been considered." And, Appendix E, Section IV, states in part, "Emergency plans shall contain, *but not necessarily be limited to*, information needed to demonstrate compliance with the elements set forth below." A self-imposed requirement or commitment that exceeds regulatory requirements may still be an essential element of advance planning or part of the overall concept of licensee emergency operations.

† For all currently licensed plants, this is Revision 1, dated 1980. Any facility receiving their initial license after a future NUREG-0654 Revision 2 is published would have to meet the requirements of that revision.

There is no standard or required method of documenting the licensing basis. It is probably fair to say that in the 1980s the expectation was that the emergency plan would serve this function, although it is probably also true that the Commission licensed many plants with emergency plans that were incomplete in that respect. In particular, commitments to regulatory guides were often well documented, but commitments to NUREG-0696, etc., were poorly documented. As the industry's philosophy regarding the level of detail found in emergency plans shifted over time, much of the licensing basis details that had been found in the initial plans were removed, sometimes relocated into other documents and sometimes not maintained at all. The current level of licensing basis documentation at most licensees is likely to create a significant challenge to any emergency planner trying to identify and understand it. The best practice would be to maintain the licensing basis in as stand-alone format as possible, with a minimum of links and references. The incorporation of design and performance information by reference can create future maintenance problems as the relied-upon design documents are deleted or incorporated into other documents, new design documents are created, documents that require periodic updating are not revised, or source documents are revised without the knowledge of the emergency preparedness department. If the relied-upon reference documents are subsequently revised without conforming changes in the emergency preparedness program, a justification should be included in the licensing basis to explain why a conforming change was unnecessary.

PLANNING STANDARDS

The Nuclear Regulatory Commission and FEMA have jointly determined that reasonable assurance continues to exist when licensee and offsite emergency response programs adequately implement the emergency preparedness planning standards.[*] The standards are broadly stated functions that, taken as a whole, describe the essential capabilities of an acceptable radiological emergency preparedness program. There is overlap among some of the planning standards, although it is unclear whether that was an intentional or accidental design feature. The current understanding of the planning standards is that the interrelationships among standards render the planning scheme ineffective if any one standard cannot be effectively implemented.

The 16 planning standards developed jointly by the NRC and FEMA represent a consensus among agency subject-matter experts as it existed in the early 1980s. The initial development process did not include input from industry or other stakeholders. Some aspects of each planning standard apply to both reactor licensees and to offsite response organizations, while others are specific to either the onsite or offsite program alone. The planning standards are found in Title 10 (Energy, NRC) of the Code of Federal Regulations, Section 50.47(b), and in Title 44 (Emergency Management, FEMA) Subchapter F, Part 350.5(a), as well as in NUREG-0654/FEMA REP-1.

In the author's opinion, the planning standards represented a new approach to emergency planning when they were created. Unlike some elements of 10 CFR 50.47 and 50.54 and Appendix E, the planning standards were not a refinement or extension of existing emergency preparedness guidance and did not derive from the previous experience of other federal agencies. There was no body of knowledge or practice that established that the planning standards formed a complete set of the essential capabilities required to respond to a radiological emergency. To the present day, there is still no definitive analytical way to demonstrate that the planning standards are truly complete.

The current regulatory position is that a lack of any function directly associated with a planning standard potentially renders emergency response efforts ineffective and must be corrected. The assumption is that any function or capability not directly associated with a planning standard either is associated with program management or is a program enhancement that is not central to the

---

[*] Other requirements related to administrative controls, auditing, assessment, and program management are found in 10 CFR 50.47 and 50.54, and in Appendix E to 10 CFR 50. These represent desirable qualities in managing an emergency preparedness program but do not directly impact the reasonable assurance finding because they do not represent operational capabilities.

response mission. A lack of an enhancement may represent a failure to follow the emergency plan but is presumed not to render response efforts ineffective. This position is not clearly stated in any guidance document. There have been no significant structural changes to the planning standards in the roughly 30 years they have been in place.[*]

Some planning standards apply to any emergency response effort, whether the response is to a natural disaster or to a technological one. Standards 4 (emergency classification scheme), 5 (notification to offsite authorities and the public), 7 (annual information to the public), 9 (radiological assessment methods), 10 (protective measures), 11 (control of radiation exposure), and 12 (contaminated injured personnel) represent capabilities that are unique to radiation and radiological releases. Analogous standards could be developed for planning and preparedness for releases of chemicals or other toxic materials and for planning for other kinds of technological hazards.

The language of the planning standards is intentionally broad, and they are difficult to implement as written. The practical meaning of the planning standards is best understood through the associated guidance documents, especially NUREG-0654/FEMA-1. Regulatory Guide 1.101 also gives insight into the planning standards, particularly Revision 0 (1975) and Revision 1 (1981).[†] Some planning standards also have associated specific requirements in Appendix E to 10 CFR 50, Section IV. Some information about the intent and boundaries of the planning standards can also be gained through review of Commission actions taken to enforce regulatory requirements from 1982 to date.

RISK-SIGNIFICANT PLANNING STANDARDS

One of the major conceptual differences between the 2001 reactor oversight program and previous programs is that the reactor oversight program is *risk informed*, not *risk based*. A risk-based program would include only those elements that meet a predetermined risk threshold and ignore all other elements; outcomes and decisions would be determined solely by the numerical results of a risk analysis. A risk-informed program means that the program uses information from risk models to prioritize inspection and oversight in combination with non-risk-based deterministic criteria, including subject-matter-expert opinion and previous experience. The deterministic criteria could include, for example, maintaining defense-in-depth capabilities and maintaining engineered safety margins greater than those determined from risk models. It also includes requiring licensees to continue to comply with Commission regulations, even when those regulations have not been demonstrated to reduce risk or increase safety.

In the emergency preparedness area, the reactor oversight program introduced the term *risk-significant planning standard*, which applies to 10 CFR 50.47(b)(4), which requires a standard emergency action level scheme; 50.47(b)(5), which requires the capability to notify offsite authorities of an emergency; 50.47(b)(9), which requires the capability to perform radiological assessments; and 50.47(b)(10), which requires the capability to recommend protective actions for the public. All other 50.47(b) standards are non-risk significant. This distinction conveys the general conclusion of the Commission staff that these four planning standards form the core of an adequate emergency response[‡] (i.e., they are necessary if not sufficient). If a licensee cannot perform these functions, then performance in the other standards is largely irrelevant because the cornerstone objective may not be met (e.g., adequate measures are not ensured to be taken to protect the health and safety of the public).

---

[*] A joint NRC–FEMA effort to revise and update NUREG-0654 was begun in 2013, with completion of the project anticipated in 2016 and implementation in 2017–2018. The overall structure of the planning standards is unlikely to change. Some outdated or ineffective planning standard elements will likely be removed. Evaluation elements will be added to reflect changes to practice, guidance, technology, and regulation that occurred between 1981 and 2013. The resulting document will not apply to existing power reactor licensees unless they voluntarily commit to the new standard or unless the Commission implements rules requiring adoption; this is considered to be highly unlikely. Whether FEMA will apply NUREG-0654 Revision 2 to the existing plans and procedures of participating offsite agencies is currently unclear.

[†] In the author's opinion, Revisions 2 through 5 of Regulatory Guide 1.101 do not accomplish the purpose for which the Regulatory Guide was originally intended and offer little value to the licensee.

[‡] FEMA does not use this terminology.

The risk-significant planning standards are used to guide inspection activities and in determining the significance of findings and violations. The direct inspection of activities associated with the risk-significant planning standards has higher priority than inspection of other activities. In enforcement, a performance deficiency associated with a risk-significant planning standard is generally evaluated as being one category of significance higher than a similar performance deficiency associated with a non-risk-significant standard.

EMERGENCY PLAN

An organization's emergency plan is intended to be a comprehensive document that describes all of the preplanning for a radiological event made by that organization. It should describe the following:

- Emergency functions to be performed by the organization
- Essential concepts of operation for performing each identified emergency function
- Staff that will perform each identified emergency function
- Equipment, facilities, and other resources that will be maintained to ensure the capability to perform identified emergency function
- Training program to ensure that the staff can perform the identified emergency functions
- Drill and exercise program to ensure that the staff can perform the identified emergency functions
- Program for reviewing, revising, and maintaining essential program documents
- Process for reviewing the effectiveness of the overall emergency preparedness program

For power reactor licensees, the site emergency plan is both an operational and licensing document. It is operational in that it documents the essential concepts of emergency operation, response capabilities, on-shift and augmenting staff, and the available equipment and response facilities. It is a licensing document because the initial (Revision 0) emergency plan is part of the site's final safety analysis report and required approval by the Commission. The initial Commission approval was documented in a safety evaluation report. After the initial Commission approval, the emergency plan was subsequently maintained by the licensee, and compliance with its requirements was inspected by the Commission.

In the author's experience, this dichotomy of function has had a direct impact on the quality of emergency plans. The licensing aspect gives licensees an incentive to make their emergency plan as non-specific as possible because of its role in inspection and enforcement. This incentive conflicts with the plan's operational purpose of describing the essential aspects of preplanning for a radiological event, which requires a high degree of detail to be useful. Each licensee decides whether to emphasize the plan as licensing document or as operational document, often resulting in a document that has good detail in some sections and poor detail in many others. Because a licensee's original plan was approved by the Commission, the level of detail in the plan also depends on the original license reviewer. Although all emergency plans were reviewed against the NRC's standard review plan, individual reviewers had wide latitude in determining when the review plan elements were satisfied. As a result, some differences in the level of detail are due simply to individual preferences as they played out during the licensing process, some reviewers having required more detail than did others.

Appendix E to 10 CFR 50, Part III, states, in part, "The plans shall be an expression of the overall concept of operation; they shall describe the essential elements of advance planning that have been considered and the provisions that have been made to cope with emergency situations ... information shall be sufficient to provide assurance of coordination among the supporting groups and the licensee." In the author's opinion, these words indicate that the Commission intended the plans to be primarily oriented toward response operations. Experience seems to show that, as a group, licensees do not understand this. A case can be made that Part III implies that no part of the licensee's emergency preparedness program can be independent of the emergency plan. Stated another way, licensees could be found in violation of this requirement if they have any emergency preparedness capability that would be routinely relied upon in an emergency but is not explicitly described in the emergency plan. The licensee cannot segregate the "plan-described" and the "maintained but not described" elements of their response program to manage or limit their regulatory exposure.

The emergency plan describes the functions the emergency response organization is capable of, the methods used to accomplish those functions, the facilities and equipment provided to accomplish those functions, and the supporting network the licensee can call upon as needed. It also includes some supporting documents that are required by Appendix E to 10 CFR 50, Part IV, such as the current evacuation time estimate and the on-shift staffing analysis that were required to be performed by December 2012, whether or not those documents are physically attached to the plan document or are separately maintained. It is not intended to include the very detailed information necessary for implementation, particularly phone lists, physical or electronic address or distribution lists, rosters, and kit or facility inventory lists. Most information in the emergency plan should not be subject to frequent or continuous revision; any information in this category found in the plan should probably be considered for relocation into a procedure, checklist, or other document.[*]

EMERGENCY PLAN IMPLEMENTING PROCEDURES

The emergency plan is intended to describe the planning effort, the background and technical justification for the choices made by the originating organization, the commitments, and the program requirements that define an emergency preparedness program. The plan does not provide the instructions for accomplishing those tasks. The specific sequences of actions for accomplishing a task, function, or goal, are found in implementing procedures. The original vision of the authors of 10 CFR 50.47, Appendix E to Part 50, and NUREG-0654 was that each program element described in the emergency plan would have one or more associated implementing procedures to provide specific directions for implementing that element. The procedures were understood as being distinct from the plan and were intended not to duplicate information found in the plan, which is why 10 CFR 50.54(q) only applies to the emergency plan.

In the author's experience, the line between the emergency plan and emergency plan implementing procedures has become blurred over the years, so current procedures often contain background, planning, and commitment information that is supposed to be in the plan. This situation was largely a result of the licensee's desire to minimize their regulatory exposure.[†] Licensees were concerned about regulatory exposure because a failure to follow the emergency plan may result in Commission enforcement; however, a failure to follow a procedure generally does not. An exception would be when the plan includes a self-imposed requirement for procedure adherence, a commitment to an external standard requiring compliance, or the failure to follow procedure diminishes the licensee's ability to implement the plan. It was in the licensee's interest to move as much information as the Commission allowed out of the emergency plan and into procedures.

---

[*] Individual data such as phone numbers and physical or electronic addresses would not normally be subject to the requirements of 10 CFR 50.54(q)(3) and 50.54(q)(4), although deleting phone numbers or discontinuing the electronic distribution of information to a particular agency would have to be reviewed for its effect on the program. Inventory check sheets for emergency kits or facilities may be subject to 10 CFR 50.54(q)(3) and 50.54(q)(4), because the deletion of previously dedicated equipment could affect the ability to perform an emergency function.

[†] One might wonder whether Commission staff contributed to the level-of-detail confusion because they allowed details to be relocated. Recall that Section IV of Appendix E to 10 CFR 50 states, in part, "The ... emergency plan shall contain ... information needed to demonstrate compliance with the elements set forth below ... [and] shall contain information needed to demonstrate compliance with the standards described in §50.47(b)." The case can be made that although relocating licensing basis and other commitment information does not reduce the effectiveness of the emergency plan, relocating such information does create a noncompliance with the quoted text from Appendix E, Section IV. This noncompliance was either not recognized at the time or was considered to be of minor significance by Commission staff.

The Commission did eventually recognize that licensee emergency plans were declining in both quality and utility. The current regulatory understanding of an *emergency plan* includes not only the plan as a stand-alone document but also any other document that contains the information or material that is required to be in the plan (and has been relocated). Because of the expanded definition of the emergency plan, some licensees have created another tier of documents below that of "implementing procedure." These are often referred to by site-specific titles such as *position information documents* or *emergency response organization job-aids*. These lower tier documents are excluded from the change review process and essentially function as pure checklists or instructions.

SELF-IMPOSED STANDARDS

Licensees need to define performance criteria for elements of their emergency preparedness program that are not required by regulation. Any performance criteria voluntarily adopted by a licensee is called a *self-imposed standard*. Examples of self-imposed standards include, but are not limited to, some contents of the site-specific final safety analysis report, NRC regulatory guides, and NUREG guidance documents to which the licensee formally commits; the emergency plan implementing procedures; INPO guidance; NEI guidance; ANSI standards; owner's group guidance;* vendor manuals; International Commission on Radiation Protection (ICRP) and National Commission on Radiation Protection (NCRP) guidance; and International Atomic Energy Agency (IAEA) guidance. The emergency plan should document all of the self-imposed standards that apply to the emergency preparedness program. A self-imposed standard for performing program elements required by regulation may be enforceable by the Commission.

CHANGING THE EMERGENCY PLAN

The Commission never intended for the emergency plan they initially approved to be the only plan a licensee ever had. It was anticipated from the start that circumstances would require licensee plans to be revised. Expression of this expectation is the regulation that requires licensees to conduct periodic reviews of the plan to ensure its continuing adequacy, performed at least annually. The plan may require updating because of plant modifications, equipment and instrument replacement, new analytical methods that are implemented, changes among offsite organizations, or as a result of drill and exercise experience. Because the number and kinds of possible changes were unpredictable, the Commission did not want to go through a formal licensing review-and-approval process for every change. Licensees generally refer to their document change process as the *50.54(q) process*, because this is the regulation that authorizes licensees to make changes to the plan and provides the acceptance criteria, and because prior to November 2011 10 CFR 50.54(q) was a single paragraph, not broken into its current subparagraphs, (1) through (5).

A two-tier approach was designed in which changes that potentially affect the planning basis are required to be approved by the Commission through the licensing process, and all other changes are implemented by the licensee and subsequently reviewed through inspection. The burden of deciding which changes affect the planning basis is placed on the licensee, who must determine whether a proposed change reduces the effectiveness of the plan by applying the criteria in 10 CFR 50.54(q). Placing this burden on the licensee, which includes a degree of regulatory risk, is intended to discourage licensees from making unnecessary changes. The Commission expects industry to take a deliberative, cautious, and conservative approach to changing their programs. The general industry assumption from the 1980s through the present day has been that reductions in effectiveness

---

* An owner's group exists for each reactor technology type: pressurized water reactors (Westinghouse, Combustion Engineering, Babcox-Wilcox, etc.) and boiling water reactors (General Electric). The reactor vendors and associated owner's groups distribute technology-specific operating experience and guidance.

(affecting the planning basis) would not be approved by the Commission; therefore, very few licensees have requested prior approval for such changes. This assumption is likely too pessimistic but is so widespread and deeply held that it is unlikely to be dispelled.

According to 10 CFR 50.54(q),[*] licensees are authorized to make changes to their emergency plan provided that the as-changed plan continues to meet the 10 CFR 50.47(b) planning standards and the requirements of Appendix E to 10 CFR Part 50, and the change does not reduce the effectiveness[†] of the emergency plan. The regulatory definition of "reduction in effectiveness" is a change that reduces a licensee's capacity to perform an emergency planning function.[‡] The regulations implemented in 2011 explicitly added this definition to regulation where it had previously only been found in Commission guidance. Regulatory Guide 1.219 (NRC, 2011f) further explains that a capacity is reduced when the function is eliminated, resources to perform the function are reduced, or the change results in a delay in accomplishing the function as compared to when it would have been accomplished before the change. The ability to perform some functions could also be reduced by changes to the sensitivity in an instrument (e.g., substitution of a less efficient detector), changes to instrument measurement range (e.g., an instrument with a range of four decades is replaced by one with a range of three decades), changes to alarms (e.g., an alarm referenced in emergency action levels has its threshold value increased), changes to calibration methods or periodicity, and other physical changes to the plant. Resources are considered to include the number of available personnel, installed and portable equipment, sources of data including means of access, means of communications, plant and emergency plan implementing procedures, plant drawings, staff training, and work areas.[§] The concept of a "reduction in effectiveness" applies to the entire emergency plan, including site-specific commitments and self-imposed standards, not to only those parts whose contents are required by regulation. The concept also applies to modifications made to the plant or to resources counted upon to implement the emergency plan when no concurrent change is made to the emergency plan.[¶]

A proposed change is not a reduction in effectiveness when the affected emergency planning function will be performed in essentially the same time frame and at the same level of performance after the proposed change is implemented as it had been previously performed. This does not mean the function has to be performed by the same emergency response organization personnel, from the same location, or using the same resources as prior to the change. Any and all of these could be changed. A change will likely be found acceptable as long as the evaluation provides sufficient evidence to conclude that the result or outcome will be essentially the same.

A robust process for changing the emergency plan would include all of the following elements:

- Identify the proposed change at the conceptual or functional level.
- Prepare the specific proposed "as changed" language for each document that must be revised to implement the change.
- Identify the document revision and date when the current means of accomplishing the function was described; if the same information is included in multiple documents, identify the revision and date of origin for every affected document.
- Identify the emergency planning functions affected by the proposed change. A single change may affect multiple emergency planning functions; if a function cannot be identified that is affected by the change, no further analysis is required.

---

[*] After December 2011, 10 CFR 50.54(q)(2).

[†] The phrase *decrease in effectiveness* was replaced in 2011 by *reduction in effectiveness*, but the meaning is unchanged.

[‡] The Commission made several attempts to communicate to licensees the staff position on the definition of *decrease of effectiveness* and its application; see *Clarifying the Process for Making Emergency Plan Changes* (NRC, 2005a, 2011b).

[§] This is not an exhaustive or complete list of resources; other considerations may apply to specific emergency planning functions.

[¶] It could be that concurrent changes should have been made to the emergency plan or procedures but that the emergency preparedness department was unaware due to failures in the intra-licensee communication processes. It may also be the case that the existing language of the plan bounds the changes being made or is non-specific enough that no document change is needed. Also see *Effect of Plant Configuration Changes on the Emergency Plan* (NRC, 2005d).

- Identify the planning or commitment basis for the current practice, facility, method, or means.[*]
- Identify the affect of the proposed change on the timing, accuracy, or other relevant performance attribute of each identified emergency planning function. Some negative effects are likely to be found acceptable provided they are small; it would be incumbent on the licensee to define what "small" or "negligible" means in each case and to provide a justification of why that degree of impact can be disregarded.
- Identify each department or working group within the station organization affected by the proposed change and ensure that those groups review the proposed change. "Affected" means they own one or more of the documents that require revision because of the proposed change, they have special skill or expertise in the subject matter related to the proposed change, or they will be assigned tasks as part of implementing the proposed change. In some cases, offsite agencies may be affected by the proposed change, and these should be given opportunity to review and comment on the proposed change.

In the above discussion, a single performance element is assumed to change. This is often not the case with actual changes, in which a single analysis package bundles together several individual changes (i.e., for a single document revision rather than one analysis for one change). In the author's experience, bundling several changes into a single evaluation creates some vulnerability to future regulatory challenge. The vulnerabilities are that the specific sentence-by-sentence, before-and-after changes may not be analyzed and that undetected differences between the conceptual change and the actual language may actually reduce the effectiveness of the plan without the reduction being identified by the reviewer. The description of changes in bundled analyses is frequently at a high or conceptual level rather than providing a specific listing of the "as changed" text of every individual change in the revision. Sometimes this occurs because the licensee believes the analysis must be done against the concept or expected outcome rather than against the actual words; more frequently, it is done because including all of the text in a substantially changed document makes the package too thick to review. Functional checklists in the review package are marked to indicate the 10 CFR 50.47(b) planning standards or emergency planning functions affected by any of the proposed changes; however, often the analysis does not identify which specific change in the bundle affects which specific planning standard or function. The result is that the package may not provide evidence that the actual text was reviewed, and a more detailed review may identify changes that are unacceptable.[†]

Licensees perform their 50.54(q) regulatory reviews using standard checklists that typically list all of the planning standards and many of the elements in Appendix E to 10 CFR Part 50. One potential issue in performing a good regulatory analysis is whether the licensee's checklist is complete in its list of emergency planning functions. Licensee checklists tend to be adequate in their listing of requirements derived from regulation. However, in the author's experience, the checklists may not prompt the reviewer to review against the current Commission-approved plan revision, against commitments, or against site-specific program elements. The checklist may also fail to direct the reviewer to use the licensing basis to establish why the function that is proposed to be changed was implemented.

Note that for more than 30 years there was no regulatory requirement to perform a regulatory analysis prior to implementing a change to the emergency plan; a licensee was simply required not to implement an unacceptable change. An explicit analysis requirement became effective in 2012.

---

[*] When changes are made to means and methods that have been in place a long time (since Revision 0 of the plan), it may not be possible to identify the original planning basis. Records may not be available or they may not be complete enough to reconstruct the original reasoning. When this occurs, licensees ought not be dissuaded from making changes as necessary; it can be acceptable to acknowledge a lack of detailed historical information and records. When there is insufficient original information, the licensee should document their best guess as to the basis for what the "before changes" means.

[†] Some unacceptable changes that may be difficult to identify have to do with the deletion or inclusion of words such as *or, and, could,* or *may* or with unit changes. Changes in the area of radiation protection may confuse radiation exposure (external, in roentgens) with dose (including internal, in rem).

The impact analysis typically compares the "as proposed" change to the "as found" current condition. The inherent assumption is that the "as found" means and methods are themselves acceptable. This may not be the case if the "as found" condition is itself the cumulative result of licensee-evaluated changes to the emergency plan that did not receive Commission approval because they were determined by the licensees not to require such approval. Licensee reviewers should be aware of *revision creep* when evaluating changes under 10 CFR 50.54(q). In this context, "creep" refers to the unanalyzed cumulative effect of multiple small changes that individually appear acceptable when compared to the "as-found" plan, but which over time deviate from the approved program and therefore do require Commission approval. Licensees who do not compare a proposed change to the most recent NRC-approved plan risk the Commission determining that a change did reduce the effectiveness of the plan based on cumulative impact. Note that the most recent plan could be years or decades old. Identifying the origin (date, document, revision, purpose) of the current planning function as part of the regulatory analysis is a practice that often aids in identifying when creep has occurred; it may not be sufficient to simply review against the current document text.

Licensees often believe that it is not possible to eliminate any existing emergency response capability without prior Commission approval. It may be possible to eliminate a capability through the 50.54(q) process when

- The capability was required by a regulation that has been changed or eliminated.
- The capability was required by a regulatory guidance document to which the licensee was committed but which has been changed to no longer require that capability.
- The capability was required by a voluntary standard to which the licensee was committed but which has been changed to no longer require that capability.

When a licensee proposes to eliminate a capability, their analysis should be sufficient to demonstrate that the capability proposed to be eliminated derived only from the document that has been changed, and there are no site-specific circumstances that require maintaining the capability.

There is some advantage to reviewing all changes to implementing procedures using 10 CFR 50.54(q) from a program management perspective. It is simpler to review all changes than it is to review some changes and not review others because the practice is easier to implement, oversee, and audit. For the most part, licensees also evaluate proposed changes to administrative procedures to ensure that commitments are maintained regarding emergency response organization and staff training, program oversight, the drill program, arrangements with offsite agencies, and the alert and notification system.

The long-time industry perspective, dating back to the 1990s, is that the Commission has been inconsistent in applying 10 CFR 50.54(q) to licensees and has often applied it too harshly. In the author's opinion, the industry has primarily struggled with making changes to their emergency plans because they did not understood the basis for the as-found condition and therefore could not ensure that the function was preserved by the proposed changes. The author believes that the lack of understanding by licensees has been real. The perception of inconsistency may be a real perception but is probably inaccurate, or at least not as significant as is generally believed by licensees. The author's experience is that the Commission has generally applied the same evaluation standard to evaluating changes to emergency plans for more than 20 years. Although the form of 10 CFR 50.54(q) changed in 2011, its essential elements and concepts remained the same; the requirements on licensees were essentially the same prior to the new rule as they were after it.

Another aspect of the 2011 regulation change that affects changes to the emergency plan is the new requirement, 10 CFR 50.54(q)(4), which states that requests by licensees for prior Commission approval of changes that are determined by the licensee to be reductions in effectiveness of the plan must be submitted as requests for an amendment to the plant's operating license. Prior to this, requests for Commission approval had been submitted by letter from the licensee to the Commission requesting a licensing review. The final licensing decision was communicated to the licensee by letter from the Office of Nuclear Reactor Regulation, with the accompanying safety evaluation report. The change to a more formal process was driven by the Commission's Office of General Counsel because the emergency plan is defined in regulation as part of the plant's final safety analysis report, which is defined in regulation as part of the plant's operating license. The Commission's process for making changes to the operating license includes public notice of the proposed changes in the *Federal Register*, provision for the public to submit comments on the proposed licensing action, provision for the public to request a hearing on the proposed licensing action, and publication of the final action in the *Federal Register*. The Office of General Counsel determined that the previous process for approving changes to the emergency plan constituted a licensing action to change the operating license that did not provide for public notice or public participation. Note that, although the licensee must first determine that the proposed change is a reduction in effectiveness, the Commission staff will perform an acceptance review of the request for a license amendment and may elect not to accept a change the staff does not believe is a reduction in effectiveness. When licensees receive approval from the Commission to make changes to their emergency plans—for example, to change emergency action level schemes—they must implement what was approved without any changes.[*] If changes to the approved document are identified as being necessary, those changes should be evaluated separately using the 50.54(q) process and implemented in a separate revision (although the revisions may be implemented successively on the same day).

A longstanding requirement for licensees to submit changes to the emergency plan to the Commission within 30 days of their effective date is found in Appendix E to Part 50, Part V, dating from the early 1980s.[†] The 2011 regulation added a new requirement that licensees also submit to the Commission a summary of the associated 50.54(q) regulatory analysis within 30 days of the effective date; the summary must contain enough information for inspectors to determine whether the licensee's conclusion that a reduction in effectiveness did not occur is justified. Nothing in the requirement would prevent a licensee from voluntarily submitting their entire analysis in lieu of creating a summary.

REGULATORY MARGIN IN THE EMERGENCY PLAN

Regulatory margin is defined as the difference between the as-found function or capability and the associated regulatory requirements. From a licensee's point of view it comes into play when licensees voluntarily elect to provide for more capability than they are required to provide by regulation. The commercial nuclear power industry trade group, the Nuclear Energy Institute, argued during the rulemaking process[‡] for the 2011 final emergency preparedness rule that licensees should only have to demonstrate that an as-changed emergency plan continues to meet Commission regulations and that any change that maintained regulatory compliance *by definition* did not decrease the effectiveness of the emergency plan, regardless of its effect on their capabilities.

The Commission disagreed with the industry's position, recognizing that the industry's interpretation would have essentially removed significant portions of their emergency preparedness programs from oversight and inspection. Licensees are already required to comply with regulations, so the industry interpretation would have practically negated the existing 10 CFR 50.54(q). The Commission believes that the regulatory margin concept applies in some areas of commercial power

---

[*] Some examples have recently been identified of licensees not having completely implemented the changes that were approved in a safety evaluation report, some examples being for approvals obtained in the 1990s. Such examples could represent violations of 10 CFR 50.54(q)(4) because the changes that were implemented were not approved by the Commission.

[†] From the early 1980s through 2015, the text also stated that implementing procedures should be submitted to the Commission within 30 days of implementation. However, the Commission removed the requirement as it applied to emergency plan implementing procedures in an administrative rule change that took effect on December 31, 2015 (NRC-2015-0239, RIN 3150-AJ69).

[‡] See the NRC Rulemaking Docket 2008-0122 via the NRC website, http://www.nrc.gov/reading-rm/doc-collections/rulemaking-ruleforum/rulemaking-dockets/2008/. Comments were made during the public comment period for the draft preliminary rule and final preliminary rule.

reactor operation but largely does not apply in emergency preparedness. Returning to Appendix E to 10 CFR 50, Part III states in part, "The plans shall be an expression of the overall concept of operation; they shall *describe the essential elements of advance planning*," and Part IV states, in part, "Emergency plans shall contain, *but not necessarily be limited to*, information needed to demonstrate compliance with the elements set forth below." It is generally the Commission's view that when a licensee elects to provide additional resources, staff, emergency preparedness equipment, or other capabilities not based in regulation or associated with standards to which they are formally committed, the licensee is describing their overall concept of operations and their site-specific advance planning. The Commission views those additional capabilities as essential emergency preparedness elements that licensees have determined for themselves to be necessary for them to have an effective emergency response program. Because the additional capabilities are self-determined to be necessary to have an effective program, changes to those additional capabilities do have to be evaluated against the basis that caused the licensee to require them.

MAINTAINING THE EMERGENCY PREPAREDNESS PROGRAM

Appendix E to 10 CFR 50, Part IV.G, requires that licensees maintain their emergency plan, implementing procedures, and equipment up to date. This is done by routinely reviewing the plan as procedures are revised or created and equipment is replaced or updated to ensure that the plan accurately describes current capabilities. At a minimum, a complete plan review should be done annually, checking references, verifying agreements with offsite support agencies and vendors, and verifying the accuracy of facility and capability descriptions.

A licensee should use experience gained in the drill and exercise program to validate, simplify, clarify, and order steps in the emergency plan implementing procedures, making each procedure as complete and easy to use as possible. Procedure changes may also result from changes to the personnel, location, or equipment needed to perform the functions described in the procedures. Although there is no explicit regulatory requirement that licensees validate their emergency plan implementing procedures, planning standard 10 CFR 50.47(b)(14) states, in part, that "periodic exercises are conducted to evaluate major portions of emergency response capabilities." In the author's opinion, it is in a licensee's interest to show that a new procedure was validated in a drill or exercise within a reasonable time after implementation. There is no accepted definition of reasonable, but a good practice would be to validate a procedure within 2 years of implementation. A good practice would be to validate all of the current emergency plan implementing procedures over an exercise cycle (currently, over 8 years) to ensure that nothing has changed that would prevent implementation.

Some licensee emergency plans include statements that drills and exercises are conducted to ensure the adequacy of procedures or to maintain the emergency response organization's familiarity with procedures. It is recommended that these licensees define the periodicity in which the procedures are tested and maintain records that show how the commitment is met. That is, they should be able to identify the procedures the requirement applies to, and for each procedure they should document the drill or exercise in which the procedure was used.

Other activities that contribute to maintaining the emergency preparedness program include after-action reports from events,* drill and exercise self-critiques, critiques of the emergency preparedness training program by trainees and site management, periodic facility surveillances, internal audits, internal and external assessments, and visits to other licensees to compare specific program elements (called *benchmarking*).

---

* Most licensees only prepare a formal evaluation report following a declared emergency. Note that the preferred term is becoming *after action report*, taken from the Homeland Security Exercise Evaluation Program (HSEEP). Licensees should also consider preparing after action reports following "near misses" in which senior reactor operators evaluate plant or owner-controlled area conditions against the emergency action levels and determine that classification is not warranted. Current practices would generally not self-identify situations in which the senior reactor operator inappropriately fails to classify an emergency condition that exists.

Some elements of the emergency preparedness program are established by engineering calculations. These include detector efficiencies; instrument alarm thresholds; flows, temperatures, and pressures that render structures and components inoperable; source term reduction factors in containment; and many default values used in radiological assessment. It would be beneficial to a licensee to maintain a list of program parameters and their associated calculations, including revisions and dates. Where only a portion of a calculation applies, this should be identified. A mechanism should exist to inform the emergency preparedness program when any calculation is revised that affects a program parameter, ensuring that the change is appropriately evaluated for its effect on emergency plan functions and any necessary conforming change is made. This evaluation should be done within a reasonable period following the calculation revision. A good practice would be to periodically review engineering calculations to ensure that the most current analytical methods have been used. In this context, the most current methods are ones that model reality more accurately than does the existing calculation. It is the author's opinion that it is currently unclear whether 10 CFR 50, Appendix E, Part IV.G, requires that a licensee committed to a particular calculation (and revision) as part of its licensing basis must make a conforming change whenever that calculation is revised.

AUDITS OF THE EMERGENCY PREPAREDNESS PROGRAM

A licensee is required to periodically perform an independent review (audit) of the emergency preparedness program, meaning the auditors do not report to the same senior executive as does the emergency preparedness department. The licensee has the option to either perform annual audits or to perform audits every 24 months with certain restrictions. A licensee must select one option, 10 CFR 50.54(t)(1)(i) or 10 CFR 50.54(t)(1)(ii); they cannot implement both simultaneously.* Whatever audit requirement is selected, it should be unambiguously documented in the site emergency plan and in applicable procedures. In either case, each audit must review at least the drill and exercise program, emergency preparedness department procedures (including, but not limited to, the emergency plan implementing procedures), the emergency response functions, and the capabilities to which the licensee is committed, in addition to evaluating the interface between the licensee and offsite authorities. Some licensees take the position that auditors are not independent if they are part of the emergency response organization; in the author's opinion, this is an unnecessarily restrictive requirement, in that individual emergency response organization members are not responsible for implementing the overall emergency preparedness program.

The annual audit option (10 CFR 50.54(t)(1)(i)) is simple to implement in that the audit is conducted routinely at about 11- to 12-month intervals. Evaluations are not needed to determine whether an audit is warranted, and no specific program monitoring activities are required between audits. The 24-month option (10 CFR 50.54(t)(1)(ii)) is more complex to implement because the additional year between formal audits is permitted only if the licensee can show that the program health has not degraded using an appropriate performance indicator scheme.† An audit is also required following a major change in the program, specifically to site personnel, procedures, equipment, or facilities; the review criteria should be sufficient to distinguish between minor changes and major ones. When the need for an additional for-cause audit is identified, it is required to be completed within 12 months of identifying the need.

---

* It is not acceptable for the emergency plan to state that the organization will perform annual audits (10 CFR 50.54(t)(1) (i)) unless a 12-month review shows that an extension to two years is acceptable (10 CFR 50.54(t)(1)(ii)). In this case, the 12-month review does not employ performance indicators or have established decision criteria.

† The decision whether or not to conduct a for-cause audit cannot be made solely on a subjective basis, the skill of the craft of the auditing organization, or only on management discretion. A licensee that does not have any measurable, objective criteria has not properly implemented 10 CFR 50.54(t)(1)(ii).

There is no Commission guidance to inform the implementation of an adequate performance indicator scheme. The intent is that the licensee must identify those attributes, tasks, and other measurable qualities associated with the emergency preparedness program that provide insight into program quality and health. They may incorporate the existing performance indicators reported to the Commission* as a part of their scheme, but they may not rely solely upon these indicators, as the Commission did not design them as comprehensive measures of program effectiveness. Licensees may include any additional indicators reported to the INPO or to any other internal or external group. There may also be site-specific indicators that measure specific attributes that are unique to the licensee's program.

Wherever possible, a performance indicator should lead program performance rather than follow it. That is, the selected indicator should tend to move from the acceptable performance band into the unacceptable performance band faster than does the overall program. When an indicator is generally predictive, necessary audits will be performed before the overall program becomes unacceptable, and corrective actions will be identified that may prevent the overall program from becoming unacceptable. When indicators lag the overall program health, there can only be corrective actions to recover the program; prevention becomes impossible. As a group, the performance indicators should measure enough aspects of the licensee program to form a reasonable basis for making the "audit/don't audit" decision. It is recommended that licensees have a basis document that justifies why the selected performance indicator scheme is sufficiently comprehensive to reliably measure the health of the emergency preparedness program. The site quality assurance department is not required to maintain the performance indicators, but the final selection of indicators should be an auditing decision, not one made by the emergency preparedness department, because it is quality assurance that will decide whether a for-cause audit is necessary.

An adequate performance indicator scheme has several attributes, without which its power of measurement is either reduced or compromised; these include the following:

- Definitions of the quantities to be measured, including all calculations as applicable
- Defined acceptable and unacceptable performance bands for individual indicators
- Defined data collection and reporting periods
- Defined reporting mechanisms and analysis periods

The individual performance bands should be chosen such that any result outside of the chosen range indicates that an audit is needed; some indicators may require both an out-of-band high and out-of-band low value, depending on the parameter they measure, similar to an instrument control chart. In addition, collective decision criteria should be developed for situations in which no single indicator is outside its control band, but the overall set of indicators collectively shows an audit is necessary.

The licensee should establish a review periodicity that ensures that adverse trends are identified in time to take corrective action. Quarterly or triennial reviews are effective in this; semiannual reviews may be acceptable but are not as desirable. Given that it takes some time to schedule, plan, resource, and initiate an audit after identifying the need, too long a review period could cause a licensee to not meet the 12-month for-cause requirement. In any case, the licensee should clearly document when the program is reviewed, whether or not it is decided to audit, and the basis for the decision. The documentation should include the performance indicator data that were considered, along with any other measures of program health that were considered.

Every audit must include an evaluation of the effectiveness of coordination between the site emergency preparedness program and offsite programs. This requirement is intended to detect issues of concern to offsite officials that have not been appropriately recognized or handled by the emergency preparedness staff and could degrade the integrated ability to protect the health and safety of the

---

* These are drill and exercise performance, emergency response organization participation, and alert and notification system reliability.

public. This review function is assigned to the independent auditors because offsite officials may be reluctant to identify issues to the licensee emergency preparedness staff if the officials feel their concerns are not being taken seriously.* The evaluation requires contact between the auditors and offsite representatives; the actual contact can be in person, by telephone, by questionnaire, or any other means that ensures the offsite representatives the opportunity to express their opinion of coordination with the licensees. Any offsite response agency relied upon to perform emergency functions in support of the licensee (i.e., those described in the emergency plan) should be considered for this evaluation; the audit should not be limited to only local and state governments. The minimum set of agencies (100% contact is required) whose coordination should be evaluated includes senior emergency management officials from each county or parish in the plume phase emergency planning zone, the senior elected governmental official in each county or parish (e.g., county judge, county commissioner), senior officials in the state emergency management agency (including tribes, as applicable, and each state where the planning zone crosses state boundaries), and senior officials in the state agency responsible for licensing radioactive material (generally either the public health agency or the environmental quality agency). The author suggests that, as a best practice, auditors should also sample from among senior officials of local and state law enforcement agencies (e.g., county sheriffs, state patrol commanders), local hospital directors, executives of ambulance services, the superintendents of local school districts, officials of nearby state parks (as applicable), representatives of the American Red Cross or Salvation Army or other private disaster services organizations, and officials of the Radio Amateur Civil Emergency Service (RACES) or other private radio organizations, among others. Although coordination issues between offsite emergency management or radiation control agencies and the licensee will generally have the largest impact on the licensee's emergency preparedness program, undetected issues with other agencies or organizations also degrade the effectiveness of the program and should be corrected. The audit report should specify which offsite agencies were contacted and generally describe their responses.

It is a good practice for audit teams to include subject matter experts in emergency preparedness in addition to qualified auditors, although it is not acceptable to employ staff from the department being audited. Most licensees routinely include one or two peer evaluators on each audit team, the peer being an emergency preparedness staff member at another licensee. When a licensee is part of a fleet, emergency preparedness staff from other fleet sites may be used as subject matter experts, although it would be beneficial to the organization to at least periodically use peers from outside of the fleet. Another good practice would be to include a peer from an offsite agency on the audit team (e.g., state or county emergency management agency, state radiation source control agency); this practice brings a unique point of view to the audit and further educates the offsite peer about the licensee.

Licensees have established qualification programs for lead auditors and auditors, generally focused on their auditing proficiency. Effective auditors also require sufficient knowledge and training in emergency preparedness so they recognize important issues and avoid insignificant, irrelevant, or unfocused issues. Although many licensees provide auditors with some subject-area proficiency, this is often informal, poorly documented, and not driven by site procedures. The required level of actual proficiency varies greatly among licensees. There is also no uniformity with regard to periodic refresher training. Although an auditor need not have the same proficiency as an emergency preparedness staff member, they do need to have more knowledge about emergency preparedness programs than do most emergency response organization members.†

---

* This should not be taken to imply that it is the licensee's responsibility to resolve every issue of concern to every offsite official. It may not be within the licensee's legal, financial, or organizational ability to address some issues, and licensee management may choose not to address some concerns. However, the licensee should be aware of the issues of concern to offsite officials and address those that immediately and directly affect the onsite or offsite ability to protect the public from a radiological emergency.

† Although licensees should generally be wary of adopting Commission documents and processes for internal use, some elements of the *Inspection Manual*, Chapter 1245, training program for emergency preparedness inspectors might be useful in developing training topics.

Commission regulations require that each offsite agency contacted as part of an audit be informed of the audit results, in at least the area of coordination with the licensee—this means the overall audit results and not solely that organization's comments and the licensee response. The licensee should clearly document the provision of audit results to offsite agencies, in a memo to file, minutes of a regularly schedule coordination meeting, a letter to each participant, or by some other readily retrievable means. It would be a good practice to inform all offsite agencies supporting a licensee of the audit results, not limiting the information to those agencies contacted by the auditor.

INSPECTIONS

The NRC ensures that licensees maintain an emergency preparedness program that meets Commission regulations and applicable self-imposed standards through the inspection process. An inspection is the direct evaluation of licensee performance, practices, or documents by a qualified Commission inspector. Most inspections are performed at licensee facilities, although some activities performed at Commission offices can be counted as inspections. In general, Commission staff at the Rockville, MD, headquarters are responsible for licensing actions and program management, while staff at the four regional offices—King of Prussia, PA; Atlanta, GA; Lisle, IL; and Arlington, TX—are responsible for inspections at licensee facilities. All emergency preparedness inspections are documented in inspection reports that are on the licensee's docket and made available to the public.

The baseline inspection program consists of the normally assigned inspection procedures, inspection hours, and inspection samples; this level of effort is the same for all licensees and is the minimum allowed by the program.* For emergency preparedness, the baseline inspection procedures are numbered 71114.*xx* and currently consist of the following:

- 01, "Exercise Evaluation," at a nominal 64 inspection hours
- 02, "Alert and Notification System Testing," at a nominal 6 inspection hours
- 03, "Emergency Response Organization Staffing and Augmentation System," at a nominal 8 inspection hours
- 04, "Emergency Action Level and Emergency Plan Changes," at a nominal 16 inspection hours
- 05, "Maintenance of Emergency Preparedness," at a nominal 12 inspection hours
- 06, "Drill Evaluation," at a nominal 15 inspection hours
- 07, "Exercise Evaluation—Hostile Action Event," at a nominal 88 inspection hours
- 08, "Exercise Evaluation—Scenario Review," at a nominal 14 inspection hours

Inspection procedures 71114.01, 71114.02, 71114.03, 71114.05, and 71114.08 are performed every 2 years; once per exercise cycle (one in four exercises), procedure 71114.07 is substituted for procedure 71114.01. The normal practice is to perform procedures 71114.01/71114.07 and 71114.08 together in one year and perform procedures 71114.02, 71114.03, and 71114.05 together in the alternate year. In rare cases, the 71114.08 procedure could be performed in the same year as the 71114.02, etc., procedures if the associated exercise was scheduled for January or February of the following year. The 71114.08 procedure is performed at Commission offices using information submitted to the Commission by the licensee as required by Appendix E to Part 50, Part IV.F(2)(b). Inspection procedures 71114.04 and 71114.06 are annual procedures. The 71114.04 procedure is generally performed by region-based inspectors and can be done at Commission offices, the licensee's location, or a combination of both;† the 71114.06 procedure is generally performed by the resident inspectors permanently assigned to the reactor site and can only be performed onsite.

---

* This assumes that inspectable activities occur. If no exercise is conducted or no changes made to the emergency plan in a given year, then the inspection procedure is not used.

† Procedure 71114.04 is performed only when the licensee makes emergency plan, emergency action level, or emergency plan implementing procedure changes that meet entry criteria for the procedure.

A *sample* is a specific inspection activity required by an inspection procedure, which meets the procedure completion criteria. Inspection procedures 71114.01, 71114.02, 71114.03, 71114.05, 71114.07, and 71114.08 have one associated sample; that is, either the procedure has been completed or it has not. The inspection activities that count toward a sample are primarily performed at the licensee's location, although some activities may be performed at Commission offices.[*] Procedure 71114.04 is required to have at least one sample per year but may have more, depending on the number of licensee documents reviewed during the inspection period. Inspection procedure 71114.06 requires three samples, one of which must be observation of a licensee exercise and one of which must be observation of the demonstration of emergency preparedness activities by licensed reactor operators during training scenarios on the plant-specific simulator.

Inspection procedure 71114.01/71114.07 is typically performed by a team of three to five inspectors. The major activity is direct observation of participant actions and activities in several emergency response facilities. These observations are supplemented and informed by reviewing applicable licensee procedures, documents generated during the exercise (e.g., personnel logs, checklists, briefing records), corrective action program entries, and recent drill and exercise evaluation reports. The inspectors observe the immediate post-exercise critique sessions in the emergency response facilities to understand the performance and program issues that are self-identified by the participants, and they observe the licensee's briefing to site executives regarding the preliminary exercise results.[†] The Commission expects that the licensees will identify at all exercise performance issues that warrant designation as a weakness; the procedure identifies this as completing the critique process. Weaknesses are generally human performance issues in which the participants inadequately implement an otherwise adequate procedure or process. It is not acceptable to limit discussion to only those weaknesses associated with emergency classification, notification to offsite authorities, radiological assessment, and the development of protective action recommendations.

Inspection procedures 71114.02, 71114.03, and 71114.05 are typically performed together by a single inspector. The major activities are reviews of licensee records and documents as described in the inspection procedures, supplemented by the direct observation of program activities, facility walk-throughs, small-scale demonstrations or task drills, and interviews with subject-matter experts and other licensee staff. This inspection focuses on the licensee's ability to identify and correct problems with emergency warning systems, the licensee's ability to staff emergency facilities, the material condition of emergency facilities, emergency response organization procedures and training, and human performance during drills and exercises. The inspector may observe siren or augmentation/callout system tests, emergency response organization training, facility inventories, communication checks, the inspection or operation of emergency response facility diesel generators, or emergency preparedness drills, if any happen to occur during the onsite inspection period.

The risk-significant planning standards are used to prioritize resources and guide sampling during inspections. In the 71114.01 procedure, inspectors are to directly observe the risk-significant activities, which generally means at the simulator control room and emergency operations facility, and inspectors are assigned to observe other exercise activities as resources and time allow. There is some emphasis on emergency worker protection being more important than other "non-risk-significant" functions, but collectively direct observation of the performance in all non-risk-significant areas has less priority. In the 71114.04 procedure, inspectors are to review essentially all emergency

---

[*] This primarily applies to inspection procedures 71114.04 and 71114.08.

[†] The briefing to site management described in inspection procedure 71114.01 was not routinely done by licensees when this procedure was implemented in 2000. Some licensees subsequently added this briefing to their normal post-exercise processes, but most did not. Most licensees only conduct this briefing after biennial exercises when NRC inspectors are onsite. The Commission cannot impose regulatory requirements through their inspection procedures; therefore, a licensee cannot be required to conduct this briefing. A licensee could elect not to brief management and send the Commission the completed evaluation report. It could be argued that this expectation on the part of the Commission distorts the evaluation process in that a licensee cannot be reasonably expected to identify all performance issues warranting entry into the corrective action program 2 to 3 days after the exercise.

plan and procedure changes associated with classification, notification, radiological assessment, and protective action recommendations, and they select a sample from among changes associated with the other standards; if time or resources are not sufficient to support additional sampling, then no changes will be reviewed in these other areas.* In the 71114.05 procedure, inspectors are to review all after-action reports for actual events. They also review all corrective action program issues associated with classification, notification, radiological assessment, and protective action recommendations and complete their corrective action program sample from the remaining issues. In the author's experience, a practical sample size is 20 to 30 corrective action reports.

The Commission also conducts supplemental or reactive inspections, which are not part of the routine baseline program. These inspections are conducted following significant plant events or to verify the adequacy of corrective actions following significant enforcement actions. The supplemental inspections that focus on a single licensee program are conducted using supplemental inspection procedures 95001 and 95002. An inspection using procedure 95001 is typically conducted following a single enforcement action for a finding of low-to-moderate safety significance; this is most often conducted by one inspector and verifies that the licensee's root cause analysis is adequate, the corrective actions (and planned future actions) align with the identified causes, and corrective actions will likely prevent recurrence of the same or similar issues. This inspection relies upon the licensee's data and analysis and focuses on internal consistency and completeness. An inspection using procedure 95002 is typically conducted when there are two or more findings of low to moderate safety significance in the same functional area or a single finding of substantial safety significance. This inspection is typically conducted by teams of two to five inspectors, led by a senior inspector. It verifies the attributes of the root cause analysis, as does the 95001 procedure, and inspectors also perform independent inspection to validate data and assumptions used in the root cause analysis. The inspectors also review both the *extent of condition* and *extent of cause analyses*[†] and may perform additional inspections to verify adequacy in the areas.

CRITIQUE PROCESS FOR DRILLS AND EXERCISES

The terms *weakness* and *deficiency* are often used interchangeably in emergency preparedness to refer to an unacceptable level of performance. Although they have similar meanings, weaknesses generally describe human performance issues, and deficiencies generally denote equipment and process problems, including inadequate procedures. A *weakness* is defined in Section 2.0(l) of the *Inspection Manual*, Chapter 0609, Appendix B, "Emergency Preparedness Significance Determination Process" (dated September 22, 2015), as performance during a drill or exercise that would have precluded effective implementation of the emergency plan had the events actually occurred. A *critique* is defined in Section 2.0(m) as a formal licensee assessment that identifies weaknesses and enters them into a corrective action system. The phrase "precluded effective implementation of the emergency plan" generally refers to degraded or deficient performance in at least one of the primary emergency functions.[‡]

---

* Experience to date indicates that there are sufficient inspection hours assigned to allow a review of virtually all changes submitted by licensees, so this restriction has been more theoretical than practical.

† *Extent of condition* refers to efforts to discover other areas of the licensee's program that have the same or similar deficient condition. After root and contributing causes have been identified, *extent of cause* refers to efforts to discover other areas of the licensee's program in which the same causes could create deficient conditions; the causal conditions may be similar to the original deficiency or could be dissimilar. A *root cause* is an underlying condition whose correction would have prevented the actual deficient condition from existing or occurring. A *contributing cause* is an underlying condition whose correction would not have prevented the actual deficient condition, but its existence increased the effect or severity of the actual condition. A *deficient condition* could be actual malfunctions of equipment, the physical state of equipment that led to that equipment being vulnerable to malfunction, inadequate procedures or processes or training, a lack of work standards or work controls, or any other physical or administrative state that does not meet Commission regulations or licensee self-imposed standards.

‡ See the discussion and list on p. 29 of *Interim Staff Guidance: Emergency Planning for Nuclear Power Plants* (NRC, 2011g).

Although planning standard 10 CFR 50.47(b)(14) has existed since the early 1980s, the Commission did not begin emphasizing the self-identification of weaknesses and deficiencies until introduction of the reactor oversight program in 2000. This was true even after the introduction of corrective action programs in the mid-1990s. The primary element of the Commission's exercise inspection program in the 1980s and 1990s was direct performance observation; at that time, inspectors identified performance issues using essentially the same performance standard as is currently employed, but without consideration of whether the licensee also identified the issue. In the author's experience, corrective actions for exercise performance at that time were largely driven by whether Commission inspectors documented an exercise weakness, not by whether the issue truly was a weakness. Weaknesses that were not documented in inspection reports rarely received formal corrective action. A licensee had to demonstrate that the inspector-identified weakness had been corrected during the next exercise (annual or biennial, depending on the year). Internal licensee evaluation reports did not identify problems as weaknesses and generally did not discuss corrective actions, and inspectors did not review licensee evaluation or after-action reports to identify recurring problems. Prior to 2000, failure-to-critique and failure-to-correct violations of 10 CFR 50.47(b)(14) were very rare. The current inspection process essentially reverses the earlier process in that inspectors now document performance problems only when the licensee does not identify them.

The current critique process for drills and exercises generally consists of an immediate post-exercise debrief between the participants and facility controllers[*] (also called a *hot wash*), a post-exercise review of performance and performance objectives by evaluators in each participating facility, an integrated cross-facility review by the group of lead facility evaluators, a meeting with senior management to review the preliminary exercise evaluation, and preparation of a post-exercise after-action report. The corrective action program entries are prepared after the lead evaluator meeting but before the after-action report is written. The meeting with management must discuss at least the drill and exercise performance indicator results, the weaknesses and deficiencies that occurred, and the corrective action program entries that were or will be made. Most licensees also discuss the scoring of exercise objectives, the most important improvement items identified, any scenario implementation issues, and any exercise control issues, and they briefly comment on the performance in each participating facility.

The reactor oversight program assumes that the drill evaluation team will present their preliminary conclusions to site management within a few days of the exercise, giving senior managers an opportunity to discuss the performance. This is intended to give organizational visibility to the drill and exercise program and provide an independent check on the preliminary significance evaluation. Experience shows that managers will often question the evaluator's conclusions and are more likely to increase the significance of issues rather than decrease them. The meeting with management is considered the endpoint of evaluation after which no additional changes are expected. To be considered as critiqued, a performance issue must be both identified and assigned the appropriate significance. Inspectors are generally free to discuss the weaknesses they observed during the drill or exercise following the management meeting.

The post-exercise meeting with senior management was a new element in the reactor oversight program, something that licensees were not doing prior to 2000. One could argue this is an example of regulation through inspection procedure because it introduced an expectation outside of regulations, although the meeting does have advantages for both licensees and inspectors. The fact that essentially all licensees immediately began holding these meetings, without any noticeable protest, does not mean that the Commission did not effectively impose a new requirement. Some licensees continue to only conduct the management meeting for biennial exercises and not for their routine drills and exercises.

---

[*] For this discussion, controllers include controllers, emergency preparedness evaluators, quality assurance or nuclear oversight evaluators, management observers, etc. Most sites do not have sufficient staff to have completely independent drill (exercise) controllers and evaluators; generally, the same individuals perform both functions.

Inspection of a licensee's critique following a biennial exercise* is unlike other Commission activities in that inspectors are constrained from discussing observed performance weaknesses until the critique process is complete. The constraint is intended to prevent confusion over whether weak performance was, or was not, evaluated by the licensee. The critique process is complete when the licensee has identified all the issues requiring corrective action[†] and there will be no subsequent reviews or changes. The anticipated corrective action program entries do not have to be written at the end of the process but there does need to be assurance they will be made rapidly (i.e., within a few days).

A critique is successful when all of the weaknesses that occurred during an exercise are identified and entered into the corrective action program. In practice, it is difficult to discern after the fact those weakness that were not identified by the exercise evaluation team; this usually requires an in-depth analysis of all exercise logs and associated procedures, forms, checklists, analyses, worksheets, etc. For an evaluated biennial exercise, the working definition of success is that the licensee identifies all weaknesses identified by the inspection team. The inspection program assumes that the licensee's evaluation team and the Commission's inspection team together will identify all weaknesses that occurred. Any weakness identified by the inspection team that is not identified by the licensee is a finding against 10 CFR 50.47(b)(14). The performance deficiency is not because of the poor performance of the emergency response organization during the exercise; rather, the deficiency is the result of the lack of a thorough and complete evaluation by the licensee's team of evaluators. Because the licensee has many more evaluators than does the Commission, the implication when inspectors find weaknesses not found by the licensee is that the licensee's evaluation process may be sufficiently flawed that it fails to identify weaknesses that occur in those exercises not observed by the Commission. Although the Commission generally accepts an error rate of as much as 10%, there should be enough licensee evaluators and enough duplication of observation to preclude an error at the level of a weakness by the collective group of evaluators. The potential flaws could include too few evaluators, a lack of subject-matter experts in evaluator positions, inexperienced plant staff assigned as evaluators, a lack of evaluator training, or over-familiarity with the program (leading to a failure to question long-standing practices that may be inadequate).

The finding is intended to focus licensee attention on their evaluation process and result in corrective actions to improve the likelihood that licensee evaluators will identify weaknesses in the future. Such an issue is always of more than minor significance because it affects the cornerstone objective— a weakness (i.e., performance at the level of a deficient or degraded emergency function) by definition affects the licensee's ability to take adequate measures to protect the health and safety of the public.

The discernment of weaknesses from less significant performance issues requires a degree of experience and professional judgment, and competent observers may disagree about whether a specific performance meets the weakness threshold. One would like to think that all observers would agree that the observed performance was not in accordance with expectations or requirements. There is probably no way to eliminate subjectivity and judgment from this kind of evaluation or to ensure that all observers come to the same conclusion on significance. The first criterion that must be met is that the participant's actions affected a significant emergency preparedness function; otherwise, a weakness cannot exist. The second criterion is that the scenario allowed the emergency preparedness function to be demonstrated or that the participant had control over whether the function could be demonstrated. The third criterion is that the function was not demonstrated during the exercise when it could or should have been, or it was demonstrated in a deficient manner.

A deficient manner might mean significant delays in performing the function until long after it was needed, a failure to completely perform the function that affected other responders or other facilities or offsite authorities, performing the function based on wrong assumptions or inputs, or inaccurate results that result in incorrect decisions by other responders. A deficient manner does

---

* This discussion also applies to the critique of licensed operator training scenarios, licensee drills, or licensee exercises other than biennial exercises that are observed by resident inspectors under procedure 71114.06.
† By definition, performance that does not rise to the level of a weakness does not require corrective action.

not refer to timing issues of no consequence, failures to circle or slash the procedure or initial the checklist, incomplete performance having no additional impact, or minor mistakes in calculation or noncompliance with procedures that do not change any subsequent action or decision. Another criterion to be considered is whether any reasonable or effective corrective action is possible to correct the observed poor performance; performance that is truly a weakness is likely to require more than brief individual coaching to correct. Evaluators may also apply an operating experience test: If the error was such that other emergency response organization members holding the same position as the poorly performing individual would clearly benefit from being warned about the error, then the performance likely was at the level of a weakness.

Some licensees create omnibus corrective action program entries following drills and exercises, in which a single entry covers all issues identified in a single response facility or all issues from the exercise. This is not a good practice; instead, it is better to document each weakness individually in a separate corrective action program entry. A good practice is identifying the issue as a "weakness requiring corrective action in accordance with 10 CFR 50.47(b)(14)" in the corrective action program statement or using other language having the same meaning. Experience suggests that when multiple performance issues are documented in a single corrective action entry the assigned corrective action significance level may not reflect the importance of all of the issues (i.e., the level may be lower than the issue would be assigned if treated separately, possibly leading to a failure to correct a condition requiring correction), the assigned corrective actions may not reflect all of the issues in the problem statement (i.e., corrective action may be incomplete), and the entry may be closed without action having been taken for every listed performance issue (again, incomplete action). Omnibus entries also reduce the licensee's ability to track and trend performance, as assigned keywords and trending codes may not cover all of the listed problems, and there is no clear connection between such codes and any individual performance issue.

The value of having the problem statement identifying the issue as a weakness is to provide another barrier to closing the issue to track and trend or to no action; the same identification should be present in the after-action report for the same reason. Omnibus corrective action program entries also create barriers to internal assessment (e.g., departmental-level assessments, audits) and external assessments (primarily by the Commission but may also include the Institute for Nuclear Power Operations and industry groups such as the Utilities Service Alliance or the Strategic Teaming and Resource Sharing [STARS] group). Barriers are created because assessments typically rely on sampling from a large population of corrective action program entries, starting from a report that gives a title or short summary of the problem statements from entries initiated over a specified range of dates—there is significant likelihood that an omnibus entry will not be selected for review when it should be selected or the assessor could expend unnecessary effort selecting all omnibus entries to ensure that no weaknesses are missed.

Inspection procedures 71114.01 and 71114.07 implicitly assume that the preliminary critique process is completed the same week as the exercise, although they cannot establish a requirement that this must occur. A licensee could elect to not conduct a post-exercise management meeting and provide the inspector their final after-action report when it is completed. The effort to expedite the management meeting is a courtesy by the licensees, one that exposes them to a certain amount of regulatory risk. There is such a large volume of exercise records to review during the evaluation phase that even a large pool of experienced evaluators is challenged to do a thorough examination in 24 to 48 hours. A short evaluation phase is even more challenging when the as-run scenario deviated significantly from the design or there were serious human performance issues (i.e., the worse the overall performance, the more time it takes to identify all of the weaknesses and look for causes). In the author's opinion, one should expect that licensees regularly fail to identify weaknesses simply because of time pressure due to such a short evaluation period.

The Commission does not require licensees to have a formal set of exercise objectives and does not inspect their content or application. The reactor oversight process does not have inspectors compare the observed performance against licensee objectives. There is no expectation that the preliminary presentation of critique results to licensee management will include a discussion of objectives that were successful, in need of improvement, or failed, although this is a common practice. A preliminary presentation that focused on objective grading would not be considered adequate if it did not also identify the specific underlying performance issues that must be corrected.

Although the discussion of drill and exercise critiques largely focuses on the biennial exercise that is directly observed by Commission inspectors, licensees should understand that the identification of weaknesses not entered into the corrective action program is not limited to evaluated activities. Inspectors perform after-the-fact reviews of drill and exercise documents and evaluations annually while validating performance indicator data, biennially as part of preparing to observe exercises (procedure 71114.01), and biennially in the alternate year as part of the inspection of correction action programs and problem identification and resolution in emergency preparedness (procedure 71114.05). Any of these reviews may reveal performance issues at the level of a weakness that were documented by licensee evaluators but not corrected.

GRADING OF EXERCISE OBJECTIVES BY PARTICIPANTS

Exercise objectives are very important to exercise design and somewhat important to exercise evaluation. Many licensees have adopted a critique process suggested by the INPO which has each response facility manager (i.e., senior participant) lead the immediate post-exercise critique and asks each facility to grade itself against the exercise objectives. Critiques using this process generally begin with a discussion of the intended timeline of events and critical decisions. The second step is discussing and grading each objective, and any other issues are discussed last. In the author's opinion, there are two problems with this approach: (1) an inherent tendency in any facility toward self-grading each objective as at least satisfactory (or the site-specific equivalent), and (2) a critique fatigue, which tends to limit the participant's collective ability to identify performance issues not associated with a specific objective. A self-grading group tends to move the critique focus away from individual performance and toward team activities. Also, groups appear to be less likely to grade objectives as failed or as performance in need of improvement when the underlying performance deficiency was the actions, or lack of actions, of a single individual.[*] Members of the participant group are rarely willing to state in public a belief that another group member failed to perform as required. The way this process is implemented at many licensees allows many individuals to be present at the critique without substantially contributing to the discussion, as they are never individually polled.

The second problem with the self-grading approach is that it tends to foster an attitude among participants that the grade counts more than the performance. That is, participants are more likely to have the perception that only graded objectives have value, making them less inclined to raise other issues. This can be a real problem if the licensee's set of objectives is poorly prepared, poorly written, or incomplete. It can also be a problem even when the licensee has a quality set of objectives if too many are not selected for evaluation (weaknesses occurring during an exercise cannot be ignored if the associated objective is not selected) or if an objective does not exist. Some licensees have very exhaustive exercise objectives that parse performance in great detail, resulting in post-exercise critiques that last as long as 2 hours; in these cases, the fatigue is physical as much as mental.

In the author's opinion, if the INPO model must be followed, the order should be revised to maintain the emphasis on individual performance. The critique leader ought to begin by asking all individuals present to discuss the strengths and deficiencies in their own personal performance. Well-trained emergency response organization members should understand their roles and responsibilities sufficiently well that they can readily discuss their actual performance against those standards without having the exercise objective to refer to. This should be done before the expected

---

[*] An additional problem is their ability to objectively critique the performance of individuals in management having the authority to adversely affect their employment.

events and results are discussed with the participants, so individuals compare their performance against the information they actually had. Informing the participants of the intended outcomes before they critique may alter their perceptions of performance and cause inaccurate comparisons to conditions they did not (perhaps, could not) know. The author believes this approach is more likely to identify actual weaknesses and deficiencies, as well as program elements in need of improvement (e.g., poor procedures, equipment issues). Each individual should be polled, giving the rest of the group a chance to agree or disagree with their comments. Only after participants have provided their own evaluations should they be informed of the intended results and asked to grade the exercise objectives.

EXERCISE EVALUATIONS BY FEMA

Although FEMA reviews and approves state and local emergency plans and procedures and provides evaluators to assess performance during drills and exercises, it does not have a formal enforcement process. This is because of the government-to-government relationship among FEMA, the states, and local jurisdictions (which may also include school districts, park districts, and in some cases other federal agencies). The FEMA Radiological Emergency Preparedness (REP) program views the states as its primary customers because it has essentially no mechanism to formally interact with the public. The FEMA process is fundamentally collaborative, rather than directive; there is no analog in the FEMA–state relationship to a Commission. FEMA lacks a mechanism to enforce compliance; it cannot revoke the ability to operate in the way the Commission can. FEMA officials, particularly the Regional Assistance Committee chairs (i.e., regional branch chiefs), might dispute this characterization, taking the position that states are not required to participate in radiological emergency planning, but those that elect to participate are bound by all of the program requirements (current revision of the *Radiological Emergency Preparedness Exercise Manual*).

The Federal Emergency Management Agency directly evaluates the performance of states and local jurisdictions in drills and exercises. As with licensees, offsite response organizations are evaluated against the commitments of their emergency plans and the requirements of their procedures, and evaluators identify deviations between expected and actual performance. These evaluation teams are typically led by the Regional Assistance Committee chairman and can be quite large, from 15 to 25 evaluators, depending on the location. It is FEMA's normal practice to evaluate several facility-only drills during the same week as they observe an integrated exercise; these drills are commonly referred to as *out-of-sequence drills* because they are not demonstrated during the integrated exercise. An out-of-sequence activity is primarily driven by the unavailability of a location during the exercise (e.g., a school used to receive evacuees that has classes during the day); it is less frequent that an out-of-sequence evaluation occurs because of limits on the number of available evaluators. Examples of out-of-sequence evaluations include interviews with school personnel, demonstrations of evacuee monitoring centers, demonstrations of vehicle monitoring, interviews with radio station personnel responsible for maintaining the emergency alert system, and demonstration of medical capabilities to treat an injured person with radioactive contamination present.

Only rarely does FEMA directly review the plans and procedures of private entities. Parties such as hospitals, ambulance services, the American Red Cross, the Salvation Army, and others are brought into the response network by formal agreements between the private entity and one or more local jurisdictions, as documented in the jurisdiction's emergency plan. These formal agreements can be referred to as memoranda of agreement or letters of agreement, or they may be contracts. FEMA provides a draft after-action evaluation report to the state that participated in the exercise within about 30 days of the exercise. This is usually the state in which the reactor site is located, although there are a few sites located along state boundaries in which one FEMA region is responsible for planning in the state on the east side of the emergency planning zone, while another region is responsible for the state on the west side. The state has 30 days to review the draft report, propose revisions, and discuss any proposed findings with the FEMA region. The state acts as an agent in dealing with FEMA when findings are proposed against local jurisdictions. The FEMA region has 30 days after receiving comments and proposed revisions from the states to issue its final after-action report, which goes to the state emergency management agency.

A Level II finding (formerly an area requiring corrective action) is required to be closed no later than the biennial exercise following the exercise in which it was identified, although there are examples of corrective actions not having been made for several consecutive exercise cycles and still being held open. The preferred method for closing a Level II finding is actual demonstration during an observed drill or exercise but not necessarily a full biennial exercise. Some findings at this level are closed based on revising or providing training or other administrative actions acceptable to the FEMA region that issued the finding.

It is FEMA's practice to inform a jurisdiction of a proposed Level I finding (formerly a deficiency) by letter before the end of the second complete week following the exercise in which the deficiency was identified. It also notifies the Commission of the Level I finding in the same time frame. If the performance that created the deficiency is not corrected within 180 days of the jurisdiction being informed, the FEMA region will inform the NRC that there is no longer reasonable assurance that adequate measures can be taken to protect the health and safety of the public in the emergency planning zone of the affected reactor site (by definition, as a Level I finding affects the ability to implement protective measures for the public). Receipt of the FEMA withdrawal of reasonable assurance starts another 180-day clock for the Commission to decide whether to issue an Order to the affected licensee to cease power operations because of the loss of reasonable assurance (see 10 CFR 50.54(s)(2)(ii) and 50.54(s)(3)). The Commission is not required to order the licensee to cease operations, only to make a decision as to whether the deficiency warrants such an Order.

In recent years, FEMA regions have tried to separate performance issues from program issues by characterizing inadequate emergency plans or procedures as *planning issues*. This term is not well defined and may not be consistently applied by all FEMA regions. Planning issues identified through the exercise evaluation process are not documented in after-action reports. It is not clear how planning issues are opened, tracked, or closed, nor does there appear to be a mechanism to inform the public about current planning issues associated with any particular jurisdiction.

It is curious that FEMA does not make its reports directly available to the public. The Agency does not have an online analog to the Commission's electronic reading room, from which current and historical FEMA documents can be obtained. FEMA provides its final after-action reports to the NRC, which enters them into its record system, then makes them publically available through the Commission website. For some sites, FEMA evaluation reports can be found for as far back as 1999.*

CORRECTIVE ACTIONS FOR EMERGENCY PREPAREDNESS ISSUES

The existence of a robust corrective action program that self-identifies problems at an appropriate threshold is one of the key assumptions of the reactor oversight program. The Commission's expectation is that licensees will take corrective actions for any problem with a promptness and thoroughness appropriate to the safety significance of the problem. Licensee corrective action program procedures often require that *conditions adverse to quality* be entered into the site's formal corrective action program and encourage entry of other problems. A condition adverse to quality is defined as a failure, malfunction, deficiency, deviation, defect in material or equipment, or nonconformance in a safety-related or important-to-safety structure, system, or component. Some equipment important to emergency preparedness is included in this definition, primarily alarms and indications in

---

* The *FEMA After Action Reports and Communication Related to Specific Emergency Exercises* page can be found at http://www.nrc.gov/about-nrc/emerg-preparedness/related-information/fema-after-action-reports.html. FEMA after-action reports may also be available from the individual states, depending on details of the state open-records laws. Interested persons should check individual state government websites.

the control room. Most emergency preparedness equipment, facilities, and programs are outside the definition; therefore, the corrective action procedures would allow most emergency preparedness problems not to be entered into the system. This is contrary to the Commission's expectation and generally contrary to licensee expectations, as well. Essentially no licensee actually limits the problems entered in their corrective action program to those required by procedure. The most common term for a problem entered into a corrective action program is a *condition report*.

As compared to other aspects of nuclear power plant operations, emergency preparedness has relatively weak corrective action requirements. The two regulations related to corrective actions are (1) planning standard 10 CFR 50.47(b)(14) and the associated Appendix E to Part 50, IV.F(2)(g), and (2) 10 CFR 50.54(t) and the associated Appendix E to Part 50, IV.G. The planning standard only requires weaknesses and deficiencies identified in drills and exercises, or training, to be corrected. Self-revealing problems or those identified through surveillances, audits, or assessments are not covered by this regulation. The Commission addresses the correction of self-revealing problems and those identified through assessments primarily through 10 CFR 50.54(q)(2), which requires the licensee to "follow and maintain the effectiveness of" their emergency plan. Almost any problem or failure of operational or regulatory significance will be associated with a requirement of the licensee emergency plan, with one of the 50.47(b) planning standards, or both. The argument can therefore be made that a licensee that does not promptly take compensatory and corrective action for most problems is not "maintaining the effectiveness of" their plan. Because failures are expected to periodically occur, it is not necessarily the failure that is of concern; the performance deficiency becomes the failure to act promptly to restore the degraded emergency function or capability. If the problem or failure results from the licensee having failed to implement a reasonable maintenance program or other controls that constitute maintenance in a traditional sense (i.e., physical or equipment), the failure to implement controls could be a separate violation of 50.54(q)(2).

The Commission's guidance on the promptness expected for taking corrective actions is found in Sections 6.1 and 6.2 of the NRC *Inspection Manual*, Chapter 0609, Appendix B, "Emergency Preparedness Significance Determination Process" (dated September 22, 2015). The guidance is that problems in classification, offsite notification, radiological assessment, or making protective action recommendations should be corrected within 90 days of identification. Problems directly related to any other planning standard should be corrected within 180 days. Other problems not directly related to any planning standard should be corrected within the subsequent 2 years. Compensatory actions to maintain emergency functions can generally be implemented rapidly; the guidance does not define "rapidly," but one might expect that the existence of such problems should be communicated to the emergency response organization within a day or two of problem discovery, and immediate actions should be taken no later than 3 or 4 days after that. Some problems may have several corrective actions assigned, with different completion times; a licensee should implement corrective actions as soon as possible rather than waiting until they are ready to completely implement all assigned actions.

The Commission requires that noncompliances with regulations be corrected, regardless of the level of effort required and regardless of the significance of the finding. A licensee cannot postpone correcting a finding simply because its significance is minor and it was not documented in an inspection report. Reasonable efforts should be made to correct problems of very low safety significance so that recurrence is unlikely, or the closure basis should provide justification for why recurrence is an acceptable condition. Corrective actions for problems of findings of moderate or greater safety significance ought to be sufficiently comprehensive to preclude recurrence of the problem. Licensees should be particularly sensitive to noncompliance with the emergency plan, recognizing this as a failure to comply with regulation. When corrective action program problem statements only document the inappropriate condition without identifying the associated violations, there is a risk the issue will be closed to no action or to track-and-trend, because the requirement to correct is not recognized.

Corrective action is also required for each individual weakness identified during drills, exercise, or training. It is not acceptable to document the weakness and wait to see if it reoccurs before taking action or to wait until the number of occurrences reaches an adverse trend threshold. Although multiple examples of a weakness can allow for a better informed cause analysis, this is not a sufficient reason to delay required corrective actions.

Licensee corrective action programs screen problems entered into the program to assign significance levels. In this context, significance is generally a combination of how completely the issue's causes must be investigated and whether the issue must be corrected to prevent recurrence. Issues of greater corrective action program significance receive a more in-depth cause analysis than issues of lesser significance. Issues can generally be categorized as non-problems, suggestions for improvement or enhancement, issues not requiring immediate action to be trended, issues requiring action not significant enough for cause analysis, issues requiring action significant enough for cause analysis, and issues requiring action to prevent recurrence and in-depth cause analysis. The lowest level of cause analysis is *apparent cause analysis*, which is done by a single evaluator without extensive research, involving perhaps a day or two of effort. The higher level of cause analysis is *root cause analysis*, which is done by a team of evaluators and may involve extensive research (and sometimes physical testing) and many man-days of effort. An apparent cause analysis may use formal methods of analysis, such as the "why tree," whereas a root cause analysis often uses multiple analysis methods, such as barrier analyses and fault trees. Both types of analysis are often documented in formal reports. The major difference between the levels of analysis often is that an apparent cause analysis stops at the *extent of condition* but a root cause analysis also establishes the *extent of cause*. The extent of condition is a determination of whether the problem is unique or affects other elements of the emergency preparedness program. The extent of cause can only be addressed after the causes of a condition are determined; it is a determination of what other emergency preparedness program elements could be degraded by the same cause (and also require correction). For example, a cause of ineffective procedures because of a lack of job–task analyses could affect the licensee's ability to perform virtually any emergency preparedness function; a cause of a lack of communication between the emergency preparedness department and plant operations could affect the ability of control room staff to classify events, notify offsite authorities and onsite employees, or to protect plant workers in the early phase of an event (before additional emergency response organization members arrive at the site during an off-hours event). Note that it is not uncommon for several causes to be identified for issues having safety significance; in this instance, an extent of cause analysis is done for each identified primary cause and potentially for each contributing cause.

In the author's opinion, licensees are more reluctant to screen an issue entered into the corrective action program as a non-problem than they should be. A non-problem is an assertion of a deficiency in equipment or a program element, when that equipment or element actually complies with applicable Commission regulation and site requirements. A non-problem differs from a suggestion for improvement, in that a non-problem generally asserts a negative condition, while an improvement item acknowledges compliance and asserts a positive benefit from the proposed change. Because licensee programs allow any employee to put any issue into the program, the program will always include non-problems. These tend to be individual perceptions of noncompliance when none exists. These perceptions may be based on incomplete situational information, a lack of knowledge about the requirement perceived not to be complied with, or an attempt to implement or influence new (internal) emergency preparedness program elements desired by the initiator. These types of issues may be appropriately closed to no action when the closure basis clearly shows that the problem statement contains conceptual or factual errors.

Some good practices to consider when creating, processing, and closing corrective action program entries include the following:

- Only include one issue or problem in a problem statement.
- Document the who, what, where, and when in the problem statement.
- Be aware that, for most issues, if the problem cannot be expressed in a few sentences then one probably does not have a clear conception of the problem.
- Avoid most acronyms.
- Avoid speculation about the why of an issue in the problem statement.
- Provide some analysis for every problem, even those not requiring an apparent cause analysis. The analysis may be simple or limited, but it shows that someone considered the apparent problem.
- Every analysis should address the why question.
- Apply the obvious question test to the analysis—is there an obvious impact or corollary if the problem statement is true that has not been considered?
- Always document why it is acceptable to close a problem to no action. If it is difficult to express this in a few sentences then closure is probably not warranted.
- Do not close a corrective action entry to actions planned to be taken.
- For each action taken, be specific in the closure about the who, what, where, and when. Documenting the why of an action is always helpful.
- When the action taken is a procedure change, new or revised training, or other product, attach a copy of that product to the package. At a minimum, provide a link to where the product is found.
- When coaching, lesson-learned e-mails, or training are the proposed actions, consider whether the same action has been taken for the same or similar issue in the previous 2 years. When the proposed action duplicates recent corrective action for similar issues, stop and first consider why previous actions did not prevent the problem from reoccurring. Do not repeat corrective actions that were previously ineffective.
- When the action taken is coaching, record who provided the coaching and the date, and briefly describe the content.
- Apply the "Grandma test" to the closure basis, particularly for closure to no action or to track-and-trend: If one described the problem to Grandma and then the proposed closure, would she find it reasonable?
- Check the closure basis against the problem statement to ensure that it addresses every contention or issue (i.e., check for completeness).

CROSS-CUTTING ISSUES

The Commission has identified aspects of licensee performance that are not specific to individual cornerstones but which affect the Commission's safety mission. These areas are human performance, the effectiveness of problem identification and resolution processes, and the maintenance of a safety-conscious work environment; within each aspect are more specific performance components. The Commission's philosophy is that problems in these performance areas are likely to manifest as the root causes of specific problems (i.e., findings and violations). Each finding of more than minor significance is evaluated to determine if a cross-cutting aspect contributed to the finding. A cross-cutting aspect is assigned a violation if the Commission finds that one of the identified performance criteria is the most likely underlying cause and the aspect reflects current performance.

The assignment of a cross-cutting aspect is necessarily a subjective process. An aspect generally reflects current performance if the associated performance deficiency occurred in the previous 2 years and subsequent corrective actions would not preclude the performance deficiency from reoccurring. Only one cross-cutting aspect can be assigned each violation. When more than one aspect may apply, the Commission chooses the one it considers to have contributed the most to the performance deficiency. The cross-cutting aspect assigned to a violation may not be the ultimate root cause because the Commission does not perform formal independent cause analyses for most findings.

The Commission and licensees will often agree on the performance deficiency underlying a finding or violation, agree that a violation of Commission regulations occurred, and disagree on the associated cross-cutting aspect or whether an aspect should be assigned at all. In part, this is because the assignment process is subjective and depends on the information known to the Commission at the time the aspect is assigned. Additional information could change the cause determination. Licensees have also been known to object to the assignment of cross-cutting aspects to manage their risk of being assigned substantive issues or themes, rather than because of technical concerns. A reactor site's licensing organization generally tracks cross-cutting assignments closely and maintains an ongoing awareness of the number of findings associated with each performance component, information that most Commission inspectors do not have ready access to. The current guidance about cross-cutting issues can be found in the NRC *Inspection Manual*, Chapter 0310, "Aspects Within Cross Cutting Areas" (dated December 14, 2014).

PERFORMANCE INDICATORS

The reactor oversight program implemented in 2000 has two components: direct inspection and the review of licensee performance indicators. A *performance indicator* is a numerical metric or statistic that objectively describes an aspect of licensee performance and is derived from a series of measurements made by the licensee. Performance indicators are reported to the Commission quarterly through a mechanism created and maintained by the NEI. Each report gives the current cumulative results for a rolling* assessment period of one to eight quarters, as assigned to each indicator.

The measurements in emergency preparedness consist of discrete comparisons of the as-observed performance or the as-found condition of equipment against a standard, so the numerical result of the measurement is always either 1 (the standard is met or the equipment is operable) or 0 (the standard is not met or the equipment is not operable). The derived statistic is the sum of the numerical results in a reporting period divided by the total number of measurements in that period, expressed as a percentage. The usual terminology in emergency preparedness is that any measurement is an *opportunity*, measurements in which the performance standard is met or the equipment operable are *successes*, and measurements in which the standard is not met or the equipment not operable are *failures*.

There are currently 17 performance indicators, of which 3 are in the emergency preparedness performance area. The performance indicators are defined in NEI 99-02, *Regulatory Assessment Performance Indicators*, Revisions 0 through 7 (2000 to 2013).[†] The guidance is maintained by the Nuclear Energy Institute, with Commission review and input, because the performance indicator program is a voluntary industry initiative, not a regulatory requirement.[‡] Additional information can be found in the NRC *Inspection Manual*, Chapter 0308, Attachment 1, "Technical Basis for Performance Indicators" (dated November 8, 2007) and Chapter 0608, "Performance Indicator

---

* *Rolling* means there is an assessment period of fixed length that advances one quarter with each successive report. The results from the oldest quarter assessed in the previous report always fall off the current assessment, and the results from the newest quarter are added to those remaining. The overall statistic is recalculated using the newly accumulated data for each report.

† Many licensees copy the guidance as written into their implementing procedures for their performance indicator program, to the extent of not even changing the word *licensee* to the name of the reactor site. The author believes the purpose of implementing procedures is to provide specific implementation instructions to site staff about how the definitions, instructions, and exceptions apply in a site-specific manner. Lengthy generic guidance may be adequately incorporated by reference; there is little to be gained by a copy-and-paste that does not translate the generic to activities that apply to each individual program.

‡ Industry essentially agreed to the performance indicator program in 1998–1999 to preempt regulatory action by the Commission. At the time, industry expected the then-developing reactor oversight program to reduce inspection efforts and result in less Commission enforcement. Because the Commission was prepared to adopt performance indicators regardless of industry agreement, industry would have had much less influence over the choice of performance indicators and their inspection if they had not taken preemptive action. In theory, any licensee can opt out of part, or all, of the performance indicator program and receive additional direct inspection, although the Commission does not have any guidance for determining what additional inspection to perform.

Program" (dated September 26, 2012). The accuracy of the performance indicator data reported to the Commission is evaluated annually by inspectors using inspection procedure 71151, "Performance Indicator Verification," at a nominal 2 inspection hours per performance indicator. The reader is referred to the current revision of NEI 99-02 for the calculational details of each indicator.

Each performance indicator is assigned significance bands to allow the results to be used in the assessment of licensee performance. These are color-coded to correspond to the colors in the significance determination process; a red band is not defined for the emergency preparedness indicators. Results in the green band are acceptable and do not require Commission action; that is, they are not considered to be the equivalent of a green significance determination process finding. Results in the white or yellow bands are considered to represent degraded performance that requires the same Commission response as an inspection finding of the same color, and they are considered as a finding of that color for purposes of the action matrix. Most licensees have established internal control bands for each performance indicator such that the indicator effectively changes color before it is reported to the Commission.

The overall philosophy for the development of performance indicators was that aspects of reactor operations related to safety that could be readily measured and reported by the licensee would be taken out of the inspection space and given to licensees, whereas the inspection program would be redirected toward aspects of reactor operations that were not readily measurable. The discussions in 1999 and 2000 were about how the commercial nuclear power industry was mature and stable and therefore capable of a higher degree of self-assessment and self-reporting than previously permitted. The general expectation was that after the initial implementation period more performance indicators would be developed, with corresponding reductions in active onsite inspections by the Commission, although this has yet to occur. There was serious consideration given in 1999 to establishing three individual statistics instead of one cumulative indicator for emergency response organization proficiency, one for each current performance component, but it was concluded there were underlying program elements that were common to each component, and that the individual sample sizes (i.e., total opportunities) were too small to be statistically significant. The alert and notification system reliability indicator was chosen because the same information was already being collected from licensees by states for annual reporting to FEMA; serious consideration was given to having licensees report sirens in some manner, either as total hours of unavailability or as the percent of time the system was available. The current alert and notification system reliability definition was accepted because Commission staff did not want to impose a new calculational method on licensees that differed from the requirements of FEMA REP-10, *Guide for the Evaluation of Alert and Notification Systems for Nuclear Power Plants.*

The performance indicator program was designed from the beginning to include a process to resolve disagreements between licensees and the Commission about the interpretation of NEI guidance. It was anticipated that these disagreements could be generic or site specific. A collaborative frequently asked question (FAQ) process was put into place. Either an individual licensee or Commission staff may generate a FAQ problem, along with a suggested solution or interpretation. The FAQ submission goes to a joint industry–Commission committee that meets quarterly. The committee evaluates the submission and decides whether to act on it. If the committee comes to an agreement on a response to the problem, it is published on the Commission's website and incorporated into the next revision of the NEI guidance. The agreed-upon response may be, and often is, different from that suggested by the initiator; it is not unusual for the committee to accept a submission and then expand its scope. If the committee cannot come to agreement after a reasonable period of discussion, the Commission is the final arbiter and may decide to implement its response without industry agreement.

Because performance indicators are reported quarterly, but their accuracy is evaluated annually, inspectors may review data from three to six quarters in an inspection, depending on the scheduling of successive inspections of the same licensee. Problems in a licensee application of performance indicator guidance are generally not identified until well after the data are reported to the

Commission. Inspectors have found instances of both false positives (reported successes that were failures) and false negatives (reported failures that were successes),* along with reported opportunities that should not have been reported. The expectation is that a licensee will enter such an issue into its corrective action program and correct the deficiency in its evaluation process that created the inaccurate information. Although the NEI guidance does not address the correction of reports that are subsequently identified as inaccurate, the reporting system does allow the subsequent revision of already-reported data. If the inaccurate information is not in a quarter that will be removed in the next assessment period, licensees are highly encouraged to make such revisions because there is a potential for future reports to be compromised by inaccurate past data for indicators with long assessment periods (i.e., eight quarters).

FINDINGS AND VIOLATIONS

The Commission's core mission is ensuring the adequate protection of public health and safety. It meets this mission, in part, by issuing regulations that govern the implementation of emergency preparedness programs and inspecting against the regulations. The Commission has created a formal citation process to document deviations from regulations, which is intended to notify licensees of deficiencies so the licensee can take actions that bring it back into compliance. The citations are contained in inspection reports that are generally made available to the public. The process is intended to inform the public of Commission efforts on their behalf and provide assurance that an adequate safety margin is being maintained.

A *performance deficiency* is a nonconforming condition or practice that does or did not meet a performance standard that applies to the licensee when the condition is reasonably within the licensee's control. A *finding* is a performance deficiency in which the applicable standard is or was self-imposed. A *violation* is a performance deficiency in which the applicable standard is or was a Commission regulation. The Commission expects that inspectors will inform the licensee about actual or potential performance deficiencies as soon as they are identified, giving the licensee the opportunity to provide additional information that pertains to the issue. The inspector provides their preliminary evaluation of the issue and its significance to licensee management at an exit interview that concludes the inspection. However, the determination that a violation exists is an agency decision, not an individual decision, and the violation does not formally exist until the licensee is notified on the docket (i.e., in an inspection report).

The Commission determined that some violations do not warrant enforcement action; these are commonly referred to as *minor violations.*† In this context, reporting the violation in an inspection report is considered an enforcement action. By Commission policy, a violation of minor significance is not documented in an inspection report; it is only verbally communicated by the inspector to licensee management. It therefore exists as of the exit interview meeting in which it is discussed with the licensee. One of the conditions for an issue to be characterized as minor is that the licensee must document the condition in the corrective action system to ensure that it is corrected. It is good practice for the licensee to note in the corrective action program problem statement that the condition also constitutes a minor violation; the corrective action program entry could be closed without restoring compliance if the persons responsible for action are not aware it has regulatory significance. A failure by the licensee to promptly restore compliance with a minor violation will lead to further enforcement action by the Commission.

---

* Any incorrectly reported performance indicator statistic can be characterized as a violation of 10 CFR 50.9(a), which requires that information provided to the Commission be correct in all material respects. In practice, this regulation is usually applied only to cases in which the reported statistic is higher (more favorable to the licensee) than its accurate value and the actual statistic falls into the white or yellow assessment band.

† For more information about minor violations, see Sections 2.2.2 and 2.3.1 of the NRC *Enforcement Policy* and *Inspection Manual*, Chapter 0612, Appendix B ("Issue Screening") and Appendix E ("Examples of Minor Issues").

SIGNIFICANCE DETERMINATION PROCESS

Most emergency preparedness findings will be evaluated using the significance determination process (see NRC *Inspection Manual* Chapter 0609, Appendix B). Entering the significance determination process requires that, first, a performance deficiency has occurred; second, the deficiency is identified as a violation of Commission regulation; and, third, the significance has a more than minor significance. There are many similarities between how reactor oversight program significance determination is performed and traditional enforcement; the major differences are as follows:

- The four categories of significance are labeled with colors instead of roman numerals, with associated descriptions* of the risk significance. From highest to lowest significance, these are
  1. Red, high safety significance
  2. Yellow, substantial safety significance
  3. White, low to moderate safety significance
  4. Green, very low safety significance
- The examples of deficiencies are not directly used to assign significance; they establish whether the associated planning standard function is unaffected, lost, or degraded. The logic flowcharts are used to establish significance, depending on the planning standard and the degree of degradation.
- Examples of lost and degraded planning standard functions are given for each of the 16 planning standards.

Each individual finding is assigned an individual significance; the process does not consider the number of findings in each category. The grouping of several findings of the same color to create a finding at a higher significance is prohibited. The assignment of a cross-cutting aspect, or lack of one, does not affect the significance of a finding. The action thresholds assigned to individual performance indicators are chosen so that a performance indicator color has approximately the same significance as does a significance determination process outcome; this allows performance indicator results of low to moderate, or higher, safety significance to be used in plant assessments.

The emergency preparedness significance determination process is summarized on two flow charts, the first (Attachment 1) for failures to implement a regulatory requirement during an event and the second (Attachment 2) for failures of the emergency preparedness program to comply with Commission requirements. Failures to implement risk-significant planning standard functions during events have significance essentially equal to the level of emergency in which the failure occurred: General Emergency, red; Site Area Emergency, yellow; Alert, white; Notification of Unusual Event, green. Failures to implement non-risk-significant planning standard requirements during an event are reduced by one significance category from that of risk-significant issues.

The significance of failures to comply with program requirements depends on the risk significance (or lack) of the associated planning standard and the degree of degradation that has occurred. No failure-to-comply finding can reach red significance, as there are no actual consequences from deficient planning; an actual deficiency at the General Emergency classification can cause protective action recommendations to offsite authorities to implement protective measures for the public. A loss of risk-significant planning standard function has yellow significance, and a loss of planning standard function is one category lower at white. Degraded functions of any planning standard have one category less significance than that of a loss (i.e., white or green). Violations of requirements that are not associated with a planning standard all have green significance because all planning standard logic decisions in the failure-to-comply flowchart are answered "no."

---

* Although the definitions each include a security component, these are omitted from the discussion because they generally do not apply to emergency preparedness. For most working purposes, the color of a finding is referred to rather than its safety significance description.

Chapter 0609, Appendix B, of the NRC *Inspection Manual* contains other information that may be useful to emergency planners. The most important may be the extensive discussion found in Section 5.14 regarding failures to critique, including the interaction between scope of drill or exercise and the critique, interaction between the drill and exercise performance indicator and the critique, the effect of inappropriate controller actions on the critique, and the critique process endpoint. Appendix B, Section 6.0, discusses the correction of weaknesses, including approximate guidelines for timeliness and criteria for evaluating the effectiveness of corrective actions. The document also describes the planning standard functions encompassed by each 10 CFR 50.47(b) standard, both the risk-significant and the non-risk-significant components (some standards contain elements of both), lists the associated implementing requirements found in Appendix E to Part 50, and lists reference documents associated with the standard.

ENFORCEMENT

The process of identifying performance deficiencies and deviations from regulations is part of inspection. *Enforcement* is the process of assigning significance to findings, communicating resulting violations to licensees, and evaluating licensees' responses to the violation. The 2006 revision of the Commission's Enforcement Policy document is available only on the Commission's website. Prior to 2006, a paper copy was distributed as NUREG-1600, *General Statement of Policy and Procedure for NRC Enforcement Actions* (NRC, 2000d). For the purposes of emergency preparedness, the policy applies to organizations holding Commission licenses, applicants for licenses, licensee contractors, and vendors supplying equipment to licensees. The policy may apply to individuals employed by a licensee in some circumstances, in addition to the licensed entity. Some violations may be considered for civil enforcement (e.g., federal court), and some may result in criminal prosecution.

Prior to April 2001, all deviations from Commission requirements were assessed directly using the Enforcement Policy. The resulting violations were assigned Severity Levels of I through IV. The policy describes Severity Level I violations as having (or could have had) serious consequences, Level II as having significant consequences, Level III as having moderate consequences, and Level IV as having less serious consequences. All violations were assessed for potential civil penalties (fines), although penalties were rarely assessed for Severity Level III or IV violations.

The current Enforcement Policy considers civil penalties when there have been two or more Severity Level I, II, or III violations in the previous 2 years (the violations are not required to be in the same performance area), when the licensee did not identify the issue, and when the licensee did not (will not) take effective corrective actions. Civil penalties will also be considered for reactor oversight program violations of white, yellow, or red significance if there were actual consequences associated with the violation. Penalties are generally not considered for Severity Level IV violations or reactor oversight program violations of green significance. In general, when the licensee both identifies the issue and promptly corrects it, the Commission will not assess a penalty. If the licensee either fails to identify or fails to correct, a penalty will be assessed; if the licensee both fails to identify and fails to correct, the penalty is doubled.

The enforcement process for non-cited violations generally concludes with issuance of the inspection report in which the licensee is formally notified of the violation, unless the licensee chooses to dispute the violation. When an issue is identified that may result in escalated enforcement, the Commission generally issues an inspection report documenting the issue and the Commission's preliminary determination of significance. The determination is preliminary because it is based on the information available to the Commission at the time the decision was made. The cover letter, often referred to as a *choice letter*, describes the options available to the licensee to provide additional information to the Commission.[*] These choices are usually (1) do nothing and the Commission will

---

[*] The Commission describes issues that have preliminarily been dispositioned as escalated enforcement as *apparent violations* until a final decision is made. An issue whose characterization is final is referred to simply as a *violation*.

make a final decision based on the information it currently possesses; (2) submit a written response on the docket within 30 days containing any additional information the licensee believes is material to the issue, including the licensee's perspective on the significance determination process; or (3) participate in a meeting to discuss any additional information the licensee believes is material to the issue, including the licensee's perspective on the significance determination process. When the meeting concerns an issue assigned a Severity Level it is called a *predecisional enforcement conference*; when it concerns a reactor oversight program issue it is called a *regulatory conference*. From a licensee's perspective, there are essentially no differences between the two categories of enforcement-related meetings. Both involve senior managers from the Commission and licensee, both discuss the facts about the issue as known to the Commission and licensee, both review the decision path the Commission used to assign its preliminary significance to the issue, and both provide the licensee opportunity to present new information about the issue. These meetings are usually held at the Commission's regional office overseeing the licensee and are open to the public, including by open-line telephone (sometimes also by webcast). The Commission's goal is to hold an enforcement-related meeting within about 30 days after issuing the inspection report that informs the licensee of the preliminary characterization. The Commission typically makes a final determination on the issue in the 2 weeks following the conference. The final decision is communicated in a *final significance determination letter* that includes a notice of violation if the issue is decided to require a citation. The final significance could be the same as the preliminary significance, less significant, or more significant, as determined from new information provided by the licensee.

TRADITIONAL ENFORCEMENT

In power reactor emergency preparedness, the Enforcement Policy is still used to assess violations having actual safety consequences, that degrade the Commission's ability to perform its regulatory oversight function, that involve willful noncompliance with requirements, and that do not have an associated performance deficiency (i.e., not reasonably within the licensee's ability to prevent). The use of the Enforcement Policy to assess significance instead of the reactor oversight program is called *traditional enforcement*,[*] as that was the process the Commission followed from 1974 through 2000. The concept of *actual consequences* is unlikely to apply to emergency preparedness activities because they do not include handling high-activity radioactive sources with a potential for radiation over-exposure and do not include operating plant equipment that can cause reactor trips or other safety concerns. The Commission's ability to perform its regulatory oversight function is affected by

- Implementation by the licensee of changes to the emergency preparedness program, emergency plan, or implementing procedures that actually decrease the effectiveness of the emergency plan
- Failures to perform 50.54(q) analyses of changes to the emergency preparedness program,[†] whether or not the changes decrease the effectiveness of the emergency plan
- Failures to submit to the Commission reports of changes to the emergency plan and implementing procedures, whether or not the changes decrease the effectiveness of the emergency plan (including reports made greater than 30 days following such changes)

---

[*] Additional information about traditional enforcement and the significance of findings may be found in SECY 99-087, *Proposed Strategy to Revise the Enforcement Policy to Address the Process for Assessing Significance and Assigning Severity Levels of Noncompliances (Including Regulatory Significance and Risk)* (NRC, 1999d), and SECY 99-219, *Proposed Revision to the Enforcement Policy to Address the Process for Assessing the Significance of Violations* (NRC, 1999c).

[†] Changes to the emergency preparedness program may include physical, administrative, financial, staffing, or other changes affecting the reactor plant or any other location under the licensee's control. When the change was not under the control of the emergency preparedness organization, it should have been evaluated for its impact on the emergency plan, and the evaluation was not done.

- Failures to report to the Commission conditions or events that constitute major losses of licensee assessment capabilities, emergency warning notification systems, or offsite capabilities
- Failures to report to the Commission complete and accurate performance indicator data in accordance with station commitments
- The provision of inaccurate or incomplete information to the Commission by any licensee employee, contractor, or vendor, regardless of whether the individual knows, or should know, that the information is inaccurate or incomplete
- Any willful noncompliance with Commission regulations by any licensee employee, contractor, or vendor

"Willful noncompliance" means the licensee employee knows the regulations that will be violated (or reasonably should know), knows that his or her action (or lack of action) will cause the regulation to be violated, and subsequently performs the action (or fails to take action) intentionally in the knowledge that the regulation will be violated. "Willful" may also refer to situations involving inaccurate or incomplete information when the individual provides the information in full knowledge that the information is inaccurate, expecting that the Commission will use the inaccurate information to come to a regulatory decision.

The significance of emergency preparedness violations dispositioned through traditional enforcement is determined by comparing the circumstances with the examples in the NRC Enforcement Policy, Section 6.6. There is some degree of subjectivity when applying these examples to actual circumstances. The examples primarily fall into two categories: (1) failures to classify, notify, or assess during actual events, and (2) failures that degrade the ability to implement a 10 CFR 50.47(b) planning standard or prevent the standard from being implemented. There is a certain amount of cross-reference between the traditional enforcement emergency preparedness examples and the emergency preparedness significance determination process. The policy recognizes that the examples are broadly written, are not exhaustive in scope, and do not address every possible situation. The examples are not limiting; that is, the policy does not prohibit Commission staff from exercising discretion in deviating from the examples (i.e., a licensee cannot appeal a deviation that results in higher than expected significance solely on the grounds the Commission did not follow the policy).

CITED AND NON-CITED VIOLATIONS

A non-cited violation is documented in an inspection report and briefly discussed in the cover letter for the report. A cited violation is generally attached to a final significance determination letter, which refers to a previously issued inspection report documenting the circumstances of the violation and the preliminary determination of significance. The final significance determination letter will discuss any changes in characterizing the issue between the preliminary and final determinations, including differences in significance. A citation states the requirement, the identified failure (i.e., the "contrary to" statement), the specific performance deficiency, and any associated cross-cutting aspect. It also includes information about the response required from the licensee and how the licensee may dispute the violation.

From a licensee's point of view, the primary difference between the two types of violations is that non-cited violations are not generally used when assessing a plant's performance, whereas cited (escalated) violations are used when assessing performance. Also, a licensee is not required to respond to a non-cited violation on the docket, but a cited violation does require a written response. The Commission normally treats Severity Level IV and reactor oversight program violations of very low safety significance (green) as non-cited violations. All other violations—Severity Levels I, II, and III and reactor oversight program red, yellow, and white—are normally cited. The Commission may occasionally waive the requirement for a written response to a cited violation when the Commission fully understands the causes of the violation, compliance was restored prior to issuance of the violation, and corrective actions have already been taken to address the issue. In general, cited violations are described as *escalated enforcement* and result in additional inspection to verify that the compliance has been restored, that the underlying causes are understood, and that corrective actions will likely prevent recurrence. The Commission verifies that compliance has been restored for non-cited violations as part of the routine baseline inspection program. A violation of low safety significance cannot be handled as a non-cited violation unless the licensee enters the violation into a formal corrective action program and restores compliance in a reasonable amount of time commensurate with its safety significance. For some violations, the issue cannot be repetitive as a result of inadequate corrective actions for previous examples. A violation that results from willful noncompliance is not normally treated as a non-cited violation, regardless of its safety significance.

APPEAL PROCESS

A licensee may appeal the Commission's assignment of a violation of any significance, whether issued under the reactor oversight program or using the Enforcement Policy. The licensee may disagree with the Commission's description of the circumstances of the proposed noncompliance, may disagree with the validity of the issue (i.e., that the performance constitutes a violation of requirements), or may disagree with the significance assigned the violation. An appeal cannot be initiated until after the Commission makes its final significance determination (i.e., the inspection report for a non-cited violation or final significance determination letter for escalated enforcement). Any additional information provided by the licensee after receipt of a preliminary significance determination is considered part of the enforcement process and should be considered in reaching the final significance determination. Additional information can be found in the NRC *Inspection Manual*, Chapter 0609, Attachment 2, "Process for Appealing NRC Characterization of Inspection Findings" (dated June 8, 2011).

A licensee must inform the Commission of an appeal in writing, within 30 days of the date of the inspection report or final significance determination letter that documents the violation. An appeal must be based on one of three possible contentions: (1) that the Commission staff incorrectly applied the significance determination process, (2) that information relevant to the issue was not considered by the Commission staff in reaching its conclusion and the information had been provided to the Commission by the licensee, or (3) there is new information not previously available that is relevant to the issue, and the licensee stated that new information would be provided prior to the Commission making a final determination. An appeal that is not based on at least one of these contentions will not be accepted or adjudicated.

The regional administrator of the NRC region that issued the finding convenes a panel of three members, two members with technical expertise (e.g., emergency preparedness) and one enforcement specialist. In general, panels consist of individuals who did not participate in the original decision, although the process only requires one person to be independent. In practice, this means that panel members are appointed from other regions because of the small number of persons in each region having emergency preparedness expertise. A consensus of the panel is required for a recommendation, meaning at least two members are in agreement. The panel's recommendation is made to the regional administrator, who makes the final decision. The Commission's goal is to complete the acceptance review and panel review and make a decision within 60 days of receiving the appeal.

LICENSING ACTIONS

Appendix E to 10 CFR 50, Parts I and II, states that the licensee's emergency plan is a part of the licensee's final safety analysis report, even when the plan is maintained as a stand-alone document. In the final safety analysis report template, the emergency plan is assigned to Chapter 13, a nomenclature that is still maintained by some licensees. The final safety analysis report is part of the reactor's operating license; therefore, changes to the licensee emergency plan are changes to the operating license and licensing basis. Licensing actions in emergency preparedness are formal determinations by the Commission that proposed changes to the licensing basis do not materially affect the existing determination of reasonable assurance and therefore may be implemented by the licensee. Proposed licensing actions generally fall into one of the following categories: (1) approval of an initial emergency plan for a new licensee, (2) changes from one emergency action level scheme basis to another, (3) proposed changes to the licensee emergency plan that the *licensee has determined* will reduce the effectiveness of the plan,* and (4) one-time requests for exemptions from specific regulatory requirements. The most common exemption request is to move a required biennial into the next calendar year because of a major natural disaster or event affecting the licensee or offsite authorities; for example, several exercises were moved into 2002 following the events of September 2001, and exercises were moved because of Hurricane Katrina in 2005 and widespread Missouri River flooding in 2011. A licensee changing from an operating reactor to a permanently defueled and decommissioning reactor currently would also use the exemption process to permanently reduce the scope of its onsite and offsite emergency preparedness programs, commensurate with the changing radiological risks.

Prior to February 2012, the licensing action process in emergency preparedness was somewhat informal, generally consisting of a letter from the licensee regulatory affairs or licensing department directly to the emergency preparedness group at Commission headquarters.† Since February 2012, all proposed emergency preparedness licensing actions are submitted as license amendment requests, as described in 10 CFR 50.4(1), 50.4(5), and 50.54(q)(4); some relevant information may be found in SECY 02-0096 (NRC, 2002e).

The Commission prepares a safety evaluation report to document its review of any request for a licensing action. The safety evaluation report describes what was reviewed, discusses technical issues that were considered, documents the requests for information made by the Commission during the review process, and provides the technical bases for recommendations for approval or disapproval of the request. The Commission issues a request for information when a licensee's submission is inadequate or incomplete or otherwise found lacking. Complex submissions, such as emergency action level scheme changes, may have several iterations of requests for information with each request and response made on the docket.

ASSESSING LICENSEE PERFORMANCE

The current regulatory oversight process for commercial power reactors is the *reactor oversight program*,‡ which became effective in 2000 after a 1-year pilot program. The previous oversight program was the *systematic assessment of licensee performance* (SALP).§ The reactor oversight

---

* The Commission may not agree that a proposed change reduces the effectiveness of the licensee emergency plan and may decline to docket the request for licensing action on the grounds the licensee may implement it through 50.54(q)(3).

† Prior to January 2006, requests for emergency preparedness-related licensing actions went to the Office of Nuclear Reactor Regulation; after January 2006, they went to the Office of Nuclear Security and Incident Response.

‡ For more information about the reactor oversight program, see *Inspection Manual*, Chapter 0308 ("Reactor Oversight Process Basis Document"); SECY 97-02, *Staff Action Plan to Improve the Senior Management Meeting Process*; SECY 97-122, *Integrated Review of the NRC Assessment Process for Operating Commercial Nuclear Reactors*; SECY 99-007, *Recommendations for Reactor Oversight Process Improvements*; SECY 99-176, *Plans for Pursuing Performance-Based Initiatives*; SECY 01-114, *Results of the Initial Implementation of the New Reactor Oversight Process*; SECY 00-0049, *Results of the Revised Reactor Oversight Process Pilot Program*; SECY 01-0114, *Results of the Initial Implementation of the New Reactor Oversight Process*; and SECY 11-0073, *Staff Proposal to Reintegrate Security into the Action Matrix of the Reactor Oversight Process Assessment Program*.

§ See *OIG Review of the NRC's Systematic Assessment of Licensee Performance Program (SALP)*, 1989; Generic Letter 92-05, *NRC Workshop on the Systematic Assessment of Licensee Performance (SALP) Program*; Administrative Letter 93-02, *Implementing the Revised Systematic Assessment of Licensee Performance (SALP) Program*, Review of revised NRC systematic assessment of licensee performance (SALP) program, *Federal Register* 60(147), 39193–39194, 1995; SECY 96-005, *Systematic Assessment of Licensee Performance*; SECY 98-218, *Suspension of the Systematic Assessment of Licensee Performance Program*; SECY 99-86, *Recommendations Regarding the Senior Management Meeting Process and Ongoing Improvements to Existing Licensee Performance Assessment Processes*; and Administrative Letter 1998-007, *Interim Suspension of the Systematic Assessment of Licensee Performance (SALP) Program*.

program combines the results of licensee-reported performance metrics (performance indicators) with direct inspection to produce an integrated assessment of licensee performance. The design goals of the reactor oversight program included the following:

- Focus Commission activities on plant problems having actual safety significance (i.e., apply safety risk information to the programs).
- Provide objective and predictable criteria for taking regulatory action against licensees.
- Integrate licensee corrective action programs into regulatory oversight processes.*
- Limit inspection to performance areas in which no alternate measurement areas are available.
- Identify performance thresholds below which no additional Commission interaction is required.
- Better distinguish between baseline (normal) and reactive (post-event or enforcement) inspections.

Licensees had a variety of issues with the SALP program, the most important of which was the subjective and somewhat arbitrary nature of the evaluation process, at least from their point of view. SALP rated each reactor site in several categories, with numerical values of 1 (most favorable), 2, or 3 (least favorable), and the site received an overall score using the same scale. The number of rating categories varied over time, but at the end (1995–1998) they included plant operations, maintenance, engineering, and plant support; emergency preparedness was a component of the plant support category. A plant's overall SALP score was not necessarily the average of individual category ratings. Licensees believed they could not predict when the Commission would take regulatory action or how severe the action would be. At the time, the Commission maintained a list of reactor licensees that received increased regulatory attention; the list was referred to as either the "troubled plant list" or the "watch list" and was reviewed every 6 months. The number of plants on the list varied over time but was generally between four and six. Licensees perceived that there was no regulatory basis for some of the additional oversight given plants on the list and no clear criteria for going onto, or being taken off, the list.

The reactor oversight program is organized with three top-level safety functions, or *strategic performance areas*: reactor safety, radiation safety, and safeguards (physical security). Below the strategic performance areas are seven safety cornerstones; four cornerstones are associated with reactor safety, two are associated with radiation safety, and one with safeguards. The Commission's philosophy is that acceptable performance in the cornerstones provides reasonable assurance that protection of the public health and safety is ensured. The cornerstones together provide the basis for regulatory assessment. Each inspection procedure is tied to a particular cornerstone. Emergency preparedness is a separate cornerstone associated within the reactor safety strategic performance area.

An individual cornerstone is either fully met or is degraded. A cornerstone is fully met when there are no associated findings during an assessment period, only findings of very low safety significance, or one finding of low-to-moderate safety significance. A cornerstone is degraded when there is more than one finding of low-to-moderate safety significance in an assessment period, or any finding of substantial safety significance.

The current method of assessing overall licensee performance is the *action matrix*, as described in the NRC *Inspection Manual*, Chapter 0305, "Operating Reactor Assessment Program" (dated December 21, 2014). A reactor site is placed in one of five columns using rules based on the number of current active escalated enforcement actions, the distribution of the active escalated enforcement actions among cornerstones, and the number of performance indicators in the white, yellow, or red

---

* Recall that the Commission required licensees to adopt formal corrective action programs from 1995 to 1996. Until the reactor oversight program was introduced, licensees largely did not get any regulatory credit for self-identifying and correcting problems.

bands. The columns are licensee response (one), regulatory response (two), degraded cornerstone (three), multiple-repetitive degraded cornerstone (four), and unacceptable performance (five). The common practice is to refer to a licensee's position by column number rather than column name. The matrix is read from left to right, with placement in column one having the least impact on the licensee and column five having the most impact. As a consequence of this assessment model, an operating licensee is always in a matrix column.

In this context, "operating" means at power, with only normal or routine outage activities. Licensees shut down for longer than 6 months may be removed from the Commission's normal assessment process with oversight performed per NCR *Inspection Manual*, Chapter 0350, "Oversight of Reactor Facilities in a Shutdown Condition Due to Significant Performance and/or Operational Concerns," or Chapter 0351, "Implementation of the Reactor Oversight Process at Reactor Facilities in an Extended Shutdown for Reasons Other Than Significant Performance Problems." The normal assessment process may not accurately evaluate the performance of a shutdown licensee because the containment and the reactor coolant system may not be intact, mitigating systems may not be available, the initiating events cornerstone may not reflect day-to-day operations, parts of the radiation safety strategic performance area may not apply, or several performance indicators become meaningless when the reactor is not at power. Past experience has shown that plants approaching a continuous year in an outage condition or those with known equipment issues expected to take a year or more to resolve are candidates for being moved into Chapter 0350 or 0351 oversight. Plants in this situation are technically no longer in the reactor oversight program; however, they generally continue to receive those reactor oversight program baseline inspections that apply to their current configuration. The supplemental inspection procedures, especially 95002 and 95003, are also used to inform development of a unique, site-specific inspection program to resolve the unusual technical issues that are preventing restart of the reactor.

A licensee that has no open findings of low-to-moderate safety significance is in column one and receives only the baseline level of inspection. A licensee with one active finding of low-to-moderate significance is in column two and receives a 95001 inspection when the they are ready to close out the issue. A licensee with two active findings of low-to-moderate significance or one finding of substantial significance is in column three and receives a 95002 inspection when they are ready to close out the issue. In the emergency preparedness area, introduction of the reactor oversight program changed the focus of inspections from facilities, equipment, and supplies to emergency functions and corrective actions.

REPORTING EVENTS OR CONDITIONS TO THE NRC

A licensee is required by 10 CFR 50.72 and 50.73 to report a variety of conditions to the NRC. To report means to make a telephone call to the NRC Operations Center in Rockville, MD,[*] generally supplemented at a later date by a written form submitted by fax or electronic means. Reports for some kinds of conditions consist of written submissions only. A report is considered to be made when the information is received or taken by a Commission operations officer. The current guidance about reporting events can be found in NUREG-1022 (Lewin, 2013). A report to the Commission is generally called a *licensee event report* and is given a tracking reference number by the operations officer. In the emergency preparedness area,

- 10 CFR 50.72(a)(1)(i) requires a report following declaration of any emergency classification to be made as soon as possible following notification to offsite authorities and not to exceed 1 hour after the declaration.
- 10 CFR 50.72(b)(1) requires a report of any deviation from the emergency plan or security plan using the authority of 10 CFR 50.54(x).

---

[*] The operations center is continually staffed.

- 10 CFR 50.72(b)(2)(xi) requires a report if notification has been (or will be) made to a government agency related to the health and safety of the public.
- 10 CFR 50.73(a)(2)(iii) requires a report of any natural phenomenon or external condition that poses a threat to the safety of the plant or hampers plant operation.
- 10 CFR 50.73(a)(2)(viii)(A) and (B) require the report of airborne or liquid radiological releases that exceed 20 times the limits of 10 CFR 20, Table 2.
- 10 CFR 50.73(a)(2)(x) requires a report of any actual threat to the safety of the plant or event that hampers plant operations, including fires and releases of toxic gas.
- 10 CFR 50.72(b)(3)(xiii) requires a report of a major loss of emergency assessment capability, offsite response capability, or offsite communications capability, including losses of the ability to operate the alert and notification system.

Several reporting requirements are duplicative, in that the phenomena, external conditions, releases, and plant events that are required to be reported would also require the declaration of an emergency condition. The report of the transportation of a radioactively contaminated patient to an offsite medical facility is required by 50.72(b)(3)(xii); such an event would cause declaration of an emergency classification under the original NUREG-0654, Appendix 1, emergency action levels, although the event was deleted from subsequent classification schemes. A deviation from the emergency plan requiring invocation of 50.54(x) likely would only occur following declaration of an emergency classification and activation of the emergency response organization. Some considerations that may apply to emergency preparedness programs include the following:

- Licensee after-action critiques for events should carefully review the elapsed time between the conclusion of notifying offsite authorities and the initiation of the notification to the NRC. The only acceptable justification for delaying notification to the NRC is if the designated control room communicator is performing a task important to plant operations and mitigating the event. A violation may be issued to a licensee even if notification to the NRC is made within an hour of a declaration if there is no justifiable reason the notification was not performed *immediately* after notification to offsite authorities. Licensee procedures that have the communicator initiate callout of the emergency response organization or perform other response-related tasks before notification to the NRC may not be acceptable.
- A condition requiring an emergency classification may still be reportable even when discovered after the condition no longer exists (i.e., the classification is not made because the emergency action level is not met at time of discovery). Events discovered 3 years or more after they existed are excluded.
- The requirement to activate the Emergency Response Data System is independent of the requirement to report the event or condition to the NRC.
- The NRC *has not been notified* in accordance with the requirement when a communicator provides information about a reportable condition to the Emergency Notification System bridge or health physics network bridge (i.e., open-line communication with the NRC following declaration of an event). The NRC *has not been notified* when the reportable information is provided to the resident inspector or a member of the NRC site response team at the control room or other emergency response facility (including the regional incident response center). The NRC is only notified when the report is taken by an authorized NRC operations officer.
- Licensees occasionally notify county sheriffs or emergency management offices of the need to use backup means of alerting the public should emergency occur. This is usually because individual offsite emergency warning sirens or other alert and notification system components (e.g., National Weather Service radio towers) are out of service or have emergent failures. For the most part, the number of out-of-service sirens is below the threshold for a major loss of offsite communications capability. Notifications to county officials of

this kind may also be required to be reported to the NRC in accordance with 50.72(b)(2) (xi). See NUREG-1022 (Lewin, 2013, p. 55).

- The report required under 50.72(a)(2) may not be fulfilled by reporting an emergency classification because of the related emergency action level.
- In the author's experience, licensees generally fail to recognize when the radiological releases commonly postulated in biennial exercises (or other drills and exercises reaching the General Emergency classification) exceed the concentrations required to be reported in accordance with 50.73(a)(2)(viii)(A).

Industry has historically struggled with making reports of major losses of assessment capability because of the lack of a clear regulatory definition. The Commission has allowed each licensee to define a major loss of capability for itself and has not required consistency among licensees. In practice, licensees have created internal procedures for use by their staff in determining whether an event or condition is reportable to the Commission, an event was determined to be reportable if it matched an example in the procedure. Licensees put the three examples listed in 10 CFR 50.72(b) (3)(xiii)—control room indication, Emergency Notification System, and offsite notification system (sirens)—into their manuals, but many failed to generate any additional site-specific examples. Because licensees often rely on the list of examples they may fail to recognize that a report is required if their list of examples is short.

After the Commission began to examine more closely whether licensees were accurately reporting all conditions requiring a report, licensees began systematically making precautionary reports to ensure compliance. This situation occurred mostly in the period from approximately 2008 to 2013. The licensees are not greatly concerned that unnecessary reports affect the availability of operations officers when significant events or emergencies occur, that such reports place an administrative burden on Commission staff, or that they negatively affect the Commission staff's ability to provide appropriate oversight. In emergency preparedness, the most common example was reporting the major loss of assessment capability when required emergency response facility ventilation or filtration systems are out of service.

DISASTER-INITIATED REVIEW

A disaster-initiated review is an administrative process between FEMA and the Commission to make decisions about the restart or continued operations of a reactor following a major event at or near the reactor site.* The authority for this process comes from the Memorandum of Understanding between FEMA and the Commission (Appendix A to 44 CFR 353). It is implemented by the NRC's *Inspection Manual*, Chapter 1601, "Communication and Coordination Protocol for Determining the Status of Offsite Emergency Preparedness," Revision 4 (dated August 27, 2013);† Part IV.V of the *Radiological Emergency Preparedness Program Manual* (FEMA, 2016); and *Disaster Initiated Review* (FEMA, 2011a). The review is intended to ensure compliance with 10 CFR 50.47(2), which states, in part, "The NRC will base its finding on a review of the Federal Emergency Management Agency findings and determinations as to whether State and local emergency plans are adequate and whether there is reasonable assurance that they can be implemented."

A disaster-initiated review presupposes that a widespread disaster has occurred affecting the emergency planning zone around a commercial nuclear power plant. The licensee may not have been materially affected by the disaster, and it does not matter whether the licensee declared an

---

* It is one of the two significant areas in which the Agency affects onsite programs, the other being the Agency's sole authority to approve the design, operation, and testing of emergency warning systems for the public operated by licensees.
† Revision 1, dated July 7, 2005, expanded the scope of the chapter to include reactors shut down because of hostile actions and having extended outages for reasons other than natural disasters. Revision 3, dated July 17, 2012, expanded the chapter to include reactors that remained at power. Prior to 2012, there was no mechanism that allowed FEMA to question the continued operation of a reactor that did not shut down.

emergency during the event. Although the disaster most likely involves the physical destruction or depletion of resources needed by offsite authorities to respond to an emergency at the reactor site, it may also include the widespread loss of the electric grid, malevolent acts at the reactor site or in the emergency planning zone, and situations (such as hostile action) that cause significant manpower and operational issues for offsite authorities.

A disaster-initiated review is always initiated by the FEMA region in which the reactor site is located, or one of the two regions for those few sites having emergency planning zones split between Agency regions. A review will not be performed unless there is a formal request from the Agency. If it cannot be readily determined by the Agency region whether the amount of offsite impairment warrants a full review, the Agency may conduct a preliminary capabilities assessment of offsite EP capabilities to determine the need for a formal assessment of continued reasonable assurance.

Although the Commission is not generally involved in licensee decisions about plant operations, a licensee attempting restart or intending to remain at power following a negative finding by FEMA may receive an Order from the Commission. Section 4.03 of the NRC *Inspection Manual*, Chapter 1601, states, in part, "A licensee is not required by NRC regulations to immediately shut down a reactor due to degraded offsite emergency response infrastructure, but the Commission can order the facility to shut down if the deficiencies in offsite EP have the potential to cause a radiological public health and safety concern." Experience suggests that the Commission will likely not allow an offline reactor to resume operations when any offsite capabilities are degraded or lost. However, the Commission is likely to allow an operating reactor to remain at power when offsite capabilities are degraded if the degraded condition can be expected to last no longer than a few hours to few days.

Bibliography

AECB, *Recommended Criteria for the Evaluation of Onsite Nuclear Power Plant Emergency Plans*. Vol. 1. *Basis Document*. Atomic Energy Control Board, Ottawa, Canada, 1997a.

AECB, *Recommended Criteria for the Evaluation of Onsite Nuclear Power Plant Emergency Plans*. Vol. 2. *Criteria*. Atomic Energy Control Board, Ottawa, Canada, 1997b.

AMS, *Glossary of Meteorology*, 2nd ed. American Meteorological Society, Boston, MA, 2000.

ANSI, *Guide to Sampling Airborne Radioactive Materials in Nuclear Facilities*, ANSI N13.1-1969. American National Standards Institute, Washington, DC, 1969a.

ANSI, *Practices for Respiratory Protection*, ANSI Z88.2-1969. American National Standards Institute, Washington, DC, 1969b.

ANSI, *Inspection and Test Specifications for Direct and Indirect Reading Quartz Fiber Pocket Dosimeters*, ANSI N322-1977. American National Standards Institute, Washington, DC, 1977.

ANSI, *Emergency Control Centers for Nuclear Power Plants*, ANS 3.7.2-1979. American National Standards Institute, Washington, DC, 1979a.

ANSI, *Facilities and Medical Care for Onsite Nuclear Power Plant Radiological Emergencies*, ANSI/ANS-3.7.1-1979. American National Standards Institute, Washington, DC, 1979b.

ANSI, *Performance Specifications for Reactor Emergency Radiological Monitoring Instrumentation*, ANSI N320-1979. American National Standards Institute, Washington, DC, 1979c.

ANSI, *Radiological Emergency Preparedness Exercises for Nuclear Power Plants*, ANSI/ANS-3.7.3-1979. American National Standards Institute, Washington, DC, 1979d.

ANSI, *Criteria for Accident Monitoring Functions in Light-Water-Cooled Reactors*, ANSI/ANS-4.5-1980. American National Standards Institute, Washington, DC, 1980a.

ANSI, *Practices for Respiratory Protection*, ANSI Z88.2-1980. American National Standards Institute, Washington, DC, 1980b.

ANSI, *Nuclear Fuel Facilities—Spent Fuel Storage Installation, Site Selection and Design of an Independent Spent Fuel Storage Installation (Water-Pool Type)*, ANSI/ANS-2.19-1981. American National Standards Institute, Washington, DC, 1981.

ANSI, *Dosimetry–Personnel Dosimetry Performance Criteria for Testing*, ANSI N13.11-1983. American National Standards Institute, Washington, DC, 1983.

ANSI, *Design Criteria for an Independent Spent Fuel Storage Installation (Dry Storage Type)*, ANSI/ANS-57.9-1984. American National Standards Institute, Washington, DC, 1984a.

ANSI, *Determining Meteorological Information at Nuclear Power Sites*, ANSI/ANS-2.5-1984. American National Standards Institute, Washington, DC, 1984b.

ANSI, *Radioactive Source Term for Normal Operation of Light Water Reactors*, ANSI/ANS-18.1-1984. American National Standards Institute, Washington, DC, 1984c.

ANSI, *Criteria for Accident Monitoring Functions in Light Water Cooled Reactors*, ANSI/ANS-4.5-1986. American National Standards Institute, Washington, DC, 1986.

ANSI, *Criteria for Emergency Radiological Field Monitoring, Sampling, and Analysis*, ANSI/ANS-3.8.5-1992. American National Standards Institute, Washington, DC, 1992.

ANSI, *Criteria for Functional and Physical Characteristics of Radiological Emergency Response Facilities*, ANSI/ANS-3.8.2-1995. American National Standards Institute, Washington, DC, 1995a.

ANSI, *Criteria for Maintaining Radiological Emergency Response Capability*, ANSI/ANS-3.8.4-1995. American National Standards Institute, Washington, DC, 1995b.

ANSI, *Criteria for Radiological Emergency Response Functions and Organizations*, ANSI/ANS-3.8.1-1995. American National Standards Institute, Washington, DC, 1995c.

ANSI, *Criteria for Radiological Emergency Response Plans and Implementing Procedures*, ANSI/ANS-3.8.3-1995. American National Standards Institute, Washington, DC, 1995d.

ANSI, *Criteria for the Conduct of Offsite Radiological Assessment for Emergency Response for Nuclear Power Plants*, ANSI/ANS-3.8.6-1995. American National Standards Institute, Washington, DC, 1995e.

ANSI, *Criteria for Planning, Development, Conduct, and Evaluation of Drills and Exercises for Emergency Preparedness*, ANSI/ANS-3.8.7-1998. American National Standards Institute, Washington, DC, 1998.

ANSI, *Determining Meteorological Information at Nuclear Power Sites*, ANSI/ANS-3.11-2000. American National Standards Institute, Washington, DC, 2000.

ANSI, *Performance and Documentation of Radiological Surveys*, ANSI/HPS N13.49-2001. American National Standards Institute, Washington, DC, 2001.

ANSI, *Determining Meteorological Information at Nuclear Facilities*, ANSI/ANS-3.11-2005. American National Standards Institute, Washington, DC, 2005.

ANSI, *Emergency Planning for Research Reactors*, ANSI/ANS-15.16-2008. American National Standards Institute, Washington, DC, 2008.

ANSI, *Nuclear Power Plant Simulators for Use in Operator Training*, ANSI/ANS-3.5-2009. American National Standards Institute, Washington, DC, 2009.

ANSI, *Determining Meteorological Information at Nuclear Facilities*, ANSI/ANS-3.11-2015. American National Standards Institute, Washington, DC, 2015a.

ANSI, *Emergency Planning for Research Reactors*, ANSI/ANS-15.16-2015. American National Standards Institute, Washington, DC, 2015b.

Arya, S.P., *Air Pollution Meteorology and Dispersion*. Oxford University Press, Oxford, U.K., 1999.

Azarm, M., Gitnick, T., Herrick, S. et al., *Risk Informing Emergency Preparedness Oversight: Evaluation of Emergency Actions Levels—A Pilot Study of Peach Bottom, Surry, and Sequoyah*, NUREG/CR-7154. U.S. Nuclear Regulatory Commission, Washington, DC, 2013.

Barto, A., Chang, Y.J., Compton, K. et al., *Consequence Study of a Beyond-Design-Basis Earthquake Affecting the Spent Fuel Pool for a U.S. Mark I Boiling Water Reactor*, NUREG-2161. U.S. Nuclear Regulatory Commission, Washington, DC, 2014.

Blumenthal, D., *DOE/NNSA Response to Radiological Releases from the Fukushima Dai-ichi Nuclear Power Plant* [PowerPoint presentation]. National Nuclear Security Administration, U.S. Department of Energy, Washington, DC, 2012.

Briggs, G.A., *Plume Rise*. U.S. Atomic Energy Commission, Washington, DC, 1969.

Brodsky, A., *Accuracy and Detection Limits for Bioassay Measurements in Radiation Protection: Statistical Considerations*, NUREG-1156. U.S. Nuclear Regulatory Commission, Washington, DC, 1986.

Buesseler, K.O., Fukushima and ocean radioactivity. *Oceanography*, 27(1), 92–105, 2014.

Bush, G.W., Executive Order 13286: Amendment of Executive Orders, and other actions, in connection with the transfer of certain functions to the Secretary of Homeland Security. *Federal Register*, 68, 10619, 2003.

Bush, G.W., Executive Order 13347: Individuals with disabilities in emergency preparedness. *Federal Register*, 69, 44573, 2004.

Bush, G.W., Executive Order 13407: Public alert and warning system. *Federal Register*, 71, 36975, 2006.

Carbajo, J.J., *Severe Accident Source Term Characteristics for Selected Peach Bottom Sequences Predicted by the MELCOR Code*, NUREG/CR-5942, ORNL TM-12229. Oak Ridge National Laboratory, Oak Ridge, TN, 1993.

Carter, J., *Statement by the President* [regarding the Kemeny Commission on the Accident at Three Mile Island]. White House, Washington, DC, 1978a.

Carter, J., *U.S. Civil Defense Policy*, Presidential Directive 41. White House, Washington, DC, 1978b.

Carter, J., Executive Order 12127: Creation of the Federal Emergency Management Agency. *Federal Register*, 44, 19367, 1979a.

Carter, J., Executive Order 12130: President's Commission on the Accident at Three Mile Island. *Federal Register*, 44, 22027, 1979b.

Carter, J., Executive Order 12148: Transfer of emergency management and response functions to the Federal Emergency Management Agency. *Federal Register*, 44, 43239, 1979c.

Carter, J., Executive Order 12241: Radiological contingency plan. *Federal Register*, 45, 64879, 1980.

Cember, H., *Introduction to Health Physics*, 2nd ed., Pergamon Press, New York, 1983, pp. 282–290.

CEOG, *Technical Justification for the Elimination of the Post-Accident Sampling System from the Plant Design and Licensing Bases for CEOG Utilities*, CENPSD-1157. Combustion Engineering Owners Group, 1999.

Clinton, W.J., Executive Order 13010: Critical infrastructure protection. *Federal Register*, 61, 37347, 1996.

CNSC, *Emergency Planning at Class I Nuclear Facilities and Uranium Mines and Mills*, Regulatory Guide G-225. Canadian Nuclear Safety Commission, Ottawa, 2001.

CNSC, *Nuclear Emergency Management*, Regulatory Policy P-325. Canadian Nuclear Safety Commission, Ottawa, 2006.

Cooper, J.R., Randle, K., and Sokhi, R.S., *Radioactive Releases in the Environment: Impact and Assessments*. Wiley, New York, 2003.

Covello, V.T., *Developing an Emergency Risk Communications (ERC)/Joint Information Center (JIC) Plan for a Radiological Emergency*, NUREG/CR-7032. U.S. Nuclear Regulatory Commission, Washington, DC, 2011a.

Covello, V.T., *Guidance on Developing Effective Radiological Risk Communication Messages: Effective Message Mapping and Risk Communication with the Public in Nuclear Power Plant Emergency Planning Zones*, NUREG/CR-7033. U.S. Nuclear Regulatory Commission, Washington, DC, 2011b.

CRS, *Emergency Management Preparedness Standards: Overview and Options for Congress*. Congressional Research Service, Washington, DC, 2005.

Currie, L.A., Limits for qualitative detection and quantitative determination. *Analytical Chemistry*, 40(3), 586–593, 1968.

Currie, L.A., *Lower Limit of Detection: Definition and Elaboration of a Proposed Position for Radiological Effluent and Environmental Measurements*, NUREG/CR-4007. U.S. Nuclear Regulatory Commission, Washington, DC, 1984.

Dabberdt, W.F., Overwater atmospheric diffusion: measurements and parameterization. *Journal of Climate and Applied Meteorology*, 25, 1160–1172, 1986.

DCPA, *Civil Preparedness Principles of Warning*, CPG 1-14. Defense Civil Preparedness Agency, Washington, DC, 1977.

Deutch, J.M. et al., *The Future of Nuclear Power: An Interdisciplinary MIT Study*. Massachusetts Institute of Technology, Cambridge, MA, 2003.

Dietzel, H. and Kriest, I., ^{137}Cs off Fukushima Dai-ichi, Japan—model based estimates of dilution and fate. *Ocean Science*, 8, 319–332, 2012.

DiNunno, J.J., Anderson, F.D., Baker, R.E., and Waterfield, R. L., *Calculation of Distance Factors for Power and Test Reactor Sites*, Technical Information Document 14844. U.S. Atomic Energy Commission, Washington, DC, 1962.

Distenfeld, C. and Klemish, J., *High Efficiency Mixed Species Radionuclide Air Sampling, Readout, and Dose Assessment System*, Report BNL-21541. Brookhaven National Laboratory, Upton, NY, 1976.

Distenfeld, C. and Klemish, J., *An Air Sampling System for Evaluating the Thyroid Dose Commitment Due to Fission Products Released from Reactor Containment*, NUREG/CR-0314, BNL-NUREG-50881. Brookhaven National Laboratory, Upton, NY, 1978a.

Distenfeld, C. and Klemish, J., *Environmental Radioiodine Monitoring to Control Exposure Expected from Containment Release Accidents*, NUREG/CR-0315, BNL-NUREG-50882. Brookhaven National Laboratory, Upton, NY, 1978b.

Dotson, L.J. and Jones, J., *Development of Evacuation Time Estimate Studies for Nuclear Power Plants*, NUREG/CR-6863, SAND2004-5900. Sandia National Laboratories, Albuquerque, NM, 2005a.

Dotson, L.J. and Jones, J., *Identification and Analysis of Factors Affecting Emergency Evacuations*, NUREG/CR-6864, SAND2004-5901. Sandia National Laboratories, Albuquerque, NM, 2005b.

Egan, B.A. and Snyder, W.H., Atmospheric dispersion: complex terrain, in *Encyclopedia of Environmetrics*, El-Shaarawi, A.H. and Piegorsch, W.W., Eds., pp. 109–124. John Wiley & Sons, New York, 2002.

Eisenbud, M., *Environmental Radioactivity from Natural, Industrial, and Military Sources*, 3rd ed. Academic Press, San Diego, CA, 1987.

Eisenhower, D.D., *Attack Warning for Civilians*, Presidential Directive 5513/1. White House, Washington, DC, 1955.

EPRI, *Environmental Radiation Doses from Difficult-to-Measure Nuclides*, EPRI NP-3840. Electric Power Research Institute, Palo, Alto, CA, 1985.

EPRI, *Deterring Terrorism: Aircraft Crash Impact Analyses Demonstrate Nuclear Power Plant's Structural Strength*. Electric Power Research Institute, Palo Alto, CA, 2002 (details withheld from the public).

Ericson, D.M., Jr., *Accident Descriptions for Emergency Response Exercise Scenarios*, NUREG/CR-0388, SAND-78-0269. Sandia National Laboratories, Albuquerque, NM, 1978.

EURATOM, *Informing the General Public About Health Protection Measures to Be Applied and Steps to Be Taken in the Event of a Radiological Emergency*, Council Directive 89/618/Euratom. European Atomic Energy Community, 1989.

EURATOM, *Off-Site Nuclear Emergency Management and Restoration of Contaminated Environments*, EUR 21927. European Atomic Energy Community, 2007.

EURATOM, *Laying Down Basic Safety Standards for Protection Against Dangers Arising from Exposure to Ionizing Radiation*, Council Directive 2013/59/Euratom. European Atomic Energy Community, 2013a.

EURATOM, *Review of Current Off-Site Nuclear Emergency Preparedness and Response Arrangements in EU Member States and Neighbouring Countries, Final Report*, ENER/D1/2012-474. European Atomic Energy Community, 2013b.

Federal Radiation Council (FRC), Radiation protection guidance for federal agencies. *Federal Register*, 25(97), 4402, 1960.

Federal Radiation Council (FRC), Radiation protection guidance for federal agencies. *Federal Register*, 29, 12056, 1964.

Federal Radiation Council (FRC), Radiation protection guidance for federal agencies. *Federal Register*, 30, 6953, 1965.

FEMA, *Guidance on Offsite Emergency Radiation Measurement Systems. Phase 1. Airborne Release*, FEMA REP-2. Federal Emergency Management Agency, Washington, DC, 1980a.

FEMA, *Joint Review of Comments on Criteria for Preparation and Evaluation of Radiological Emergency Response Plans and Preparedness in Support of Nuclear Power Plants*, FEMA REP-4. Federal Emergency Management Agency, Washington, DC, 1980b.

FEMA, *National Contingency Plan*. Federal Emergency Management Agency, Washington, DC, 1980c.

FEMA, *Outdoor Warning Systems Guide*, CPG 1-17. Federal Emergency Management Agency, Washington, DC, 1980d.

FEMA, *Report to the President—Radiological Emergency Planning and Preparedness in Support of Commercial Nuclear Power Plants*. Federal Emergency Management Agency, Washington, DC, 1980e.

FEMA, Operative guidance memoranda and related documents dating from 1980 to 1990:

Radio Transmission Frequencies and Coverage, Guidance Memorandum 4, April 1, 1980.

Standard Regional Reviewing and Reporting Procedures for State and Local Radiological Emergency Response Plans, Guidance Memorandum 16, August 7, 1980.

Conducting Pre-Exercise and Post-Exercise Activities, Guidance Memorandum 17, January 8, 1981.

Agreements Among Governmental Agencies and Private Parties, Guidance Memorandum 5, Revision 1, October 19, 1983.

Foreign Language Translations of Public Education Brochures and Safety Messages, Guidance Memorandum 20, October 19, 1983.

Regional Advisory Committee Coordination with Utilities, Guidance Memorandum 8, Revision 1, October 19, 1983.

Acceptance Criteria for Evacuation Plans, Guidance Memorandum 21, February 29, 1984.

Radiological Emergency Preparedness for Handicapped Persons, Guidance Memorandum 24, April 5, 1984.

Guidance on NUREG-0654/FEMA-REP-1 and 44 CFR 350 Periodic Requirements, Guidance Memorandum PR-1, October 1, 1985.

FEMA Action to Pilot Test Guidance on Public Information Materials and Provide Technical Assistance on Its Use, Guidance Memorandum PI-1, October 2, 1985.

Federal Response Center Site Selection Criteria for Peacetime Radiological Emergencies, Guidance Memorandum FR-1, November 20, 1985.

Medical Services, Guidance Memorandum MS-1, November 13, 1986.

Protective Actions for School Children, Guidance Memorandum EV-2, November 13, 1986.

FEMA Action to Qualify Alert and Notification Systems Against NUREG-0654/FEMA-REP-1 and FEMA REP-10, Guidance Memorandum AN-1, April 21, 1987.

Staff Support in Evaluating REP Exercises, Guidance Memorandum EX-2, July 15, 1985; Revision 1, August 11, 1987.

Clarification of Selected Provisions of Guidance Memorandum MS-1, Medical Services, February 9, 1988.

Managing Pre-Exercise and Post-Exercise Meetings, Guidance Memorandum EX-3, February 26, 1988; amended, March 7, 1988.

The Ingestion Exposure Pathway, Guidance Memorandum IN-1, February 26, 1988.

Medical Services and Radiological Monitoring Guidance, September 19, 1988.

Guidance on Ingestion Pathway Exercises, December 7, 1989.

Remedial Exercises, Guidance Memorandum EX-1, July 15, 1985; Revision 1, December 14, 1989.

Distribution and Use of the Generic Ingestion Pathway Brochure Entitled "Radiological Emergency Information," January 12, 1990.

FEMA, Federal radiological emergency planning and preparedness. *Federal Register*, 47, 10758, 1982.

FEMA, *Dynamic Evacuation Analysis: Independent Assessments of Evacuation Times from the Plume Exposure Pathway Emergency Planning Zones of Twelve Nuclear Power Stations*, FEMA REP-3. Federal Emergency Management Agency, Washington, DC, 1983a.

FEMA, *Standard Guide for the Evaluation of Alert and Notification Systems for Nuclear Power Plants*, FEMA-43. Federal Emergency Management Agency, Washington, DC, 1983b.

FEMA, *Exercise Evaluation and Simulation Facility Evacuation Events Models, Part I: PREDYN Users Guide*, FEMA REP-6. Federal Emergency Management Agency, Washington, DC, 1984a.

FEMA, *Exercise Evaluation and Simulation Facility Evacuation Events Models, Part II: Users Manual for the Interactive Dynamic Network Evacuation Model*, FEMA REP-7. Federal Emergency Management Agency, Washington, DC, 1984b.

FEMA, *Exercise Evaluation and Simulation Facility Evacuation Events Models, Part III: Application of the I-DYNEV System*, FEMA REP-8. Federal Emergency Management Agency, Washington, DC, 1984c.

FEMA, *A Guide to Preparing Emergency Public Information Materials*, FEMA REP-11. Federal Emergency Management Agency, Washington, DC, 1985a.

FEMA, *Guide for the Evaluation of Alert and Notification Systems for Nuclear Power Plants*, FEMA REP-10. Federal Emergency Management Agency, Washington, DC, 1985b.

FEMA, *Guidance on Offsite Emergency Radiation Measurement Systems. Phase 2. The Milk Pathway*, FEMA REP-12. Federal Emergency Management Agency, Washington, DC, 1987.

FEMA, *Guidance on Offsite Emergency Radiation Measurement Systems. Phase 3. Water and Non-Dairy*, FEMA REP-13. Federal Emergency Management Agency, Washington, DC, 1989.

FEMA, *Guidance on Offsite Emergency Radiation Measurement Systems. Phase 1. Airborne Release*, FEMA REP-2, Revision 2. Federal Emergency Management Agency, Washington, DC, 1990.

FEMA, *Principles of Warning and Criteria Governing Eligibility of National Warning System (NAWAS) Terminals*, CPG 1-14. Federal Emergency Management Agency, Washington, DC, 1991a.

FEMA, *Radiological Emergency Preparedness Exercise Evaluation Methodology*, FEMA REP-15. Federal Emergency Management Agency, Washington, DC, 1991b.

FEMA, *Radiological Emergency Preparedness Exercise Manual*, FEMA REP-14. Federal Emergency Management Agency, Washington, DC, 1991c.

FEMA, *Guidance for Developing State, Tribal, and Local Radiological Emergency Response Planning and Preparedness for Transportation Accidents*, FEMA REP-5, revised. Federal Emergency Management Agency, Washington, DC, 1992a.

FEMA, *National Warning System (NAWAS) Operations Manual*, CPG 01-016. Federal Emergency Management Agency, Washington, DC, 1992b.

FEMA, *Radiological Emergency Preparedness (REP) Program Brochure*, FEMA L-225. Federal Emergency Management Agency, Washington, DC, 1992c.

FEMA, *Statements of Consideration for FEMA REP-14 and FEMA REP-15*, FEMA REP-18. Federal Emergency Management Agency, Washington, DC, 1992d.

FEMA, *Evacuation Time Study Review Guide (Checklist)*, RG REP-05, revised. Federal Emergency Management Agency, Washington, DC, 1993.

FEMA, *Emergency Alert System*, CPG 01-40. Federal Emergency Management Agency, Washington, DC, 1996a.

FEMA, *Emergency Alert System—A Programmatic Guide for State and Local Jurisdictions*, CPG 01-41. Federal Emergency Management Agency, Washington, DC, 1996b.

FEMA, *Guide for All-Hazard Emergency Operations Planning*, SLG-101. Federal Emergency Management Agency, Washington, DC, 1996c.

FEMA, *Radiological Emergency Preparedness (REP) Program Brochure*, FEMA REP-14. Federal Emergency Management Agency, Washington, DC, 2000.

FEMA, Federal policy on use of potassium iodide. *Federal Register*, 67(7), 1355–1357, 2002a.

FEMA, Radiological emergency preparedness: exercise evaluation methodology. *Federal Register*, 66, 47526, 2002; corrections published in *Federal Register*, 67, 20579, 2002b.

FEMA, *Joint Field Office Activation and Operations, Interagency Standard Operating Procedure,* Version 8.3. Federal Emergency Management Agency, Washington, DC, 2006.

FEMA, *Developing and Maintaining Emergency Operations Plans*, 2nd, ed., CPG-101. Federal Emergency Management Agency, Washington, DC, 2010.

FEMA, *Disaster Initiated Review*, FEMA Standard Operating Guide. Federal Emergency Management Agency, Washington, DC, 2011a.

FEMA, *REP/HSEEP Exercise Integration Handbook*. Federal Emergency Management Agency, Washington, DC, 2011b.

FEMA, *Threat and Hazard Identification and Risk Assessment Guide*, 2nd ed., CPG-201. Federal Emergency Management Agency, Washington, DC, 2013.

FEMA, *Radiological Emergency Preparedness Program Manual*, FEMA P-1028. Federal Emergency Management Agency, Washington, DC, 2016.

FEMA/NRC, Memorandum of understanding between FEMA and NRC for incident response. *Federal Register*, 45(243), 82713, 1980.

FEMA/NRC, Memorandum of understanding between FEMA and NRC for incident response, revised. *Federal Register*, 50, 15485, 1985.

FEMA/NRC, Memorandum of understanding between FEMA and NRC for incident response, revised (44 CFR 353 Appendix A). *Federal Register*, 58, 47997, 1993.

GAO, *Stronger Federal Assistance to States Needed for Radiation Emergency Response Planning*, Report to Congress. U.S. General Accountability Office, Washington, DC, 1976.

GAO, *Areas Around Nuclear Facilities Should Be Better Prepared for Radiological Emergencies*, EMD-78-110. U.S. General Accountability Office, Washington, DC, 1979.

GAO, *Emergency Preparedness: Current Emergency Alert System Has Limitations, and Development of a New Integrated System Will Be Challenging*. U.S. General Accountability Office, Washington, DC, 2007.

GAO, *Emergency Preparedness: Improved Planning and Coordination Necessary for Modernization and Integration of Public Alert and Warning System*, Report to Congress. U.S. General Accountability Office, Washington, DC, 2009a.

GAO, *National Preparedness: FEMA Has Made Progress But Needs to Complete and Integrate Planning, Exercise, and Assessment Efforts*, Report to Congress. U.S. General Accountability Office, Washington, DC, 2009b.

GAO, *Emergency Preparedness: FEMA Faces Challenges Integrating Community Preparedness Programs into Its Strategic Approach*, Report to Congress. U.S. General Accountability Office, Washington, DC, 2010.

GAO, *Emergency Preparedness: NRC Needs to Better Understand Likely Public Response to Radiological Incidents at Nuclear Power Plants*, Report to Congress. U.S. General Accountability Office, Washington, DC, 2013.

GAO, *Emergency Preparedness: Opportunities Exist to Strengthen Interagency Assessments and Accountability for Closing Capability Gaps*, Report to Congress. U.S. General Accountability Office, Washington, DC, 2014.

Gavila, F.M., *Hydrated vs. Dehydrated Silver Zeolite: A Response to an Event at LaCrosse Boiling Water Reactor (BWR) in March 1986 During Air Sampling Activity Utilizing Silver Zeolite*. F&J Specialty Products, Ocala, FL, 2003a.

Gavila, F.M., *Technical Performance Specification for Radioiodine Collection Cartridges Containing TEDA Impregnated Charcoal and Silver Zeolite Media*, Revision 21. F&J Specialty Products, Inc., Ocala, FL, 2003b.

GCRP, *Basic Radiological Principles for Decisions on Measures for the Protection of the Population Against Incidents Involving Releases of Radionuclides*. German Commission on Radiological Protection, 2014 (English translation).

Gifford, F.A., The area within ground-level dosage isopleths. *Nuclear Safety*, 4(2), 91–92, 1962.

GSA, Radiological incident emergency response planning, fixed facilities and transportation: interagency responsibilities. *Federal Register*, 40(248), 1975.

GSA, *Federal Response Plan for Peacetime Nuclear Emergencies (Interim Guidance)*. Federal Preparedness Agency, General Services Administration, Washington, DC, 1977.

Hatch, M.C. et al., Cancer near the Three Mile Island nuclear plant: radiation emissions. *American Journal of Epidemiology*, 132(3), 397–412, 1990.

Hatch, M.C. et al., Cancer rates after the Three Mile Island nuclear accident and proximity of residence to the plant. *American Journal of Public Health*, 81(6), 719–724, 1991.

Health Canada, *Recommendations on Dose Coefficients for Assessing Doses from Accidental Radionuclide Releases to the Environment*. Radiation Protection Group, Health Canada, Ottawa, 1999.

Hessheimer, M.F. and Dameron, R.A., *Containment Integrity Research at Sandia National Laboratories—An Overview*, NUREG/CR-6906, SAND2006-2274P. Sandia National Laboratories, Albuquerque, NM, 2006.

Howe, G.R., Risk of cancer mortality in populations living near nuclear facilities. *JAMA*, 265(11), 1438–1439, 1991.

IAEA, *Advances in Radiation Protection Monitoring*, IAEA-SM-229/103. International Atomic Energy Agency, Vienna, Austria, 1979.

IAEA, *Preparedness of Public Authorities for Emergencies at Nuclear Power Plants*, 50-SG-G6. International Atomic Energy Agency, Vienna, Austria, 1982a.

IAEA, *Preparedness of the Operating Organization (Licensee) for Emergencies at Nuclear Power Plants*, 50-SG-O6. International Atomic Energy Agency, Vienna, Austria, 1982b.

IAEA, *Emergency Preparedness Exercises for Nuclear Facilities: Preparation, Conduct, and Evaluation*. International Atomic Energy Agency, Vienna, Austria, 1985.

IAEA, *Conventions on Early Notification of a Nuclear Accident*. International Atomic Energy Agency, Vienna, Austria, 1986.

IAEA, *On-Site Habitability in the Event of an Accident at a Nuclear Facility.* International Atomic Energy Agency, Vienna, Austria, 1989.

IAEA, *Planning for Cleanup of Large Areas Contaminated As a Result of Nuclear Accident.* International Atomic Energy Agency, Vienna, Austria, 1991a.

IAEA, *Principles for Establishing Intervention Levels for the Protection of the Public in the Event of a Nuclear Accident or Radiological Emergency,* Revision 1. International Atomic Energy Agency, Vienna, Austria, 1991b.

IAEA, *Accident Management Programmes in Nuclear Power Plants: A Guidebook.* International Atomic Energy Agency, Vienna, Austria, 1994a.

IAEA, *Guidelines for Agricultural Countermeasures Following an Accidental Release of Radionuclides,* Report 363. International Atomic Energy Agency, Vienna, Austria, 1994b.

IAEA, *Intervention Criteria in a Nuclear or Radiation Emergency,* STI/PUB 900. International Atomic Energy Agency, Vienna, Austria, 1994c.

IAEA, *Defense in Depth in Nuclear Safety, A Report by the International Nuclear Safety Advisory Group,* INSAG-10. International Atomic Energy Agency, Vienna, Austria, 1996a.

IAEA, *International Basic Safety Standards for Protection Against Ionizing Radiation and for the Safety of Radiation Sources,* Safety Series No. 115. International Atomic Energy Agency, Vienna, Austria, 1996b.

IAEA, *Nuclear and Radiation Safety: Guidance for Emergency Response,* IAEA Bulletin 38. International Atomic Energy Agency, Vienna, Austria, 1996c.

IAEA, *Generic Assessment Procedures for Determining Protective Actions During a Reactor Accident,* IAEA-TECDOC-995. International Atomic Energy Agency, Vienna, Austria, 1997.

IAEA, *Planning the Medical Response to Radiological Accidents.* International Atomic Energy Agency, Vienna, Austria, 1998.

IAEA, *Basic Safety Principles for Nuclear Power Plants, 75-INSAG-3 Rev. 1, A Report by the International Nuclear Safety Advisory Group,* INSAG-12. International Atomic Energy Agency, Vienna, Austria, 1999a.

IAEA, *Generic Procedures for Monitoring in a Nuclear or Radiological Emergency,* IAEA TECDOC-1092. International Atomic Energy Agency, Vienna, Austria, 1999b.

IAEA, *The International Nuclear Event Scale: For Prompt Communication of Safety Significance,* Pamphlet 99-00305/FS-05. International Atomic Energy Agency, Vienna, Austria, 1999c.

IAEA, *Generic Procedures for Assessment and Response During a Radiological Emergency,* IAEA TECDOC-1162. International Atomic Energy Agency, Vienna, Austria, 2000.

IAEA, *Planning and Preparing for Emergency Response to Transport Accidents Involving Radioactive Material.* International Atomic Energy Agency, Vienna, Austria, 2001.

IAEA, *Emergency Notification and Assistance, Technical Operations Manual,* EPR-ENATOM 2002. International Atomic Energy Agency, Vienna, Austria, 2002a.

IAEA, *Planning and Preparedness for Emergency Response to Transport Accidents Involving Radioactive Material.* International Atomic Energy Agency, Vienna, Austria, 2002b.

IAEA, *Preparedness and Response for a Nuclear or Radiological Emergency, Safety Requirements.* International Atomic Energy Agency, Vienna, Austria, 2002c.

IAEA, *Method for Developing Arrangements for Response to a Nuclear or Radiological Emergency.* International Atomic Energy Agency, Vienna, Austria, 2003.

IAEA, *Implementation of Severe Accident Management Programmes in Nuclear Power.* International Atomic Energy Agency, Vienna, Austria, 2004.

IAEA, *Generic Procedures for Medical Response During a Nuclear or Radiological Emergency.* International Atomic Energy Agency, Vienna, Austria, 2005a.

IAEA, *Preparation, Conduct and Evaluation of Exercises to Test Preparedness for a Nuclear or Radiological Emergency.* International Atomic Energy Agency, Vienna, Austria, 2005b.

IAEA, *IAEA Safety Glossary: Terminology Used in Nuclear, Radiation, Radioactive Waste and Transport Safety.* International Atomic Energy Agency, Vienna, Austria, 2006a.

IAEA, *Manual for First Responders to a Radiological Emergency.* International Atomic Energy Agency, Vienna, Austria, 2006b.

IAEA, *Arrangements for Preparedness for a Nuclear or Radiological Emergency.* International Atomic Energy Agency, Vienna, Austria, 2007.

IAEA, *Severe Accident Management Programmes for Nuclear Power Plants.* International Atomic Energy Agency, Vienna, Austria, 2009.

IAEA, *Criteria for Use in Preparedness and Response for a Nuclear or Radiological Emergency.* International Atomic Energy Agency, Vienna, Austria, 2011a.

IAEA, *Generic Procedures for Response to a Nuclear or Radiological Emergency at Research Reactors— Training Material*. International Atomic Energy Agency, Vienna, Austria, 2011b.

IAEA, *Communication with the Public in a Nuclear or Radiological Emergency*. International Atomic Energy Agency, Vienna, Austria, 2012a.

IAEA, *Operations Manual for Incident and Emergency Communication*. International Atomic Energy Agency, Vienna, Austria, 2012b.

IAEA, *Actions to Protect the Public in an Emergency Due to Severe Conditions at a Light Water Reactor*. International Atomic Energy Agency, Vienna, Austria, 2013.

IAEA, *Advances in Small Modulator Reactor Technology Developments, A Supplement to: IAEA Advanced Reactors Information System (ARIS)*. International Atomic Energy Agency, Vienna, Austria, 2014.

IAEA, *Method for Developing a Communication Strategy and Plan for a Nuclear or Radiological Emergency*. International Atomic Energy Agency, Vienna, Austria, 2015a.

IAEA, *The Fukushima Daiichi Accident*. Technical Volume 5. *Post-Accident Recovery*. Annex IV. *Comparative Analysis of Remediation Strategies and Experience After the Fukushima Daiichi and Chernobyl Nuclear Accidents*. International Atomic Energy Agency, Vienna, Austria, 2015b.

IARC, Ionizing radiation, Part 1: x- and gamma (γ)-radiation, and neutrons. *IARC Monographs*, 75, 78, 2000.

ICRP, *Recommendations of the International Commission on Radiological Protection*, ICRP 26. International Commission on Radiological Protection, Ottawa, Canada, 1977a.

ICRP, *The Principles and General Procedures for Handling Emergency and Accidental Exposures of Workers*, ICRP 28. International Commission on Radiological Protection, Ottawa, Canada, 1977b.

ICRP, *Principles for Handling Emergency and Accidental Exposures of Workers*, IRCP Report 28. International Commission on Radiological Protection, Ottawa, Canada, 1978.

ICRP, *Limits for the Intake of Radionuclides by Workers, Part 1*, ICRP 30. International Commission on Radiological Protection, Ottawa, Canada, 1979.

ICRP, *Limits for the Intake of Radionuclides by Workers, Part 2*, ICRP 30. International Commission on Radiological Protection, Ottawa, Canada, 1980.

ICRP, *Limits for the Intake of Radionuclides by Workers, Part 3*, ICRP 30. International Commission on Radiological Protection, Ottawa, Canada, 1981.

ICRP, *Protection of the Public in the Event of Major Radiation Accidents: Principles for Planning*, ICRP 40. International Commission on Radiological Protection, Ottawa, Canada, 1984.

ICRP, *1990 Recommendations of the International Commission on Radiological Protection*, ICRP 60. International Commission on Radiological Protection, Ottawa, Canada, 1991.

ICRP, *Principles for Intervention for Protection of the Public in a Radiological Emergency*, IRCP Report 63. International Commission on Radiological Protection, Ottawa, Canada, 1992.

ICRP, *Protecting People Against Radiation Exposure in the Event of a Radiological Attack*, IRCP Report 96. International Commission on Radiological Protection, Ottawa, Canada, 2005.

ICRP, *Application of the Commission's Recommendations for the Protection of People in Emergency Exposure Situations*, IRCP Report 109. International Commission on Radiological Protection, Ottawa, Canada, 2009a.

ICRP, *Application of the Commission's Recommendations to the Protection of People Living in Long-Term Contaminated Areas After a Nuclear Accident or Radiation Emergency*, IRCP Report 111. International Commission on Radiological Protection, Ottawa, Canada, 2009b.

IEC, *Radiation Monitoring Equipment for Accident and Post-Accident Conditions in Nuclear Power Plants*. Part 1. *General Requirements*, IEC 60951-1. International Electrotechnical Commission, Geneva, Switzerland, 1988a.

IEC, *Radiation Monitoring Equipment for Accident and Post-Accident Conditions in Nuclear Power Plants*. Part 2. *Equipment for Continuously Monitoring Radioactive Noble Gases in Gaseous Effluents*, IEC 60951-2. International Electrotechnical Commission, Geneva, Switzerland, 1988b.

IEC, *Radiation Monitoring Equipment for Accident and Post-Accident Conditions in Nuclear Power Plants*. Part 3. *High-Range Gamma Dose Rate Monitoring Equipment*, IEC 60951-3. International Electrotechnical Commission, Geneva, Switzerland, 1989.

IEC, Application of the Commission's recommendations for the protection of people in emergency exposure situations, IRCP Report 109. *Annals of the ICRP*, 39(1), 1–110, 2009.

IEEE, *Performance Specifications for Reactor Emergency Radiological Monitoring Instrumentation*, IEEE N320. Institute of Electrical and Electronics Engineers, Piscataway, NJ, 1993.

IEEE, *Standard Criteria for Accident Monitoring Instrumentation for Nuclear Power Generating Stations*, IEEE 497. Institute of Electrical and Electronics Engineers, Piscataway, NJ, 2002.

INPO, *Emergency Preparedness Program Review*, INPO 85-014, revised. Institute of Nuclear Power Operations, Atlanta, GA, 1991.

INPO, *Emergency Preparedness Drill and Exercise Manual*, INPO 88-019. Institute of Nuclear Power Operations, Atlanta, GA, 1998.

INPO, *Emergency Preparedness Manual*, INPO 08-007. Institute of Nuclear Power Operations, Atlanta, GA, 2008.

INPO, *Guidelines for Training and Qualification of Emergency Response Personnel*, INPO 09-006. Institute of Nuclear Power Operations, Atlanta, GA, 2009.

Jablon, S., Hrubec, Z., and Boice, Jr., J.D., Cancer in populations living near nuclear facilities: a survey of mortality nationwide and incidence in two states. *JAMA*, 265(11), 1403–1409, 1991.

Jeffries, D.F., Fission product radionuclides in sediments from the North-East Irish Sea. *Biological and Hydrographical Consequences of Pollution*, 17(1), 280–290, 1968.

Jorgensen, B., *The Theory of Dispersion Models*. Chapman & Hall, London, 1997.

Kennedy, J.F., Executive Order 11089—Assigning emergency preparedness functions to the Atomic Energy Commission. *Federal Register*, 28, 1839, 1963.

Kocher, D.C., *Derivation of Effective Resuspension Factors in Scenarios for Inhalation Exposure Involving Resuspension of Previously Deposited Fallout by Nuclear Detonations at the Nevada Test Site*, DTRA-TR-09-15. Defense Threat Reduction Agency, Fort Belvoir, VA, 2009.

Koren, H., *Handbook of Environmental Health*. Lewis Publishers, Boca Raton, FL, 2003.

Kot, C.A., Lin, H.C., van Erp, J.B., Eichler, T.V., and Wiedermann, A.H., *Hazardous Material Accidents Near Nuclear Power Plants: An Evaluation of Analyses and Approaches*, NUREG/CR-3548, ANL-83-53. U.S. Nuclear Regulatory Commission, Washington, DC, 1983.

Kouts, H.J.C., Apostolakis, G., Kastenberg, W.E. et al., *Special Committee Review of the Nuclear Regulatory Commission's Severe Accident Risks Report (NUREG-1150)*, NUREG-1420. U.S. Nuclear Regulatory Commission, Washington, DC, 1990.

Kratchman, J. and Sullivan, R., *Public Comment Analysis and Adjudication: Supplement 3 to NUREG-0654/ FEMA REP-1, "Guidance for Protective Action Strategies,"* NUREG-2112. U.S. Nuclear Regulatory Commission, Washington, DC, 2011.

Leggett, R.W., Dickson, H.W., and Haywood, F.F., *A Statistical Methodology for Radiological Surveying*. International Atomic Energy Agency, Vienna, Austria, 1979.

Lewin, A., *Event Reporting Guidelines*, NUREG-1022, Revision 3. U.S. Nuclear Regulatory Commission, Washington, DC, 2013.

Lin, C.C., *Radiochemistry in Nuclear Power Reactors*, NAS-NS-3119. National Academy Press, Washington, DC, 1996.

Lindsey, C.G. and Glantz, C.S., *Method to Characterize Local Meteorology at Nuclear Facilities for Application to Emergency Response Needs*, NUREG/CR-3882, PNL-5155. Pacific Northwest National Laboratory, Richland, WA, 1986.

Lorenz, R.A., Collins, J.L., Malinauskas, A.P., Kirkland, O.L., and Towns, R.L., *Fission Product Release from Highly Irradiated LWR Fuel*, NUREG/CR-0772. U.S. Nuclear Regulatory Agency, Washington, DC, 1980.

Luckas, J.J., Vandenkieboom, J.J., and Lehner, J.R., *Assessment of Candidate Accident Management Strategies*, NUREG/CR-5474. U.S. Nuclear Regulatory Commission, Washington, DC, 1992.

Ludwick, J.D., *The Iodine Collection Efficiency of Activated Charcoal from Hanford Reactor Confinement Systems: Methyl Iodide Retention by Activated Charcoal*, Report BNWL-1046. Pacific Northwest National Laboratory, Battelle–Northwest, Richland, WA, 1969.

Maeck, W.J., Hoffman, L.G., Staples, B.A., and Keller, J.A., *An Assessment of Offsite, Real-Time Dose Measurement Systems for Emergency Situations*, NUREG/CR-2644, ENICO-1110. U.S. Nuclear Regulatory Commission, Washington, DC, 1982.

Marcus, C.S., Administration of decorporation drugs to treat internal radionuclide contamination: medical emergency response to radiologic incidents. *RSO Magazine*, 9(5), 9–15, 2004.

Mauchline, J. and Templeton, W., Dispersion in the Irish Sea of the radioactive liquid effluent from Windscale Works of the U.K. Atomic Energy Authority. *Nature*, 198, 623–626, 1963.

McGinnity, P. et al., *Radioactivity Monitoring of the Irish Environment, 2010–2011*, RPII 12/02. Radiological Protection Institute of Ireland, Dublin, 2012.

McGuire, S.A., Ramsdell, Jr., J.V., and Athey, G.F., *RASCAL 3.0.5: Description of Models and Methods*, NUREG-1887. U.S. Nuclear Regulatory Commission, Washington, DC, 2007.

McKenna, T.J. and Glitter, J.G., *Source Term Estimation During Incident Response to Severe Nuclear Power Plant Accidents*, NUREG-1228. U.S. Nuclear Regulatory Commission, Washington, DC, 1988.

Meinke, W.W. and Essig, T.H., *Offsite Dose Calculation Manual Guidance: Standard Radiological Effluent Controls for Boiling Water Reactors*, NUREG-1302. U.S. Nuclear Regulatory Commission, Washington, DC, 1991.

Meroney, R.N., Dilution of Hazardous Gas Cloud Concentrations Using Vapor Barriers and Water Spray Curtains, paper presented at Second Asia-Pacific Symposium on Wind Engineering, Beijing, China, June 26–29, 1989.

Mikkelsen, T. and Desiato, F., Atmospheric dispersion models and pre-processing of meteorological data for real time application. *Radiation Protection Dosimetry*, 50(2-4), 205–218, 1993.

Molenkamp, C.R., Bixler, N.E., Morrow, C.W., Ramsdell, J.V., and Mitchell, J.A., *Comparison of Average Transport and Dispersion Among a Gaussian, a Two-Dimensional, and a Three Dimensional Model*, NUREG/CR-6853. U.S. Nuclear Regulatory Commission, Washington, DC, 2004.

Mosser, J., *EPA's Response to Fukushima Japan Nuclear Emergency* [PowerPoint presentation]. Center for Radiological Emergency Management, Office of Radiation and Indoor Air, Washington, DC, 2011.

Napier, B.A., *Alternative Conceptual Models for Assessing Food Chain Pathways in Biosphere Models*, NUREG/CR-6910, PNNL-15872. Pacific Northwest National Laboratory, Richland, WA, 2006.

Napier, B.A., Fellows, R.J., and Krupka, K.M., *Radionuclide Behaviors in Soil and Soil-to-Plant Concentration Ratios for Assessing Food Chain Pathways*, NUREG/CR-7120, PNNL-20979. Pacific Northwest National Laboratory, Richland, WA, 2012.

National Research Advisory Committee on the Biological Effects of Ionizing Radiation, *The Effects on Populations of Exposure to Low Levels of Ionizing Radiation*. National Academy of Sciences, Washington, DC, 1980.

National Research Council, *Radiochemistry in Nuclear Power Reactors*. National Academies Press, Washington, DC, 1996.

National Research Council, *Distribution and Administration of Potassium Iodide in the Event of a Nuclear Incident*. National Academies Press, Washington, DC, 2004.

NBS, *Maximum Permissible Body Burdens and Maximum Permissible Concentrations of Radionuclides in Air and in Water for Occupational Exposure*, Handbook 69. National Bureau of Standards, Washington, DC, 1959.

NCI, *Cancer in Populations Living Near Nuclear Facilities*, GPO 017-042-00276-1. National Cancer Institute, Bethesda, MD, 1990.

NCI, *Surveillance, Epidemiology, and End Results Cancer Statistics Review, 1975–2003*. National Cancer Institute, Bethesda, MD, 2006.

NEA, *Protection of the Population in the Event of a Nuclear Accident: A Basis for Intervention: A Report*. Nuclear Energy Agency, Organization for Economic Cooperation and Development, Paris, 1990.

NEA, *Short Term Countermeasures After a Nuclear Emergency, Proceedings of an NEA Workshop, June 1994, Stockholm, Sweden*. Nuclear Energy Agency, Organization for Economic Cooperation and Development, Paris, 1995.

NEA, *Chernobyl Reactor Accident Source Term [The]. Development of a Consensus View*, NEA 219. Nuclear Energy Agency, Organization for Economic Cooperation and Development, Paris, 1996.

NEA, *Agricultural Aspects of Nuclear and/or Radiological Emergency Situations*, NEA 486. Nuclear Energy Agency, Organization for Economic Cooperation and Development, Paris, 1997.

NEA, *Inspection of Licensee Activities in Emergency Planning*, NEA/CNRA/R(98)2. Nuclear Energy Agency, Organization for Economic Cooperation and Development, Paris, 1998.

NEA, *Methodologies for Assessing the Economic Consequences of Nuclear Reactor Accidents*, NEA 2228. Nuclear Energy Agency, Organization for Economic Cooperation and Development, Paris, 2000a.

NEA, *Monitoring and Data Management Strategies for Nuclear Emergencies*, NEA 2108. Nuclear Energy Agency, Organization for Economic Cooperation and Development, Paris, 2000b.

NEA, *Experience from International Nuclear Emergency Exercises*, NEA 3138. Nuclear Energy Agency, Organization for Economic Cooperation and Development, Paris, 2001.

NEA, *Strategic Aspects of Nuclear and Radiological Emergency Management*, NEA 6387. Nuclear Energy Agency, Organization for Economic Cooperation and Development, Paris, 2010.

NEA, *Practices and Experience in Stakeholder Involvement for Post-Nuclear Emergency Management*, NEA 6994. Nuclear Energy Agency, Organization for Economic Cooperation and Development, Paris, 2011.

NEA, *The Fukushima Daiichi Nuclear Power Plant Accident: OECD/NEA Nuclear Safety Response and Lessons Learnt*, NEA 7161. Nuclear Energy Agency, Organization for Economic Cooperation and Development, Paris, 2013.

NEA and Commission of the European Communities, *Proceedings of a Joint NEA/CEC Workshop on Emergency Planning in Case of Nuclear Accident: Technical Aspects*. Nuclear Energy Agency, Organization for Economic Cooperation and Development, Paris, 1989.

Neeb, K.-H., *Radiochemistry of Nuclear Power Plants with Light Water Reactors*. Walter de Gruyter, Berlin, 1997.

NEI, *Severe Accident Issue Closure Guidelines*, NEI 91-04, Revision 1. Nuclear Energy Institute, Washington, DC, 1994.

NEI, *Regulatory Assessment Performance Indicator Guideline*, NEI 99-02, Revision 0. Nuclear Energy Institute, Washington, DC, 2000.

NEI, *Regulatory Assessment Performance Indicator Guideline*, NEI 99-02, Revision 1. Nuclear Energy Institute, Washington, DC, 2001a.

NEI, *Regulatory Assessment Performance Indicator Guideline*, NEI 99-02, Revision 2. Nuclear Energy Institute, Washington, DC, 2001b.

NEI, *Methodology for Development of Emergency Action Levels*, NEI 99-01, Revision 4. Nuclear Energy Institute, Washington, DC, 2003.

NEI, *Regulatory Assessment Performance Indicator Guideline*, NEI 99-02, Revision 3. Nuclear Energy Institute, Washington, DC, 2005.

NEI, *Nuclear Energy Statistics*. Nuclear Energy Institute, Washington, DC, 2006a.

NEI, *Regulatory Assessment Performance Indicator Guideline*, NEI 99-02, Revision 4. Nuclear Energy Institute, Washington, DC, 2006b.

NEI, *Regulatory Assessment Performance Indicator Guideline*, NEI 99-02, Revision 5. Nuclear Energy Institute, Washington, DC, 2007.

NEI, *Methodology for Development of Emergency Action Levels*, NEI 99-01, Revision 5. Nuclear Energy Institute, Washington, DC, 2008.

NEI, *Assessment of On-Shift Emergency Response Organization Staffing and Capabilities*, NEI 10-05. Nuclear Energy Institute, Washington, DC, 2009a.

NEI, *Methodology for Development of Emergency Action Levels—Advanced Passive Light Water Reactors*, NEI 07-01. Nuclear Energy Institute, Washington, DC, 2009b.

NEI, *Regulatory Assessment Performance Indicator Guideline*, NEI 99-02, Revision 6. Nuclear Energy Institute, Washington, DC, 2009c.

NEI, *Guideline for the Development of EP Drill and Exercise Threat-Based Scenarios*, NEI 06-04, revised. Nuclear Energy Institute, Washington, DC, 2010.

NEI, *Development of Emergency Action Levels for Non-Passive Reactors*, NEI 99-01, Revision 6. Nuclear Energy Institute, Washington, DC, 2012a.

NEI, *Diverse and Flexible Coping Strategies Implementation Guide*, NEI 12-06, Revision 0. Nuclear Energy Institute, Washington, DC, 2012b.

NEI, *Guideline for Assessing Beyond Design Basis Accident Response Staffing and Communications Capabilities*, NEI 12-01. Nuclear Energy Institute, Washington, DC, 2012c.

NEI, *Guidelines for Evaluating Emergency Plan Changes Under 50.54(q)*, NEI 11-03. Nuclear Energy Institute, Washington, DC, 2012d.

NEI, *Guidelines for Implemention of NRC EP Rule Changes and Interim Staff Guidance*, NEI 11-05. Nuclear Energy Institute, Washington, DC, 2012e.

NEI, *Regulatory Assessment Performance Indicator Guideline*, NEI 99-02, Revision 7. Nuclear Energy Institute, Washington, DC, 2013.

NEI, *Reportable Action Levels for Loss of Emergency Preparedness Capabilities*, NEI 13-01. Nuclear Energy Institute, Washington, DC, 2014.

NFPA, *Recommended Practice for Disaster Management*, NFPA 1600. National Fire Protection Association, Quincy, MA, 1995.

NFPA, *Standard on Disaster/Emergency Management and Business Continuity Programs*, NFPA 1600, revised. National Fire Protection Association, Quincy, MA, 2004.

Nixon, R., Executive Order 11490—Assigning emergency preparedness functions to federal departments and agencies. *Federal Register*, 34, 17567, 1969.

Nourbakhsh, H.P., *Estimate of Radionuclide Release Characteristics into Containment Under Severe Accidents*, NUREG/CR-5747, BN-NUREG-52289. Brookhaven National Laboratory, Upton, NY, 1993.

NRC, *Guide and Check List for the Development and Evaluation of State and Local Government Radiological Emergency Response Plans in Support of Fixed Nuclear Facilities*, NUREG 75/111. U.S. Nuclear Regulatory Commission, Washington, DC, 1974.

NRC, *Emergency Planning for Nuclear Power Plants*, Regulatory Guide 1.101, Revision 0. U.S. Nuclear Regulatory Commission, Washington, DC, 1975a.

NRC, *Reactor Safety Study: An Assessment of Accident Risks in U.S. Nuclear Power Plants*, NUREG 75/014, WASH-1400 ("Rasmussen Report"). U.S. Nuclear Regulatory Commission, Washington, DC, 1975b.

NRC, *Assumptions Used for Evaluating the Potential Radiological Consequences of a Radioactive Offgas System Failure in a Boiling Water Reactor*, Regulatory Guide 1.98. U.S. Nuclear Regulatory Commission, Washington, DC, 1976a.

NRC, *Calculation of Releases of Radioactive Materials in Gaseous and Liquid Effluents from Light-Water-Cooled Reactors*, Regulatory Guide 1.112. U.S. Nuclear Regulatory Commission, Washington, DC, 1976b.

NRC, *Emergency Planning for Nuclear Power Plants*, Regulatory Guide 1.101, Revision 1. U.S. Nuclear Regulatory Commission, Washington, DC, 1977a.

NRC, *Guide and Checklist for the Development and Evaluation of State and Local Government Radiological Emergency Response Plans in Support of Fixed Nuclear Facilities*, NUREG 75/111, Supplement 1. U.S. Nuclear Regulatory Commission, Washington, DC, 1977b.

NRC, *Methods for Estimating Atmospheric Transport and Dispersion of Gaseous Effluents in Routine Releases from Light-Water-Cooled Reactors*, Regulatory Guide 1.111, Revision 1. U.S. Nuclear Regulatory Commission, Washington, DC, 1977c.

NRC, *Planning Basis for the Development of State and Local Government Radiological Emergency Response Plans in Support of Light Water Nuclear Plants*, NUREG-0396, EPA-520/1-78-016. U.S. Nuclear Regulatory Commission, Washington, DC, 1978a.

NRC, *Standard Format and Content of Safety Analysis Reports for Nuclear Power Plants*, Regulatory Guide 1.70, Revision 3. U.S. Nuclear Regulatory Commission, Washington, DC, 1978b.

NRC, *Atmospheric Dispersion Models for Potential Accident Consequence Assessments at Nuclear Power Plants*, Regulatory Guide 1.145. U.S. Nuclear Regulatory Commission, Washington, DC, 1979a.

NRC, *Contents of the Offsite Dose Calculation Manual*, Generic Letter 79-006, Revision 1. U.S. Nuclear Regulatory Commission, Washington, DC, 1979b.

NRC, *Draft Emergency Action Level Guidelines for Nuclear Power Plants*, NUREG-0610. U.S. Nuclear Regulatory Commission, Washington, DC, 1979c.

NRC, *Emergency Plans Submittal Dates*, Generic Letter 79-050. U.S. Nuclear Regulatory Commission, Washington, DC, 1979d.

NRC, *Estimates for Evacuation of Various Areas around Nuclear Power Reactors*, Generic Letter 79-067. U.S. Nuclear Regulatory Commission, Washington, DC, 1979e.

NRC, *Follow-Up Actions Resulting from the NRC Staff Reviews Regarding the TMI-2 Accident*, Generic Letter 79-040. U.S. Nuclear Regulatory Commission, Washington, DC, 1979f.

NRC, *Follow-Up Actions Resulting from the NRC Staff Reviews Regarding the TMI-2 Accident*, Generic Letter 79-051. U.S. Nuclear Regulatory Commission, Washington, DC, 1979g.

NRC, *Nuclear Incident at Three Mile Island*, Bulletin 1979-05, Supplements A–C. U.S. Nuclear Regulatory Commission, Washington, DC, 1979h.

NRC, *Nuclear Incident at Three Mile Island*, Information Notice 79-016. U.S. Nuclear Regulatory Commission, Washington, DC, 1979i.

NRC, *Offsite Dose Calculation Manual*, Generic Letter 79-003. U.S. Nuclear Regulatory Commission, Washington, DC, 1979j.

NRC, *Population Dose and Health Impact of the Accident at Three Mile Island Nuclear Station*, NUREG-0558. U.S. Nuclear Regulatory Commission, Washington, DC, 1979k.

NRC, *Radioactive Release at North Anna Unit 1 and Lessons Learned*, Generic Letter 79-052. U.S. Nuclear Regulatory Commission, Washington, DC, 1979l.

NRC, *TMI-2 Lessons Learned Task Force Status Report and Short-Term Recommendations*, NUREG-0578. U.S. Nuclear Regulatory Commission, Washington, DC, 1979m.

NRC, *Upgraded Emergency Plans*, Generic Letter 79-063. U.S. Nuclear Regulatory Commission, Washington, DC, 1979n.

NRC, *Clarification of TMI Action Plan Requirements*, NUREG-0737. U.S. Nuclear Regulatory Commission, Washington, DC, 1980a.

NRC, *Clarification of NRC Requirements for Emergency Response Facilities*, Generic Letter 80-034. U.S. Nuclear Regulatory Commission, Washington, DC, 1980b.

NRC, *Criteria for Preparation and Evaluation of Radiological Emergency Response Plans and Preparedness in Support of Nuclear Power Plants*, NUREG-0654, FEMA REP-1, Revision 1. U.S. Nuclear Regulatory Commission, Washington, DC, 1980c.

NRC, *Emergency Plan*, Generic Letter 80-094. U.S. Nuclear Regulatory Commission, Washington, DC, 1980d.

NRC, *Emergency Planning*, Generic Letter 80-108. U.S. Nuclear Regulatory Commission, Washington, DC, December 9, 1980e.

NRC, *Emergency Preparedness*, Generic Letter 80-093. U.S. Nuclear Regulatory Commission, Washington, DC, 1980f.

NRC, *NRC Action Plan Developed As a Result of the TMI-2 Accident*, NUREG-0660. U.S. Nuclear Regulatory Commission, Washington, DC, 1980g.

NRC, *Possible Loss of Emergency Notification System with Loss of Offsite Power*, Bulletin 1980-15. U.S. Nuclear Regulatory Commission, Washington, DC, 1980h.

NRC, *Post TMI Requirements, NUREG-0737*, Generic Letter 80-90. U.S. Nuclear Regulatory Commission, Washington, DC, 1980i.

NRC, *Request for Information Regarding Evacuation Times*, Generic Letter 80-60. U.S. Nuclear Regulatory Commission, Washington, DC, 1980j.

NRC, Statement of interim policy: nuclear power plant accident considerations under the National Environmental Policy Act of 1969. *Federal Register*, 45, 40101, 1980k.

NRC, *TMI-2 Lessons Learned*, Generic Letter 80-061/80-062. U.S. Nuclear Regulatory Commission, Washington, DC, 1980l.

NRC, *Transmittal of Information on NRC Nuclear Data Link Specifications*, Generic Letter 80-024. U.S. Nuclear Regulatory Commission, Washington, DC, 1980m.

NRC, *Accidental Actuation of Prompt Public Notification System*, Information Notice 81-34. U.S. Nuclear Regulatory Commission, Washington, DC, 1981a.

NRC, *Commission Approval Guidance on EOF Location and Habitability*, COMJA-80-37. U.S. Nuclear Regulatory Commission, Washington, DC, 1981b.

NRC, *Emergency Action Levels for Light Water Reactors* [draft], NUREG-0818. U.S. Nuclear Regulatory Commission, Washington, DC, 1981c.

NRC, *Emergency Planning and Preparedness for Nuclear Power Reactors*, Regulatory Guide 1.101, Revision 2. U.S. Nuclear Regulatory Commission, Washington, DC, 1981d.

NRC, *Function Criteria for Emergency Response Facilities*, NUREG-0696. U.S. Nuclear Regulatory Commission, Washington, DC, 1981e.

NRC, *Functional Criteria for Emergency Response Facilities*, Generic Letter 81-017. U.S. Nuclear Regulatory Commission, Washington, DC, 1981f.

NRC, *Guidelines for Preparing Emergency Procedures for Nuclear Power Plants*, NUREG/CR-1977. U.S. Nuclear Regulatory Commission, Washington, DC, 1981g.

NRC, *Joint Review of Comments: Criteria for Preparation and Evaluation of Radiological Emergency Response Plans and Preparedness in Support of Nuclear Power Plants*, NUREG-0742, FEMA Report 4. U.S. Nuclear Regulatory Commission, Washington, DC, 1981h.

NRC, *Methodology for Evaluation of Emergency Response Facilities*, NUREG-0814. U.S. Nuclear Regulatory Commission, Washington, DC, 1981i.

NRC, *Post-TMI Requirements for the Emergency Operations Facility*, Generic Letter 81-010. U.S. Nuclear Regulatory Commission, Washington, DC, 1981j.

NRC, *Report to Congress on Status of Emergency Response Planning for Nuclear Power Plants*, NUREG-0755. U.S. Nuclear Regulatory Commission, Washington, DC, 1981k.

NRC, *Atmospheric Dispersion Models for Potential Accident Consequence Assessments at Nuclear Power Plants*, Regulatory Guide 1.145, Revision 1. U.S. Nuclear Regulatory Commission, Washington, DC, 1982a.

NRC, *Calculation of Reactor Accident Consequences* (CRAC-2 Report). U.S. Nuclear Regulatory Commission, Washington, DC, 1982b.

NRC, *Clarification of Emergency Plan Exercise Requirements*, Information Notice 82-044. U.S. Nuclear Regulatory Commission, Washington, DC, 1982c.

NRC, *Post-TMI Requirements*, Generic Letter 82-05. U.S. Nuclear Regulatory Commission, Washington, DC, 1982d.

NRC, *Submittal of Copies of Documentation to NRC—Copy Requirements for Emergency Plans and Physical Security Plans*, Generic Letter 82-019. U.S. Nuclear Regulatory Commission, Washington, DC, 1982e.

NRC, *Supplement 1 to NUREG-0737—Requirements for Emergency Response Capability*, Generic Letter 82-33. U.S. Nuclear Regulatory Commission, Washington, DC, 1982f.

NRC, *Clarification of TMI Action Plan Requirements*. Supplement 1. *Requirements for Emergency Response Capability*, NUREG-073. U.S. Nuclear Regulatory Commission, Washington, DC, 1983a.

NRC, *Criteria for Protective Action Recommendations for General Emergencies*, Information Notice 83-28. U.S. Nuclear Regulatory Commission, Washington, DC, 1983b.

NRC, *Defective Emergency-Use Respirator*, Information Notice 83-021. U.S. Nuclear Regulatory Commission, Washington, DC, 1983c.

NRC, *Event Notification Information Worksheet*, Information Notice 83-34. U.S. Nuclear Regulatory Commission, Washington, DC, 1983d.

NRC, *Final Environmental Statement Related to the Operation of the Teton Uranium ISL Project*, NUREG-0925. U.S. Nuclear Regulatory Commission, Washington, DC, 1983e.

NRC, *NRC/FEMA Operational Response Procedures for Response to a Commercial Nuclear Reactor Accident*, NUREG-0981, FEMA-51. U.S. Nuclear Regulatory Commission, Washington, DC, 1983f.

NRC, *Safety Evaluation of Emergency Response Guidelines*, Generic Letter 83-022/83-023. U.S. Nuclear Regulatory Commission, Washington, DC, 1983g.

NRC, *Analysis of Emergency Staffing for Nuclear Power Plants*, NUREG/CR-3903. U.S. Nuclear Regulatory Commission, Washington, DC, 1984a.

NRC, *Design Basis Threat and Review of Vehicular Access Controls*, Information Notice 84-007. U.S. Nuclear Regulatory Commission, Washington, DC, 1984b.

NRC, *Emergency Worker Doses*, Information Notice 84-40. U.S. Nuclear Regulatory Commission, Washington, DC, 1984c.

NRC, *Exercise Frequency*, Information Notice 84-005. U.S. Nuclear Regulatory Commission, Washington, DC, 1984d.

NRC, *Physical Qualification of Individuals to Use Respiratory Protective Devices*, Information Notice 84-24. U.S. Nuclear Regulatory Commission, Washington, DC, 1984e.

NRC, Statement of policy on NRC response to accidents during the transportation of radioactive material. *Federal Register*, 49, 12335, 1984f.

NRC, *Emergency Communication System Monthly Test*, Information Notice 85-44. U.S. Nuclear Regulatory Commission, Washington, DC, 1985a.

NRC, *Errors in Dose Assessment Computer Codes and Reporting Requirements Under 10 CFR Part 21*, Information Notice 85-052. U.S. Nuclear Regulatory Commission, Washington, DC, 1985b.

NRC, *Event Notification*, Information Notice 85-078. U.S. Nuclear Regulatory Commission, Washington, DC, 1985c.

NRC, *NRC/FEMA Operational Response Procedures for Response to a Commercial Nuclear Reactor Accident*, NUREG-0981, FEMA-51, revised. U.S. Nuclear Regulatory Commission, Washington, DC, 1985d.

NRC, Policy statement on severe reactor accidents regarding future designs and existing plants. *Federal Register*, 50(153), 32138, 1985e.

NRC, *Revised Emergency Exercise Frequency Rule*, Information Notice 85-055. U.S. Nuclear Regulatory Commission, Washington, DC, 1985f.

NRC, Statement of policy on Emergency Planning Standard 10 CFR 50.47(b)(12). *Federal Register*, 50, 20892, 1985g.

NRC, *Timely Declaration of an Emergency Class, Implementation of an Emergency Plan, and Emergency Notifications*, Information Notice 85-080. U.S. Nuclear Regulatory Commission, Washington, DC, 1985h.

NRC, *Delayed Access to Safety-Related Areas and Equipment During Plant Emergencies*, Information Notice 86-055. U.S. Nuclear Regulatory Commission, Washington, DC, 1986a.

NRC, *Emergency Communications Systems*, Information Notice 86-097. U.S. Nuclear Regulatory Commission, Washington, DC, 1986b.

NRC, *Information for Licensees Regarding the Chernobyl Nuclear Plant Accident*, Information Notice 86-033. U.S. Nuclear Regulatory Commission, Washington, DC, 1986c.

NRC, *NRC On-Scene Response During a Major Emergency*, Information Notice 86-018. U.S. Nuclear Regulatory Commission, Washington, DC, 1986d.

NRC, *Offsite Medical Services*, Information Notice 86-098. U.S. Nuclear Regulatory Commission, Washington, DC, 1986e.

NRC, *Problems with Silver Zeolite Sampling of Airborne Radioiodine*, Information Notice 86-043. U.S. Nuclear Regulatory Commission, Washington, DC, 1986f.

NRC, Safety goals for the operation of nuclear power plants. *Federal Register*, 51, 28044, 1986g.

NRC, Safety goals for the operation of nuclear power plants; policy statement; republication. *Federal Register*, 51, 30028, 1986h.

NRC, Statement of policy on Emergency Planning Standard 10 CFR 50.47(b)(12) [Medical Services]. *Federal Register*, 51, 32904, 1986i.

NRC, Statement of policy: safety goals for the operations of nuclear power plants. *Federal Register*, 51, 28048, 1986j.

NRC, *Unanalyzed Post-LOCA Release Paths*, Information Notice 86-060. U.S. Nuclear Regulatory Commission, Washington, DC, 1986k.

NRC, *Continuous Communications Following Emergency Notifications*, Information Notice 87-058. U.S. Nuclear Regulatory Commission, Washington, DC, 1987a.

NRC, *Design of an Independent Spent Fuel Storage Installation (Dry Storage)*, Regulatory Guide 3.60. U.S. Nuclear Regulatory Commission, Washington, DC, 1987b.

NRC, *Emergency Response Exercises*, Information Notice 87-054. U.S. Nuclear Regulatory Commission, Washington, DC, 1987c.

NRC, *Standard Format and Content for Emergency Plans for Fuel Cycle and Materials Facilities* [draft for comment], NUREG-0762, revised. U.S. Nuclear Regulatory Commission, Washington, DC, 1987d.

NRC, *Availability of FDA-Approved Potassium Iodide for Use in Emergencies Involving Radioactive Iodine*, Information Notice 88-015. U.S. Nuclear Regulatory Commission, Washington, DC, 1988a.

NRC, *Criteria for Preparation and Evaluation of Radiological Emergency Response Plans and Preparedness in Support of Nuclear Power Plants*. Supplement 1. *Criteria for Utility Offsite Planning and Preparedness*, NUREG-0654, FEMA REP-1. U.S. Nuclear Regulatory Commission, Washington, DC, 1988b.

NRC, *Individual Plant Examination for Severe Accident Vulnerabilities—10 CFR 50.54(f)*, Generic Letter 88-20. U.S. Nuclear Regulatory Commission, Washington, DC, 1988c.

NRC, *Confidentiality of Exercise Scenarios*, Information Notice 89-46. U.S. Nuclear Regulatory Commission, Washington, DC, 1989a.

NRC, *Emergency Response Data System*, Generic Letter 89-15. U.S. Nuclear Regulatory Commission, Washington, DC, 1989b.

NRC, *Failure of Senior Reactor Operators to Classify Emergency Events Properly*, Information Notice 89-72. U.S. Nuclear Regulatory Commission, Washington, DC, 1989c.

NRC, *Implementation of Programmatic Controls for Radiological Effluent Technical Specifications in the Administrative Controls Section of the Technical Specifications and the Relocation of Procedural Details of RETS to the Offsite Dose Calculation Manual or to the Process Control Program*, Generic Letter 89-01. U.S. Nuclear Regulatory Commission, Washington, DC, 1989d.

NRC, *Task Action Plan Item I.D.2, Safety Parameter Display System*, Generic Letter 89-06. U.S. Nuclear Regulatory Commission, Washington, DC, 1989e.

NRC, *Information on Precursors to Severe Accidents*, Information Notice 90-74. U.S. Nuclear Regulatory Commission, Washington, DC, 1990a.

NRC, *Response to False Siren Activations*, Information Notice 90-034. U.S. Nuclear Regulatory Commission, Washington, DC, 1990b.

NRC, *Severe Accident Risks: An Assessment for Five U.S. Nuclear Power Plants*, NUREG-1150. U.S. Nuclear Regulatory Commission, Washington, DC, 1990c.

NRC, *Emergency Response Data System (ERDS) Implementation*, NUREG-1394. U.S. Nuclear Regulatory Commission, Washington, DC, 1991a.

NRC, *Emergency Telecommunications*, Generic Letter 91-014. U.S. Nuclear Regulatory Commission, Washington, DC, 1991b.

NRC, *Issuance of a Revision to the EPA Manual of Protective Action Guides and Protective Actions for Nuclear Incidents*, Information Notice 91-72. U.S. Nuclear Regulatory Commission, Washington, DC, 1991c.

NRC, *Reactor Safety Information for States During Exercises and Emergencies*, Information Notice 91-033. U.S. Nuclear Regulatory Commission, Washington, DC, 1991d.

NRC, *Shift Staffing at Nuclear Power Plants*, Information Notice 91-077. U.S. Nuclear Regulatory Commission, Washington, DC, 1991e.

NRC, *Site Area Emergency Resulting from Loss of Non-Class 1E Uninterruptible Power Supplies*, Information Notice 91-064. U.S. Nuclear Regulatory Commission, Washington, DC, 1991f.

NRC, *Emergency Planning and Preparedness for Nuclear Power Reactors*, Regulatory Guide 1.101, Revision 3. U.S. Nuclear Regulatory Commission, Washington, DC, 1992a.

NRC, *Emergency Response Information Requirements for Radioactive Materials Shipments*, Information Notice 92-062. U.S. Nuclear Regulatory Commission, Washington, DC, 1992b.

NRC, *Emergency Response Resource Guide for Nuclear Power Plant Emergencies*, NUREG 1442, FEMA REP 17, revised. U.S. Nuclear Regulatory Commission, Washington, DC, 1992c.

NRC, *Implementation Date for the Revision to the EPA Manual of Protective Action Guides and Protective Actions for Nuclear Incidents*, Information Notice 92-038. U.S. Nuclear Regulatory Commission, Washington, DC, 1992d.

NRC, *Intersystem LOCA Outside Containment*, Information Notice 92-036. U.S. Nuclear Regulatory Commission, Washington, DC, 1992e.

NRC, *Limited Participation by NRC in IAEA International Event Scale*, Generic Letter 92-09. U.S. Nuclear Regulatory Commission, Washington, DC, 1992f.

NRC, *Problems with Emergency Ventilation Systems for Near-Site Emergency Operations Centers and Technical Support Centers*, Information Notice 92-032. U.S. Nuclear Regulatory Commission, Washington, DC, 1992g.

NRC, *Revised Protective Action Guidance for Nuclear Incidents*, Information Notice 92-08. U.S. Nuclear Regulatory Commission, Washington, DC, 1992h.

NRC, *Site Area Emergency Resulting from Loss of Non-Class 1E Uninterruptible Power Supplies*, Information Notice 91-064, Supplement 1. U.S. Nuclear Regulatory Commission, Washington, DC, 1992i.

NRC, *Classification of Transportation Emergencies*, Information Notice 93-007. U.S. Nuclear Regulatory Commission, Washington, DC, 1993a.

NRC, *Effect of Hurricane Andrew on Turkey Point Nuclear Generating Station and Lessons Learned*, Information Notice 93-053. U.S. Nuclear Regulatory Commission, Washington, DC, 1993b.

NRC, *Emergency Response Data System Test Program*, Generic Letter 93-01. U.S. Nuclear Regulatory Commission, Washington, DC, 1993c.

NRC, *Fire at Chernobyl Unit 2*, Information Notice 93-071. U.S. Nuclear Regulatory Commission, Washington, DC, 1993d.

NRC, *Implementation of Engineering Expertise on Shift*, Information Notice 93-81. U.S. Nuclear Regulatory Commission, Washington, DC, 1993e.

NRC, *Modification of the Technical Specification Administrative Control Requirements for Emergency and Security Plans*, Generic Letter 93-07. U.S. Nuclear Regulatory Commission, Washington, DC, 1993f.

NRC, *Unauthorized Forced Entry into the Protected Area at Three Mile Island Unit 1 on February 7, 1993*, Information Notice 93-94. U.S. Nuclear Regulatory Commission, Washington, DC, 1993g.

NRC, *Unauthorized Forced Entry into the Protected Area at Three Mile Island Unit 1 on February 7, 1993*, NUREG-1485. U.S. Nuclear Regulatory Commission, Washington, DC, 1993h.

NRC, *Distribution of Site-Specific and Site Emergency Planning Information*, Administrative Letter 94-007. U.S. Nuclear Regulatory Commission, Washington, DC, 1994a.

NRC, *Effect of Hurricane Andrew on Turkey Point Nuclear Generating Station and Lessons Learned*, Information Notice 93-053, Supplement 1. U.S. Nuclear Regulatory Commission, Washington, DC, 1994b.

NRC, *Facility Operating Concerns Resulting from Local Area Flooding*, Information Notice 94-027. U.S. Nuclear Regulatory Commission, Washington, DC, 1994c.

NRC, Final rule: protection against malevolent use of vehicles at nuclear power plants. *Federal Register*, 59, 38900, 1994d.

NRC, *Intersystem LOCA Outside Containment*, Information Notice 92-036, Supplement 1. U.S. Nuclear Regulatory Commission, Washington, DC, 1994e.

NRC, *Revision of the NRC Core Inspection Program for Annual Emergency Preparedness Exercises*, Administrative Letter 94-16. U.S. Nuclear Regulatory Commission, Washington, DC, 1994f.

NRC, *Control Room Staffing Below Minimum Staffing*, Information Notice 95-23. U.S. Nuclear Regulatory Commission, Washington, DC, 1995a.

NRC, *Emergency Preparedness Position (EPPOS) on Acceptable Deviations from Appendix 1 of NUREG-0654 Based Upon the Staff's Regulatory Analysis of NUMARC/NESP-007, "Methodology for Development of Emergency Action Levels."* U.S. Nuclear Regulatory Commission, Washington, DC, 1995b.

NRC, *Emergency Preparedness Position (EPPOS) on Requirement for Onshift Dose Assessment Capablity.* U.S. Nuclear Regulatory Commission, Washington, DC, 1995c.

NRC, *Emergency Preparedness Position (EPPOS)-2 on Timeliness of Classification of Emergency Conditions.* U.S. Nuclear Regulatory Commission, Washington, DC, 1995d.

NRC, *NRC Participation in World Use of the International Nuclear Event Scale*, SECY 95-098. U.S. Nuclear Regulatory Commission, Washington, DC, 1995e.

NRC, *Relocation of Selected Technical Specifications Requirements Related to Instrumentation*, Generic Letter 95-10. U.S. Nuclear Regulatory Commission, Washington, DC, 1995f.

NRC, *Results of Shift Staffing Study*, Information Notice 95-048. U.S. Nuclear Regulatory Commission, Washington, DC, 1995g.

NRC, *Severe Accident Natural Circulation Studies at the INEL*, NUREG/CR-6285, INEL-94/0016. U.S. Nuclear Regulatory Commission, Washington, DC, 1995h.

NRC, *Status of Implementation Plan for Closure of Severe Accident Issues, Status of the Individual Plant Examinations and Status of Severe Accident Research*, SECY-95-004. U.S. Nuclear Regulatory Commission, Washington, DC, 1995i.

NRC, *Criteria for Preparation and Evaluation of Radiological Emergency Response Plans and Preparedness in Support of Nuclear Power Plants*. Supplement 2. *Criteria for Emergency Planning in an Early Site Permit Application*, NUREG-0654, FEMA REP-1. U.S. Nuclear Regulatory Commission, Washington, DC, 1996a.

NRC, *Criteria for Preparation and Evaluation of Radiological Emergency Response Plans and Preparedness in Support of Nuclear Power Plants*. Supplement 3. *Criteria for Protective Action Recommendations for Severe Accidents*, NUREG-0654, FEMA REP-1. U.S. Nuclear Regulatory Commission, Washington, DC, 1996b.

NRC, *Emergency Preparedness Position (EPPOS) on Emergency Planning Information Provided to the Public*. U.S. Nuclear Regulatory Commission, Washington, DC, 1996c.

NRC, *Failure of Tone Alert Radios to Activate When Receiving a Shortened Activation Signal*, Information Notice 96-019. U.S. Nuclear Regulatory Commission, Washington, DC, 1996d.

NRC, *Final Amendments to 10 CFR Part 50 Relating to the Frequency of Emergency Planning Exercises at Nuclear Power Plants*, SECY 96-060. U.S. Nuclear Regulatory Commission, Washington, DC, 1996e.

NRC, *Generic Environmental Impact Statement for License Renewal of Nuclear Plants: Main Report*, NUREG-1437, Vol. 1. U.S. Nuclear Regulatory Commission, Washington, DC, 1996f.

NRC, *Potential Containment Leakage Paths Through Hydrogen Analyzers*, Information Notice 96-013. U.S. Nuclear Regulatory Commission, Washington, DC, 1996g.

NRC, *Reconsideration of Nuclear Power Plant Security Requirements Associated with an Internal Threat*, Generic Letter 96-02. U.S. Nuclear Regulatory Commission, Washington, DC, 1996h.

NRC, *Response Coordination Manual*, NUREG/BR-0230. U.S. Nuclear Regulatory Commission, Washington, DC, 1996i.

NRC, *Standard Review Plan for the Review of Safety Analysis Reports for Nuclear Power Plants*, NUREG-0800 (formerly NUREG-75/087), Draft Revision 3. U.S. Nuclear Regulatory Commission, Washington, DC, 1996j.

NRC, *Additional Information Regarding the Federal Policy on Potassium Iodide*, SECY 97-124A. U.S. Nuclear Regulatory Commission, Washington, DC, 1997a.

NRC, *Deficiencies in Licensee Submittals Regarding Terminology for Radiological Emergency Action Levels in Accordance with the New Part 20*, Information Notice 97-34. U.S. Nuclear Regulatory Commission, Washington, DC, 1997b.

NRC, *Elevation of the Core Damage Frequency Objective to a Fundamental Commission Safety Goal*, SECY 97-208. U.S. Nuclear Regulatory Commission, Washington, DC, 1997c.

NRC, *Failure to Provide Special Lenses for Operators Using Respirator or Self-Contained Breathing Apparatus During Emergency Operations*, Information Notice 97-66. U.S. Nuclear Regulatory Commission, Washington, DC, 1997d.

NRC, *Inspection Manual*. Chapter 1601. *Communication Protocol for Assessing Offsite Emergency Preparedness Following a Natural Disaster*. U.S. Nuclear Regulatory Commission, Washington, DC, 1997e.

NRC, *Offsite Notification Capabilities*, Information Notice 97-005. U.S. Nuclear Regulatory Commission, Washington, DC, 1997f.

NRC, *Plant Restart Discussions Following Natural Disasters*, Administrative Letter 97-003. U.S. Nuclear Regulatory Commission, Washington, DC, 1997g.

NRC, *Proposed Federal Policy Regarding Use of Potassium Iodide After a Severe Accident at a Nuclear Power Plant*, SECY 97-124. U.S. Nuclear Regulatory Commission, Washington, DC, 1997h.

NRC, *Results of Emergency Planning for Evolutionary and Advanced Reactors*, SECY 97-020. U.S. Nuclear Regulatory Commission, Washington, DC, 1997i.

NRC, *Rulemaking Plan for Emergency Preparedness Requirements for Permanently Shutdown Nuclear Power Plant Sites 10 CFR Part 50.54(q) and (t); 10 CFR 50.47; and Appendix E to 10 CFR Part 50*, SECY 97-120. U.S. Nuclear Regulatory Commission, Washington, DC, 1997j.

NRC, *Commonwealth Edison Company's Proposal to Centralize Its Emergency Operations Facility Functions at Its Corporate Offices*, SECY 98-274. U.S. Nuclear Regulatory Commission, Washington, DC, 1998a.

NRC, *Emergency Preparedness Position (EPPOS) on Emergency Plan and Implementing Procedure Changes*. U.S. Nuclear Regulatory Commission, Washington, DC, 1998b.

NRC, *General Site Suitability Criteria for Nuclear Power Stations*, Regulatory Guide 4.7, Revision 2. U.S. Nuclear Regulatory Commission, Washington, DC, 1998c.

NRC, *Information Likely to Be Requested If an Emergency Is Declared*, Information Notice 98-008. U.S. Nuclear Regulatory Commission, Washington, DC, 1998d.

NRC, *Modifications to the Safety Goal Policy Statement*, SECY 98-101. U.S. Nuclear Regulatory Commission, Washington, DC, 1998e.

NRC, *NRC's 1998 Report to Congress on the Price-Anderson Act*, SECY 98-160. U.S. Nuclear Regulatory Commission, Washington, DC, 1998f.

NRC, *Nuclear Fuel Cycle Facility Accident Analysis Handbook*, NUREG/CR-6410. U.S. Nuclear Regulatory Commission, Washington, DC, 1998g.

NRC, *Problems with Emergency Preparedness Respiratory Protection Programs*, Information Notice 98-020. U.S. Nuclear Regulatory Commission, Washington, DC, 1998h.

NRC, *Results of the Revised (NUREG-1465) Source Term Rebaselining for Operating Reactors*, SECY 98-154. U.S. Nuclear Regulatory Commission, Washington, DC, 1998i.

NRC, *Staff Options for Resolving a Petition for Rulemaking Related to a Reevaluation of the Policy Regarding the Use of Potassium Iodide by the General Public After a Severe Accident at Nuclear Power Plant*, SECY 98-61. U.S. Nuclear Regulatory Commission, Washington, DC, 1998j.

NRC, *Acceptable Programs for Respiratory Protection*, Regulatory Guide 8.15, Revision 1. U.S. Nuclear Regulatory Commission, Washington, DC, 1999a.

NRC, *Federal Bureau of Investigation's Nuclear Site Security Program*, Information Notice 99-016. U.S. Nuclear Regulatory Commission, Washington, DC, 1999b.

NRC, *Proposed Revision to the Enforcement Policy to Address the Process for Assessing the Significance of Violations*, SECY 99-219. U.S. Nuclear Regulatory Commission, Washington, DC, 1999c.

NRC, *Proposed Strategy to Revise the Enforcement Policy to Address the Process for Assessing Significance and Assigning Severity Levels of Noncompliances (Including Regulatory Significance and Risk)*, SECY 99-087. U.S. Nuclear Regulatory Commission, Washington, DC, 1999d.

NRC, *Alternative Radiological Source Terms for Evaluating Design Basis Accidents at Nuclear Power Reactors*, Regulatory Guide 1.183. U.S. Nuclear Regulatory Commission, Washington, DC, 2000a.

NRC, *Emergency Planning for Indian Point 2 and Other Co-Located Licensees*, SECY 00-228. U.S. Nuclear Regulatory Commission, Washington, DC, 2000b.

NRC, *Final Amendments to 10 CFR 50.47; Thereby Granting in Part Two Petitions for Rulemaking (50-63 and 5063a); Relating to a Reevaluation of Policy on the Use of Potassium Iodide for the General Public After a Severe Accident at a Nuclear Power Plant*, SECY 00-040. U.S. Nuclear Regulatory Commission, Washington, DC, 2000c.

NRC, *General Statement of Policy and Procedure for NRC Enforcement Actions*, NUREG-1600. U.S. Nuclear Regulatory Commission, Washington, DC, 2000d.

NRC, *Modifications to the Reactor Safety Goal Policy Statement*, SECY 00-77. U.S. Nuclear Regulatory Commission, Washington, DC, 2000e.

NRC, *NRC Emergency Telecommunications System*, Regulatory Issue Summary 00-11. U.S. Nuclear Regulatory Commission, Washington, DC, 2000f.

NRC, *Review of the Tokai-Mura Criticality Accident and Lessons Learned*, SECY 00-085. U.S. Nuclear Regulatory Commission, Washington, DC, 2000g.

NRC, Consideration of potassium iodide in emergency plans. *Federal Register*, 66(13), 5427, 2001a.

NRC, *Expanded NRC Participation in the Use of the International Event Scale*, SECY 01-070. U.S. Nuclear Regulatory Commission, Washington, DC, 2001b.

NRC, *Policy Issues Related to Safeguards, Insurance, and Emergency Preparedness Regulations at Decommissioning Nuclear Power Plants Storing Fuel in Spent Fuel Pools*, SECY 01-100. U.S. Nuclear Regulatory Commission, Washington, DC, 2001c.

NRC, *Rulemaking Plan: Revision of Appendix E to 10 CFR Part 50*, SECY 01-192. U.S. Nuclear Regulatory Commission, Washington, DC, 2001d.

NRC, *Rulemaking Plan: Revision of Appendix E, Section IV.F.2, to 10 CFR Part 50, Concerning Clarification of Emergency Preparedness Exercise Participation Requirements for Co-Located Licensees*, SECY 01-131. U.S. Nuclear Regulatory Commission, Washington, DC, 2001e.

NRC, *Status of Potassium Iodide Activities*, SECY 01-208. U.S. Nuclear Regulatory Commission, Washington, DC, 2001f.

NRC, *Technical Study of Spent Fuel Accident Risk at Decommissioning Nuclear Power Plants*, NUREG-1738. U.S. Nuclear Regulatory Commission, Washington, DC, 2001g.

NRC, *Update of Evacuation Time Estimates*, Regulatory Issue Summary 01-16. U.S. Nuclear Regulatory Commission, Washington, DC, 2001h.

NRC, *An Approach for Using Probabilistic Risk Assessment in Risk-Informed Decisions on Plant-Specific Changes to the Licensing Basis*, Regulatory Guide 1.174, Revision 1. U.S. Nuclear Regulatory Commission, Washington, DC, 2002a.

NRC, *Challenges to Licensee's Ability to Provide Prompt Public Notification and Information During an Emergency Preparedness Event*, Information Notice 02-25. U.S. Nuclear Regulatory Commission, Washington, DC, 2002b.

NRC, *Changes to NRC Participation in the International Nuclear Event Scale*, Regulatory Issue Summary 02-01. U.S. Nuclear Regulatory Commission, Washington, DC, 2002c.

NRC, *Current Incident Response Issues*, Regulatory Issue Summary 02-16. U.S. Nuclear Regulatory Commission, Washington, DC, 2002d.

NRC, *Direct Final Rule on Electronic Maintenance and Submission of Information*, SECY 02-0096. U.S. Nuclear Regulatory Commission, Washington, DC, 2002e.

NRC, *Ensuring a Capability to Evacuate Individuals, Including Members of the Public, for the Owner Controlled Area*, Information Notice 2002-14. U.S. Nuclear Regulatory Commission, Washington, DC, 2002f.

NRC, *National Guard and Other Emergency Responders Located in the Licensee's Controlled Area*, Regulatory Issue Summary 02-21. U.S. Nuclear Regulatory Commission, Washington, DC, 2002g.

NRC, *NRC Response Technical Manual*, NUREG/BR-0150, Revision 5. U.S. Nuclear Regulatory Commission, Washington, DC, 2002h.

NRC, *Revised Draft NUREG-1633 and Public Information Brochure on Potassium Iodide for the General Public*, SECY 02-089. U.S. Nuclear Regulatory Commission, Washington, DC, 2002i.

NRC, *Status of Proposed Amendments to Emergency Preparedness Regulations in 10 CFR 50 Appendix E*, SECY 02-130. U.S. Nuclear Regulatory Commission, Washington, DC, 2002j.

NRC, *Clarification of NRC Guidance for Modifying Protective Actions*, Regulatory Issue Summary 03-12. U.S. Nuclear Regulatory Commission, Washington, DC, 2003a.

NRC, *Control Room Habitability*, Generic Letter 03-01. U.S. Nuclear Regulatory Commission, Washington, DC, 2003b.

NRC, *Emergency Planning and Preparedness for Nuclear Power Reactors*, Regulatory Guide 1.101, Revision 4. U.S. Nuclear Regulatory Commission, Washington, DC, 2003c.

NRC, *Evaluation of Nuclear Power Reactor Emergency Preparedness Planning Basis Adequacy in the Post-9/11 Threat Environment*, SECY 03-165 (not currently available to the public). U.S. Nuclear Regulatory Commission, Washington, DC, 2003d.

NRC, *Methods and Assumptions for Evaluating Radiological Consequences of Design Basis Accidents at Light-Water Nuclear Power Reactors*, Regulatory Guide 1.195. U.S. Nuclear Regulatory Commission, Washington, DC, 2003e.

NRC, *Proposed Amendments to 10 CFR Part 50, Appendix E Relating to (1) NRC Approval of Changes to Emergency Action Levels (EAL) Paragraph IV.B. and (2) Exercise Requirements for Co-Located Licensees, Paragraph IV.F.2*, SECY 03-067. U.S. Nuclear Regulatory Commission, Washington, DC, 2003f.

NRC, *Use of NEI 99-01, "Methodology for Development of Emergency Action Levels," Revision 4, Dated January 2003*, Regulatory Issue Summary 03-18, Revision 4. U.S. Nuclear Regulatory Commission, Washington, DC, 2003g.

NRC, *Consideration of Sheltering in Licensee's Range of Protective Actions*, Regulatory Issue Summary 04-13. U.S. Nuclear Regulatory Commission, Washington, DC, 2004a.

NRC, *Emergency Preparedness Issues: Post 9/11*, Regulatory Issue Summary 04-15. U.S. Nuclear Regulatory Commission, Washington, DC, 2004b.

NRC, *Final Amendments to 10 CFR Part 50, Appendix E, Relating to (1) NRC Approval of Emergency Action Levels Paragraph IV.B, and (2) Exercise Requirements for Co-Located Licensees Paragraph IV.F.2*, SECY 04-211. U.S. Nuclear Regulatory Commission, Washington, DC, 2004c.

NRC, *Memorandum of Agreement on the Interagency Modeling and Atmospheric Assessment Center*, SECY 04-221. U.S. Nuclear Regulatory Commission, Washington, DC, 2004d.

NRC, *Problems Associated with Back-Up Power Supplies to Emergency Response Facilities and Equipment*, Information Notice 04-19. U.S. Nuclear Regulatory Commission, Washington, DC, 2004e.

NRC, *Use of NEI 99-01, "Methodology for Development of Emergency Action Levels," Revision 4, Dated January 2003*, Regulatory Issue Summary 03-18, Supplement 1. U.S. Nuclear Regulatory Commission, Washington, DC, 2004f.

NRC, *Clarifying the Process for Making Emergency Plan Changes*, Regulatory Issue Summary 05-02. U.S. Nuclear Regulatory Commission, Washington, DC, 2005a.

NRC, *Consideration of Sheltering in Licensee's Range of Protective Actions*, Regulatory Issue Summary 04-13, Supplement 1. U.S. Nuclear Regulatory Commission, Washington, DC, 2005b.

NRC, *Denial of a Petition for Rulemaking to Revise 10 CFR Part 50 to Require Offsite Emergency Plans to include Nursery Schools and Day Care Centers*, SECY 05-045. U.S. Nuclear Regulatory Commission, Washington, DC, 2005c.

NRC, *Effect of Plant Configuration Changes on the Emergency Plan*, Information Notice 05-019. U.S. Nuclear Regulatory Commission, Washington, DC, 2005d.

NRC, *Emergency Response Planning and Preparedness for Nuclear Power Reactors*, Regulatory Guide 1.101, Revision 5. U.S. Nuclear Regulatory Commission, Washington, DC, 2005e.

NRC, *Emergency Preparedness and Response Activities for Security-Based Events*, Bulletin 2005-02. U.S. Nuclear Regulatory Commission, Washington, DC, 2005f.

NRC, *Endorsement of Nuclear Energy Institute (NEI) Guidance "Range of Protective Actions for Nuclear Power Plant Incidents,"* Regulatory Issue Summary 05-08. U.S. Nuclear Regulatory Commission, Washington, DC, 2005g.

NRC, *Failure to Maintain Alert and Notification System Tone Alert Radio Capability*, Information Notice 05-06. U.S. Nuclear Regulatory Commission, Washington, DC, 2005h.

NRC, *NRC Incident Response and the National Response Plan*, Regulatory Issue Summary 05-13. U.S. Nuclear Regulatory Commission, Washington, DC, 2005i.

NRC, *NRC Incident Response Plan (IRP)*, NUREG-0728, Revision 4. U.S. Nuclear Regulatory Commission, Washington, DC, 2005j.

NRC, *Review of Operational Programs in a Combined License Application and Generic Emergency Planning Inspections, Tests, Analyses, and Acceptance Criteria*, SECY 05-197. U.S. Nuclear Regulatory Commission, Washington, DC, 2005k.

NRC, *Use of NEI 99-01, "Methodology for Development of Emergency Action Levels," Revision 4, Dated January 2003*, Regulatory Issue Summary 03-18, Supplement 2. U.S. Nuclear Regulatory Commission, Washington, DC, 2005l.

NRC, *Criteria for Accident Monitoring Instrumentation for Power Plants*, Regulatory Guide 1.97, Revision 4. U.S. Nuclear Regulatory Commission, Washington, DC, 2006a.

NRC, *Denial of a Petition for Rulemaking to Codify Federal Emergency Management Agency GM-EV-2, "Protective Actions for School Children," into Emergency Planning Regulations in 10 CFR Part 50*, SECY 06-228. U.S. Nuclear Regulatory Commission, Washington, DC, 2006b.

NRC, *Emergency Preparedness for Daycare Facilities within the Commonwealth of Pennsylvania: Update on Staff Actions and Request for Commission Approval for Related Staff Actions*, SECY 06-101. U.S. Nuclear Regulatory Commission, Washington, DC, 2006c.

NRC, *Emergency Preparedness Issues: Post 9/11*, Regulatory Issue Summary 04-15, Supplement 1. U.S. Nuclear Regulatory Commission, Washington, DC, 2006d.

NRC, *Endorsement of Nuclear Energy Institute Guidance "Enhancements to Emergency Preparedness Programs for Hostile Action,"* Regulatory Issue Summary 06-12. U.S. Nuclear Regulatory Commission, Washington, DC, 2006e.

NRC, *Good Practices for Licensee Performance During the Emergency Preparedness Component of Force-on-Force Exercises*, Regulatory Issue Summary 06-02. U.S. Nuclear Regulatory Commission, Washington, DC, 2006f.

NRCC, *Guidance on Requesting an Exemption from Biennial Emergency Preparedness Exercise Requirements*, Regulatory Issue Summary 06-03. U.S. Nuclear Regulatory Commission, Washington, DC, 2006g.

NRC, *History of the Emergency Notification System and Options to Provide Confirmation of Authority/ Identity of a Caller*, SECY 06-0173. U.S. Nuclear Regulatory Commission, Washington, DC, 2006h.

NRC, *Improving Response Capabilities Through the Use of an Incident Response Electronic Library*, Regulatory Issue Summary 06-21. U.S. Nuclear Regulatory Commission, Washington, DC, 2006i.

NRC, *Results of the Review of Emergency Preparedness Regulations and Guidance*, SECY 060-200. U.S. Nuclear Regulatory Commission, Washington, DC, 2006j.

NRC, *Siren System Failures Due to Erroneous Siren System Signal*, Information Notice 06-28. U.S. Nuclear Regulatory Commission, Washington, DC, 2006k.

NRC, *Clarification of NRC Guidance for Emergency Notifications During Quickly Changing Events*, Regulatory Issue Summary 07-02. U.S. Nuclear Regulatory Commission, Washington, DC, 2007a.

NRC, *Clarification of NRC Guidance for Maintaining a Standard Emergency Action Level Scheme*, Regulatory Issue Summary 07-01. U.S. Nuclear Regulatory Commission, Washington, DC, 2007b.

NRC, *Meteorological Monitoring Programs for Nuclear Power Plants*, Regulatory Guide 1.23, Revision 1. U.S. Nuclear Regulatory Commission, Washington, DC, 2007c.

NRC, *Options and Recommendations for the Responsibility for Future Replenishment of Potassium Iodide*, SECY 07-078. U.S. Nuclear Regulatory Commission, Washington, DC, 2007d.

NRC, *Revision of NUREG-0654, Supplement 3, "Criteria for Protective Action Recommendations,"* SECY 07-225. U.S. Nuclear Regulatory Commission, Washington, DC, 2007e.

NRC, *State of the Art Reactor Consequence Analyses (SOARCA)*. U.S. Nuclear Regulatory Commission, Washington, DC, 2007f.

NRC, *Tactical Communications Interoperability Between Nuclear Power Licensees and First Responders*, Information Notice 07-12. U.S. Nuclear Regulatory Commission, Washington, DC, 2007g.

NRC, *Annual Update on Emergency Preparedness Activities*, SECY 08-168. U.S. Nuclear Regulatory Commission, Washington, DC, 2008a.

NRC, *Clarified Requirements of Title 10 of the Code of Federal Regulations Section 50.54(Y) When Implementing 10 CFR Section 50.54(X) to Depart from a License Condition or Technical Specification*, Regulatory Issue Summary 08-26. U.S. Nuclear Regulatory Commission, Washington, DC, 2008b.

NRC, *Delegation of Commission Authority to Staff to Approve or Deny Emergency Plan Changes That Represent a Decrease in Effectiveness*, SECY 08-024. U.S. Nuclear Regulatory Commission, Washington, DC, 2008c.

NRC, *Review of NUREG-0654, Supplement 3, "Criteria for Protective Action Recommendations for Severe Accidents,"* NUREG/CR-6953/SAND2007-5448P. Sandia National Laboratories, Albuquerque, NM, 2008d.

NRC, *State of the Art Consequence Analyses—Reporting Offsite Health Consequences*, SECY 08-029. U.S. Nuclear Regulatory Commission, Washington, DC, 2008e.

NRC, *Use of NEI 99-01, "Methodology for Development of Emergency Action Levels," Revision 5, Dated January 2008*, Regulatory Issue Summary 03-18, Supplement 2. U.S. Nuclear Regulatory Commission, Washington, DC, 2008f.

NRC, *Annual Update on Emergency Preparedness Activities*, SECY 09-152. U.S. Nuclear Regulatory Commission, Washington, DC, 2009a.

NRC, *Communications Between the NRC and Reactor Licensees During Emergencies and Significant Incidents*, Regulatory Issue Summary 09-10. U.S. Nuclear Regulatory Commission, Washington, DC, 2009b.

NRC, *Emergency Response Data System Upgrade from Modem to Virtual Private Network Appliance*, Regulatory Issue Summary 09-13. U.S. Nuclear Regulatory Commission, Washington, DC, 2009c.

NRC, *Evaluation of Radiological Consequence Models and Codes*, SECY 09-051. U.S. Nuclear Regulatory Commission, Washington, DC, 2009d.

NRC, *Hostile Action-Based Emergency Preparedness Drills*, Information Notice 09-19. U.S. Nuclear Regulatory Commission, Washington, DC, 2009e.

NRC, *National Response Framework*, Information Notice 09-01. U.S. Nuclear Regulatory Commission, Washington, DC, 2009f.

NRC, *Non-Power Reactor Licensee Notifications to the NRC During an Incident*, Information Notice 09-31. U.S. Nuclear Regulatory Commission, Washington, DC, 2009g.

NRC, *Proposed Rule Related to Enhancements to Emergency Preparedness Regulations, 10 CFR 50*, SECY 09-007. U.S. Nuclear Regulatory Commission, Washington, DC, 2009h.

NRC, *Recommendation for Future Replenishment of Potassium Iodide*, SECY 09-041. U.S. Nuclear Regulatory Commission, Washington, DC, 2009i.

NRC, *Annual Update on Emergency Preparedness Activities*, SECY 10-139. U.S. Nuclear Regulatory Commission, Washington, DC, 2010a.

NRC, *Proposed Revision to the Memorandum of Understanding Between the Federal Emergency Management Agency and the Nuclear Regulatory Commission*, SECY 10-099. U.S. Nuclear Regulatory Commission, Washington, DC, 2010b.

NRC, *Annual Update on Emergency Preparedness Activities*, SECY 11-146. U.S. Nuclear Regulatory Commission, Washington, DC, 2011a.

NRC, *Clarifying the Process for Making Emergency Plan Changes*, Regulatory Issue Summary 05-02, Revision 1. U.S. Nuclear Regulatory Commission, Washington, DC, 2011b.

NRC, *Criteria for Preparation and Evaluation of Radiological Emergency Response Plans and Preparedness in Support of Nuclear Power Plants. Supplement 3. Guidance for Protective Action Strategies*, NUREG-0654, FEMA REP-1, revised. U.S. Nuclear Regulatory Commission, Washington, DC, 2011c.

NRC, *Development of an Emergency Planning and Preparedness Framework for Small Modular Reactors*, SECY 11-152. U.S. Nuclear Regulatory Commission, Washington, DC, 2011d.

NRC, *Final Rule: Enhancement to Emergency Preparedness Regulations*, SECY 11-053. U.S. Nuclear Regulatory Commission, Washington, DC, 2011e.

NRC, *Guidance on Making Changes to Emergency Plans for Nuclear Power Reactors*, Regulatory Guide 1.219. U.S. Nuclear Regulatory Commission, Washington, DC, 2011f.

NRC, *Interim Staff Guidance: Emergency Planning for Nuclear Power Plants*, NSIR-ISG-1. U.S. Nuclear Regulatory Commission, Washington, DC, 2011g.

NRC, *Near-Term Report and Recommendations for Agency Actions Following the Events in Japan*, SECY 11-093. U.S. Nuclear Regulatory Commission, Washington, DC, 2011h.

NRC, *Prioritization of Recommended Actions to Be Taken in Response to Fukushima Lessons Learned*, SECY 11-137. U.S. Nuclear Regulatory Commission, Washington, DC, 2011i.

NRC, *Proposed Minor Revision to Management Directive 5.12, "International Nuclear Event Scale Participation,"* SECY 11-105. U.S. Nuclear Regulatory Commission, Washington, DC, 2011j.

NRC, *Recommendations for Enhancing Reactor Safety in the 21st Century: The Near-Term Task Force Review of Insights from the Fukushima Dai-Ichi Accident*, U.S. Nuclear Regulatory Commission, Washington, DC, 2011k.

NRC, *U.S. Environmental Protection Agency Revisions to the Protective Action Guidance Manual*, SECY 11-078. U.S. Nuclear Regulatory Commission, Washington, DC, 2011l.

NRC, *Annual Update on Emergency Preparedness Activities*, SECY 12-149. U.S. Nuclear Regulatory Commission, Washington, DC, 2012a.

NRC, *Entergy Operation's Request to Relocate the River Bend Station Backup Emergency Operations Facility*, SECY 12-097. U.S. Nuclear Regulatory Commission, Washington, DC, 2012b.

NRC, *Failure to Properly Augment Emergency Response Organizations*, Information Notice 12-18. U.S. Nuclear Regulatory Commission, Washington, DC, 2012c.

NRC, *Modeling Potential Reactor Accident Consequences*, NUREG/BR-0359. U.S. Nuclear Regulatory Commission, Washington, DC, 2012d.

NRC, *NRC Enforcement Policy*. U.S. Nuclear Regulatory Commission, Washington, DC, 2012e.

NRC, *RASCAL 4: Description of Models and Methods*, NUREG-1940. U.S. Nuclear Regulatory Commission, Washington, DC, 2012f.

NRC, *Stakeholder Feedback Regarding Emergency Preparedness Rule Implementation*, SECY 12-129. U.S. Nuclear Regulatory Commission, Washington, DC, 2012g.

NRC, *State-of-the-Art Reactor Consequence Analyses (SOARCA) Report*, NUREG-1935. U.S. Nuclear Regulatory Commission, Washington, DC, 2012h.

NRC, *Annual Update on the Status of Emergency Preparedness Activities*, SECY 13-110. U.S. Nuclear Regulatory Commission, Washington, DC, 2013a.

NRC, *Deficiencies with Effluent Radiation Monitor System Instrumentation*, Information Notice 13-13. U.S. Nuclear Regulatory Commission, Washington, DC, 2013b.

NRC, *Emergency Action Level Thresholds Outside the Range of Radiation Monitors*, Information Notice 13-01. U.S. Nuclear Regulatory Commission, Washington, DC, 2013c.

NRC, *History of the Use and Consideration of the Large Early Release Frequency Metric by the U.S. Nuclear Regulatory Commission*, SECY 13-029. U.S. Nuclear Regulatory Commission, Washington, DC, 2013d.

NRC, *Request to Change Approval Authority for Emergency Plan Changes*, SECY 13-079. U.S. Nuclear Regulatory Commission, Washington, DC, 2013e.

NRC, *State-of-the-Art Reactor Consequence Analyses Project*, NUREG/CR-7110. Sandia National Laboratories, Albuquerque, NM, 2013f.

NRC, *Risk-Informed, Performance-Based Radiological Emergency Response Program Oversight*, ADAMS Accession No. ML13274A531. U.S. Nuclear Regulatory Commission, Washington, DC, 2014.

NRC, *Enforcement Discretion Not to Cite Certain Violations of Section V of Appendix E to 10 CFR Part 50*, Enforcement Guidance Memorandum 2015-003. U.S. Nuclear Regulatory Commission, Washington, DC, 2015a.

NRC, *NRC Incident Response Program*, Management Directive MD-8.2. U.S. Nuclear Regulatory Commission, Washington, DC, 2015b.

NRC, *Options for Emergency Preparedness for Small Modular Reactors and Other New Technologies*, SECY-15-0077. U.S. Nuclear Regulator Commission, Washington, DC, 2015c.

NRC, *Protective Action Recommendations for Members of the Public on Bodies of Water*, Regulatory Issue Summary 15-11. U.S. Nuclear Regulatory Commission, Washington, DC, 2015d.

NRCP, *Radiological Factors Affecting Decision Making in a Nuclear Attack*, NRCP Report 42. National Council on Radiation Protection and Measurements, Bethesda, MD, 1974.

NRCP, *Protection of the Thyroid Gland in the Event of Releases of Radioiodine*, NRCP Report 55. National Council on Radiation Protection and Measurements, Bethesda, MD, 1977.

NRCP, *Population Monitoring and Radionuclide Decorporation following a Radiological or Nuclear Incident*, NRCP Report 166. National Council on Radiation Protection and Measurements, Bethesda, MD, 2010a.

NRCP, *Responding to a Radiological or Nuclear Terrorism Incident: A Guide for Decision Makers*, NRCP Report 165. National Council on Radiation Protection and Measurements, Bethesda, MD, 2010b.

NRCP, *Decision Making for Late Phase Recovery from Major Nuclear or Radiological Incidents*, NRCP Report 175. National Council on Radiation Protection and Measurements, Bethesda, MD, 2014.

NSC, *United States Civil Defense Policy*, NSDM 184. National Security Council, Washington, DC, 1972.

Nuclear Emergency Response Headquarters, *Additional Report of the Japanese Government to the IAEA, Second Report*. Government of Japan, Tokyo, 2011.

NUMARC, *Methodology for Development of Emergency Action Levels*, NUMARC/NESP-007, Revision 2. Nuclear Management and Resources Council, Washington, DC, 1992.

Obama, B., *National Preparedness*, Presidential Policy Directive 8. White House, Washington, DC, 2011.

OECD, *The Chernobyl Accident Source Term*. Organization for Economic Cooperation and Development, Paris, France, 1996.

Pasquill, F., The estimation of the dispersion of wind borne material. *Meteorology Magazine*, 90(1063), 33–49, 1961.

PDH, *Cancer and Morbidity around TMI*. Pennsylvania Department of Health, Harrisburg, 1985.

Perry, R., *Evacuation Decision Making and Emergency Planning*. National Technical Information Service, Springfield, VA, 1980.

Povinec, P.P., Sykora, I., Holy, K., Gera, M., Kovacik, A., and Brestakova, L., Aerosol radioactivity record in Bratislava/Slovakia following the Fukushima Accident—a comparison with global fallout and the Chernobyl accident. *Environmental Radioactivity*, 114, 81–88, 2012.

Povinec, P.P., Hirose, K., and Aoyama, M., *Fukushima Accident: Radioactivity Impact on the Environment*. Elsevier, Amsterdam, 2013.

Pratt, W.T., Mubayi, V., Chu, T.L., Martinez-Guridi, G., and Lehner, J., *An Approach for Estimating the Frequencies of Various Containment Failure Modes and Bypass Events*, NUREG/CR-6595, BNL-NUREG-52539, Appendix A. Brookhaven National Laboratory, Upton, NY, 2004.

Presidential Commission, *Report of the President's Commission on the Accident at Three Mile Island*. White House, Washington, DC, 1979.

Reagan, R., Executive Order 12472—Assignment of national security and emergency preparedness telecommunications functions. *Federal Register*, 49, 13471, 1984.

Reagan, R., Executive Order 12656—Assignment of emergency preparedness responsibilities. *Federal Register*, 53, 47491, 1988a.

Reagan, R., Executive Order 12657—Federal Emergency Management Agency assistance in emergency preparedness planning at commercial nuclear power plants. *Federal Register*, 53, 47513, 1988b.

Reagan, R., Executive Order 12658—Establishes the President's Commission on Catastrophic Nuclear Accidents. *Federal Register*, 53, 47517, 1988c.

Robert T. Stafford Disaster Relief and Emergency Assistance Act, Public Law 93-288, amended by Public Law 10-106-390, October 20, 2000.

Robertson, D.E., Cataldo, D.A., Napier, B.A., Krupka, K.M., and Sasser, L.B., *Literature Review and Assessment of Plant and Animal Transfer Factors Used in Performance Assessment Modeling*, NUREG/CR-6825, PNNL-14321. Pacific Northwest National Laboratory, Richland, WA, 2003.

Rogovin, M. and Frampton, G.T., *Three Mile Island: A Report to the Commissioners and to the Public*, NUREG/CR-1250, Vols. I and II. U.S. Nuclear Regulatory Commission Special Inquiry Group, Washington, DC, 1980.

Romander, C.M. and Cotton, J.D., *Mechanics of a Highway Accident at Wichita, Kansas, Involving Natural Uranium Concentrate*, NUREG/CR-0992. U.S. Nuclear Regulatory Commission, Washington, DC, 1979.

Sailor, V.L. et al., *Severe Accidents in Spent Fuel Pools in Support of Generic Issue 82*, NUREG/CR-4982. U.S. Nuclear Regulatory Commission, Washington, DC, 1987.

Salmonson, B.J., Hoffman, L.G., Honkus, R.J., and Keller, J.H., *Guidance on Offsite Emergency Radiation Measurement Systems. Phase 3. Water and Non-Dairy Food Pathway*. Westinghouse Idaho Nuclear Company, Idaho Falls, 1984.

Seibert, P., Uncertainties in atmospheric dispersion modeling and source determination, in *Proceedings Informal Workshop on Meteorological Modelling in Support of CTBT Verification*, Vienna, December 4–6, 2000.

Sejkora, K., Temporal Comparison of Atmospheric Stability Classification Methods, paper presented at Tenth NUMUG Meeting, Wilmington NC, June 29–30, 2005.

Shair, F.H., Sasaki, E.J., Carlan, D.E., Cass, G.R., and Goodin, W.R., Transport and dispersion of airborne pollutants associated with the land breeze–sea breeze system. *Atmospheric Environment*, 16(9), 2043–2053, 1982.

Silberberg, M., Mitchell, J.A., Meyer, R.O., and Ryder, C.P., *Reassessment of the Technical Bases for Estimating Source Terms, Final Report*, NUREG-0956. U.S. Nuclear Regulatory Commission, Washington, DC, 1986.

Sjoreen, A.L., Ramsdell, Jr., J.V., McKenna, T.J., McGuire, S.A., Fosmire, C., and Athey, G.F., *RASCAL 3.0: Description of Models and Methods*, NUREG-1741. U.S. Nuclear Regulatory Commission, Washington, DC, 2001.

Skupniewicz, C.E. and Schacher, G.E., Parameterization of plume dispersion over water. *Atmospheric Environment*, 20(7), 1333–1340, 1986.

Slade, D.H., Ed., *Meteorology and Atomic Energy*, TID-24190. U.S. Atomic Energy Commission, Washington, DC, 1968.

Smith, R.B., A *K*-theory of dispersion, settling and deposition in the atmospheric surface layer. *Boundary-Layer Meteorology*, 129, 371, 2008.

Snell, W.G. and Jubach, R.W., *Technical Basis for Regulatory Guide 1.145, "Atmospheric Dispersion Models for Potential Accident Consequence Assessments at Nuclear Power Plants,"* NUREG/CR-2260. U.S. Nuclear Regulatory Commission, Washington, DC, 1981.

Soffer, L., Burson, S.B., Ferrell, C.M., Lee, R.Y., and Ridgely, J.N., *Accident Source Terms for Light Water Nuclear Power Plants*, NUREG-1465. U.S. Nuclear Regulatory Commission, Washington, DC, 1995.

Spangler, T.C. and Johnson, V.S., The dispersion of offshore pollutant plumes into moderately complex coastal terrain. *Atmospheric Environment*, 23(10), 2133–2141. 1989.

Steinmeyer, K.P., *Manual of Respiratory Protection Against Airborne Radioactive Materials*, NUREG/CR-0041, Revision 1. U.S. Nuclear Regulatory Commission, Washington, DC, 2001.

Stratton, W.R., *A Review of Criticality Accidents*, Report LA-3611. Los Alamos Scientific Laboratory of the University of California, Los Alamos, NM, 1967.

Strom, D.J. and Stansbury, P.S., Minimum detectable activity when background is counted longer than the sample. *Health Physics*, 63(3), 360–361, 1992.

Sugano, T. et al., Full-scale aircraft impact test for evaluation of impact force. *Nuclear Engineering and Design*, 140, 373–385, 1993.

Sullivan, R., Jones, J., LaChance, J., Walton, F., and Weber, S., *Emergency Preparedness Significance Quantification Process, Proof of Concept*, NUREG/CR-7160, SAND2012-3144P. Sandia National Laboratories, Albuquerque, NM, 2013.

Sutter, S.L., *Accident Generated Particulate Materials and Their Characteristics—A Review of Background Information*, NUREG/CR-2651, PNL-4154. Pacific Northwest National Laboratory, Richland, WA, 1982.

Thielen, H., Brücher, W., Martens, R., and Sogalla, M., Advanced atmospheric dispersion modelling and probabilistic consequence analysis for radiation protection purposes in Germany, in *Air Pollution Modeling and Its Application XVII*, Borrego, C. and Norman, A.-L., Eds., pp. 664–666. Springer, New York, 2007.

Till, J.E. and Meyer, H.R., Eds., *Radiological Assessment, A Textbook on Environmental Dose Analysis*, NUREG/CR-3332, ORNL-5968. U.S. Nuclear Regulatory Commission, Washington, DC, 1983.

Tokuhata, G.K., *Impact of TMI Nuclear Accident upon Pregnancy Outcome, Congenital Hypothyroidism, and Mortality*. Pennsylvania Department of Health, Harrisburg, 1981.

Travis, R.J., Davis, R.E., Grove, E.J., and Azarm, M.A., *A Safety and Regulatory Assessment of Generic BWR and PWR Permanently Shutdown Nuclear Power Plants*, NUREG/CR-6451, BNL-NUREG-52498. Brookhaven National Laboratory, Upton, NY, 1997.

Truman, H.S., Executive Order 10312—Providing for emergency control over certain government and non-government stations egaged in radio communication or radio transmission of energy. *Federal Register*, 16, 12452, 1951.

Truman, H.S., Executive Order 10346—Preparation by federal agencies of civil defense emergency plans. *Federal Register*, 17, 3477, 1952.

Turnbull, J.A. and Beyer, C.E., *Background and Derivation of ANS-5.4 Standard Fission Product Release Model*, NUREG/CR-7003, PNNL-18490. Pacific Northwest National Laboratory, Richland, WA, 2010.

Turner, D.B., *Workbook of Atmospheric Dispersion Estimates*. U.S. Department of Health, Education, and Welfare, Cincinnati, OH, 1970 (*Turner's Workbook*).

Turner, D.B., *Workbook of Atmospheric Dispersion Estimates*, revised. U.S. Environmental Protection Agency, Research Triangle Park, 1973 (*Turner's Workbook*).

Turner, D.B., *Workbook of Atmospheric Dispersion Estimates: An Introduction to Dispersion Modeling*, 2nd ed. Lewis Publishers, Boca Raton, FL, 1994 (*Turner's Workbook*).

UIC, *Safety of Nuclear Power Reactors*, Nuclear Issues Briefing Paper 14. Uranium Information Centre, Melbourne, Austrlia, 2006.

Unterweger, M.P., Hoppes, D.D., Schima, F.J., and Coursey, J.S., *Radionuclide Half-Life Measurements*. National Institute of Standards and Technology, Gaithersburg, MD, 1992.

Urbanik, T.E. and Jamison, J.D., *State of the Art in Evacuation Time Estimate Studies for Nuclear Power Plants*, NUREG/CR-4831. U.S. Nuclear Regulatory Commission, Washington, DC, 1992.

Urbanik, T.E., Desrosiers, A., Lindell, M.K., and Schuller, C.R., *Analysis of Techniques for Estimating Evacuation Times*, NUREG/CR-1745. U.S. Nuclear Regulatory Commission, Washington, DC, 1980.

U.S.–Canada Power System Outage Task Force, *Final Report on the August 14, 2003, Blackout in the United States and Canada: Causes and Recommendations*, 2004.

USAEC, *Theoretical Possibilities and Consequences of Major Accidents in Large Nuclear Power Plants*, WASH-0740. U.S. Atomic Energy Commission, Washington, DC, 1957.

USAEC, *Calculation of Distance Factors for Power and Test Reactor Sites*, TID-14844. U.S. Atomic Energy Commission, Washington, DC, 1962.

USAEC, *Guide to the Preparation of Emergency Plans for Production and Utilization Facilities*. U.S. Nuclear Regulatory Commission, Washington, DC, 1970.

USAEC, *Assumptions Used for Evaluating the Potential Radiological Consequences of a Steam Line Break Accident for Boiling Water Reactors*, Regulatory Guide 1.5. U.S. Atomic Energy Commission, Washington, DC, 1971.

USAEC, *Assumptions Used for Evaluating the Potential Radiological Consequences of a Fuel Handling Accident in the Fuel Handing and Storage Facility for Boiling and Pressurized Water Reactors*, Regulatory Guide 1.25. U.S. Atomic Energy Commission, Washington, DC, 1972a.

USAEC, *Assumptions Used for Evaluating the Potential Radiological Consequences of a Pressurized Water Reactor Radioactive Gas Decay Tank Failure*, Regulatory Guide 1.24. U.S. Atomic Energy Commission, Washington, DC, 1972b.

USAEC, *Onsite Meteorological Programs*, Safety Guide 1.23. U.S. Atomic Energy Commission, Washington, DC, 1972c.

USAEC, *Assumptions Used for Evaluating the Potential Radiological Consequences of a Loss of Coolant Accident for Boiling Water Reactors*, Regulatory Guide 1.3, revised. U.S. Atomic Energy Commission, Washington, DC, 1974a.

USAEC, *Assumptions Used for Evaluating the Potential Radiological Consequences of a Loss of Coolant Accident for Pressurized Water Reactors*, Regulatory Guide 1.4, revised. U.S. Atomic Energy Commission, Washington, DC, 1974b.

USDHEW, *Radiological Health Handbook*, Publication 2016, revised. U.S. Department of Health, Education, and Welfare, Rockville, MD, 1970.

USDHS, *Homeland Security Presidential Directive 5: Management of Domestic Incidents*. U.S. Department of Homeland Security, Washington, DC, 2003a.

USDHS, *Homeland Security Presidential Directive 7: Critical Infrastructure Identification, Prioritization, and Protection*. U.S. Department of Homeland Security, Washington, DC, 2003b.

USDHS, *Homeland Security Presidential Directive 8: National Preparedness*. U.S. Department of Homeland Security, Washington, DC, 2003c.

USDHS, *National Response Plan*. U.S. Department of Homeland Security, Washington, DC, 2004.

USDHS, *Federal Guidelines for Requesting Potassium Iodide (KI) from the Strategic National Stockpile (DRAFT)*. U.S. Department of Homeland Security, Washington, DC, 2005.

USDHS, *National Response Framework*. U.S. Department of Homeland Security, Washington, DC, 2008a.

USDHS, *Nuclear/Radiological Incident Annex to the National Response Framework*, revised. U.S. Department of Homeland Security, Washington, DC, 2008b.

USDHS, *Homeland Security Exercise and Evaluation Program (HSEEP)*. U.S. Department of Homeland Security, Washington, DC, 2013.

USDOE, *Radiation Protection of the Public and Environment*, DOE Order 5400.5. U.S. Department of Energy, Washington, DC, 1993.

USDOE, *Radiological Emergency Response Health and Safety Manual*, DOE/NV/11718-440. U.S. Department of Energy, National Nuclear Security Administration, Washington, DC, 2001.

USDOE, *FRMAC Assessment Manual*. Vol. 1. *Methods*, SAND2003-1071P. Sandia National Laboratories, Albuquerque, NM, 2003.

USDOE, *Comprehensive Emergency Management System*, DOE Order 151.1C. U.S. Department of Energy, Washington, DC, 2005a.

USDOE, *FRMAC Laboratory Analysis Manual*. U.S. Department of Energy, Washington, DC, 2005b.

USDOE, *FRMAC Monitoring Manual*. Vol. 1. *Monitoring Group Operations*. U.S. Department of Energy, Washington, DC, 2005c.

USDOE, *FRMAC Monitoring Manual*. Vol. 2. *Radiation Monitoring and Sampling*. U.S. Department of Energy, Washington, DC, 2005d.

USDOE, *Departmental Radiological Emergency Assets*, DOE Order 153.1. U.S. Department of Energy, Washington, DC, 2007.

USDOE, *FRMAC Assessment Manual*. Vol. 2. *Pre-Assessed Default Scenarios*, SAND2010-2575P. Sandia National Laboratories, Albuquerque, NM, 2010a.

USDOE, *FRMAC Operations Manual*, Rev. 3, DOE/NV/25956-980. U.S. Department of Energy, National Nuclear Security Administration, Washington, DC, 2010b.

USEPA, *Manual of Protective Action Guides and Protective Actions for Nuclear Incidents*, EPA-520/1-75-001. U.S. Environmental Protection Agency, Washington, DC, 1975.

USEPA, *Protective Action Evaluation*. Part I. *The Effectiveness of Sheltering-in-Place as a Protective Action Against Nuclear Accidents Involving Gaseous Releases*, EPA 520/1-78-001A. U.S. Environmental Protection Agency, Washington, DC, 1978.

USEPA, EPA Policy Statement: Planning basis for emergency responses to nuclear power reactor accidents. *Federal Register*, 45, 2893, 1980a.

USEPA, *Manual of Protective Action Guides and Protective Actions for Nuclear Incidents*, EPA-520/1-75-001, revised. U.S. Environmental Protection Agency, Washington, DC, 1980b.

USEPA, *An Estimation of the Daily Average Food Intake by Age and Sex for Use in Assessing the Radionuclide Intake of Individuals in the General Population*, EPA 520/1-84-021. U.S. Environmental Protection Agency, Washington, DC, 1984a.

USEPA, *An Estimation of the Daily Food Intake Based on Data from the 1977–1978 USDA Nationwide Food Consumption Survey*, EPA 520/1-84-015. U.S. Environmental Protection Agency, Washington, DC, 1984b.

USEPA, Radiation protection guidance to federal agencies for occupational exposure. *Federal Register*, 52(17), 2822, 1987.

USEPA, *Limiting Values of Radionuclide Intake and Air Concentration and Dose Conversion Factors for Inhalation, Submersion, and Ingestions*, Federal Guidance Report Number 11, EPA-520/1-88-020. U.S. Environmental Protection Agency, Washington, DC, 1988.

USEPA, *Manual of Protective Action Guides and Protective Actions for Nuclear Incidents*, EPA-400-R-92-001. U.S. Environmental Protection Agency, Washington, DC, 1992.

USEPA, *External Exposure to Radionuclides in Air, Water, and Soil*, Federal Guidance Report Number 12, EPA-402-R-93-081. U.S. Environmental Protection Agency, Washington, DC, 1993.

USEPA, *PAG Manual: Protective Action Guides and Planning Guidance for Radiological Incidents*. U.S. Environmental Protection Agency, Washington, DC, 2013.

USFDA, Accidental radioactive contamination of human food and animal feeds: recommendations for state and local agencies. *Federal Register*, 47(205), 47073, 1982.

USFDA, *Preparedness and Response in Radiation Accidents*, FDA 83-8211. U.S. Food and Drug Administration, Washington, DC, 1983.

USFDA, Radionuclides in imported foods—levels of concern. *Federal Register*, 51, 23155, 1986.

USFDA, Accidental radioactive contamination of human food and animal feeds: recommendations for state and local agencies. *Federal Register*, 63, 43402, 1998.

USFDA. *Guidance: Potassium Iodide As a Thyroid Blocking Agent in Radiation Emergencies*. U.S. Food and Drug Administration, Washington, DC, 2001.

USFDA, *Supporting Document for Guidance Levels of Radionuclides in Domestic and Imported Foods*. U.S. Food and Drug Administration, Washington, DC, 2004.

Walker, J.S., *Three Mile Island: A Nuclear Crisis in Historical Perspective*. University of California Press, Berkeley, 2004.

Wallace, J.M. and P.V. Hobbs, *Atmospheric Science*, 2nd ed., Section 9.5.2. Academic Press, Burlington, MA, 2006.

Walsh, C. and Jones, J.A., *Atmospheric Dispersion from Releases in the Vicinity of Buildings*, Report NRPB-W16. National Radiation Protection Board, United Kingdom, Chilton, U.K., 2002.

Weinstein, E.D., Bates, E.F., Adler, M.V., and Gant, K.S., *Guidance for a Large Tabletop Exercise for a Nuclear Power Plant*, NUREG-1514. U.S. Nuclear Regulatory Commission, Washington, DC, 1995.

White House, *U.S. Civil Defense Policy*, National Security Decision Directive 23. White House, Washington, DC, 1982a.

White House, *U.S. Civil Defense Policy*, National Security Decision Directive 26. White House, Washington, DC, 1982b.

White House, *U.S. Civil Defense*, National Security Decision Directive 259. White House, Washington, DC, 1987.

White House, *Civil Defense*, National Security Directive 66. White House, Washington, DC, 1992.

Whiteman, C.D., *Mountain Meteorology: Fundamentals and Applications*. Oxford University Press, Oxford, U.K., 2000.

Whittaker, E.L. and Heck, R.D., *An Evaluation of an Activated Charcoal Filter for the Collection of Gaseous Airborne Iodine*, Intralaboratory Technical Report 6. Southwestern Radiological Health Laboratory, Las Vegas, NV, 1965.

WHO, *Health Implications of Nuclear Power Production, Report of a Working Group, Brussels*. World Health Organization, Copenhagen, 1978.

WHO, *Nuclear Power: Health Implications of Transuranic Elements*. World Health Organization, Geneva, Switzerland, 1979.

WHO, *Nuclear Power: Accidental Releases—Principles of Public Health Action*. World Health Organization, Copenhagen, 1982.

WHO, *Nuclear Power: Accidental Releases—Practical Guidance for Public Health Action*. World Health Organization, Copenhagen, 1987.

WHO, *Derived Intervention Levels for Radionuclides in Food: Guidelines for Application After Widespread Radioactive Contamination Resulting from a Major Radiation Accident*. World Health Organization, Geneva, Switzerland, 1988.

WHO, *Nuclear Accidents—Harmonization of the Public Health Response*. World Health Organization, Copenhagen, 1989.

Wilson, W.B., England, T.R., and La Bauve, R.J., *Extended Burnup Calculations for Operating Reactor Reflood Reviews*, NUREG/CR-3108. Los Alamos National Laboratory, Los Alamos, NM, 1983.

WOG, *Post Accident Sampling System Requirements: A Technical Basis*, WCAP-14696 and WCAP-14986-P. Westinghouse Owners Group, Buchanan, NY, 1998.

Zelac, R.E., Cameron, J.L., Karagiannis, H., McGrath, J.R., Sherbini, S.S., Thomas, M.L., and Wigginton, J.E., *Consolidated Guidance: 10 CFR Part 20—Standards for Protection Against Radiation*, NUREG-1736. U.S. Nuclear Regulatory Commission, Washington, DC, 2001.

Index

For Product Safety Concerns and Information please contact our EU
representative GPSR@taylorandfrancis.com
Taylor & Francis Verlag GmbH, Kaufingerstraße 24, 80331 München, Germany

9 781032 242279